JU~~DY~~ ALWA ~~CON~~ROVERSY

HERE'S HOW HOW THEY WERE REVIEWED BY SOME OF THEIR CONTEMPORARIES— AND HOW THEY SAW THEMSELVES

"Judy Garland was a star at seventeen, a legend at twenty-seven, and a corpse at forty-seven. Sadly, she was trapped by her talent. She had a drug problem that her abusive mother initiated and sanctioned at MGM. She tried to get over the rainbow with the help of five husbands, seeking to replace her meek homosexual father whom she adored. Little did we know, Judy began to die the day she was born."

—Jane Ellen Wayne

"Judy Garland struggled with her sexuality, and with her meteoric rise to stardom with the fear of discovery and rejection and banishment that was sure to follow. To millions, she was Dorothy, the girl next door who traveled over the rainbow. Yet her life was a careening roller coaster of emotional turmoil, addiction, tempestuous marriages, and, for romantic solace, other women. She was intense, headstrong, and explosive, possessed of an insatiable desire to please. While still a teenager, she claimed that her life was 'absolute chaos.'"

—Axel Madsen

"Even at the age of ten, I thought a lot about boys. It wasn't about sex. I wanted someone to love me. As I set out in life as a little girl, I was always searching for love. I developed one crush after another, some lasting no more than a week, if that. Nothing really worked out except I always ended up getting my heart broken."

—Judy Garland

"Judy was like a whirlpool. She just sucked everyone into the experience."

—Sid Luft

"*Judy Garland was never a conventional film star, nor, really, a beauty, and her singing voice had its rough edges, especially in later years. Yet something about Garland made both sexes want to put their arms around her and protect her from the world.*"

—Eric Braun

"*Her rich, controlled vibrato, emotionally, was devastating. She launched into Over the Rainbow—the planned conclusion of the show—and the crowd went berserk. People were scrambling down the aisles now, crowding around the stage, yelling and screaming. Her voice broke on the first phrase—the hind of a sob—then she was the brave little girl facing the troubles of the world, but still pleading: 'Why, then, oh why can't I?' And when she finished, the roar was deafening.*"

—Christopher Finch,
Carnegie Hall, April 23, 1961

"*Back then, I became a thing, not a person, and I never intended to become a legend. I was not really prepared for the fame that descended, much less the notoriety. I would have been better off if I had gone to school like a normal girl, attended the senior prom, cheered the football team, married its captain, settled down, and had three children. I became a star, one of the biggest, but I never succeeded as a person.*"

—Judy Garland in 1967
(two years before her death)

"*Since her death in 1969, Judy Garland has become a gay icon, if not the gay icon. Indeed, she had a big gay following when she was alive. William Goldman castigated the 'flutter of fags' in the audience at the Palace in the summer of 1967 in Esquire magazine, while Time spoke disparagingly of the 'boys in tight trousers' who came to see her perform. It has been suggested that homosexuals of the closet era identified with her because she put up with the same demeaning jokes and dismissive remarks that they suffered.*"

—Nigel Cawthorne

"*There will never be another Judy Garland. She was one of a kind. When Judy sang, she had the power to make you feel great sadness and great happiness.*"

—Ann Miller

Too Many Damn Rainbows

Judy Garland & Liza Minnelli

What is Blood Moon Productions?

"Blood Moon, in case you don't know, is a small publishing house on Staten Island that cranks out Hollywood gossip books, about two or three a year, usually of five-, six-, or 700-page length, chocked with stories and pictures about people who used to consume the imaginations of the American public, back when we actually had a public imagination. That is, when people were really interested in each other, rather than in Apple 'devices.' In other words, back when we had vices, not devices."

—The Huffington Post

Award-Winning Entertainment About
American Legends, Hollywood Icons, and the Ironies of Fame.

www.BloodMoonProductions.com

JUDY GARLAND &
LIZA MINNELLI

TOO MANY DAMN RAINBOWS

DARWIN PORTER & DANFORTH PRINCE

JUDY GARLAND & LIZA MINNELLI
TOO MANY DAMN RAINBOWS

Darwin Porter and Danforth Prince

www.BloodMoonProductions.com

Manufactured in the United States of America

ISBN 978-1-936003-69-3

Covers & Book Design by Danforth Prince

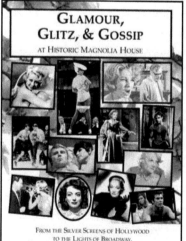

THIS BOOK IS DEDICATED

To anyone who ever expressed his or her love for Judy Garland, the world's greatest entertainer. This book records a roundup of their memories—or nightmares—of the most turbulent performer in the history of American Show Business.

A WORD ABOUT PHRASEOLOGIES

Since we at Blood Moon weren't privy to long-ago conversations as they were unfolding, we have relied on the memories of our sources for the conversational tone and phraseologies of what we've recorded within the pages of this book.

This writing technique, as it applies to modern biography, has been defined as "conversational storytelling" by *The New York Times*, which labeled it as an acceptable literary device for "engaging reading."

Some people have expressed displeasure in the fact that direct quotes and "as remembered" dialogue have become a standard—some would say "mandatory"—fixture in pop culture biographies today.

Blood Moon is not alone in replicating "as remembered" dialogues from dead sources. Truman Capote and Norman Mailer were pioneers of direct quotes, and today, they appear in countless other memoirs, ranging from those of Eddie Fisher to those of the long-time mistress (Verita Thompson) of Humphrey Bogart.

Best wishes to all of you, with thanks for your interest in our work.

Danforth Prince, President,
Blood Moon Productions

CONTENTS

Chapter Ten, Page 261

EASTER PARADE
In A Vaudeville-Inspired Remake of *Pygmalion*, Judy, Sometimes Wearing a
Bonnet, Plays A Showgirl Getting Mentored By An Older Pro (Fred Astaire)
With An Axe To Grind.

WORDS & MUSIC
Fluffy, Athletic, & Fun, Judy Shakes Her Way Through a
Song & Dance Memorial to Rodgers & Hart

MARIO LANZA
America's Caruso Lusts for Food, Drink, and Judy

SYLVIA SYDNEY & CARLETON ALSOP
Judy Steals Her Best Friend's Husband

IN THE GOOD OLD SUMMERTIME
The Strange Love of Van Johnson & Keenan Wynn, & How MGM Tried to Fix It.

ANNIE GET YOUR GUN
Judy Fucks It Up

Introducing MGM's Newest Villain
DORE SCHARY

"The film career of Judy Garland has come to an end."
—Motion Picture Magazine, 1950

Chapter Eleven, Page 291

Though She's Way Too Big A Name for Off-Broadway, Judy
--Addicted, Overweight, and Exhausted--
Dysfunctionally Portrays A Farm Girl in
SUMMER STOCK

Deep Diving and Cranking Things Up with
SID LUFT

BING! & FRANK!
(Making Music & Sometimes Love with Crosby & Sinatra)

ROYAL WEDDING
Furious, Judy Gets Disinvited.
Jane Powell Replaces Her as its Female Lead

Touring the U.K. and In the Mood for
LONDON'S PALLADIUM
Judy Spurs, Cajoles, and Needles Her Manager/Escort to Set Up a Booking

Chapter Twelve, Page 323

Saddled With a Reputation as a
Temperamental, Drug-Addicted Über Diva,
JUDY ENTERS HER CONCERT YEARS
Zing! Went the Strings of Their Hearts
in L.A., San Francisco, and at The Palace in NYC

THE SID & JUDY SHOW
Fistfights & Brawls with Unlucky Motorists,
Work Colleagues, & With One Another

HELL AT HOLMBY HILLS
Sid, Judy, and Their Entourage Battle Suicide Attempts,
Unstable Income, Spontanous Combustions, and the IRS

ETHEL GUMM & THE BIRTH OF LORNA
Alienated and Embittered, Judy's "Stage Mother from Hell"
Departs Angrily for the Land of Oz.

THE DUKE AND DUCHESS OF WINDSOR
Invite the Lufts for Society Gossip & Overspending in Palm Beach

A STAR IS BORN
The Cinematic Celebration of a Man That Got Away

Chapter Thirteen, Page 353

GETTING AWAY FROM IT ALL
Sid & Judy's Brouhahas on the Côte d'Azur

"IT'S A SNAKE PIT"
Judy's Review of the French "Rest Clinic" to which she's Temporarily Committed

20,000 Screaming Fans Attend the Opening of
A STAR IS BORN
The End of an Era, It's the Last Great Star-Studded Premiere in Tinseltown

JUDY GOES BALLISTIC
The Convoluted Academy Awards Of 1954

PACKING IT IN WITH THE RAT PACK
Very Cool, Very Hip, Very Vegas

JUDY'S AFFAIR WITH PRINCE ALY KHAN
Cosmopolitan, Spectacularly Promiscuous, and Unimaginably Rich,
He's a Direct Descendent of the Prophet Mohammed

PAUL NEWMAN, *The Helen Morgan Story*, &
THE THREE FACES OF EVE
Judy: *"It's a tacky little film noir that no one will see."*
Joanne Woodward Makes It Her Own and Later, Wins an Oscar.

Chapter Fourteen, Page 389

BITTER AND BROKE, JUDY
Records Albums & Entertains Random Beaux,

Begins a "Dazzling" Seven-City Tour but Sours It by Cutting the Ending Short

Crafts TV Specials for Ford Motor Co. &
Ronald Reagan's General Electric Theater,

Complains about Her Failing Marriage,

"Does Vegas,"

Hires Alan King as Her "Warm-Up" Act,

& Moves Sid and Her Children to Scarsdale.
Liza: *"I didn't fit in."*

She Attempts Multiple Suicides & Self-Mutilations,

Profoundly Alienates the Owners of a Major Nightclub in Brooklyn,

and Opens another act at The Dominion Theatre in London.

"Liza, take your mother's advice. Follow me as the best example of what not to do."
—Judy Garland

FALLING IN LOVE AGAIN, & AGAIN, & AGAIN
Eddie Fisher, Douglas Fairbanks, Jr., Glenn Ford

PARIS: LE PALAIS DE CHAILLOT
How do you say "Judy" in French?

IS THIS ANY WAY TO RUN A MARRIAGE?
Management Changes: Luft is Out; Begelman In

OF COURSE, SHE'S AN EMOTIONALLY DAMAGED WRECK
But Critics Insist "Her Pipes Are Better Than Ever"

PARTIES AT THE WHITE HOUSE
Jack! Jackie! Bobby! Ethel!

JUDGMENT AT NUREMBERG
Crimes Against Humanity

CARNEGIE HALL
"Judy! Judy! Judy! Becomes a Mantra for Thousands of Her Fans

Chapter Seventeen, Page 479

WHY DID JUDY DEFINE 1961 AS HER BEST YEAR?
Read About It Here

AMERICAN PIE
Judy Tours the U.S.

STEVIE PHILLIPS
As the Suicidal Diva's Handler, She Asks,
"What's a Nice Girl Like Me Doing in a Place Like This?"

GAY PURR-EE!
In an Animated Cartoon, Judy Talks Like a French Pussy.
"Sir Lancelot" (Robert Goulet) Plays a Horny Tomcat.
& Hermione Gingold Stars as "Mme Rubens-Chatte"

TV MAGIC
with Frank (Sinatra) & Dean (Martin)

LIZA Gets Cast as Anne Frank in a High School Play

GAY MEN ADORE HER
Judy Reinforces Her Status as a Quasi-Religious Icon

A CHILD IS WAITING
(and Waiting, and Waiting, and Waiting)
With the Collaboration of Bonny Burt (Lancaster),
Who Plays a Child Therapist and Hospital Administrator

Chapter Eighteen, Page 505

THE SLAMMING OF DOORS & THE GNASHING OF TEETH
As a Business Team and as a Marriage, "Sid and Judy" Become Unglued

JUDY KIDNAPS HER CHILDREN
Sid Pursues Them in the U.S. & British Courts

THE LONELY STAGE
It's the Only Place Where Judy Can Go On Singing

SLUGFEST AT THE SAVOY
Miss Garland vs. Mrs. Begelman

HANDLING JUDY
Sexually Liberated, Sardonic, & Sophisticated,
Dirk Bogarde Has Greatness Thrust Upon Him.

CRASH DIETS & TOO MANY PILLS
Judy Collapses at Lake Tahoe, then Rallies in Chicago

TWO JACKS (Paar and Kennedy) AND A JUDY
Enigmatic, Thin-skinned, and Mercurial, Jack Paar, as a TV Host,
Is Like "Little Lord Fauntleroy With a Switchblade."

JOURNEY BACK TO OZ
Liza Puts Her Best Foot Forward

Chapter Nineteen, Page 533

CBS-TV, THE SMILING COBRA & THE JUDY GARLAND SHOW
Spectacularly Dysfunctional, & Despite More of Judy's Widely Publicized
Suicide Attempts, 26 Episodes of Her Prime-Time TV Show
Get Stressfully Broadcast.

EXPLOITED AGAIN. WAS IT SABOTAGE?
Again and Again, CBS Denies Judy the Chance to Configure Her Show
the Way She Wants.
"I wanted Noel Coward as a guest on my show, but instead they give me
a Hillbilly Banjo Troupe and all the wrong advisors."

Judy is Presented with Evidence of
MAJOR EMBEZZLEMENTS FROM HER MANAGERS.
But Viewing Them as Vital to the Success of Her TV Series,
She Refuses to Confront Them.
"Okay, so Freddie and David took $300,000 from me. I stand to make $24 mil-
lion. I can deal with these crooks after the show gets successfully launched"

LIZA DANCES UP A STORM,
HELPS HOLD HER MOTHER TOGETHER,
AND BECOMES A THEATRICAL PERSONALITY IN HER OWN RIGHT.

GOSSIP FROM BEYOND THE LITTLE BLACK BOX
Barbra! Peggy Lee! Lena! Phil Silvers! Robert Goulet! Vic Damone!
Steve & Eydie! Bobby Darin! George Maharis!
& Judy's Backlot Intrigue With Other Guests on Her Show!

Chapter Twenty, Page 581

HOW CBS-TV'S *"THE JUDY SHOW"* STAGGERED
DYSFUNCTIONALLY ONWARD
"I've met The Devil, and his name is James Aubry"
—Judy's reference to the director of CBS

LEGALESE, SEX, & CONTRACT DISPUTES
Between the Sheets with Hollywood's Super Lawyer, Greg Bautzer

French Airs With Louis Jourdan,
A "Fart Fest" With Martha Raye, and
Ongoing Conflicts (*Carnival!*) With Liza

MORE ABOUT MEL TORMÉ (Hint: It Ended Badly)
Collaborations with Bobby Cole & Lionel Bart.

LIZA IS "FANTASTICK"
on the Road in Mineola, Miami, & Westport

MARK HERRON, JUDY'S AMBITIOUS 4th HUSBAND
He Isn't Perfect, But Neither Is Judy

MADNESS IN MELBOURNE: AN AUDIENCE IN REVOLT.
Judy's Soggy, Suicidal, Drug-Soaked Recovery in Hong Kong

INTRODUCING PETER ALLEN
Kangaroo Hopping With The Boy From Oz

Chapter Twenty-One, Page 621

SUICIDE & ARSON ATTEMPTS
DRUG ABUSE & SELF-MUTILATIONS

WIDELY PUBLICIZED ÜBER-DRAMAS
With Princess Margaret, Patricia Kennedy, Frenemies from the Old Days,
and Happenstance "Objects of Her Erratic Affections"

UNHARMONIOUS DISCORDS WITH LIZA

A CALIFORNIA D-I-V-O-R-C-E FROM SID, &
A Spontaneous (4th) Marriage at a Tacky All-Night Chapel in Vegas.

WEDDING BELL BLUES
More About Mark

JUDY! JUDY! JUDY!
Garfreaks and Their Musicological Feuds

PROMISCUOUS RONDELAYS WITHIN JUDY'S ENTOURAGE
"But it's the '60s, dahling..."

IS IT THE BEGINNING OF THE END?
As a Singer, Judy Flops in Cincinnati, Then Gets Hired as
"A Dysfunctional, Devouring Stage Mother" in a biopic of Jean Harlow

For Judy & Liza: What Becomes a Legend Most?
BLACKGAMA

Chapter Twenty-Two, Page 653

LIZA BECOMES A RED MENACE ONSTAGE,
A CABARET SENSATION AT THE PLAZA,
A RECORDING STAR (LIZA! LIZA! LIZA!)
AND A COMPETITIVE THREAT TO HER MOTHER.
Judy Considers Suing Her When Their Battles Escalate.

Judy Screens *The Wizard of Oz* for Her Children
"I think it's too scary for Kids."

JOHN CARLYLE GOES UNDER THE RAINBOW WITH JUDY
Before Seducing Her Husband

GOSSIPY CHITCHAT & SOCIAL HORROR
With Hedy Lamarr, Christopher Isherwood,
Angela Lansbury, & the Ex-Husband of Lana Turner.

Meanwhile, Peter Allen (now, Liza's Husband & Judy's Son-in-Law)
Becomes a Piano-Playing Staple at THE PLAYBOY CLUBS

HELL HATH NO FURY LIKE A PILL ADDICTED MEGA-DIVA SCORNED
Judy Trashes Her Dressing Room (Again)

The I.R.S. Gets Red, White, & Blue with Judy

MARK HERRON FINDS LOVE AT LAST
But After Multiple Fist Fights, It Isn't With Judy.

LOVE IS PAIN
The Sad and Tawdry Saga of Tom Green

THE VALLEY OF THE DOLLS
Pretentious, UnFunny, and Trashy,
It's Another Nail in Judy's Professional Coffin

OVERMEDICATED, EXHAUSTED, & MENTALLY UNSTABLE,
JUDY STAYS CAMERA-READY FOR CLOSEUPS
at Concert Gigs in Westbury (Long Island), The Palace (NYC),
Camden (NJ), Boston (Twice), Columbia (MD), Chicago, Cleveland,
Detroit, Indianapolis, Las Vegas, Holmdel (NJ),
& (with Horrible After-Effects) BALTIMORE

SAUCY AND SOPHISTICATED: TALK-TV INTERVIEWS WITH
Dick Cavett, Merv Griffin, Mike Douglas, & Johnny Carson
"On the Air, She's the Female Equivalent of Dean Martin...When He's Drunk"

"Garland's Onstage Pizzaz Still Holds"
UNTIL IT DOESN'T

"SHE'S A SCHEMING, INCOHERENT MESS."
After Another Aborted Stab at Finding a Writer
for Her Memoirs, Judy Unleashes New Horrors on Tom Green,
& Calls In an Anonymous Bomb Threat to a Broadway Theater.

THE MILE-HIGH CLUB: JUDY'S BRAWL AT 30,000 FEET
Nineteen Expensive & Embarrassing Hours of In-Flight Misery

FAMILY, FAMILY, FAMILY
Judy Lashes Out at Her Children

HEARTBREAKER: Two Months with John Meyer.
In London, Judy Becomes the Talk of the Town

MICKEY DEANS
The Man Who Wanted to Get Away, But Couldn't

DEATH OF AN ICON
"Judy Garland Was a Star in Her Final Role"
—NY Daily News

We Remember Judy Garland

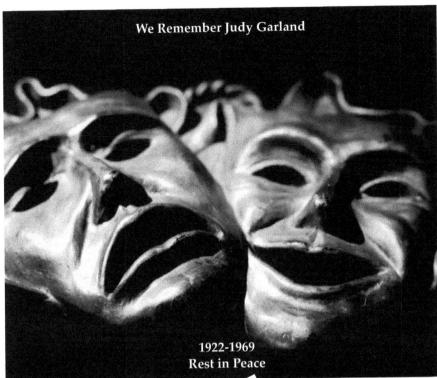

1922-1969
Rest in Peace

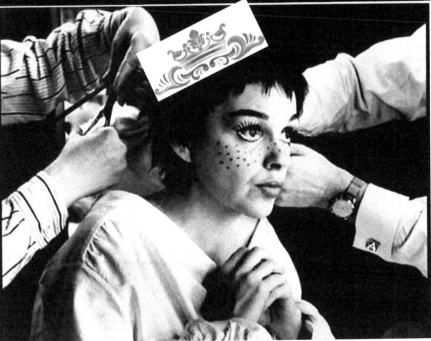

BORN IN A TRUNK

UNWANTED AND ALMOST ABORTED, BABY JUDY
DISLIKES HER MOTHER, ADORES HER FATHER, AND
SHINES ONSTAGE, EVEN AS A TWO-YEAR-OLD

"I was born to sing and to take people's minds off their troubles for awhile if I can."

—Judy Garland

"Youth isn't all it's cracked up to be. There are so many terrible things to find out about."

—Judy Garland

"If you think being Judy Garland is rough, imagine what it was like grow-ing up as Frances Gumm. It was brickbats thrown at me that I could never erase from my memory. One time when I was only eight years old, they threw cheese at me and a rotten tomato. One critic called me 'a pathetic ornament left over from the dying days of vaudeville.' But I showed the bastards."

—Judy Garland

Frances Gumm, later Judy Garland, was not "born in a trunk," but she well could have been. Both of her parents were vaudeville troupers.

Her father, Francis Avent Gumm, nicknamed Frank, was born in 1886 into Southern gentry in the little hamlet of Murfreesboro in Tennessee hill country, fifty miles southeast of Nashville. His ancestors, mostly Irish, were among the early settlers of the state—in fact, a neighboring village was named Gumm after their family.

Sadly, both of his parents died when he was twelve, and his older sister had to assume the burden of rearing the family.

Like his future daughter, Judy Garland, young Frank grew up wanting to become a professional singer. He began by becoming the lead singer in the church choir. On an impulse when he was only twelve, he ran away from home to join a minstrel show. For years, he carried around a photograph of him snapped in blackface, imitating Al Jolson, with a ukulele under his arm.

There was later speculation that he was frequently molested by other male performers during this vagabond period of his youth.

`A stocky, healthy, and fairly good-looking teenager, he eventually returned home finding his family in dire financial straits. To earn money, he rode the rails back and forth to Chattanooga. The boy soprano had morphed into a sweet baritone, warbling such favorites as "Danny Boy" or "After the Ball" before he passed the hat among passengers.

His hard-working sister had put aside enough money to send him to the Sewanee Military Academy, a private preparatory institution.

`Wanting to continue his education, he had no more money. Luck came his way when the richest man in his hometown, George M. Darrow and his wife, Tempe, took an interest in him. Frank was a frequent visitor at their home, Oak Manor, an elegant Italianate villa with a dozen bedrooms. Black servants presented seven courses nightly. Darrow told Frank, "I was a poor boy from Nebraska, who just happened to marry into money."

In time, Darrow defined himself as the boy's godfather.

Frank turned thirteen in 1899, and Darrow generously agreed to finance his term at Sewanee, an Episcopalian boy's school attached to the University of the South, about sixty miles southeast of Murfreesboro. Sewanee was set high on the Cumberland Plateau, some eight hundred feet above sea level.

He recalled his months spent there as "the happiest time of my life," and it was also the setting where he came into his sexuality and developed a lifelong attraction to teenage boys, something that would remain with him long after he became an adult. Word soon spread through the dorms that he liked to "service" his fellow students. Even late at night, boys in their underwear could be seen coming and going from his room. His roommate had moved out.

After only two years, he dropped out when his sister called him to return home to help his impoverished family. He heeded her call and returned to his hometown, where he was hired at the local Town Hall as a court reporter.

For four years, he held onto this boring job as a stenographer until he could take it no more. He relocated

Upper photo, **Frank Gumm** in 1926, two years after the birth of Judy and deeply involved in his same-sex affair with another man.

(lower photo) a late-in-life photo

2

to the town of Tullahoma, Tennessee, a resort and health spa some forty miles to the southeast of his hometown. He joined a barbershop quartet and got bookings at weddings, anniversary parties, and receptions.

He still held onto his dream of becoming a vaudeville singer, and one day he decided to leave Tennessee behind him. He joined the vaudeville circuit, traveling from town to town, sleeping in seedy hotels and often having to move on after only a one-night gig.

In the autumn of 1911, he settled in the logging town of Cloquet, Minnesota, where he got a job managing two small movie houses, the Bijou and the Diamond. He lasted in that post for only nine weeks before he was forced to leave town.

He'd developed a reputation for seducing teenage boys he hired as ushers. He packed up and fled late one night, heading twenty miles east to Superior, Wisconsin.

It was here that he met his future wife, Ethel Marion Milne.

***

Born in 1893, Ethel Marion Milne became the mother of the future Judy Garland. She was Canadian, the daughter of Scottish parents, her father, a railroad worker, crossed the border and headed south in 1888, settling into the Great Lakes district. There, he got married and started a family.

Ethel was the first of eight children, and she inherited her limited musical talent from her parents. Her mother played the piano, her father the violin. For a while, both of Ethel's parents toured in a medicine show, hawking a foul-tasting laxative.

As a teenager in Superior, she landed a job playing the piano to provide background music for the silent flickers shown at the Orpheum movie house.

Rather stout, she stood less than five feet tall, with very black eyes that were a wee bit crossed. In her late teens, she was interested in finding a beau, perhaps getting married one day, but she was not popular and found no one who wanted to date her.

She was rather plain looking, but "I could paint a face on myself." Like her future daughter, Judy, she did not watch her diet. When Frank met her, she was rather plump, always ordering second helpings at the family table and doubling down on desserts.

At the time she met her future husband, she was only twenty, although later in life, she "shaved" three years off her age.

Frank, age twenty-nine, arrived on the doorstep of her parents, John and Eva Milne, who ran a small boarding house in town. Eva

Frank Gumm, amicable, congenial, nonconformist, and adored by his daughter, the future superstar, Judy Garland.

rented him a room. The next night he walked Ethel down to the theater for her gig.

Unlike most homes in the area, this was not a devout Christian family, since Ethel's father was an avowed atheist.

Superior was a boisterous little port on the western shore of Lake Superior. As they passed along, a lot of boatmen were already drunk on the streets. Ethel liked Frank right away and managed to get him a part-time job at the Orpheum. He sang Irish ballads while reels of film were being changed in the booth overhead. "By the Light of the Silvery Moon" became his theme song.

As she later said, "It was his Irish smile that drew me to him, that and his eyes. They were dark brown and flecked with green."

Sometimes, the audience yelled out requests, as they would do at the concerts of his future daughter, Judy. "The Old Rugged Cross" was one of his crowd-pleasers.

One of Frank's most popular songs was "You Made Me Love You, I Didn't Want to Do It." That reflected his feelings for Ethel. Until he met her, he had planned to remain a bachelor for life, since his sexual interests did not center on a woman. But she changed all that.

He began to date Ethel, and, since funds were low, that meant a drink and a hot dog at the local tavern, which showcased live entertainment of the kind Frank performed.

There was talk of marriage, but suddenly one night when she came home, she found he'd checked out of her parents' boarding house and fled

Displayed above is a vaudeville theatre more ornate and elaborate than the dusty, rundown "frontier town" venues managed by **Frank and Ethel.** Inset photo shows a publicity photo of Judy's parents, already deeply disillusioned with each other, from one of their acts.

town, without leaving a forwarding address. As she later said, "That was my first heartbreak, the first of many to come."

The theater owner, her boss, tried to explain what had happened. One of the ushers claimed he was "bringing sexual assault charges."

"I don't want to hear such gossip," she flatly told him.

Frank had joined a traveling vaudeville circuit and played in twenty-eight states, often with one-night gigs. Tiring of that, he left his fellow performers in Portland, Oregon, where he got a job managing a local theater, the Crystal on Killingsworth Avenue.

That lasted for only a few weeks before what was becoming a pattern repeated itself. Two of the ushers complained to the theater owner that Frank, on several occasions, had tried to fondle them when they were in the dressing room changing into their gold-braided uniforms.

With money saved, he returned to Superior in October of 1913. He got a job singing, this time at the Parlor Theater. He soon learned that Ethel was now playing piano at the Lyric Theatre nearby.

Her parents were no longer taking in boarders, and he found lodgings elsewhere. When his romance with Ethel was re-ignited, she asked few questions about where he'd been or even why he'd left town without telling

Left photo: Vaudeville was the rage, an escape from the workaday humdrum that marked the lives of millions during the peak of the industrial age. Here's the front cover of a racy *belle epoque* "instruction manual" for how to break into show business

Middle photo: **Ethel Gumm** in 1925 as a vaudevillian, Virginia Lee, half of an act she organized, alongside her husband, Frank, and billed as the "Sweet Southern Singers."

Right photo: **AND THEN THERE WAS CAGNEY: James Cagney,** the latter-day "Ultimate vaudevillian," playing a "hoofer" in the biopic of George M. Cohan, *Yankee Doodle Dandy.* Released during the darkest year of World War II (1942), it lightened the spirits of Americans with elaborate song-and-dance numbers and memories of happier times.

her.

Soon, they were planning to get married, and they applied for a license. He carried it around for a month, as if hesitating to marry her.

One night, he confessed to her that he was worried the he could not satisfy a woman, but she assured him she would be patient and understanding. She also confessed that she was still a virgin.

Their wedding took place January 22, 1914, and it was attended by her parents, although her father didn't believe in church weddings, suggesting they could have more easily gotten married at Town Hall. "You kids don't need all this religious mumbo-jumbo."

On their two-day honeymoon, they spent most of the time rehearsing a vaudeville act, deciding to bill themselves as "Jack and Virginia Lee, and go on the road, as "Sweet Southern Singers."

After months of touring, Ethel announced one night that she was pregnant. They decided that very evening to settle down in the town where they were appearing at the time. It was Grand Rapids, Minnesota.

He got a job managing the New Grand, one of a duo of movie houses in town. As manager, he hired Ethel to play the piano for the silent movies he booked. In addition to running the theater, he also sang in his rich Irish brogue.

The local *Herald-Review* praised his performances, calling them "clean, decent, and fun for the entire family."

Grand Rapids was only eighty miles northwest of Superior, so Ethel on occasion could visit her parents. Frank, for reasons of his own, refused to return there.

With enough money coming in, Ethel and Frank purchased a house of their own to raise a family. On September 24, 1915, Ethel gave birth to her first child, an 8 ½ pound girl she named Mary Jane Gumm. [*She later changed her name to Suzanne.*]

Only two nights after delivering her child, Ethel joined Frank on stage, singing two big hits from 1915: "The Old Gray Mare" and "There's a Broken Heart for Every Light on Broadway."

By 1917, their vagabond life was coming to an end. On July 4, the birth date of the famous showman George M. Cohan, a second daughter arrived. She received the name of Dorothy Virginia, nicknamed "Jimmy"—later spelled "Jimmie."

Her birth delayed Dr. Hirsh who was to make an Independence Day speech in the town square.

The following day, Frank, in a private confab with Ethel, told her, "That's going to be the last time you give birth. I don't want any more kids, certainly no more girls, perhaps a boy. If so, I'll name him Frank Junior."

After the second birth, Frank would often not come to her bed for weeks at a time, although she complained that she was at her sexual peak. He preferred a smaller bedroom, about the size of a pantry, down the hall.

To the public, he presented a smooth, polished façade of a Southern gentleman, dressed in white suits and shoes. Glib and witty, his outgoing personality won many admirers. At home, he was moody and sulking, a man unfulfilled and bored with family life. On occasion, he threw a temper fit. Sometimes, he'd leave Ethel and his assistant manager to run the theater and set on out mysterious trips to Chicago, never revealing why he went there.

When he returned home after one long weekend in Chicago, Ethel told him he'd have to handle their daughters and the theater, since she was leaving for an extended visit with her parents in Superior. Once there, and in a confidential talk with her mother, she confided, "After five years of marriage, I'm not getting what I want from a husband, He doesn't fulfill me, and I long to be loved."

Eva Milne assured her, "You'll get used to it. Most married women after a few years come to realize that their dream of a dashing knight on a white horse was merely to grace their dreams. It's not realistic to expect any more from a man. I don't. The most important thing is to concentrate on being a good mother instead of some sexpot of a wife."

***

Love entered Frank's life when a medical student, Marc Rabwin, arrived at his theater in Grand Rapids in June of 1920. Handsome, charming, and outgoing, the tall, well-built young man was only nineteen years old. At school, he was known to make feminine hearts flutter, even though he bunked with a homosexual roommate, Bill Thomas, a football player.

He was only a freshman at the University of Minnesota Medical School. To support himself, he spent the summer selling some fifty Western films throughout the state, going from town to town, movie theater to movie theater.

His father advised him to skip remote Grand Rapids, which lay near the Canadian border. "Some jerk named Frank Gumm runs it, a real bastard. The town has just one theater and only 4,000 residents."

For some reason, Marc decided to go there anyway. Arriving in town, he walked down the main street, heading for the new Grand Theatre, carrying a suitcase full of movies. His first meeting with Frank was right before the two o'clock afternoon silent picture was about to start. Frank was not only taking tickets but selling freshly popped corn.

After the last ticket holder came in and the show began, he turned his full attention to Marc. Perhaps seeing how strikingly good looking he was, he handed him a fresh bag of popcorn.

"The guy held my hand for a long time," Marc later told his homosexual roommate at the university after his return that fall. "I had a hard time retrieving my palm. That guy really was switched on by me. We talked for about a half hour and really bonded. When I had to take a leak, he directed me into the men's room, taking the urinal next to mine. I guess he liked what he saw. He asked me to come home with him and his family after closing hour and spend the night."

That night, after Ethel and the Gumm Sisters went home, Marc and Frank shut down the theater and went to a late-night tavern catering to sailors. "We talked and talked. By the time I got to his house, everyone was asleep. He invited me to sleep with him in this small room with a three-quarter bed. I knew what was coming. He really gave me a good time. You see, I love to be body worshipped—and a lot of people won't do that—especially girls."

The next morning, Frank told Ethel, "Marc is the son you never gave me."

Planning to stay only one night, Marc spent two weeks with the family. Ethel kept her distance from him, but the daughters liked him a lot, ending up calling him "Uncle Marc."

Within three days, Frank took him shopping, buying him two new suits and a pair of alligator shoes imported from Miami.

When the Gumm girls were set to perform a skit inspired by *Uncle Tom's Cabin*, Marc helped them with their makeup and costumes. Jimmy, the younger sister, was cast as Little Eva. Suzanne, in blackface, was Topsy with corkscrew curls.

***

When Marc had to go back on the road, Frank bid him a tearful goodbye. The young man promised weekend visits twice a month, and both of them plotted a summer vacation, exploring the wilds of neighboring Canada.

He kept his promise, on many a weekend arriving on a Friday night and leaving Monday morning. On Sunday mornings, he and Frank didn't emerge from the bedroom until noon.

One weekend was different from all the others. Marc arrived at the Gumm home to find a very distraught Frank in conflict with Ethel. "She's pregnant again," Frank confided after calling Marc aside. "We don't want the kid. You're studying to be a doctor. Can't you help us get rid of it?"

"I probably could, but I won't," he said. "I just can't do it. I'm opposed to abortion."

After a long talk that night, Frank agreed to let Ethel carry the infant to term. But once Marc left to return to the university, he and Ethel plotted to get rid of the child—first, by her swallowing some powerful, foul-tasting laxative; second by driving along bumpy country roads where she bounced up and down hard on the back seat, in rhythms that accentuated the lurches and potholes.

Nothing seemed to work, and

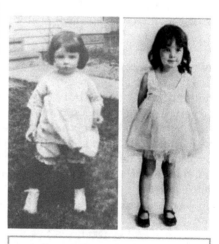

Born an unwanted child, **Baby Frances Gumm** later said, "The first three years of my life were the happiest I would ever know, the only tranquil period I ever had."

the couple finally gave up. "Maybe it'll be born a boy," he said. "All we need is another girl."

Without ever knowing it, Marc may have spared the life of one of the world's greatest entertainers, Judy Garland.

***

At 5:30am, Frances Ethel Gumm came into the world on June 10, 1922 at the Grand Rapids Hospital, weighing seven pounds. Delivered by Dr. H. E. Binet, "she arrived kicking and screaming," the doctor said, "This one resisted leaving the cozy womb to face life on the outside."

The next day, she was driven to her modest new home at the corner of Second Avenue and Fourth Street.

In time, as the baby grew up, she would be written about in newspapers across the globe. But the first mention of her in a paper occurred on July 19 when the local paper (Grand Rapid's *Herald-Review*) carried notice of her baptism at the local Episcopal Church.

Although she'd entered the world showing off the power of her lungs, Frances, as a little snub-nosed and homely baby, rarely cried.

Frances came to despise her mother, but she adored her father and crawled up on his lap whenever possible. When Marc arrived, he showered the infant with love, perhaps aware that were it not for him, she would not have been there.

He also visited for the Christmas holidays when Frances—nicknamed "Baby" or "Babe"—was just two years old, making her first appearance on the stage. On December 26, 1924, at the New Grand, the little tot came out onto the stage with a dinner bell and sang "Jingle Bells" in a surprisingly loud voice. She then rang the dinner bell and was greeted with thunderous applause, which she relished. Then she sang it again…and again…and again until Frank rushed out onto the stage, grabbed her, and hauled her off as applause reached a crescendo.

Frances got her first review, published in *The Herald-Review*: "The work of Frances Gumm, a two-year-old baby, was a genuine surprise. The baby girl was heard by everyone in the house."

***

Frank might have had his Marc, although Ethel could never understand how a young man with "matinee idol looks" would spend any time with her "dowdy husband with the middle age spread."

"I'm having my own torrid affair. It's with Valentino, on the screen," she said. "I think this Latin lover is the sexiest man on the planet, and I often dream of him. Charlie Chaplin is fun to watch with all his crazy antics, but who would want to go to bed with him? Give me Rudi any day."

The time eventually came for Marc and Frank to say goodbye, as he would soon be departing for California where he would be employed as a doctor in a Los Angeles hospital.

9

Before he left, Frank and Marc toured for a month through the wilds of Northern Canada.

The two lovers wrote to each other frequently. Marc urging Frank to pull up stakes in Minnesota and head west to sunny California.

Frank began to think seriously about a move west.

Otherwise, business as usual continued at the New Grand, with Frances becoming one of the Gumm Sisters. She would soon be the star attraction.

Occasionally, Ethel deserted her piano to sing a solo, perhaps "I'm Saving It for a Rainy Day."

As Frances grew older, it appeared that she was the only real talent in the act.

In an article entitled, "There Will Always Be Another Encore," Judy remembered herself as a little girl. "Daddy had a wonderful voice, but my mother didn't sing well, and she played the piano very badly. They had a lousy act. And we kids were awful, too. Mother was untalented but very touching. She was a very lonely and determined woman."

Even as a little girl, Frances called her mother Ethel. After Ethel had delivered what Frances thought was a horrible performance at the theater, she turned on her mother at the dinner table and said, "You stink, Ethel!"

Judy Garland would later remember the slap that immediately followed. It was so hard it knocked her down. "It wasn't until I married that bum, Sid Luft, that I got a slap to equal that of Ethel."

The Gumm Sisters didn't always go over," Frances said. "Sometimes we got 'bombs' thrown at us—in this case, rotten tomatoes and eggs. Even if the audience hated us, our little trio would join hands at the end of our act and gracefully bow to an audience as it booed us."

When summer came, Frank drove his wife and children on a working vacation to the West, making vaudeville stage appearances in some of the country's most obscure towns, most of which were eager for almost any form of entertainment.

"I did those horrible Egyptian belly-rolls in Arabian harem balloon pants and a lot of bracelets and spangles," the future Judy Garland recalled. "My sisters wore Spanish costumes with those funny hats with little balls hanging around the brims and toreador pants, singing, 'In a Little Spanish Town.'"

In the fourth year of her life, Frances went out on stage on June 9, 1926 to entertain an audience in Devil's Lake, North Dakota. That was followed by shows in Harve, Shellby, Kalispell, and Whitefish, all towns in Montana. Heading for Washington State, the Gumms went on stage in Cashmere and Leavenworth.

At long last, they reached Los Angeles, where Frank disappeared for three days in Palm Springs with Marc. On July 10, they opened at the Erlanger's Mason Theatre on the same bill with the more famous Duncan Sisters. Marc attended the show for a reunion with Ethel and her girls.

A week later, all the Gumms were back in Grand Rapids, performing once again at the New Grand.

***

Having bid farewell to Marc, this time in California, Frank, back in Minnesota, became intrigued with Bob Grant, the captain of the basketball team at the local high school. At age seventeen, he was tall and handsome, with a muscular but lean body. On his father's side, he had Indian blood.

At Danny's Bar, where the small gay colony in Grand Rapids gathered, he told the other patrons that he had fallen for Bob when he was covering sports for the *Herald-Review.* "I saw him in the communal shower—and I was a goner."

After writing two or three sports stories about him, predicting he'd become one of the state's star athletes, he was a most welcome visitor at the home of his parents, Jeffrey and Betty Grant. They seemed unaware of what was going on and were pleased that such a prominent citizen was taking an interest in their son. When Bob got his driver's license, Frank bought him a second-hand Ford, and frequently gave him presents, including clothes, a watch, and sports gear. Parents were a lot more innocent in those days.

Bob often dined with the Gumms, and the sisters, including Frances, "adored" him. Soon, they were calling him "Uncle Bob." Frank often took him on long trips, ostensibly searching out the best college for him in the Great Lakes region. One weekend, he took him to Chicago where a friend of his, a gay photographer, took nude pictures of the teenager.

One night in October of 1926, Frank slept over at the Grant household, sharing Bob's bed. When they did not come down for breakfast the next morning, Betty went upstairs to retrieve them because Bob was due at school.

None of the doors were locked, and she had a habit of just barging into the bedrooms of any of her children. Such was the case when she opened the door to Bob's bedroom to discover Frank fellating her son.

She became hysterical and Bob's father struck Frank, bloodying his nose. He fled from the house, as the Grants began threatening to call the local police chief.

That very day, Frank placed his assistant manager in charge of the New Grand. At home, he told Ethel, Frances, and his other two daughters to pack all their things. He said they were heading for Los Angeles. "In sunny California, we'll find a new life," he promised them.

That night, before their morning departure, Frank and Ethel performed their Sweet Southern Singing act and the Gumm Sisters did their routine. It became their farewell show to Grand Rapids.

The next morning, they hit the road for the long trek across the country. Along the way, Ethel assured Frances that she was going to take her around from studio to studio to see if she might become a child star in pictures like Baby Peggy.

BABY
PEGGY

in

"*The*
FLOWER GIRL"

produced by
CENTURY FILM Co.
distributed by
UNIVERSAL

Baby Frances Gumm
(later known as Judy Garland)

Baby Peggy
(later known as Diana Serra Cary)

BREADWINNING BABIES: At least some of her parents' stage ambitions for **Baby Frances** (left photo) derived from her physical likeness to one of the silent era's most wildly popular child stars, **Baby Peggy** (right), the focal point of *The Flower Girl (1924)*.

So during the bleak days of the Great Depression, when Baby Frances began showing an almost alarming stage talent, her parents rushed her into an up-front-and-centered position on stage with "The Gumm Sisters" and began plotting what they hoped would be a lucrative career in show-biz.

12

THE ROAR OF THE CROWD

JUDY, AS "BABY GUMM DROP," GETS HOOKED ON SHOW-BIZ

"The roar of the crowd—that wonderful, wonderful sound ringing in my ears—convinced me I was born to perform."

—Judy Garland

Leaving Grand Rapids late in October of 1926, Frank in his Buick touring car headed west with Ethel and his three dancing, singing daughters, the Gumm Sisters. He knew that his friend, Marc Rabwin, was waiting for him on the West Coast. Two years before, he had obtained his medical degree.

After the last lap, through the searing heat of the desert, the Gumm family headed down Holly-wood Boulevard on their way to the Rabwin home for lunch, as agreed.

But first, Ethel demanded they stop at the newly built Grauman's Chinese Theatre, the creation of showman Sid Grauman. She got out of the car in front of the theater for a look outside. Cuddled in her arms, Frances was still asleep but woke up in the glare of sunlight.

Years later, movie star Judy Garland would step into the glare of Kleig lights, as she made her way into the theater.

California Dreamin': To starstruck newcomers like the Gumm family, from the frigid winters of provincial Minnesota, **Grauman's Chinese Theatre** looked like this shortly after its construction in 1927.

Clad in mink and in towering high heels, she would wave and blow kisses at her adoring fans.

Already, some major stars had embedded imprints of their hands and feet in cement in front of the theater, a tradition that would follow for years ahead, stretching down the block, including the imprints of Judy Garland.

As Frank came up beside her, Ethel said, "It's not just a theater. It's a grand cathedral."

Gossip columnist Hedda Hopper later wrote of the Gumm's arrival in Tinseltown: "Ethel and Frank Gumm and the Gumm Sisters, including the future star, Judy Garland, arrived in Hollywood like a flock of hungry locusts driven by the gale winds of their prompting, ruthless mother. One look into the eyes of this woman told you what was on her mind. 'If I can get this kid of mine on the screen, I might just hit it big.' She took the little creature, her young daughter, scarcely old enough, and trained her like a buck sergeant, drilling her to shuffle through a dance step and sing a song. She robbed Judy of her childhood, instructing her to keep the waves in her hair, the pleats in her dress, and the pink polish of her little nails."

At the Rabwin home, a festive Mexican luncheon prepared by their South of the Border cook awaited them. Frank was obviously overjoyed to be with Marc again. But he was disappointed to learn that he had not been able to find an available theater in Frank's meager price range in Los Angeles. [Frank's entrepreneurial dream involved running all aspects of a theater, everything from determining what movies would appeal, managing its food and beverage services, hiring organists to provide the musical accompaniments to silent films, even bringing in between-reel song and dance acts that included the Gumm Sisters.] He had taken a week off from the hospital and would drive Frank to outlying towns, looking for a theater to lease. Frank had instructed him, "As a rental, it has to be cheap. I've got to hang on to my money."

Later that afternoon, Marc escorted the family to their lodgings in a seedy hotel in the downtown area to check them in.

All the Gumms would have to share one small room, with use of a hallway bathroom. Later, after seeing some of the other tenants, Ethel concluded her fellow roomers were "either a whore or a drunk."

On their first night at the hotel, Frank disappeared with Marc and didn't return until morning. Later that day, they set out together to find a theater. After four days of fruitless searching, Marc suggested they head for Lancaster, a very small town (population 500) which lay sixty miles northeast of Los Angeles, a desert outpost 2,350 feet above sea level. It was separated from the metropolis by the San Gabriel Mountains. To its east lay the Mojave Desert, inhabited by scorpions and rattlesnakes, its most dramatic vegetation being the Joshua Tree (yucca). Rabbits scampered among the screwbean and mesquite bushes, and temperatures in summer reached 120°F. The San Andreas Fault cut directly through the center of the town.

Marc had arranged for Frank to meet the owner of the theater, Whitley Carter, who was also the town mayor. He had constructed a 500-seat theater, a seat for every resident of the town. The townspeople mocked him, calling it "Carter's Folly."

The theater only became half-full on Saturday afternoon when two matinee westerns were shown, luring real cowboys from the desert or mountains.

Celluloid cowboys also passed through the town, stopping over, since many silent films were shot nearby in Red Rock Canyon.

The theater had become dilapidated, and the present lease would not expire for six months. But once Frank saw the Antelope Valley Theatre had a stage, he agreed to rent it.

Eager to find a renter, Carter had lowered the price, making it "real cheap."

Since it was the only theater for many miles around, its manager could sell tickets for fifty cents each. *[In Grand Rapids, he got only a quarter per seat.]*

After their deal was signed and sealed, Frank and Marc headed back to Los Angeles, opting to spend the night together at a small roadside motel ten miles from the city limits of Los Angeles.

Later that night, Marc delivered Frank some devastating news. He was dating a young woman from Hollywood and planned to get married. To soften the blow, he agreed to drive to Lancaster every other weekend to be with Frank.

As it turned out, Marc would fall in and out of love several times before eventually wedding Marcella Bennett in 1934.

While Frank and Marc were away together, Ethel enrolled her three daughters in a dance school run by Ethel Meglin, who also directed a dance troupe, the "Meglin Kiddies Dancers."

After auditioning the Gumm Sisters, she signed them to a training program and agreed to try to secure bookings for them. She was especially charmed by Frances. "That is one talented cutie pie," she told Ethel, "but you should get rid of that awful name of Frances. As for your older daughters, forget it. They'll never make it."

With her daughters, Ethel toured the various studios, including MGM, the future home

What Baby Frances saw in **Lancaster, California**, the year of her arrival there.

of Judy Garland. In the days before the advent of sound recording for film, "rubber-neckers" were regularly allowed into the studios to watch films being shot.

Within just a few days, the Gumm Sisters got to see Marion Davies, the mistress of the press baron, William Randolph Hearst, filming a scene. On another day, they witnessed John Gilbert emoting, and got to shake the hand of Lon Chaney. From a distance, they also watched Lillian Gish execute a scene from her latest movie, *Auntie Laurie.*

On March 17, 1927, Ethel was able to arrange the first booking for her daughters in Los Angeles. They sang and danced at the Biltmore Hotel in Hollywood, entertaining at a luncheon for members of the Al Malaikah Temple Shrine. Each girl was paid fifty cents. The same fee prevailed when they were summoned back to the Biltmore on May 4, performing for the Kiwanis Club.

When it seemed that the Gumms would be living in Los Angeles for another six months, they moved into a house at 3154 Glen Manor in West Hollywood.

It was a stressful time for them during their search for money and careers, with home life always being sacrificed. Whenever Marc was free, he called Frank, who dropped whatever he was doing to run off with him.

Night after night, Ethel and Frank engaged in epic battles. Frances and her sisters heard the violent clashes, but they didn't dare to interfere in any way.

In the spring of 1927, the Gumm Sisters, with Ethel, moved to the bleak desert town of Lancaster. Frances would not only celebrate her fifth birthday there, but her eleventh as well. Of course, much of that time was spent with Ethel driving her daughters across the San Gabriel Mountains into Los Angeles seeking performance gigs for her daughters.

From the beginning, Frances found the desert air laden with dust and pollen, which made her hay fever all

In Hollywood, in the aftermath of the Great Depression, many stage mothers, including Ethel Gumm, dreamed of augmenting their family's meager incomes with acting gigs for their children, talented or not. As such, a widely recognized venue for training, development, and promotion of young wannabe stars involved enrollment in Meglin's Dance Studios. Run by Ethel Meglin as the premier training ground for "juvenile actors and dancers" in L.A.,, it had proven its merit through the development of child stars who had included Lorraine Grey, Virginia Grey, Maureen O'Connor, Jane Withers, June Lang, and the spectacularly successful Shirley Temple.

Pictured above is a scene from *Roaring Lead* (1933). The high-stepping dancers in the foreground were billed as the **"Meglin Kiddies Dancers."** The trio of dancing cowboys in back, completely forgotten today, included **Ray Corrigan, Robert Livingston, and Max Terhune.**

the worse. Sometimes, she'd wake up at night and scream, "I can't breathe."

In their theater, the New Lancaster, all five of the Gumms made their theatrical debuts. Frank and Ethel came on first, singing such favorites of the 1920s as "Bye Bye Blackbird" and "When the Red Red Robin Come Bob, Bob Bobbin' Along." They were followed by the Gumm Sisters.

The local newspaper, *The Ledger-Gazette,* reviewed their performance: "The little daughters completely won the hearts of the audience with their songs and dances."

For the big July 4 celebration that year, the entire family sang "Rocky Mountain Moonlight," written by Ethel.

In November of that year, Frank changed its name to the Valley Theatre as his daughters premiered their new act, "The Kinky Kid Parade." Frances came out in blackface, impersonating Al Jolson singing "Mammy" in *The Jazz Singer* (1927), one of the first films with sound.

She also pioneered a new routine in which she jumped out of a big hat box and performed a wild Charleston as the audience roared its approval. The dance was all the rage among flappers of the 1920s, as depicted on-screen by Joan Crawford. Frances had another routine in which she appeared in an Egyptian harem costume. "I had to do these horrible *Arabian Nights* belly rolls," she said.

A skeptical rancher, after riding his horse into town to see the show,

The Valley Theatre—formerly owned by the father of Judy Garland—depicted above as it looked shortly before it was torn down.

It was here that Frances Gumm, in harem pants, performed the Egyptian belly roll.

The Gumm Sisters in 1925, 1933, and 1934. It quickly became clear that "Baby Gumm Drop" (Judy) was the star of the trio.

17

gave his verdict: "That Frances Gumm is no girl—that's a fucking midget if you ask me."

On July 17, 1927, at the Valley Theatre, France made her debut as a solo performer, as her sisters watched from the wings. They weren't jealous that Frances was getting all the attention, as neither of them liked performing and kept hoping that in a few years some handsome young man would propose marriage and haul them away.

It was on that night, watching Frances onstage, that both Ethel and Frank agreed that "A Star Is Born."

"All my life I'd heard warblers on stage, but never a sound coming from a little girl like Frances," Frank said. "There was a certain magic to her strong, clear voice that could be heard in the balcony. It combined the pathos of an older woman with the sweet innocence of a little girl. She belted out a song with a high, throbbing sound, a sort of no-holds-barred soprano. Her voice was heart-breaking, or at least a heart about to burst. Even more remarkable was the audience. They wanted to protect her."

Dashing cowboy star **Fred Thomson** is depicted above with "America's sweetheart," **Mary Pickford.**

He was the object of Judy's first crush on a film star.

FRED THOMSON

In time, Judy Garland would meet most of the major movie stars in Hollywood and become friends with some of them, even lovers. But her first encounter with a movie star occurred when she was six years old in Lancaster.

Fred Thomson was one of the leading cowboy stars of silent pictures, ranking up there with Tom Mix and William S. Hart.

He rode into town one afternoon on his beautiful white horse, "Silver Lake," hitched the animal to a post outside Frank's theatre, and introduced himself to Frank and Frances. Her father had booked all his movies, and Frances had seen him on the screen many times. [He had played Mary Pickford's husband in The Love Light (1921) the year before she was born. In 1926 and again in 1927, he was the second highest-grossing star at the box office.]

He later invited Frances to ride with him on his horse, Silver Lake, as they headed toward Red Rock Canyon, where his latest western was being shot.

She once confessed, "I had a schoolgirl crush on him even at my tender age. I couldn't wait to grow up to marry him. Too bad. He was soon to die young."

[In early December of 1928, Thomson stepped on a rusty nail in his stable

18

and contracted tetanus, which was not properly diagnosed by his doctors. He died on Christmas Day, 1928. He was only thirty-eight years old.]

***

Along with her sisters, Frances was hauled back and forth in 1928, either to perform in Los Angeles at a children's hospital ward—or in a Christmas Show dressed as Cupid singing "I Can't Give You Anything But Love, Baby." That number led to the *Los Angeles Record* calling her "The Sophie Tucker of Tomorrow."

As the world would soon learn, Judy Garland was not only a great singer, but could dance as well. However, she would often be asked how she learned to act.

Later in life she recalled, "I never went to Actors Studio like Marlon Brando and a host of others. I learned to act by sitting in my father's theater in Lancaster and watching the stars of that day emote. My favorites were John Barrymore, Lillian and Dorothy Gish, Mary Pickford, Greta Garbo, John Gilbert, and Gloria Swanson. I stole from these greats."

***

Ethel and her three daughters almost weekly set out in their battered old Buick to cross the San Gabriel Mountains into Los Angeles, where they lodged in their rented apartment. They performed at school parties, benefits, weddings, even a Shriner's luncheon.

Sometimes, they joined one of Ethel Meglin's productions of the Meglin Kiddies. She still ran her School of Dance and had become a good friend of Ethel Gumm.

The two Ethels became confidants. The mother of the Gumm Sisters told Meglin, "Don't worry about the husband I left behind in Lancaster. He's glad to get rid of me. He's quite busy at night. He hires handsome teenage boys as ushers—you know, those who can fulfill his sexual needs."

In 1928, a career highlight for Frances and her sisters occurred when they were asked to perform for KFI Radio in Los Angeles, a gig that lasted from August to October. On their first show, the sisters sang "You're the Cream in My Coffee" and, as a tribute to cowboy star William S. Hart, "There's a Long, Long Trail A-Winding."

As she commuted back and forth between Lancaster and Los

The Gumm Sisters (Frances on the left) made their film debut in 1929 in *The Big Revue* as the advent of sound hit Hollywood.

19

Angeles, Frances complained to Frank, "Ethel winds me up and sends me out there to perform, which I do. Then she locks me in the closet." Of course, she didn't mean that literally.

[Actually, whenever she wanted to punish Frances, Ethel would leave her locked in a room and go away, telling her, "I'm not coming back. You've seen the last of your mother."

She usually returned five or six hours later, finding her daughter crying and almost hysterical. "Serves you right," was Ethel's oft-repeated refrain.]

The Gumm Sisters capped 1928 by starring with 115 of the Meglin Kiddies in an All-Star Revue at the newly built Shriner Auditorium in Los Angeles in front of 6,000 spectators. Frances got to meet a newly emerging star, Joan Crawford. Backstage, she rapturously told Crawford, "I learned to do the Charleston by watching you in *Our Dancing Daughters* (1928)."

Frances Gumm had morphed into **Judy Garland** around the time she signed her first contract with Metro-Goldwyn-Mayer.

After the show, a young man appeared to escort Crawford home, and she introduced him to Frances. "Little girl, this is Clark Gable."

That was Frances' first meeting with Gable. Years later, when she was more famous and he was King of Hollywood, she would sing him her famous song, "Dear Mr. Gable."

Frances would also meet that event's other performing artists, too, including Myrna Loy, cowboy star Tom Mix, and the Mexican actress with the porcelain skin, Dolores Del Rio. She also met actress Billie Dove, who introduced her to the aviator-producer Howard Hughes backstage. Hal Roach's "Our Gang" members flirted with the older Meglin Girls."

Frank usually made it obvious that Frances was his favorite child, even though he'd lobbied to have her aborted. "She is such a little thing, frail and delicate, and she grows more beautiful every year. All that applause doesn't go to her head. She remains good-natured and loving. Nothing spoiled about her. She's a true Daddy's Girl. But she doesn't like Ethel. Neither do I."

***

In Lancaster, Frank and Ethel had little time to make close friends, only passing acquaintances. That changed when their neighbors, Will and Laura Gilmore, entered their lives. Ethel and Laura were the first to become friends, often shopping together at J.C. Penney's or at the local grocery store. Frank liked her, too, and agreed to let Laura and her children into the movie house for free.

Will Gilmore, a railroad engineer, was working at the time in San Diego and didn't return until three weeks later. Laura invited Frank over to meet her husband over dinner.

For Ethel, it must have been love at first sight. A graduate in engineering at the University of Nebraska, he was of mixed Irish and Indian blood, and seemed like a matinee idol with his good looks, broad shoulders, jet-black hair, and aquiline features.

The two couples soon became the town's "foursome," meeting for dinners and bridge games. Like the Gumms, the Gilmores also had three children. When the two broods met, they liked each other and often played games together.

At first, it seemed like an ideal situation of two compatible couples finding companionship in a small town.

Problems arose, however. First, it became obvious that Ethel was powerfully attracted to Will. The second problem arose when Laura suffered an almost deadly stroke and was confined to a wheelchair for the remainder of her short life.

Even though loving to Ethel, Will had a violent streak in him, as he was given to temper fits and sudden outbursts. Once, when a stray, starving dog tried to invade his chicken pen, he took a rake and embedded its teeth into the poor animal's back. Screeching in pain, it ran away with the rake still stuck in him and died, bleeding to death, on Main Street.

With Frank busy at the theater, Ethel often invited Will over to dinner with her daughters. From the beginning, Frances detested him and was forced to eat with "this mean man."

She later claimed, "He criticized everything about me—my appearance, the dress I wore, my table manners, even attacking my performances at Dad's theater. Ethel often joined in. One night when he didn't like what I said to my mother, he threw a glass of milk in my face at table, and I ran screaming to my room."

One day Frances was playing hide-and-seek with the Gilmore kids on their back lot. In the far corner stood a two-story shed.

Frances snuck in to hide out and decided to climb the stairs. So involved were Will and Ethel that they took no notice of her until she came upon him mounting her, with her mother urging him on.

A sudden noise from her attracted their attention. He shouted at her, "Get the hell out of here, you little bitch."

She ran in horror and would remember that afternoon for the rest of her life. She shared this discovery of her mother's adultery with no one, especially not with Frank, who may have known about it. He could hardly complain, as he was seducing teenage boys.

Little did Frances know at the time, but Will Gilmore would eventually become her stepfather.

***

In March of 1929, the Gumm family underwent a dramatic change.

Ethel took Frances and her other two daughters with her, as they packed up and headed south to Los Angeles, leaving Frank to fend for himself in Lancaster. Ethel's lover, Will Gilmore, with his paralyzed wife, Laura, had already settled in Los Angeles.

On March 1, an item appeared in Lancaster's local paper:

"Mrs. Frank Gumm and her three daughters leave next week for Los Angeles, where they will reside indefinitely in order that the girls may pursue special studies. They will spend their weekends in Lancaster, and Mrs. Gumm will return to play the piano in her husband's theater. Mr. Gumm will continue to reside in the family home on Cedar Avenue."

Their new home in the city would be in a very modest second-floor apartment at 1814 South Orchard, near Vermont Avenue and Washington Boulevard, close to the theater district.

Judy Garland looked back on those early years: "It wasn't Baby Gumm who ended up on the casting couch," she told tap-dancing star, Ann Miller. "It was Ethel herself. She was still an attractive woman, and she wanted us to get gigs so much, she would put out. In other words, she prostituted herself for us, especially for me, but they did not make me like her any more."

Judy also confessed that it was at this time that she began her life-long addiction to pills. "I was complaining of being tired all the time because of our rugged schedule. Ethel started giving me pep pills. But I would be so high strung that I was too jazzed up to go to sleep when it came time. So she gave me sleeping pills."

By April of that year, Frances continued to appear in the Meglin Kiddies Revue, which began to feature a solo act from her.

She developed an exit strategy for herself, disappearing behind the curtain but not before performing a back kick and a flounce of her small rear end. She labeled it as a farewell to her wildly appreciative audience. The first time Louella Parsons, the era's leading gossip maven, saw her perform, she suspected the Baby Gumm might be a midget.

In addition to her loud singing, she added different movement to her act, even doing cartwheels, back bends, flips, and splits. She often performed in emerald green harem pants suitable for a sultan's favorite in a court from the *Arabian Nights* of long ago—that is, if the sultan were a child molester.

Ethel enrolled her daughters in another theatrical school, Mrs. Lawlor's Professional School on Hollywood Boulevard. Here, Frances met two very young male stars who would become her friends. They were Donald O'-Connor and a pint-sized Mickey Rooney.

Three years younger than Frances, O'Connor was a native of Illinois born into a family of vaudeville performers. He told Frances that he'd been hauled out onto the stage when he was only thirteen months old. "My dad held me up by the back of my neck and ordered me to 'dance, kid, dance.'"

He later suffered the loss of his father in Brockton, Massachusetts, after he had a heart attack on stage. As Donald was always traveling from town to town, he had even less schooling than Frances.

Years later, O'Connor claimed, "I had this young crush, a powerful one at that, on Baby Gumm, but I expressed my love in a rather bizarre way."

He was no doubt referring to the night he was backstage with her in a vaudeville theater.

Frances herself remembered the incident. "Donald, that dear boy, asked me if I had ever seen a boy's penis, and I told him I had not. He then unbuttoned his pants and took out his little penis, which looked like a worm to me. It was not hard. Frankly, I thought it was sorta pathetic, and I asked him to put it back in his pants. Better than that, he taught me how to play jacks."

In the late 1930s, O'Connor became part of a young Hollywood set who hung out together. Not only O'Connor, but others formed a kind of unofficial club, chiefly Ann Rutherford, Mickey Rooney, Jackie Cooper, and Bonita Granville, each of whom was destined to become a star.

In later life, O'Connor jokingly asked Judy if she'd like him to expose himself to her again, promising, "It's much bigger now."

"Keep it in your pants," she told him.

Rooney would play a far greater role in Judy's life. Born Joseph Yule in Brooklyn, he was two years older than Frances. Like O'Connor, he, too,

Yesterday's wannabes, where are they today? Depicted above is part of the student body of **the Lawlor school** in 1934.

Two views of Judy's schoolmate, young **Donald O'Connor.**

Brash and bold, he decided to show Judy what little boys conceal in their pants.

had made his first stage appearance at an early age—seventeen months in his case.

"At Ma Lawlor's School, I was known as a profane little hoodlum," Mickey said. "She was a tall, lean, no-nonsense schoolmarm type with a background in show biz."

He went on: "The boys and girls in our class were a horny bunch. Instead of studying arithmetic or history, we sent love notes to each other. Everybody—the girls, too—were checking each other out. I adopted that old motto, 'If you're not near the girl you love, love the girl you're near.'"

"My first note to Frances Gumm, who was then of tender age, was simple and rather blunt—'Wanna fuck?'"

"Yes, I was one tough little rutabaga. I figured if I talked tough and used foul language, I would indeed be tough in spite of my size. I don't think Frances was too impressed with me."

"She later came to view me as the most talented actor in the history of the cinema, stealing every scene from her."

"I'm glad Frances changed her name like I changed my name to Mickey Rooney. Gumm was the wrong image—sticky, soft, chewy, *tutti-frutti*. Garland, on the other hand, was full of joy—it smelled of pine needles and sounded like sleigh bells and tasted like Christmas pudding."

He remembered the first time he ever saw Frances perform. It was at the Pantages Theatre in Hollywood. "She plants both feet wide apart, almost as if she were challenging the audience. Then she sang 'Zing! Went the Strings of My Heart' with the kind of verve that made our heartstrings, all ninety of us from the Lawlor School, go *bing, ding, ping, ring, ting,* and *zing.*"

One night after school, a lot of us kids got together," Judy recalled. "We played this game I'd never heard of called 'Post Office.' In a 1964 interview with *McCalls* magazine, she revealed "The future Mickey Rooney planted a great big gooey wet kiss with tongue on me."

The magazine editor edited her confession, phrasing it in more polite terms.

***

Ironically, movies in the 1920s had often featured musicals with no sound. But when talking pictures came in, especially beginning in 1929, musicals with sound became all the rage. Studios such as Warners began to film musical shorts, usually from ten minutes to as much as eighteen.

Thus, Frances Gumm, on June 11, 1929, made her film debut with her sisters, singing "That's the Good Old Sunny South. "It was shot at the Tec Art Studios in Hollywood for Mayfair Pictures. The two-reel short ran for eighteen minutes and had its premiere in August at the Fox Belmont Theatre in Hollywood. Frances had just turned seven.

The Big Revue was set in a glitzy night club with an all-boy orchestra and a trio of Gumms. "The camera fell in love with me, the beginning of a life-long affair, and I loved it back," Judy Garland remembered.

Although not naming her, one reviewer remarked on how talented

Frances was, claiming, "She was in complete and natural command of both the lyrics and her movements."

One gig followed another as Ethel kept getting engagements for her daughters. On July 16, they opened at the Bishop Theatre in Bishop, California, performing for 400 patrons.

Frances sang and danced with her sisters and then performed a solo act warbling "Wear a Hat With a Silver Lining," and "Little Pal." The local paper cited Baby Frances' "particular appeal because of her diminutive size and few years."

In mid-August, Frances and the Meglin Kiddies, billed as "56 Clever Tots," appeared on a bill with Stepin Fetchit at the Loew's State Theatre in Los Angeles.

Fetchit's reputation has undergone massive attacks by today's standards, but young Frances found him quick-witted and intelligent. Born in Key West, Florida, in 1902, he became one of the most controversial actors in the history of cinema.

Barry Monush wrote: "Fetchit's stock portrayal of a slow-talking, wide-eyed, shuffling, almost moronic black man in countless supporting parts of the 1930s has made his name synonymous with Hollywood's insensitive, racist attitude towards African-Americans." Over the course of his career, he worked with Janet Gaynor, Shirley Temple, Will Rogers, and, of course, the future Judy Garland.

By November, Frances and her fellow Gumms were signed by their mother to appear in a trio of "Vitaphone Kiddies" shorts for Video Varieties, a subsidiary of Warners. Formatted in two-color Technicolor, filming took place at the First National Studios in Burbank.

Directed by Roy Mack, the first was *A Holiday in Storyland,* billed as "a fantasy of childhood dreams in the glowing hues of the rainbow." All three Gumms sang "Where the Butterflies Kiss the Buttercups Goodnight," and Frances performed her first-ever on-screen solo, "Blue Butterfly."

The second short, *The Wedding of Jack and Jill,* also directed by Mack, was a ten-minute reeler, using an array of beautiful ragdolls from around the globe. The Gumms, as the talented "Video Vitaphone Kiddies," provided royal entertainment for the wedding of John Pirrone (later John Perri) and Peggy Ryan, who would soon become a frequent teen screen co-star of Donald O'Connor.

In this short, Frances sang a solo, "Hang on to a Rainbow," the first time she used "rainbow" in a song. All three Gumms sang "The Wedding of Jack and Jill." The cast, dressed to kill, was hailed for appealing to both kiddies and adults.

The final short, *Bubbles,* was billed as a romp through a child's land of dreams,

Frances Gumm worked on the same bill with **Stepin Fetchit,** who was hired as a comical foil for many films. On screen, he often portrayed dim-witted servants and farmers who were radically unlike his real-life personality.

with the Gumms singing "The Land of Let's Pretend." Each of them portrayed a "Moon Maiden."

For Baby Gumm, her close-up remains the only film strip that survives today. Much of the footage of these shorts has been lost to history. However, the soundtracks remain intact.

***

Later called "Black Tuesday," October 29, 1919 dawned pretty much like any other day. But by that afternoon, some stockholders were making suicidal jumps from skyscraper windows on Wall Street. The Stock Market crash roared in, and a great depression settled over the land.

Hollywood was negatively affected, of course, but not devastated as many companies—even banks—were. More than ever, a depressed America, hovering on the brink of financial disaster, desperately needed entertainment to escape its woes.

All of this occurred at the time Hollywood was converting to sound. That trend affected Frank in his Lancaster movie house, too.

As Hollywood learned to talk, some of the greats of the silent screen had too heavy an accent. Fade outs were Vilma Banky and Pola Negri. Gloria Swanson could talk, but her role as a reigning screen vamp faded into

SELLING PANIC WRECKS STOCK EXCHANGE; NEW YORK FRENZIED

WILDEST DAY IN HISTORY OF MARKET RUINS SCORES; LOSSES TO BE IN BILLIONS

During the prolonged anguish that swept across America in 1929, "Baby Gumm Drop" and her sisters were called upon, through their hoofing and singing, to lighten the spirits of a nation that seemed to be spinning out of control.

In the lower right-hand corner of the **"Black Tuesday"** photo-montage assembled above, **the Gumm Sisters** seem earnest, endearing, and surreal as, onstage and in vaudeville halls, they tried to amuse and bemuse their crisis-soaked audiences.

history.

Amazingly, Hollywood's top two box office attractions, Wallace Beery and Marie Dressler, reigned briefly as box office champs. William Haines, a star in silent pictures, was tops at the box office until he refused to abandon his male lover.

Janet Gaynor, a lesbian, and Charles Farrell, who was gay, provided romance on the screen. New stars were on the way, including Jean Harlow, who set girls rushing to buy peroxide.

Germany's "Blue Angel," Marlene Dietrich, was seducing her co-star, Gary Cooper, in *Morocco* (1930), a talkie. Then-lovers Clark Gable and Joan Crawford were each on the dawn of major stardom in the 1930s.

Ethel viewed the coming of talking pictures as a possible bonanza for Frances. Whereas before, she could dance on the silent screen, now the world would get to hear her powerful singing voice, too. "I think she'll become a sensational entertainer," she accurately predicted.

***

On March 4, 1930, Ethel entered Frances into the Eighth Annual Los Angeles Evening Express "Better Babies Exposition" at Paramount Studios. Her hope was that it would encourage talent scouts to arrange a screen test for her daughter. Although Frances came in second, all she got from the contest was a porcelain doll. It was presented to her by Mary Pickford, whose own screen career was fading with the advent of the Talkies.

Bookings that paid very little included a gig in June when the sisters billed themselves as "The Hollywood Starlets Trio." They performed before the Knights of Pythius and at the Million Dollar Theatre in Los Angeles.

On July 4, Ethel's daughters performed at the famous Hotel Del Coronado in San Diego, where Frances once again met Joan Crawford and Clark Gable. A reviewer for the *San Diego News* wrote, "Frances Gumm is a feisty little miss who sang a solo in a surprisingly powerful voice—and all but stopped the show."

That August, Frank premiered his daughter's film, a one-reel short musical, *The Wedding of Jack and Jill* (1930), in Lancaster. He got to see his offspring sing and dance on the screen for the first time. During that summer and fall, the sisters appeared in revues in Hollywood at the Roosevelt Hotel or at the Pantages Theatre of Lowe's State.

At every performance, Ethel kept hoping a talent scout would be in the

Judy, left, with child actor **John Perri** in 1928, dressed for a short musical film whose footage has been lost forever, on the Warner Brothers lot in Hollywood.

audience and single her daughters out for a screen test. That didn't happen, and they ended up instead with low-rent bookings at Walker's Department Store, where their paycheck was a voucher for three pairs of shoes.

Back in Lancaster, in dire need of money, Ethel opened a small dancing school. It attracted twenty pupils, most of them girls, since boys who danced were viewed as "sissies."

When in Los Angeles, Ethel still lobbied for a screen test for her daughters and continued to get rejected by such studios as Paramount and MGM. "Shirley Temple came along and grabbed the spotlight I wanted for my Frances."

During that time in Lancaster, Frances grew more and more alienated, discovering that girls in school resented her. Years later, she said, "Those who lived there were like the desert at their doorstep—harsh, bitter, and barren. As for Ethel, she did nothing but create chaos and fear. She promoted my talent as a singer, yet resented me, perhaps out of jealousy since she'd failed as a singer herself. I finally concluded that what was keeping me from stardom was my link to my older sisters, who on their best nights were hideously mediocre, with no star quality whatsoever."

During the painful years of the early 1930s, before stardom arrived, Judy Garland blamed Ethel for everything that went wrong in her life. This resentment was exposed by author Norman Zierold in his book *The Child Stars:* "Ethel Gumm was a most intriguing figure of the entertainment world, a stage mother who chose to fulfill her own dreams and fantasies through the careers she planned for her daughters. Her obsession became ever more resolute and all embracing. The mother love she felt expressed itself through that enactment."

Frances and Ethel even fought over her wrists, her mother calling them "virtually deformed, awkward, large, and ugly." Judy Garland ignored this, and her wrists became part of her act, emphasized in front of millions as, for example, whenever she slung a microphone cord over her shoulder.

Yet the big breakthrough into show business just didn't happen the way she fantasized. In 1930, demoralized and alert to the ravages of the Depression, Ethel and her daughters gave up their apartment in Los Angeles and moved back to Lancaster.

Once there, her fights with Frank resumed night after night. When Ethel could stand it no more, she fled back to Los Angeles and again into the arms of Will Gilmore. His paralyzed wife, Laura, was soon to die. More and more, he pressed Ethel to divorce Frank and marry him.

It was always with a deep longing that she told him goodbye after a few days for a return to her dull life with Frank.

Frank, too, saw his real love, Dr. Marc Rabwin, only on occasion. In the meantime, he had taken up with two of the leading athletes at the local high school, one excelling in football, the other in basketball. They came and went freely from his theater, often bringing their girlfriends. For that privilege, they visited Frank in the afternoon for an extended session in his office, backstage.

Naturally, at any showing at his theater, they were invited to devour all the popcorn and candy they wanted, and each of them was given a new bicycle.

As she grew older, Frances was confronted with tales of her father's attraction to teenage boys. She responded in anger, often calling the bearer of such claims "a dirty liar."

Then a false rumor was spread that the Gumms were a Jewish family, which had no basis in fact.

Writing for the *Los Angeles Mirror,* Paul Coates tried to decipher the Ethel vs. Frances relationship.

Ethel and Frank Gumm, miserably unhappy in their marriage but "keeping up appearances."

He never lived to see Frances, his favorite daughter, become a star.

> *"They were a familiar sight around Hollywood auditions in the early 1930s. While Frances Gumm, a pert, wide-eyed child sang, Mamma accompanied her on the piano. Mrs. Gumm was a tenacious stage mother. And it finally paid off. Her little girl was a big star. Nobody can really know what caused this deep and terrifying resentment of each other. Judy's life has been marked by success and tragedy. Undoubtedly, her mother's relentless driving was at least partially responsible for her success. But that same relentless driving could also be completely responsible for the tragedy this young artist has known. Miss Garland was never a child. At three years old, she was already a veteran theatrical property, first to her mother, then to MGM. It was a shocking and abnormal upbringing, and it was bound to have unhappy repercussions."*

Judy, in years to come, surprised an interviewer when she confessed, "I never wanted to be a singer. I wanted to be a dramatic star like my favorite actresses at the time: Bette Davis, Margaret Sullavan, and Norma Shearer. My favorite males were Spencer Tracy, Clark Gable, Robert Donat, and Charles Boyer. I didn't intend to marry until I was thirty, and I wanted my future husband to be a combination of those four guys."

***

Months after the Wall Street crash, the Depression engulfed Lancaster. To attract customers, Frank lowered the price of admission from fifty cents to thirty-five cents, with seats in the back row selling for only fifteen cents. Even so, attendance declined.

That dwindling revenue at the box office caused him to become delinquent in his rent. The theater owner warned him that when his lease came up for renewal, it would not be renewed.

There was another reason: Word was spreading about his addiction to teenage boys, and often, behind his back, he was widely defined as a "pansy" within the homophobic society at large.

Both Frank and Ethel never informed their daughters about their financial woes, but their costumes and travel expenses ate into the Gumm family budget. Often, a gig paid so little money, that Ethel spent more on the performance of her daughters than she got paid. Still, she persisted in keeping them in the competition for show biz bookings.

The year 1931 opened with the Gumm Sisters continuing to perform with "The Meglin Kiddies," although all of them were growing tired of that.

They became familiar faces at the Pantages Theatre in Los Angeles, but also went south to San Diego for appearances at the Savoy Theatre too.

For a while, at least, Frank's theater in Lancaster remained their principal performance venue.

That July, the Gumm Sisters appeared in Maurice Kusell's "Stars of Tomorrow," a juvenile revue, at the Wilshire Ebell Theatre in Los Angeles. The trio performed song-and-dance numbers such as "Putting' on the Ritz," and Frances starred in solo numbers that included "A Plantation Melody." The performers were accompanied by an eight-piece orchestra.

Around that time, Frances was signed by the Dunlap Talent Agency, whose other clients included James Cagney. She would become the agency's first child performer, and executives viewed her as a formidable rival to the fast-emerging Shirley Temple. She was re-christened "Frances Gayne" and promised bookings for radio, stage, and screen, but Frank protested that his daughter was too young and broke the contract.

He did allow her to go to an audition at Universal on August 15, but executives there chose not to hire her.

For the rest of the year, Frances, in a move away from the Gumm Sisters, billed herself as "Baby Marie Gumm" or else as "Francis Gayne. "For You, For You" became one of her favorite songs, as well as "Sweet and Lovely."

***

Frances launched 1932 by performing on January 23 at the famous Cocoanut Grove night club in the Ambassador Hotel. After she became Judy Garland, this became one of her famous night spots, and she would often show up with both her gay and straight husbands. As well as her lover *du jour*, be it Frank Sinatra, Peter Lawford, Tyrone Power, Artie Shaw, or Orson Welles.

For her first-ever gig there, she appeared at a "Tea Dance" backed up by Jimmie Grier and his Orchestra. The manager claimed, "The future Judy Garland back then was just a skinny little girl with this Ethel Merman voice, truly astounding. I feared, however, that our audience was too sophisticated for little girl entertainers, since we were booking the best bands and the top singers in America."

[In 1958, Judy would make a spectacular "comeback" at the Grove, and also would use the occasion to introduce her daughter, Liza Minnelli.]

On August 5 of that year, in spite of all their struggles, the Gumm Sisters still did not have much name recognition, and the marquee at the Cabrillo Theatre in San Pietro billed them as "The Gum Sisters."

On August 25 at the Paramount Theatre in Los Angeles, they were the backup act for the star of the night, comedian Fuzzy Knight, a forgotten name today.

The appearance is only significant in that it marked their first review in *Variety*. It read: "Gumm sisters, harmony trio, socked with two numbers. Selling end of trio is the ten-year-old sister with a pip of a lowdown voice. Kid stopped the show but wouldn't give more. She adamantly refused an encore, even though the loudly clapping audience demanded it."

To cap 1932 and to launch themselves into 1933, Baby Gumm was singled out for special attention in Maurice Kussel's *Juvenile Christmas Revue* at the Million Dollar Theatre in Los Angeles. The critic for the *Los Angeles Record* pronounced her solo performance astonishing, claiming that "her singing knocks one for a loop. Her dancing is snappy and clever, and she handles herself on stage like a veteran pro."

On April 7, 1933, Frances returned to the Cocoanut Grove Night Club to appear at the "Little Club Event." A scout for KFI Radio asked her to appear onstage singing with Al Pierce and His Gang. She eagerly accepted, hoping that if she could not break into the movies, she might in time become a singer on radio.

She was still struggling to come up with the right name, thinking that the day might soon be approaching when she would break from her sisters and go solo.

In May, she relaunched herself with a new name, "Alice Gumm," using it for her appearance at the Garfield Theatre in Alhambra, California. But by June, she was back to starring as part of the Gumm Sisters trio when they performed at the Alexandria Hotel in downtown Los Angeles.

On June 10, Frances celebrated her eleventh birthday when she and her sisters went to West Lake in California to appear at its annual spring "Dance & Frolic." They were billed as "The Gum Sisters." More and more booking agents were urging them to get rid of "that sticky name," and come up with a more marquee-friendly logo for their act.

From mid-June to early in July, the sisters returned to Radio KFWB in Los Angeles with their *Junior High Jinx Show,* in which they got rave reviews from the *Los Angeles Examiner.*

In the summer of 1933, Ethel once again moved her daughters back to Los Angeles, renting a modest address for them at 2605 Ivanhoe Drive. Her two older daughters had already told her that one day—sooner than later—they wanted to get married, settle down, and get out of show business. Long in advance of that, Ethel already knew that only Frances was star material.

On July 17, the Gumm Sisters starred at the Hillcrest Theatre in Los Angeles, where Frances did a solo, warbling "Rain, Rain, Go Away."

After her performance, Ben Piazza came backstage and introduced himself as a casting agent for Metro-Goldwyn-Mayer. He promised he'd arrange for the studio to give her a screen test. "But the bastard never called us," she said.

What followed was a seven-day booking, beginning on July 20, at the Warner Brothers Downtown Theatre, where they were billed once again as "The Gum Sisters." When Frances complained to the manager, he said, "Who gives a damn? Better than if I'd billed you as 'The Glum Sisters.'"

At long last, the Gumms traveled north to San Francisco for a booking at the Golden Gate Theatre from August 2 to 6. Ethel played the piano as the sisters went through their familiar routine. Frances provided "the verve and punch" of the show, finding her sisters rather lackluster. "Their hearts just weren't in it," she lamented.

The next morning, *Variety* gave the sister act their second review:

"With Mama Gumm at the piano, three girls of assorted sizes sing in mediocre style and voice with the majority of burden falling to the youngest one, a mere tot, who lustily shouted three numbers, decidedly not of her type. And much toooo looooooooong."

Her sisters more or less ignored the attack, but Frances was "badly depressed." Her pain was relieved somewhat when the trade paper, *Junior Professional,* wrote: "This remarkable tot has twice the charm and genuine ability of all child movie stars put together."

In the *San Francisco Chronicle,* George C. Warren wrote: "The Gumm Sisters harmonize and have a strong-voiced small woman, who imitates and sings in a big way."

That is the first time Frances had ever been called a woman in print. Not for the first time, the reviewer must have thought she was a midget.

***

At the end of August, Ethel secured a week-long booking for her daughters at the Warner Brothers Downtown Theatre in Los Angeles. Once again, the manager got the billing wrong, billing them as "the Drumm Sisters."

` The act received its third review in *Variety:*

"The Gumm Sisters, three harmonious warblers, feature Mother Gumm accompanying them on the piano. Two of the sisters are grownup, while the third is a precocious little juve whose mild attempts at comedy add nothing to the offering."

As a footnote in movie history, Mickey Rooney and Judy Garland ap-

Like Judy, **Mickey Rooney**, who would star with her in ten movies, was propelled from birth almost directly into show-biz.

Here's young Mickey, as a "hoofer in training" in the vaudevillian style of James Cagney.

peared on the same stage for the first time on October 21, under the direction of their acting coach, nicknamed "Ma Lawlor." At the Hollywood Conservatory Auditorium, Lawlor's Hollywood Professional School Recital was staged. Both Judy and Mickey were just years away from becoming box office champs at MGM.

Before he left the theater that night, Mickey gave Frances a long and passionate kiss, and would continue to do so for years to come.

Although only thirteen years old, he had become a self-admitted sex addict. "I lost my virginity when I was ten years old to a girl named Ann who was eleven."

"At the beginning of puberty, I wanted to get laid time and time again. I had money in my jeans, and if I wanted it, I got it. No romantic illusions— just pure, raw sex."

"When I turned fourteen, I remained that age for the next thirty years."

As he set out from the Vine Street Elementary School, six wives, including the sultry Ava Gardner, lay in his future, as did such luscious girlfriends as Lana Turner, Betty Grable, Gene Tierney, stripper Tempest Storm, and even the widowed Norma Shearer, then the reigning Queen of MGM.

***

With Ethel and his daughters gone most of the time, Frank became more aggressive in his pursuit of teenaged boys. Since he had the home to himself, he invited groups of them over for beer parties, taking them one by one into his bedroom while the other boys drank and "cut up" in his living room, listening to loud music on the radio.

Biographer Gerald Clarke claimed, "In the high school locker room, two of the athletes, Steve Castle and Lyle Hatley, bragged about Frank performing oral sex on them, neglecting giving them a description of how they made him beg. Since they were doing the same thing with the track coach, no one doubted that they were telling the truth. At the Valley Theatre, the two boys strolled through the door without paying while their friends were lining up at the box office."

Word soon spread that if a boy wanted free admission and popcorn, he should "submit to a blow-job" from Frank. He was also known to sit in the rear of the theater, providing no patrons were nearby, and masturbate several of the boys one after another.

The townspeople, at least some of them, became aware of all this, but such activities went on for months. Occasionally, there was a complaint filed with the sheriff. One outraged woman charged that Frank had made inappropriate advances to her fifteen-year-old son. The sheriff called on Frank at the theater, but he denied all accusations, claiming that he was happily married and the father of three beautiful daughters. Back then, the sheriff was naïve enough to fall for that line of reasoning.

In the 1960s, a Hollywood writer, John Roth, drove north from Los Angeles to Lancaster to interview the long-retired sheriff there. He was hoping to write an article about the origin of the Gumm Sisters.

The sheriff met with Roth and expressed nothing but contempt for Judy Garland's father. "He was a god damn queer who had this thing for teenage boys, corrupting them. He gave blow-jobs to some of our finest young boys—and got away with it. I didn't know until much later just how many boys he seduced. I was a bit naïve about queers in those days, and, like most things, his perverted acts caught up with him. I had to run the bastard out of town."

"Most of the boys went along with his scheme, and there were few complaints, at least at first. Not only did he let boys into his theater for free, but he gave most of them a five-dollar bill. That was big money back then. Many guys had to work all day for fifty cents. You could just imagine what a kid would do for five dollars. Apparently, there was no attempt at sodomy. You might not believe this, but I didn't know until years later what sodomy was."

***

Frank wasn't the only one enjoying sexual intimacies in the back row of the Valley Theatre in Lancaster. So was his eleven-year-old daughter, Frances. She had developed a strong attraction to boys, which became a life-long passion, gradually replacing teenagers with grown-up men.

Years later, Judy Garland was very candid with her gay friends, such as actors Roddy McDowall and Lon McCallister, who always seemed to be cast as that innocent-looking farm boy next door.

One night at dinner at McDowall's home, she discussed her early experiences with boys after the two actors told of their own early attraction to boys.

"Back when I had that awful dumpy name of Frances Gumm, I fell in love with a boy name Glenn Reed, who was two years older. We got better acquainted in the back row of my dad's movie house. No major stuff, just heavy petting. He was a great kisser. Of course, I had no experience to compare him with. It was years later that I painfully learned that he was also servicing Dad. Frank paid him to sing with me on stage at the theater. Glenn and I shared our dream of growing up in a few years and going on the vaudeville route as a singing duet, warbling love songs. Our singing at Dad's theater went over pretty big, and at the end of our act, he gave me a big kiss, as the audience applauded."

"When Valentine's Day came, he paid fifty cents for my Valentine, whereas most boys were shelling out only a nickel or a dime for their girls."

As Judy admitted, "I wasn't faithful to Glenn. I was also carrying on with Charles Murphy, an usher at the theater. He had the most adorable buckteeth, a regular Bugs Bunny. Backstage one night in the dressing room, he performed oral sex on me. As you've probably heard from the rumor mill, it's still my favorite form of sex."

McCallister and McDowall listened intently to her drunken revelations.

"Charles did not ask me to reciprocate, although I think I would have tried if requested," she said. "He masturbated while he did the dirty deed.

34

It seemed that Frank shared my taste in boys. Sometimes he took Charlie away with him for a weekend in Los Angeles. I never asked what they did."

Other boys were starting to show an interest in Frances, particularly Edward White, the son of the town's hardware store owner. He would arrive at my doorstep and walk with me to school carrying my books. All I got from him was a quick kiss on the lips. But he soon was lured away by the lead cheerleader. I lost him, the first of many men I'd lose to sexier women over the years—or, in my case, lose to sexy men."

"I also developed a crush on Buddy Welch, who sat across from me in class," she confessed. "Instead of listening to our boring teacher, I looked at Buddy. He stood five feet, six inches, a perfect size for me. He had blonde hair and cat-green eyes. He was the only boy in school who wore purple or pink shirts, sometimes sunflower yellow. Those were the favorite colors of his Mexican mother, and sometimes the boys beat him up for being a sissy."

"I had dinner at his home. His mother prepared enchiladas. Once we went on our bikes toward the Red Rock Canyon, and his mother, Maria, packed us a picnic lunch. Afterward, we found a spot in the shade and got kissy-feely. He wanted me to play with his thing, a first for me."

***

By 1934, the Gumm Sisters and Ethel were spending less and less time in Lancaster, leaving Frank to run his failing theater.

In Los Angeles, the Gumm Sisters were becoming better known, making appearances at such prestigious venues as the Paramount Theatre or the Orpheum.

Frank and Ethel put a down payment on a house at 2671 Lakeview Terrace at Silver Lake, outside Los Angeles.

When mainstream bookings became rare in Los Angeles, because of the massive array of talent assembled in that city, Ethel accepted singing engagements for her daughters as far north as Seattle and as far east as Idaho. She concluded one of those tours with a swing through San Francisco, where they starred at the Fox Theatre.

In Lancaster, Frank moved out of their home and rented a seedy, unheated shack with an outdoor toilet on the slummy side of town. He was barely holding on to the Valley Theatre and fell increasingly behind in his rent. He reputation grew worse. The choir master at his church asked him to drop out after two teenage boys complained he'd tried to molest them. He became more reckless in his pursuits as attendance dwindled at the Valley Theatre. Instead of paying the rent, he spent a lot of his box office receipts paying young teenage boys to submit to fellatio.

By April, Ethel drove her girls south to San Diego, where Frances was billed as "Baby Gumm," as part of the entertainment at the Gilmore Circus. She sang the politically incorrect "Why Darkies Are Born."

Before returning to Los Angeles, she sang another inappropriate song, "That's What a Darkie Is," which would enrage African Americans if performed today.

Back in Los Angeles, Frances had a long overdue reunion with her father, and was alarmed by his failing health. It is not known just how much she knew of her father's bad reputation in Lancaster. All she said was, "I love him more than ever and miss him all the time."

At Silver Lake, on June 10, she celebrated her twelfth birthday.

Later that month, Ethel came up with a daring plan that Frank opposed, but she overrode his objections. She planned to drive her daughters across country for the 1934 World's Fair in Chicago, hailed at the time as a celebration of "A Century of Progress." She hoped to pay their travel expenses by appearing at clubs along the way.

Their first booking was at the Blakeland Inn in Denver, where she found it had been raided the night before by the police, who shut it down for illegal gambling. Since that night at least, the joint was closed to the public, the club's owner ordered the Gumms to perform the following night for his friends, ten men in all.

He assigned Frances, the star of the show, her own dressing room, and Ethel fussed away within the room she shared with her other two daughters, who were complaining about their costumes. The owner of the club came to Frances' dressing room and exposed himself to her, ordering her to go down on him.

She was terrified and trembled and began to cry. He buttoned his pants and left quickly.

Finally, after much difficulty, Ethel and the Gumm Sisters arrived in Chicago for their booking at the Old Mexico Night Club on the periphery of the fair grounds. They were hired for a three-week engagement but given only a thirty-five dollar advance. As her money ran low, Ethel kept asking for another advance. Finally, at the end of the booking, she learned that the club had gone bankrupt. She demanded money from the owner, but he warned that if she persisted, she would find herself at the bottom of the lake.

Out of funds, Ethel began to cash the first of the $300 in travelers' checks that Frank had given her. At the last minute, as they were packing to flee from Chicago, Jack Cathcart entered their lives. He had played the trumpet on the same bill as the sisters and was impressed with their talent.

A tall man in his twenties, with wavy hair, he looked like the typical All-American cleancut youth. He told Ethel that a musical trio had just been fired nearby at the Oriental Theatre, where the audience had booed their act. He suggested that Ethel rush over right

away and talk to the manager.

Coincidentally, that manager had dropped into the Old Mexico recently, and he'd been impressed with the singing, dancing Frances; less so with her sisters. In desperate need of a fill-in act, he hired the Gumm Sisters on the spot to appear on a bill headlined by the comedian George Jessel as the master of ceremonies.

Not familiar with their act, Jessel just assumed by their name that they were childhood comedians. "Now, ladies and gentlemen, I give you the Gumm Sisters. Rhymes with glum and dumb." The audience laughed loudly but quieted down for the opening of their act.

For the second show, he introduced them and, without their permission, he changed their name: "Ladies and gentlemen, I give you 'The Garland Sisters.' A sensational act of three pretty little singing and dancing girls."

After he heard Frances sing, he said, "That little girl sings like a woman whose heart is broken."

The comedian may have taken the name from the movie on the same bill. Carole Lombard was starring in *Twentieth Century*, and the character she played was "Lily Garland." It was also said that Jessel took the last name from his friend, the drama critic, Robert Garland.

In 1954, Jessel appeared in Hollywood at the world premiere of *A Star Is Born* at the Pantages Theatre. He came before the microphone and addressed the fans assembled outside the theater. "I think I can tell you folks assembled here that it was I who named Judy Garland. Not that it would have made any difference—you couldn't hide talent like that even if you called her 'Tel Aviv Windsor Shell.' You know, I first met her when she was known as Frances Gumm, and it wasn't the kind of name such a sensitive girl like her should have. So I called her Judy Garland, and I think she's a combination of Helen Hayes and Al Jolson, and maybe Jenny Lind and Sarah Bernhardt."

Actually, Jessel only named the act Garland. Judy took her first name from the popular Hoagy Carmichael song, "Judy."

LEWIS & GORDON
IN ASSOCIATION WITH
SAM H. HARRIS

present

GEORGE JESSEL

in

the JAZZ SINGER

AN AMERICAN COMEDY DRAMA
BY SAMSON RAPHAELSON
STAGED BY ALBERT LEWIS

This is a rare advertisement hawking a "road show" production of *The Jazz Singer*, which had opened as a play on Broadway in 1925.

It starred **George Jessel,** who always took credit for inventing a stage name for Frances Gumm: Judy Garland.

Jessel was slated to star in the play's 1927 film adaptation, but the role was signed to Al Jolson instead.

As part of a technological revolution, it included several audio and musical sequences, thereby defining itself as the first "Talkie" in the history of movie-making.

Frances' rendition of the song, "Bill," brought down the house as she sat wrapped in a shawl atop a piano, rendering the popular song Helen Morgan sang in *Show Boat* (1936).

Before the newly christened Garland Sisters headed back to California, Jessel got them a few more bookings at theaters in the Chicago area.

Judy's sister, Suzanne, hated to leave Chicago because of the presence there of Jack Cathcart, who had taken her swimming every day in Lake Michigan. Frances thought he had fallen in love with her. Ironically, years later, their paths would cross when Suzanne divorced her first husband and married him.

En route to California, the Gumms recouped their travel expenses with appearances in such towns as Milwaukee and three stops in Missouri, including Kansas City.

Back home again, the sisters used their new name of Garland for their engagement at Grauman's Chinese Theatre, which at the time was screening *The Count of Monte Cristo* (1934).

Booked for a week beginning on November 1, Judy was singled out for her singing and also acclaimed for "her hoofing." The other sisters were dismissed as "mere background."

On December 7, using the familiar name of the Gumm Sisters in Lancaster, the girls made their farewell appearance at the Valley Theatre. Many of the townspeople, even those who had turned against Frank, came out to hear them and wish them well.

The following day, they starred as the Garland Sisters again at the Wilshire-Ebell Theatre in Los Angeles. *The Times* claimed that the youngest member of their team practically stopped the show with her "mature voiced singing."

The sisters closed out 1934 with an appearance at the Hollywood Playhouse. A critic from the *San Francisco Call-Bulletin* was in Hollywood, and he wrote that Judy was "the talk of the town, as much a sweetheart of the stage as Shirley Temple is on the screen."

On New Year's Eve, as they gathered to celebrate the arrival of 1935, both of Judy's older sisters warned her that in the coming months, the act would break up as they no longer wanted to perform in vaudeville.

She didn't seem in the least bit disappointed. "That's okay by me. I, too, am tired of singing on the stage. In the coming year, I plan to become Judy Garland, movie star."

In 1936, after "dumping my two untalented sisters," fourteen-year-old Judy Garland planned to "Take Hollywood by storm,"

38

JUVENILE JUDY

JUDY'S ADOLESCENCE IN GOLDEN-AGE HOLLYWOOD

RAGING HORMONES, PREDATORY INSIDERS, AND MURKY MOTIVES OF EVERYONE AROUND HER

"I cried and applauded all the way to California."

—Judy Garland

For a one-week booking whose debut was scheduled for Christmas Day, 1934, Ethel drove her daughters to San Francisco for an engagement at the Curran Theatre. They were part of a 60-member show, *Irving Strouse's Vaudeville Frolics*. The sisters were billed as "Frances Garland and Her Sisters," or alternatively as the "Frances Garland Trio." It was obvious to Ethel that little Frances had become the family breadwinner.

When the gig was over, they were eager to return to Hollywood, where a screen test had been scheduled for January 10 at the financially strapped Universal Studios. Although it was too costly for their limited budget, ex-

Built in 1922, San Francisco's **Curran Theatre** (left photo) evolved into one of the grandest dowager theaters of the West Coast. It was famously used as the site of interior and exterior scenes of Bette Davis' *All About Eve* (1950).

In 1934, when she was 12, Judy and her sisters were among the five dozen players putting on its *Vaudeville Frolics* Christmas Show. The right-hand photo depicts some of what Judy saw from its stage. Inset photo shows Judy in 1935.

ecutives were moving ahead to make *The Great Ziegfeld* (1936), hoping that all those sexy showgirls would skyrocket them out of red ink. The sisters were scheduled to appear in the film as one of Ziegfeld's vaudeville acts—that is, if they pulled off the screen test.

Their test was a success, and Frances was praised for her powerful voice. Back home, they couldn't afford to wait around for filming to begin, so they performed any gig that popped up. They were called back to Universal to sing at producer Carl Laemmle's sixty-eighth birthday celebration at the studio.

Still no movie deal. To their disappointment, Universal couldn't finance *The Great Ziegfeld* and consequently, they sold its film rights to MGM.

In the revised script, now under control of a different set of administrators, the Garland girls were dropped. Star roles went to William Powell as Ziegfeld, with support from Myrna Loy, Spencer Tracy, and Luise Rainer, whose memorable performance brought her an Oscar. The movie itself walked off with the gold for Best Picture. Frances was broken-hearted that she didn't get to appear in the star-studded extravaganza.

Then, for a period of about a week, beginning on March 7, the sisters appeared in a return engagement at the Paramount Theatre in Los Angeles. Their combined salary was $110 a week. "We've come up in the world," Frances (Judy) said. "I remember when we sang in a show for fifty cents each."

In their fifth review in *Variety*, the critic wrote: "Girl (meaning Judy) looks like a good bet for pictures and should make rapid headway." He did point out, however, that she "should be coached more proficiently in singing in a foreign tongue."

In the final days of March, the weather felt like summer, as Ethel marched her girls into the headquarters of Decca Records in Los Angeles. The sisters had been scheduled to make three test records.

Decca wanted to see if they had a possibility of becoming recording artists. Judy sang her best rendition of Helen Morgan's "Bill," sounding like a much more mature artist. The trio sang "Moonglow," and their rendition of "On the Good Ship Lollipop," which became a favorite when Shirley Temple performed it on screen.

The executives at Decca rejected the Garland Sisters, and the three test records disappeared in a junk heap somewhere.

In early April of 1935, the Gumm family relocated into a house at 842 Mariposa Avenue, near the studio of 20th Century Fox, the domain of Darryl F. Zanuck and the show-biz home of Little Miss Shirley Temple.

As the accumulated weight of Frank's sex offenses grew and as profits diminished from his long-past-its-prime Valley Theatre, he pulled up his roots in the desert outpost of Lancaster and wangled his way into a new management contract with a potentially more profitable theater in Lomita, California, only twenty miles from Los Angeles. Hoping to capitalize off his youngest daughter's growing reputation, he renamed it the Garland Lomita Theatre.

On May 15, Ethel got her daughters a return engagement at the Paramount Theatre in Los Angeles. They were so successful that the manager extended their booking for another two weeks.

A critic singled Judy out, writing, "She is about as talented an entertainer as one could imagine."

She got a rave for her tender rendition of "Eyli, Eyli" ("My God, My God"), whose dirgelike notes she sang in the song's original Yiddish. Popular on the vaudeville circuit, and originally written in 1896, she had learned it for presentations at branches of the B'nai B'rith.

Variety wrote, "The Garland Sisters are the hits of the program. Little Frances Garland seems to have been mysteriously overlooked by local talent scouts because this remarkable youngster has an amazing amount of talent for both stage and pix shows."

The critic for the evening *Los Angeles Herald-Express* wrote:

> *"Not your smart, adult-aping prodigy is this girl, but a youngster who has the divine instinct to be herself on the stage along with a talent for singing, a trick of rocking the spectator with rhythms and a capacity for putting emotion into her performance that suggests what Sarah Bernhardt must have been at her age. It isn't the cloying, heavy sentiment her elders so often strive for on the vaudeville stage, but simple, sincere feeling that reaches the heart."*

FAMOUS LAKE TAHOE RESORT—1937

***

Unknown at the time, the gig from June 15 to July 26, 1935 would be life-changing for the Garland Sisters. Its venue, the Cal-Neva Lodge, stood directly on the border that separated California from Nevada. In fact, the state line ran directly through its dance floor.

During rehearsals, Judy insisted, "No more Baby or Babe, no more Frances. I will only answer to Judy." She found her new name "peppy."

Her favorite refrain from the Hoagy Carmichael song was, *"If she seems like a saint, and you find out she ain't, it's Judy."*

A stay at the Lodge seemed like a vacation, as they swam during the day and performed before gamblers at

Views of the infamous **Cal-Neva Lodge** snapped as publicity photos in the late 1930s.

Built in 1926 and scandalously associated with, among many others, Clara Bow, it's credited with controversial links to Frank Sinatra, Marilyn Monroe, and Sam Giancana.

It was also the entertainment venue that propelled Judy Garland to "juvenile stardom" in 1935.

night. Years later, Judy learned that she had lodged in the same bungalow occupied by Marilyn Monroe shortly before her tragic, scandal-soaked death in 1962.

The previous summer, at the World's Fair in Chicago, Mary Jane (now Suzanne) Gumm had fallen for a young musician, Jack Cathcart. But at the Cal-Neva, she met Lee Kahn, a saxophone player for the Jimmy Davis Orchestra. Their love affair began that very night, even though her mother warned her that "All musicians are whoremongers."

At the end of their gig, Suzanne and Kahn agreed to continue dating in Los Angeles. From the Cal-Neva, Ethel intended to drive to Kansas for another gig before heading back to Los Angeles, and she rushed her daughters through their final packing. But after driving for twenty miles, Jimmie remembered she'd left all their stage hats and all their sheet music on the top shelf of her bedroom closet.

Her mother was forced to retrace their route back to the Lodge. Since Jimmie's hair was in curlers and Suzanne was moping over her temporary separation from Kahn, Judy was sent inside to retrieve their music and their hats.

"Bones" Remer, the manager and bouncer, spotted Judy, informing her that there were some major show-biz players in the casino showroom, and suggested that she audition for them.

At first, she was worried that Ethel, with her sisters, would become even more irritated and impatient in that scorching hot car and that they'd drive away and leave her behind. But she decided to run the risk.

The coven of men gathered in the showroom included cigar-smoking Harry Cohn, the boss at Columbia Pictures. With him were two composers, Harry Akst and Lew Brown.

On stage in front of them she said, "I need someone to play the piano. Does anyone know how to play 'Dinah'?"

Akst rose to his feet. "I do. I wrote the damn thing."

Before her mini-concert ended, the composer had accompanied her through three more songs, including "Zing! Went the Strings of My Heart."

Bones turned to Cohn. "So, what do you think?"

"Can't use her. No use for fat little girls."

Both songwriters, however, found her

Mean-spirited **Harry Cohen** (right), head of Columbia Pictures, depicted here in 1934 with **Clark Gable** during the filming of his Oscar-winning performance in *It Happened One Night* with Claudette Colbert.

Although Cohen, who was at the Cal-Neva at the time of his first introduction to Judy, was cruelly dismissive, his music-industry cohorts that day prevailed in recognizing her as a "hot new discovery."

terrific. Al Rosen, a talent agent from Hollywood, said nothing until the end. Then he went backstage to introduce himself.

At this point, Ethel entered the building to find out what had happened to Judy.

"I'm a lean, mean, and hungry Hollywood agent," Rosen told her, "and I want to make a movie star out of this amazing little girl with a voice from the gods."

They exchanged cards, but Ethel, during the continuation of their drive toward their gig in Kansas, predicted "Nothing will come of it."

***

By June 8, the sisters were singing and dancing at Frank's Lomita movie house, just in time for Judy to celebrate her thirteenth birthday. She always had bad memories of Lomita and its "scorching heat, its poisonous snakes, and desolation. This bleak outpost was so terrible my sisters and I withdrew into ourselves just to stay alive. It was in such stark contrast to the green friendliness of Minnesota, and we just couldn't adjust to it."

Six days after their first appearance, they would co-star on the bill with Frankie Darro, a former child star in silent pictures. Their father was screening Chapter One of his new movie serial, *Burn 'Em Up Barnes*. Now seventeen years old, he made a personal appearance on the stage.

Their show with Darro would mark the last performance of Frank's daughters at their father's movie house.

Darro seemed enchanted by Jimmie. Ethel caught them in the back seat of her Buick, doing some "heavy petting." He protested, "But Mrs. Gumm, I'm gonna marry her!"

The hottest of the dog days of August had come to scorch Los Angeles when a call came in from MGM. The studio wanted the Garland Sisters to make a film short, beginning the next day, which was August 12.

Entitled *Le Fiesta de Santa Barbara*, it would feature an all-star cast and be shot in Technicolor. The sisters would be seen only briefly singing "La Cucaracha." A lineup of stars would appear in the movie, even Gary Cooper. Both Buster Keaton and Harpo Marx each appeared in cameos along with several

Upper photo: **Frankie Darro,** the former child star that Ethel Gumm caught "making out" with one of her older daughters.

Lower photo: a poster promoting the film series that made him briefly famous.

other big-name stars.

The sisters performed their number and headed south again.

The short has been preserved and released on CD alongside the 1936 film *Libeled Lady*, starring Jean Harlow, Myrna Loy, Spencer Tracy, and William Powell.

It marked the last formal appearance of the Garland Sisters, an act that faded into vaudeville history.

Like her older sister, Jimmie wanted to retire from show business and get married. "I want a new profession," she told Judy. "Housewife and mother. I've had it with show business. Suzy and I are bolting. You're on your own, kid."

Suzanne was planning to marry Lee Kahn, with whom she'd fallen in love at the Cal-Neva Lodge that previous summer.

"That's fine for you two," Judy said. "As for me, I want to make the name of Judy Garland known around the world."

Jimmie's parting words to her were "Most dreams of stardom are only to be dreamed. You've been in show biz long enough to know that."

The local paper, the *Lomita Progress*, announced, "The Garland Sisters, daughters of Frank Garland of the Lomita Theatre, recently fulfilled a six-week vaudeville engagement at the Cal-Neva Lodge, Lake Tahoe. This week, the trio was broken up by Dan Cupid when he

Upper photo: **The Gumm Sisters** in 1934 and *lower photo* in 1942, after the breakup of their act and the abandonment of their careers by Jimmie and Suzanne.

One of them poignantly admitted, "Show-biz ain't for everybody."

waltzed in, claiming Suzanne as the bride of Lee Kahn, orchestra leader at Tahoe."

The paper also announced the engagement of Virginia (known variously as Jimmy or Jimmie) to movie star Frankie Darro. "Frances, the third sister, is only twelve years old, so it will be a while before Dan Cupid knocks on her door."

[Jimmie's engagement to Darro was later broken off. Ironically, it would be Judy, not Jimmie, who would become intimate with the young star.]

***

[About eighteen years later, on February 27, 1953, Judy was sent a newspaper article from the Ledger-Gazette *back in Lancaster. Her father's Valley Theatre — long abandoned by Frank in favor of greener pastures — had been reduced to a burnt-out shell. A fire had almost completely destroyed the building where Frank had made love to teenage boys, Frances had indulged in heavy petting, and the*

44

Gumm Sisters had entertained locals on stage. The article noted, "This is where the film star, Judy Garland, got her early start in show business."]

***

Long after Frank had stopped making love to Marc Rabwin, the men remained the best of friends and saw each other frequently. Still a bachelor as he approached his thirty-fourth birthday, Marc had met and fallen in love with twenty-six-year-old Marcella Bennett, the executive secretary for producer David O. Selznick. She was said to be the only person on his staff who could deal with his volcanic temper.

Only six weeks after meeting her, Marc proposed marriage, jokingly quipping, "I'll have to get the approval of all five Gumms."

When a date could be agreed upon, Marc and Marcella arrived at the home of Frank and Ethel, where she met them and their daughters, including Judy.

It is not known for sure, but Marcella perhaps had no idea of Frank's former sexual involvement with her husband-to-be.

After dinner, Judy sang three songs accompanied by her mother on the piano. "She's adorable," Marcella said. "What a voice. She should be in the movies. She's a *Wunderkind.*"

Soon after their marriage, Marc and Marcella gave a housewarming party to which Judy was invited as an entertainer. As a popular doctor, Marc had a lot of show biz connections, especially a talented young screenwriter (later producer and director) Joseph L. Mankiewicz, who was employed by MGM.

At the party, Judy enthralled a lot of show biz veterans, each agreeing that she "should be in pictures," a familiar refrain for Judy at this point in her young life. Regrettably, the one friend Marc wanted to hear Judy sing, Mankiewicz, had to cancel at the last moment.

When Mankiewicz returned to Hollywood, Marc called him. "Joe, I want you to go with me to the Paramount Theatre to hear this marvelous little girl sing. She is truly amazing."

Sitting in the front row, Marc and Joe heard Judy sing "Stormy Weather" and "Be Still, My Heart," giving it her best Helen Morgan rendition.

Before going backstage to meet Judy, Mankiewicz said, "My God, she's a pint-sized Mickey Rooney. She mugs, she grimaces, she's got all the right stage movements—and that voice! She sings

Joe Mankiewicz (right) is shown here in this publicity still from 20th Century Fox, some eighteen years after his inaugural meeting with then 13-year-old Judy.

He's directing camera angles on the set of the ill-fated and disastrously overpriced *Cleopatra* (1963).

Our favorite quote from Mankiewicz? "The difference between life and the movies is that a script has to make sense, and life doesn't."

with a deeply felt emotion and conviction. She just throws herself into a song, giving it her all."

Backstage, the twenty-five-year-old screenwriter, born in Wilkes-Barre, Pennsylvania, met the "almost thirteen-year-old" Judy Garland.

Mankiewicz was already an established writer at MGM, having written a big hit, *Manhattan Melodrama* (1934), starring Clark Gable, William Powell, Myrna Loy, and Mickey Rooney. He was currently writing screenplays for *Forsaking All Others* (1934), for Joan Crawford and Clark Gable, and *Reckless* (1935) for Jean Harlow and William Powell, who were off-screen lovers.

The introduction went well, and it seems unlikely that there was any physical attraction between them at the time. [*A torrid love affair lay in their future.*] But he assured her that he would show up the following night with "someone special from MGM."

The following evening, Mankiewicz and Ida Koverman—nicknamed "Kay"—arrived at the Paramount to hear Judy sing. Koverman later said, "I know talent when I see it, and she's bursting with it. At thirteen, she's too old to be a child star and too young for late teenage roles. She's also a tiny thing." [*Judy stood only four feet, eleven and a half inches.*]

"I promise I'll do what I can," Koverman told Mankiewicz. "But I think she'll be a hard sell for Mayer." She went on to say that she'd be on the lookout for a role in which Judy might thrive, "perhaps as the plump little sister of one of our young female stars."

Judy realized that she might present a dilemma for most casting directors. "I should have been a star at six, certainly no later than eight. I could have done those Shirley Temple roles—only better. No longer a child wonder with a big voice, I've now arrived at what is called 'the in-between age.'"

As Mayer's executive secretary, and "the guardian of the gate" (i.e., his office), Koverman was said to be the force that actually ran MGM. She'd come to work for Louis B. Mayer in 1928 when talkies were just getting started. Before that, she'd been the confidential secretary of Herbert Hoover during his run for president.

At MGM, she'd been the driving force behind launching the careers of major stars who included the songbird Jeanette MacDonald, her teammate, Nelson Eddy, and such other actors as Leatrice Joy and Jean Parker.

Koverman's most notable achievement

A late in life photo of the formidable personal secretary to Louis B. Mayer, **Iva Koverman** (1876-1954), whom insiders claimed "damn near ran the studio."

She's credited by modern feminists as a crucial but frequently unrecognized power broker in the discovery and steerage of Clark Gable, Robert Taylor, and Judy Garland, and a voice of reason that often soothed the frequently ruffled feathers of her imperious boss.

was persuading Mayer to hire Clark Gable. Jack Warner had rejected him because "his ears are too big."

She'd also been instrumental in reviving the adult careers of child stars who included both Mickey Rooney and Jackie Cooper. Later, she'd give both Judy and Elizabeth Taylor a push toward stardom, too, and help morph Robert Taylor into a major-league movie star, too.

Judy and Ethel had already met talent agent Al Rosen. At the time, her mother predicted they'd never hear from him again. As was the case of many of her other predictions, she was wrong about Rosen, too.

After his return to Hollywood from the Cal-Neva, he began working to wangle Judy an audition at MGM. Just as he was on the verge of contacting Koverman, he was happily surprised that she'd already seen her on stage at the Paramount Theater and had been impressed with her talent.

MGM wasn't the only door Rosen knocked on. As Judy recalled, "Al toured me all over Southern California. I think I had an audition at every studio. The reaction was always the same. 'She isn't *any* age. She isn't a child wonder, and she isn't grown up.'"

"That was exactly my own appraisal, but Al didn't give up easily," Judy said. "He was definitely small time, competing with the big guys at William Morris. He needed a star that would keep a roof over his head, and he believed I might be the one. But it would take work. "

"At MGM, a teenager or very young woman was regarded as a menace to the industry and fit only to be stuffed into a barrel unless she could be turned into a glamour girl. That came true especially with the gals I got to know there—Lana Turner, first, followed by Hedy Lamarr, then Ava Gardner, and ultimately, Elizabeth Taylor."

Her life was made even more difficult "because Rosen and Ethel launched World War II before Hitler did" (Judy's words). Rosen refused to let Ethel accompany Judy to auditions, and bitterly fought with her over how to launch her into movies.

"I always sided with Rosen," Judy said.

After Judy became a star, many people claimed that they had arranged her first audition with Mayer. Perhaps in some way most of them indeed played a role, but most of the credit goes to Koverman, who set up the appointment.

Cinema history was made when Judy Garland met Louis B. Mayer, who was at the peak of his power, reigning over Metro-Goldwyn-Mayer, the largest and most prestigious studio in Hollywood. It boasted "more stars than there are in heaven," an array of talent that featured Norma Shearer, Joan Crawford,

Blessed with formidable social skills and able, in some cases, to use her charm as a weapon, Judy could usually comport herself well in the demanding presence of MGM's studio chief, **Louis B. Mayer.**

Clark Gable, Greta Garbo, Jean Harlow, Hedy Lamarr, and Lana Turner, with Elizabeth Taylor on the horizon.

Mayer was hailed as "the Merchant of Dreams," committed to family-friendly movies that even young children could enjoy. He rejected scripts with references to sex, drunkenness, homosexuality, prostitution, or anything else Mayer considered "unsavory." Privately, he had his own sexual secrets with a noted fondness for "young maidens." In years to come, Judy would claim that Mayer molested her during her first two years at his studio.

Mayer was born in 1884 in that part of the Russian Empire now known as Ukraine. Emigrating to America, he became a junk dealer, hauling a wheelbarrow around to pick up scrap metal in the neighborhood.

Abandoning that business, which he viewed as degrading, he opened his first movie theater way back in 1907 when films were in their infancy. In Haverhill, Massachusetts, his theater business grew and grew, and by 1914, he was in the film distribution business. In Boston, his first big break came when for $25,000, he acquired the rights to D.W. Griffith's controversial *The Birth of a Nation* (1915).

In 1918, he had formed his own production company. In a major career move in 1924, he joined with partners Marcus Loew and Samuel Goldwyn to form Metro-Goldwyn-Loew (later, Metro-Goldwyn-Mayer).

Teamed with "the Boy Wonder," Irving Thalberg, the dynamic duo turned out some of the greatest films in the history of cinema.

His golden year was 1939, when he distributed two classics, *Gone With the Wind* and *The Wizard of Oz*. He became the first American to earn a million dollars a year and was credited for the discovery of stars who included Hedy Lamarr, hailed as the most beautiful woman in the world.

He wasn't always good at predicting who would be a star and who didn't have "what it takes." For example, he predicted that Clark Gable would be "just a flash in the pan."

Finally, Rosen got what he wanted: MGM would audition Judy Garland.

Ethel was away when the phone rang. Frank was there to pick up the receiver. Rosen told him he'd be at their home within thirty minutes to take Judy to MGM where they wanted to see her within the hour. At the time,

When **Judy** received Louis B. Mayer's unexpected summons to haul herself off to his office within thirty minutes for an interview, she was unprepared, uncoiffed, and looked like a tomboy—something like how she appears in this publicity still from *Pigskin Parade* (1936).

Ironically, her look that afternoon corresponded to Mayer's preference for unsullied, all-American girl-next-door types, because—even though he was seriously angry with one of his staff members that day—he hired her anyway.

along with her dog Waffles, she was playing in their backyard in sneakers and jeans. With her Buster Brown haircut, she looked like a tomboy.

Frank called to her. "We've got to go. I know you're a mess, but MGM wants you...*NOW!*"

Rosen was waiting at the gate, and he took Judy into the office of Koverman, who had already heard her sing at the Paramount Theatre

Koverman agreed to go into a nearby studio and listen to Judy, as Frank accompanied her on the piano. After three numbers, she confronted him. "You're not very good. I'll ring for Roger Edens. He's MGM's music arranger and vocal coach. Judy will need him if she's accepted."

How could she have known? Edens, who used to be the pianist for Ethel Merman, would become a major influence during her years at MGM. He played for her as she sang "Zing! Went the Strings of My Heart."

"Mayer should hear this," Koverman said and phoned her boss. He was angry that day, feuding with Irving Thalberg. "A girl singer—just what I need," he said, sarcastically, yet Koverman prevailed.

Mayer eventually invited Rosen, Frank, Judy, and Edens into his all-white office, where he was perched on a raised, altar-like dias behind his oversized desk. Everything was in white, including the piano in the corner.

After three songs, Judy looked at Mayer, but could detect no reaction. What she didn't know is that he never showed emotion before a contract was signed.

Suspecting that Mayer was about to reject his daughter, Frank took her hand and escorted her out of the office.

A surprise call came in the next morning, summoning Judy once more to MGM. This time, she was carefully groomed and dressed for her appearance before the formidable studio chief.

When Mayer came in, Koverman suggested that Judy sing that old Yiddish favorite, "Eyli, Eyli."

At the end of the number, tears had formed in Mayer's eyes. He rose from his desk, and dismissed everyone in the room, but not before thanking Judy. He made no commitment, not even, "We'll be in touch."

Two days later, an anxious Frank and Judy urgently waited for a signal from Rosen. Ethel had returned home and was furious that she, too, had not been invited to MGM.

Finally, Rosen called with news: "Mayer is ready to sign Judy to a seven-year contract. Bring her to the studio right away." Before ringing off, he barked "and don't bring that damn wife of yours!"

***

On September 16, Judy, accompanied by Frank, signed her first contract with Metro-Goldwyn-Mayer. Her initial salary was $100 a week, with option renewals (or dismissals) at six-month intervals. The contract was for a duration of seven years, which, at its conclusion, would have her drawing $1,000 a week.

Since she was a minor, the contract had to be approved by the Los Angeles Superior Court. On September 27, a judge issued his approval.

Judy was ordered to drop out of "Ma Lawlor's" School for Actors and to enroll in MGM's "Little Red Schoolhouse." Complete with a front porch and a rocking chair, it stood on MGM's grounds in Culver City. An inspector from the Los Angeles Board of Education supervised the curriculum and its teachers.

Five days a week, from nine in the morning until lunchtime, Judy attended the classes, which were typical of any junior high school in America at the time.

Mickey Rooney was enrolled in her class but seemed more intrigued by the budding starlets than with English grammar. He and Judy bonded closely, beginning their legendary friendship.

"It was widely rumored at the time that I was the culprit who took her virginity. I was not. That was a lie. To be frank, I found Judy a wonderful person, but, as a sexual object, and as my coming years would show, I was more likely to get an erection with MGM's stars of the future, notably Lana Turner and Ava Gardner. My alltime sexual adventure was in the company of actor Donald ("Red") Barry. One weekend we took turns bedding sixteen young Japanese girls."

Judy was thrilled to learn that she'd be attending classes with Freddie Bartholomew, a London-born actor two years younger than her. "I admired Freddie's performance in *David Copperfield* (1935)." Freddie would soon become one of her boyfriends.

"As for boys my own age, there was Jackie Cooper, who was my exact age," Judy said. "I had first seen him when he co-starred with Wallace Beery in that tearjerker *The Champ* (1931). I really developed a crush on him."

Years later, Judy remembered Lana Turner and Rooney raising their hands to go to the toilet. "Actually, I found out they were not going to take a crap—or a leak—but they'd sneak behind the schoolhouse and smoke cigarettes."

Afternoons for Judy were spent with her vocal coach, Roger Edens, who was later credited with "creating" Judy Garland. If he didn't do that, he certainly polished her singing, especially her phrasing.

He would remember her as "this chunky little girl in a navy middy blouse, with dark eyes hungry for love, or at least approval from adults. My disappointment at her looks

In a behind-the-scenes context loaded with sharks, nay-sayers, and in some cases, sexual predators, vocal coach **Roger Edens** is pictured above with Judy during one of her early rehearsals at MGM. He treated her kindly, to some degree like the supportive, well-meaning (gay) uncle of a young starlet's dreams.

faded when she opened her mouth to sing. As talented as she was, she needed a lot of work, and I felt I was the man to do it for her."

"Even at the age of thirteen, she had this unbelievable control, full of power in the high register and shimmering warmth in the low. Her rendition of 'Zing! Went the Strings of My Heart' touched my own heart."

"A lot of older men at MGM made passes at the little starlet—not me! I was very open about being a homosexual and didn't conceal that from anyone, including Mayer himself. I would later write songs just for Judy."

After becoming used to the classroom and vocal coaching aspects of her association with MGM, Judy was sent to its makeup department. Orders had come down from Mayer himself that he was "sending over an ugly duckling that I want turned into a graceful swan."

In the pursuit of Mayer's directive, Judy's encounter with one of the makeup artists at MGM, Philip Parkes, was devastating. He was considered one of the best in the business, "a vicious queen who hated women but could make them look incredibly beautiful."

At their first meeting, he looked her up and down. "I felt like a slab of beef being inspected," she recalled. He was so blunt in his appraisal of her physicality that she burst into tears.

"You have a stubby neck that seems to melt into your shoulders—no neck at all, in fact. That pug nose…impossible. It'll have to be fixed. Your teeth will have to be capped or else the cameraman will not be able to take closeups of you. Your legs are too long for your body, and those wrists…my oh my. What can I say? Mayer calls you his little hunchback, and I see why. You have a curvature of the spine. If I can transform you into something acceptable for a close-up, it will be my biggest challenge to date."

Then, MGM's publicity department advised her that on October 26, she was to sing on the NBC Radio Network—her first major exposure to a nationwide audience. She was to meet with Arthur Freed, one of Hollywood's leading producers of musicals, with the understanding that he'd select the proper song for her. Later that day, she and Freed rehearsed his "Broadway Rhythm."

Years later, Freed said, "Some child actors are like artists. They're wonderful until they improve, and then they improve into failures. Over

Arthur Freed claimed that "Judy Garland could learn a song faster than anybody I ever knew. Musicians loved working with her."

In addition to fourteen movies he shot with Judy, he also produced *Singin' in the Rain*, and (as directed by one of her husbands, Vincente Minnelli), *An American in Paris* and *Gigi*.

the years, I've noted few exceptions to that. Shirley Temple never made it as an adult. But Judy did. So did Elizabeth Taylor. Margaret O'Brien, no way. Many child stars have a quality of innocence and reality that you can believe. But they lose that except in rare cases. Judy is the prime example of a child star who made it as an adult performer. And what an artist. She became a god damn legend."

At the requested time, Ethel drove her talented daughter to the KFI Studios in Hollywood, where they met Wallace Beery, that grizzly old actor who was the host of the *Shell Château Hour*. After giving Judy a sloppy wet kiss—he was fond of little girls—he told her that they'd go on the air at 6:30PM.

Her favorite films starring Beery were the trio he'd made with Jackie Cooper (*The Champ* and *The Bowery*) and Robert Louis Stevenson's *Treasure Island* (1934).

On the air, he told his listeners that Judy was twelve years old (actually, she was thirteen) and MGM's rising new star.

Although at the time, she knew nothing about it, the publicity department had given Beery a news tip: "This little girl will soon be co-starring with Robert Montgomery in *This Time It's Love*.

[That picture was never made.]

Carefully coached by Freed, Judy delivered a memorable rendition of *Broadway Rhythm*. She was so good that Beery asked her if she'd come back on the show again.

But backstage during all this "was the boy of my dreams, Jackie Cooper. We were soon dating."

***

On November 16, Judy, driven to the KFI Studios in Los Angeles by Ethel, arrived in time for her second appearance on the *Shell Château Hour* hosted by Wallace Beery.

At one point, Ethel had to go to her car to retrieve something from the trunk. While she was gone, a call from Dr. Rabwin came in from the Cedars of Lebanon Hospital for Ethel, so Judy took it instead.

In a calm voice, so as not to alarm her, he informed her that Frank had become suddenly stricken at his theater in Lomita and had been rushed by ambulance to the hospital where Marc Rabwin happened to be the

Judy's debut on the **Shell Chateau Hour** was promoted with slogans defining her as the "twelve-year-old wonder singer" and broadcast nationwide. Listeners found her endearing.

Alongside her and on the air were comedian Patsy Kelly, tennis champion "Big Bill Tilden" (later arrested on charges of boy pedophila), and operatic tenor, Allan Jones.

It was a lot for a thirteen-year-old to handle.

chief surgeon.

"We've diagnosed him with a virulent case of spinal meningitis. I don't think he's going to make it, as he's too far gone. I'll call throughout the day and keep giving you bulletins. I put a radio in his room so he can hear you sing. Give it your all, as I know you will."

She was called to go on the air, and she did, singing her heart out with her familiar song, "Zing! Went the Strings of My Heart."

By the time Judy reached the hospital, Frank had drifted into a coma. When she returned home, Ethel had nothing to say.

The following day was her birthday. Judy tried to sleep, but couldn't. Dr. Rabwin alerted the family that Frank had died at 3PM

Unknown to both Ethel and Judy, he had planned a surprise party for Ethel. Completely unaware that anything was wrong, guests with presents began arriving at 5PM. Judy accepted their presents but had to turn the guests away. This was no time for a celebration.

Without telling Judy where she was going, Ethel left the house and remained absent for three days. Judy later found out that she was with the widowed Will Gilmore, her lover. The way was now paved for their marriage, since his wife, Laura, had already passed away.

Frank's funeral was conducted Wednesday morning, November 22, at Forest Lawn's Little Church of the Flowers in Glendale. Boyd Parker, the rector at St. Paul's Episcopal Church in Lancaster, drove south to preside. He seemingly had forgiven Frank for molesting his teenage choir boys.

Dr. Rabwin was at the funeral, telling Judy, "Frank was like a father to me."

[Ironically, Dr. Rabwin would show up at Judy's own funeral in 1969, He was the only person attending who knew her when she was a girl.]

Never having attended a funeral before, Judy was horrified at the open casket, as strangers peered in at the corpse of her father, many of whom didn't really know him. She begged Ethel to close the lid of the coffin, which she finally did.

As she remembered years later, "I couldn't cry at my Dad's funeral. I was ashamed since I couldn't fake it. Eight days later, I locked myself in my bedroom and cried for fourteen hours. The person closest to me had gone."

"I never confronted Ethel in the months that followed, but in a way, I blamed her for my father's early death. All those fights, really violent arguments, and her adulterous affair with Will Gilmore, I think contributed to his death. He was forced to turn elsewhere for the love and satisfaction she didn't give him, and that got him into a lot of trouble, as I learned later."

In 1939, as she sat through the first complete showing of *The Wizard of Oz* at MGM, she said, "My greatest regret is that Frank didn't get to see me play Dorothy."

Author Barry Kehoe wrote: "By the usual standards, Frank Gumm was a failure. Forced to move from town to town, thinking he could do anything he wanted and get away with it, he ultimately self-destructed. He was a success only to himself. He was charming, enigmatic, mysterious.

He had a way about him, a charm, a jolly quality. He was all this to Frances. If she, too, became self-destructive and failed to become a great person, it was because she repeated her father's tragedy. It was enough for her that he, above all others, paid delightful attention to her: This had been enough to see her through."

Judy recalled, "His funeral was the worst day of my life. The worst thing that ever happened to me. I would spend the rest of my life searching for him."

After the funeral, she came back home, realizing that for her, she no longer had a home to return to. With both of her sisters gone, and with only Ethel left there, she felt more lonely than she'd ever felt in her life. "Being locked up with Ethel, who was gone most of the time with Gilmore, was like no home at all. Guess I'll have to make MGM my home."

Author Christopher Finch wrote; "Hollywood destroyed Judy Garland's childhood by trivializing it into oblivion, a process that started the day MGM's publicity department first turned its attention on her. She lacked the stability and security to resist the relentless erosion of fact and, eventually, she came to believe many of the myths invented for her. The studio invented a surrogate childhood for her to escape to, thus destroying any hopes she might have had of finding roots and stability. The pills and morphine and the rest of the junk would eventually finish the job, blurring whatever survived of the fictionalizing process—but, to all intents and purposes, the truth was buried the day her father died. Eventually, the happy times and all of the successes were obliterated, to be replaced by a catalogue of comic disasters."

***

Judy ended 1935 on a sad note because of the death of her father, which overrode any joy she felt from signing that seven-year contract with MGM. According to the terms of the contract, she could make outside recordings.

Once again, because of the publicity generated about her, she was summoned back to Decca Records for another recording session. She'd rehearsed two numbers, "All's Well," and "No Other One." The recording took all day, and Ethel thought she was "perfect."

Judy wasn't so sure and expressed doubt over the choice of songs. So did the executive at Decca who, for the second time, refused to sign her as a recording artist.

Today, the records would have a curiosity value on the market, but they appeared to have been either lost or destroyed.

In the final hours of this fast-fading year, the publicity department ordered her to pose for shots with Mickey Rooney. No picture at that time had been planned to star them, although one would be forthcoming. Publicists wanted the shots of them to promote the news of their signing with the studio.

In one solo shot, there is a haunting look in the eyes of Judy, perhaps a lingering sadness from the loss of Frank Gumm.

Frank had left Ethel $2,500 in unpaid bills, a $150 stock certificate, and exactly $235.31 in the bank. Even so, she believed that Judy would soon be a star, and she was so confident that she rented a house at 190 South MaCadden, close to Culver City.

The house came with a swimming pool, a status symbol in Hollywood. When Judy bonded with other stars at MGM, including Rooney, her Saturday afternoon swim parties became a fixture in her life.

From Monday to Saturday, she reported to MGM for her morning school lessons and afternoon sessions with her musical director, Roger Edens.

"Mayer wanted to get his money's worth out of me," Judy said. "With no film in mind for me, he had me perform at private parties for his stars." One night, she was sent over to the home of Jeanette MacDonald, a former chorus girl who later became a singing sensation when teamed with Nelson Eddy in a string of movie operettas such as *Naughty Marietta* (1935)

At the end of three numbers, MacDonald approached her. She didn't thank her, but said, "You dear little girl," and seemed to size up her figure. "Well, not so little. I don't know your future as a singer, perhaps…and only *maybe*…a belter like Ethel Merman."

"This diva then announced dinner for her guests," Judy said. "I was not included. She didn't even offer me a plate of food in the kitchen, and I went home hungry. What a bitch!"

***

One morning in her class at the Little Red Schoolhouse, Judy was introduced to Deanna Durbin, another singer, this one from Winnipeg, Canada, who was still known as "Edna

Jeanette MacDonald, MGM's singing sensation of the 1930s, cultivated the image of an above-reproach *prima donna*.

That was wildly inaccurate, as she had begun her show-biz career as a high-priced "escort" in Manhattan in the 1920s.

"My co-stars were either old enough to be my father or queer," she said, the latter a reference to her onscreen partner, Nelson Eddy.

After her marriage to actor Gene Raymond, MacDonald and her new husband accompanied Mary Pickford and her new husband, Buddy Rogers, on a honeymoon holiday in Hawaii.

"Gene spent more time in bed with Buddy than with me," Jeanette later complained.

Judy Garland frequently mocked MacDonald as a "Silly horse talking away with wood peg Eddy—with all that glycerine running down her Max Factor makeup."

Mae."

She was much slimmer and prettier than Judy, who would later claim that they became good friends. "I was never jealous of her."

That seems unlikely because in a few months, Mayer had a dilemma: Which girl singer should I keep?"

Their voices were different: Whereas Judy specialized in swing, Deanna was a talented lyric soprano. "If anything," Judy said, "Jeanette Mac-Donald should be the one 'Edna Mae' was likely to replace."

Early in 1935, MGM writers were at work on a screenplay depicting the life of the celebrated opera star, Ernestine Schumann-Hein. Deanna was set to play her as a young girl, with the star herself taking over as an adult.

After hearing Deanna sing only once, Mayer decided she was a "mature soprano," and he signed her for a provisional try-out of six months. However, Schumann-Hein took ill, and her bio pic was never made.

Mayer now faced two very different singers, with no roles for either of them. "Teenage brat" roles had not yet come into vogue.

As Judy said, "You have to be either eight years old or eighteen to get a movie role."

Mayer decided to make a musical short with the two of them. "I'll keep the winner and let our option expire on the loser."

Entitled *Every Sunday*, Judy co-starred with Durbin in this two-reel musical short shot in 1936 when Judy was fourteen years old. Felix Feist directed Deanna and Judy in the story of how two young singers perform to save the bandshell concerts that the town

Are you really up-to-date on Hollywood History? Find Out by Answering these Questions about

DEANNA DURBIN

(Judy's Competitor and Frenemy)

For four years in the 1930s, who was the most famous teenager in the world, and Hollywood's best-paid female entertainer?
Answer: Deanna Durbin

What did Hitler, Stalin, Mussolini, Churchill, and FDR have in common?
Answer: Deanna Durbin was their favorite singer.

In 1940, as Nazi bombs were destroying wide tracts of urban London, what was the reaction, in print, of Lord Rothermere, publisher of The Daily Mail?
Answer: "What England needs now is more Deanna Durbin movies!"

council wants to shut down. Judy came out with a dirty face, holding an apple and delivering a song in her role as the "Queen of Transelvania." Other clips from it display Judy rendering a waltz into a swing ballad. She was joined near its end by Deanna, who lilts away in an operetta style that evokes Jeanette MacDonald. Excerpts from this short film tribute to small-town America still exist, and Judy, of course, is astonishing.

Billed as MGM's newest singing sensation, Judy was shipped to New York for a promotional appearance. She celebrated her fourteenth birthday there but felt morbid that Frank was no longer alive to bring her the birthday cake as he always had.

Because of the publicity Judy was receiving, Decca Records decided to give her another chance. She was booked to record at their main head-quarters at 50 West 57th Street, backed up by the Bob Crosby Orchestra.

She sang "Stompin' at the Savoy" and "Swing, Mr. Charlie." Crosby objected to having his name appear on a label with such "an unknown singer," and it was removed.

FEROCIOUS INNOCENTS, IMPLACABLE COMPETITORS

Deanna Durbin with Judy Garland in *Every Sunday (1936)*

Within a year, Judy would sign a long-term contract with Decca.

Joe Pasternak saw the short and wanted Judy to star in his upcoming *Three Smart Girls,* but Mayer refused to release her to Universal. In the meantime, MGM had carelessly let Deanna's six-month contract expire, so Pasternak hired her instead for a film that became in international success.

"Working with Deanna, I was stunned that she had only one eyebrow," Judy later claimed. There was no separation of hair in the middle above her nose. An MGM makeup artist was summoned to remove some hair. The word was out: Our musical short would determine which gal singer MGM would retain."

"Deanna and I, at least on the surface, put up a good show that we were friends, not deadly enemies. I even accepted an invitation to attend a party at her home. Her best friends were horrible to me. I heard them gossiping about me not too far away from where I stood. One claimed that I would never be an actress. Another said that she'd heard I could not sing, and yet another claimed I was too fat. I stormed out of the party in tears."

One day, Mickey Rooney wandered into the MGM commissary for lunch and was surprised to see Judy and Deanna eating with Clark Gable and Robert Taylor.

"There was a lot of flirting going on between those two horndogs and those underaged gals," Rooney said. "Call the cops."

"Judy would soon start dating, and the word got out. She went from boy to man and back to boy again. I understood going out with guys her own age, but older men?"

"A lot of people thought I was the one who took her virginity, but I wasn't," Rooney said, his second denial. "I won't name the geezer who did, but he should be ashamed of himself. So many people told Judy she was unattractive that she turned from one guy to another, obviously to re-assure herself that she was desirable."

"Did I ever get around to seducing Judy? How do I know?" he said in an interview in 1977. "It was so long ago. Girls, girls, girls—and women, too—my memory grows dim."

Every Sunday was screened for Mayer, and he had to make up his mind: A singer at home with jazz and swing, or else a diva-in-the-making who could do classical lieder and opera. While hesitating to make a choice, he was told that MGM's option with Deanna had expired, and that Universal had signed her, a smart move since the young singer would make millions for that studio. _

"Hiring Deanna was the greatest move I ever made," Joe Pasternak said. "With Deanna, one hit musical followed another, and she rescued Universal from bankruptcy."

In 1946, Deanna was the second highest-paid woman in the United States, just behind Bette Davis. The following year, with Davis in sudden decline at Warners', Deanna became the highest-salaried woman in America.

But as the 1940s came to an end, Deanna just disappeared, moving to France to live with her third husband, Charles Henri David, who produced both American and French movies.

She faded into Hollywood history, and came back into the news only at the time of her death at ninety-one in April of 2013.

Pasternak would later move over to MGM, at which time he would produce several of Judy's movies in the 1940s. "Judy and Deanna were two different types of singers," he said. "When I saw Judy, I wanted to sing and dance with her. When I saw Deanna, I wanted to kiss her and fall in love with her."

***

In her fourteenth year, and still waiting for Mayer to give her her big break, Judy entered into her "boy crazy" period.

"I wanted to die if I weren't in love with some boy—or, in many cases—some older man. They came and went from my life. Some of the older men were quite brutal to me in their desires, but I gave in to them because I felt, for some insane reason or another, that I needed to be pun-ished."

"I don't know how I got through that period of what is known as the terrible teens," she said. "Growing up is so hard to do. I went wild trying to have a good time. Many people who met me during this period expected me to be in braids and gingham like Dorothy. Instead, they got me, a lusty little vixen in high heels. Every day I was seeing Norma Shearer, on occa-sion before her untimely death Jean Harlow, Joan Crawford, Hedy Lamarr, and Lana Turner, each a glamour girl. I wanted to be one, too."

***

At long last, Judy made her feature film debut in *Pigskin Parade* (1936), cast as "Sairy Dodd." It was not for MGM but for 20th Century Fox and produced by Darryl F. Zanuck, the power behind all those hit Shirley Temple movies. Shooting began in August of 1936, on one of the hottest days in Los Angeles' recorded history.

In the late 1930s, football movies were all the rage, and *Pigskin Parade* spoofed them. In a mistake, the coaches at Yale invite small-time Texas State University instead of the University of Texas, to play against them in its big Armistice Day football game.

TSU has a new coach, "Slug" Winters (Jack Haley). His wife, Bessie (Patsy Kelly), seems to know more about football than he does. Gags galore, songs, and occasionally football come together in this hilarious send-up of America's favorite pastime.

When their star player is injured, Slug and Bessie set out to find his replacement. They stumble across an Arkansas hillbilly (Amos Dodd, portrayed by Stuart Erwin) in a melon patch, tossing melons as far as a football field to his little sister, Sairy (Judy).

In this burlesque of the sport, football recruiters immediately want to meet him, but first they have to tangle with Sairy. She calls out to them in her hillbilly twang, "Y'all stop for melons? I can sing! I can sing! Wanna hear me?"

That would come later. Right now, their attention focuses on getting Amos enrolled at Podunk U. to face off against those snooty Yale footballers on the gridiron.

As it turns out, Judy is allowed to sing three songs, each mediocre, but in a high-voltage voice as evoked by "The Texas Tornado." She also sings "It's Love I'm After" to another singer, handsome, masculine Tony Martin, who was married at the time to movie star Alice Faye.

In later years, Judy recalled, "Tony was older than me, but I thought he was the cat's pajamas. If memory serves, I think I had an occasional one-

Two views of Judy, before and after her "show-biz transformation" in **Pigskin Parade** (1936).

In the upper photo, from early in the film, Judy appears in a style replicated three years later in *The Wizard of Oz*, with braids and a shapeless gingham dress. Despite her protests, the director wanted makeup that would emphasize her freckles.

The lower photo is a still from the movie's finale. Although Judy has been cleaned up and glamourized, she still evokes an adolescent who's be-bopping in a nightclub long after her designated bedtime.

night stand with him in the early 40s when I was married to David Rose."

Its director was David Butler, a veteran of the film industry, having starred in two D.W. Griffith movies and also in the 1927 Academy Award-winning picture, *7th Heaven*. At Fox, he would direct some thirty films, including four with Shirley Temple. In time, he would work with such singing stars as Bing Crosby and Doris Day.

Known as the "Queen of the Wisecracks," Brooklyn-born Patsy Kelly befriended teenage Judy, inviting her to share her dressing room. "Patsy was the only one in the cast who was really nice to me—maybe a little too nice. I later found out why. She dug me."

"She became the first of the Hollywood dykes who went after me. She never concealed her lesbianism, even telling *Motion Picture* magazine that she was in a loving relationship with actress Wilma Cox. Later, as her screen career diminished, she lived as a personal assistant with the bisexual Tallulah Bankhead."

SCREEN JUVENILES

AUGUST 1937

25¢

JUDY GARLAND M-G-M sensation

Judy Garland Looks Back Over 10 Years in the Show Business
also features on Deanna Durbin · Shirley Temple · The Mauch Twins

The *New York Times* was not the only media outlet to focus on Judy in the aftermath of *Pigskin Parade*.

Here, in 1937, the year after its release, she was featured as a musically gifted "cover girl" in the August, 1937 issue of **Screen Juveniles.**

On the set, Judy was introduced to Jack Haley, a vaudevillian, comedian, and radio host, who also sang and danced, and who'd been cast as the lesser team's frantic coach. She'd get to know him far better when he was cast as "The Tin Man" in *The Wizard of Oz*.

He'd heard about the death of her father, and he was most empathetic, telling her that he had lost his own father when he was only six months old in 1899 when he'd drowned in a shipwreck off the coast of Nova Scotia.

For his performance as the backwoods melon tosser and "diamond in the rough" football genius, Erwin was nominated for an Oscar as Best Supporting Actor of the Year.

In reference to the plot, as articulated by a critic at *Newsweek*. "There is more horseplay (in this movie) than football."

Pigskin Parade marked Judy's first review in *The New York Times*:

"In the newcomer category is Judy Garland, twelve or thirteen now, about whom the West Coast has been enthusing (sic) as a vocal find. She's cute, not too pretty, but a pleasingly fetching personality who certainly knows how to sell a pop."

"The critic said I wasn't all that pretty," Judy lamented, "and he was damn right. I was this fat little pig in pigtails. I could only hope that Mayer would not see this film, or else it'll be my last screen role."

"I hated myself in it," she said. "That damn director, David Butler, wouldn't let me see the rushes, where I might have improved myself. I didn't want my freckles to show. He did. I used to fret over them until I learned that Katharine Hepburn, Joan Crawford, and Myrna Loy also have freckles."

"After seeing myself on the screen, I could only hope to be afflicted with amnesia. I dreamed of looking like a glamour girl, but came across as freckled, fat, and with a snub nose—in other words, just little ol' kick-the-can Baby Gumm."

"I went home and cried myself to sleep that night."

As a mature actor, **Jackie Coogan** both starred with and married the actress who became the pin-up favorite of World War II, **Betty Grable.**

Long after the tribulations of Coogan's years as cruelly exploited child actor, they're seen together as young romantics in *College Swing* (1938).

Two years later, Zanuck considered making a sequel to *Pigskin Parade,* calling it *Corn-Husking Musical,* in which Judy would be given a major singing role, playing Sairy Dodd again. A month later, he changed his mind and canceled it.

In another failed opportunity, Judy was set to star in *Born to Dance* (1936), with music by Cole Porter. Her co-star would be Buddy Epsen, but her part was written out. The role went instead to five-year-old Juanita Quigley. The movie ended up starring James Stewart and tap-dancing Eleanor Powell.

***

The famous feud between Judy Garland and Betty Grable began on the set of *Pigskin Parade.* Grable had been cast as Laura Watson, who is romanced by "Chip" (Johnny Downs), the star player at TSU. Director David Butler assigned Grable a solo to sing called "It's Love I'm After." She photographed extremely sexy but had a very limited vocal range.

However, at the last minute, Judy joined the cast and took over the singing. Butler eliminated Grable's solo from the final cut. "There went my dream, at least for the moment," Grable lamented. "I lost my big chance to Miss Piggy."

Grable was dating Jackie Coogan (not to be confused with Jackie Cooper). Coogan had exploded into fame when he co-starred with Charlie Chaplin in *The Kid* (1921).

At the time he met Judy on the set of *Pigskin Parade,* he was front-and-center in the news, in every case, a disaster report.

Only months before, Coogan, age twenty, had been the sole survivor of a horrific automobile crash that occurred in eastern San Diego County.

Four passengers in the car with him, including his father, actor John Henry Coogan, Jr., were returning from a dove hunt across the border in Mexico, with his father driving along the highway near Pine Valley, California. The Coogan party faced a roaring oncoming vehicle and Coogan *père,* to avoid a head-on collision, swerved and rolled down an embankment. Although police pulled young Coogan from the wreckage, his father and everyone else in the vehicle were killed.

As Coogan told Judy, years later, when he turned twenty-one, he and his attorney went to collect the earnings generated by his extended stint as a child actor, estimated at four million dollars.

To his undying regret, however, the bank manager informed him that awful afternoon that his mother and his new stepfather, Arthur Bernstein, had squandered his fortune on custom-made automobiles, "a ton" of jewelry, furs, and luxury trips. Before he'd married Coogan's mother Bernstein had been a financial adviser to the family. In court, his mother told the judge, "No promises were ever made to give Jackie anything. He was such a bad boy."

[In 1938, a year after he learned about the stolen funds, Coogan sued his mother and Bernstein and was awarded just $126,000, all that remained from his earnings. Falling on hard times, he visited Charlie Chaplin, his former director, who gave him a check for $1,000.

His legal predicament led to the enactment of the California Actor's Bill in 1939. Commonly referred to as "The Coogan Bill," it was designed to protect child actors like Judy and Coogan, or Jackie Cooper and Shirley Temple. It mandated that a child actor's employer set aside fifteen percent of all their earnings to a trust.]

Jackie Coogan, who became Judy's friend and boyfriend, easily identified with her traumas as a child actor.

In the photo above, he appears with "The Tramp," **Charlie Chaplin** in the silent-movie tearjerker, *The Kid* (1921)

Though very few of them were aware of **Jackie Coogan's** long links with vintage Hollywood, fans of late-night TV best remember him as Uncle Fester on the frequently re-run 64 episodes of the 1962-64 TV series, *The Addams Family.*

Grable had met Coogan at a beach outing at Santa Monica when he was romantically involved with RKO starlet, Lucille Ball.

"I was very attracted to him," Grable told the gay actor, Cesar Romero. "It wasn't exactly love, but there was an appeal there. I knew I could take him from that flat-chested Ball creature."

[Ironically, Grable would later have an affair with Desi Arnaz, Ball's future husband.

As Grable told Romero, "My motto is 'so many men, so little time.' Even when

I became engaged to Jackie, I was still playing around, and I think he was, too."

She candidly confided, "I'm the trucker's delight."

She was referring to her secret nighttime passion of working the truck stops. Mart Martin, the biographer, wrote: "Betty Grable preferred rough men of the truck driver or bartender type—and especially liked to fellate them," a sexual pleasure also preferred by Romero.

Later, Grable told Romero, "You and I both have fallen big time for Desi Arnaz."

Even during her engagement to Coogan, Grable was slipping around and getting seduced by Mickey Rooney. "The trouble with Mickey," she confided to Romero, "is that most of his growth went into his balls—and not to a more vital part of his anatomy.]

One afternoon on the set of *Pigskin Parade*, Cooper dropped in to pick up Grable, who was shooting a scene. He met Judy and flirted with her, and asked for her phone number, which she gave him. To her, he was still a big star, and she was flattered by his attention.

"Don't tell Betty I asked for your number," he told her.

"Agreed. We'll keep it our secret."

Judy later admitted that she started secretly dating Coogan "because I wanted to get back at Grable, who was snubbing me."

The following afternoon, when Grable was busy, Coogan waited for Judy a block from the entrance gate to Fox. Once inside his car, she was driven to this beach house a friend of his owned at Malibu.

She later told her newly minted friend, Bonita Granville, "I was the ugly duckling on the set of *Pigskin Parade*. Not only did I have to compete with Grable and those luscious legs of hers, but with Arline Judge too."

Judge would go on to marry seven times, including to Dan Topping, who in time became president and part owner of the New York Yankees. He would later marry Lana Turner after Judge divorced him. In the wake of divorces from two subsequent husbands, Judge married Topping's brother, Henry.

Details are missing, but that afternoon at Malibu, Coogan performed oral sex on Judy. Like Grable herself, it was his favorite form of sex.

Some observers wondered how such a teenaged girl could go out with so many men. After Frank's death, Ethel moved more and more into the orbit of Will Gilmore and eventually married him. Since he and Judy didn't like each other, Ethel receded from Judy's life, at least for the moment.

"I became boy crazy," Judy claimed once again. "Let me correct myself—boy AND man crazy. Many of my dates were with much older men. Nothing wrong with a little seasoning in a man."

Judy and Betty both moved toward super stardom. Their jealousy of each other often raged—and not just over their attraction to the same men. In press report after press report, Grable's allure was promoted far more lavishly than Judy's charm.

A typical account came from Fred Majadalany in the *Daily Mail*: "There are musical comedy queens with more pronounced gifts—girl singing ones like Kathryn Grayson, clowning ones like Betty Hutton, and dancing ones like Judy Garland. But Miss Grable's slippers are the ones from which the most champagne *would be drunk in open competition."*

***

Judy had met Jackie Cooper before, even attending school with him. "He made me swoon both in person and on the screen when I'd seen him in all those Hal Roach *Our Gang* comedies."

Roach had sold Cooper's contract to MGM in 1931. That was followed with him co-starring with Wallace Beery in three pictures. "That old bastard was a big disappointment to me," Cooper said. "He always accused me of being a scene-stealer and bitched about how hard it was to work with a child actor."

Judy managed to get an invitation to Cooper's fourteenth birthday party.

At Cooper's birthday bash, Judy was the aggressor, making her intentions known. He asked her out on a date the following night, and she remembered it well.

"His mother, I learned, and my mother, Ethel, approved of our dating," Judy said. "It seemed harmless enough. Since he was too young to drive—I was nine months older than him—he came to my house in a chauffeur-driven limousine. In the back seat with this darling boy, I felt like Lady Vere de Vere."

"I'd messed around with boys in the back row of my father's theater in Grand Rapids, but this was a real grown-up date. At the end of the evening, we agreed to date again the following Saturday. He gave me a real good night kiss. I didn't know fourteen-year-old boys could kiss like that. He must have been taking lessons from someone."

On their second date, Cooper had his chauffeur drive her to the beach at Malibu. He had brought a blanket.

He was later candid about what happened that night. "We never took off all our clothes. She wanted to have sex orally. We did each other. Although I'm rumored to be the guy who took her cherry, I was not. I later found out who that culprit was. Judy and I confined ourselves and all of our subsequent dates to the oral arts. I was willing to go much further, but she feared getting pregnant."

Soon, "Jackie & Judy" were seen having lunch together at the Brown Derby, where

Jackie Cooper as a child star in *Skippy* (1931)

WOMEN WE LOVE: Joan Crawford, the then-greatest diva in Hollywood.

64

older stars would stop by their table to greet them. "They looked like such a cute, adorable couple," said Rosalind Russell. "Oh, the glories of young love."

They were spotted playing tennis, going swimming, and emerging together from a movie house on Hollywood Boulevard.

"At the time I was dating Judy, I was getting the real thing from Miss Joan Crawford," Cooper said. "I would visit her after dropping Judy off."

"Going out with Jackie was like counting daisy petals or reading poetry," Judy claimed.

She told Robert McIlwaine of *Modern Screen,* "Jackie is awfully smart, and he loves music as much as I do. We spent many evenings just listening to records. Sometimes we go out dancing together. The only objection I have about him is that he likes to smoke this big, stinking old pipe. He likes fun as much as I do, and we're the first to get into things and the last to sign off."

"My affair with Crawford lasted six months," Cooper confessed. "I'd slip into her house after midnight. She was one wild woman. She would bathe me, powder me, cologne me. Sometimes, she'd stand nude before a full-length mirror, except she wore a wide-brimmed hat and towering high heels, a style known in Hollywood in those days as 'Joan Crawford fuck-me shoes.'"

"During the day, I'd listen to my buddies brag about some pimply faced fourteen-year-old gal they'd seduced. Little did the jerks know that I, Jackie Cooper, was screwing the Love Goddess of the Silver Screen."

Publicity photo stressing the all-round wholesomeness of **Judy Garland**'s dates with **Jackie Cooper.**

They were anything but wholesome.

Hot, heavy, and then in the news: **Jackie Cooper** with Judy's rival, **Bonita Granville**, on the cover of *Movie Life* magazine.

"In those days, Crawford wasn't the only older woman I seduced," Cooper said. "There were at least half a dozen of my mother's friends I bedded. They were bored with their husbands and welcomed a hot seventeen-year-old into their beds."

His friend, William Smith, backed up his boast. "Cooper was a smart kid, a smart little son of a bitch. I'll tell you something about him: He could always get the broads. I once caught him in bed with an older woman who'd been a vaudeville star."

One night when I arrived at Crawford's house, I found out that Clark Gable had left only a half hour earlier," Cooper said. "I was at first reluctant to take sloppy seconds until she whispered a secret to me, telling me my penis was bigger than the King of Hollywood's."

By January of 1938, Judy told Gladys Hall of *Motion Picture Magazine,* "Jackie and I are still good friends, and he's part of our gang. We get together at each other's homes on Saturday afternoons for a pool part. He's got another girl now, my friend, Bonita Granville."

"Word got out that I dumped Judy for starlet Bonita Granville," Cooper said. "That wasn't true. She dumped me when Billy Halop came along. He was an older man at sixteen. I once showered with Billy at the gym. His cock looked bigger than mine. Maybe that was the attraction for Judy."

"Even after we stopped dating, Judy got me to serve as her beard. I'd pick her up like we were going out on a real date. But I'd deliver her to the home of that horndog, the bandleader, Artie Shaw. Then I'd come back at midnight, pick her up, and take her back home."

"Don't feel sorry for me," he said. "After delivering Shaw's 'piece' for the night, I headed over to shack up with her rival, Deanna Durbin. We were making a movie together called *That Certain Age* (1938). If not Durbin, then Joan Crawford. I was growing up."

Months later, Cooper learned who took Judy's virginity. He was amazingly frank in discussing Hollywood sex in its golden days.

"I found out who deflowered both Betty Grable and Judy Garland," he claimed. "Both gals were only fifteen at the time. For Betty, it was movie gangster George Raft, and for Judy it was Spencer Tracy. Both of those bastards should be arrested for child molestation."

***

As 1936 came to an end, Judy remembered it as an endless lineup of photo sessions, interviews, vocal lessons, and singing performances at parties or benefits.

Late in the year, MGM finally commissioned a scriptwriter to create a role for Judy in *Broadway Melody of 1937*. *[Because of production delays, its title was later changed to* Broadway Melody of 1938.*]*

It would also mark the end of a year that had been the most promiscuous period of her young life.

Who deflowered Judy Garland when she was fifteen?.

Depicted above is **Spencer Tracy** as he appeared in *Fury* (1936)

CHAPTER FOUR

BABY GUMM DROP BECOMES PROMISCUOUS
(Because Divas Grow up Fast in Hollywood, Dah-ling!)

HER INCREASING NUMBERS OF
MALE FRIENDS AGREE THAT

JUDY IS HIP, CHARMING, & INCREASINGLY FAMOUS

THOUGH STILL UNDERAGED,
SHE GETS BIG TIME MOVIE ROLES

*LISTEN, DARLING, EVERYBODY SING, 'CAUSE
THOROUGHBREDS DON'T CRY DURING BROADWAY
MELODIES ESPECIALLY WHEN*
LOVE IS ABOUT TO FIND ANDY HARDY

"Judy Garland gets into the hearts of people. She interprets a lyric as very few people in our business ever do. It takes people like Fred Astaire, Frank Sinatra, Bing Crosby, and Julie Andrews to interpret lyrics. Judy had—and has—her own style and sang her way into the hearts of an audience—and everybody backstage, too."
— Producer Arthur Freed

"Let's rename it 'Andy Hardy with a hard-on.'"

—Lana Turner, in reference to Mickey Rooney during his filming with Judy of *Love Finds Andy Hardy*

Even as late as 1937, Louis B. Mayer still hadn't decided "what to do with the little Miss Plump." He wanted her to lose weight, and he ordered the manager of the MGM commissary to give Judy only a bowl of chicken soup when she came in, regardless of what she ordered.

She didn't see how a bowl swimming with noodles and matzo balls would take off many pounds. He heard her complaint and revised his order with a command that the kitchen staff put only one matzo ball in her soup.

Ignoring Mayer's advice, she slipped around and feasted on chocolate malts and Hershey Bars. "I was addicted to any form of chocolate."

"It seemed to me that Metro was far more interested in how you looked than if you had any talent," she claimed. "In my early days at MGM, Benzedrine had come on the market, and everybody was taking it. If it had any harmful effects, we didn't know it. Nobody thought it was bad for you. One thing it did do was kill your appetite. We learned later it was speed."

"The studio doctor also prescribed Dexedrine to keep my weight down."

"Mayer thought he was raising me," Judy lamented. "He was just dreadful. He had a theory that he was all-powerful, and he ruled by fear. What better way to make a young person behave than to scare the hell out of her every day?"

Instead of casting Judy in a movie, Mayer still used her to entertain at parties. He ordered her to sing at Clark Gable's birthday party in 1936, Roger Edens was still her vocal coach, and he created her first hit song to sing at the party.

It was her tribute to the King of Hollywood, who was making his disastrous film, *Parnell,* at the time. As a teenage girl with a crush, she sang "Dear Mr. Gable, You Made Me Love You (I Didn't Want To Do It)."

At the end of her song, it was obvious that Gable was very moved. When he approached and kissed her, the guests who had showed up at his birthday bash applauded wildly. Mayer was so impressed

*"Who wouldn't love **Clark Gable**, the subject of my first real love song, an ode to my desire for him? He boasted he'd had every big female star at MGM. But can you believe it, he never had me. He thought I was too young."*

—Judy Garland

with how the song went over, he ordered that it be inserted into the upcoming production of *Broadway Melody of 1938*.

Decca Records had Judy record it, and the song became a big hit.

She later recalled, "Clark was one of the finest men I ever knew, a truly gentle man. Years later, just before his death, he told me, 'Judy, I had a birthday the other day—and I hid. I was afraid you'd jump out at me and sing that song again.'"

Mayer's executive secretary, Ida Koverman, had a specially designed charm bracelet made for Judy and instructed Gable to present it to her as a gift. Miniature musical instruments dangled from its chain—a tiny piano, a horn, drums, a violin, and other tokens, including a little book which contained a note in the smallest of print: "Dear Judy, from your fan, Clark Gable."

She kept the bracelet for years. "To keep from starving, I had to sell my diamonds, but I held onto that bracelet given to me so long ago."

Broadway Melody of 1938 was a hit, but stardom was still a couple of years away for Judy Garland.

What's wrong with this picture? It's the combination of mismatched costumes: Despite her vocal razzmatazz, Judy looks like a carefully chaperoned teenager at her first prom. She's been positioned against a backdrop of showgirls wearing semi-transparent outfits as decadent and sophisticated as the era would allow.

"I must confess, the song reflected my real sentiments about Gable," she said. "I did have this powerful crush on him, and I couldn't wait to grow up so I could become his gal. Then one day at the studio, he introduced me to Carole Lombard. My dream was dashed. You know what happened: I got the consolation prize, his best friend, Spencer Tracy."

Mayer named Jack Cummings as producer of *Broadway Melody of 1938*, and he selected the noted director, Ruth Del Ruth, to cast the picture, where the two major stars, heartthrob Robert Taylor and tap-dancing Eleanor Powell, had already been hired as the leads.

This was Judy's first time to be helmed by a major director, who by now was a Hollywood veteran, having begun his career with Mack Sennett in 1915. By 1929, he'd made the first color film for Warners, *The Desert Song*. That was the same year *Broadway Melody* was introduced, becoming Best Picture of the Year. That movie was the harbinger of *Broadway Melody of 1938*.

Del Ruth was more than a director of glitzy musicals, and he also made dramas. In 1931, he'd helmed the first version of Dashiell Hammett's *The Maltese Falcon*, with Ricardo Cortez. In pre-Code Hollywood, it dealt with sexual innuendo, including Bebe Daniels bathing in the nude, overt references to homosexuality, and one instance of cursing.

Before Judy, he'd also helmed Bette Davis, Ginger Rogers, James Cagney, Edward G. Robinson, Eddie Cantor, and James Stewart, becoming the second highest-paid director in Hollywood.

The supporting cast of *Broadway Melody of 1938* included Sophie Tucker, George Murphy, Binnie Barnes, Buddy Ebsen, Robert Benchley, and Billy Gilbert. Lyrics were by Arthur Freed, and musical arrangements were by Judy's faithful friend and musical coach, Roger Edens.

Cast as a Broadway producer, Steve Raleigh, always short of cash, Robert Taylor falls for a horse trainer, Sally (Eleanor Powell). She's both an extraordinary tap dancer and also the owner of a champion racehorse, Stargazer.

Upper photo: **Judy with a lollipop and Sophie Tucker,** playing her mother, in *Broadway Melody of 1938*.

Lower photo: **Tucker,** as a "red hot mama" during her vaudevillian heyday around 1925.

As a subplot, retired showgirl, Sophie Tucker, operates a theatrical boarding house, and she's trying to find a way for her daughter, Betty Clayton (Judy), to break into show business. It was said of Betty that "she was born in a dressing room and raised in a trunk."

"All the girls were swooning over Bob Taylor with his pretty-boy looks," Judy recalled. "Most of them were out of luck. Roger Edens, who often attended all-male parties, told me that Taylor used to show up with John Gilbert—that is, when he wasn't messing around with Greta Garbo or Marlene Dietrich."

Born in 1886 in Ukraine, Sophie Tucker emigrated to America and later became one of America's leading vaudeville artists. Billed as "The Last of the Red Hot Mammas," she was known for her comical and risqué songs.

"Miss Sophie was my mother on-screen and off," Judy said. "I just adored her. She taught me every trick she'd learned on stage and also how to peddle a song. She really knew how to put over a song herself."

"Sophie often discussed her career highlights, such as when in 1926, she sang at the London Palladium in front of George V and Queen Mary. She wowed them singing 'Some of These Days.'"

"She predicted that one day I'd sing at the London Palladium, too," Judy said.

"Sophie was horribly depressed at what was happening to her people in Nazi Germany," Judy said. "One of her most moving songs was, 'My Yiddische Momme,' and she learned that Hitler had banned it for its sympathetic treatment of Jewish culture."

At the end of *Broadway Melody*'s filming, Tucker told Mayer, "If handled right, Judy will become a superstar. I'll predict she'll be the next Red Hot Momma."

Judy did, indeed, become a superstar, but not the Red Hot Momma that Tucker had envisioned.

Other than the tribute to Gable, Judy's splashy big number was with rubber-legged Buddy Ebsen. In that scene, Ebsen arrives in a limousine, opens the rear door, and out emerges Judy. Then, as a dancing duo, they perform a delightful number together. "I taught Judy how to do the shim-sham shimmy," Ebsen later boasted.

"Buddy was in white tie and tails, and he was the tallest man on the planet. I think his legs alone measure six feet. I looked like this dancing dwarf beside him in my white organdy frills and ankle socks."

"He was such a talent, but he was the most homophobic actor I ever met, always attacking homosexual men and calling them pansies. I don't know what his damn problem was."

Judy's future co-star, George Murphy, recognized Judy's talent. "All of us who watched her perform knew immediately that she had something extra, a magnificent quality. Her voice could make you laugh and cry almost at the same time. There was no one like her. She soon would pass Deanna Durbin. Judy could do anything and do it in a way that was just… Judy."

At the film's release, Judy was touted as "the greatest little hot singer since the first Talkie" and hailed as a "startling phenomenon." *Song Hits* predicted, "The kid has a noncancelable reservation on the Stardust Express."

Bosley Crowther in *The New York Times* asserted that, "Judy Garland is Metro's answer to Deanna Durbin," and praised her "amazing precocity."

With the release of her latest movie, her star began to rise in the Hollywood Heaven. But, as she said, "It didn't rise fast enough for me, and Deanna Durbin over at Universal was practically The Milky Way."

***

In 1937, and again in 1938, both *The Hollywood Reporter* and *Variety* reported that Judy had been cast in films, but as time marched on, they were never made—at least not with her.

In a bizarre footnote to the casting of the blockbuster *Gone With the Wind*, it was reported that David O. Selznick considered casting Judy as one of Scarlett O'Hara's younger sisters. The role went instead to her friend, Ann Rutherford.

Then, in 1937, in another odd bit of casting, MGM made plans to film *The Sarah Bernhardt Story*, with Judy cast as the young Bernhardt. Regrettably, plans for it were shelved.

In 1938, nearing the end of his life, novelist F. Scott Fitzgerald wrote a screenplay, *The Captured Heart*, that was based on a short story that he had written, and which had appeared in 1929 in the *Saturday Evening Post*. Mayer briefly considered this story of three teenagers to be cast with Mickey Rooney, Judy, and Freddie Bartholomew.

Mervyn LeRoy—famously noted for launching the career of Lana Turner—planned to cast Judy and Shirley Temple in a movie, *Topsy & Eva*. The script resurfaced in the late 1940s and died a quick death.

In an equivalent footnote that never materialized, Judy might have been reteamed with Sophie Tucker in *Molly, Bless Her*. Had it been made, Judy would have played the young Marie Dressler, with Tucker cast as the mature star. Dressler, of course, was the famous character actress who had been one of the superstars of the silent era and made a dramatic comeback in the early 1930s when she reigned briefly as a box-office champion in *Min and Bill* (1930) and in *Dinner at Eight* (1933).

Upper photo: Judy at work in 1937 on the set of **Jack Oakie College**, a nationwide radio show built on the premise that college life and college students were relentlessly fun.

Lower photo: Comedian **Jack Oakie** lampooning Mussolini in this publicity photo from Charles Chaplin's *The Great Dictator* (1940).

***

Judy's second daughter, Lorna Luft, wrote: "Professionally, Roger Edens 'created' Judy Garland. He recognized not only my mother's extraordinary musical gifts, but also her emotional sensitivity. It was his gifts as a composer and arranger that gave my mother the chance to shine on camera. He worked hard to get her to stop belting out numbers like a miniature Ethel Merman and start singing like Judy, the fourteen-year-old who missed her father and longed for a boyfriend. Without Roger, we might never have had 'Over the Rainbow,' or at least not the way we remember it."

From January to June of 1937, a perfect showcase opened for Judy to refine her art, under Edens' guidance on the radio show *Jack Oakie's College*. On one of its first episodes she appeared with comedian George Jessel, who had given her the name of Garland.

A highlight of the show occurred on April 20, when she sang "Johnny One Note" to a nationwide audience only six days prior to its Broadway opening in the musical *Babes in Arms*.

The broadcast for the CBS network became a showcase for her, and she worked smoothly with Oakie, using her appearances to try out new material.

One number, among others, went over very big. She aped her mentor, Sophie Tucker, singing "Some of These Days," belting it out like The Red Hot Momma herself.

Born in Sedalia, Missouri, in 1903, Oakie was a character actor on stage and screen, and in the 1930s and '40s, he made eighty-seven films. The most notable was when he was cast as Napoloni in Chaplin's *The Great Dictator* (1940), for which he received an Oscar nod for Best Supporting Actor.

Other song highlights for Judy included when she introduced "Dear Mr. Gable, You Made Me Love You," to a nationwide audience. She also sang such hits as "Alabamy Bound," "They Can't Take That Away From Me," "Look for the Silver Lining," and "Singin' in the Rain."

"Radio was one thing, and a good thing for me, but I was raring to go before the camera. Come on, Mayer, send me the scripts."

She never said that to him di-

Three young stars, **Mickey Rooney** (left), **Judy Garland**, and **Robert Sinclair** star in the frankly hokum race track story, *Thoroughbreds Don't Cry*.

Whereas Sinclair got lost in the screen debris of yesterday, the other two were destined for screen glory.

Francis X Bushman, depicted above as the star of the silent version of *Ben-Hur* (1925), was a matinee idol, sometimes as the focal point of scenes considered unacceptably "steamy" back in the Pre-Code Era.

Bushman, fallen from his days of glory, remained working Hollywood as a less celebrated actor. He played an uncredited, very minor bit part with Judy in *Thoroughbreds Don't Cry*.

73

rectly, but he must have heeded her command. At long last, she began to get bigger roles.

***

For a 1937 release, a horse track melodrama entitled *Thoroughbreds Don't Cry,* Judy and Mickey Rooney were cast in their first picture together. It also reteamed Judy with Sophie Tucker, except this time, instead of playing her daughter, she was cast as her niece, Cricket West.

For presentation within *Thoroughbreds Don't Cry,* Arthur Freed wrote two songs for Judy, "I've Got a New Pair of Shoes," and "Sun Showers." Only the former made the final cut.

Cricket is a wannabe actress who lives in her aunt's boarding house. One of their roomers is Timmie Donovan (Rooney), a highly skilled "midget sized" jockey known for his daring "come from the back" wins on the racetrack.

The plot thickens when cash-poor Sir Peter Calverton (C. Aubrey Smith) arrives on the scene with his grandson Roger (Ronald Sinclair) and their prize-winning horse "The Pookay." They are hoping to win the grand prize to save the family estate in England. The grandson role was intended for Freddie Bartholomew, but he was not available.

Donovan is compromised when his no-good gambler father, "Click" Donovan (Charles Brown), shows up. He claims he is dying and desperately needs an iron lung. He urges his son to throw the race so that his gambling bet to win would get him the medical treatment he so desperately needs. Of course, at the end, his deception is exposed.

As a cinematic footnote, Francis X. Bushman, the faded star of silent pictures [especially famous for his starring role in MGM's *Ben-Hur* (1925)], appears in *Thoroughbreds Don't Cry* as an uncredited racing steward.

Its director, Alfred E. Green, began his career as an actor in 1912, graduating to directing feature films by 1917. In time, he would direct some of Hollywood's biggest stars, notably Mary Pickford, Wallace Reid, Barbara Stanwyck, Colleen Moore, and Bette Davis in *Dangerous* (1935), which won her a Best Actress Oscar. He was married at the time to Vivian Reed, the silent film actress.

His direction to Judy was "Be perky, be vivacious, a playful innocent, and have a lot of 'Zing.'"

In reference to when Rooney first worked with Judy, he claimed she was overly concerned with her looks. "Judy was an American beauty in more ways than one. She had marvelous, warm eyes that invited you to share her secret mirth

Louis B. Mayer spotted the on-screen chemistry of **Judy Garland and Mickey Rooney** in *Thoroughbreds Don't Cry*—and ordered that a script be written in which this "dynamic duo" could co-star.

and a cute little nose that wrinkled when she laughed. She had an expressive, generous mouth that hardly ever uttered a line that wasn't funny, or in her later years, outrageous or filled with feeling. If I had not been tainted with the same Hollywood notions about who was beautiful and who was not, I would have fallen in love with her."

Rooney took Judy to the first screening of *Thoroughbreds*. Years later he claimed, "I think that was the night that the movie star known as Judy Garland was born. One day, they should make a movie about her during that period, perhaps call it *A Star Is Born*." *[Ironically, David Selznick was producing a movie with that title starring Janet Gaynor around the same time.]*

"If our picture did nothing else," Rooney continued, "it launched Mickey Rooney (that was the name I had been given) and Judy as a screen team."

Mayer himself was in the audience at one of the early screenings of *Thoroughbreds*. Legendary for his show-biz savvy, he became aware of the on-screen chemistry of Rooney and Judy. That very week he ordered his script department to begin work on a movie that would co-star them again. *Thoroughbreds*, however, would mark the only time that Judy got star billing over Rooney.

It made a minor profit, even though *Newsweek* denounced it as "frankly hokum." Bosley Crowther of *The New York Times* noted that Judy "provided puppy love interest."

"**Louella Parsons** would spend decades writing about my troubled life," Judy said.

"Things were cleared up when she first met me. I was a young girl. Up to then, she thought I was a midget because my voice had such power.:"

***

The reigning gossip columnist of Hollywood, Louella Parsons, arrived at MGM to interview Sophie Tucker. Director Green made it a point to also introduce her to Judy as "MGM's rising new star."

It was the first time Judy had been asked about her private life, at least by a reporter who might put it in print.

"Boys are the last thing on my mind. I don't plan to get married until I'm twenty-four, at least. Marriage and children might play in my future, but right now, I have a movie career to launch."

After that, she rushed to her dressing room, where the former child actor, Frankie Darro, was waiting for her. He'd already removed his clothing. As he confessed later to Rooney, "Judy and I kept everything oral. You know, fear of having to have an abortion."

Judy had known Darro for years, attending classes with her at MGM's Little Red Schoolhouse, but seeing much more of him when he "heavy dated" her sister, Jimmie.

In time, Jimmie ditched him to marry musician Robert Sherwood.

In *Thoroughbreds*, Darro had a small role as "Dink" Reid.

Judy had always had a crush on him, and during the filming of their movie, she aggressively pursued him. On their first date, they became intimate, but according to what he told Rooney, their lovemaking never went beyond the oral stage.

Author Nigel Cawthorne wrote: "Judy was bonking another child actor, Frankie Darro, and there were others where sex was concerned. She was a free spirit, though she wrote a lot of lovelorn poetry. This may have been because, outside of the closed world of the movie lot, she was completely out of her depth."

"When a boy asked her to be his date at a fraternity pledge party at USC, she wore a slinky evening dress with a slit up the side and a white fox stole—the sort of thing a starlet might wear to a premiere. Her date took one look, discovered he had a headache, and ran."

Apparently, Darro did not take Judy's virginity. After a separation of three months, when he re-entered her life, she was fifteen. "I've lost my cherry," she told him, "if that's the right expression. We can do it now, the old-fashioned way."

***

In 1937, production began on *Everybody Sing*, Judy's third film.

Around this time, Ethel decided to fire Judy's agent, Al Rosen, who had worked hard to launch her career and to hire talent representative Jesse Martin instead.

Before it was renamed, the film's working title had been *The Ugly Duckling*, a reference to Judy's character. As her new agent, Martin strenuously protested to Mayer that it would "completely demoralize your star and destroy her confidence before the camera."

He must have been convincing, because the title was briefly changed to *Swing Time* before the producer Harry Rapf and the director Edwin L. Marin agreed on *Everybody Sing*.

Screenwriter Dalton Trumbo, later to be denounced by the House Un-American Ac-

Judy (above, left) with "Funny Girl," **Fanny Brice** in *Everybody Sing.*

Whereas Judy is fine-tuning her comedic sense and spoofing Little Lord Fauntleroy, Brice is satirizing her own *schtick,* her long-time gig as "Baby Snooks."

76

tivities Committee, worked on the script with several others, but was not credited.

On June 10, Judy celebrated her fifteenth birthday by hosting a pool party. To it, she invited Freddie Darro, Mickey Rooney, Bonita Granville, Ann Rutherford, and other guests. She also invited the object of her crush, Freddie Bartholomew, but he had another engagement.

Back to work on *Everybody Sing*, she met first with director Marin, who would, between 1932 and 1951, helm fifty-eight movies, employing stars who included Eddie Cantor, John Wayne, Peter Lorre, Anna May Wong, George Raft, Bela Lugosi, Randolph Scott, and Hoagy Carmichael.

Marin introduced Judy to the cast, billed in this order: Alan Jones, Fanny Brice, Judy Garland, Reginald Owen, Billie Burke, Reginald Gardiner, Lynne Carter (hailed as MGM's new glamour starlet), and Monty Woolley.

Judy met and bonded with them, becoming life-long friends with Brice.

A forgotten star today, singer and actor Alan Jones was known for his work in musicals and for his performance as the straight man in such Marx Brothers comedies as *A Night at the Opera* (1935). *[Jones' most famous role was as Gaylord Ravenal in* Show Boat *(1936) opposite Irene Dunne. Around the time he worked with Judy, he recorded "The Donkey Serenade" for RCA Victor, which became its third best-selling single. He also became the father of pop singer Jack Jones.]*

Fanny Brice, born in Manhattan in 1891, was a legend by the time Judy worked with her. She was most famous as the creator and star of the radio comedy series, *The Baby Snooks Show*. Her husbands included the professional gambler Nicky Arnstein, who served fourteen months in Sing Sing for wiretapping, and Billy Rose, the songwriter and stage producer.

Everybody Sing marked Judy's introduction to Billie Burke, who would go on to be cast as Glinda, the Good Witch of the West in *The Wizard of Oz*. Famously married to Florenz Ziegfeld from 1914 to 1932, she became a film favorite for her quavering and high-pitched aristocratic voice, and for her portrayal of spoiled, dim-witted society matrons.

Burke had once been a clown for the Barnum & Bailey Circus. She'd first appeared on the screen in *Peggy* (1915) and went onto be cast as Katharine Hepburn's mother in Hepburn's screen debut, *A Bill of Divorcement* (1932).

In a few months after working with Judy, producer David O. Selznick offered Burke the role of Aunt Pittypat in *Gone With the Wind* (1939). After she rejected it, he cast Laura Hope Crews—who executed it brilliantly—instead.

Judy also worked with two famed character actors, both with the first name of Reginald—Owen and Gardiner. "With first names like that, they had to be from England," she quipped.

[Reginald Owen's best-known role was that of Ebenezer Scrooge in a film adaptation of Charles Dickens' classic, A Christmas Carol *(1938). He also starred in crime thrillers both as Sherlock Holmes and also as Holmes' faithful assistant, Dr. Watson.]*

The "other Reginald" in the cast, Reginald Gardiner, would in time star in about a hundred movies, beginning in 1927 in Alfred Hitchcock's silent film, *The Lodger, A Story of the London Fog* (1927). A Londoner, he gained his most acclaimed exposure as Schultz in Chaplin's *The Great Dictator* (1940).

Character actor Monty Woolley had a small role in *Everybody Sing* as Jack Fleming. *[Known for his orgies with Cole Porter, and for his distinctive white beard, Woolley was one of the most notorious homosexuals in the industry. He later angered Porter when he took a black lover and sustained a long-lasting affair with him.]*

In *Everybody Sing*, the character Judy played was also named Judy, a girl born into the dysfunctional Bellaire theatrical family. She is expelled from her music class when she jazzes up Mendelssohn's "Spring Song," adapting it into "Swing, Mr. Mendelssohn."

She goes home to deal with the rest of her family, including her ditzy mother (Billie Burke) and her father (Reginald Owen), a frustrated playwright.

Her beautiful older sister (Lynn Carter) has the hots for the family's singing cook (Alan Jones). Olga, the family's maid (Fanny Brice), is adrift in memories of her own long-ago theatrical career in her native Russia.

When *Everybody Sing* was released, although many audiences applauded Judy's rendition of "Melody Farm," *The New York Times* was not impressed with any of the movie's music. According to one of their critics, whether it was on a Chinatown bus, in a night club, in a bedroom, or in any other setting, "One comes away with a positive hatred of the human larynx."

Film Weekly praised Judy, claiming, "Anyone who stands up to Miss Brice...is very good, indeed."

During the filming of *Everybody Sing*, MGM considered casting Judy as a young Fanny Brice in *The Fanny Brice Story*, and upcoming melodrama scheduled for a release in 1938. It was never made. However, in the mid-1950s, producer Ray Stark, Brice's son-in-law, wanted to have Judy portray his mother-in-law in a bio pic, but never followed through with it. Brice had died in 1951.

[Thirteen years after Fanny Brice's death, Barbra Streisand brought her story to the Broadway stage in the hit 1964 musical, Funny Girl, *for which she won an Oscar. Streisand reprised her characterization of Fanny Brice in the play's 1975 film sequel,* Funny Lady. *]*

***

After the completion of *Everybody Sing*, MGM flew Judy east to New York City for a personal appearance on the mammoth stage of Loew's State Theater before a packed audience. Outside, and for the first time, the name **JUDY GARLAND** appeared in six-foot letters, even though she was little known at the time.

Roger Edens, her vocal coach and mentor, flew to Manhattan with her. He recalled: "Here was this unknown, fifteen-year-old alone for the first time on an enormous stage, nervous, and singing much too loudly. The audience was coughing, and a baby started crying. People laughed at the baby, and Judy stopped her song, laughed, and started again. That one thing steadied her, and she wrapped the audience up from then on. She has been able to handle an audience ever since."

Variety applauded too. "Youngster is a resounding wallop in her first vaudeville appearance as Judy Garland. Apparent from outset girl is no mere flash but has both personality and skill to develop into a box-office wow in any line of show business. Applause was solid, and she encored twice. Finally begging off with an ingratiating and shrewd thank you speech."

***

At one of her father's movie houses, Judy had grown up watching Spencer Tracy on the screen emote with a bevy of leading ladies such as Jean Harlow, Bette Davis, Joan Bennett, Colleen Moore, Fay Wray, Myrna Loy, or Loretta Young. Young said, "He makes women feel warm and wanted, but there is no flattery about him."

Even as a young girl, Judy proclaimed him her favorite actor on the screen. "Spencer Tracy was a bit stocky and looked like an average Joe," Judy said years later. "But there was something mesmerizing about him. He projected strength and intelligence on the screen and looked like an honest bill of goods. In some ways, he reminded me of my father, and perhaps I transferred the love I had for Frank onto Tracy."

Judy was only thirteen and in Hollywood when she first met Tracy. They both appeared on comedian Frank Fay's Sunday night radio show devoted to featuring "undiscovered stars." Most of the wannabe actors who appeared on the show remained undiscovered except for Judy.

"Spencer was very kind to me and praised my singing voice," she recalled. "Somehow, as we waited backstage and talked, I felt safe and comfortable with him. He gave me pointers about the business and warned me about Hollywood wolves. He also warned me about studio chiefs who were child molesters, notably Louis B. Mayer and Darryl F. Zanuck."

Tracy told her, "Zanuck once had little Miss Shirley Temple in his office and exposed himself to her. Never, never, go into one of their offices alone."

Tracy and Judy didn't meet again until she celebrated her fifteenth birthday on June 10, 1937, when he showed up to have a slice of her pink birthday cake ordered by Mayer's assistant, Iva Koverman.

Shirley Temple in 1935. History and the #MeToo movement have revealed that she, along with Judy, each faced molestiation issues from studio chiefs at a young age.

By now, Judy had told many people at MGM that he was her favorite actor. "I know I sang that song to Clark Gable, but Tracy has always been number one in my book."

Coming together with him again, he smiled down at her as he sampled her birthday cake. "You're growing up, little girl," he said. "I hear that you like me blown up like a horse's ass on the silver screen. But you never sang a love song to me like you did to my pal, Clark Gable. He's always getting the girl instead of me."

Gallantly, Judy responded, "Whereas Gable is the man a girl develops a crush on, Spencer Tracy is a man she elopes with."

"Is that an invitation?" he asked. "Don't tempt me. There are laws, you know. And there's a slight difference in our ages," he said. "I was born in 1900."

A dressing room encounter of **Spencer Tracy with Judy.**

His "dating" of the very young starlet caused Hollywood gossips to deplore their "April/October" romance.

That makes you twenty-two years older than me," she said. "That's hardly unusual for Hollywood."

"Come to think of it, you're right. In some cases out here, there's a thirty or forty year difference."

As the other guests faded away, he came up with an idea. "Let's have dinner tonight. Have Edens call your mother and tell her you're working late at the studio. I know this wonderful place, a little hideaway in San Fernando Valley."

"Good. I'm starved to death," she said. "They work me all day and only give me a cup of soup. Originally, it was a bowl—now it's a damn cup."

Amazingly, in the days and weeks ahead, and despite the objections of Mayer, Tracy started dating her in public. They were seen together at the Cocoanut Grove, at Ciro's, and at Billy Wilkerson's Café on Sunset Strip. Whereas at the café, they cuddled together, at Ciro's, they had been seen holding hands.

"It was bound to happen," Judy confided to her giggling girlfriends.

She was referring to the night Tracy escorted her to an apartment in West Hollywood. It was a secluded, secretive place with a back entrance, a hideaway maintained jointly by both Gable and himself for off-the-record trysts.

As Tracy's biographer, Larry Swindell, revealed, "People in Hollywood started to talk, and gossip columnists speculated that Tracy might be leaving his wife. At MGM, the PR department issued a denial."

Judy admitted that she was flattered that one of the biggest stars in Hollywood took "a fatherly interest in me." Privately, she told Rooney,

"Although Spencer can have a string of Hollywood beauties, he wants me."

Judy was right. Over the course of his film career, Tracy would become known for his seductions of, among others, Loretta Young, Joan Bennett, Ingrid Bergman, Myrna Loy, and Joan Crawford, who claimed, "Spence is a very disturbed man. He is a mean drunk and a bastard." Other affairs featured Nancy Davis (later Reagan), Paulette Goddard, Gene Tierney, and Grace Kelly before she became a princess.

In the world's most definitive list of Hollywood seductions, biographer Mart Martin listed a young Judy Garland as among Tracy's many conquests.

Once, during lunch with Myrna Loy, Judy confessed, "Intercourse was painful at first, but Spencer assured me that I'd get used to it—and, dammit, he was right. I began getting more pleasure out of it and often turned to older men because they were usually better at sex than some awkward boy. Yet some of the boys I dated in the late 1930s were very, very experienced. They really knew what to do. It's called growing up in Hollywood. A boy or a girl learns early."

Though it's reminiscent of a photo still from Spencer Tracy's best known films, *Boys Town* (1938), this is the actor with his real-life son, one over whom he frequently anguished.

Much was confused and enigmatic about **Spencer Tracy**—as anyone in Hollywood who knew about his deep descents into depression and his alcoholic binges understood.

When he was asked about his relationship with Judy, Tracy brushed aside the questions: "It's nobody's god damn business. Write anything you want. Make up something. Hell, I don't care. An actor owes it to his fans to give a good performance. What he does when the shades are drawn is private—and should remain so."

Close friend James Cagney said, "We didn't know what was going on with Spence and his wife Louise. One night, he'd show up at Romanoff's with her, then he'd show up the next night with one of the MGM starlets, notably Judy Garland, who was then only fifteen."

On many an occasion, Tracy returned to that hideaway in West Hollywood, which was sometimes also visited by his friend, fellow actor Pat O'Brien.

"I never knew who I might find Spencer with," O'Brien said. "Often, it was Judy Garland. One night he was with Marlene Dietrich. I asked him, "What are you doing here?"

Dietrich answered for him. "We're discussing wired bras, darling."

Another of Tracy's biographers, Bill Davidson, wrote, "Sober, he [*Tracy*] was a Hollywood god, the greatest actor of his era. Drunk, he was an animal, wallowing for weeks in a Brooklyn bathtub, sober, he couldn't kill the chickens on his farm. Drunk, he tried to murder his own brother. He could be truculent and ugly or witty and charming, viciously cruel to some, and extravagantly kind to others. He was a voracious womanizer

81

who pursued glamorous stars and prostitutes with equal fervor. He was a lifelong
insomnia victim, wracked with insecurities and self-doubts. Hollywood's publicity mills spun a thick veil of secrecy
around their 'erratic superstar.'"

According to Mickey Rooney, "One
night, Judy told me that Spencer drove her
across the border into Mexico, where she
underwent her first abortion. Long before
future Tracy biographies caught on to him,
I knew Spencer also liked boys when he
wasn't chasing after MGM's glamour gals.
When Freddie Bartholomew and I starred
with him in *Captains Courageous* (1937), he
propositioned both Freddie and me. I
turned him down, but Freddie went away
with him to God only knows what fate. I
was too polite to ask Freddie afterward."

**Spencer Tracy & Katharine
Hepburn**: Though they got along
passably well, their romance was
one of the biggest hoaxes in Hollywood.

Richard A Leetzman, co-author of *The
Life and Times of Mickey Rooney*, wrote: "By
the time Judy had turned fifteen, Mickey
Rooney claimed that the older Spencer
Tracy was regularly seducing Judy. He said that she had told him that, and
just about everyone else at the studio knew about it. He said the seductions
lasted three years. She was a victim of one of Hollywood's many predators.
Mickey said that everyone on the inside knew what Tracy was like. The
public had no idea."

In time, Tracy's longest lasting relationship was with the bisexual actress, Katharine Hepburn. Their best friend, director George Cukor, told
his associates, "Kate and Spence are having an affair that's referred to as
platonic."

Within a few years, Tracy would play the lead in *Dr. Jekyll and Mr. Hyde*
(1941). He was so lovable and personable on screen that most of his fans
didn't know he had a sort of split personality, like the Robert Louis Stevenson character he was playing on the screen.

Tracy and Judy bonded for life, and she also became a "special friend"
of Hepburn.

Some of Tracy's associates who worked with him strongly disap-
proved of his affair with Judy. In 1940, Claudette Colbert co-starred with
Tracy and Gable in *Boom Town*. She told her fellow co-star, Hedy Lamarr,
that she was very opposed to a man in his forties dating a fifteen-year-old
Judy. "Poor little Judy," Colbert said. "She should not even be in the same
room with Tracy without a chaperone."

***

"After Spencer Tracy deflowered me," Judy told Ann Rutherford,

"Billy Halop sauntered into my life, a living, breathing, macho boy, the gang leader of the *Dead End Kids* in all those movies."

"He was only two years older than me, but very experienced. When he first took me to bed, I could tell he'd done that before. He was far better than Spencer, who was rather drunk most of the time."

"Billy was rightly proud of his equipment, and he sure knew what to do with it. I know it sounds crude, but he said it so sweetly when he called me his 'piece.'"

"In bed, he came on to me like gang-busters," she said. "But otherwise, he was very sweet, a real gentleman. I mean opening doors for me, pulling up a chair, standing up when I went to the powder room, even bringing me orchid corsages."

A writer for the *Hollywood Reporter* queried Halop about his dates with Judy. "She is one of my weaker moments." He didn't stop long enough to explain just what he meant by that.

As Mickey Rooney so bluntly revealed, "I once went out on a double date with Halop and Judy. The hot little number in the front seat with me was none other than Lana Turner—god damn... the knockers on that gal."

"Together, the four of us drove to a remote part of Santa Monica Beach right before midnight. I had brought blankets. There, under the moonlight, with the sound of the Pacific in our ears, Halop and I—him with Judy and me with Lana— did the dirty deed."

Judy told Rooney that at one point, she and Halop considered eloping to Tijuana and getting married.

Upper photo: **Billy Halop,** ringleader of the Dead End Kids, each a precursor of the 1950s era "good kids gone bad" cult best evoked a few years later by James Dean.

Lower photo: A poster for one of the many street-life sagas swirling around the young tough-guy sagas that starred **the Dead End Kids.**

"We later thought better of it, for one good reason: We were very young. She had a lot more boys to plow, and I had other young pieces to bring joy to," Halop claimed.

At the time Judy dated Halop, he was filming *Angels with Dirty Faces* (1938) starring James Cagney. Halop told Judy, "Cagney plays all these tough gangsters on screen, but actually, he's a song-and-dance man. He told me he got his start in show business dressed as a drag queen in Manhattan, claiming he made a beautiful woman, and he even showed me a picture of himself in heavy makeup and a gown. I think he wanted to make it with me."

"I'm still a child," Judy said, "but I've been around Hollywood long enough to know that in private, actors are rarely what they appear on screen."

***

After Judy and Halop broke up, they saw each other infrequently and never in a romantic way. When World War II erupted, he joined the U.S. Army, returning safely to postwar Hollywood. But with the exception of a fleeting involvement in *Gas House Kids* (1946) on Poverty Row, those juvenile roles he'd been good at had faded into the distant past.

From reports at the time, he had become an uncontrolled alcoholic, going through four marriages.

Desperate for money, he became a registered nurse at St. John's Hospital in Santa Monica.

He did get a final gig, appearing on TV as a cab driver and close friend of Archie Bunker in the hit TV series, *All in the Family.*

In 1976, Halop died young at the age of fifty-six after suffering a heart attack.

***

Around the same era that Judy dated Halop, she was seen out and about with the musician, Robert Sherwood. Sherwood was a friend of Groucho Marx, who staged "*musicales*" at his private home and sometimes invited as many as fifty guests. Sherwood attended every one of them, usually escorting Judy. It was never explained why she was going out with her brother-in-law, as Sherwood was married at the time to her sister Jimmie.

Marx just assumed the couple were having an affair, telling some of his closest friends, "Let's not judge Judy. She's not the only sister in the world who has made it with her brother-in-law. Happens all the time."

His assumption could have been completely wrong that she was sleeping with the musician, whom she called "Dear Bobby."

"We were drawn to each other because of our mutual love of music," she said.

Actually, it was more than that. As Gerald Clarke and other writers have revealed, Judy had developed a secret crush on the handsome, blonde-haired Sherwood. It had begun the moment Jimmie brought him home for dinner. Apparently, Judy managed to conceal her fascination for her sister's new beau.

After some time went by and Jimmie announced plans to marry the young musician, Judy reportedly burst into tears. She tried to explain, telling Jimmie, "Those were tears of joy for you."

***

"I'm bubbling over with joy," Judy proclaimed when MGM gave her

84

the script for her next movie, *Listen, Darling* (1938), a musical comedy.

Freddie Bartholomew would be her romantic interest. She'd had a crush on this handsome young English actor since he'd enrolled in her "Little Red School" on the grounds of MGM.

"I've been chasing after him, and now I think I'll nab him," she vowed.

The director, Edwin L. Marin, of her last picture would helm her again in *Listen, Darling*. Supporting players would include Mary Astor and Walter Pidgeon. Marin had already selected well-known players for the film's lesser roles: Alan Hale, child actor Scotty Beckett, Gene Lockhart, and Charley Grapewin. Unashamedly configured as a "feel-good movie," it would almost break even at the box office.

Judy's faithful coach, Roger Edens, was its musical arranger. Once again, he guided her through "Zing! Went the Strings of My Heart," plus two other songs, "Ten Pins in the Sky," and "On the Bumpy Road to Love."

Judy portrayed "Pinkie" Wingate, who schemes with her friend, Buzz Mitchell (Bartholomew), to keep her mother Dottie (Mary Astor) from marrying the sourpuss schoolmaster (Gene Lockhart). The teenagers search for the right man for her, finding him in Richard Thurlow (Walter Pidgeon).

Astor recalled, "In silent films, I'd played romantic leads, but now I had begun a new phase in my career. I called it 'Mothers for Metro.' In time, I'd play Judy's mother again in *Meet Me in St. Louis.* Judy was a sheer joy to work with. Only problem was that suddenly, in the middle of a take, no matter how serious, she'd burst into giggles. But oh, that voice!"

The entertainment journalist, Cecilia Ager, visited the set and heard Judy sing. She later compared her singing to the piano playing of George Gershwin. "The two of them could oxygenate a room."

See it with a song in your heart!

LISTEN DARLING

Freddie BARTHOLOMEW
Judy GARLAND

Mary ASTOR · *Walter* PIDGEON
ALAN HALE · SCOTTY BECKETT
A METRO-GOLDWYN-MAYER Picture

Judy tried to cover up her romantic involvement with child actor **Freddie Bartholomew,** but he was more frank about it later on:

"I certainly was in love with Judy Garland, and I know that she was in love with me, in spite of the fact that both of us were younger than springtime."

"I felt like her hit song, 'Zing! Went the Strings of My Heart.'"

Soon after her appearance in *Listen, Darling,* Astor would celebrate a sort of comeback, since her peak year was around the corner. It came in 1941 when she appeared in two acclaimed films—*The Big Lie,* starring Bette Davis. *[Astor won an Oscar as Best Supporting Actress.]* Later she contributed to the history of cinema through her portrayal of the scheming femme fatale, Brigid O'Shaughnessy, in *The Maltese Falcon* opposite Humphrey Bogart.

The Canadian actor, Walter Pidgeon, was on the dawn of greatness, which would occur during World War II in such films as *Blossoms in the Dust* (1941) and *Mrs. Miniver* (1942), for which he was nominated for a Best Actor Oscar in these memorable movies with Greer Garson.

Judy found out later that he led a secret gay life.

Another Canadian, Gene Lockhart, was usually cast into character roles, and he often played villains. During the course of his long career, he appeared in an astonishing 300 movies, including a role as the Dauphin's chief counselor in *Joan of Arc* (1948), starring Ingrid Bergman.

During the filming of *Listen, Darling*, a veteran performer, Charley Grapewin, played Judy's beloved uncle, Joe Higgins. He befriended Judy and Bartholomew during the shoot. He came to Judy's dressing room to bid her adieu, telling her he planned to drift off into retirement. She was sorry to see him go, and later urged him to come out of retirement for a final performance as Dorothy's uncle in *The Wizard of Oz* (1939).

Reviews of *Listen, Darling* were lukewarm. *Stage* magazine defined it as "a feeble fable." Others dismissed it as a "charming little trifle."

Variety wrote: "A lightweight offering that will sneak through on the lower sections of double bills, it has little to offer aside from three good song numbers handled capably by Miss Garland, who presents them in style."

Light, escapist fun, *Listen Darling* (1938) united **Mary Astor** (who would play Judy's mother again a few years later in *Meet Me in St. Louis*) with eight-year-old **Scotty Beckett** (foreground, left) and the well-established, fourteen-year-old child star **Freddie Bartholomew.** At the time, he was the second-most-popular child in America after Shirley Temple.

He would soon be eclipsed by **Judy Garland**, and then fade altogether from the screen scene.

As for Judy, she'd be cast in *The Wizard of Oz* a year later.

Critic Frank S. Nugent wrote, "In this winsome picture, little Judy Garland has a fresh young voice which she uses happily on the film's melodies."

When Judy read that, she said, "Talk about damning with faint praise."

***

Unless you regularly watch *Turner Movie Classics,* Freddie Bartholomew is relatively unknown today, but in the 1930s, he was a household name, at least to the movie-going public.

"Of all the child stars of Hollywood, he was the most ruthlessly exploited," Judy accurately proclaimed.

She was always full of rage about what happened to "my Freddie," as she called him. "His image as Little Lord Bartholomew just didn't suit him."

She was referring to one of his most famous performances as *Little Lord Fauntleroy* (1936), a film in which he co-starred with C. Aubrey Smith, Dolores Costello, and a very young Mickey Rooney. An interconnected medley of Victorian snobbery and melodrama, it was the story of a New York boy who suddenly finds himself "rediscovered" as a British lord.

In 1934, David O. Selznick had discovered the cute child actor in England and cast him in the 1935 film adaptation of Charles Dickens' *David Copperfield.*

Selznick brought him to Hollywood, where MGM gave him a seven-year contract. Estranged from his parents, he was accompanied by his beloved guardian, "Aunt Cissy."

In that familiar Dickens classic, Freddie held his own against a formidable array of talent: Basil Rathbone, Lionel Barrymore, Maureen O'Sullivan, and W.C. Fields.

That film was followed by his performance in the film adaptation of Tolstoy's *Anna Karenina* (1936), in which he played the son of Greta Garbo. *[Garbo had previously played the lead in an earlier (1927) film adaptation of Anna Karenina. Released under the title* Love, *it was cast with Philippe De Lacy as Karenina's young son.*

In 1936, Bartholomew was reunited with Mickey Rooney and joined by Jackie Cooper in The Devil Is a Sissy, *followed the next year by a major role in the film adaptation of Rudyard Kipling's* Captains Courageous. *In that, he appeared with Rooney again, this time with Spencer Tracy in the lead, cast as a Portuguese fisherman.*

"That film took a year to make," Freddie claimed. "For a kid, it was like one long outing as it was shot off the coasts of Florida and Catalina Island in California. When shooting ended, I cried like a baby, as I said my goodbyes."

By now, he had become the highest-paid child actor in Hollywood, topped only by Shirley Temple. "I envied the paychecks of those two," Judy said.]

Freddie Bartholomew and Judy Garland presented almost contradictory stories of how their dating was going. Whereas Judy more or less asserted that she had pursued him, and that he didn't pay her much attention, Bartholomew confessed to Rooney, "I was madly in love with Judy. At first, she didn't take me seriously because I was two years younger than she was, and she didn't want to appear to be robbing the cradle. In the Little Red Schoolhouse at MGM, I brought her a different flower every day—a gardenia on Monday, a rose on Tuesday, and so on. Our actual dating began harmlessly enough with me taking her to a movie on Hollywood Boulevard."

When Judy was quizzed about her dating Freddie, she was rather dismissive. "My involvement with Freddie was just a publicity stunt," she claimed. "You know, Sonja Henie and Tyrone Power, Wayne Morris and Priscilla Lane. It didn't mean a thing. We posed for publicity pictures, and he escorted me to a premiere or two. We're just friends."

Actually, she was trying to conceal that they were having an affair, which might have caused a scandal because of their tender ages.

She was also trying to cover up one of Freddie's darkest secrets, which she later shared with Rooney. "Mickey and I could discuss the most personal details. I expected Freddie to make love like Billy Halop. But he was a bit kinky, preferring to suck my toes while he masturbated—not very fulfilling, I must say."

"Judy and I showed up at together at Louis B. Mayer's beach house in Santa Monica," Freddie said. "Every Sunday, he invited a crowd of young stars over to watch new movies. Judy and I held hands throughout any showing. Being next to her in the dark was one of the greatest feelings in the world. I wanted to marry her within a few years and have only two children."

[*Like so many stars before him, Freddie soon learned that fame and fortune meant trouble. Many of his friends, including Judy and Mickey Rooney, watched painfully as Freddie lost all his earnings as a child performer. The same fate— through different means—had already happened to their mutual friend, Jackie Cooper.*

"Freddie lived with his guardian, Aunt Cissy, and he had struck it rich," Rooney said. "His parents in England had deserted him when he was just a tiny kid. His dad was a one-legged ne'er-do-well named Cecil. When he and his wife found out that Freddie was pulling in big bucks as a movie star, they headed to Hollywood to try to cut in on the cash flow. Suddenly, these bastards wanted their kid back."

This led to years of litigation, settlements, renewal of court cases. One of the settlements called for Freddie's $4,000-a-week salary to be divided—ten percent to his parents, five percent to each of his sisters, and another ten percent to Aunt Cissy to provide for his support. The rest would go into a trust fund until he came of age.

Even so, that settlement led to further suits and countersuits, with Freddie ending up with no money after paying off some $100,000 in legal fees. The judgment was viewed as "harshly unfair," especially the provision that Freddie was responsible for the welfare of his older sisters.

In World War II, after he became a gangly six-footer, Freddie Bartholomew enlisted in the U.S. Air Force. When the war ended, back in Hollywood, he found that acting roles had almost disappeared. To make a living he became an advertising executive on Madison Avenue in Manhattan.

He shared a reunion with Judy, who had by now become a superstar. "We chatted about the hell we, as child actors, were subjected to. She wished me well, and I extended my best wishes to her new husband and her."

Her last words to him were, "As long as Hollywood remembers Clara Bow, they will remember Freddie Bartholomew."]

***

Over a giggly lunch in the MGM commissary with girlfriends Ann Rutherford and Bonita Granville, Judy confided the details of her latest romantic entanglement.

"I'm rather fickle," she confessed. "I'm still messing around with Freddie (Bartholomew), but I'm also going out with Buddy Pepper. We're having a wild fling and going all the way. I've nicknamed him 'Hot Pepper'—he's that good—although 'Firecracker' might be more apt. I'm warning you two, stay away from him. I've staked him out for myself."

She was only fifteen when she'd taken up with him, a talented musical prodigy, whom she defined as "the best piano player in the world." He and Jackie Cooper, her former beau, had pooled their resources and rented a hideaway apartment in West Hollywood, for a cost of forty-five dollars a month.

It was the setting where they took their changing array of girlfriends. As Judy wisecracked, "Buddy and Jackie each popped out of the womb with an erection."

Born in La Grange, Kentucky, Pepper—seven months older than Judy—still retained some traces of a Southern accent. Without any piano instruction, he began to play the piano at the age of five. Two years later, he was onstage as an entertainer at his hometown theater.

At the age of eight, he and Florence Krausse formed a child vaudeville act, billing themselves as "Buddy and Florence Pepper."

He didn't like his family's birth name (Starkey) and from that point on billed himself as "Buddy Pepper."

He tried to work for RKO as a teenager but was rejected. He tried again months later and got cast at Universal in *That Certain Age* (1938), co-starring Deanna Durbin and Jackie Cooper. He and Pepper bonded and—despite the fact that they were underaged—plotted the logistics of a sex life. Hence, the secret apartment to which Judy was invited on several occasions.

She'd been attracted to Pepper ever since he'd enrolled in Ma Lawlor's acting class.

Buddy Pepper with Judy Garland near the beginning of their brief affair and long musical collaboration and friendship.

On some lists of "famous Kentuckians," despite his genuine hard work and talent, Pepper is listed mainly because of his long connections with Judy.

Judy's seventeenth birthday party was at her home. **Buddy Pepper** is at the keyboard, **Mickey Rooney** is behind Pepper, and **Jackie Cooper** is seated directly to the right of **Judy,** who is standing at the photo's left edge.

His big break came from Paramount when he was cast in *Seventeen* (1940), starring Jackie Cooper. Buddy played "Johnnie Watson" in this melodrama based on the Booth Tarkington novel.

After making *The Wizard of Oz*, Judy had gone to the set where *Seventeen* was being shot. While Buddy was appearing on camera, one of the other supporting players, Peter Lind Hayes, flirted with her and asked her out on a date. She found him handsome and charming and agreed to set one up, providing he kept it secret from Pepper. "Buddy and I aren't going steady, but I don't want to flirt with other men in front of him."

For her trysts with Pepper, she used a "beard" in the shape of her girlfriend, Betty O'Kelly. Once she traveled to Lake Arrowhead with Betty for what she described to Ethel as an innocent touristic visit. What Ethel didn't know was that two "young adult males," one of whom was Pepper, accompanied them.

Judy's affair with Pepper was widely gossiped about along the Hollywood grapevine, largely because of the age of these two *ingénue* stars.

Peter Lind Hayes, vaudevillian, radio personality, comedian, and early boyfriend of Judy Garland, shown here in a comedy schtick with his stage partner and wife, **Mary Healy.**

A long time heavy-hitter in game shows and talk radio, he, with his wife, from their home in New Rochelle, NY, broadcast a weekday breakfast conversation show on New York radio station 710 WOR.

When he was asked about his intimacies with Judy, Pepper said, "She laughs more than anybody else, and she cries more than anybody else—that's all I have to say."

Judy's fling with Pepper was brief. After the Japanese attack on Pearl Harbor, he joined the U.S. Army and became an entertainer for the troops, singing and playing the piano in remote outposts in Alaska and northern Canada, where soldiers were stationed in the bitter cold. The Air Transport Ferrying Command named him one of its top three entertainers.

He kept in touch with Judy throughout the war and also managed to compose songs, including Duke Ellington's "What Good Would It Do?"

In 1943, Pepper and songwriter Inez James composed the music for *Mister Big* starring Judy's friend, Donald O'Connor.

Discharged from the Army in

Girls, girls, girls, all of them safely packaged in MGM's family-friendly way, greeted **Mickey Rooney** in this publicity pic for *Love Finds Andy Hardy*.

Left to right are **Judy, Ann Rutherford, and Lana Turner.**

October of 1945, he headed to Hollywood to resume his career. Judy was the first person he called, and they renewed their friendship, but not their romance.

After that, the most time they would spend together would be in 1951 when he accompanied her on a six-month tour of Europe.

***

To Judy's changing array of men and boys could be added the name of Peter Lind Hayes, whom she'd met on the set of *Seventeen* (1940) through her friendship with Jackie Cooper, its star. A native of San Francisco and seven years older than her, Hayes was a vaudeville entertainer, songwriter, and later a film and TV actor.

She was flattered by the attention of this fully grown man and not one of the juveniles she'd been dating, or in some cases "shacked up" with.

She was seen on several occasions at the Grace Hayes Lodge, which happened to be owned by Hayes' mother. Her son provided musical entertainment there three or four nights a week, and a few times he got Judy to sing two or three songs.

On another night onstage at the Lodge, she and Hayes were seen together dancing a wild jitterbug. The next morning, a male guest from the audience called the Los Angeles Board of Education to report that an underage Judy had been dancing all night with an older man in a night club. No action was taken. On yet another occasion, a guest claimed he saw Hayes, with Judy, disappearing into his bedroom at the Lodge after midnight.

In an interview, Judy denied dating Hayes. "He's just a friend, a very nice person. But I can't even speak to a man, in his case a fellow entertainer, without the gossip columnists having me madly in love with him. People reading all this must think I'm boy-crazy."

With the understanding that Judy felt like an ugly duckling throughout most of her adolescence, she was doubly threatened by the hundreds of beauties MGM was cranking out of its studios.

One of the most visible and breathlessly promoted was **Lana Turner**, depicted in the photo above as publicity for her minor role in *They Won't Forget* (1937).

After she walked down the sidewalk, her breasts bouncing in a brief but pivotal scene at the film's opening, she became known as "The Sweater Girl."

♥ LANA ★
TURNER
HEARTS & DIAMONDS TAKE ALL

DARWIN PORTER & DANFORTH PRINCE

MEET LANA TURNER, the focal point of Blood Moon's comprehensive biography, *Hearts and Diamonds Take All.* It demonstrates that luscious, lovely Lana was a lot more than a girl who knew how to wear a sweater.

"I rarely go out. Most nights I'm home practicing my singing, learning my lines, or just listening to music on the radio."

That's what Judy wanted her growing list of fans to believe.

"The latest rumor I read is that I'm carrying on with this musician, Leonard Seuss. It's not true. I've known him for more than a decade, since we were kids. He's like a brother to me. He sometimes comes over for dinner cooked by my mother. At seventeen, he's the sole support of his own mother, and I admire him so much for that."

If a glare could kill, **Judy** (seated at a soda shop) would be dead by "hate vibes" from **Lana Turner** (standing). The object of their shared interest is Andy Hardy (aka **Mickey Rooney**).

[Judy's affair with Hayes had a short life. He met fellow entertainer Mary Healy and married her in 1940. It evolved into one of Hollywood's most successful unions, lasting until his death in 1998. By 1946, he and Mary opened the Copacabana in Manhattan and, as time went by, they graduated from radio presentations to gigs on TV. During one of those gigs, they originated the ad slogan, "See the U.S.A. in a Chevrolet" before Dinah Shore took it over.

By then, Judy had made not only more conquests, but marriages, too.

But first, she had to make her first Andy Hardy movie with one of her best friends and all-time supporters, Mickey Rooney.]

***

Mayer decided to cast Judy in her first Andy Hardy film, *Love Finds Andy Hardy* (the fourth in the Andy Hardy series) alongside Mickey Rooney, the series' staple teenager. Shooting was scheduled to begin during May of 1938.

Mayer wanted Andy Hardy pictures to represent a wholesome (fantasy-based) interpretation of the American family, "even though I've got three young whores in the lead roles." *[He was referring to Lana Turner, Mickey Rooney, and Judy.]*

According to Mayer, "I want Judge Hardy to be a paragon of wisdom and fatherly virtue. And I want Andy to be not too serious, but filled with energy, a wholesome boy who is charming and engaging and always willing to turn to his father for advice when he gets into a jam Andy Hardy movies should stand for God, Motherhood, Respect for one's father, and apple pie."

The young stars were directed in the most installments of the series by George B. Seitz, a Boston-bred playwright, screenwriter, and film actor born in 1888. He'd helmed his first movie, *Perils of Pauline*, back in 1914. At this point in his career, he was deeply familiar with Rooney's antics.

When Judy met him, she was surprised by the director's odd style of dress. He wore a blue suit with yellow accessories that included his tie, shirt, and gloves. His head was crowned with a wide-brimmed Panama hat, and he also wore purple socks and yellow shoes with chartreuse shoelaces.

At MGM, more than 200 wannabee starlets had auditioned for the role of Cynthia Potter, the small town's bubble-headed flirt. Lana Turner won out as the ingénue who tempts and tangles with Andy. She wants to kiss him, but he already has a girlfriend, Polly Benedict, as portrayed by Ann Rutherford.

Andy's attempt to resist Cecilia causes him to question his own masculinity. He turns to his father, Judge Hardy (Lewis Stone). "D'ya think there's anything wrong with a guy that don't want a girl to kiss him all the time?" Andy asks.

A very young Judy plays Betsy Booth, the helpful (and romantically available) girl next door. Befriending Andy, she sympathizes with his problems. At the prom, as the film's musical climax, she's persuaded to sing three jazzy numbers, winning the hearts, once again, of Judy fans on and off the screen.

Mickey Rooney became widely recognized in a role opposite **Spencer Tracy** in *Boys Town* (1938).

Tracy played his fatherly guidance role with all the toughness of a cop and all the sensitivity of an (honorable) priest.

The actress, Cecilia Parker, was cast as Marian Hardy, Mickey's sister, a role she would repeat in eleven films within the series. Before that, she had been John Wayne's leading lady in the first singing cowboy movie, *Riders of Destiny* (1933). After that, she appeared with Greta Garbo in *The Painted Veil* (1934).

Rooney later claimed that Judy was terribly jealous of Lana's beauty.

Lana felt at ease in the role of "that red-headed vampire. "I was a juvenile *femme fatale*. I'd rather kiss than kibbutz."

Love Finds Andy Hardy was selected for preservation in the United States National Film Registry by the Library of Congress as being "culturally, historically, or aesthetically significant." One writer observed that during its course, "Garland sang, Rooney mugged, and Stone pontificated, while Lana was whining, pouting, dimpling, and winking."

By now, Lana was skilled at evaluating camera angles, making her almost as adept as Joan Crawford. "I taught her what I knew about acting, and she was a fast learner," Rooney said to Busby Berkeley. "Privately, I taught her how to make love to a man's balls. She'd never done that before. And, as the Mexicans say, I've got a big pair of *cojones* in spite of my small size."

The kissing scenes between Rooney and Lana, as innocuous as they might be, encountered some minor trouble from movie censors. Rooney denounced "These blue noses. Lana and I were like a couple of aging virgins. The scenes were left in the final cut and appear harmless today."

Rooney was girl crazy not only on the screen, but in real life, too. Writer Jane Ellen Wayne claimed, "Mayer tried to keep all his child actors in line, like any father figure," Wayne wrote.

Critical of his young star's womanizing, Mayer grabbed him by his collar and shook him. "Listen to me. I don't care what you do in private, but don't do it in public. Your fans expect you to be Andy Hardy. You're the United States. You're the Stars and Stripes. Behave yourself. You're a symbol."

Rooney's film career was about to soar. His breakthrough role came in 1938 when he starred opposite Spencer Tracy in *Boys Town*. For that performance, Rooney was awarded with a special Juvenile Oscar. Mayer later proclaimed that *Boys Town* was his favorite of all the films released by MGM.

By 1939, hailed as the biggest, grandest, and most prestigious year in the history of Hollywood, Rooney became the number one box office attraction. Laurence Olivier hailed him as "the greatest actor of them all."

For his performances as Judge Hardy, gray-haired Lewis Stone earned lasting screen fame. In 1929, he'd been nominated for a Best Actor Oscar for *The Patriot,* and he'd been Greta Garbo's leading man in both silent films and talkies, including *Queen Christina* in 1933.

Andy Hardy's mother, Fay Holden, came from England after a spell in Canada. She would appear in fifteen of the sixteen Andy Hardy movies. She was always reliable, but never more than that.

Judy's friend, Ann Rutherford, had starred in Westerns with Gene Autry and John Wayne. In Andy Hardy films, one after another, she was cast as his sweet and forever patient girlfriend, Polly Benedict. Her greatest screen fame came when David O. Selznick cast her as Scarlett O'Hara's sister in *Gone With the Wind.*

Lana Turner, on the dawn of a fabulous career as a sultry blonde beauty throughout the 40s, was cast as Andy Hardy's temptation.

"I had a bad reputation," she later revealed. "I figured that if I had the name, why not play the game? Boys! Boys! Boys! I couldn't get enough of them."

"Judy Garland," Lana continued, "appeared as an innocent on camera—what a joke! She was getting as much as I did. Many of our lovers were the same. Mickey told me my knockers were much more succulent than Judy's."

During the shoot, Maxine Marx, daughter of Chico, visited the set and soon after encountered Judy crying in the women's room. She asked what the matter was and offered to help in any way.

"The picture I was in before this was called *The Ugly Duckling,* a title that referred to me, before its name was changed," Judy said. "Compared to Ann and Lana, I'm ugly."

"You have your own kind of beauty," Maxine assured her, "and you've got more talent than all the other MGM starlets. You can even hold your own on the screen against Mickey Rooney."

In *Love Finds Andy Hardy,* Judy got to sing "It Never Rains But What It

Pours." She also recorded "Meet the Best of My Heart" and "In Between." Variety praised her voice, claiming she was destined to find a particular niche in future MGM movies.

Motion Picture even stated that she "takes top honors, even beating out Rooney."

Time wrote, "Hollywood's number one box office star is not Clark Gable, Errol Flynn, or Tyrone Power, but a rope-haired, kazoo-voiced actor with a comic-strip face, Mickey Rooney, known heretofore for his mugging and overacting."

The *Herald Tribune* claimed that Judy Garland "sings her musical numbers, and they are catchy, but they have no place in this sort of show. Miss Garland is the least effective of the young players; Ann Rutherford and Lana Turner are better."

The early Andy Hardy films were such a bonanza at the box office that they led to thirteen sequels, ending with a final installment, *Andy Hardy Comes Home*, in 1958, which flopped. Judy would appear in several more of them in the early 1940s. One critic wrote, "The Andy Hardy films gave an inflated impression of what people hoped America really was, with Rooney always cast as the anxious, hyperactive, and girl-crazy teen."

Lana Turner's long friendship with Judy, which over the years would wax and wane both hot and cold, began on the set of *Love Finds Andy Hardy.*

Their relationship had hardly begun when each of them embarked on the pursuit of Artie Shaw, both of the young starlets wanting to marry the dashing bandleader.

When the two starlets first bonded, Judy said, "You and I have something in common. From what I hear, each of us lost our virginity at age fifteen. Word gets around."

The same could be said of Rooney. "We were just teenagers, but Lana, Judy and I were doing what comes naturally."

Gossip was also spread that Judy and Rooney were having an affair. "At least that's what the columns of that day reported. They keep saying that about Mickey and me," Judy said. "They must have me mixed up with Lana. The gossip upsets me, it really does, because there's not a bit of truth in it. Mickey and I are swell friends, and he's full of fun. I enjoy working with him. Outside the studio, we rarely see each other. We're pals—that's all!"

One day, Lana abruptly ended her affair with Rooney. "It's been great," she told him. "You're a lot of fun. But it's time to move on."

He later revealed, "At the time, I thought she'd outgrown me and wanted other guys like attorney Greg Bautzer. But months later, at a fund raiser, I ran into her, and she told me the truth."

"Do you know you put me in a family way?" she asked, referring in modest terms to her pregnancy.

"I was stunned," Rooney told Judy. "She never told me at the time. Had she done so I might have insisted she have our kid. Of course, aborting the child made sense. It protected our careers and, besides, we were just children ourselves."

He later learned that Eddie Mannix, known as "The Fixer" at MGM, had arranged for Lana's abortion through the studio doctor, Edward Jones. Previously, Mannix had warned Mayer that Rooney was "a loaded gun ready to go off."

"Eddie worked in publicity for the studio," Mervyn LeRoy said. "Most of his job involved suppressing scandal. He even covered up crimes such as murder. He kept the secrets of the stars, even protecting our beloved but pregnant Lana."

Howard Strickling, one of the directors of MGM's Publicity Department, said, "Our job was to publicize our new stars. But both Lana and Mickey were their own self-generating publicity machine. As time went by, our main job with them was to keep their names out of the gossip columns."

In 1991, when Rooney published his autobiography, *Life Is Too Short,* he revealed for the first time that Lana had aborted their child many decades before. She was furious, and at one point called her lawyer to suggest a lawsuit for libel. He wisely advised her not to sue.

When Rooney heard of her denial, he said, "Of course, she denied it. Why not? I would expect no less of her. But I stand by my story."

"All I can say is that if it didn't happen, it was the most beautiful, the most realistic, dream I ever had. MGM gals in those days, including Judy, were taught to deny any scandals."

***

The 1930s were coming to an end, and the greatest war in human history loomed.

Judy never read the newspapers, except for the entertainment section, and thoughts of oncoming battles were far from her mind.

By the decade's end, she would fall in love with two men and even her first husband, plus have a number of other affairs, too. On top of all that, she would play the lead in a movie that would immortalize her.

Frumpy? Funereal? Inappropriate for the Warmth of Southern California? Perhaps It Was the Wrong Look for a Jiving, Be-bop Teenager

"My mother, Ethel Gumm, and Louis B. Mayer, wanted to keep me a little girl forever," Judy said.

"But when I turned sixteen in 1938, I posed for this publicity picture, wearing what was fashionable—even chic—for an adult woman."

LANDING IN OZ

DOROTHY & TOTO MEET THE WIZARD

SKIPPING WITH FAIRYTALE CHARACTERS ALONG A ROAD MADE FROM SIMULATED YELLOW BRICKS, 17-YEAR-OLD JUDY EMBODIES & DEFINES THE AMERICAN CENTURY'S "ULTIMATE CLASSIC."

BABES IN ARMS

JUDY'S UNDERAGED AFFAIR WITH ARTIE SHAW.

MORE ABOUT MICKEY ROONEY

INTRODUCING OSCAR LEVANT & OTHER MEN THAT GOT AWAY

MGM's TREACHERY FROM WITHIN

FIXERS EDDIE MANNIX & HOWARD STRICKLING COLLUDE WITH JUDY'S "SPY IN THE HOUSE OF LOVE," BETTY ASHER

"REMEMBER ME TO *THE BARKLEYS OF BROADWAY*"

AFTER MULTIPLE FITS OF PIQUE, JUDY GETS REPLACED BY GINGER ROGERS.

"*When I was a very young gay man and was first meeting other gay men I did not understand why there was a big portrait of Judy Garland in their homes so often. All I knew her for was 'The Wizard of Oz'. When I was a more experienced gay man and a bit more cynical, I still didn't get the adulation. I just thought she was an emotionally messy and victimy queen of perpetual angst, booze, and tranquilizer-driven romantic drama. But now? I get it. It's the vulnerability, the raw emotion; I see why people adored her and why gay men bow at the Judy altar. Once you live a little, love a little, get dumped a time or two, get your heart broken and feel like shit for breaking someone else's you realize there's a Judy Garland in us all but most of us hide it.*"

—Steve Kerry

Author Frank Baum wrote *The Wonderful World of Oz* in 1900, and it would become a popular classic, creating a fantasy world of memorable characters such as the Cowardly Lion.

Throughout the 20th Century and beyond, *The Wizard of Oz* survived to enchant each new generation.

It had a forty or so year history of being a popular stage or cinematic release. At the time of its purchase, MGM also acquired the rights to previous adaptations, including a Broadway musical and silent film such as one released in 1925 with comedian Oliver Hardy as The Tin Man.

Even before MGM acquired the rights, Louis B. Mayer pondered the obvious question: What child actress would play Dorothy Gale? The success of the movie seemed to ride on that.

Shirley Temple was the obvious choice, but she was under contract to Darryl F. Zanuck at 20th Century Fox. In her autobiography, *Child Star,* Temple in 1988 revealed what was going on behind the scenes. Zanuck was offered a deal. "If he'd lend me to play Dorothy, he would lend him Jean Harlow and Clark Gable to star in a picture. "

"Gable and I would have been a flashy trade, *Fortune* magazine in its first scientific opinion poll had just declared me the national favorite of all women stars. Clark Gable was the most popular among males. The trade deal collapsed when Harlow died on June 1, 1937, while filming *Saratoga* with Gable."

Temple claimed, "I was the right age to play Dorothy. Judy Garland was far older and, in fact, she married only a year after *Oz* was released."

First published in 1900, when **Frank Baum**, its author, was turning forty-four, it inspired thirteen sequels. Before it was released as a movie with Judy Garland, it had already sold a million copies. By 1956, it had sold three million copies in multiple languages.

After Baum's death, his son told a reporter that he had recited "whimsical stories" to his children—almost as a "litmus test" for their viability—before they were inserted into the context of his books.

Mervyn LeRoy was named as its producer, and at the time, he was under an MGM contract that paid him the almost unheard-of salary of $6,000 a week. "When I came aboard, the word was out that MGM could not adequately cast the movie with live actors, only animated cartoon figures. But I figured that if Walt Disney could reproduce humans in his cartoons, we can reproduce cartoons with humans."

A former newspaper boy on the streets of San Francisco, LeRoy over the course of a long career was one of the most successful motion picture directors in the business. However, in the case of *The Wizard of Oz,* he would be the producer, not the director.

He was instrumental in the careers not only of Judy Garland, but of Clark Gable, Lana Turner, Robert Mitchum, and Loretta Young. Among his more notable films were such pictures as *Little Caesar, I Am a Fugitive from the Chain Gang, Anthony Adverse, Random Harvest, Thirty Seconds Over Tokyo,* and *Quo Vadis.*

After the proposal with Shirley Temple fell through, LeRoy then considered casting Deanna Durbin as Dorothy. She was making millions for Universal, and that studio did not want to release her. MGM then looked to its own child star, Judy Garland. At sixteen, soon to be seventeen, she was hardly a child anymore, and she was dating men much older than herself at the time.

Mayer named Arthur Freed associate producer, and he later exaggerated his role in the acquisition of the rights. "From the beginning, I wanted Judy to play Dorothy before Mayer and LeRoy endorsed the casting."

Before any specific actor was assigned to a part, the search for a director was on. The first man cited was Norman Taurog, but his name was soon deleted. LeRoy and Mayer hired Richard Thorpe, who actually shot two weeks of footage before he was fired.

The gay director, George Cukor, was brought in, and he was horrified when he sat through the rushes.

Thorpe had accessorized Judy with a curly haired blonde wig (inadvertently evoking Mary Pickford) and had applied too much showgirl makeup. "I ordered her back to makeup and told the people there to turn her into a little girl from Kansas."

From the beginning, it was made clear that Cukor was only a stand-in director, and that he would be gone when a full-time director was hired. Actually, Cukor was glad to be on his way, as he did not like fantasy films and absolutely loathed working with children.

At last the director was found. He was Victor Fleming, who in 1939 would helm two of the

Judy developed a schoolgirl crush on **Victor Fleming** during his direction of *The Wizard of Oz.*

Fleming's association with the film was brief: She threw a farewell party for him when he was reassigned to take over the direction of *Gone With the Wind* from George Cukor.

greatest films ever made in the history of Hollywood. *The Wizard of Oz* and *Gone With the Wind.*

A son of California, he started out as a photographer—in fact, he was the chief photographer of President Woodrow Wilson in 1918 when the Treaty of Versailles, ending World War I, was drawn up in Paris.

Before *The Wizard of Oz*, he had, among other achievements, directed four films starring Clark Gable. Many critics felt that Gable had adopted Fleming's macho persona in his screen roles. In 1932, he and Gable came together when they made *Red Dust*, starring Jean Harlow.

He showed up on the set of *The Wizard of Oz* and demanded to see the rushes of what little amounts of footage had already been shot. After sitting through the screening in disgust, he ordered Freed to toss "this garbage in the dump. We'll start all over again."

At the age of fifty-five, Fleming was still a dashing, handsome man, very virile and, in the words of Judy, "Very very sexy. I immediately developed a crush on him, and I flirted outrageously with him, but he didn't seem attracted to sixteen-year-old girls, unlike some other men I knew."

"He did find my breasts too big and sent me off to makeup and the wardrobe department. My growing breasts were bound and corseted, my tits encased in what was known as a 'love corset.'"

She was still a schoolgirl and would have to follow child labor laws, which mandated that three hours of every day had to be devoted to lessons.

Before the rest of casting began, LeRoy put scriptwriters and musician to work on the words and music for *The Wizard of Oz*. Most of the script was written by Noel Langley, Florence Ryerson, and Edgar Alan Woolf. Music was to be by Harold Arlen, lyrics by Yip Harburg, and musical adaptation by Herbert Stothart.

During the course of a long career, Arlen—a native of Buffalo, New York—composed some five-hundred songs, none more famous than "Over the Rainbow," which has been voted the number one song of the 20th Century. By 1929, he'd composed the celebrated song, "Get Happy," a Judy Garland classic, sung at almost every one of her concerts, and "The Man That Got Away."

The idea for the music of "Over the Rainbow" was said to have oc-

The Scarecrow (**Ray Bolger**, left), **Judy**, and The Tin Man (**Jack Haley**) went off together to see *The Wizard of Oz*. "Long after I'm gone, I will be remembered as The Scarecrow," Bolger said.

According to Haley, "My greatest problem as The Tin Man was to keep my *[toxic, aluminum-based]* makeup from melting and running into my eyes to blind me."

curred to Arlen as he was driving through rain on his way home. The rain stopped and a glorious rainbow formed over Los Angeles just as the sun went down.

He called Yip Harburg, who was to write the lyrics. After listening to the music, he wasn't sold on it. "Save it for Nelson Eddy. It's not for a little girl from Kansas. Too big, too broad, too operatic. Come to think of it, it might be ideal for Jeanette MacDonald."

Years later, Harburg said, "How wrong I was. The lyrics of that song may be heard two hundred years from now."

Harburg was also known for writing the lyrics to such hits as "April in Paris," "It's only a Paper Moon," and that Depression Era favorite, "Brother, Can You Spare a Dime?"

"Yip had strong feelings about religion," Judy said, "and he was always trying to make an atheist out of me."

One of the hardest jobs was getting the brilliant colors right in the scenes set in Oz and the sepia tones correct in the scenes in Kansas. Hal Rosson, the former husband of the doomed Jean Harlow, was one of the best cinematographers in the business, and he was hired and performed brilliantly.

"I want to be beautiful," Judy told her gay costume designer, Adrian, who created her dress and slippers. "But I probably won't be."

"Not to worry, you will be a lovely Dorothy, wide-eyed, innocent, and a creature with searching eyes taking in the wonders on the other side of the rainbow," Adrian said.

Judy would take star billing, but there were four difficult male roles, beginning with the Wizard of Oz himself. The other character parts included The Tin Man, the Scarecrow, and the Cowardly Lion. The Tin Man wanted a brain; the Scarecrow a heart, and the Cowardly Lion courage.

Ray Bolger originally was offered the role of The Tin Man, but objected to it, saying "I'm known as 'rubber legs' and I need to have movement."

LeRoy agreed with that assessment and decided that Bolger would be better as the Scarecrow. He then cast Buddy Ebsen, Judy's former dancing partner, as The Tin Man.

In his stiff metallic costume, Ebsen was unable to sit down. His face was also sprinkled with aluminum dust. Later, he found it hard to breathe, and he was rushed to the nearest hospital. There, his

To announce the movie in advance of its release, MGM's publicity department assembled its key players into a mock confrontation. Depicted from left to right are **Ray Bolger, Frank Morgan, Bert Lahr, Jack Haley, and Judy Garland. Toto**, an affable, well-trained Cairn terrier, stands in the foreground.

life was saved when he was hooked up to an iron lung. *The Wizard of Oz* would be wrapped before he was released from the hospital.

Jack Haley, who had worked with Judy before, was a last-minute replacement as The Tin Man. He had to fit into that metal suit and also had to undergo a vigorous session in the makeup room where the "artists" there had nearly killed Ebsen. Instead of metal dust, they assured him that aluminum paste would be safe. It was not. He came down with a serious eye infection and had to be hospitalized. Fleming had to shoot around him until he recovered.

In *Oz,* Haley was also seen in a double role, the part of a worker in Kansas and the farm owned by Dorothy's Uncle Henry.

One day, when Haley returned to work, John Haley, Jr., then aged five, showed up and was introduced to Judy. The teenager could not have imagined that she was meeting her future son-in-law, who would marry Liza Minnelli one day after Judy was dead.

Bert Lahr was cast as The Cowardly Lion. He had long been in show business, starting out in vaudeville, working the burlesque circuit. By the 1920s, he was seen on Broadway. In *Oz,* he was cited for his brilliant rendition of "If I Were King of the Forest."

"I might have lacked courage as the lion, but it took a hell of a lot of courage to get into that damn lion's costume. It was hotter in there than the hottest furnace room in hell. I felt like a stevedore carrying the entire boat. After *Oz,* I became typecast as a lion. Problem was, there weren't many parts for a lion."

Another show biz vet, Ray Bolger, became famous for his dancing during his portrayal of the Scarecrow. Every morning, before his performance on any given day, he had to endure at least two hours in makeup. "The coats of makeup they put on me permanently lined my face, making me appear older than I was. When I showed up to work with Judy years later on *The Harvey Girls,* I could tell she was shocked by my appearance. Blame it on that fucking makeup in *Oz.*"

Bolger would go on to star with Liza Minnelli in *That's Dancing* (1987), a film written by her husband at the time, Jack Haley, Jr.

Several actors competed for the role of The Wizard. It was first offered to W.C. Fields. But he and Mayer could never come to terms on salary. LeRoy then pitched the role to Ed Wynn, who rejected it because the part was "too small."

Wallace Beery heard that the part was up for grabs, and he phoned Mayer but was told, "You're wrong for the role."

Finally, it was offered to yet another show biz veteran, Frank Morgan.

A New Yorker born in 1890, Morgan was one of Hollywood's leading character actors, having made his screen debut in 1916.

"From what I observed, Frank was drunk most of the time," Judy recalled. "He was always toting around a black briefcase, which actually held a sizable stash of liquor. But all that alcohol didn't seem to interfere with his acting."

"He once told me, 'You're growing up, girl. It's time Dorothy learned to drink. How about a nip with me?'"

She turned him down, but later agreed with his final advice to her: "The only way to get through life, to tolerate its humiliations, is to be fortified with alcohol."

In *The Wizard of Oz,* Morgan also played five other roles — the carnival huckster "Professor Marvel"; the gatekeeper of The Emerald City; the coachman of the carriage drawn by "The Horse of a Different Color"; a guard at the Emerald City who initially refuses to let Dorothy and her companions in to see The Wizard; and Oz's scary face projection.

Morgan became known for the most part through his depictions of comical, befuddled men such as he was when he starred as Jesse Kiffmeyer in *Saratoga* (1937) alongside co-stars Clark Gable and Jean Harlow, who died right before finishing the picture.

After working with Judy, he went on to star in *The Shop Around the Corner* (1940).

As William Grogan, he lost his pain in drink in *The Human Comedy* (1943). In *The White Cliffs of Dover* (1944), he was cast as Irene Dunne's father. He played the king in *The Three Musketeers* (1948) and James Stewart's devoted buddy in *The Stratton Story* (1949).

In two of his last films, he starred with Clark Gable, cast as a gambler in *Any Number Can Play* (1949) and as a fire chief in *Key to the City,* which was released in 1950 after his death.

Ironically, Judy and Morgan were teamed once again in 1949 to film *Annie Get Your Gun,* where Judy was cast as Annie Oakley and Morgan as Buffalo Bill. But Mayer fired her, and Morgan died on September 18. He was replaced by Louis Calhern.

"I loved the Old Geezer, Charles Grapewin," Judy said of the actor who played her Uncle Henry down on the farm in Kansas. Clara Blandick was cast as her dowdy Auntie Em.

Grapewin had befriended Judy when he co-starred with her in *Listen, Darling* and *Broadway Melody of 1938.* He'd been born four years after the Civil War ended, and, as a young man, he'd traveled the world as part of the Barnum & Bailey Circus. He was also in the original Broadway production of *The Wizard of Oz* in 1903.

For the most part, Judy got along with what she called "The Three Hams," referring to Bolger, Haley, and Lahr. "They were tricksters, however, trying to

The widowed wife of showman Flo Ziegfeld, **Billie Burke**, a once-fabled beauty, reinvented herself as a befuddled *comedienne* in the 1930s and became famous for portraying dim-witted, high-society ladies.

In *The Wizard of Oz*, she was cast as Glinda, the Good Witch of the North, a character satirized by cross-dressers and drag queens ever since.

The designer, Adrian, gave her butterfly wings, a regal crown, and a gown crafted from delicate pink tulle sprinkled with "northern stars" and frosty snow crystals.

steal every scene from Dorothy. When we pranced down that Yellow Brick Road, I practically ended up in back of them."

"I was too shy to complain, but our director, Victor Fleming, wasn't."

From his perch in a boom over the set, he shouted down at them, "Listen, you fucking screen hogs, cut the shit! What in hell do you bums think you're doing? Judy is the god damn star going down that Yellow Brick Road. You creeping little pricks are mere supporting players. So get it right this time!"

Before Billie Burke was cast as Glinda, "The Good Witch," both Fanny Brice and Beatrice Lille were considered for the role, then rejected. At the age of fifty-four, Burke seemed ideal to play the "ageless" Glinda, the screen sorceress.

Oz marked Burke's second role in a film with Judy. She had been a fabled beauty back in the days when she'd been married to showman Florenz Ziegfeld.

To her fairytale costume, Adrian added a butterfly effect, giving her wings. She fitted the script's description of her character: "Her hair was a rich red in color and fell in flowing ringlets over her shoulders. Her dress was pure white, her eyes were blue, as they looked at Dorothy." L a t e r , she denied that she had ever played a witch. "I was cast as a fairy."

[Coincidentally, Judy's second husband, Vincente Minnelli, would direct Billie Burke as Elizabeth Taylor's mother-in-law in Father of the Bride *(1950) and its sequel,* Father's Little Dividend *(1951). Each film starred Spencer Tracy as Elizabeth's father.]*

Gale Sondergaard, later to be blacklisted during the McCarthy "witch hunt," was originally cast as the Wicked Witch. During her audition, she was promised that the Evil Queen would be lovingly evocative of the one in Walt Disney's *Snow White and the Seven Dwarfs.* "But when Fleming wanted to turn me into an ugly old hag, I bowed out," she said.

After Sondergaard bolted, Margaret Hamilton revealed what happened next: "I was in need of money at the time. I had already done six pictures for MGM, and my agent called, telling me that I was wanted for a role in *The Wizard of Oz,* which had been a favorite fairytale since I was four years old. I asked him what part I was wanted for. He replied, 'The Witch, naturally. What else?'"

On the set, she bonded with Judy and became her closest friend during filming. From the very first take, in her grotesque makeup and witch costume,

Reflecting later on her physically dangerous role as The Wicked Witch of the West, **Margaret Hamilton** said, "Wise men tell us we can't go home again, but Dorothy did. And she did it for all of us. That's why *The Wizard of Oz* is so special...and will remain so."

with a broom and a wide-brimmed cone-shaped hat, she was a triumph. In fact, she is today ranked among the fifty top screen villains of all time.

A former kindergarten teacher, she was employed as a character actress for seven years before she was hired as the Evil Witch of the West. Often, she played a gossipy spinster.

In *The Wizard,* she was cast in a double role as Miss Alma Gulch, and she is seen briefly as an unidentified flying witch during the tornado that transported Judy over the rainbow.

"Even as a young woman, I was known as 'Mag the Hag' because of my prominent nose. My father wanted to have it altered by plastic surgery, but I preferred to keep my nose and make it a trademark in character roles as a gossipy bitch. That nose worked for me. In my next picture, *My Little Chickadee* (1940), with Mae West and W.C. Fields, I was no competition for Mae, who never wanted a prettier woman than herself in one of her films."

In the movie, although it was Hamilton's character of the Wicked Witch who threatened Dorothy with danger, it was Hamilton herself who ran the greater chance of being injured or killed during filming. An accident occurred in a scene clouded with smoke and fire where she is supposed to disappear into the blaze. A trap door had been installed for her quick exit out of camera range.

Alas, the blaze erupted too soon. Her broom and her hat caught on fire, and her green copper-based makeup melted, causing second- and third-degree burns to her face and hands. She was rushed to the hospital, where she spent six weeks in recovery before reporting back to work.

Hamilton's stand-in and stunt double, Betty Danko, also suffered an on-set accident in February of 1939. With Hamilton out of commission, it was Danko who made the fiery entrance into Munchkinland. During the "Surrender Dorothy," skywriting sequence, at the Emerald City, Danko sat on a smoking pipe designed to look like the witch's broomstick.

Fleming ordered a third take, but as it unfolded, the pipe exploded, injuring her and requiring two weeks in the hospital. Her legs were permanently scarred. A stunt double, Alice Goodwin, had to finish the broom-riding stunt for her.

As the witch, Hamilton delivers one of cinema's most immortal lines, as she threatens Dorothy, "I'm going to get you, my pretty, and your little dog, too."

She was referring to Toto, who entered screen immortality as one of filmdom's most famous canines, ranking up there with Lassie and Rin-Tin-Tin.

In many scenes in *The Wizard of Oz* (1939), including close-ups of those dancing feet in the ruby-red slippers, that is not Judy Garland, but one of her two stand-ins, dancer Caren Marsh.

[*Judy's other stand-in was Bobbie Koshay. During filming, Judy, according to California law, had to be in MGM's schoolhouse four hours a day and wasn't always available for filming. Whereas Caren was used for close-ups of those dancing feet, Koshay was used in any shot where Garland's face wasn't visible. That included tumbling into a sloppy pig pen or being borne aloft by the "Winged Monkeys." Koshay also had to appear climbing out of a balloon and leaping onto the platform below to retrieve Toto, who had escaped.]*

Caren's feet are seen dancing down the Yellow Brick Road before Judy calls on The Wizard. A native daughter of Hollywood, Caren, a talented tap dancer, was three years older than Judy.

Ironically, when she wasn't needed on the set of *Oz*, Caren rushed over to work as an extra on MGM's other 1939 classic, *Gone With the Wind,* starring Clark Gable, Vivien Leigh, and Olivia de Havilland.

Caren also doubled for Judy in *Ziegfeld Girl* (1940), a movie co-starring Lana Turner and Hedy Lamarr. Caren said that Judy worried about having to compete on the screen with those two fabled MGM beauties.

Like Marsh, Koshay was given a replica gingham dress, blouse, and a pair of Ruby Slippers. She spent far more time on the set than Marsh did. She had to stand under hot lights until the camera was ready and last-minute changes were made to the set. "I was always called in for any dangerous stunt. MGM couldn't afford risking life or limb of Judy."

It is Koshay who opens the door but steps out of the frame for Judy to walk into a Technicolor Munchkinland. And it is Koshay who taps her heels together three times at the end of the movie that brings her back over the rainbow and safely back to Kansas.

A native daughter of Colorado, Koshay was twelve years older than Judy. A champion swimmer, she became a member of the 1928 United States Olympic Team.

She told Judy that she had gotten married to Jack Harcourt Wilson in June of 1936, but the union was annulled in October. She warned Judy about an early marriage. "As husband material, Jack could be a double for Dracula." Two years after standing in for Judy, she married for a second time, this time to Richard Allen Perkins, a union that lasted until her death in 1975 at the age of sixty-five.

"My ruby red slippers were slightly larger than Judy's, because my feet were bigger," Koshay said. "In some scenes, Judy's feet became

Which is the real Dorothy?　　(left) Judy's stunt double and stand-in, **Bobbie Koshay,** (center) **Judy Garland** herself; and (right photo), Judy's "dance double," **Caren Marsh**.

swollen, so she had to use my slippers."

"At the end of the movie, I should have secretly slipped out of the studio with a pair," Koshay said. "If so, I could have been fixed for life."

After her stint as Judy's "dancing double," Caren Marsh went on to appear in a number of Hollywood musicals and was even a leading lady in Westerns. Her pictures included *Best Foot Forward* (1943) where she worked with Lucille Ball, and in *Night and Day* (1946) with Cary Grant. Her last film was *Adventures of Don Juan* (1948) starring Errol Flynn, where the swashbuckler took notice of her. That would be her last movie.

On July 12, 1949, she boarded a flight from Albuquerque shortly before dawn. As it approached the airport in Burbank, it crashed. Thirteen passengers of the 48 people aboard the flight survived, including Caren, who was badly injured. Her left foot was crushed. Doctors considered amputation, but she held on, wanting to save her foot, although told, even if it were saved, she would never dance again. After several operations, her foot was saved, and she took rehabilitation exercises for years, even becoming a dance instructor.

In 1950, she wed Bill Doll, the press agent for Mike Todd, married at the time to Elizabeth Taylor. Caren spent the last decades of the 20th Century attending *Oz* festivals, conventions, and the final gathering of the original cast and crew.

Still lively and high-spirited, with an entourage of loyal friends and fans, Caren was found living quietly in Palm Springs, one of the last survivors not only of *tte Wizard of Oz,* but of *Gone With the Wind,* too.

On April 6, 2020, she celebrated her 101st birthday.

* * *

COULD IT BE?
A SHOE FETISH IN MUNCHKINLAND?
WHATEVER HAPPENED TO THE RUBY SLIPPERS?

For years, Debbie Reynolds, the spunky, durable and entrepreneurial female star of, among other Hollywood Classics, *Singin' in the Rain* (1952), collected movie memorabilia, with the intention of one day opening a museum on Hollywood Boulevard, but she never got financing for it.

She did, however, raise enough money to open a hotel, casino, and showroom in Las Vegas. On one of its lower floors, in glass-fronted exhibit cases, she proudly displayed her memorabilia. It included a dress worn by Scarlett O'Hara in *Gone With the Wind* (1939), and Charlie Chaplin's bowler hat. Debbie's hotel and casino operated until 1997.

After that, in need of cash, she organized an auction of her memorabilia. For only $300, she had purchased from MGM the original pair of ruby slippers worn by Judy during the early footage of *The Wizard of Oz,* footage which its replacement director, Victor Fleming, had deemed unusable and had rejected.

Fleming also objected to the original pair of ruby slippers, the ones later acquired by Debbie, finding them too fanciful, too ornate, and "like something that a princess might wear in *Arabian Nights."* Instead, he commissioned a streamlined (at least in their contours and overall design) version.

At Debbie Reynold's auction, her "early prototype" version of the slippers sold for $510,000, and the "country cousin" gingham dress worn by Judy throughout most of the film sold for $910,000.

[At the same auction, the white dress worn by Marilyn Monroe in The Seven-Year Itch *(1955) sold for an astonishing $5,520,000.]*

In 2011, at an unrelated sale, the simplified Ruby Slippers worn by Judy in footage used for *The Wizard's* final cut were sold to a private buyer for $690,000.

***

The story of the casting of the Munchkins became part of Hollywood legend and lore. Story after story, really tall tales, have been told about their off-screen antics during the making of *The Wizard of Oz.*

LeRoy claimed, "The wee little folk gave me my alltime biggest headache. No, that is too kind. They were a pain in the ass. I had to import midgets—call them dwarfs—from all over America and even had to turn to Europe in my search for these little devils. When I still needed more, I had to cast kids as adults."

The Munchkins, to the everlasting regret of its manager, were housed at a hotel in Culver City. "They behaved like a pack of drunks during a wild convention in Las Vegas," LeRoy claimed. "After two of them fell into the toilet bowls, I had to hire a female and a male attendant to hold onto them whenever they went to take a crap."

"The manager and staff of the hotel were enraged," LeRoy said. "Night after night, the Munchkins were wild, at times running up and down the hallways in the nude. These little jerks had no inhibitions whatsoever. Orgies were staged every night. Three of the homo ones tried to hold down a room service waiter and rape him."

"I'd rather have them making love than erupting into fights every night. I could just imagine the bill for damages I was going to get at the

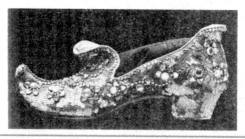

Left photo: the (unused) Ruby Slipper prototype. Though they never appeared in *The Wizard of Oz'* final cut, they sold for $510,000 at the auction of Debbie Reynold's memorabilia in 1998.

Right photo: "the real deal," **the simplified Ruby Slippers** as depicted in the film. In 2011, they sold in an unrelated auction for a reported $690,000.

108

end of their stay. On some nights, things got so out of control that the Culver City Police had to be called in to keep these evil bastards from killing each other. One night, a German midget got into an argument with a Polish Jew (also a midget) and almost castrated him. Apparently, they got into a fight over the merits and dangers of circumcision."

"I was delighted when Fleming told me the last scene with the damn Munchkins had been shot," LeRoy said.

For the most part, Judy got along with the Munchkins, although she had a few nasty encounters. "I was always getting my ass pinched," she claimed.

Some of the little guys were fond of lifting up Judy's dress to see what they could see. Others bragged about their sexual prowess, telling her they weren't small all over.

Some of the female midgets revealed that they worked as prostitutes in Europe. An import from Amsterdam said: "It's no secret that many men prefer young girls to older women. Even though I'm almost thirty, I still dress up every night as a twelve-year-old."

Years later during a TV interview with NBC host Jack Paar, Judy said, "Those Munchkins were a pile of little drunks, intoxicated all the time. Sometimes, they had to be rounded up in butterfly nets."

It wasn't just the Munchkins with whom Judy experienced unwelcome sexual encounters. Others she endured came from one of her greatest promoters, Arthur Freed himself. During the filming of *The Wizard of Oz,* he summoned her into his office to discuss her upcoming film, *Babes in Arms* (1939). Mayer had already designated him as its producer.

At the time, she was unaware of one of his sexual fetishes, although she was to learn later that it was the subject of gossip around MGM.

She later told Mickey Rooney and others what had happened that afternoon during her private meeting with Freed. "Instead of discussing *Babes in Arms,* Arthur unzipped his fly and exposed himself to me. After a few awkward moments, he put his thing back in his pants, and nothing else was said about it. And that was that. I assumed that he wanted me to perform oral sex on him, but he didn't insist."

In their search for 124 actors who might be suited to portray "**The Munchkins**," a nationwide search was launched. Carnivals and circus owners were contacted, and ads were placed in newspapers. Mervyn LeRoy considered casting Mickey Rooney as one of them, but he was "too tall."

Another child star, Shirley Temple, had a similar experience, as she revealed in her 1988 autobiography, *Child Star*. She was only twelve years old when Freed, in the privacy of his office, exposed himself to her. "Being innocent of the male anatomy at the time, I giggled. He threw me out of his office."

In addition to the Munchkins, the "Winkies" and the "Winged Monkeys" also had to be cast, prepped, rehearsed, and costumed. The Winkies were slaves of the Wicked Witch, who used them as her guards. Under the harsh lights needed for filming in Technicolor, actors sweated under the almost unbearable conditions in their heavy felt costumes. A few of them passed out in the heat.

Another menace for Dorothy were the grotesque Winged Monkeys, who wreaked havoc in the Haunted Forest.

Wearing heavy makeup and costumes, animal impersonators were hired for the roles. Pat Walshe talked to Judy, who noticed that his wings had been clipped in a way that wasn't replicated by the other monkeys. The told her, "The Witch Bitch had my wings clipped to make sure I wouldn't fly away, and that she could keep me in servitude."

At least three pairs of ruby slippers were crafted—one for Judy, the other two for the stand-ins. They were covered in red satin lined with cream-colored kid leather. A total of 2,300 sequins were sewn onto each pair, each leather bow fitted with forty-five rhinestones, two bugle beads, and a trio of costume jewels. Inspired by the technicalities of the Technicolor process, sequins were either colored crimson or deep burgundy to maximize their shimmering shade of ruby. Several different prototypes were crafted and manufactured before a relatively simple version was used in the final cut.

The script called for Dorothy, The Tin Man, the Scarecrow, and the Cowardly Lion, "to follow the Yellow Brick Road." Consequently, one had to be created. The film's original director, Richard Thorpe, had commissioned a road constructed from yellow-painted bricks. Fleming had it ripped apart and rebuilt with yellow Masonite tiles, which, when filmed, gave off the il-

Arthur Freed with Judy Garland. He showed her sketches of routines she'd have to perform.

Then, in the privacy of his office, he unzipped and showed her something else, too.

The **Winged Monkeys** wreak havoc on poor Dorothy in the Haunted Forest. Men with very tiny physiques donned hair suits and facial masks to portray their menacing armies. To assist MGM's costume designers, a call went out to anyone who might offer to sell an embalmed body of a condor, if its wings were still attached.

lusion of gleaming marble.

The Emerald City, decorated with green glass spires, was the film's largest set.

In February of 1939, word reached the set of *The Wizard of Oz* that George Cukor had been fired from *Gone With the Wind*. As his replacement, Mayer immediately hired Fleming, even though he hadn't yet finished his direction of *The Wizard*. Consequently, Fleming abandoned *Wizard* to direct Scarlett O'Hara, Rhett Butler, Butterfly McQueen, and others, and was replaced on the set of *The Wizard of Oz* with King Vidor.

It was Vidor who, therefore, directed the sepia-toned scenes set in Kansas, including Judy's delivery of "Over the Rainbow" and the tornado scenes that swept her away.

A close friend of Fleming, Vidor chose not to take credit for his contribution to *The Wizard* until after the death of Fleming in 1949, a dozen years after *Wizard* was wrapped and released.

After many grueling months, and at long last, it was time for *The Wizard's* first sneak preview. Mayer himself selected the theater in San Bernardino where it would be previewed. Other test markets included the Strand Theatre in Oconomowoc, Wisconsin, Kenosha, also in Wisconsin, and at a theater on Cape Cod in Massachusetts.

Audiences responded favorably, but the film ran fifteen minutes overtime, and Mayer ordered that it be cut. Among a few other scenes he wanted to end up on the cutting room floor was Judy's rendition of "Over the Rainbow."

"I don't like our heroine singing this dreamy ballad in a barnyard of horseshit."

Fortunately, saner minds prevailed, and Arthur Freed, among others, convinced the studio chief to retain the song in the final cut. Judy would spend the rest of her life singing "Over the Rainbow."

She was not alone in recording the Harold Arlen song, but hers became the most popular rendition. Other singers who, in her footsteps, recorded versions of their own included Frank Sinatra, Ella Fitzgerald, Doris Day, Tony Bennett, and Sarah Vaughan.

To promote the film, Mayer ordered Judy and Mickey Rooney, who was not in the picture, to go on a massive publicity tour to promote *The Wizard*.

Yip Harburg said,

There's no place like home: Judy, as Dorothy, awakens in Kansas after her dream about Oz, its Wizard, and her friends and adventures there.

Anyone in the audience who had ever studied Freud in college immediately began analyzing his theories about the nature of dreams.

111

"MGM treated Judy like a commodity to be exploited. She was used to the hilt—unwisely and unhumanely. The studio wanted every ounce of her blood."

On August 17, 1939, Judy and Rooney performed seven shows a day at the Capitol Theatre in Manhattan, each of them between screenings of *The Wizard of Oz.* In one day alone, the box office sold 37,000 tickets to enthusiastic audiences.

Variety called it "Grade-A entertainment from a tousle-haired young man and a cute, clean-cut girl with a smash singing voice and style."

When Rooney had to fly back to Hollywood to begin work on another picture with Judy, she stayed on. Her *Wizard* co-stars, Bert Lahr and Ray Bolger, filled in for Rooney.

"I made more money during this live show at the Capitol than I was paid to be Dorothy," Judy recalled.

After performing their show on August 31, Judy woke up the next morning to learn that Nazi Germany had invaded Poland, and that England and France had declared war on Germany.

"All the talk was of war, war, but in show biz we carried on entertaining, putting up a good front," Judy said. "But we knew that American lives eventually would be changed forever."

***

SHOWBIZ JUDY ARRIVES IN THE BIG APPLE: Grand Central Station, NYC, August, 1939. Judy, with Mickey Rooney, each visible near the foreground of this press and PR picture, were greeted with raving adulation and a formible corps of police officers to protect them.

Judy got the best reviews of her life as *The Wizard of Oz* opened in theaters throughout the land. *Film Daily* claimed that "MGM has given its deepest lion roar." *The Hollywood Citizen* said, "Judy Garland is rosy-cheeked, starry-eyed, and more alluring than a glamour girl."

The New York Times found Judy as Dorothy "a pert, fresh-faced miss with wonder-lit eyes of a believer in fairy tales." *The New York Post* joined in the praise, viewing Judy's Dorothy as "perfect."

Amid the raves, there were occasional attacks, some reviewers finding Judy "too old" to play Dorothy. *The New Yorker* labeled *The Wizard* as "a real stinkeroo." *The New Republic* claimed, "The film has Judy Garland and Technicolor, but weighs like a pound of fruitcake soaking wet."

The Wizard of Oz has withstood the test of time, the hardest test for any movie.

In a 2009 retrospective in San Francisco, *The Chronicle* labeled *The Wizard* "one of the greatest in cinema history." Judy's skipping down the Yellow Brick Road with her unlikely assortment of companions was viewed as one of the most iconic moments in the history of film.

A massive undertaking, *The Wizard of Oz* was one of the most expensive films ever made to that point in time, costing $2.8 million. Most people thought it was a major hit, but in reality, MGM suffered a loss of $1.4 million, which it would not recoup until a decade later.

A lot of its initial loss derived from the fact that at almost every showing, the audience consisted of "an ocean of kids" who paid half-price, or less, than the cost of an adult ticket.

The Wizard launched Judy into stardom, and MGM rewarded her with an increase in salary. It was a wise move: From it, she would morph into one of the biggest box office attractions in America.

Over the years, literary sleuths have detected forty differences between scenes in the movie and descriptions in the Baum novel.

It was nominated for Best Picture but lost to David O. Selznick's *Gone With the Wind*. Other losers that year were *Dark Victory*, *Ninotchka* (during which "Garbo Laughed"), *Love Affair*, *Mr. Smith Goes to Washington*, *Stagecoach*, *Of Mice and Men*, *Wuthering Heights*, and *Goodbye, Mr. Chips*.

Judy was given an honorary Oscar as Best Juvenile Performer of the Year, receiving it for her performances in both *The Wizard* and for *Babes in Arms*, which she made later in 1939 with Mickey Rooney.

The Wizard walked off with the gold for Best Music and Original Score (awarded to Herbert Stothart). An award for Best Musical Original Song ("Over the Rainbow") went to Harold Arlen and Yip Harburg.

The film was also nominated for Best Art Direction (Cedric Gibbons and William A. Horning) and Best Special Effects (A. Arnold Gillespie and Douglas Shearer).

In 1956, *The Wizard of Oz* was re-released and was seen by millions who watched it on the CBS Television Network. According to the Library of Congress, it's the most-watched film in cinematic history.

***

WHATEVER HAPPENED TO TOTO?

The Cairn terrier, "Toto" (whose original name was Terry), became immortalized when she appeared opposite Judy Garland in *The Wizard of Oz*. Together, they went over the rainbow.

The Wizard was Toto's only credited role, though in her lifespan of eleven years, she appeared in sixteen different movies.

Years before working with Judy, she starred with Shirley Temple in *Bright Eyes* (1934), one of the dog's first screen roles.

In the same year that Toto worked with Judy, she also appeared in George Cukor's *The Women* as the "Fighting Dog" at a beauty shop. The stars of that film were Norma Shearer and Joan Crawford, along with an all-female cast.

Many fans over the years thought Toto was a male. Not so. She became the mother of another screen dog, Rommy, who starred in such films as *Reap the Wild Wind* (1942), directed by Cecil B. DeMille. Stars included Ray Milland, John Wayne, and Paulette Goddard.

During the filming of *The Wizard*, Toto had a terrible accident when one of the Winkie Guards stepped on her foot, breaking it. Judy took her home and nursed her back to health. She fell in love with the dog and tried to buy her from her trainer, Carl Spitz, but he refused. At the time, he was getting $125 a week for her services, the equivalent of $2,200 in the currency of 2020.

Before showing up with Toto, Spitz had read *The Wonderful Wizard of Oz*, noting whatever tricks or mannerisms Toto would need to perform, and then training her accordingly.

Toto's last film role was *Tortilla Flat* (1942), starring Spencer Tracy and Hedy Lamarr. It reunited her with *Oz* director Victor Fleming and with Frank Morgan, who had portrayed The Wizard.

Toto died on September 1, 1945 as World War II came to an end. Spitz buried her on his ranch in Studio City. In 1958, the grave was destroyed during the construction of the Ventura Freeway.

A permanent memorial of Toto was built in June of 2011 at Los Angeles' Hollywood Forever Cemetery. Fans of Dorothy and Toto

Judy and Toto: The REAL stars of the picture

114

still show up with flowers.

Even before the filming of *Oz,* the German-born Spitz became known as the best dog trainer in Hollywood. *[He had provided the St. Bernard used in* The Call of the Wild *(1935), starring Clark Gable and Loretta Young.]* Having emigrated to America as an adult in 1926, he had trained police and military dogs in Germany during World War I.

When World War II broke out, Spitz—a patriotic American citizen— set up America's War Dog Program for the training of, and caring for, dogs involved in or affected by the conflict.

Spitz himself has earned at least a footnote in the history of cinema, and a major chapter in the training and compassionate treatment of dogs. He lived until the age of eighty-two. He was buried in Glendale's Forest Lawn Memorial Park Cemetery.

***

Jazz's finest clarinetist in the "Big Band" era of the late 1930s and early 40s, Artie Shaw spearheaded one of the nation's most popular bands. Along with Glenn Miller and Harry James, he was a household name.

Judy had fallen in love with Shaw's music before she met the man himself. On her record player, she had heard his rendition of Cole Porter's "Begin the Beguine" countless times.

Born on Manhattan's Lower East Side, Artie Shaw grew up in a Jewish family, his father both a dressmaker and a photographer. The family moved to Connecticut, where Shaw's natural introversion was deepened by rampant anti-Semitism. With his savings, he bought a used saxophone when he was thirteen. Three years later, he decided his talent lay in the clarinet. At sixteen, he left home to tour the country with a local band.

Beginning in 1925, and lasting for more than a decade, he played his clarinet with many different bands and orchestras, recording such hits as "It Don't Mean a Thing If It Ain't Got That Swing," "Stardust," and "Rosalie."

He told his fellow musicians that he wished he'd been born a Gentile. He seemed free of racial prejudice, and in time he would have a torrid affair with Lena Horne.

He backed Bessie Smith, hung out with Count Basie, and inspired Ray Charles. He even hired Billie Holiday as his band's lead vocalist. His was the first white band to employ a full-time black singer. He toured the segregated South with Holiday, but she eventually dropped out, demoralized by the racial prejudice she encountered in, among others, Alabama and Mississippi.

In 1936, when she met her idol during a visit to Manhattan with Ethel, Judy was only fourteen. She had been booked to sing over MGM's radio station (WHN) and to record for Decca.

During her two-week visit, John Mercer, the singer and composer, agreed to escort Judy and Ethel to the ballroom of the Hotel Lexington , where Judy wanted to hear Shaw and his band and to meet him, admitting that she'd developed a powerful crush on him.

115

Leaving her mother to talk to Mercer, Judy paraded backstage to introduce herself to Shaw. "Hi, I'm Judy Garland, a singer for Metro. I wanted to meet you and tell you you're the greatest."

"How old are you, little girl?" he asked.

"Fourteen, but I'm growing up fast," she answered.

"I'm delighted to hear that a girl as young as you appreciates me and my 'sweet swing band.' Most of the people who come to my concerts are music morons. I'm experimenting with music and backed up by only a rhythm section and a string quartet. I call it 'Third Stream,' inspired by Igor Stravinsky."

"And I'm inspired by you," she gushed. "You're very good looking, unlike that Paul Whiteman who's so ugly. No one, and I mean no one, can play the clarinet like you. From your lungs emerges magic."

Handsome, responsive, insanely popular, and prone to mysterious absences during crucial moments of his show-biz career, **Artie Shaw** was the hippest man in the business of big bands.

"If you don't stop complimenting me, I'll start to believe you."

"All that talent you have, and being gorgeous to boot," she said.

"Sweetie, all that flattery will go to my head, and I'll become stuck up."

He suddenly gave her a big hug, telling her "to grow up and come back for me."

And then he was gone, leaving her dazed.

Time would pass before they would meet again.

***

Shaw saw Judy again in February of 1938 when he joined well-wishers after her spectacular publicity appearance at Loew's State Theater in Manhattan. Following greetings from Sammy Cahn and Saul Chaplin, two songwriters, Shaw suddenly appeared before her. He kissed her lightly on the lips, sending "electricity through my body."

"What magic! What a voice for a little girl," he said. "You're going to be a big star. Forget Deanna Durbin. You'll be telling her, 'Eat my dust, bitch.'"

"Oh, Artie, Artie, so glad to see you."

"I'm on my way to the airport, but I shall return, perhaps sooner than you think. It's all your god damn fault. Why don't you grow up faster so that I can deflower you without getting arrested?"

After another kiss on the lips, with a slight flicker of his tongue, he was gone from her life again.

***

116

In Los Angeles, on February 10, 1939, Judy visited Palomar, the largest dance hall in the West. Shaw and his band were performing there. In front of thousands, Artie Shaw collapsed onstage and had to be rushed to Cedars of Lebanon Hospital. For five days, he remained in a coma, his doctors diagnosing it as a malignant leucopenia, a form of leukemia.

It's been suggested that **Artie Shaw** had a knack for (and obsession with) convincing famous and beautiful celebrities to marry him.

The left photo shows him after his 1940 wedding to **Lana Turner**. The right photo depicts him after his 1945 marriage to **Ava Gardner.**

With a temperature of 105 degrees, he drifted close to death.

When he regained consciousness, the first face he saw was Judy's, hovering near his bedside. Her face was gleaming yet filled with distress. "It showed me she really cared if I lived or died," he said. She had visited him every day in the hospital, praying that he would emerge from his coma unscathed.

After Shaw recovered and was released, his first public outing—and the first time he escorted Judy anywhere—was on a Sunday afternoon when they attended a party at the home of Dorothy Lamour, the "Sarong Girl."

There, Judy was introduced to Cary Grant and his lover, actor Randolph Scott. Years later, in the 1950s, she would urge Grant to sign on as her co-star in *A Star Is Born* (1954).

At the party, she also met producer Samuel Goldwyn, who told her, "I should have signed you before that shithead Mayer did."

As Grant was talking to Shaw on the terrace, Grant asked, "Isn't Judy, who is adorable by the way, a bit young for you?"

"It's not what you think," Shaw answered. "It's a harmless relationship like a big brother, little sister. She has this crush on me, but she'll get over it in a few weeks. Hasn't anyone ever developed a crush on you?"

"Sure," Grant answered. "Charles Laughton."

Near sunset, Lamour, accompanied by a pianist, sang "Moonlight and Shadows," which Shaw had recorded with Peg La Centra more than a year before. After she finished, Judy took her place and sang "Over the Rainbow."

World War II icon **Betty Grable**—Judy's competiton for the affections of Artie Shaw

Before the party ended that night, Lamour pointedly suggested to Shaw that he hire Judy as his girl singer. He answered "She's a little girl, but she's a belter like Ethel Merman, which is not what I want for my band. I hire only café singers who don't make so much noise."

That night, after exiting from Lamour's home, Shaw drove Judy to his place. That was the first time he seduced her.

The next day, with Rooney during lunch in the MGM commissary, she confessed what had happened. "My schoolgirl crush had turned into a violent crush—it's that serious. I am madly, desperately in love. I may even give up my career for him."

When Ethel learned that her seventeen-year-old daughter was dating a much older musician, a profession she loathed, she demanded that she break it off.

Judy had no intention of doing that, and begged Jackie Cooper to pretend to be dating her. He would pick her up, drop her off at Shaw's home, and then spend hours with his own current girlfriend, Bonita Granville.

Then, at the end of the evening, Cooper would drive by Shaw's house, retrieve Judy, and deliver her back. He did this for several weeks until he told Judy, "I'm tired of being your beard."

After that, Judy pretended to be spending the night with Jimmie, her sister, or with some other girlfriend.

After he was fully recovered, Shaw was booked into the Los Angeles Coliseum, where his band entertained 26,000 fans. Judy occupied a place of honor in the front row.

After that, Shaw starred in his first film, *Dancing Co-Ed*. One afternoon, in walked his co-star, eighteen-year-old Lana Turner.

He delayed calling Judy for three days, but on the fourth day, he did, complaining that he'd had serious business to tend to. "How about slipping out to see me tonight?"

"I'm your girl."

The next day, again in a conversation with Rooney, she declared, "I'm going to marry Artie Shaw, even though he hasn't asked me yet. So good-looking, so hard to catch. All the babes are after him."

"Including Betty Grable?" he asked.

"She's bigtime competition for me," she answered.

"You're younger than her and more talented," he assured her. "Of course, she does have those legs."

At the time, Grable was involved in a merry-go-round of show-biz intrigue. Simultaneous with her divorce proceedings from Jackie Coogan, she had launched an affair with Artie Shaw and was also having occasional trysts with the Cuban bandleader, Desi Arnaz, too, before he got involved with Lucille Ball.

Until now, Grable had for the most part starred in B pictures, often portraying a college student. Stardom, however, was around the corner. Soon, she'd replace Alice Faye in *Down Argentine Way* (1940), her first major Hollywood role.

Grable's marriage to Jackie Coogan had ended dramatically and horribly. He came home drunk one night, finding her asleep in their bed. She woke up screaming after he gave her what he called "a piss cocktail" and urinated in her face. The next day, she told Shaw what had happened and announced, "I'm filing for divorce."

In reference to Shaw's love affair with Judy, Frank Sinatra told him, "You're moving from a girl like Judy Garland to an experienced dame like Grable."

Shaw said, "What I dig about Judy is her innocence. She worships me...inflates my ego. I imagine that she's my daughter. That's a big turn-on for me."

"Whatever turns you on..." Sinatra said. "A lot of men fantasize about seducing a young gal."

[He was years away from marrying Mia Farrow.]

Judy was far more serious about Shaw than he was about her. She told Rooney, "He's been married twice before—in fact, one of those marriages was annulled. I know I'm the right gal for him. I'll make it last. We'll grow old together."

"Dorothy has her fantasies," the worldly wise Rooney chided her.

Shaw had appearances scheduled on the East Coast for his band. She spent a final night in his arms before he flew off to New York.

In November of 1939, Judy read in *Variety* that Shaw had rigorously rounded up the members of his band at the Hotel Pennsylvania in Manhattan, but then instructed them to find other gigs. With the understanding that he was walking away from a fortune in future bookings, he told them that he planned "to disappear. I don't know when, or if, I'm coming back. But I've had it."

And then he was gone from the music scene.

Judy didn't know where to phone him or even if she'd ever see him again. However, three days later, he phoned. "ARTIE!" she almost shouted into the phone. "Where in hell are you? I've been going out of my mind."

He told her he was hiding out in this seedy little roadside motel on the outskirts of Little Rock, Arkansas. "Last night, racing through Virginia in a blinding snowstorm, I veered off the road into a big ditch and almost killed myself," he said.

He also informed her that he could not return to Hollywood because his home had been staked out by reporters and photographers. He revealed that he was on his way to Acapulco and that he'd return to Hollywood "when the heat was off."

"I want you, girl," he told her. "I need you, and I've got to have you. I know I'm an older man, and you're a very young girl. But the Goddess of Love doesn't always make people in the same age bracket fall in love."

As she revealed to Rooney, "Those were the words I'd been waiting to hear. I promised him I'd wait for him, counting the days."

Unknown to Judy, Shaw, in time, returned to Hollywood but didn't call her. She didn't even know he'd returned from Mexico until weeks later.

Judy would always remember that morning back in 1940 when Ethel, with a certain glee, rushed into her bedroom to awaken her with an over-sized headline: ARTIE SHAW ELOPES WITH LANA TURNER.

She screamed before bursting into tears. "But Artie's in love with ME!

The son of a bitch! He told me he loved me—and only me!"

Two days later, an enraged Ethel managed to get Shaw on the phone, where he denied he'd ever had sex with her (underaged) daughter.

Judy stayed in her room for the next three days, surviving on her always-reliable pills, which she consumed to help her recover from heartbreak. She later said, "Every girl I've talked to has gone through what I'm going through right now. That is, experiencing their first major heartbreak. Finding Mr. Right is so hard to do."

Through the Hollywood grapevine, Judy soon learned that she was not alone in her heartbreak: All the promises made to Betty Grable were just empty words, too, and her dilemma was even more difficult than Judy's. Before abandoning her, Shaw had impregnated her. On her own, Grable opted for an abortion. She recovered from it and from her broken affair rather quickly and was soon dating Tyrone Power and Victor Mature, two of the most sought-after men in Hollywood.

Grable was also slipping around and having a torrid affair with Desi Arnaz, the Cuban bandleader during his pre-Lucille Ball days. She also resumed her affair with an old flame, George Raft.

Much later at MGM, Shaw made three points clear, as he understood them, to Arthur Freed:

- *"I was never in love with Judy. I knew from the beginning that I was not the man to skip along with her down the Yellow Brick Road."*
- *"Grable's a whore, giving blow jobs to drivers at truck stops."*
- *"Lana struck me as more refined, more of a lady, but after we broke up, she told me that in 1942 alone, she went out with 150 servicemen she met at the Hollywood canteen."*

In 1943, Grable morphed into the number one box office star in America, and the reigning pin-up queen of World War II. That was the prelude to Grable marrying bandleader Harry James in 1943.

[Artie Shaw would live to the ripe age of ninety-four, dying on December 30, 2004 at Thousand Oaks, California. He had expressed a burning desire to see the New Year come in.

Shortly before he died, he told close friend Jan Curran, "I was married eight times, even to that sultry brunette, Ava Gardner, before Frankie got her. I even married the author of that bodice ripper, Forever Amber *(Kathleen Winsor). I had a longer run with Evelyn Keyes, Scarlett O'Hara's younger sister. All were mistakes. What I should have done is marry Judy Garland."]*

***

One of the major influences in Judy's career, Arthur Freed, had gone to see the Broadway production of *Babes in Arms* in 1937. It featured lyrics by Lorenz Hart and book by Richard Rodgers.

He thought it would be ideal for an MGM musical that once again teamed Judy Garland with Mickey Rooney. He pitched the idea to Louis B. Mayer, who designated him as its producer, setting a budget of $600,000.

After directing (and choreographing) all those lavish musicals for Warners, Busby Berkeley was assigned to direct it and, along with Freed, to select a supporting cast.

Freed had steadily built up a good reputation, and he would soon be known for "bringing Broadway to Hollywood" in the shape of Roger Edens (Judy's vocal coach), with Vincente Minnelli, Adolph Green, and (among others) Betty Comden. Freed would eventually play a big role in the careers of not only Judy, but Frank Sinatra, Gene Kelly, Lena Horne, Ann Miller, and Kathryn Grayson, too.

After a talented cast was selected for this late 1930s *schmaltz* fest, *Babes in Arms* became the best of that genre of *"Kids, let's put on a show!"* musicals that flourished in the early 1940s.

Its theme is about the death of vaudeville, focusing on two old showbiz pros, Joe Moran (Charles Winninger) and his wife, Florrie (Grace Haynes). They're desperately trying to make a comeback with reprises of tried-and-true acts on the road, leaving their son Mickey Moran (Rooney) at home. Feeling rejected, he enlists Patsy Barton (Judy) to sing in his peppy new show. It includes Judy with her rendition of, among other numbers, "Good Morning."

The BIG SHOW COMES TO BROADWAY

Mickey **ROONEY** *Judy* **GARLAND**
BABES in ARMS

CAPITOL'S BIG SHOW *Starts* **TODAY**

Babes in Arms made millions at the box office and was one of the most lauded films of **1939**, a year hailed as the greatest in the history of motion pictures.

It saw the release of both *Gone With the Wind* and *The Wizard of Oz.*

[Years later, that song was reprised and made even more famous in the hit film, Singin' in the Rain *(1952) with Gene Kelly, Debbie Reynolds, and Donald O'Connor.]*

Its opening scene was later defined as "juvenile anarchy." The action begins as Don Brice (Douglas McPhail) sings "Babes in Arms," leading a parade of young people carrying what look like revolutionary slogans and torches to light a bonfire in the town square.

The town busybody, Martha Steele (Margaret Hamilton), and her nephew—Jeff Steele (Rand Brooks), who's home from a military school—file a complaint demanding that these unruly kids get exiled like juvenile delinquents to a work farm. Judge Black (Guy Kibbee) is more sympathetic, and the kids are allowed to put on their show.

At a soda fountain, Mickey and Patsy meet a has-been child star, Baby Rosalie Essex (June Preisser), who is older now and trying to make a comeback. *[Preisser's performance was an obvious send-up of an "aging" Shirley Temple who at that point in her career was desperately trying to do the same thing. Reportedly, at the time, Temple was "insanely jealous" of Judy. Temple's reign as a box office princess would soon fade into cinematic history.]*

Another memorable number focuses a spotlight on Judy, who, as Patsy, sings, "I Cried for You."

[In the same film, long before it became politically unacceptable, she also sang, "Daddy Was a Minstrel Man," with Mickey Rooney, both of them in blackface. Rooney also led his gang in a rendition of "God's Country." It included the quirky line, "We've got no Duce, we've got no Führer, we've got Garbo and Norma Shearer. Rooney and Judy also included a song that satirized FDR and Eleanor Roosevelt. After the President's death in 1945, the sequence was cut, only to be restored before its re-release in the 1990s.]

WHEN FDR'S "NEW DEAL" WAS STILL NEW

In which of their films did Rooney and Garland perform a musical number that (gently) satirized then-President Franklin Roosevelt and his First Lady, Eleanor?

ANSWER: **Babes in Arms.** Their imitation of the then-President and his controversial First Lady was instantly recognizable to movie audiences across the country.

Surprisingly, although *Babes in Arms* had been a hit Broadway musical, only two numbers were retained from its original stage version. They included "Where Or When," sung by Judy, and "The Lady Is a Tramp," whose melody was relegated to background music. *[That song later become one of Frank Sinatra's biggest hits.]*

Judy and Rooney also sang "I Wish I Were in Love Again," and "I'm Just Wild About Harry." For their efforts, Roger Edens and George Stoll were nominated for an Oscar for the year's Best Musical Score.

In the 1930s, Berkeley had become famous for his kaleidoscopic musical numbers featuring showgirls in extravagant costumes. His choreographies were more modest in *Babes in Arms*.

He was also drinking heavily, having recently survived three grueling courtroom trials. In September of 1935, he had been driving, drunk, along the Roosevelt Highway outside Los Angeles. Without signaling, he suddenly changed lanes and immediately ran headlong into one vehicle and sideswiped another, killing two passengers and seriously injuring five others, including himself. He was tried twice for second-degree murder, having arrived at the first trial on a stretcher. Both cases ended in hung juries. A third trial declared him not guilty. He was acquitted and set free.

Two views of the lead actors in *Babes in Arms*.

"My romance with Judy," Rooney claimed, "was played out only on the screen."

Having bonded so well with Margaret Hamilton on the set of *The Wizard of Oz*, Judy was happy to renew her friendship with the "Wicked Witch." Cast as a priggish and mean-spirited society do-gooder out to punish the kids, Hamilton's newest role was also unattractive.

June Preisser had broken into films through her skill as an acrobat. She and her sister, Cherry, had toured America and Europe with their acrobatic feats, even entertaining George VI in London. Preisser made her film debut in *Dancing Co-Ed (1937)*, starring Artie Shaw and Lana Turner. She later appeared again with Rooney in more Andy Hardy movies.

If the love triangle laid out in the plot of *Babes in Arms* were distilled into a single photo, this would be it.

Despite the fact that **June Preisser** (left) plays a spoiled, scheming, rich-kid blonde with flashy seductive powers, **Judy** (right) wins **Mickey Rooney** (center) in the end.

Guy Kibbee as the kind-hearted judge had launched his career with vaudeville performances aboard Mississippi riverboats. He'd dreamed of being a leading man, but he eventually settled for character roles instead, often in memorable movies such as *Captain Blood* (1935) and *Mr. Smith Goes to Washington* (1939).

A vaudeville actor, Winniger was best known for his performance as the captain in the musical stage version of *Show Boat*. He later repeated that role in its 1936 film version. The same year that he worked with Judy, he also made *Destry Rides Again* (1939) with Marlene Dietrich and James Stewart. He would later play Judy's father in the upcoming *Ziegfeld Girl* (1941).

Both Judy and Rooney complained that "Busby nearly killed us, working us around the clock with his alcoholic perfectionism."

"Metro had Mickey and me working day and night," Judy said. "They gave us pep pills to keep us on our feet long after we were exhausted. Then, they'd take us to the studio hospital and knock us out cold with sleeping pills. Mickey was sprawled on one bed and me on another. Then, after four hours, they'd wake us up and give us pep pills so we could work another seventy-two hours straight."

The premiere of *Babes in Arms* unfolded at Grauman's Chinese Theatre on Hollywood Boulevard on October 10, 1939. For the occasion, Judy told MGM that, "I want to look as glamourous as Joan Crawford, so I want Adrian to design my gown."

There was some resistance to that at first, but she finally got her wish.

She later lamented, "Anywhere else in the world, once you have graduated from high school, have celebrated your nineteenth birthday, and drive a car, you automatically step out of the Junior Miss class. But in Hollywood, people won't forget how you look when you were that age. I can't spend the rest of my life looking like Dorothy."

Escorted by Rooney, they arrived at Grauman's to the sound of loud applause. Later, several reporters asked, "Whatever happened to

Dorothy?"

She pressed her feet and hands in a slab of wet cement on the Hollywood Walk of Fame, becoming the 74th star to do so.

That was a signal that she had finally "arrived." Both *The Wizard of Oz* and *Babes in Arms* would find a place among the Top Ten Box Office Draws of the Year. She and Bette Davis, then at the peak of her career, would be the only women on that coveted list.

The next morning, the *Hollywood Reporter* asserted, "Judy Garland does Judy Garland, which is enough for any ticket buyer."

Nearly all the reviews that night centered on the bravura performance of Rooney. Although she was his friend, Judy resented the lavish praise heaped on him, often to her detriment. One critic said, "a laurel should be placed on Rooney's head. He ran away with the picture, and Judy Garland was nice with her singing."

"I would not exactly call it a rave for me," she said, after reading that.

Another reviewer noted Judy's dilemma at having to get noticed alongside "an old hand like Mickey Rooney pulling every mugging trick in show biz out of the bag."

Although rumors of a romance between the two young stars appeared in many newspapers, Judy denied them. "Mickey and I are just good friends, but we don't see each other after work." Privately, she told Freed, "Mickey is far too short for me."

Some critics were hostile to Rooney, one reporter comparing his performance to "an overstimulated robot bouncing about hysterically."

With zip, dash, and exuberance, *Babes in Arms* became one of the big hits in Hollywood's most competitive year. Rooney was nominated for a Best Actor Oscar, but he, along with Clark Gable playing Rhett Butler, lost to the English actor, Robert Donat, for *Goodbye, Mr. Chips,* in which he co-starred with Greer Garson.

***

Now in her late teens, Judy was seeking more and more independence from both her mother and from MGM. She was also becoming more and more addicted to drugs as a means of keeping her going.

The *Hollywood Reporter* claimed, "Mickey Rooney's exploits probably will have to be shaved to a more conventional mode of life, since the studio is putting him under its thumb, but good. They're also keeping a watch on Judy Garland, now that she's having dates and driving her own bus." *["Bus," in this case, was a reference to her own car.]*

Between 1938 and 1940, she dated increasing numbers of men. Some of her liaisons led to extended affairs, others were as simple as one-night stands. She was photographed with Walter Doniger, a screenwriter for MGM, and also with Barron Polan, an assistant producer to Mervyn LeRoy whom she'd met during the filming of *The Wizard of Oz*. She also became fleetingly involved with Clark Liddell, a sophomore at the University of Southern California.

After the huge acclaim of *The Wizard of Oz* and the big financial success

124

of *Babes in Arms,* Judy rose to the ranks of one of MGM's top money makers like Mickey Rooney. Louis B. Mayer ordained that Eddie Mannix and Howard Strickling, both from MGM's publicity department, needed to assign a "spy" to report on what Judy did every day after she left MGM.

Relatively unknown outside Hollywood, Strickling and Mannix were called "The Fixers," meaning their job was to cover up or tone down any scandal, present or past, in which MGM stars were entrapped. Their main concerns were bisexuality, homosexuality, unwanted pregnancies, or abortions, many of them performed even if a particular star were married. Some actors, as could be expected, caused them more trouble than others. A particularly vexing star was Mickey Rooney, who once accused Strickling of "kissing Mayer's ass."

Other trouble came from Joan Crawford, Clark Gable, Wallace Beery, Jeanette MacDonald, Nelson Eddy, and, most definitely, Spencer Tracy. Van Johnson and June Allyson would bring future problems.

Born in 1896 in the coal-mining region of West Virginia, Howard Strickling eventually drifted to Hollywood, where he became head of publicity for MGM during its golden heyday in the late 1920s until the 1960s, when MGM was the most powerful movie studio in the world. He also became the chief publicist for such films as *Gone With the Wind* and *The Wizard of Oz.*

Strickling's phone was often ringing "with another brush fire for me to put out" (his words). "Those calls that came in at three in the morning were the worst to deal with."

It might be Marlene Dietrich (not an MGM star), telling him that she had come home to discover the nude (and dead) body of John Gilbert.

Perhaps it was Jean Harlow informing him that William Powell had made her pregnant, or Loretta Young calling to make the same charge against Clark Gable, who had seduced her on location during the filming of *Call of the Wild* (1935). Since she was a devout Catholic, abortion was out of the question. Instead, she carried her child to term, and—at some later, "safer" date—officially adopted her baby daughter.

One of Strickling's biggest secrets involved Joan Crawford's long-ago status as a prostitute and porn star in the 1920s. Another potentially career-killing secret involved the screen diva and singing star Jeanette MacDonald, who also spent a period of her early (she hoped forgotten) life as a prostitute.

Maybe it was Spencer Tracy on the phone, charged with raping a

Eddie Mannix (left), **Clark Gable** (center), and **Howard Strickling** in the aftermath of Carole Lombard's tragic death in an airplane crash in 1942.

If something looked suspicious or potentially embarassing to MGM's profits, these were the "fixers" who handled it.

sixteen-year-old girl. In that case, the mother dropped charges when Strickling made a cash settlement. *[To Strickling's horror, Tracy continued his three-year-old affair with teenaged Judy.]*

Strickling also handled murders, covering up the suspicious death of Paul Bern, married to Jean Harlow at the time. Strickling also tidied up the murder of Ted Healy (creator of *The Three Stooges*), who had been killed by Wallace Beery. Gable himself had killed a pedestrian in a hit-and-run incident when he was drunk at the wheel.

Rougher around the edges than Strickling, Eddie Mannix, born in 1891 in Fort Lee, New Jersey, was a very different type of man, From lowly beginnings as a bouncer at the Palisades Amusement Park, he rose from the ranks to become the general manager and vice president of MGM.

A former thug with mob connections in his native New Jersey, Mannix was placed in charge of abortions. He arranged them, among many other stars, for Judy, for Lana Turner, and for Jeanette MacDonald.

Whereas Mannix became Mayer's strong arm, handling many of the studio's "dirty assignments," Strickling, five years younger, was more of a "smoothie." It was Mannix in particular who was charged with concealing the bisexuality of Greta Garbo and, later on, Van Johnson's homosexuality.

Mannix would eventually discover that Judy, in addition to the medications that MGM doctors were prescribing, had access to a stash of illegal drugs from a female pusher linked to gangster Lucky Luciano. Mannix hired another mob member to threaten her, telling her he'd torture and toss her to her death from a clifftop. *[Even thought that scared her away, Judy found others to do her bidding.]*

Despite the fact that he was married to a former Ziegfeld Follies showgirl, Toni Lanier, Mannix sustained many affairs during the course of his career as a Hollywood "fixer." In the early 1950s, with Mannix's blessing, his wife launched an affair with George Reeves, the original TV Superman.

Something went very wrong, however. Mannix, so it was rumored, eventually had Reeves murdered. The resulting scandal became the plot of *Hollywoodland* (2006), co-starring Ben Affleck as Reeves and Diane Lane as Mrs. Mannix.

To spy on Judy, Mannix and Strickling enrolled Betty Asher, another employee of MGM's publicity department. In almost no time at all, Asher became Judy's constant companion, her *confidante* in all matters personal, her secretary, her private "fixer," her wardrobe mistress, her best friend… and, oh yes, her lover, too.

Asher was twenty-two at the time, Judy only eighteen. Instead of trying to cure Judy of her addiction, she encouraged her constant pill popping.

Adding to the Byzantine nature of all this, and unknown to Judy at the time, Asher was also one of Mannix's mistresses. She was also sustaining an affair with composer David Rose, whom Judy would marry in 1940.

To complicate matters even further, Asher began an affair with Artie Shaw right after he walked out on Judy. As the bandleader claimed, "She arrived on my doorstep on Friday afternoon and didn't leave my bedroom until Monday morning."

With her winning personality and a certain charm, Asher was instructed (and configured) as a buffer between Judy and the rest of the world.

From Day One, sometimes referred to in code as "Judy's shadow," she relayed to Mannix what Judy was doing and with whom. He would then incorporate her findings into his reports for Mayer.

Even Ethel used Mayer's power over Judy to threaten her if she misbehaved. "I'll tell Mayer on you, and he'll cancel your contract." Those became familiar threats.

Since Asher was well-connected in Hollywood, she was invited to a lot of A-list parties, often taking Judy with her. She was the daughter of Ephraim Asher, a producer for Carl Laemmle. Her brother was the producer/director William Asher, who in the 1950s helped launch the hit TV series *I Love Lucy.*

As Judy's maid of honor, **Betty Asher** appears as partly visible on the far right of this wedding photo from the Garland/Minnelli marriage.

Third from left in the photo is MGM's dogmatic and controlling chief, **Louis B. Mayer,** a frequently traumatizing factor in her young life.

Her brother, William, later admitted, "Betty was bisexual, and she fell hopelessly in love with Judy even though spying on her." He also vouched for his sister's affairs with David Rose and Artie Shaw.

One cannot be certain, but it appears that it was Asher who introduced Judy to the art of lesbian love. Years after Judy's death, Mickey Rooney admitted, "Judy was not a bona fide lesbian. Actually, she preferred men. But if no man were available, she would sleep with a woman. The people at MGM, including Mayer himself, knew this about Dear Judy. But Mayer ordered Strickling and Mannix to 'keep it quiet.'"

In his book, *The Fixers,* E. J. Fleming wrote about Mannix and Strickling, and of many of their cover-ups for MGM stars.

"Judy Garland and Betty Asher were photographed all over Los Angeles, shopping, dining, and walking hand in hand. The couple was obvious to MGM workers, and questions were raised about Judy's actual sexual preferences. Asher and Garland were on-again, off-again lovers for years."

Over the years, several close friends of Judy claimed that she may not have been a lesbian, but that she preferred oral sex, finding women in her experience better at the performance of that act than men.

Of course, sexual experimentation had been a feature of the movie colony since films began in the West. It burst into full flower in the 1920s, and was suppressed somewhat in the 1930s, only to come back on a massive scale during the turbulent war years of the 1940s among the men and women who won the war. Hundreds of books detailed this change in the way Americans had sex during those years, when a soldier on battlefields didn't know if he would be alive the following day.

In the summer of 1939, as she was finishing *The Wizard of Oz,* Judy met and fell in love with a most unlikely man, piano-playing Oscar Levant, who was sixteen years older than her. He was both a concert pianist, composer, and music conductor. His signature song was "Blame It on My Youth" (1934).

She admitted, "I wasn't drawn to his beauty. His sad eyes and droopy face were compared to that of an aging basset hound. It was his quick wit and offbeat charm that drew me to him. He delivered the best one-liners in show biz. He said things like, 'I think a lot of Leonard Bernstein, but not as much as he does.' My favorite of his lines came in the 1950s when he heard that Marilyn Monroe had become of member of the Jewish faith. Oscar said, 'Now that she's kosher, Arthur Miller can eat her.'"

Between 1929 and 1948, he composed music for nearly two dozen movies, some songs from which made the Hit Parade.

"I was immediately attracted to Oscar and threw myself at him, but he kept postponing having sex with me. After all, we had something in common, as both of us were addicted to prescription drugs. Borrowing a line from Mae West, I told him he could 'come up and see me sometime,' but I added something: 'I hope that sometime is tonight.' He didn't show up."

"I wrote him love poems, I called late at night and asked him if I could come over. He turned me down, later telling Arthur Freed that 'Judy is throbbingly emotional.'"

"He did send me letters. He's so intelligent, so brilliant. In the days when I was struggling and feeling blue, he wrote once or twice a week. Each letter made a lot of common sense, and they would inspire me to carry on. I vowed always to keep his letters and read them in one of my darkest moments. I have them in my desk drawer, all tied with a red ribbon."

The reason that Levant did not rush to bed Judy was that he was falling in love with June Gale, one of the singing Gale Sisters. He would marry her in 1939, which led to their having three children. Their union lasted until he died in 1972 at the age of sixty-five of a heart attack. He had always been a heavy smoker.

"My whole life story is that of the man that got away," Judy recalled. "In fact, in one of my most popular songs, I sang about it. But whereas men aren't trustworthy, my little fellas never desert me. They are my pills to which I have given nicknames: 'Yellow Jackets,' 'Redbirds,' and 'Bluejays.'"

If Judy and Levant had gotten married, they would have had at least something in common. One night in the 1950s, news came

Oscar Levant as a bohemian pianist in *An American in Paris* (1951).

"Could you believe it?" Judy asked. "I actually fell for this cynical, sarcastic bastard. A lot of good it did me."

over the radio of a new suicide attempt by Judy.

Levant turned to his poker-playing buddies. "Judy is two up on me on suicide attempts, but I'm three up on her in nervous breakdowns...or is it the other way around?"

Levant was looking forward to working with Judy on a musical, *The Barkleys of Broadway*, released in 1949 with Fred Astaire.

According to Levant, "Judy had appeared for wardrobe tests, and even taken home a gown she was to wear in an opening scene," Levant said. "But on the day of the shoot, she was absent. No one could get her on the phone. In desperation, Arthur Freed and Louis B. Mayer went to her house and found her there sulking in her bedroom. She absolutely refused to do the movie. Finally, giving up, Freed cast Ginger Rogers instead, reuniting the RKO dancing duo of the 1930s."

[During the week that followed, despite the fact that she'd been fired, Judy showed up on the set in that gown that had been designed for her first appearance in the movie. Levant approached her, and she hugged and kissed him, assuring him, "We're going to make a great movie together. I'm ready now to face the camera."

Having witnessed that disconnect from reality, Rogers, horrified and detesting confrontations, fled to her dressing room.

Freed was finally called to the set, and he had to lead a loudly protesting Judy out of the studio. Chuck Walters, the film's director, appeared and was notified of the incident. "I've suspected it for months: Judy Garland is out of her fucking mind."

Levant was still around years later to watch Judy on her weekly television show. He later gave his opinion. "Her voice became wobbly, and she had depleted herself by taking off too much weight too quickly. But she's a vocal sorceress whose range—at its best—has a deep, interior vibrancy. Strangely enough, her medium and soft palates are not interesting. She has no great variety of expression. She's more Sarah Bernhardt than Eleonora Duse. Judy has become the singing version of the novelist, F. Scott Fitzgerald."]

All of Judy's fears and neuroses bubbled to the surface after she was cast as Fred Astaire's dance partner in MGM's **The Barkleys of Broadway** (1949).

After days of terrified defiance, she was fired, and her role was transferred to Fred Astaire's tried-and-true dance partner, Ginger Rogers.

It was the tenth, and last, musical Rogers ever made with Astaire,. It was the only one they made together at MGM (the others had all been at RKO), and the only one they ever made together in color.

***

During the time Judy was chasing after Levant, a stalker appeared in her life, as one has with so many female stars.

Robert Wilson, a nineteen-year-old who lived in Buffalo, New York, had fallen in love with the screen image of Dorothy. He had seen *The Wizard of Oz* twenty times, sometimes at the rate of three screenings a day, in a local movie house. He had some money, and with it, he set out for California with a plan to kidnap her and take her to a remote cabin on Lake Tahoe, a site that his father rented every year.

The March 9, 1940, issue of the *Los Angeles Examiner* broke the story— JUDY GARLAND KIDNAP PLOT LAID TO LOVE. Regretting what he was about to do, Wilson had turned himself over to the police at Culver City.

When interviewed by a reporter from the *Examiner,* Wilson confessed "Every time she wiggles that little pug nose of hers, I fall more in love with Dorothy. She is my dream girl." He also confessed what he had planned to do to Judy after he locked her away in that lakeside hideaway, but the writer could not print that in a family newspaper.

***

Somehow, Judy quickly got over her crush on Levant. It had taken a lake of tears to recover from Artie Shaw, but she had moved on from Levant after a day or so. The two of them would remain friends for years to come.

A handsome, dashing star had entered her life, the actor, Robert Stack. She told him, "I've just gone through a platonic affair with Oscar Levant. I hope that's not what you're contemplating.

"That's the last thing I have on my mind," he assured her.

PANAMA CITY PILOT
FOIL PLOT TO KIDNAP JUDY GARLAND
WHO WOULD WANT TO KIDNAP JUDY GARLAND? The possibility outraged and terrified her fans. Although it ended with a whimper, not a bang, the story was run around the country, including within the March 9, 1940 edition of this newspaper in northern Florida.

DOROTHY JOINS THE SHOW-BIZ RAT RACE

AS A PILL-POPPING *INGÉNUE,* SHE GRINDS OUT FILMS, SONGS, AND DANCE ROUTINES

LIFE BEGINS FOR ANDY HARDY WHEN HE MEETS A DEBUTANTE & STRIKES UP A BAND. MICKEY ROONEY'S BABE ON BROADWAY MORPHS INTO A ZIEGFELD GIRL NAMED JUDY GARLAND

PHOTOGENIC FRENEMIES: LANA TURNER, HEDY LAMARR, AND BONITA GRANVILLE.

DATE MATES: ROBERT STACK, FORREST TUCKER, & YOUNG JFK

POOL PARTIES WITH JUDY'S FUTURE FIRST HUSBAND, DAVID ROSE

"Judy got around and tried to make men fall in love with her, and she was quite successful at it."
— Director Charles ("Chuck") Walters

One lazy Sunday afternoon,

Robert Stack had a late luncheon beside his pool with Rock Hudson and Lauren Bacall at the time they were filming *Written on the Wind* (1956).

For some reason, the talk turned to Judy Garland, as Stack seemed in a nostalgic mood. He spoke of how he'd met and dated her before he joined the U.S. Navy as an aerial gunnery officer and instructor.

He was both an actor and a sportsman, known as an avid polo player and shooter. At the age of sixteen, he'd become a member of the All-American Skeet Team, and later set the world records in skeet shooting, becoming a National Champion.

At the age of twenty, he visited the Universal lot, where he met Joe Pasternak, who was immediately struck by his good looks and deep, commanding voice. "How would you like to be in pictures?" the producer asked.

"I could go for it if I'm allowed to make love to the leading lady?" Stack said.

The next day, he was given a screen test opposite starlet Helen Parrish, a friend of Judy's, and Pasternak was impressed at how he came across on the screen. The next day, he cast him in *First Love* (1939), in which he made movie history by giving Deanna Durbin her first screen kiss.

When the movie opened, Judy and Ann Rutherford went to see it. After they left the theater, Judy raved about Stack's "male beauty. I wish I'd been up there on the screen instead of Durbin getting kissed by that hunka man. He'll be in my dreams tonight, and he'll do more than dream."

Coincidentally, Iva Koverman, Louis B. Mayer's private secretary, came up with the idea that Stack and Judy, each now within the MGM stable, would make an ideal couple. She arranged for Judy to meet him on the set where he was filming *The Mortal Storm* (1940), co-starring James

While they were dating, **Robert Stack** and **Judy** were spotted roller skating and dancing at various venues in Los Angeles.

Later, Stack introduced her to his well-referenced new friend from Massachusetts.

That friend later became a Navy Lieutenant, and later, President of the United States.

Stewart and Margaret Sullavan. Stack played a young man who joins the Nazi party.

Judy was immediately attracted to him, three years her senior. She found him "charming and personable—and oh those looks, oh that voice." He invited her for dining and dancing with him at the Trocadero that night.

To Judy's disappointment, he called her in the early evening with news that the date had to be canceled because he'd been ordered to work late at the studio. "If you'll forgive me, how about tomorrow night?"

Even though dressed and ready to go out that night, she concealed her disappointment and was ready and waiting for him the following night, too.

When he picked her up, Judy was delighted to learn that he was taking her to an exclusive party at Pickfair, the then-famous and very opulent residence of Mary Pickford and her husband, Buddy Rogers, a musician.

The event was definitely A-List, as Judy circled the room, meeting and greeting

Pool parties associated with Judy Garland often turned into photo ops for MGM.

Depicted above are the guests culled from MGM's "baby crop" at a party hosted by its studio chief, **Louis B. Mayer** who appears as a "referee" at the right side of this photo.

Other than **Judy** (third from left), the other two top box offices draws included **Deanna Durbin** (far left) and **Mickey Rooney** (fourth from left).

"the cream of Hollywood." The guests included her "Dear Mr. Gable," to whom she'd sung her hit song. Also present were James Stewart, Norma Shearer, Katharine Hepburn, Cary Grant, Myrna Loy, and William Powell. Charlie Chaplin invited her out onto the terrace, where, as she later told Stack, "He made a pass at me."

"He likes little girls, the younger the better," Stack told her.

Back in the main parlor, Judy met an aging Mary Pickford, who was most gracious. "You were such a dear in *The Wizard of Oz*. You pulled off the role to perfection. I admit I'm a bit jealous. In my day, I would have been offered the role of Dorothy, but time has passed me by."

"You would have been terrific," Judy graciously assured her.

Before re-depositing Judy off at her home later that night, Stack gave her a long, lingering kiss, and she invited him to her pool party the following Sunday afternoon. "Bring your bathing trunks," she said.

He showed up at two o'clock and had a reunion with Helen Parrish, the starlet he had appeared with in his screen test. He then met some of Judy's friends: Jackie Cooper, Bonita Granville, Mickey Rooney, and rising starlets Linda Darnell and Betty Jane Graham.

Ethel was away with Will Gilmore that night, and Judy had the house to herself. After all the guests had left, Stack invited her to a hidden-away restaurant in the canyon, and she was back at home by eleven. She asked him in for a sleepover.

It was the first time he seduced her. As he later told Bacall and Hudson,

"I did not take her virginity. Some lucky guy beat me to it. He taught her well. She knew her birds and bees."

"After that night, we had many a rendezvous, but it was not any of that 'going steady' crap," he said. "Whereas she was dating a lot of other men, I had a horny brigade after my ass, too, including Howard Hughes. In fact, I played the field for years to come before settling down."

It wasn't until 1956, the year he made *Written on the Wind,* that Stack finally married Rosemarie Bowe.

As Judy got to know him, she said, "I loosened him up. At first, I found him a bit stuffy and conservative."

Some of their evenings were very modest, including going to Schwabs Drugstore for chocolate malts and listening to records on the jukebox. They went to see the great Katharine Cornell perform onstage in *No Time for Comedy.* Once, they were seen holding hands at the Tail of the Cock restaurant.

On another occasion, Stack—loaded up with jawbreakers and licorice drop—took her to see *Honky Tonk* (1940), starring Clark Gable and Judy's rival, Lana Turner. *[There were rumors of an affair between those stars.]*

Judy told Stack that she yearned to be in an adult role like Lana's, but that Mayer had, to her chagrin, as-signed her to yet another Andy Hardy movie.

One of their dates was different from the others, and it became one of the most memorable of her life. It involved a dinner-date Stack or-ganized for her at the Brown Derby, with the understanding that he'd bring along a new friend he'd recently met—the young John F. Kennedy, who had been living in London. His wealthy and influen-tial father, Joseph, had, until re-cently, been the controversial U.S. Ambassador to the Court of St. James's.

["I was practically ignored for the rest of the evening," Stack admitted years later to Hudson and Bacall. "I was considered the Lothario of Holly-wood, but nothing like Jack. He could just look at a girl, and she'd go to bed with him."]

After dinner, Kennedy and Judy sat together in the car's back seat as Stack drove them to a hide-away he maintained at Whitley Ter-race, between Cahuenga and

Robert Stack (left) formed an immediate friendship with young **John F. Kennedy** when he first arrived in Hollywood.

Stack jokingly said, "Jack was the only man in Tinseltown better looking than me, and all the hot tamales on the West Coast took no-tice. He really needed a date book. I've known him to have sex in the afternoon with a woman, sex at cocktail time, sex after din-ner, and even a sleepover after midnight. Each with a different woman."

"Most of the great male stars of Hollywood, including Clark Gable, have passed through my life," Stack said. "Gable was a man's man, but liked a lot of different women on the side. But he was nothing compared to Jack. I was also introduced to Bobby Kennedy, but he didn't need the number of gals Jack did. One gal a day was enough for Bobby."

Highland in the Hollywood Hills. It was a jumbled series of apartments built against a stone wall, each flat with a balcony overgrown with wisteria.

Off the living room was a tiny bedroom with barely enough space for a double bed. It rested under a low, five-foot ceiling. Fastened to the walls and ceiling were flags from nations around the world, with the notable absence of Japan's Rising Sun and Germany's Nazi Swastika. Later, jokingly, Stack quipped, "I helped Jack with his geopolitical studies, teaching him which flag belonged to which nation."

"Jack took 'house guest privilege' and invited Judy into my 'chamber of seduction.' Some of the most beautiful women in Hollywood, including an Oscar winner, had already been seduced in that low-ceilinged room. They were gone for about half an hour before I took my turn with her.. I hate to have it called sloppy seconds."

"When I came out, Jack was on the phone talking long-distance to his dad…at my expense," Stack claimed.

"Both JFK and I were too drunk to drive, so I phoned a cab to take Judy home and gave her a twenty-dollar bill for the fare. For some odd reason, my rich friend, JFK, never carried any dough with him. He was versatile in his taste of women— blondes, redheads, brunettes, young ones, mature ones, all sizes and shapes."

[Remarkably, that night in Stack's hideaway marked the beginning of her life-long friendship with JFK. In 1960, she actively supported him in his run for the presidency. After he was installed in the Oval Office, if he were in a depressed mood, he sometimes called her and asked her to sing "Over the Rainbow" to him over the phone.

A few years after Kennedy's assassination (November of 1963), Judy said, "Whenever I sing about the man that got away, I'm always thinking of Jack."]

In 1946 Hollywood, the hottest two dates in town were **Robert Stack and Jack Kennedy**, or so claimed Judy Garland, who found both of these handsome young men "adorable and more." Stack served as *[his words]* "Jack's guide to the hottest pussies in Hollywood."

When JFK became president and saw very little of Stack, the actor talked about the time he had spent with Jack during the 1940s. "I think he inherited all this womanizing from his father, Joseph P. Kennedy. He bragged about his father's conquests—not just Gloria Swanson, everybody knew about that—but Constance Bennett, Evelyn Brent, Nancy Carroll, Betty Compson, Viola Dana, Phyllis Haver, even Marion Davies and, surprise of surprises, Greta Garbo."

Stack claimed that "Old Joe's ways rubbed off on his son. Joe sorta denigrated Rose and rubbed her nose in his affairs. I think Jack did that to Jackie, even after he got to the White House. There was a big difference, though, between Joe and Jack. After a few weeks of philandering, Joe always came back with expensive presents for Rose. Jack didn't even bring Jackie flowers."

***

Judy met Dan Dailey on the set of *The Mortal Storm* when she stopped by for lunch with her current flame, Robert Stack.

Later in his career, during a movie-making stint with Twentieth-Century Fox, Dailey became famous for the musicals he made with Betty Grable, especially *Mother Wore Tights* (1947). But before that, when he was linked to MGM, that studio assigned him minor parts in dramas that included *Susan and God* (1940) and later, *The Mortal Storm* (also 1940), in which, like Stack, he played a Nazi.

When Judy was dating **Dan Dailey** and they danced together, Judy said, "On the floor I came up to his crotch."

"That made it convenient for me," Dailey said.

"I can't think of two men less likely to be Nazis," Judy said. "They were as American as apple pie. Two great guys. While waiting for Bob to finish a scene, I started chatting with Dan."

"When he learned that Bob and I were only casually dating, he asked me out, so I gave him my phone number. He called the next day."

She had a vague professional link to him: Whereas he had appeared in the onstage musical version of *Babes in Arms* in 1937, she had been the star of its film adaptation two years later.

Another link was that both of them had been active during the dying days of vaudeville and minstrel shows. According to Dailey, "I did anything for a buck—caddy on the golf course, shoe salesman, a performer on a South American cruise line."

Later, still on the set of *The Mortal Storm,* Judy met with her sister, Suzanne, who had a small uncredited role in it.

News about Judy's simultaneous romances with Stack and Dailey ended up in the gossip columns of both Hedda Hopper and Louella Parsons. "Hedda had me practically walking down the aisle with Dailey, and Louella had me ready to exchange vows with Stack. None of the gossip was true. I had no intention of marrying either one, although if Bob had asked me, I would have said yes."

"When I met Dan, he was coming down from his marriage to Esther Rodier. In 1942 he married Elizabeth Hofert, with whom he had a son."

Although Judy's affair with Dailey continued during their performances together in *Ziegfeld Girl* (1941), he was deeply upset by events that followed his designation as one of the leads in the film musical *For Me and My Gal* (1942).

"Eleanor Powell, who was near the end of her career, was to be my co-star. We'd been in rehearsal for some of the dance scenes. Eleanor and I arrived together on the set one morning. Arthur Freed was waiting there to greet us."

"You're fired!" Freed told them. "I've recast the picture with Judy Garland and Gene Kelly."

"Although It wasn't Judy's fault," Dailey said, "I resented her, MGM, and especially Gene Kelly."

Years after Judy's dating of Dailey, she encountered Betty Grable at a Hollywood party. According to Grable, "I don't know if you ever knew this, but Dan also goes for the guys, especially young dancers. He's also a cross-dresser, always stealing apparel from my wardrobe."

Judy was not around to mourn the tragic suicide of Dailey's son in 1975. Dailey's final screen appearance was *The Private Files of J. Edgar Hoover,* in which he was cast as Clyde Tolson, the gay lover of the F.B.I. director. In 1978, at the relatively young age of 62, he died of anemia after complications that followed hip replacement surgery.

***

Although the 1940s morphed into a decade of upheaval in Judy's life, she would shoot to major-league stardom. She hired a new agent. Frank Orsatti, and he immediately got Mayer to raise her salary to $500 a week. But he didn't stay around long. The powerful theatrical agent, Leland Hayward, paid $25,000 to let him take over Judy's representation.

In January of 1940, as the decade roared in, she began making regular appearances as a radio personality on the *Pepsodent Show Starring Bob Hope*. She became so popular that he invited her back again and again. As their friendship deepened, she uncovered more and more rumors about Hope, particularly his mysterious first marriage and his constant womanizing. According to his frequent co-star, Bing Crosby, "Bob is a fast man with a squaw, but tight fisted with a buck,"

Occasionally, Hope seduced from the top of the A-list. *[Noteworthy conquests included Betty Hutton, Dorothy Lamour, Paulette Goddard, Janis Paige, and Marilyn Maxwell.]* Yet more frequently, he seemed to prefer overnight quickies with anonymous pickups.

Judy had been warned that Hope might come on to her, but he did not, telling Crosby, "Judy is not my type. I prefer a more whorish type of gal."

Whenever they were on the air together, Hope engaged in an easy banter with Judy before she launched into one of her numbers. During one of their public exchanges she lamented, "I'm not old enough to play glamour girls, but I'm too

RADIO DAYS Upper photo: **Judy** as she appeared in 1940, the year she became a staple on (lower photo) *The Pepsodent Show Starring* **Bob Hope.**

old to play with dolls."

On the air, he retorted, "I hope I'm never too old to play with dolls."

Throughout the early part of 1940, MGM never really developed a script for her. In the interim, she recorded some songs for Decca, including "I'm Nobody's Baby," that hit song from 1921, and "Buds Won't Bud."

Because of the Oscar she'd won for her performance in *The Wizard of Oz*, she hoped for star billing in her next picture, *Andy Hardy Meets a Debutante* (1940). She was disappointed, however, when she was billed in seventh position on that film's posters and advertising materials.

Much about this newest film in the Andy Hardy series was familiar to the cast and its legions of fans. What made it different from its predecessors was that most of the action takes place in New York City.

Cecilia Parker was cast as Marion Hardy, Andy's sister, who was always having complications with a boyfriend. Parker had been signed by MGM because her looks evoked Greta Garbo. *[Previously, Parker had portrayed Garbo's sister in The Painted Veil (1954).]* Parker would go on to star in eleven Andy Hardy movies.

Preview audiences filled out cards with their reactions to the latest **Rooney/Garland** vehicle.

"Isn't it about time Andy Hardy fell for Judy?" asked one fan.

In a way that was eerily equivalent (or "inbred"), the director of *Andy Hardy Meets a Debutante*, George B. Seitz, would helm eleven of the Hardy movies, too.

Its plot? In New York, Andy becomes enchanted with a young socialite, Daphne Fowler (Diana Lewis). At the time, the actress was married to the MGM star, William Powell.

Once again, Judy played Betsy Booth, who nurtures her long-enduring crush on Andy. By the final reel, he realizes "There's no place like home," and he turns to Judy, giving her her first on-screen kiss—a modest one—as Andy.

The film did well at the box office and generated good reviews. "That means I'll be teamed with Mickey again in some more fluff," Judy said.

Most of its reviews were kind, *Time* finding Judy "growing prettier every year." Bosley Crowther of *The New York Times*, however, lamented that "All Andy Hardy movies are beginning to look alike."

***

In August of 1940, Judy gave an interview with the magazine, *Movie Mirror*. In it, she admitted to hanging out with a "gang" of young men and women. Although its center of attention was Mickey Rooney, still a reigning box office champion, many others of that "gang" were fairly new to Hollywood, each yearning for a big break.

Judy regularly invited "my bunch" over for weekends. In her home, they found a radio in every room blasting out music at high volumes. "I think music should be very, very loud," she said. In addition to Rooney, arriving every weekend with their bathing suits were Bonita Granville, Helen Parrish, Robert Stack, Jackie Cooper, Linda Darnell, Bob Shaw, Jack Hopkins, and Forrest Tucker.

Ever since she'd seen Tucker in the briefest of swimwear, Judy had wanted to date him, although he was on the verge of marrying Sandra Jolley, "For six glorious weeks, the hunka man was yours truly's," Judy claimed.

Their first of many nights out together was at the Cocoanut Grove, where she paid the tab, since Tucker was low on funds.

Since Ethel was absent most of the time and involved with her new husband, Judy eventually invited Tuck to spend the evening with her, with the understanding that he'd slip out the next morning at dawn, before Ethel arrived to prepare her breakfast and to see her off to MGM.

"During my first night out with Tuck, a reporter discovered us and wrote about it, calling us the male/female version of Mutt and Jeff. He towered over me at six feet, five inches. Other than that blonde Viking god, Sterling Hayden, Tuck was the tallest actor in Hollywood."

Three years older than her, Tucker had been a farm boy from Indiana. He had thick, wavy blonde hair, and although he drank too much, he delighted Judy.

During the era he dated her, he was filming *The Westerner* (1940), starring Gary Cooper. In it, as a powerfully built farmer, Tucker clashed with the hero in a fight scene with Coop.

He told her that he was not suited, like Tyrone Power or Robert Taylor, for any pretty boy roles. Instead, he was on the lookout for roles that might have been played by youthful reincarnations of Victor McLaglen, Wallace Beery, or Ward Bond.

Two views of **Forrest Tucker** (upper photo) in *F-Troop* (1965-67) and (lower photo) with **Rosalind Russell** in *Auntie Mame.* (1958).

"Anyone who went to bed with Tuck could never stop talking about it," Judy said. "He called his thing 'The Chief.' That penis of his should be immortalized in cement on Hollywood's Walk of Fame. I didn't know men came in that size."

James Bacon, the Hollywood columnist, said, "Tuck's big cock was the chief attraction at the Lakeside Golf Course. He would lie down nude, and pass out, drunk, on a massage board. People would come and go, getting a preview of it. When he paraded around jaybird naked, he got a lot of *oooooohs* and *aaaaaaaaahs*."

Bacon added, "He was going with little Judy Garland, but Tallulah Bankhead and Joan Crawford, two others of his conquests, might have handled his equipment more easily than Little Dorothy."

Although Tuck eventually ran off to get married, Judy encountered him again when MGM borrowed him to co-star with Spencer Tracy and Katharine Hepburn in *Keeper of the Flame* (1942).

"To get that role, I had to put out for Spence," he confessed to her.

"Been there, done that," Judy responded.

"And during the making of that film, my director, George Cukor, rendezvoused every afternoon at three o'clock with me and 'The Chief' in my dressing room."

"Since I'm a girl, I never had to worry about ending up on Cukor's casting couch," Judy answered

***

One halcyon afternoon in Hollywood in 1940, about a year before America entered World War II, the battlefields of Europe appeared far, far away. No one seemed to be thinking about the Annexation of Poland, the Fall of France, the Siege of Stalingrad, or the Blitz of London.

MGM producer, Arthur Freed, an uncredited associate producer of *The Wizard of Oz*, drove Vincent Minnelli, a New York stage designer and director, to the studio lot where Freed was producing a musical, *Strike Up the Band*. Directed by Busby Berkeley, its stars were the reigning box-office champ Mickey Rooney, and America's singing sensation, Judy Garland.

Minnelli remembered Mickey as "a pint-sized bundle of energy, boyish and

June Preisser appears ready to not only strike up the band, but to steal Mickey Rooney's heart from her puppy-love rival, Judy, in this ode to American cheer on the eve of World War II.

cocky just like he was in those Andy Hardy movies. He was the most talented actor in Hollywood. The son of vaudevillians, he first appeared on the stage at the age of two—that's what Freed told me."

Judy soon emerged from her dressing room for a rehearsal with Mickey. "Glad to meet you, Mr. Minnelli," she said, paying him very little attention, as she seemed distracted.

He offered glowing praise for her performances a Dorothy in *The Wizard of Oz,* for which she gratefully thanked him. Then she surprised him by saying, "That was then and this is now. Mickey and I have got to make this turkey a hit. Arthur told us he needs your help. We don't know where Busby is…maybe drunk somewhere."

Then she turned and left for the rehearsal hall with Mickey.

Her introduction to Minnelli was otherwise uneventful. Although she would soon forget him, he would never forget her "emotional intensity."

Freed then asked Minnelli to design one of the film's musical sequences. The director's imagination went to work at once, finding inspiration in a bowl of fresh fruit.

From that, he devised a memorable sequence of the film. According to the plot, Mickey, in the role of a band leader, would direct cartoon figures dressed in tuxedos but with heads molded into replicas of fruit, including both strawberries and avocados. Cast members disguised as apples would become fiddlers; oranges would play trumpets and horns; and bananas would play the woodwinds, etc.

MGM's technicians went to work at once, devising the music and choreography, which was then filmed with Mickey directing this *tutti-frutti* band. It eventually morphed into one of the highlights of the film, winning praise from both *Variety* and Louis B. Mayer himself. "This Minnelli fag must be some kind of genius to come up with a novelty like that," Mayer said. "I think we'll find work for him as a musical director."

Minnelli was remembered a week later when tap-dancing Ann Miller visited Judy's dressing room. *[According to Judy at the time, ""Ann knew more about what was going on in Tinseltown than either Hedda or Louella."]*

"I think Minnelli is one of the ugliest men I've ever seen," Judy said. "He has the face of a baby dinosaur, with long, mascara'd lashes, and big but droopy eyes.

Razzmatazz, big band glitz, and young love, all rolled into one feel-good film that strikes up audience expectations for more **Judy and Mickey Rooney** romances.

141

He's rather effeminate, with a slight stammer, and he's shy. And he regularly wears more makeup, including lipstick, than you do."

"The word in New York is that he's a real flamer," Miller said. "You'll be perfectly safe in any picture he directs. More than likely, he'll be chasing after either your leading man or the boys in the chorus."

"I find him a creep," was all Judy said before turning to the gossip of the day.

***

The plot of *Strike Up the Band* is relatively simple. Rooney, cast as Jimmy Connors, is a high school drum player who dreams of becoming part of a bigtime dance band. He and his girl pal, Mary Holden (Judy), get permission from the school principal to put on a show to pay for their musical instruments. The show is a hit.

The famous bandleader, Paul Whiteman, cast as himself, stages a contest for the best high school band in the country. You might figure out who wins.

Other than Rooney, the only star in the cast with whom Judy had worked before, was June Preisser. Cast as a rich blonde transfer student and a narcissistic *prima donna,* she performs some remarkable acrobatic stunts onstage.

George and Ira Gershwin, along with Roger Edens, supplied the lyrics and music. Songs included "Strike Up the Band" and a moving "Our Love Affair," sung by Judy. It brought an Oscar for Edens and Arthur Freed. Judy and Rooney also performed a show-stopping conga.

The New York Times, which more or less dismissed Judy as "nice," heaped lavish praise on Rooney. "Roll out the red carpet and stand by. The boy is here again, the Pied Piper of the Box Office, the eighth or ninth wonder of the world, the kid himself—in short... Mickey Rooney."

Daily Variety asserted that "Rooney now ranks as one of the screen's greatest personalities."

He was sent to New York on a publicity tour. There, he received an invitation from Norma Shearer to visit her in her suite. Now in the twilight of her film career, the widow of Irving Thalberg had ruled as the Queen of MGM in the 1930s.

"She didn't want me to take her out—she had James Stewart for that. She just wanted my body." In a memoir, he graphically wrote: "There I was on her living room couch, my pants by my ankles, and Norma on her knees."

When Mayer learned of their affair, he ordered Rooney to break it off at once.

Rooney emerged, however, with the best dressing room at MGM. When Shearer departed from the studio forever, she turned it over to him.

At the time, Rooney was receiving ten bags of fan mail every week; Judy less than half a bag. He published one of his fan letters:

"Dear Mr. Rooney,
I loved you in Strike Up the Band *with Judy Garland. I've seen all of your pictures. You're absolutely wonderful. I guess I've been in love with you since I saw your first movie. I'll always love you, I guess, and who knows, maybe someday we can meet.*
Yours forever,
Bruce."

***

Even though he was deeply enmeshed in a romance with Bonita Granville (there was even talk of marriage), Jackie Cooper continued an occasional secret rendezvous with Judy. Apparently, Granville never caught on to the fact that Cooper and Judy had quietly resumed their affair.

Years later, Cooper discussed his long-ago "secret" trysts during the 1940s with Judy Garland: "One afternoon at one of Judy's pool parties, Bonita was there, too. But when I went into the kitchen, Judy was alone. She came on to me, asking me to return after I drove Bonita home. It was on that night that Judy and I resumed the affair we'd begun when we were just kids."

Judy promised Cooper that she'd keep their affair a secret from Bonita. "Frankly, I think Judy got off on all this intrigue," he said. "I indulged her but felt guilty about it. We were often in Bonita's company, at a pool party, or whatever, and at those events, Judy virtually ignored me. Sometimes, I'd visit Judy after a date with Bonita."

"I asked myself, what is Judy trying to prove?" The same question could be asked of me. Was I trying to audition for the role of a two-timer? Yet, in spite of some dark feelings, I always kept answering Judy's summons, at least until her marriage to David Rose. Finally, I did put a stop to it."

"Even if she did get married, I didn't think she would remain faithful," Cooper concluded. "That's not who she is. She is a young woman who lives for the moment. I don't think she viewed adultery as a sin—that's Judy for you. But let's face it: I was no better."

One night, she told me, "Temptation is not something to resist, but to give in to."

Mayer had lots of spies, and he learned of Judy's series of affairs. In addition to issuing personal warnings, he called in Louella Parsons. Known for her ability to either break or advance a Hollywood career, she wrote in her column, "Judy Garland's boss, who knows what's best for the lovely girl, has requested that she curtail her night club adven-

Two legs of one of Judy's early love triangles: **Bonita Granville with Jackie Cooper** in *Syncopation* (1942).

143

tures."

According to Judy, "Mayer wants to turn me into the girl next door—innocent, endearing Dorothy. But that is not who I am. I don't want to sit home at night. I want to get out and discover the world. Men are part of the world, wouldn't you agree?"

***

Perhaps it was their joint love of music that drew Judy into the orbit of David Rose, who was twelve years her senior. Handsome but rather shy and reserved, he was also married. [*He was separated from the comedian Martha ("Big Mouth") Raye, whom he had married in 1938. Their divorce had not become final.*]

Born in London in 1910 to Jewish parents, Rose had moved to Chicago when he was only four years old. He studied music, which led in time to his playing the piano on local radio stations. Eventually, he relocated to Hollywood, where he became a composer, songwriter, pianist, and orchestra leader.

Judy met him at the NBC Studios when she was making appearances as a radio singer for the Bob Hope Show. Rose had been a friend of Artie Shaw.

Songbird Margaret Whiting told Rose that Judy was hysterical because of the loss of Shaw and that she was afraid she could not go on.

That afternoon, his mother had dropped off a chocolate cake for the boys in his band. There was still a big slice left, so he decided to take it to Judy's dressing room, perhaps to console her. "He could not have made a better choice," said Whiting. "The way to Judy's heart was any form of chocolate."

As she devoured his mother's chocolate cake, she accepted his invitation to dinner. That night, over plates of food, he talked music to her. In time, he helped her with her Decca recordings, one aspect of her career not controlled by MGM. He soon became one of her mentors and morale-boosters, advising her about vibrato, cadences, and her phrasing.

As their romance deepened, Ethel found out about it. "Not another goddamn musician!" she shouted at Judy. "Both of your sisters married one of those bums. NOW YOU! You'd think Artie Shaw might have taught you a lesson about music men. Besides, technically at least, Rose is still married to that part-time lesbian, Martha Raye."

Ethel wasn't alone in objecting to Judy's involvements with Rose. Mayer hated the idea, too. He gave every appearance of wanting Judy as a permanent and ongoing fixture within the Andy Hardy films, maturing her way through additional sequels until she and Rooney were old enough to step into the parents' roles, following, perhaps with a sense of irony, in the footsteps of the elderly Lewis Stone and Fay Holden.

[*Mayer might have had a secret reason for detesting Rose. Years before, Mayer had lustily pursued Jeanette MacDonald. To his chagrin and enduring wrath, she had dumped him for Rose.*]

Mayer told Judy, "Right now, you're America's sweetheart, and big box office. Do you want to give that up for some damn cast-off *[a reference to Rose]* of a vulgar comedian? *[a reference to Martha Raye.]*"

As a means of maneuvering around Ethel, Judy planned escapes on weekends with her girlfriend Betty O'Kelly. She departed with her for a week's vacation on Lake Arrowhead. What Ethel didn't know at the time was that Rose and pianist Buddy Pepper, Judy's old flame, went along too. Whereas O'Kelly was sleeping with Pepper, Judy shared her room with Rose.

Not all of Judy's friends opposed the romance. Their mutual friend, songwriter Harold Arlen, told Judy, "David can listen to a Sibelius concert while writing an arrangement in E-flat for Irving Berlin. Rose is a good choice for you, gal."

After a few weeks, Rose expressed concerns to his boss, Tony Martin,

MGM publicity photo announcing **Judy's engagement to David Rose.**

"Privately," she told Mickey Rooney, "I need two things to get through life: Pep pills and David Rose."

about Judy's mental and physical state. "She's overly medicated, underfed, and much too overworked, sometimes putting in eighteen hours a day. She has a hearty appetite but lives in fear of getting fat. She'll eat anything chocolate. Malts are her preferred drink, but instead of malts, she consumes cup after cup of black coffee every day and smokes four packages of cigarettes."

Rooney was familiar with Rose's work. "He made a name for himself by playing pop music as if it were a symphony. His best-known work was 'Holiday for Strings.' My mother was the most disappointed when I told her that Rose and Judy might get married."

"I always thought, dear, that one day you and Judy might tie the knot," his mother had said.

Judy told Rooney, "I don't think a girl has to be madly in love with the man she marries. It's more important that he be madly in love with *her.*"

When Rooney heard that Judy was becoming engaged to Rose, he arrived at her home unannounced: "I don't know what I would have done that day if she'd told me that instead of marrying Rose, she really wanted to marry me. When I left, she gave me a long, wet, and very meaningful kiss, and I wished her good luck. God knows what would have happened if she and I had gotten married. We could have made an incandescent couple, no doubt about that. Maybe we could have gone off like Roman candles, lighting up the sky. Instead, in time, I got sultry, stunningly beautiful Ava Gardner, and what a disaster that was for me."

As Judy grew more intense with her romance, she referred to Rose as

"Mr. Sunshine. He can make me laugh. He cheers me up and brings me chocolate desserts. I need him. More than I need someone to fall in love with, I need someone to fall in love with ME."

She celebrated with Rose when she signed a new MGM contract. It stipulated that she'd receive $2,000 a week for three years, $2,500 a week for the two years following, and $3,000 for the final two years—a total of $680,000 for seven years.

One night after midnight, Ethel drove past Rose's home and was surprised to see Judy's car parked in his driveway. Judy had sworn to her mother that she was spending the night with her friend, Patsy O'Kelly.

After she returned home, Ethel phoned Rose, and he picked up the receiver. "If you don't have my daughter delivered here in fifteen minutes, I'm calling the law on you, you fucking child molester."

Within ten minutes, Judy herself pulled into their driveway. The argument that followed was the most violent of their relationship. At one point, Judy picked up a heavy ceramic lamp and threw it in the direction of her mother's face.

Although Lorna Luft, Judy's second daughter, never met Rose she claimed years later, "I've always thought that mother married David to assert her independence and to escape from my grandmother's control. She was sick to death of being treated like 'little Dorothy' by everyone around her. When you're eighteen, it isn't much fun to be treated as if you were twelve, even if everyone does think you're cute."

IRISH EYES ARE SMILING:

Both of these photos illustrate some aspect of Judy's role in Little Nellie Kelly.

Top photo: With **George Murphy** (later a Senator from California).

Lower photo with **Douglas MacPhail** (left) and again, Murphy.

***

As a change of pace, Judy was allowed to distance herself from scene-stealing Mickey Rooney when producer Arthur Freed cast her in Little Nellie Kelly (1940), her first star role. It was based on a 1922 musical comedy by George M. Cohan.

In an unusual bit of casting, she had a dual role as both the wife of Jerry Kelly (George Murphy) and later, as his daughter. She marries him and emigrates to America over the objections of her father, portrayed by Charles Winniger.

Winniger was best known for his performance as Captain Andy Hawks in the original Broadway production of *Show Boat* in 1922. He would soon play Judy's father once again in *Ziegfeld Girl*.

According to Judy, "The part of Nellie Kelly was my first adult role and a big challenge for me. It included my first really grown-up kiss—those smooches with Mickey Rooney didn't count. It was also the only time I'd perform a death scene on screen."

"After George Murphy and I made love on the screen, I felt embarrassed and couldn't face him. He kidded me, saying, 'I felt I was in Tennessee with my child bride.'"

Nellie dies in childbirth, a scene Judy played so evocatively that she had the crew in tears. Later in the film, she re-emerges as the daughter of a New York City policeman (Murphy).

She had first worked with song-and-dance man Murphy in *Broadway Melody of 1938*. "I called her Grandma with all the affection in the world, not in a mocking sense," he said.

For more than two decades, between 1930 and 1952, Murphy had appeared in many big-budget silver screen musicals. After that, fascinated by politics, he emerged as a U.S. Senator from California. Ronald Reagan, who was his best friend, and for reasons known only to himself, referred to Murphy as "John the Baptist."

Although he later relented, Mayer, at first, loudly objected to the script of *Little Nellie Kelly*, protesting, "We can't have MGM's baby having a baby on screen." In that film, character actor Barry Fitzgerald was originally cast as Judy's father, but producer Freed objected and replaced him with Winniger.

Freed also made some other changes before filming began. None was as major as firing Busby Berkeley as the director and replacing him with Norman Taurog, who was sometimes critiqued as "uninspired."

Taurog had an impressive record as a director. During the course of his long career, he directed 180 movies, including *Skippy* (1931), for which he won a Best Director Oscar. He received a Best Director nomination for *Boys Town* (1938) with Spencer Tracy. Jackie Cooper, Judy's sometimes beau, portrayed his nephew.

Judy met Taurog when he was filming test scenes for *The Wizard of Oz*, but as a candidate for that film's director, he was later dismissed. He did go on to helm six Dean Martin movies and a total of nine for Elvis Presley.

Near the end of his career, Taurog said, "I'm ashamed of those Elvis films—nothing but a bunch of horny girls, a few crappy adventures, some of the King's most uninspired songs, weak plots, bad acting. Blame it on that shithead, Co. Tom Parker."

In *Little Nellie Kelly,* Judy grows up with her loving father (George Murphy) and develops a love interest in Dennis Fogarty (Douglas McPhail). A handsome actor and singer, McPhail had previously worked with Judy on *Babes in Arms*. *Little Nellie Kelly* would be his second to last movie.

In December of 1944, he committed suicide.

In *Little Nellie Kelly,* as the character she played marched down Manhattan's Fifth Avenue in St. Patrick's Irish Day Parade, Judy sang "It's a Great Day for the Irish," which became one of her biggest hits. She also sings "Singin' in the Rain" more than a decade before Gene Kelly made it more famous in that song's namesake movie, *Singin' in the Rain* (1952). She also does a solo of "A Pretty Girl Milking Her Cow." Regrettably, her magnificent rendition of the Irish ballad, "Danny Boy," ended up on the cutting room floor.

A lot of critics called *Little Nellie Kelly* "a bit of Blarney." *Variety* wrote: "Judy Garland romps through the role of Nellie Kelly in grand style, emphasizing her stature as a topnotch actress with plenty of wholesome charm and camera presence."

In contrast, *The New York Times* wrote: "It's a long and drawn-out battle of the sexes and an overly sentimental story of an Irishman's love for his daughter. In a double role, Garland does her best, but even her beguiling exuberance and her sweet way with a ballad cannot entirely overcome the deficiencies of the story."

Although Judy was dating David Rose three or four nights a week, she managed to fit in an affair with Johnny Mercer, too, even though he had a wife, Ginger. A native of Savannah, Georgia, Mercer had long been one of her favorite songwriters and singers.

In a career that lasted from 1930 to 1975, he'd receive nineteen Oscar nominations for Best Original Song, winning four of them. Of the many songs he wrote, his biggest hits were "Moon River," "Days of Wine and Roses," "Autumn Leaves," and "Hurray for Hollywood."

At the age of thirty-one, Mercer fell madly in love with Judy. A reporter claimed, "He was so besotten with her that he wandered around in a lovesick daze."

Their affair began soon after Bob Hope introduced them and got them to record the song, "Friendship," by Cole Porter in April of 1940.

"I was attracted to Mercer's music, not his beauty," Judy said.

One writer at the time described Mercer as having a face "that was round and homely, with a huge gap-toothed grin which looked as if it has been stolen from a Hallowe'en Jack-o-Lantern."

Mercer's friend, Hoagy Carmichael, referred to him as "the bouncy butterball from Savannah."

One night he gave her the music to two of his songs which he wanted to hear her sing, "Jeepers Creepers" and "You Must Have Been a Beautiful Baby."

During some of the quiet evenings they spent together at her home, he described his years in Georgia as a teenager growing up in the Jazz Era, and his empathy for Bessie Smith, Ma Rainey, and Louis Armstrong.

His father had owned the first car to ever appear on the streets of Savannah. Young Mercer used to drive it recklessly through the town's historic core. He told her he'd often wander down to Savannah's riverfront to hear the fishermen and streetcart vendors singing in a patois known as "Geechee," *[an Afro-Caribbean creole dialect also known as Gullah]* as they pushed their carts up and along the streets.

Mercer often visited the home of his friend, Bing Crosby, for hard-drinking parties. One drunken night, Crosby asked Judy to sing his first big hit, "I'm an Old Cowhand from the Rio Grande."

Judy told Mickey Rooney that "Bing came on to me one night, but I did not intercept the pass. His lead-in line was 'It's obvious you like musicians. Why not let me audition?'"

She never took him up on that offer, but later, she'd perform on the radio with him.

During another, even more drunken, party hosted by Crosby, Mercer, right before midnight, launched into a venomous tirade in which he denounced everybody in the room, sparing Judy. The next day, he sent out apologies.

She said, "I soon found out that Mercer had hidden rages. He could go for days and be fine. But then, he'd bubble over, spilling out his hatred. Fortunately, he never turned on me during the time we dated—quite the opposite. He worshipped me."

***

It was bound to happen. At a party, Judy came face to face once again with Artie Shaw, the bandleader who had broken her heart by running off and marrying Lana Turner. "What a bastard," she said to him. "I'll never forgive you."

"Let bygones be forgotten," Shaw answered, looking over at Mercer, who was chatting with friends at the piano. "It seems you've recovered and 'discov-

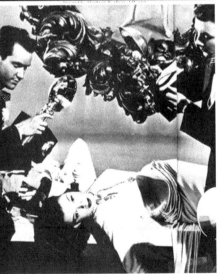

In this publicity shot for **Ziegfeld Girl,** MGM wanted to prove that Dorothy, her pigtails, and her gingham sundress had "really and truly" been been left behind in Kansas.

ered' Johnny Mercer and, from what I hear, my buddy David Rose, too."

"I'm soon going to be making a movie with your soon-to-be ex-wife, Lana," Judy shot back. "She'll tell me what happened between you two fellahs. I hear your marriage ended the day you got back from your elopement in Vegas. She's got Clark Gable now, even though he's saddled with Carole Lombard. How complicated, these Hollywood affairs."

"Frankly, I don't see much future in your romances with either David Rose or Johnny Mercer," Shaw said. "Your boy Johnny, especially when he's drunk, is always raving about my male beauty. He calls me his 'handsome bastard.' I think there's a little faggotry in him. He tags along any time I have to take a piss."

"It must be wonderful to be admired by so many beautiful women...and men, too," Judy retorted.

"It wouldn't have worked out between us," he said. "So just forget about me."

"After our brief chat tonight, I'm left wondering what I ever saw in you in the first place."

Two weeks later, Judy walked out on Mercer. An ode he'd written to impossible love, "Old Black Magic," had been inspired by her.

Months later, when someone asked her about Mercer, Judy responded, "He had a certain hush puppy charm."

***

Flo Ziegfeld had been the most flamboyant showman in the American theater. Night after night, he glorified "The American Girl" (or the American concept of beauty) in glittering, glamorous settings, with an armada of female pulchritude attired in artfully outrageous costumes. His *Ziegfeld Follies*, a lavish

None of them realized it at the time, but (top to bottom) **Lana Turner, Hedy Lamarr, and Judy Garland** would each morph into some of the highest-grossing (and most notorious) glamour gals in the entertainment industry.

In gauchely flamboyant "chiquita" costumes, the three reigning queens of MGM—**Hedy Lamarr** (left), **Judy Garland, and Lana Turner** —are camera ready for their show-stopping number, "Minnie from Trinidad."

annual revue, attracted vast audiences during their heyday [*roughly speaking, from 1907 To 1931*]. In his glory years, he seduced as many of his actresses as he could get around to.

MGM's plan involved shooting *Ziegfeld Girl* as a sequel to an earlier film, *The Great Ziegfeld* (1936), which had starred William Powell as the show biz impresario, and which had brought a Best Actress Oscar to Luise Rainer.

In contrast to the original, its sequel would no longer include a character impersonating Flo Ziegfeld himself, but would focus on the lives of three female performers in the follies.

Filming of *Ziegfeld Girl* was scheduled to begin in 1938 with the leads played by Joan Crawford, Eleanor Powell, and Margaret Sullavan, but filming was delayed when there was a reorganization shuffle of everything associated with the original script. Crawford, Powell, and Sullavan were out and replaced with a new and younger cast. In the new lineup, now examining the lives of three female performers (but with no male actor cast into the role of Flo Ziegfeld himself), Judy Garland would be billed over Hedy Lamarr and Lana Turner. The male lead was assigned to James Stewart, cast as a lovesick truck driver.

In preparation for her role, Judy worked feverishly with drama coach Lillian Burns, claiming, "I don't want to blow my chance. This could be a biggie. I'm terrified. With my looks and body, I have to compete with two of the most beautiful women at MGM."

Producer Pandro S. Berman hired Robert Z. Leonard to direct, and he employed Roger Edens, Judy's vocal mentor, along with six other men, to create the music and lyrics. Of the three female leads, Judy would be the most memorable, singing, "I'm Always Chasing Rainbows," and telling Leonard off-camera,, "That's the story of my life."

Singer Tony Martin, on whom Judy still had a crush, performed one of the most splendid numbers, "You Stepped Out of a Dream," surrounded by stunningly costumed beauties.

Judy was cast as Susan Gallagher, plucked from a small town vaudeville act for her debut on Broadway as part of *Ziegfeld Follies*. The most dramatic role of the many women in the cast went to Lana Turner as Sheila Regan, the doomed, alcoholic star. Judy's love interest in the movie is Sheila's brother, Jerry Regan, played by Judy's former boyfriend, Jackie Cooper.

Hedy Lamarr was cast as Sandy Kolter, who is discovered by accident when she accompanies her violinist husband, Franz (Philip Dorn) to rehearsals.

Charles Winninger plays Judy's vaudevillian father, Pop. The cast is rounded out by the prissy Edward Everett Horton, Paul Kelly, Eve Arden, and Dan Dailey (another ex of Judy's).

Judy lamented, "I am surrounded by glamour to the right of me and to the left of me—and not a drop for Judy."

Even though he got star billing, Stewart felt his role of a truck driver, Gilbert Young, was actually that of a supporting player. He goes to prison for stealing to buy expensive baubles demanded by Sheila (Lana).

William Anthony McGuire had written the script for the original Oscar-nominated *The Great Ziegfeld,* (1936), and he was called back to write a new script, but he died before shooting began in September of 1940.

Censors from the Breen Office cracked down on many of the lines from *Ziegfeld Girl's* 1940 script. In what they considered a generous concession, however, they allowed the character played by Dailey to refer to Sheila as a "tramp."

As filming advanced, Lana, Judy, and Hedy became very competitive, and the set crackled with intrigue. At one point, Judy complained to Leonard. "When Lana bounces by, the electricians whistle; when Hedy sweeps in, the grips stare lasciviously. But when I go by, it's 'Hi, Judy!'"

One day, Joe Pasternak, the film producer, perhaps during the period when he was debating whether he should officially migrate over to MGM, visited the set. On site, he closely observed the interactions of Judy, Hedy, and Lana. "Judy didn't realize how much talent she had or that she had more to offer than Hedy or Lana, or even Joan Crawford. Judy never believed that she had the strength, I mean feminine strength. She felt she was a failure in her private life. Talk about failures! In their private lives, Lana, Hedy, and Joan were each disastrous, despite their triumphs on the screen."

Mickey Rooney arrived to visit Judy on the set. Although Lana did not exit from her dressing room to see him that day, he talked animatedly to Judy, his frequent co-star.

"If I looked like Lana," she said with more than a touch of envy, "I could have any man I wanted. Mostly I have to dream about them: Clark Gable, Tyrone Power, Errol Flynn, even Robert Taylor—I mean especially Robert Taylor. Lana represents the epitome of female beauty. As for me, men call me pretty and give me a pat on the chin."

On the set, although Judy and Lana pretended to be friends, Judy could hardly mask her jealousy. Lana had already snatched Artie Shaw from her arms, and now she was making a play for Tony Martin.

Judy's biographer, Gerald Clarke, wrote, "If Lana Turner could club-hop every night, why couldn't Judy? She was tired of being regarded as the kind of girl a boy might safely take home to the family. What she wanted was to be a seductress, a temptress who could look into a man's eyes and cause him to reel with lust and longing, abandoning everything for just one delirious night with her. She wanted to smile at Artie Shaw, as Turner had done, and cause him to tootle to her tune and her tune alone. She wanted, in short, to be Lana Turner."

At last, Judy was working with producer Pandro S. Berman, who, during his reign at RKO, had produced the Fred Astaire/Ginger Rogers musicals and was a prime fixture in the rise of Katharine Hepburn at the studio. He'd also just released such classics as *Gunga Din* and *The Hunchback of Notre Dame* in 1939. Judy later referred to Berman as "a darkly handsome dynamo, gruff and irascible."

Berman felt he really had to succeed in producing *Ziegfeld Girl* as a means of proving to Mayer that he could make spectacular films for Metro, the same way he had for RKO. He told Judy, "Pull this one off, baby, and you'll have a breakthrough film. If you do, it will mean only starring roles for you in your future."

For creation of the film's lavish gowns, Berman hired the well-known costume designer, Adrian, knowing that he'd devise some of the most spectacular outfits ever seen on a movie screen.

Adrian opted to dress Lamarr in "high camp" costumes long before that term was invented. In her most famous scene, she appears in show-stopping headgear so heavy she could hardly walk, despite instructions from the director to appear, at least, to "float down the steps."

Hedy later lamented to Lana, "I couldn't see where I was going because of the blinding lights. To keep me from falling over with that elaborate headdress, a board was fastened to my back and my bosom was taped from behind. I felt like some religious penitent in the 10th Century walking in a torture procession."

Busby Berkeley was hired as choreographer for the spectacular musical numbers. Lana met Berkeley just at the time that his outsized musical numbers, which had enthralled Depression-era audiences, were becoming *passé*. She culled a lot of smart performance tips from him, especially about how to present herself regally as a showgirl. According to Lana, "Garland detested him, but I found him very sympathetic and deeply troubled."

At the beginning of the film, Sheila (Lana) was working as an elevator girl. She is plucked "out of the elevator shaft" to become a glamorous showgirl, and the movie traces her rise and fall through lavish production numbers in which she struts like a peacock.

She was assigned many dramatic moments, including one in which she's beaten up by a former boxer. In another, she accidentally plunges from the stage into the footlights in full view of the (horrified) opening night audience. There's even a sickbed scene during which it becomes clear that her illness is a result of chronic alcoholism.

After Sheila is fired from the Follies, she goes from bad to worse. To survive and to pay her liquor bill, she's forced to sell her jewelry, after which she's reduced to populating the seediest and filthiest of speakeasies.

Many critics lamented the fact that *Ziegfeld Girl* had been shot in black and white. An oft-repeated line in reviews was that the movie "screamed out for Technicolor."

According to James Stewart, "Lana Turner should have had star billing instead of being in fourth position. My role as her bootlegging boyfriend should have assigned me to fourth place, following Judy Garland and Hedy Lamarr. Any number of actors could have played my part. However, on reflection, it did have the greatest fringe benefits of any movie being shot at MGM," he told Cary Grant, Henry Fonda, and others.

No doubt, Stewart was referring to his seduction of both Hedy and Lana during the filming of *Ziegfeld Girl*. Its director, Robert Z. Leonard, said, "I know for a fact that Stewart spent three hours in Hedy's dressing room one afternoon when I didn't need them on camera. And I saw him driving away from the studio an hour or so later with Lana. They returned the next morning in the same car. There was little doubt he'd spent the night with her, and that satisfied grin on his face proved my case. Poor Judy missed out."

The New York Times wrote: "Judy Garland, with her head-over-heels excitement, counts for something."

Newsweek claimed, "Garland sings and dances her way enthusiastically from tank-town vaudeville to the New Amsterdam Theatre."

By the time *Ziegfeld Girl* was released, Judy, at least temporarily, had something else on her mind. The *Hollywood Reporter* announced that on May 28, 1941, Judy and David Rose were engaged with plans to be married that September.

***

After *Ziegfeld Girl*, Judy had hoped to be given more starring roles, where she would be the chief focus. To her regret, she was assigned to two back-to-back pictures for 1941, each starring Mickey Rooney.

The first was *Life Begins for Andy Hardy*, his most mature role to date. In it, portraying an eighteen-year-old, he proclaims, "I am a man."

Judy, cast once again as Betsy Booth, still harbors a crush on Andy, as they cope with the pitfalls of life in New York City.

Right before her nineteenth birthday, Judy was called to the studio to record three songs for the movie—"Easy to Love," "The Rosary," and "Abide with Me." To her regret, all three of them never made the movie's final cut. All that did was her singing "Happy Birthday" *a cappella*.

On Sunday afternoon, June 15, a garden party was hosted at her home to celebrate her engagement to David Rose. An amazing six-hundred guests were invited, and the Bobby Sherwood Orchestra was hired for the event.

With Rose immaculately dressed and groomed, she appeared looking her most dazzling as she stood at the door greeting guests and, for the most part, receiving their kisses. She hugged James Stewart in uniform [*he was on leave and at home*], as well as Ann Sothern, Eleanor Powell, Joan Crawford, and George Murphy. Ethel had invited Hollywood reporters and photographers, and Judy posed for pictures in a billowy gossamer pink gown with a diamond brooch.

Jackie Cooper showed up with Bonita Granville. [*Apparently, she was still unaware of her boyfriend's seductions of Judy.*] Another former beau, Freddie Bartholomew, arrived with Jane Withers. Johnny Mercer and his wife, Ginger, hugged and kissed Judy. Like Granville, Ginger didn't seem to know about her husband's recent adultery with Judy.

John Payne and Ann Shirley were guests, and Judy met him for the first time, later proclaiming, "That is the single sexiest man on Planet Earth." As she told Ann Rutherford, "I wanted to trade off David for Payne. Do you think Shirley would like to make a deal?"

Arriving late were Lana Turner and Tony Martin. In another aside to Rutherford, Judy said, "Some girls have all the luck," referring to Lana's entrapment of Martin.

Once again, George Seitz was to direct another Andy Hardy movie. He rounded up as many familiar faces as he could. Lewis Stone and Fay Holden were cast as Rooney's parents, and Ann Rutherford was cast as Polly Benedict, the same part she'd played in *Love Finds Andy Hardy.*

The movie marked Judy's farewell appearance in an Andy Hardy movie. Although she'd go on to co-star in more films with Rooney, she was glad to say goodbye to the little town of Carvel.

Like all Andy Hardy movies to that point, the latest serial made money at the box office. *The New York Times* claimed that Rooney still maintained his "boyish gusto, and once again, poor Judy as Betsy Booth is still mooning over the cruelly unattentive Andy."

Picturegoer maintained that "There is no more accomplished actress on the screen today than Judy Garland."

On reflection, she said, "I was nineteen and getting married yet portraying a fifteen-(sic) year-old lovesick kid. That really called for some acting."

***

Two familiar authority figures, producer Arthur Freed and director Busby Berkeley, teamed Mickey Rooney and Judy together again in *Babes on Broadway* (1941). It was another of those formulaic "kids putting on their own show" films in the tradition of *Babes in Arms* (1939) and *Strike Up the Band* (1940).

Although politically incorrect by today's standards, the movie ends with a minstrel

Family Circle reviewed **Judy Garland and Mickey Rooney in Babes on Broadway** as "back with a bang. The film is well done enough to make it a great musical. Highlights are the scenes of the two transported by imagination in imitations of famous stars."

show that included most of the players wearing blackface.

Judy was still rueful that in her previous film, except for a short rendition of "Happy Birthday," her songs had all been excised. Freed made up for that in *Babes on Broadway*. Judy's featured songs included "Babes on Broadway," and, in tandem with Rooney, a tune crafted by Barton Lane, "How About You?"

One of the show-stopping numbers is Rooney's appearance in drag, performing the song, "Bombshell from Brazil." He does an iconic impersonation of the outrageous Carmen Miranda, mimicking her as the "*chick-chika-boom*" girl.

Despite Berkeley's objection, Freed imported Vincente Minnelli to work with Judy and Rooney, most pointedly for a routine in which they impersonate the idiosyncrasies of famous theatrical personalities. It was Judy's second meeting with Minnelli, and she recalled, "I was no more impressed with him than when I met him for the first time. I certainly didn't view him as anyone I wanted to hook up with. Besides, my mind was on my upcoming marriage to David Rose."

For *Babes on Broadway*, Minnelli created a haunted theater sequence in which the pair paid tribute to the "ghosts with greasepaint."

Mickey impersonates Richard Mansfield in his signature role of *Cyrano de Bergerac*, followed by Judy as the actress Fay Templeton performing "Mary's a Grand Old Name." As Sir Harry Lauder, Rooney sings "She's Ma Daisy," followed by Judy as Blanche Ring doing her memorable number, "I've Got Rings on My Fingers." As Sarah Bernhardt, Judy sings "La Marseillaise," ending with the duo performing "Yankee Doodle Boy" with Rooney as George M. Cohan.

The New York Times commented on Rooney's impersonations, ruling that he was "very bad" as Sir Harry Lauder and only "fair" as Cohan. They went on to say, "His impersonation of a hillbilly idiot is exaggerated but fun."

Berkeley didn't like the impersonation numbers, and when Minnelli saw the rushes, he admitted, "We weren't very good in those sequences, now, were we?"

The world was at war, and as a feel-good musical, *Babes on Broadway* included a sequence where angel-faced children fleeing from war-torn England appear, many of them teary-eyed.

Fred F. Finklehoffe created all these roles, including Judy's character of Penny Morris and Rooney's as Tommy Williams, both of them a Broadway hopeful who staged a show. Judy even managed to get Berkeley to cast her two sisters, Suzanne and Jimmie, as part of the MGM studio chorus in the "Babes on Broadway" number.

In a change-of-pace role in *Babes on Broadway*, Oscar winner **Fay Bainter** plays a theatrical agent with a sharp eye, seeking out new talent and finding it in **Mickey Rooney and Judy Garland.**

A strong supporting cast was rounded up for the character roles. Fay Bainter, in the third lead, played Miss Jonsey Jones; child star Virginia Weidler played Jo Conway; and Ray McDonald was Ray Lambert. He appears graceful and nimble in a brief tap-dance. The future movie star, Donna Reed, appears briefly as Jonsey's secretary.

Bainter as a theatrical agent, "discovers" the "Three Balls of Fire" (i.e., Rooney, Richard Quine, and Ray McDonald).

On the set, Judy made a special point of meeting all the supporting players and talking to them between takes. Some of them would work with her in future pictures, including Fay Bainter in *Presenting Lily Mars* (1943).

In 1938, Bainter had a dual honor of winning a Best Supporting Actress Oscar for *Jezebel* starring Bette Davis. She was also nominated that same year for the Best Actress Oscar for *White Banners*.

Cast as producer Thornton Reed, character actor James Gleason made a career out of playing tough-talking, world-weary guys with a secret heart of gold. He'd made his film debut in 1922, starring with Constance Talmadge in *Polly of the Follies*. He also co-wrote *The Broadway Melody* (1929), winning an Oscar for Best Picture of the Year and cast with Anita Page and Bessie Love as two sisters.

Donald Meek as Mr. Stone was a native of Glasgow. He was best known for his role in *You Can't Take It With You* (1938) with James Stewart, and for *Stagecoach* (1939) with John Wayne.

Judy had several talks with one of the leading child stars of the 1930s and '40s, Virginia Weidler, who played Jo Conway. Born in 1927, she was younger than Judy and had made her first film appear-

Character actor **Donald Meek** told Judy, "Every day when I get up, I look into the mirror to confront the best-looking actor who ever hit Hollywood. I get by on male beauty alone."

Child star **Virginia Wiedler** is pictured holding Toto, Judy's beloved dog from *The Wizard of Oz*.

As a minor league child performer, she told Judy, "I'm leaving the business when I turn eighteen."

And she did.

The long-faced, balding **James Gleason,** with his pencil-thin mustache, showed up in more than 100 movies in three decades.

At the time he worked with Judy, he'd already reached the pinnacle of his career in *Meet John Doe* (1941), with Barbara Stanwyck and Gary Cooper.

ance in 1931, eventually working with Gary Cooper, George Raft, Norma Shearer (playing her daughter in *The Women,* released in 1939.) In *The Philadelphia Story* (1940), she played Dinah Lord, the nutty younger sister of Katharine Hepburn. She had also worked with Clark Gable and with Myrna Loy in *Too Hot to Handle* (1938), and with Bette Davis in *All This and Heaven Too* (1940).

She never tried to make it as an older actress, disappearing into retirement, never to be heard from again. Her brother, George, married Doris Day in 1946. *[It was his first marriage, her second.]*

During the shoot, Freed more or less kept an open door policy. One afternoon, in walked an agent with a four-year-old girl wearing a kilt. "Show him what you can do," the agent instructed the child.

The four-year-old raced over to Freed's desk and tugged at his shirt. "Oh, please, mister, don't send my brother to the chair. Don't let him fry!"

Freed was so taken with the girl that he ordered that a scene should be written into the screenplay for her.

He had discovered Margaret O'Brien, the leading child star of the 1940s and Judy's future co-star in *Meet Me in St. Louis* (1944).

The acerbic critic, Alexander Woollcott, cast as himself in *Babes on Broadway*, was known for his articles in *The New Yorker* magazine and for his devastating critiques of Broadway shows. *[He was the inspiration for the cantankerous character in the play* The Man Who Came to Dinner *which was adapted into a 1941 starring Monty Woolley, Bette Davis, and Ann Sheridan.]*

When he was introduced to Judy, Woollcott looked at her skeptically and asked, "Are you for real, girl?"

She later said, "I found him obnoxious."

At its opening in Manhattan, lines formed down the street. Even so, Howard Barnes of the *New York Herald Tribune* suggested that "Rooney and Judy are getting a bit on in years to be designated as babes, but they have not lost their shrewd showmanship in their passages through adolescence."

Time magazine noted that Judy was "intensely aware of her co-star's propensity for stealing scenes, and she nearly takes the picture from him. Rooney can't sing, but Judy sure can in her sure-fire number, 'Waiting for the Robert E. Lee.'"

Babes on Broadway made nearly four million dollars at the box office, which virtually assured that Mayer would cast Rooney with Judy again.

Reviews were mostly positive, *The New York Times* noted its high points, even though they condemned it as "a dull and overly long potpourri of comedy, drama, third-rate jokes, and music. It is basically the story of youngsters who hang out in the Times Square theatrical district, hoping for the big break, which will open the gates to the pearly white highway of the show world."

As the press found out later, Judy had bolted during the filming of *Babes on Broadway* to elope with David Rose.

PRESENTING LILY MARS &
AN AFFAIR WITH TYRONE POWER
A FAMOUS PSYCHIATRIST EVALUATES JUDY FOR MGM,
THEN DELIVERS AN ALARMING DIAGNOSIS

JUDY GETS MARRIED!
ENRAGING BOTH HER MOTHER &
LOUIS B. MAYER

AMERICA GOES TO WAR
WITHIN DAYS AFTER BOMBS DESTROY PEARL
HARBOR, JUDY ENTERTAINS U.S. TROOPS, THEN
CHURNS OUT "HOME & HEARTH" FILMS LIKE
ME AND MY GAL & GIRL CRAZY

"GIRL TROUBLE"
JEALOUS EXCHANGES WITH
AVA GARDNER & JUNE ALLYSON

"With her life, as with her songs, she gave us love—and hope."
—Adela Rogers St. Johns

"Judy turned to drugs because she was in pain and because drugs made her feel good. As one of the MGM kids, she'd been treated for most of her life to magical, instant solutions to everything...She could never escape herself, so she was always on the run."
—Mickey Rooney

Carol Craig, in the June 1941 issue of *Motion Picture* magazine, wrote: "Don't class Judy Garland among the kiddies any longer. A big girl going on nineteen, she's the same age as Deanna Durbin, and old enough to know what she wants. Like getting married."

When Mayer read that, he was furious. He had already boycotted Judy's engagement party to Davis Rose. That Monday morning, he summoned her to his office and practically demanded she postpone the very thought of marriage. "I want to do some more pictures with you and Rooney, and I want you to keep up that innocent little Dorothy image for at least three more years. If I have any whore roles to cast, there's always Lana Turner."

"I'm in love with David, and he loves me, too," she answered. "Not only that, but he helps me be a better singer."

"From what I hear, you're getting plenty of sex from all our resident studs," he said. "Why settle for just one piece of meat?"

"Oh, please Mr. Mayer, don't put it that way."

"Likewise, I have the same problem with Mickey Rooney—I'm sure he's had you…perhaps often. But his fans are still flocking to the Andy Hardy movies. If he gets married, truckloads of teenage girls, will desert the films. And making things worse, he's a serial seducer. He'll probably desert his bride on their wedding night and run off with some wench!"

At home, Ethel was even more violently opposed than Mayer was to her marrying Rose. Ironically, her hatred of musicians had intensified, as she'd watched her two older daughters marry musicians unsuccessfully.

Ethel told Judy, "I wish you could find a man who digs a slide rule instead of a slide trombone. Now you're dragging in some horn tootler and piano pounder."

Columnist Louella Parsons speculated, "I wonder what will happen when Dave Rose gets his final divorce decree. Judy is frankly in love with him, even though MGM feels it's mere infatuation. Still, Judy is a young woman of strong will. If she decides to marry Rose, I doubt if someone will change her mind."

In the weeks before her marriage, Judy and Rose were sometimes seen double dating with Tony Martin and Lana Turner. By now, Judy had recovered from her heartbreak over "that other musician," meaning Artie Shaw, although perhaps she had not fully forgiven Turner for running off and marrying him as part of one of Hollywood's shortest and most disastrous marriages.

The foursome was seen dining and dancing along the Sunset Strip. Their favorite hangout was Billy Berg's Night Club in San Fernando Valley, especially if Billie Holiday were appearing there.

Nearly all of Judy's friends pointedly noted the difference in their ages, as she had just turned nineteen and Rose was thirty-one, still waiting for his divorce from Martha Raye.

Rose and Judy had planned to get married in September, but one night on an impulse, when he was finally legally free to marry, they decided to elope to Las Vegas. Ethel had at last relented to Judy's wishes, and she and her husband, Will Gilmore, flew with them to the gambling mecca.

At 1AM on July 28, 1941, they stood before a justice of the peace and were married.

The next day, the *Hollywood Reporter* noted, "In Las Vegas, Judy Garland became Mrs. David Rose, thereby twisting the tails of newshounds here who were assured that the deal would not come off until September. We wish happiness for both of them—they're great kids."

Judy's elopement took MGM by surprise since she had not finished shooting *Babes on Broadway* with Rooney. Only an hour after her marriage she sent a telegram to producer Arthur Freed.

"Dear Mr. Freed. I am so very happy. David and I were married this AM. Please give me a little time, and I will be back and finish the picture with one take on each scene. Love, Judy."

Sourly, he adamantly refused to give her more time and insisted that she return to MGM early that Monday morning.

Arriving at the studio, she told a reporter, "Even if I wasn't allowed a honeymoon, Dave and I are the happiest couple in the world.

Mayer never reconciled himself to her marriage and remained furious at her for disobeying him. At the Academy Awards presentations, he assigned Judy "to a table in Siberia," not letting her join the studio's money-makers at the upfront tables. Perhaps feeling sorry for her, columnist Hedda Hopper deliberately seated herself at the table with Judy and Rose.

"I just floated into my marriage to Judy," Rose said. "Somehow, it seemed right at the time."

Since Rose's former home was too small, and because Judy never wanted to live under the same roof as Ethel ever again, they began looking for a place to live. A real estate agent rented them the former residence of the doomed Jean Harlow. The place looked like it had been decorated by MGM's prop department with lots of gilt, brocades, and satins *à la Trianon*.

In 1964, Judy reflected on her first husband. "David and I were very much in love. Our marriage gave me a chance to get away from my mother and the domination of the studio. But MGM muscled in and tried to humiliate him, and even kept him from working. He couldn't battle such a big, powerful

Depicted above is **Judy** newlywed **with David Rose**. She told the press, "This is no ordinary Hollywood romance. It's the real thing. It will be my one and only marriage, unlike most of my friends."

studio. We had a wonderful marriage until my professional life tore me one way and David another. Our happiness lasted less than a year and a half and ended in divorce. I was tired, and the regiment at Metro wouldn't let me stop working long enough to be really married."

As Judy admitted, she knew nothing about cooking, cleaning, and doing laundry. Her mother lived nearby, visiting frequently to run the house for her, even cooking meals for Rose when Judy wasn't at home, which was most of the time.

Although Judy had desperately wanted to escape from the tight-fisted control of her mother, Ethel became more or less the *chatelaine* of her household. Often, when she was tied up at the studio, Rose dined with Ethel.

Betty Asher, MGM's watchdog, was still spying on Judy and reporting directly to MGM's "Fixer," Eddie Mannix. At this point, Judy still trusted her. Asher was the first to learn that Rose had impregnated her.

Word soon reached Mayer. "My little hunchback is driving me crazy. She wants to completely ruin her image and become a god damn baby factory. Order her to have an abortion. Work it through her mother. She'll force her to do it."

Mayer was right. Mannix reached Ethel that afternoon, informing her of Mayer's mandate and agreeing to set up an appointment with MGM's abortion specialist. Before Judy returned home that evening, Ethel met with Rose and informed him of the studio's demand. At first, he objected until she accused him of trying to destroy Judy's career.

Both of them, therefore, presented a united front when Judy came home. She never really forgave her husband for siding with Mayer and Ethel.

As she told Asher, "Our marriage really began to unwind that night. I locked my bedroom door and cried myself to sleep."

Two days later, Ethel drove her to a secret address, a clinic in a small suburb outside Los Angeles where abortions were performed for stars affiliated with MGM.

Judy's friends, her co-workers and some outside observers, noted that in the weeks that followed, she would suddenly break into tears and flee from the set, retreating, sobbing, to her dressing room.

Author Anita Loos was no friend of Judy's. She said, "A lead star at the age of twelve, Judy Garland was a compulsive weeper. There are some characters who simply cannot endure success, and Judy is one of them. She loved to pace the alley, stopping all and sundry to whimper about some alleged affront. 'Nobody loves me!' she would lament. She was persecuted by Mayer, her family neglected her, and even her servants ignored her. Judy's mental atti-

Judy with Ethel Gumm.

Things were not as idyllic as this cheery photo might have implied.

162

tude may have been pathetic, but it turned her into a great bore. I had little interest in a character ruled by petulance."

There was room in their new home's garden for Rose to install 780 feet of track for his miniature railroad. After bringing it to working order, he invited Judy for a ride, but she soon came to resent his obsession with "that damn toy rail line. I thought I married a musician, but he seemed to have entered the wrong profession. He wanted to be a train engineer."

His locomotives were fueled with coal, which generated steam to turn the pistons. His obsession with miniature railroads dated back to when he was seven.

Night after night, after they'd each returned from the studio and finished dinner, she wanted to spend a quiet evening with him, listening to music and then retiring early to make love. Instead, after dinner, he put on his railroad cap and was out riding the rails until sometime after midnight.

***

Producer Arthur Freed had seen the Kern and Hammerstein Broadway musical, *Very Warm for May,* and thought it might be a vehicle to star Judy Garland. Although it had flopped in New York as a stage play, Freed thought "My Unit," as he called it, might make it a silver screen hit if it could also feature co-stars Marta Eggerth, the Hungarian singer, and dancer Ray McDonald.

MGM's story department soon let it be known, however, that it was too similar to *Babes in Arms,* and Freed decided to make *For Me and My Gal* instead, scheduling it for a release in 1942.

[To that end, he hired Fred Finkelhoffe to tweak—along with two other writers—the screenplay. Finkelhoffe had been the chief writer

Honolulu Star-Bulletin 1st EXTRA

WAR!
OAHU BOMBED BY JAPANESE PLANES

SAN FRANCISCO, Dec. 7.—President Roosevelt announced this morning that Japanese planes had attacked Manila and Pearl Harbor

Following the Japanese attack on America's Pacific fleet at Pearl Harbor **(December 7, 1941),** Judy became one of the first Hollywood stars to entertain U.S. troops, many about to embark to the Pacific.

Appearing in four shows a day, she sang in five midwestern towns over a three week period.

163

of Judy's previous hit, Strike Up the Band *(1940).]*

America entered World War II in December of 1941 (Pearl Harbor), an event that transformed the priorities of the United States. Reacting to this for commercial reasons (and as a genuine reflection of his own patriotism, too), Mayer ordered additional infusions of feel-good Americana into the script of *For Me and My Gal* (1942). Its plot focused on two vaudeville dancers and a singer during World War I.

Freed had originally cast Judy with George Murphy as the male lead. Murphy had already portrayed both her husband and her father in *Little Nellie Kelly,* and they worked well together.

Later, however, Freed saw Gene Kelly portraying a heel in the Broadway production of *Pal Joey,* and offered him the romantic (male) lead in *For Me and My Gal.* Simultaneously, he, demoted Murphy to third place in the star lineup as the "other" male dancer, the one hoping to win Judy's love.

With trepidation, Kelly reported to work for his first day at MGM, because, as he admitted, there was already "bad blood" between Louis B. Mayer and himself. Mayer, who had also seen Kelly in *Pal Joey* on Broadway, had loudly assured him that, in accordance with Freed's wishes, no screen test would be required before a contract was issued for his promised role in *For Me and My Gal.*

However, two months later, MGM brusquely notified Kelly that the studio's perceptions had changed, and that a screen test would be required after all.

Hot-tempered, Kelly fired off a letter to Mayer, attacking him. He

For Me and My Gal, Marching Off to War:

George Murphy. left, and **Gene Kelly** hold a chipper and cheerful **Judy** aloft against a silhouette of soldiers marching ominously off to war—in this case, World War I, even though the intent was clearly about morale-boosting in the aftermath of Pearl Harbor.

Don't be fooled by these happy faces beaming out from the finale of *For Me and My Gal.* As career prospects for **Gene Kelly** (right) grew brighter, those for **George Murphy** (left) grew dimmer.

Murphy harbored deep resentment of Kelly, telling Judy, "I've ended up playing the *schnook* who loses the girl, namely you. I despise him for taking my role. My days as a song-and-dance man are almost over.

ended the letter with this line: "I'm sorry I won't work for you because you lied. I'd rather dance in a saloon."

In the meantime, in a murky act of Hollywood intrigue, David O. Selznick signed Kelly to a contract, and subsequently sold half of that contract to MGM. That deal gave Mayer 50% control over Kelly, at least until the end of filming *For Me and My Gal.*

With Ethel, Judy, too, had seen Kelly emoting in *Pal Joey* on Broadway. After his performance, she headed backstage to congratulate him on his performance, inviting him to join her party at the Copacabana. Kelly accepted but was disappointed to discover that the context was neither intimate nor private: He and Judy would be seated at a table with twenty other people.

As he was dancing with her, he suggested that they split. She agreed, and they escaped through a rear door, after she instructed a waiter to inform Ethel that she'd run off "to paint the town red with Gene Kelly."

When she returned to her hotel suite at 3AM, Ethel was waiting up for her. "Where have you been?"

Feeling defiant and independent, Judy turned on her. "We did what any twenty-eight-year-old man does when dating a teenaged girl." Then she stormed into her bedroom and locked the door behind her.

Somehow, despite the cheesecake costume and showgirl pose, **Judy**, in this publicity still from *For Me and My Gal*, still manages to look like the kind of girl a soldier might introduce to his Mom.

Back in Hollywood, the filming of *For Me and My Gal* occurred during April and May of 1942. At that time, the war against Nazi Germany and the Empire of Japan was going very badly for the Allies.

With Busby Berkeley directing, Judy was billed above the title—a solo listing—for the first time in her career. "No more second fiddle to Mickey Rooney," she said.

Freed told her, "After the war, I predict that the public will soon tire of Mickey, and you'll become a far bigger star than he ever was."

In *For Me and My Gal,* Judy was cast as Jo Hayden: Kelly played Harry Palmer; and Murphy portrayed Jimmy K. Metcalfe. Supporting players featured Marta Eggerth as Eva Minard; Ben Blue as Sid Simms; Richard Quine as Danny Hayden (Judy's brother killed in the war); Keenan Wynn as Eddie Melton; and singer Lucile Norman as Lily Duncan. She sings "The Doll Shop" with Murphy; "Tell Me;" and the very memorable "Till We Meet Again."

Loaded with songs, many of them oldtime ballads, *For Me and My Gal* depicts a love triangle among three vaudevillians whose lives are changed by the oncoming world war. Each is determined, one day, to be billed as a star at The Palace Theatre in New York City.

Two of Judy's alltime favorites were "When Johnny Comes Marching Home" and "It's a Long Way to Tipperary." The title song of *For Me and My Gal* was performed as a duet by Judy and Gene Kelly.

The duo also sang "When You Were a Tulip," an old favorite. Judy also sang an even more popular longtime favorite, "Pack Up Your Troubles." *[For their work on it, Roger Edens and George Stoll were Oscar-nominated for Best Scoring of a Musical.]*

Judy went over big in the number, "Bullin' the Jack," she executed with Kelly. Clad in shorty-shorts, she won the attention of a critic from *Time* magazine, who cited her for her "horse-race legs."

Throughout the picture, she encouraged Kelly all the way. He had grave doubts about the artistic merits of movies, considering himself a stage actor and dancer. He predicted that *For Me and My Gal* would be a colossal flop. "When I saw the final cut, I was appalled at myself blown up on the screen twenty times."

Judy tried to keep the peace among the principals. Kelly had never been a fan of Berkeley's exaggerated dance routines in those musicals of the 1930s, and, as Judy remembered, there was almost a fight every day.

Budapest-born Marta Eggerth, a major-league diva from "The Silver Age of Operetta," was cast as "the other woman," vying with Judy for the affection of Kelly. She would play a similar role in Judy's next picture. She'd arrived at MGM with impressive credentials. Franz Lehár, Robert Stolz, Oscar Straus, and Fritz Kreisler had each composed works specifically with her in mind.

A Canadian, Ben Blue, cast as Sid Simms, had two big numbers, "A Sailor's Hornpipe," and "What Are You Gonna Do for Uncle Sam?" This actor/comedian usually played a bald-headed dumbbell with a goofy expression.

Keenan Wynn, an American character

Europa! Europa!

Marta Eggert—Judy Garland's female rival in *For Me and My Gal*—was as much of a *Wünderkind* in Central Europe as Judy was in the U.S.

Born in Hungary in 1912 during "the Silver Age of Operetta," she made more than 40 films in five languages, including "leading diva" roles whose music was written especially for her by Franz Lehár.

After her marriage in 1936 to the Polish-born tenor, Jan Kiepura, they became collectively known as Europe's *Liebespaar* (Love Pair), drawing crowds and rave reviews in performances of operas, including *La Bohème*, in theaters stretching from Vienna to Chicago.

Eggert died in Rye, New York, in 1966 at the age of 101, a spectacularly cosmopolitan oddity with a respected involvement in Hollywood musicals.

actor with a particularly expressive face, had been assigned the minor part of Eddie Melton. He 'd play an important role in Judy's life as the man who introduced her to actor Van Johnson, her co-star and one of her closest friends. Wynn and Judy would work together a few years later on her picture *The Clock* (1945).

During the shoot, Judy and David Rose invited Gene Kelly and his wife, actress Betsy Blair, over for dinner. Kelly and Blair had married in 1941.

Blair later recalled in a memoir that after dinner, Rose invited Kelly and her for a ride on his miniature railroad and noted that Judy had been "absently indulgent of her new husband."

For its review of *For Me and My Gal*, *The New York Times'* Bosley Crowther wrote: "Judy Garland is a saucy little singer and dances passably. She handles such age-flavored ballads as 'After You've Gone,' and 'Smiles' with music hall lustiness. The songs are good, the story maudlin—that is the long and short of it. But maybe that was vaudeville."

Judy had lost a lot of weight, and many reviewers commented on that, several noting that she appeared "thin and frail," another referring to her as "bony-faced."

Time noted, "In this nostalgic re-evocation of vaudeville's Golden Age, and the sweeter, simpler times of World War I, Miss Garland and Mr. Kelly do a notable job. She is well graduated from being a female Mickey Rooney and is one of the best song pluggers in the business."

The *New York Daily News* wrote that "Judy Garland has developed enormously as an actress and entertainer since her last screen assignment. She projects the old melodies charmingly, and she dances with grace."

The *New York Herald Tribune* claimed, "Baring the corny aspects of the continuity of the film, Judy Garland turns in a warm, persuasive, and moving portrayal of a diffident hoofer and singer who loves a heel, played by newcomer Gene Kelly. Good guy George Murphy is kept waiting for her in the wings."

Judy's favorite review appeared in the *Tacoma Times:* "When you start picking the best entertainers in show business, you wouldn't be too far off the beam were you to head the list with Judy Garland, who will still be

By the time Judy was invited to banter and sing on the **Chase & Sanborn Hour**, the venue was already hugely popular nationwide as a radio-based variety show.

The poster above promotes Pre-Code film star **Joan Blondell** as a subject of interest five years before Judy appeared on the show.

It was conceived as a morale builder broadcast from a U.S. military base filled with soldiers on the verge of being shipped off to war zones in the Pacific.

around after ninety percent of the so-called stars of stage and screen have been relegated to a permanent dim-out."

For Me and My Gal was a hit at the box office. It made Gene Kelly a movie star and was yet another money-maker that advanced both Judy's film career and her star power.

***

On Sunday, December 7, 1941, Judy, with David Rose accompanying her, was appearing on NBC's weekly radio show, *The Chase & Sanborn Hour,* a 60-minute broadcast that ran at prime time on Sunday nights between 1929 and 1948. The program that night was live from Fort Ord, a military base outside Monterey, California. Edgar McCarthy and his wisecracking puppet, Charlie McCarthy, were on the bill with her.

In the middle of her song, "Zing! Went the Strings of My Heart," the program was interrupted by a news bulletin from Honolulu. Air and Sea Forces of the Empire of Japan had attacked Pearl Harbor, bombing extensively, killing thousands of military personnel and sinking naval vessels.

Stunned, Judy was told to return to the broadcast and complete the show. To that effect, she struggled valiantly, interrupted by frequent news bulletins from Hawaii.

It was announced that President Roosevelt would address Congress in the morning, and so he did, declaring that "December 7, 1941, was a date that would live in infamy." He asked and got a Declaration of War from the U.S. Congress. On December 11, after Nazi Germany joined its ally, Japan, in declaring war on America, the United States announced that it was joining in the battle for Europe, too.

Before leaving Ford Ord, Judy was made an honorary corporal in Company H of the 1st Medical Regiment.

From January 21 to February 9 of 1942, Judy become one of the first Hollywood movie stars to entertain troops across America. Having just completed filming of *For Me and my Gal,* she began a personal appearance tour, singing to soldiers before they were shipped out to the battlefields of Europe.

For a period of three

Whereas Betty Grable became the pin-up girl of World War II, **Judy** morphed into its unofficial "G.I. Sweetheart."

In many ways, she represented the girl next door, or perhaps the girl who soldiers had left behind before they went off to get wounded, become disabled,, or die.

weeks, she appeared to wild applause on stages in training installations across the Midwest [*Fort Custer, Jefferson Barracks, Camp Robinson, and Camp Wolters*]. It was a grueling schedule that called for her starring in four shows a day, singing a dozen songs at each show, including the inevitable "Over the Rainbow." Her tour ended in Mineral Wells, Texas, after she developed a case of strep throat.

About eighteen months later, beginning in Washington D.C. and scheduled from September 8 to mid-October of 1943, Judy embarked on a second high-voltage, morale-building, personal appearance tour that took her through fifteen American cities. In each of the sites, she sold war bonds (a billion dollars were raised during the course of that tour) and sang in front of an estimated seven million Americans. In each city she visited, she was featured as the star of a two-hour parade.

She was joined by Lucille Ball, Fred Astaire, James Cagney singing "Yankee Doodle Dandy," and Mickey Rooney.

At every stopover, Judy sang the Irving Berlin favorite, "You're in the Army, Mr. Jones." Later, after singing to the men, she visited them, especially in hospital beds. She talked to them, listening to their stories, and even made phone calls to family members who were astonished to hear Judy Garland on the other end of the line. She assured the wounded's loved ones that Johnny was safe and all right.

***

Tyrone Power was a handsome, dashing, box office champ at 20th Century Fox. The night he met Judy, he said, "I think I fell in love with her when I saw her in *For Me and My Gal.*"

He was twenty-eight when he was introduced to her at the Brentwood home of actor Keenan Wynn and his wife, Eva Lynn Abbott. Judy was still married to David Rose but separated from him. Likewise, Power and the French actress Annabella, who'd been married in 1939, were estranged, and she was out of town.

Tyrone Power with his wife, **Annabella** in 1943.

The French actress and the American matinee idol were bisexuals. Judy began an affair with him, calling it "a high-intensity romance."

According to Judy, "There was trouble in Paradise. Ty refused to divorce her, even though he admitted to me that he had fallen out of love with her."

Wynn and Judy had become friends when he'd worked with her on *For Me and My Gal.* He invited her to a party at his home, and she arrived alone, as did Power.

He certainly wasn't in need of a date, as he was avidly pursued by both men and women throughout Hollywood. He had already sustained intimacies with men who included Howard Hughes and Errol Flynn, and with women such as Betty Grable, Rita

Hayworth, Joan Crawford, and Loretta Young.

Spotting Judy standing alone in a far corner of the room, Power approached her and introduced himself. "I know who you are, Mr. Power," she said. "I've swooned over you in so many movies....*The Mark of Zorro, Blood and Sand...*"

He immediately began relating how beautiful she'd been in *For Me and My Gal.* "I was absolutely mesmerized."

She admitted "that's music to my ears" She later said, "I could not believe it. Here I was standing next to the fist-fighting, sword-wielding, swashbuckling hero himself."

The following night, Power was seen slipping into Judy's new apartment on Sunset Boulevard. Their months-long affair began that night and continued even when she moved into her new home in Bel Air.

As she admitted frankly to Mickey Rooney and others, "I have found the perfect lover in Ty. We are ideal for each other, and both of us have a fondness for oral sex."

She was deeply disturbed, however, that he was still married to Annabella, and there was no talk of divorce. She had heard persistent rumors that the French actress was a lesbian and that indeed her union with Power was a "lavender marriage." She was told that he was an avid bisexual. Nonetheless, she began showing up at the Fox commissary for lunch with him, their arms linked, much to the surprise of all the other guests, who turned and stared as if not believing their eyes.

Then, the day after a mutually affectionate appearance Judy made with Power in the MGM commissary, Mayer summoned her to his office. He warned her to break off this burgeoning romance with the star from Fox Studios "at once."

"But I'm in love with him," she protested.

"Bullshit!" Mayer shot back. "You're in love with his face on the cover of *Photoplay.* He was Howard Hughes' boy, and still might be for all I know. He had this fling with Errol Flynn, and there have been countless others. Betty Grable had been known to bring soldiers back from the Hollywood Canteen for a three-way with him."

"That is mere gossip," she said. "Hollywood is the most gossipy town on the planet. The things you're saying do not apply to the Ty I know."

Power's best friend and confidant was Watson Webb, who kept abreast of the blossoming affair between Power and Judy Garland. [*A film editor credited for his work on more than 30 movies between 1941 and 1952, and later, a philanthropist, Webb was a partial heir to branches of both the Vanderbilt and Havemeyer families.*] "For the short time it lasted, Ty was nuts about Judy. She was Dorothy all grown up. She was now a seductive, sexy woman of wit, intelligence, and charm. Ty confessed that of all his seductions, she was the most compliant in bed. Yes, she'd go around the world on him, something he adored."

"He and Judy became not mere lovers, but soulmates."

As one writer put it, "Ty Power and Judy Garland were celebrators of everything romantic, from the wistful music of Rachmaninov to the elegiac, doom-shrouded verse of A.E. Houseman."

Power's biographer, Fred Lawrence Guiles, wrote: "Judy Garland believed she was homely and about as sexy as ZaSu Pitts. One of her ways of dealing with that was to make herself available to the most attractive men she could find, taking them to bed. She had a long string of affairs in that endeavor, which were nearly always successful at the beginning, because she was, in reality, extraordinarily attractive both in and out of bed."

"When it came to men, Judy made the rounds," said Charles, ("Chuck") Walters, a film director. "She was no Lana Turner or Betty Grable, but she knew how to make men fall for her. She was pretty good at pulling off that trick. Although she wasn't really one of MGM's glamour girls, she was enormously appealing in her own right."

During this period when America was at war, Power contemplated joining the Marines, feeling that it was his patriotic duty. Judy urged him not to. "You're at the peak of your career, in heavy demand at Fox. MGM even wanted you to play Ashley Wilkes in *Gone With the Wind* (1939). Who knows what will happen if you disappear from the screen? You might come home from the Marines to find that a lot of younger guys have replaced not only you but the likes of Robert Taylor and Clark Gable, too."

"What a gloomy prospect," he said.

"What man or woman wouldn't fall in love with Ty Power?" asked Darryl F. Zanuck, his boss at Fox. "If I weren't hopelessly heterosexual, I would have fallen in love with him myself. He and I strip down and go naked into a steambath at the studio every day. I can vouch for him—he is one hell of a good-looking son of a bitch."

Power warned Judy that he might not make the ideal husband, admitting that he had "flaws. I know that both men and women are attracted to me, and I don't like to frustrate them by holding off a sexual encounter. If I'm feeling horny at the time and I like the person, I'll oblige. Henry Fonda mockingly calls me 'Miss Roundheels.'"

She didn't seem to let that revelation sink in. "My love affair with Ty, brief though it was, was the most idyllic of my life," she told her roommate Betty Asher. [*Even at this late date, she did not know that Asher had been hired to spy on her for MGM. Asher had also been instructed to sabotage her romance with Power.*]

Then came devastating news from him. He had joined the U.S. Marines and was to report to Camp Pendleton for boot camp on January 2, 1943. "On my final night with him, I clung to him desperately. I cried for days after that morning I had to tell him farewell."

Before leaving, he gave her a copy of his favorite novel, *Forever*, by Mildred Cram. It was the

FOREVER

When Tyrone Power gave a copy of this novel about a heart-rending affair that extends to points beyond the grave, Judy thought it was just for her...

To her rage, she later learned that he had also given copies to other lovers with the same (false) sense of committed passion.

171

story of a young man and women who vow to love each other for eternity. And indeed, they do, dying in the same car accident and making their love eternal.

When he returned from the war, Power told her that he wanted her to star with him in a film adaptation of this romantic, mystical tale. *[Judy didn't know at the time that he had given that same novel to a number of other women with the same vow.]*

While Power was serving in the Marines, Annabella was keeping her own fires burning through numerous affairs—one with an English actor, another with a pilot in the U.S. Air Force, and yet another with the scion of a prominent family in Manhattan...plus other beaux, too.

During Power's absence, Judy was informed by her doctor that she was pregnant. That put heavy pressure on her, as she knew she could not face the scandal of having been impregnated by a married man. She contacted Power and urged him to divorce Annabella and marry her right away.

He had often spoken of having a son to carry on the theatrical legacy of himself and his father, Tyrone Power, Sr., a famous English-born actor who had died in 1931. *[Tyrone, Jr., eventually named his future son Tyrone Power III.]*

The Marine promised Judy that during an upcoming weekend furlough, he'd have a confrontation with Annabella in Washington, D.C., about a divorce. Annabella, perhaps with the intention of creating maximum drama, demanded that Judy fly to Washington to face the news with him.

She checked into a hotel and waited and waited. The phone never rang. All she got from Power was a telegram informing her: "ANNABELLA ADAMANT. NO DIVORCE."

Devastated, Judy flew back to Hollywood in tears.

There, she placed an emergency call to Eddie Mannix, MGM's "Fixer." He quickly arranged for her to have an abortion the following day.

[Although she didn't tell either David Rose or Ethel, Betty Asher was fully aware of what was going on. Asher reported the news to Mayer's office. He was furious that Judy was trying to break up Power's marriage and that she'd gone so far as to get pregnant by him. "When will my little hunchback ever learn?"]

Steve Watkins, a fellow Marine, bunked with Power. "I was with him the night he got the news that Judy had aborted their son. He just knew it was a boy. He cried that night, and I comforted him as best I could because I loved him dearly. I tried to convince him that he didn't need some untrustworthy woman but a loyal comrade who would always have his back."

"He was worried about resuming his film career after the war. I assured him he had something to fall back on. My father had died and left me a large estate in Maryland. I told him I could take him there, and that we could spend the rest of our lives in luxury, riding horses, going swimming, whatever we wanted to do. He would never have to work another day in his life. Alas, he turned me down."

After Power left to serve in the Marines, Judy wrote him long letters, pouring out her love for him. Asher, however, told her, to Judy's horror, that Power made it a point to mockingly read her letters out loud to other Marines in his barracks.

[*Actually, Power was a private person and never shared any of Judy's letters. Asher, however—as a spy for MGM charged with sabotaging Judy's affair—continued to propagate that falsehood with a certain zeal, in part, perhaps, because she was in love with Judy herself.*

According to Asher's brother, "My sister loved Judy at the same time she was betraying her to MGM."

When letters from Power arrived at their apartment addressed to Judy, Asher destroyed them.]

Unknown to Judy, Power was transferred for a while to San Diego, where he could more easily commute to Los Angeles on a weekend pass. For some reason on his first leave, he chose to stay behind, going to a local bar he had heard about.

There, he met Smitty Hanson, who, at the age of eighteen, was both virile and attractive. He was also a hustler. When Power picked him up that night and hauled him back to a hotel room he'd rented, little did either of them know that this was the beginning of a life-long affair. It would be interrupted whenever Power went away for film shoots on location. Once, they were separated for a period of two years, but they always linked up with each other again.

"Tyrone Power was a sweetheart of a man," Hanson said. "A dear, dear fellow. Over the years, I would sneak away with him, usually to this secret address he had in Palm Springs. He knew I was a hustler, but he was a gentleman about it. He didn't openly give me money but would slip it into my shirt pocket."

"After he died, a reporter asked me about him. I said he was basically homosexual who married on occasion and went with a woman from time to time. Incidentally, Judy Garland was my favorite entertainer, and he talked about her a lot when he wasn't discussing Lana Turner and that conniving bitch, Linda Christian, who was just in it for the money."

Long after their affair ended, according to Judy, "Almost to the end, I still had had hopes that when Johnny Came Marching Home—Ty in this case—he'd fall into my arms. We could start afresh. No such luck. Right after the war ended, the minute he got back, he fell into the arms of that blonde bitch, Lana Turner."

For years after the end of his affair with Judy, Power remained married to Annabella. Their union remained legally binding until their divorce in 1948.

[*Until the divorce was finalized, their union was marked with long separations, but while it lasted, he invited Annabella to the Champagne Room of El Morocco nightclub in Hollywood. As Power entered the room, he spotted Judy at a table with a half-dozen other guests, one of whom was Peter Lawford. She seemed to be laughing and telling stories to amuse the other guests.*

Later in the evening, Power walked past her table en route to the men's room, but she didn't look up, even though he knew she was aware of his presence.]

Judy recalled her affair during World War II with Power. "He was different *from all my other lovers. It was no small affair. The hurt still lingers. I never loved any man as deeply as I loved Tyrone. Forget David Rose. Forget Artie Shaw, and you can definitely write off my future husbands. It was Ty who stole my heart. Fortunately, Joseph Mankiewicz came along to save me."]*

***

In 1942, David Rose was inducted into the U.S. Army and stationed at the Culver City Motion Picture Air Force Base. He was allowed two weekend passes a month, which he'd use to return home for reunions with Judy.

"My wife was hardly a recluse when I was away," he recalled. "I'd come back and find her throwing a raucous party. Even though we had only a short weekend together, we were rarely alone at those times—a quick session in the bed—and that was that."

"Over the course of our short marriage, her drug dependencies and a threat of suicide every now and then had taken their toll on our marriage."

Privately, she complained to Mickey Rooney, "Dave can't satisfy me in bed. No wonder Martha Raye divorced him."

"On my quickie weekends home, even if I slipped out the door, I don't think anyone would notice me," Rose said. "Not even Judy."

A fellow soldier, Richard Stevens, a native of Indiana, later told a reporter, "I was in love with David Rose all through my Army days. To my ever-lasting regret, he always resisted my sexual advances but not the friendship I offered. He needed and wanted love, and he got plenty from me...not from Judy."

"A few times, he took me home with him, where I met Judy," Stevens said. "She seemed relatively indifferent and was a bit hostile to me. I expected Dorothy, but got this rather witty, sophisticated woman who drank too much at parties. She was no innocent, but a woman of the world. There were rumors that she was having a number of affairs and was a visitor at the Hollywood Canteen where she met a lot of soldiers."

"At one of her parties, I noticed that Dave often stood in the corner, nursing a drink," Stevens said. "He was never part of the scene. Mickey Rooney was a feature at these parties, and he and Judy would entertain. Unlike your typical show-biz personality, Dave was very shy. I wish he had turned to me for sex, but he never did. I slept near him at night, and sometimes I could hear him masturbating."

"I felt that he needed my love and support. I always had his back. The saddest day in my life came when we said goodbye for the final time. My parents had died, and I'd inherited the farmstead in Indiana. He promised to write or call me, but I never heard from him again."

Rose did make one contact in the Army that he did hear from—Red Skelton. By 1948, Skelton hired him for his TV show, and Rose worked there for twenty years. He would marry again and have two daughters, dying at the age of eighty on August 23, 1990, when his life with Judy was but a distant memory.

Rose's breakup with her came early in 1943 but received little notice in the press because he was in the Army. The couple seemed to simply

174

have drifted apart.

After his exit from her life, she moved out of the (rented) Jean Harlow home and into another (also rented) house owned by Broadway star Mary Martin.

Elsa Maxwell, the society *duenna* and party giver, delivered her opinion about it in *Photoplay:* "I don't know what David Rose did or didn't do that was wrong. But I do know that Judy at this time was completely unfitted to be a wife. One time I arrived with dinner guests at her house and found her having din-

Professional hostess and society maven **Elsa Maxwell** getting tipsy and gossiping, perhaps viciously, with **Cole Porter** (right) and the philanthropist, **William Rhinelander Stewart,** about everybody in show biz.

ner in bed. David was not home. She had completely forgotten about her invitation. Those two never kept an engagement book. Sometimes, they would discover that they had asked separate groups of friends over on the same evening."

On June 8, 1944, Judy announced "I'm rid of David and those damn trains, always going somewhere but never arriving anywhere."

Their final divorce decree would not become final until June of 1945, when World War II was still raging in the Pacific.

In April of 1964, Judy reflected on her first marriage: "Dave and I broke up for personality reasons. Our personalities were so different. We could barely agree on anything. Yet we wanted to please each other so badly that these differences rarely came out in the open. I would agree with him because I didn't want to hurt him. He did the same thing for me. We tried to change for each other. We tried to make ourselves over from the inside out. But you can't do that. You can't change the real you. You can only pretend to. So, there was a constant heaviness that hung in the air."

***

After Louis B. Mayer sat through Ava Gardner's screen test, he concluded, "This Tarheel cracker can't act, can't sing, can't dance, and she has a 'spittin' cotton' accent, but she's terrific! Sign her!"

On her first week as she wandered through the Metro lot, she spotted Mickey Rooney, MGM's top box office draw. He was performing a scene for *Babes on Broadway* (1941), a film that co-starred Judy. In full drag, he was impersonating Carmen Miranda, that "Bombshell from Brazil." With a basket of fruit resting on his head, he wore a bodice blouse with falsies, a splashy rainbow-colored skirt, and platform high heels. His face was adorned with false eyelashes, rouge, and lots of Victory Red lipstick coated his lips. "Don't you think I look gorgeous!" he asked Busby Berkeley.

Gardner watched in amazement as he performed this difficult number. When the director yelled "Cut!" he walked over and introduced himself.

"Hi, I'm Mickey Rooney. Who might you be, you lovely thing, you?"

In a voice that Rooney characterized as "dripping molasses," she said, "I'm Ava Gardner from North Carolina. Mayer wants me to become a big movie star."

Later that day, Rooney had lunch with Judy in the commissary. "I've met the gal I'm gonna marry," he said. "My heart almost stopped beating when I saw her. I'm in love."

"The hell you are," she said. "You're just horny as hell and want to get your rocks off—that's all it is."

"No, this is the real thing," he claimed.

She was not convinced.

During the next few days, he showered Gardner with flowers and boxes of candy, as well as invitations to go out with him, dancing and dining. Finally, he wore down her resistance, and she agreed to go out with him to the Cocoanut Grove.

Judy and Gardner were the same age, and both of them would wed men older than they were. In both cases, Mayer opposed their marriages, especially for Judy and Rooney. "I won't be able to cast you as kids in any more Andy Hardy movies. You would no longer be convincing as teenagers. There would go our box office receipts."

Mickey Rooney with **Ava Gardner** in the 40s, around the time of their marriage.

Rooney told Judy, and later inserted something equivalent into a memoir, "My North Carolina hillbilly has big brown nipples which, when aroused, stand out like some double-long California raisins."

"If you marry this Gardner heifer, you'll be out screwing around with some other dame before the honeymoon is over—I know you, you horny little bastard."

"I'll be faithful," Rooney assured his boss.

"Cut the crap!" Mayer said. "I'm no fool. I know what I'm talking about. I've seen many a lovesick fool come and go with disastrous results. Take John Gilbert swooning over that lesbian, Greta Garbo. I've lived through their adulteries, their abortions, their rages, and their cheating hearts. Here's some advice for you: Why not take on Lana yourself?"

"She's already aborted my child," he confessed.

"Then try Hedy Lamarr. But don't get married."

Rooney and Gardner socialized with David Rose and Judy when they were still man and wife at least twice a week to talk about marriage, each afraid that the ire of Mayer could destroy their careers. "Mickey was completely gone for Ava like I'd never seen him before," Judy said. "When I met Ava, I thought she was lovely but, oh my god, how naïve. She struck

176

me as some gal who had just come back into the house after slopping the hogs."

At first, Judy urged Gardner and Rooney to defy Mayer and run off and get married. But then she began to sense a change in Gardner, telling Rose, "Ava is a fast learner. Almost overnight, she's gone from this naïve little hick girl into a scheming starlet like Lana Turner."

On another evening, Gardner confirmed Judy's suspicions about her. "My intention is to marry a tall, dark, and handsome type—take Robert Taylor, for example," Gardner said. "Not some sawed-off runt like Mickey. But he *is* MGM's box office champ. When we go out, all the photographers want to take our picture, a great way for me to get known in this town. The other night at Ciro's, we double-dated with Errol Flynn and this little whore."

"I sat next to Errol," she said. "While talking to Mickey, his hand under the table was practically masturbating me. I want to be free. I could have run off with Flynn that night, ditching Mickey."

"Mickey has his faults, I'll agree," Judy said. "He's 'ON' all the time, always performing on and off the camera. For a wife, that might get exhausting after a while. Wed to him, you might never get any rest."

"I want lots of publicity," Gardner said. "That way, directors will know who I am. Let's face it, I'm one beautiful doll."

"That you are," Judy agreed.

"Once I become a star in the MGM stable, I won't need Mickey anymore and can dump the little fart."

"A sure fire road to stardom," Judy said, not completely disguising the cynicism in her voice.

Defying Mayer, Gardner and Mickey were married on January 10, 1942, in the obscure location of Ballard, California. Mayer felt their marriage would not get publicity there, and Mickey could still play innocent Andy Hardy. After lodging many protests and even threatening Rooney's film career, Mayer had finally given up and allowed Mickey to enter into what the studio chief felt would be a disastrous marriage.

Back from a brief honeymoon, Rooney brought Judy up to date: "Ava turned out to be the last surviving virgin in Hollywood. Once I broke her in, she couldn't get enough. I was tender but tremendous in bed. It was all night long, as we performed our own symphonies—some Bach, some Brahms, throw in Beethoven...hell, the whole gang, even Ravel. On our honeymoon, I'd play golf during the day and return for an early dinner where it was early to bed to practice Mozart."

As Judy had recognized in advance, Gardner's marriage to Rooney seemed doomed almost from the beginning.

As Mayer had so accurately nailed him, he began a series of adulterous affairs after his wedding. "The marriage lasted about as long as my union with David Rose," Judy said.

"Ava and I saw each other during the coming years, but it was never a friendship—too much rivalry," Judy said. "After Mickey, Ava played the field and then up and married that heartbreaker, Artie Shaw. Even though I'd gotten over Artie, I still harbored some resentment about her running off with him and getting married, something I had failed to do. No woman under the circumstances can completely conceal her resentment."

"Later, to my regret, when I made *The Clock* (1945) with Robert Walker, I learned that he was secretly running around with Ava," Judy said.

Ava Gardner and Frank Sinatra were very much in love when this photo was taken. But their marriage, characterized by adulterous affairs on both their parts, ended in divorce.

"Ava accompklished what I failed to to," Judy said. "She married Artie Shaw."

"Years later, I shacked up with Frank Sinatra during Ava's marriage to him. "I gave Ava a dose of her own medicine."

***

Based on a novel by Booth Tarkington, *Presenting Lily Mars* was originally scheduled as a drama to star Lana Turner. But Louis B. Mayer ordered that it be turned into a musical for Judy. It was the story of a stagestruck small town girl who dreams of Broadway stardom.

For her performance, Judy was given MGM's most glamourous treatment, her hair lightened and stylishly coiffed. She was dressed and gowned by the *couturière*, "Irene." When Judy posed in her new wardrobe, before three full-length mirrors, she told the designer, "I am no longer Andy Hardy's Betsy Booth."

Producer Joe Pasternak, who had bolted from Universal, where he had made a star out of Deanna Durbin, was put in charge of MGM's *Presenting Lily Mars*. He told Judy that he had wanted to work with her years ago when he shot *Three Smart Girls,* but that MGM had refused to release her, and that subsequently, he had chosen Durbin instead.

Judy found that reassuring, and she and Pasternak would work together in her future. "Judy was explosive and unpredictable," the producer said. "Durbin was much more staid. Every picture with Judy would turn into an event. You never knew what was going to happen on the set."

Norman Taurog, who had helmed Judy in the melodrama, *Little Nellie Kelly,* was hired to direct her again. "He appreciated my talent, and I responded to his direction," she said.

This was also the first time Judy worked with Chuck Waters, the Brooklyn-born director and choreographer who would have an enormous impact on her future career, helming her in such pictures as *Easter Parade* (1948).

Discounting Mickey Rooney, Van Heflin became Judy's first romantic leading man. In *Presenting Lily Mars,* he played Broadway director John Thornway, whom Judy, cast in the title role of Lily Mars, pursues for a break on Broadway. Of course, as anticipated, there would be a major roadblock in the form of reigning diva Isobel Rekay (Marta Eggerth), the singing sensation from Hungary. *[She had previously co-starred in Judy's* For Me and My Gal*].*

"Eggerth was too high brow for me," Judy said. "We avoided each other both on and off the screen."

She found Heflin a very accomplished actor. He had won a Best Supporting Actor Oscar for his role in *Johnny Eager* (1942), in which he had co-starred with Robert Taylor and Lana Turner.

In Judy's latter-day appraisal, she said, "Van was talented but, as a romantic leading man, he just didn't make it as a dashing, handsome star. He looked earnest and dependable, but there was just no charisma. Don't tell him I said that."

Enraged, Isobel walks out of Thornway's production and the role goes instead to Lily. But at the last minute, he concludes that she is not seasoned enough, and she ends up in a bit part near the end. However, by the following season on Broadway, she has become Mrs. John Thornway and a star, a "double dream come true."

Three strong performers were cast into key role: Richard Carlson as Owen Vail; Spring Byington as Mrs. Mars; and Fay Bainter as Mrs. Thornway.

Judy's songs included "Tom, Tom, the Piper's Son," "Every Little Movement," "When I Look at You," "Russian Rhapsody," "Where There's Music," "Three O'Clock in the Morning," and "Broadway Rhythm" backed up by the Tommy Dorsey Orchestra.

When he saw the final cut, Taurog said, "Judy is both a sparkling *comedienne* and a moving dramatic actress."

The orchestras of both Tommy Dorsey and Bob Crosby were called in for lavish production numbers. Dorsey

Center photo: "As my leading man, **Van Heflin** was a nice guy, but had no sex appeal."

Lower photo: **Judy:** "When I saw this publicity picture of me, I said, "Where did that Ugly Duckling of yore go?"

was billed as "The Sentimental Gentleman of Swing" because of his smooth-toned trombone playing. He was the younger brother of bandleader Jimmy Dorsey. Tommy's hit single was "I'll Never Smile Again."

Bob Crosby always lived in the shadow of his older brother Bing (Crosby), with whom Judy would work, frequently, in her future. In 1940, Bob had hired as his "girl singer" teenager Doris Day. He was best known for his group "The Bob-Cats," a New Orleans-inspired Dixieland jazz octet.

The New York Times referred to Judy as "fresh, pretty, perky, totally disarming, and gifted." Yet it suggested that MGM should let her grow up. Its rival, the *Herald-Tribune* wrote, "That juvenile darling, Judy Garland, goes to Broadway before you can say 'Jake Shubert,' marries a great producer, and is soon seen swaying in black tulle in a super-sumptuous musical staged by the super lucky fellow."

Photoplay asserted, "If ever there was a shining example of young lady stampedes to fame. It's Judy, who proves herself capable of the heavy assignment given her."

***

As biographer Fred Lawrence Guiles described Joseph L. Mankiewicz, "He was an imperious man who could have stepped inside Napoléon's boots during the retreat from Moscow and very possibly turned a monumental defeat into a triumphant victory."

"Joe," or "Josephus," as Judy called him, was the complete opposite of Tyrone Power, yet he was the tonic she needed to recover from yet another man who had gotten away. When Joe had first met her, she was a performing child, and he had been amazed at her powerful voice. When he came together with her again late in 1942, she was still recovering from a mental breakdown she had after aborting Power's child.

Thirteen years older than Judy, Joe was no raving beauty like Power, yet he was ruggedly handsome, with a winsome smile and a dynamo personality plus a reputation for having had most of his leading ladies fall in love with him.

He'd married his second wife, the Austrian actress, Rose Stradner, at the time Judy was filming *The Wizard of Oz*. She'd given Mankiewicz two sons, but around the time he reunited with Judy, Rose was shipped to the Menninger Clinic in Topeka, Kansas, where she was confined to (and remained in) a mental ward.

At MGM, Joe was viewed as a kind of Renaissance-era *Wünderkind*—a director, screenwriter, and producer. He was the brother of Herman J. Mankiewicz, also a screenwriter, who had won an Oscar for co-writing Orson Welles' *Citizen Kane*.

A future leading lady of Joe's, Anne Baxter, told author Darwin Porter, "Every one of us gals fell for Joe when he directed us. He had dancing eyes that saw the world with his own special kind of vision. He never gave a woman a bad direction but was always right on target about how a role should be played. Even when he took you to bed, he still kept directing

180

you into what to do, and he was always right, bringing the greatest pleasure to both of us."

When he started secretly dating a very young Judy, Mankiewicz was celebrating his great success with *The Philadelphia Story* (1940), starring James Stewart, Katharine Hepburn, and Cary Grant. He had also had another big success with Hepburn in *Woman of the Year* (1942), in which she was first teamed with Spencer Tracy.

After her first week of seeing Joe, Judy confided in Mickey Rooney when they came together to co-star in another movie, *Girl Crazy.* "Joe is the most wonderful man in the world," she claimed.

"Sorry to hear that," Rooney shot back. "I thought I was."

When Louis B. Mayer heard that Joe was dating "my child star," he summoned him to his office. "Come on now, fellow, you are a married man, and Judy could be your daughter."

"Not unless I got someone pregnant when I was thirteen," he responded.

"You're also a married man, and there could be a scandal," Meyer said. "Since your wife is away, why not shack up with Joan Crawford again? She's always available, and you're making a movie with her." *[The studio chief was referring to* Reunion in France *(1942) in which Crawford starred with John Wayne, seducing him—to her disappointment—off screen.]*

"I'm in love with Judy, but it's the love a man can have for his pet animal," Mankiewicz claimed.

"Whatever it is, drop her—and that's an order. She is our property, and I want to protect her career."

Joe did not obey Mayer's command and continued to see Judy privately. "I was a troubled man at the time with my wife in an asylum," he said. "Judy made me laugh with her wit and her charm. For a while, at least, she made me forget about Rose. She came along in my life at the right time, when I was looking for someone or something to fill those lonely hours before dawn."

"Judy was wild, always acting on instinct," he said. "She was a great bed partner, she had an endearing smile, and would sing 'Over the Rainbow' to me every night. She was of the age when a girl, just emerging from her teens, needs molding. I was the man for the job."

Joe really cared for Judy, and he began to sense how troubled she was, always pill popping and haunted by demons. She felt that Mayer and Ethel had combined forces to deny her a childhood. He noticed a disturbing tendency in the way she embellished stories. In several instances she related, she had taken the experience of someone else and told it as if it had happened to her.

During a visit to Los Angeles, Dr. Karl Menninger, the most famous psychiatrist in America, was introduced to Judy by Joe. His wife, Rose, was his patient in Topeka.

Joe asked Judy to communicate with him for an hour, and she did. Later, the doctor told Joe that she needed immediate treatment. He even suggested the impossible in that she should attend his Kansas clinic for a period that might stretch on for a year.

"She is a very damaged little person," he told Joe. "Her problems go way back to her childhood. The mother is a horrible influence on her. She's an addict and on a path of self-destruction, and, if she doesn't get help soon, she'll never live to see forty, much less fifty. She desperately needs to be cured."

For Judy to take a year out from a burgeoning career that was about to explode into super stardom was out of the question. When Joe presented the idea to her, she responded with, "That is about the most ridiculous idea I've ever heard, and I've heard some winners."

Eleanor Roosevelt, the most famous woman in the world at the time, in Topeka, Kansas with **Dr. Karl Menninger** in 1959.

Even then, Menninger warned Judy's mentors at MGM that she was desperaely in need of psychiatric counseling.

She did agree, however, to spend an hour every morning, five days a week, with Dr. Ernst Samuel, a former colleague of Dr. Sigmund Freud himself, and perhaps the best-known psychiatrist in Southern California. A former president of the Berlin Psychoanalytic Society, he'd fled from the Nazis in the late 1930s and set up a practice in Los Angeles. There, his couch had been visited by some of the leading stars of Hollywood, both male and female.

Columnist Adela Rogers St. Johns said: "Dr. Samuel knew more secrets of Hollywood stars than I ever found out. It would shock fans to learn how many male stars engaged in homosexual affairs, at least in their younger days., revelations that would amaze you. I'm sure he learned that virtually all actresses cheated on their husbands, often with lesbian friends as well as men."

After a few sessions with Dr. Samuel, Ethel began to see a change in her daughter. As her own marriage to Will Gilmore was collapsing, she turned more and more to trying to run Judy's life.

Judy had become increasingly self-assertive, one night yelling at Ethel, "I've had enough of your crap!"

Her mother was urging her to stop seeing Joe Mankiewicz. "You want to run my love life? You? A god damn expert, after two failed marriages? You've raised two older daughters, each in a disastrous marriage themselves…or out of it, as the case may be. Why don't you shut your god damn fucking trap!"

Judy had a short attention span, and she soon began missing appointments with Dr. Samuel, a fact he reported to Joe. "She should be a screenwriter like yourself. She invents stories. I don't think she has ever told me the truth in any session."

Judy admitted to her sister, Jimmie, that that was true. "In every session, I badger him with a pack of lies. I told him that my father used to force sex on me like Rita Hayworth's father used to do to her. I also claimed

182

the same thing about Will Gilmore during his marriage to Ethel. I told the shrink I've had lesbian affairs with Marlene Dietrich and Greta Garbo… and especially with Joan Crawford. I also told him that Mayer, too, forced sex on me when I was thirteen."

"I paid a price for my affair with Judy," Mankiewicz claimed. One afternoon in Mayer's office, he confronted both the studio chief and a raging, shouting Ethel. "Both of them not only wanted me to vow never to see Judy again, but they wanted me to stop sending her to a psychiatrist."

Charges flew back and forth until Joe could stand it no more. He turned on Mayer: "You're a sick old man and a sexual pervert yourself. Judy told me how you used to fondle her little breasts."

"GET OUT!" Mayer shouted at him. "To hell with your contract. Don't darken the gates of MGM ever again. No one, but no one, talks to me like that."

[Mankiewicz was immediately hired by Darryl F. Zanuck at Fox and went into pre-production on The Keys of the Kingdom *(1944) starring Gregory Peck as a Scots-born missionary priest in China.]*

One night at 3AM, Judy placed an urgent call to Joe announcing that she was pregnant. Although she was a known liar, he believed her this time. They had not always practiced birth control.

He decided it would be better if they slipped out of town and hid out for a while in a friend's apartment in Manhattan until she could be tested.

In a private railroad compartment, they rode the rails across America. Judy later recalled, "It was a honeymoon, the only honeymoon Joe and I would ever have."

In Manhattan, the test results came in revealing that Judy was not pregnant.

Joe left at once for Topeka, telling her that he had to be at the clinic since his wife was being released the following day. After that, he never answered her calls and tossed her letters to him into the fireplace.

Eventually, he sent her a telegram which read: "IT'S OVER! GET ON WITH YOUR LIFE AND LET ME GET ON WITH MINE."

[Moving over to Fox turned out to have been a smart career move for Joe Mankiewicz. His greatest pictures lay before him, including Best Director Oscars for A Letter to Three Wives *(1949), starring Kirk Douglas, among others, and* All About Eve *(1950), co-starring Bette Davis and Anne Baxter. He would also direct a notorious epic he*

Judy's first impression of **Joe Mankiewicz** was as a tweedy, pipe-smoking professorial type, who had been accepted at Columbia University at the age of fifteen.

According to Judy, "Joe was as smart as Artie Shaw thought he was. And he was just as witty as Oscar. I'm referring to Oscar Wilde, not Oscar Levant."

would forever regret, Cleopatra *(1963), starring Elizabeth Taylor and Richard Burton.*

When Rose returned from the asylum, Joe remained her husband until her death in 1958.

He married Rosemary Matthews in 1962 and was still married to her at the time of his death in 1993.]

***

Since Judy and Mickey Rooney were still top money-makers for MGM, Mayer decided to dust off a property from the story department and co-star them together once again. Featuring music by Ira and George Gershwin and a young Ginger Rogers, *Girl Crazy* had been a hit on Broadway in 1930. Two years later, RKO had adapted it into a film with Burt Wheeler, Dorothy Lee, and Robert Woolsey.

When MGM purchased the rights, their plan involved a sweeping transformation into a vehicle for their top dancers, Eleanor Powell and Fred Astaire, but that movie never got made.

An array of talented supporting players included the very accomplished Nancy Walker along with Frances Rafferty, Gil Stratton, Robert E. Strickland, "Rags" Ragland, and Guy Kibbee, backed up by the Tommy Dorsey Orchestra.

Fred Finklehoffe, one of the co-authors of the screenplay for Judy's *Me and My Gal,* was hired to create a completely revised script.

The crew consisted of familiar faces to Judy: Producer Alfred Freed, Director Busby Berkeley (later replaced by Norman Taurog), and as her music director, Roger Edens.

The dance director and choreographer, Charles ("Chuck") Walters, worked with Judy on her dance numbers. She also dated him two or three times. "He was brilliant as a choreographer," she told June Allyson, who was making her film debut in *Girl Crazy.* "But as a man to get giddy about, forget it."

As the film's director, Berkeley was not in top form, experiencing what he called "personal demons." He and Judy clashed from the beginning. "I felt he had this big black bull whip and was lashing me every day with it," she told Freed. "I worked with him for two weeks, and I wonder if I will make it for another day with him at the helm."

That and other reasons led to his dismissal. He was replaced by Judy's previous director, Norman Taurog.

Film historian Frank N. Magill said, "Taurog's work reflected the beginning of a new style in film musicals in that the songs were used for the development of the movie's characters instead of just routinely being thrown in for diversion, often having nothing to do with the plot."

In addition to Judy's big "I've Got Rhythm," number, staged by Berkeley before his firing, Judy also sang "But Not for Me," "Embraceable You," and "Bidin' My Time."

As for plot, the film opens with Danny Churchill (Rooney) cast as a philandering playboy at Yale University. His major is "girls and more girls!" Infuriated, his father takes him out of Yale and ships him out west to the all-male Cody College of Mines and Agriculture, a school facing serious financial difficulties and the possibility that if will soon be shut down by the state's governor when the term ends.

Along the way, Rooney meets Ginger Gray (Judy), the local postmistress. Their relationship gets off to a rough start, but he falls for her. To save the school's finances, they stage a Wild West Rodeo musical, which evolves into a big hit. *[By now formulaic, this plot device had been repeated, to the point of fatigue, in several Garland-Rooney pairings of their recent past.]*

Mickey angers Judy when he crowns not her, but the governor's daughter, cast with Rafferty, as "Queen of the Rodeo." But Judy forgives him when she learns that his motive involved keeping on the good side of the governor and saving the school from foreclosure. After the rodeo, the college is flooded with new applicants—especially, girls wanting to storm this all-male bastion of young college guys.

Showtime & Hee-Haw at the Rodeo

Judy and Mickey—two urban kids—maintaining the illusion that they're country singers in *Girl Crazy.*

During the shoot, Judy's health fell into serious decline, her weight dropping to ninety-four pounds. Dr. Marc Rabwin, who remained a dear family friend, ordered her to bed for three weeks.

Rooney was very disturbed by her declining physical condition. "She'd take four pills, then another four, and so on until she's lost count of just how many of those little devils she swallowed. I loved her dearly, but she blamed everybody else for her condition—her mother, Mayer, the studio itself. She didn't want to take the blame for killing Judy Garland, the Judy Garland the whole world loved."

"We had a big hit, MGM grossing $3.7 million for *Girl Crazy,*" Rooney said. "Yet that was never reflected in our paychecks: I got $68,000, Judy $28,000. I also got a bonus of $25,000, she got no bonus at all. In my career so far, I had not earned one million dollars. This should lay to rest all the bullshit people write about how I pissed away millions of bucks. I should have taken Judy by the hand and gone to Mayer and demanded $10 million each."

Girl Crazy became one of the big hits of 1943, a war-ravished year when most studios, including MGM, were turning out a grim roster of mostly battlefield and war movies.

The New York Times wrote, "The immortal Mickey Rooney is an entertainer to his fingertips. Judy Garland sings and acts like an earthbound angel to temper his brashness. Well, they can do almost anything they wish, and we'll like it in spite of ourselves."

Also in reference to *Girl Crazy*, the *New York Herald Tribune* stated, "Rooney and Garland are almost the whole show. Miss Garland looks very sweet as an out-of-doors girl. She holds up her half of the show, doing for the music what Rooney does for the story."

Time magazine claimed, "If Judy Garland were not so profitably good at her own game, she would obviously be a dramatic cinema actress with profit to all."

***

After a successful appearance on Broadway, June Allyson signed a contract linking her career to Metro-Goldwyn-Mayer in 1943. Shortly thereafter, she was cast with Rooney and Jody in *Girl Crazy*. She was assigned a song, "Treat Me Rough."

"I played a 'Betty Hutton' type, a little tough," she said.

Before facing the camera, she hung out on the set watching Judy perform with Rooney. At the time, she was reluctant to introduce herself.

On the morning of the shoot, as she was waiting at a bus stop for public transport to Culver City, a chauffeur-driven limousine pulled up at the corner. Judy Garland, in the back seat, rolled down the window. "Allyson, get your ass in the car. The light's about to change!"

Startled, Allyson recognized Judy and got in with her before Judy said, "I recognize you as that girl who was hanging out on the set yesterday and the day before. Spying on us, right?"

"I'm sorry, Allyson said. "It's all so new to me. I go one-on-one with Mickey today, and I'm terrified. I threw up this morning."

"Don't worry," Judy said. "Mick will help you get through it."

Allyson noted that Judy was attired in slacks. Beginning the following day, she would adopt the same attire of "a girl in pants."

That morning marked the beginning of a long-term friendship between the two stars. They soon discovered they had much in common, and they would often discuss

To most of **June Allyson**'s fans, she's not immediately recognizable in this picture where she's interacting with **Mickey Rooney** in *Girl Crazy*.

It was her first Hollywood film, and MGM had not yet established the "girl next door" image that caused her to be typecast, for years to come, as "America's Sweetheart."

their difficult childhoods. "Judy would tell me stories that made me tear up, and then I would follow with tales of my own that made her shed a tear or two. We became soulmates."

"We should have been jealous of each other, but we really weren't." Allyson said. "Even when the subject of men came up. She didn't object when I started dating her former husband, David Rose. Also, I fixed her up with two rising young stars at MGM, Peter Lawford and Van Johnson. Of course, in those cases, I don't know whether she should thank me or not."

"June and I were *confidantes*, telling naughty stories about our secret affairs, all the things we were up to when night blanketed Tinseltown," Judy said.

When he heard that his new star, June Allyson, was dating Judy's divorced husband, Mayer summoned her to his office, demanding that she drop Rose. Whereas Judy had defied him, Allyson, newer on the lot and with less of a profit-generating history, was afraid to stand up to him. That evening, she broke off her relationship, telling the composer that it was "all off" between them.

Later in life, Allyson recalled that "Judy was the only person I could tell about my secret affair with Desi Arnaz behind Lucille Ball's back. If truth be known, it was Desi who took my virginity, not my first husband, Dick Powell, as I had so loudly maintained."

Like Judy, she, too, had dated Robert Stack, and—as he'd done with Judy—Stack led her to the bed of the then-rising politician, John F. Kennedy. "I went for him," Allyson confessed, "but he aimed higher. Later, I slipped around and shacked up with Ronald Reagan, too."

Judy was startled, even a bit envious, at how suddenly movie stardom came to Allyson. After starring opposite Van Johnson in *Two Girls and a Sailor* (1944), she was on her way to becoming the American archetype of "The Girl Next Door" and "America's Sweetheart" in an era when thousands of embattled G.I.'s were overseas and desperately homesick.

When she met with Judy, she said, "I'm not doing so bad for little Miss Eleanor Geisman, born in the Bronx."

Allyson tried to explain her sudden appeal to Louella Parsons: "I have big teeth. My eyes disappear when I smile. My voice is funny, Madame Bull Frog. I certainly can't sing like Judy Garland. I don't dance like Cyd Charisse, certainly not like Ann Miller. But women identify with me. And while men desire Betty Grable, they take me

"After *Girl Crazy*," **June Allyson** claimed, "MGM tried to pit Judy and me against each other for film roles. Some producer would say to me, 'You know that if you don't behave yourself, we've always got Judy. We'll give her the role because she can do anything.' And then they'd say to Judy, 'If you don't behave yourself, we've got this new kid on the block, June Allyson, and she can step right into your shoes.'"

home to meet mom."

She was excited late one Saturday afternoon when she visited Judy's home. "Your David (Rose), Peter Lawford, and John Kennedy were just steps up to the man I'm going to marry, Dick Powell. He's a bit older than me, and Mayer is against it, *but I'm going to marry Dick Powell.* Mayer said he will put me on suspension if I do. But I'm saying 'I do' in spite of his threat."

Before she left that day, Allyson told Judy, "I have an awful confession to make, and those gossip columnists would go batshit if they find out. But I can tell you. In my heart of hearts, I'm a nympho. I can't help myself. Men turn me on. I just hope that Dick will be an understanding husband."

***

As early as 1940, MGM considered filming *Thousands Cheer* as a vehicle for Judy in her first glamour role. The project was shelved but revived again in 1943 when Mayer green-lighted it as a morale booster for U.S. servicemen and their families on the homefront.

Instead of Judy, Producer Joe Pasternak and Director George Sidney cast songbird Kathryn Grayson in the lead opposite Gene Kelly. He plays a low-ranking G.I. (a private) who's pursuing the daughter of his commanding officer. Supporting players included Mary Astor, John Bole, Ben Blue, and Frances Rafferty.

Both Mickey Rooney and Judy would appear only briefly as guest stars. During Rooney's brief appearance, he impersonated Clark Gable and Lionel Barrymore as inspired by their 1938 film, *Test Pilot.*

Judy's shining moment in *Thousands Cheer* was her number "The Joint is Jumpin' at Carnegie Hall" where she was accompanied by conductor/pianist José Iturbi making his film debut. Other guest stars included Lena Horne singing "Honeysuckle Rose," judged by the American Film Institute as among the Top One Hundred songs of the Twentieth Century. Also popping up in this musical were Red Skelton, Eleanor Powell, Lucille Ball, Donna Reed, and child star Mar-

In *Thousands Cheer*, **Judy**—one of thirty stars who appeared in it—coaxes classical pianist Jose Iturbi into accompanying her delivery of a morale-building boogie-woogie.

garet O'Brien.

Music derived from a wide range of composers, including both Ira and George Gershwin, Max Steiner, Jerome Kern, Irving Berlin, and Richard Rodgers. Kelly's star moment came when he danced with a mop to the music of "Let Me Call You Sweetheart."

The New York Times defined this midwar morale booster "a grab bag of delights." *Thousands Cheer* earned $3.8 million at the box office. It was nominated for three Oscars: Best Cinematography, Best Score, and Best Art Direction.

During the shoot, Judy's love life seemed to have tanked until she received a call from a former beau, Robert Stack, on leave from the U.S. Navy.

He recalled, "When this old sailor returned from the service and phoned his former girlfriends, I found they had moved on to other loves. But Judy came through for me. In fact, she said, 'Robert Stack can put his shoes under my bed anytime, day or night.'"

***

With the war over and movie stars returning from the battlefields of Europe and Asia, Hollywood entered its post-war years. Any although Judy didn't make all (or many) of the films envisioned and proposed for her, she was on the verge of filming one of the milestones of her career.

In addition to that, additional handsome lovers and even a not particularly handsome future husband loomed in her immediate future.

Many critics maintain that Judy Garland never looked better, certainly never more glamourous, than she did late in 1942 and early in 1943. Some fans thought this dance scene in **Presenting Laura Mars** was just as dazzling as anything Lana Turner appeared in at around the same time.

IF THE FATES AND JUDY'S SCHEDULE HAD ALLOWED

In the mid-1940s, as a crowd-pleaser, Judy Garland was hot and in demand, with a voice that could melt steel (or the hardest hearts), and a twenty-something physicality that stopped the cameras. The question was, "how many movies could MGM maneuver her into without causing her to either break down or lead to impossible scheduling conflicts? Here is an abbreviated layout of movies which, for one complicated reason or another, contained "JUDY' ROLES THAT GOT AWAY."

"If Metro could have put Judy in every single film they made, they would have."

—June Allyson

190

LAVENDER HIP

JUDY PALS AROUND WITH GUYS WHO PLAY AROUND IN
GAY GOLDEN AGE HOLLYWOOD

MEET ME IN ST. LOUIS, BABY!

THE CINEMATIC TRIUMPH OF NOSTALGIA-SOAKED AMERICANA

WATCHING THE CLOCK

JUDY SLOGS THROUGH A WARTIME LOVE STORY
AS HER CO-DEPENDENT CO-STAR,
ROBERT WALKER,
GETS SUICIDAL OVER JENNIFER JONES

MORE ZIEGFELD FOLLIES

THIS TIME, IT'S THE VERSION RELEASED IN 1946

JUDY IS SOMETIMES A GOOD GIRL,
AND SOMETIMES SHE'S A BAD GIRL, TOO,
BUT WHEN THE WAR ENDS, SHE BECOMES FAMOUS AS
A HARVEY GIRL

"Judy Garland often wanted to please, but she could also be strong-willed, independent, and even defiant. She was making millions for MGM, and she knew she had Louis B. Mayer by the balls."

—Joseph Mankiewicz

"Judy wanted to enjoy the extraordinary life of a movie star, for which she was basically unsuited. Her talent had matured much more quickly than her mind. On the one hand, she wanted to enjoy affairs with both men and women; on the other hand, this led to further confusion, because she felt guilty about them. In effect, she managed to worry about not worrying."

—Author David Shipman

"Judy is a Gemini, and that confers on her a twin personality. She could be the sweetest thing who ever walked onto a sound stage. When crossed, or even when she viewed something as crossing her, she could become a raging tarantula. Back in the late 1930s, MGM had sold her as Betsy Booth in those Andy Hardy films and also as Dorothy in The Wizard of Oz. She was the complete opposite of those two characters."

—Vincente Minnelli

"Sounds to me like another one of those god damn dewy ingénue pieces of shit,"

—Judy Garland, after hearing Vincente Minnelli's inaugural description of *Meet Me in St. Louis*

Judy as a major-league cover girl during the closing months of World War II.

Here she is on the cover of *LIFE* in their December, 1944 edition. Credited for her morale-building during the darkest years of the war, she wears her hair and lipstick in a style that's **"VICTORY RED."**

In Hollywood, June Allyson phoned Judy to extend an invitation to a small dinner party she was hosting Saturday night, attended by two of her newly minted male friends, the rising star at MGM, Van Johnson, and Keenan Wynn, the character actor who had starred with Judy in *For Me and My Gal.*

"Sounds like a double date to me," Judy answered. "Which are you fixing me up with? I've got to tell you. It can't be Wynn. He's a fun guy but not my type. I'll take Van. To judge from his photographs, he's quite handsome."

She was aware that Wynn had married the former stage actress, Eva Lynn Abbott, in 1939. "Will Keenan's wife be there?"

"No way," Allyson answered. "You see, Keenan and Van are secret lovers."

"Aha!," Judy said. "How do I fit into this happy arrangement?"

"Mayer has heard the rumors that Van is a homosexual, and he's ordered him to be seen out on the town dating females," Allyson said. "We need you to go out with him, hit all the high spots, get photographed in the newspapers and magazines."

"Since I'm not deeply involved right now, I'll go for that," Judy said.

That Saturday night at Allyson's home became memorable in Judy's life. It would mark the beginning of Judy's life-long friendship with Van. "The four of us had a hell of a good time," she said.

She found the freckle-faced, red-haired actor "a delight." He was equally drawn to her, especially her wit and charm.

Lavender undercurrents in *Easy to Wed* (1946):

Two views of its male stars (long-time off-screen lovers **Keenan Wynn and Van Johnson**) interconnecting with (upper photo) **Lucille Ball** and (lower photo) other forms of physicality.

On Broadway in 1939, Van Johnson had appeared in the musical, *Too Many Girls.* In 1940, he was cast in its film adaptation. On Broadway, he was also the understudy for Gene Kelly in *Pal Joey*.

In the early 1940s, Van formed a relationship with Wynn when they'd appeared in minor parts in *Somewhere I'll Find You* (1942), starring Lana Turner and Clark Gable, who at the time were having an affair.

Mayer had cast Johnson and Allyson—in the first of their eventual five screen teamings—in the light-hearted wartime musical, *Two Girls and a Sailor* (1944). He ordered his publicity department to promote them as "America's Sweethearts." Allyson would become "the girl next door," with Van hyped as her male counterpart.

In the evenings that followed, Judy and Van were seen together at all the hot spots; dancing together at the Cocoanut Grove and dining at Chasen's.

"I wasn't jealous," Wynn said, "sitting at home with my wife while Van and Judy had fun. I think Van plugged her two or three times, but for the most part it was platonic. They became great friends."

Later in life, Wynn recalled, "I think her going out with Van marked the beginning of Judy's reputation as a 'fag hag.' For the rest of her life, she always hung out with a gay crowd. She could let her hair down, gossip with the guys, laugh, tell dirty jokes, and sing hit songs from musicals at the piano. In time, gay men adopted Dorothy's 'Over the Rainbow' as their virtual theme song."

"Van and I suspected that Judy made up some of the tall tales she hilariously relayed," Wynn claimed. "But who cares? Why let truth intrude into a good story?"

Within the ranks of MGM, Judy became a charter member of "The Freed Unit," a core group of musicians and dancers who were instrumental in churning out all those MGM musicals. Most of the guys were gay, but not Arthur Freed himself.

As they were increasingly seen out and on the town together, Judy and Van were written up as "the lovebirds," much to the delight of Mayer, who wanted Van to be portrayed as heterosexual.

Allyson also dated Van, and soon, his supposed heterosexual lifestyle was promulgated even further. *[Ironically, in reality, Allyson was a nymphomaniac, and he was a serial seducer of young men. According to Van,*

Although they'd be mismatched in a real-life dating scene, **Van Johnson and June Allyson**, appear here in the fifth of the six movies in which they co-starred together as "America's Sweethearts," in *Too Young to Kiss* (1951).

To modern-day gays and lesbians, what is remarkable is the energy that the studio spent to conceal Johnson's preference for men and Allyson's nymphomania (for men), all throughout the years of Johnson's most intense romantic bonding with Keenan Wynn.

"U.S. servicemen are returning in droves from the battlefields, and many are settling in Los Angeles. June and I have our pick — one, two, or three — every night if we wish."]

"Van and I attended plays together at the Pasadena Playhouse," Judy said. "It was party party. And the Freed guys liked to throw costume parties. I remember Van came as Captain Blood, a swashbuckler like Errol Flynn, and I came dressed as Jeanette MacDonald in an operetta. Keenan went with us dressed like Billie Burke, describing himself as 'The Good Fairy' from *The Wizard of Oz.*"

Judy was amazed at how rapidly Van rose to stardom at MGM. His breakthrough came in the wartime drama, *A Guy Named Joe* (1943), co-starring Spencer Tracy and Irene Dunne.

During the months it took to film it, Van suffered a serious car accident on Hollywood Boulevard that nearly killed him. That led to a metal plate being inserted in his head, and left him with forehead scars that makeup could not completely hide.

Chuck Walters, a prominent choreographer and dance coach, was legendarily well-suited for the fragile egos and dance-related insecurities of A-list stars, including Judy Garland.

He's shown here in a publicity photo of an aging **Joan Crawford**, rehearsing her in routines for *Torch Song* (1953).

Tracy, according to Van, had fallen in love with him and refused to finish the picture with another actor. Consequently, the entire production was delayed until Van returned from the hospital.

On his first date with Judy since the accident, Van described Tracy's romantic involvement with him. Judy reacted by saying, "So he got around to you, too. He took my cherry when I was fifteen."

"He's been wonderful promoting my career," Van said. "A young, struggling actor has to do what he has to do."

Judy was pleased to see Allyson and Van click as a screen team in a series of pictures in the mid-1940s. Each movie generated profits despite negative reviews from the *National Lampoon*. In 1946, it "defined" Van as the worst actor of the year, along with Allyson, who was referred to as the worst actress of the year.

Chuck Walters, a master choreographer and later director, was a key player in the Freed Unit. He had dated Judy on occasion, but she soon learned that he preferred dating any of several male dancers instead. *[Judy also learned that Vincente Minnelli had seduced Walters when he'd helmed him in a seven-month run on Broadway (1936-37) of* The Show Is On.

In the years that followed, Walters directed her in Easter Parade *(1948) and in* Summer Stock *(1950). He would also direct Allyson and Peter Lawford in* Good News *(1947).]*

Walters would become a major mentor in Judy's career, usually rehearsing her behind the scenes. Growing up in Anaheim, he said he had always wanted to be a dancer, and he finally fled from his home in California and moved to Manhattan. In 1933, he danced with Imogene Coca in *New Faces*.

Then he met an even more important choreographer, Robert Alton, and they fell in love. [*Around the same time, Dorothy Kilgallen, in her popular newspaper column that focused on Broadway, referred to Walters as looking like "the brunette version of the Duke of Windsor."*]

In Hollywood, Walters began a long-term relationship with John Darrow, who had been a juvenile star in silent films of the 1920s. Judy was a frequent visitor to the couple's lavishly decorated villa in Malibu, often finding herself the only woman in a party of thirty, even forty, men.

Minnelli was and had always been a bit jealous of Walters. Nonetheless, on occasion, he called on him for help and advice. That included when he needed inspiration and help in the staging of "The Night They Invented Champagne" in the hit musical *Gigi* (1958), a picture starring Leslie Caron and Louis Jourdan, the French actor.

Before her 1945 marriage to Dick Powell, Allyson had a fling with an English actor, Peter Lawford, when he was under contract to MGM. She complained to Judy, "He's bisexual and prefers only oral sex."

"Pass him on to me," Judy said. "Unlike you, it's my favorite sexual expression."

"Okay," she said. "But you must not let Keenan Wynn find out that Peter is also having an affair with Van Johnson."

"Oh, Hollywood..." Judy answered. "Everybody's screwing everybody else, especially one's boyfriend."

***

Producer Arthur Freed and director Vin-

Judy as the girl next door, **with Tom Drake,** as the boy next door, who—according to the plot—just happened to be studying to be a lawyer. He had a bright future, and was secretly but madly in love with Esther (i.e., Judy).

Meet Me in St. Louis was Tom Drake's largest, meatiest, and most widely publicized role.

On the Trolley, singing about the Trolley, Judy starred in this ode to small-town America during the peak of its industrial expansion.

As a calculated gambit, *Meet Me in St. Louis* fell on fertile soil. World War II was still raging, and audiences were eager for reminders of a less anguished and more wholesome overview of the American identity.

cente Minnelli teamed up to produce one of Judy's three most memorable movies, *Meet Me in St. Louis* (1944), released in the final full year of World War II. *[Nazi Germany and the Empire of Japan surrendered the following year.]*

A halcyon and frothy musical, it returned viewers to St. Louis in 1903 as that city prepares for a World's Fair.

Judy had star billing over an impressive cast. She plays Esther Smith, who falls in love with "the boy next door," John Truitt (Tom Drake).

In time, *Variety* defined it as one of Hollywood's all-time box office champions, representing a financial triumph for MGM, topped only by *Gone With the Wind* (1939).

Meet Me in St. Louis represented the pinnacle of Judy's star power, and she introduced two songs that she would continue to sing in concerts for the rest of her life. "Have Yourself a Merry Little Christmas" (which at some parties became as indispensable as eggnog), and "The Trolley Song."

The movie was adapted by Irving Brecher (its chief writer) and Fred F. Finklehoffe, based on a series of short stories by Sally Benson first published in *The New Yorker* magazine under

Margaret O'Brien played Judy's little sister, Tootie, in *Meet Me in St. Louis.*

"I knew that MGM was planning to turn her into its version of Shirley Temple in the 1930s," Judy said. "I had to watch her like a hawk, fearing she'd steal the picture from me. She was sickly sweet and could she ever cry."

the title of *5135 Kensington*, the (fictional) address in St. Louis of the Smith family. The collection was later adapted into a novel entitled *Meet Me in St. Louis.*

[Although Finkelhoffe had worked on previous Judy pictures, most of the scriptwriting fell on Brecher because Finkelhoffe bolted, having accepted another assignment before it was completed.]

The Smith family is the focus of the script, and each member of the cast was carefully vetted by Minnelli.

Filmed on the back lot of MGM, the setting replicated St. Louis as it looked in 1903, evocative of a painting by Thomas Eakin. Minnelli would be working in Technicolor for the first time.

"When I first pitched the plot to Judy, she

looked at me as if I were committing armed robbery," Minnelli said.

"Sounds to me like another one of those god damn dewy *ingénue* pieces of shit," she said.

She lodged strenuous objections to playing a seventeen-year-old girl. "Dorothy is dead and gone. I buried her when I made *Presenting Lily Mars*. I want glamourous, grown-up roles, but here I am again, playing Betsy Booth in one of those Andy Hardy stinkers."

"When he first heard of me being cast in the role, even Joe Mankiewicz sent word, 'This picture will set back your career twenty years.'"

What finally made up her mind about accepting the role of Esther was that she was broke. Will and Ethel Gilmore had been in charge of her money, spending most of it on themselves or else investing it in disastrous business ventures.

She was deeply in debt to the Internal Revenue Service. Bankers were threatening to foreclose on her home. She was also, if she rejected the part, facing suspension from MGM. Therefore, she had no choice but to go ahead with *Meet Me in St. Louis*.

The eccentric Dorothy Ponedel was assigned to create Judy's makeup. "Bring her on," she said. "I created the Marlene Dietrich look in the 1930s. But in Marlene's case, I had a lot to work with. From what I've seen of Judy, I've been assigned a less than perfect girl, one with irregular teeth. Caps are called for, and I've got to do some-

Here, the dutiful daughter, **Judy**, helps her mother get dressed for a party. This was the second time **Mary Astor** had played Judy's mother, the first being in *Listen, Darling* (1938).

The film was a celebration of turn-of-the 20th Century St. Louis and of small-town America before the ravages of the 20th Century.

In an old-fashioned kitchen, **Mary Astor** (left) as the Smith family's matriarch, argues with their cook/housekeeper/overseer, Katie, as played by **Marjorie Main**, about the degree of spiciness of this year's batch of homemade catsup.

thing about the shape of that impossible nose. I'll raise her eyebrows and make her bottom lip fuller, and I'll use tweezers to rid her of that Simian hairline."

The score had been written by Ralph Blane and Hugh Martin, with music directed by George Stoll. Its dance director was Chuck Walters, and George Folsey was the chief cameraman. Musical adaptation was by Judy's ever-faithful Roger Edens.

Freed told Minnelli that in five years, Blane and Martin would be as famous as Rodgers and Hart.

Minnelli spent sleepless nights agonizing over the casting of Judy's supporting players, wanting each actor to be letter perfect and on cue. "I wasn't going to depend on makeup. I wanted the characters to already look like the people they would portray, especially all members of the Smith family, including her mother, father, sisters, and brother."

From the beginning, Judy feared that she'd be upstaged by the emerging child star Margaret O'Brien in her scene-stealing role of "Tootie." Fifteen years younger than Judy, O'Brien had been signed by MGM at the age of four. She became one of the most popular child stars in cinema history, filling the shoes outgrown by Shirley Temple over at Fox.

The daughter of a circus performer, O'Brien had her breakthrough role in the film *Journey for Margaret* (1942). Her most memorable role would be as Judy's feisty but fragile little sister, Tootie, in *Meet Me in St. Louis.*

O'Brien and June Allyson became known as MGM's "Criers," shedding tears on command. According to O'Brien, "I wanted to cry better than June, and she tried to cry better than me. When I couldn't cry on cue, my mother, Gladys, taunted me and claimed she was calling makeup to give me false tears. Then I'd think to myself, 'They'll say I'm not as good as June,' and I'd start to cry."

The patriarch of the Smith clan is the crotchety Alonzo Smith, played by veteran actor Leon Ames. He puts his family into an uproar when he announces at table that all of them might be relocating to New York so that he can accept a promotion within his company.

Ames was often cast as a father figure, a bit stuffy and exasperated by the younger generation. He was on the dawn of his most famous role, that of district attorney Kyle Sackett in the *film*

Vincente Minnelli coaching a sometimes uncooperative **Judy** for her role in *Meet Me In St. Louis.*

During the first three weeks of filming, Judy grew impatient with his demands for retake after retake *[in one instance, as many as seventeen takes in a row]* before she satisfied him.

"He made me feel I could not act. We often had cross words."

noir, *The Postman Always Rings Twice* (1946), co-starring Lana Turner and John Garfield.

[Other Smith family roles would be awarded to veteran character actor Harry Davenport as the eccentric Grandpa. Actress Joan Carroll played Agnes, another one of Judy's sisters, and the role of her brother "Lon" (who was Princeton bound) went to Henry H. Daniels, Jr.

Outside of the family circle, yet still a part of it, was Katie, the no-nonsense family cook and maid, cast with Marjorie Main. She had become famous in the movies playing raucous, rough, and cantankerous women.

When filming Meet Me in St. Louis, *Main was on the dawn of her break-through role as Ma Kettle in* The Egg and I *(1947), starring Claudette Colbert and Fred MacMurray. Main and Percy Kilbride virtually stole the picture from those two established stars. Ma and Pa Kettle got such rave reviews that Universal cast them in a long-enduring series of adventures which rescued the studio from bankruptcy.*

Robert Sully was cast as Warren Sheffield, whom Judy's sister, Rose, wants to marry. Her competition is June Lockhart in the role of Lucille Ballard.

Chill Wills, as always, made a striking (and very macho) appearance as Mr. Neel, the man who delivers ice. Although he was mostly known for his roles in Westerns, he also became the voice of Francis the Talking Mule in a series of comedies. In Giant *(1956), starring Rock Hudson, James Dean, and Elizabeth Taylor, Wills played "Uncle Brawley."*

Cast as Colonel Darly, Hugh Marlowe is remembered today chiefly for his performance as the playwright in All About Eve *(1950), starring Bette Davis and Anne Baxter.*

Darryl Hickman, as Johnny Tevis, was uncredited as "neighborhood boy."]

Mary Astor tried to convince her that the very demanding Minnelli knew what he was doing and was only concerned with how she would come across. "Listen to him, Judy, it's for your own good," the older actress cautioned the younger one.

It didn't help relations between Judy and Minnelli when Tom Drake told her that the director found Lucille Bremer "right on the mark," rarely requiring a retake.

Minnelli's exact words were, "Lucille delivers her lines with sincerity. You believe her, whereas Judy seems to be mocking the lines in the script."

During the filming of *Meet Me in St. Louis,* Judy began a pattern of behavior that would in time lead to her dismissal from MGM. She would arrive later and later, often keeping cast and crew idling for anywhere from three to four hours—that is, when she showed up at all. Some days she called in sick.

June Lockhart, waiting to do a scene with Judy, claimed that she stayed in her dressing room for four hours before finally emerging to face the camera. "When she did, she didn't know her lines and seemed to be in some drugged-out state."

Minnelli liked to rehearse his cast, but often, Judy would bolt from the set, driving her car toward the entrance. Minnelli alerted the security guards to block her and force her to come back.

But as the days went by, Judy began to come around, Minnelli claiming, "She put as much into her scenes of drama as she did her musical numbers. She was trusting my directions more and more."

On the set, Gladys O'Brien hovered over her daughter Margaret, aided also by an interfering aunt who seemed to want to direct the picture herself. "Gladys was a stage mother from hell, reminding me of Ethel and all her worst traits," claimed Judy. "Margaret even had to get her permission to go to the toilet."

One scene called for Margaret to become hysterical and run out the front door and knock down the snowmen in the front yard. But she was feuding with her mother that day and could not cry, which she usually did at any director's command.

Gladys came over to Minnelli and gave him some instructions. "If you want her to cry, threaten that you're going to kill her pet dog. Describe a gruesome death."

Reluctantly, he followed her advice and confronted the child actress. He told her he was going to kill her dog and make the animal's death as painful as possible. "You'll hear him yelping in agony."

Reacting in horror, Margaret burst into tears. Minnelli called for action, and the scene was pulled off in one take—except Margaret could not stop crying for the next hour.

Minnelli felt guilty about his deception and for causing the young girl such pain. "My direction of Margaret and Judy in the famous cakewalk scene came off much smoother."

O'Brien had nothing but praise for Judy. "She did indeed treat me like I was her little sister. During the shoot, I lost my front teeth and a dentist put in artificial ones. In one very exuberant scene, my teeth seemed to fly out of my mouth and hit Judy in the face."

The Halloween scene was the most unusual, the most horrific, and the most controversial in the movie. In the costume department, Minnelli selected a man's coat which he ordered Margaret to wear inside out. She also wore pajama bottoms and a derby.

Makeup was told to smear her face with burnt cork. *Time* magazine later wrote, "Margaret O'Brien's self-terrified Halloween adventures richly set against the firelight, dark streets, and the rusty confabulation of fallen leaves, bring this section of the film very near the first-rate."

Minnelli was flabbergasted when the film ran too long, and the Halloween scene was set to end up on the cutting room floor. Over his almost hysterical protests, it was saved at the last minute.

Belcher recalled Minnelli coming into his office, "bawling like a baby." Freed and Mayer wanted to cut out the Halloween sequence.

"That scene is why I signed on in the first place," he said.

Belcher agreed it should be retained and went to see Freed about it. The producer listened, then burst into fury. "Who in the fuck do you think you are? You're just a hired hand. I'm the damn producer! You get your sodomized ass out of my office."

The Halloween scene was shown before a preview audience to rave reviews, so Freed and Mayer agreed to retain Tootie's trick-or-treating *tour de force*.

While Minnelli was still involved in the final editing, Judy celebrated her twenty-first birthday. He presented her with a metallic evening bag, which she cherished.

"I thought Judy was one of the best actresses I've ever come across, both technique wise and innately. She was just fabulous in comedy or tragedy. She had a very brittle type of humor that you would expect to find on people who had been around for years and years, like John Barrymore. It's a sophistication you don't find in average people. It's the genius type of sophistication, all this when she was only twenty-one."

That was Drake's assessment to the press. Privately, he had a different point of view, which he shared with one of his lovers, Van Johnson. "Judy was a real hellcat. She went after me like a tigress, and at first, I resisted. One night, she forced me into sex, and it was a complete disaster. I was turned off by her and just couldn't perform. She mocked my failure. A man never forgives an insult like that."

Ironically, Van had been considered for Drake's role himself, but he evaluated the part as too small.

"Minnelli had better luck with me than Judy did," Drake claimed. "At least I could satisfy him when he serviced me, although personally, I found his looks repulsive. I went for good-looking guys like Van or Peter Lawford."

When Louis B. Mayer sat through the final, edited cut of *Meet Me in St. Louis,* he told Iva Koverman, his secretary, and some other aides, "That fag, Vincente Minnelli, has done what no other director has ever done. He has made my little hunchback look beautiful."

***

In spite of all the trouble he had during the production of *Meet Me in St. Louis,* especially with Judy, Arthur Freed nonetheless called it "my favorite film."

Judy's favorite song from it was "Boys and Girls Are Like You and I" by Rodgers and Hammerstein, but Freed had to cut it when the movie ran too long.

After watching the final cut, Judy walked over to Freed and said, "Arthur, remind me not to tell you what kind of picture to make."

One reviewer claimed, "*Meet Me in St. Louis* evoked an era when a suitor arrived on the doorstep of his lady-in-waiting with a ten-pound box of Page & Shaw Candies."

Another critic noted, "The picture is a marvelous re-creation of the gaslight era with men in straw boaters and ice cream trousers, the women in gowns of flowing creations. The set decorations were perfectly in style of what an upper middle-class home looked like in the Middle West of America in those bygone days."

Time magazine claimed, "The real love story is not between Judy and the boy next door, but between a happy family and a way of living. Will it be New York or St. Louis, the hometown of the Smith family?"

Life magazine topped all its competitors by featuring Judy on its edition of December 11, 1944. Brecher and Finkleshoffe were nominated for an Oscar for Best Screenplay.

"The Trolley Song" was nominated for Best Song, but lost the Oscar to that sentimental favorite, "Swinging on a Star," which was featured in the movie *Going My Way,* starring Bing Crosby.

Like Judy before her, O'Brien received an Oscar for "Outstanding Child Actress of 1944." Her maid later stole the Oscar statuette and disappeared. It did not resurface until forty years later.

In 1959, *Meet Me in St. Louis* was remade for television, starring Jane Powell, Jeanne Craine, Patty Duke, Walter Pidgeon, Ed Wynn, Tab Hunter, and Myrna Loy.

***

Dan Loper was a dancer at MGM, part of the "Freed Unit," and he later became a well-known fashion designer. Even though he was a homosexual, he had formed a liaison with the Brooklyn-born actress, Ruth Brady.

She had been discovered in a beauty pageant in Atlantic City and later appeared on Broadway before being offered an MGM contract.

Late one afternoon, Loper suggested to Judy that she should get on better terms with Minnelli, and she reluctantly agreed. He set up a double date with Minnelli, who escorted Judy to dinner along with Loper and Brady.

Over dinner that night, Judy found Minnelli quite different from how he appeared while directing a picture. He was most personable and supportive of her, later saying, "I was amazed at her self-deprecating wit. I felt she was very vulnerable, and I had the feeling I wanted to protect her."

That night was followed by four more dinner dates and an evening of music and dancing at the Cocoanut Grove.

Two nights after their evening at the Grove, Minnelli phoned Judy, telling her that Loper was sick and that their pre-arranged double date would have to be cancelled. "We don't always have to go out with Don and Ruth, do we?" she asked. "What about the two of us meeting for dinner tonight?

He quickly agreed and arrived at her house at 7:30PM, and from there, drove with her to a sea-fronting restaurant in Malibu. Later during the course of that moonlit night, they strolled hand in hand along the beach.

Three days later, after yet another dinner together, he invited her to spend the night with him, and she accepted. By now, Minnelli had become alarmed by her reliance on amphetamines followed by sedatives to put her to sleep.

During the next few days, she told her *confidante,* Mary Astor, what had happened: "He treated me like I was his daughter, a case of incest. In the missionary position, he's lousy, but not in the oral arts. For the moment, he's filling a void in my life until someone more dashing comes along."

Regardless of whatever romantic feeling Minnelli had for Judy, he had a professional motive for dating her. When reports of his homosexuality reached Mayer, Minnelli was summoned to his all-white office for a tongue-lashing.

"If you want to stay with us, you've got to start dating beautiful women — or else!"

Minnelli promised he would. He began taking out his assistant, Marion Herwood Keyes. As it became clear that they were incompatible, they dated only a few times. Keyes later told friends, "We never made it in the sack, and his kisses lacked passion — more like what a brother might kiss his sister good night. On the cheek, that is."

As Minnelli grew more attached to Judy, he met with Freed to talk it over. The producer was amazingly frank and candid: "What do you plan to do for sex if you marry her? Continue to make pictures and seduce good-looking actors, like you did Tom Drake, on the casting couch?"

"I would be marrying her mainly as a means of keeping up appearances," Minnelli confessed. "We wouldn't have to pledge fidelity to each other. Sex would be the least important part of our relationship. Of course, she would be free to pursue the Hollywood hunks she's so fond of."

"If those terms are suitable to Judy, I see no reason you might not go ahead," Freed said, disguising the mocking tone in his voice. "It sounds like wedded bliss."

Freed's voice then became cautionary: "Frankly, I think that such an arrangement, although common in this town, would be a disaster. From what I've observed, Judy demands a lot of sex. Forrest Tucker might have been a better candidate for her. Some starlets tell me he can go five or six times a night, exercising that monster between his legs that he affectionately calls 'The Chief.'"

When the rest of the cast filming *Meet Me in St. Louis* heard about the strengthening bonds between Judy and Minnelli, they were shocked. Most of them reacted negatively. Roger Edens referred to them as "The Odd Couple. They're about as believable as Clark Gable falling for Louella Parsons, or Betty Grable running off with Gabby Hayes."

Darryl Hickman, who had only a brief appearance in *Meet Me in St. Louis,* claimed, "The bonding of those two makes no sense to me. I can't imagine Minnelli having sex with a woman."

"I think Judy views Minnelli as a father figure," said her music director, George Stoll. "He's almost twenty years her senior. I was told that her real father was fluttery as a butterfly in the wind. Maybe she wants to become Daddy's Little Girl all over again, reverting to her previous self-image as Frances Gumm — at least within the privacy of their bedroom."

Hank Moonjean, Minnelli's sometimes collaborator, weighed in too: "Vince is ninety-eight percent female and two percent male. Take the way he walks...or should I say 'prances?' The way he dresses like a lily in spring, all made up. He smokes like Bette Davis. Just because he gets Tom Drake to drop his pants every afternoon doesn't mean he's a homo. He could be checking Tom for crabs."

Judy's makeup artist, Dorothy Ponedel, dismissed accusations of homosexuality. "Minnelli isn't a homosexual, but a man who keeps connected to his feminine side, which makes him a great director for Judy."

Mary Astor warned Judy about getting involved with Minnelli. "Darling, I've been in this business a long time, and I've seen the boys come and go. Any girl should beware of a man who shows up in green eye shadow and ruby red lipstick. Tom Drake visits him in the afternoons, and a grip once told me that he had discovered Vince down on his knees servicing Tom. If you marry Minnelli, the two of you will be the most talented misfits in Hollywood."

She later told Freed, "It's hard for me to believe that Judy is going from the super masculine Joe Mankiewicz to the super feminine Minnelli. That would be the equivalent of her dropping Robert Taylor and replacing him with Edward Everett Horton, that jittery-voiced Nervous Nellie."

In spite of all the alarms raised, Judy accepted Minnelli's invitation to move in with her. She explained the move to Astor. "What I feel for Vince is not what I felt for Tyrone Power or for Artie Shaw. It's not passion, but he fulfills some need I have, and he gives me confidence as an actress and singer. That's the real reason I fell in love with him." Then she paused: "Perhaps love is the wrong word. He did one thing for me, and that was to make me beautiful on the screen. He even claims that I'm as lovely as Lana Turner, Rita Hayworth, or Betty Grable."

***

Some close friends of Judy's, close but gossipy, suggested that her plan to marry Minnelli was all part of a greater scheme. For public consumption, she would be wed to a not-so-closeted homosexual. Their marital links would provide a cover for both of them to carry on adulterous affairs.

Even while she was dating him, she took time out to sustain an affair with that former "Boy Genius," Orson Welles. Seven years her senior, he was a boy no more.

At the age of twenty-five, he'd written, produced, directed, and starred in *Citizen Kane,* a film obviously inspired by the flamboyant life of press baron William Randolph Hearst. [*Since its release in 1941, it has consistently been hailed as one of the greatest films ever made.*]

Unlike Minnelli, Welles was an imposing figure of a man, standing at least six feet three, with flashing green eyes and a reputation for gargantuan appetites and a tendency to gain weight.

On radio, he was known for his gloriously resonant speaking voice. "A heroic tenor" since puberty, he had deliberately trained his voice down to a bass baritone.

Like Judy herself in years to come, Welles would wage a running battle with weight gain, swinging between periods of binge eating and crash diets accessorized with drugs and corsets which gave the impression that he was slimmer than he actually was, at least during his early film roles.

After she met Welles at a Hollywood party and he flirted with her outrageously, Judy was flattered that he had come on to her. Welles shared his home with superstar Rita Hayworth, hailed as the love goddess of the world. "Even though Rita was waiting, Orson still wanted me," Judy told Mary Astor. "I seemed to have graduated from my ugly duckling period, and, I exaggerate, but I feel more like I'm on the road to becoming a *femme fatale* any day now. Move over, Lana."

Before she became more formally committed to Minnelli, Welles would visit Judy's house at least three nights a week. He always brought large bouquets of flowers, which he carried in the back of his car. One night he visited her, he was so distracted by an upcoming film project that he left the flowers in his car, forgetting about them and the love note, addressed to Judy, that was tied to them.

Later in the evening, after Welles' returned to his home, hearth, and wife (Rita Hayworth), she saw the bouquet in his car and assumed they were for her. After hauling them inside, she passed them over to Shifra Harna, her assistant. After uncovering Welles' love letter to Judy from the masses of foliage, Shifra took the flowers away and quietly destroyed the message intended for Judy.

One night at Ciro's, Joseph Cotten, who had starred in *Citizen Kane,* served as Welles' "beard," concealing that Welles was actually at the restaurant as part of a date with Judy. During their time together, she noticed that Welles consumed eight double brandies in quick succession and still remained upright and articulate.

That night, the gay gossip columnist, Mike Connolly, intercepted Judy on her way to the powder room. Seriously tipsy, he indiscreetly asked her, "Do you mind marrying an effeminate man like Minnelli?"

"I wouldn't be the first," she shot back. "Lynn Fontanne is married to Alfred Lunt, and that pair seems to be doing just fine. Now get out of my way. I've got to take a leak."

She told a different story in a dialogue with Astor the next day. "Orson makes up for Vince's inadequacies."

During her long conversations with Welles, she found him very frank in assessments of his life. "When I was younger, I was the Lillie Langtry of the homosexual set," he confessed to her. "Everybody wanted me, male and female. I always seduce actors and make them fall in love with me. Don't ask me why."

He also told her that he lost his virginity when he was nine to three of his female cousins.

"I'm like Casanova in the sense that I'm willing to wait under a window until the object of my affection arrives home, even as late as 4:30AM. I'm a romantic fellow."

Born in Wisconsin, Welles was a teenage prodigy who evolved into an actor, film director, writer, and producer. In 1937, with John Houseman, he co-founded, with the sponsorship of money made available by Roosevelt's New Deal, Manhattan's Mercury Theatre, an avant-garde repertory company.

The following year during a broadcast through the branch of the Mercury Theatre devoted to radio broadcasts , he generated a nationwide panic that followed in the wake of his narration of a science fiction script based on H.G. Welles' novel, *The War of the Worlds.* His voice and the events he was relaying sounded so realistic and urgent that thousands upon thousands of listeners interpreted it as a news broadcast announcing a Martian invasion. They fled from their homes in panic, causing traffic jams, accidents on bridges and on highways, and leading to general mayhem and hysteria.

Although Welles admitted that he would probably never make another movie as prestigious as *Citizen Kane,* he said that he was "always stewing" with new ideas. With Judy, he discussed his latest concept for a movie, *The Lady from Shanghai,* eventually released in 1947, and suggested that she should play the lead.

Interpreting it as an opportunity to escape from the frothy musicals of her recent past, and to prove her abilities as a budding Sarah Bernhardt, Judy responded that she'd be thrilled.

[Whereas Welles went on to make The Lady from Shanghai, *it starred not Judy, but his estranged and alienated wife, Rita Hayworth.]*

Orson Welles (left) and love goddess **Rita Hayworth** at their wedding ceremony in Santa Monica (1943), as witnessed by **Joseph Cotten.**

The wedding—broadly publicized in every form of media available at the time—occurred less than two years before Welles' adulterous fling with Judy Garland.

When Walter Kerr, theater critic for the *New York Herald Tribune,* wrote "Orson Welles is the youngest has-been actor & director in Hollywood," Judy wondered if in a few years, the same would be said about her.

She was not good at keeping her dates straight, and one night, she invited both Welles and Minnelli to her home for dinner.

Minnelli pulled into her driveway first. Quickly realizing what she'd done, and with the understanding that Welles was scheduled to arrive at any minute, she jumped into Minnelli's car and announced that she wanted, immediately, to invite him out to dinner because she'd burnt the dinner she had planned, and that her kitchen was filled with smoke from the meal she had ruined.

Minnelli and Judy disappeared before Welles arrived, as planned. Judy's maid apologized for her, reciting that she had had to rush to her sister's house because of a medical emergency.

In reference to her brief sexual fling with Welles, Judy said, "It was short but sweet, and we remained friends for life."

[Thus, a reference to Judy Garland can be added to Orson Welles' impressive list of romantic conquests: Lucille Ball, the French actress Corrine Calvet, the African-American singer Eartha Kitt, composer Marc Blitzstein, Geraldine Fitzgerald, Marlene Dietrich, actor Francis Carpenter, Marilyn Monroe, Dolores Del Rio, actor Jack Carter, Maria ("Cobra Woman") Montez, heiress Gloria Vanderbilt, ballerina Vera Zorina, actor-producer John Houseman, Lena Horne, actor Hilton Edwards, a concubine of the Pasha of Marrakesh, and dozens of women and young catamites in the brothels of Singapore and Shanghai.

As Welles' former assistant claimed, "You didn't get one-night stands with Orson. You got afternoon stands, before dinner stands, and after dinner stands."

Divorcing him, Rita Hayworth told the press: "I adore enormous men, but I just can't take his genius any more."]

***

By now, living with Minnelli, Judy admired and respected him, although she wasn't thrilled with his performances between the sheets. Her bolting from Ethel's influence and dominance had infuriated her mother. Two days after changing her address, a messenger hand-delivered a venomous letter to Minnelli from Ethel.

In it, she accused him of "being a sexual degenerate, preying on innocent little girls. Until now, I thought you were a gentleman—that is, until you kidnapped my daughter to use for your own sick smut. This puts you in the ranks of all the other sleazeballs in this town. Frankly, I think charges should be brought against you. You definitely should be investigated, as I suspect you have had a long history of child molestation."

He wrote back: "Judy wants a quickie divorce from David Rose in Mexico, but I want to go through the courts in California because in many instances, a Mexican divorce has been invalid. When she is finally free from Rose, I have every intention of marrying her and raising a family. I can offer her a stabilized life. She has told me horrible stories about you, and I have no respect for you as a mother. The story is in: You are an unfit mother. Please stay away from us. I also learned that you and your husband have squandered Judy's hard-earned money. Haven't you done enough damage? Let her go. It is because of you that she has become addicted to pills. You should be ashamed of yourself."

Judy's co-workers knew that she hated her mother, blaming her for her life's pain and setbacks. In Hollywood circles, Ethel Gumm Gilmore was often compared to the formidable "Mama Rose" who exercised such a strong (some say, "corrosive") influence over her daughters, actress June Havoc and stripper Gypsy Rose Lee.

After the first week of having Judy under his roof, Minnelli became more acutely aware of her sudden mood swings. He attributed it to her dependence on drugs. "She would be almost giddy with happiness one moment, but within the hour, her mood could shift drastically. She would become melancholy and depressed. I tried to get her off pills, and for a day or so she gave them up. But the tiniest little setback would drive her to pill-popping again."

"She promised me time and time again that she would give up pills tomorrow," Minnelli claimed. "She would parrot Scarlett O'Hara's line from *Gone With the Wind,* saying 'Tomorrow is another day.'   But tomorrow never came, and she came to rely on those little dolls, which she called pills, more than ever."

Long before Minnelli began to photograph and make her look beautiful for *Meet Me in St. Louis,* Judy had been sensitive about her looks, figuring she didn't measure up to MGM's stable of beauties, notably Hedy Lamarr and Lana Turner.

As she moved deeper into her relationship with Minnelli, she discovered that he, too, was deeply concerned with his own looks. One night he told Judy, "We must not have children. Imagine having a son or daughter who looks like me."

By 1950, Judy told Van Johnson, "Vince is a lousy husband but a brilliant director. I'm not sure why I married him. The only good thing that came out of our marriage was my daughter, Liza. It was not sex that brought us together, but his ability to make a bigtime star of me. I will always be grateful to him for making me look glamourous up there on the screen in glorious Technicolor."

"Sometimes he would provoke an argument with me, especially on weekends," Judy claimed. "It was just an excuse to run off with his longtime lover, Lester Gaba. He'd moved to the Coast and bought this beautiful home in the Hollywood Hills just to be close to Vince."

[On Broadway, as a romantic couple, Minnelli and Gaba were often referred to as "Lester & Lester" because Minnelli's birth name had been Lester before he changed it to Vincente.]

MGM's songbird, Kathryn Grayson, once said, "Minnelli is so ugly I can't bear to look at him. Judy certainly did not marry him for his looks. Let's face it: She'd had some beautiful men before him, notably that living doll, Tyrone Power. Some people claimed that Minnelli's small head reminded them of baby dinosaur. He was so effeminate and all that eye shadow and lipstick added to the effect of a mincing queen."

Let's face it," Judy once said to Gene Kelly and others. "Vince is as gay as a May Day parade. I'm sure he comes on to you. That must make Lester [Gaba] jealous."

"He gets up early to spend an hour at his vanity table," Judy said. "He does everything but false eyelashes. He doesn't need them."

June Allyson, Judy's longtime friend, also weighed in on the mating rituals of Judy and Vincente Minnelli. "He was so wrong for Judy, totally, totally wrong. How did she put up with him for so long? More to the point, why did she ever marry a man like that? He didn't love her the way a man can love a woman. But he sure loves Lester Gaba."

Before marrying Minnelli, she had discussed a possible union of them as a couple with Arthur Freed. "I made a big mistake marrying David Rose, and I don't want this to become mistake number two. I'm not going to become a housewife and settle down, cooking dinner to have ready when hubby comes home from work. One reason I'm marrying him is to get him to direct my future musicals. I think we can make great pictures together, and, to me, that's a good enough reason for marriage."

Freed went to Mayer and told him he felt Judy's upcoming marriage to Minnelli would be a "steadying influence on her." What he didn't tell Mayer but told Roger Edens was, "Vince will find all the sex he wants with dancers from my Freed Unit. Most of them are gay anyway and will surely shack up with Vince, if only for career advancement."

Several Hollywood insiders suggested that the only thing Minnelli had in common with Joe Mankiewicz, Judy's former lover, was that both of them were "part Pygmalion and part Svengali. Both men had a talent for molding exceptional actresses, providing that the candidate had the innate talent to begin with," Freed said.

Privately, Mayer approved of Judy's upcoming marriage. "She'll make a man out of Minnelli. When he shacks up with a real woman, he'll give up those chorus boys and fags. His trouble is that he never met the right woman. Any right-minded female of the species can cure any man of homosexual tendencies."

Early in their relationship, Minnelli learned that Judy had not seen the first two musicals he'd directed. So he arranged a double feature screening at MGM. He had directed the 1943 musical, *Cabin in the Sky*, with an all-black cast, starring Ethel Waters, Eddie ("Rochester") Anderson, and Lena Horne. The music was supplied by Louis Armstrong and Duke Ellington and his orchestra.

The second feature he'd directed was *I Dood It*, released the same year, starring Red Skelton and tap-dancing Eleanor Powell.

Minnelli told Judy, "The movie should have been called 'The Battle of Two Black Divas, Hazel Scott and Lena Horne.'" The picture had also starred John Hodiak, who would go on to become Judy's leading man in *The Harvey Girls* (1946).

Jimmy Dorsey and his orchestra supplied the music. Judy had been delighted with Butterfly McQueen since she'd seen her in *Gone With the Wind* (1939). In *I Dood It*, "She was just precious as Annette." Minnelli told Judy. "But believe it or not, Butterfly has a bigger ego than either Scott or Horne."

When he began living with Judy, Minnelli tried to bring her more closely into his orbit and spark her with an interest in paintings and antiques. Through him, she began to meet an entirely different set of friends, many from the literary and theatrical worlds of New York. She already knew Harold Arlen and both Ira and Lee Gershwin.

One night, she found herself in a dialogue with the famous author, Dorothy Parker, whom Judy later called "the most sophisticated woman I have ever met."

"One of the many quotes I'm famous for," Parker told her, is: "Scratch an actor and you'll find an actress." In reference to her second husband, the actor/writer Alan Campbell, Parker said, "Believe me, darling, I know what it's like being married to a homosexual."

She issued a warning: "Because you know Vince, you're likely to meet the playwright Elmer Rice. He'll probably make a pass at you, but don't intercept it. Elmer is the world's worst lay."

"One weekend, Minnelli invited William Saroyan, the novelist and playwright, to their home as a house guest. Judy was unfamiliar with his work, and he gave her a copy of *The Human Comedy*, published in 1943, to read.

A few weeks later, Judy—through Minnelli—was delighted to meet the gay composer, Cole Porter. [*During the summer of 1938, her former love, Artie Shaw, had recorded his biggest hit, 'Begin the Beguine.' Shaw had told her, "After releasing Cole's song, I became a sort of weird, jazz-band-leading, clarinet-tooting, jitterbug-surrounded symbol of American Youth."*]

Porter told her how much he'd adored her recording of his hit song,

"Friendship," which she and Johnny Mercer, her lover at the time, had recorded. *[Porter would eventually compose the music for one of Judy's upcoming films,* The Pirate *(1948), which Minnelli would direct.]*

One particular evening at the Minnelli/Garland household involved the spectacularly theatrical arrival of the African American diva, Josephine Baker. Minnelli had previously worked with her on *Ziegfeld Follies* in 1936. She wore a burgundy-colored velvet suit trimmed in sable. With her was a handsome Italian count and two well-groomed dogs.

During her conversation with Judy, Baker related stories of co-starring with Bob Hope and Fanny Brice in the Broadway production of *Follies.* "I'm aware that you, too, made a picture with Brice," Baker said. "I don't know about you, but after my experience with her, I think Brice is the biggest bitch on Broadway."

For years, Judy had heard outrageous stories about Baker, and was eager to meet her. Biographer Stephen Papich wrote, "In Paris, she strolled down the Champs-Elysées with a bejeweled panther on a leash and a sheik by her side. Heads turned as the crowd cheered her on. Once, Herman Goering aimed a pistol at her head over dinner. She made love to the Crown Prince of Sweden in his private railway car. At fourteen, she saw strikebreakers burn down her home, and a few years later, she was the star of the *Folies Bergère* in Paris. She was with Charles De Gaulle at the Arc de Triomphe upon the Liberation of Paris in 1944."

He continued: "Josephine Baker was a legend in her own time. This fabulous black woman, who began her career in show business as the wardrobe mistress to Bessie Smith, made millions and lost them just as easily during one of the most glamourous and exciting lives ever lived."

A producer and choreographer, Papich would later work with not only Judy herself, but with Mae West, Susan Hayward, and Marilyn Monroe.

Papich claimed that after meeting her, Baker adopted the famous "Judy Garland Plan," as it came to be known in Hollywood. "Whenever Judy was dissatisfied with something, she began pitting one associate on a set against another—the 'divide and conquer' routine. Then, whenever everyone on the set was up in arms against everyone else, she would waltz in, exceedingly happy and, amid the chaos that she had created, set about to

A friend of Dorothy and a friend of Judy Garland, **Josephine Baker** appears here during her Jazz Age heyday in Paris, wearing her famous "Banana Costume."

Baker credited at least some of her business success to her adoption of the "Judy Garland Plan."

211

right the wrongs."

On another night, elegantly groomed and beautifully dressed, Lena Horne, arrived at the Minnelli/Garland home. In 1942, she'd been the first black woman to have signed a long-term contract with a major studio like MGM. After that, however, she repeatedly objected to the roles assigned to her. Most often they involved an appearance as a café singer in a vignette. As an "self-standing" clip, it could easily be edited out of a reel of celluloid before its screenings in the Deep South. "I longed for a serious role in a mixed-cast movie," she lamented.

At the age of sixteen, before moving on to Hollywood, Horne was seen in the chorus line at the Cotton Club in Harlem.

After Judy met her, she referred to Horne as "The Bronze Venus." Horne herself preferred her moniker as "The Sepia Hedy Lamarr."

Judy congratulated her on her performance in *Cabin in the Sky* (1934). "Vince had to cut my best scene," Horne said. "It was of me singing 'Ain't It the Truth' while taking a bath. It was too hot for the censors."

Horne would soon be working with Judy in the *Ziegfeld Follies of 1946*, although shooting began in 1944.

After a night with Horne, Judy agreed with that society gadabout and party-giver, Elsa Maxwell, who said, "Lena is a honeypot for the bees."

A number of high-profile lovers seemed to agree with Maxwell's assessment: Duke Ellington, Harry Belafonte, David Janssen, Paul Robeson, and boxer Joe Lewis.

Glamourous **Lena Horne,** an *haute* nightclub star (and later, social activist) singing "Stormy Weather" in *Cabin in the Sky* (1943), accompanied by bandleader **Cab Calloway**.

Horne discussed the difficulties and benefits of working on *Cabin in the Sky* (1943). "Ethel Waters detested me. She was hard on other girl singers, especially if they were young or more attractive than she was. She's no beauty, as you know."

But she praised Minnelli, claiming that she was his *protégée*. "He loves to make a woman beautiful, and he adores dressing them."

At first, Judy harbored a resentment of Horne because she'd had an affair with Artie Shaw, the bandleader who had broken Judy's heart.

During the crafting of *Cabin in the Sky*, Horne was also alleged to have had an affair with Minnelli. And as the years rolled on, both Ava Gardner and Judy would be accused of having had a lesbian affair with Horne. [*At*

MGM's
ZIEGFELD FOLLIES
GREATEST PRODUCTION SINCE THE BIRTH OF MOTION PICTURES !

WOULD FLO ZIEGFELD HAVE DEFINED JUDY GARLAND AS A CONTENDER FOR HIS FOLLIES?

MGM's ZIEGFELD FOLLIES
Judy to Toto: "I guess we aren't in Kansas any more!"

Surrounded by men posing (before they break into dance) as reporters and photographers, Judy was cast in MGM's **Ziegfeld Follies** as an actress who has already proven herself in Oscar-winning dramas. At the beginning of the film, it's revealed that now, as a change of pace, she desperately wants to try some sexier roles.

One of her scenes was conceived as a spoof on her real-life competitors: Greer Garson, Katharine Hepburn, and Greta Garbo.

Columnist Hedda Hopper witnessed Judy's delivery of that scene, and later filed a report:

"The corkscrew Judy ties herself into while getting her picture taken will have you rolling. She gets a touch of Hepburn's 'Rally...Rally...,' plus Garbo's 'I tank I go home' in her impersonations.'"

Is that (gasp!) Dorothy? Scantily clad and showing herself off in semi-transparent glitter as a CHORINE?

Auntie Em would DIE!!

least Frank Sinatra thought so and bruited it loudly and often through the entertainment community.]

At the time Judy entertained Horne, she was perhaps unaware that she, like Judy herself, was also having an affair with Orson Welles.

***

Judy had already co-starred with Hedy Lamarr and Lana Turner in *Ziegfeld Girl* (1941). Her latest offer came when producer Arthur Freed asked her to execute a satirical skit in its sequel, *Ziegfeld Follies* (1944). Because of long production delays, it was finally released as *Ziegfeld Follies of 1946.*

The series had begun with William Powell impersonating the showman, Flo Ziegfeld, in *The Great Ziegfeld* in 1936. In this latest rendition, Powell (as the ghost of Ziegfeld) is in Heaven looking down at his Follies, imagining how he would cast it today with the current crop of MGM stars.)

Freed asked Minnelli to direct it, although he got a lot of help from Roger Edens for his musical adaptations. Robert Alton for his dance direction, and Lennie Hayton for his musical direction.

Appearing in various skits were Gene Kelly, Fred Astaire, Lucille Ball, Lucille Bremer, Kathryn Grayson, Lena Horne, James Melton, Victor Moore, Red Skelton, Esther Williams in a water ballet, Edward Arnold, Cyd Charisse, Hume Cronyn, William Frawley, Robert Lewis, Virginia O'Brien, and, among others, Keenan Wynn.

At the time, the English actress, Greer Garson—based on her wartime hits such as *Mrs. Miniver* and *Random Harvest* (1942, and *Madame Curie,* released the following year—was still the reigning Queen of MGM. An elegant and striking red-haired beauty, Garson took herself very seriously.

Edens had collaborated with Kay Thompson on a satirical cameo in which Garson would satirize herself. *[Thompson, who hailed from St. Louis, Missouri, was an influential, behind-the-scenes author, composer, musician, actress, and singer in Hollywood. She was destined to become Judy's lifetime friend, mentor, and possibly, according to rumors of the day, her lesbian lover.]*

Garson was invited to the home of Freed, where Kay and Edens rehearsed a prototype of the skit in front of the English actress and her mother.

When it was over, Garson, without saying a word, rose, took her mother's arm, and exited from the house.

The next day, Kay, Freed, and

Greer Garson with Walter Pidgeon in what might have been her greatest role in one of the greatest movies ever made about World War II, *Mrs. Miniver.*

214

Edens decided to replicate the cameo skit within the context of *Ziegfeld Follies of 1946*. It was suggested as a change of pace from Judy's "tried-and-true" portrayals of Dorothy Gale, Betsy Booth, and the other *ingénue*, small-town girl roles she had played.

Kay Thompson never got the credit she deserved for this opportunity for Judy to showcase, in just a few well-choreographed minutes, her acting, comedic, and singing skills. Film critic Rex Reed later wrote, "Kay introduced the first rap song forty years before Harlem did."

The only other skit in the film that rivaled Judy's involved Lucille Ball cracking a whip at eight chorus girls portraying "panthers."

Years later, Judy claimed, "This skit made me the 'Camp Madonna,' although the word 'camp' had not been invented at the time. It also solidified my relationship with the gay community, who had been in love with me since *The Wizard of Oz*. In those closeted days, gay men secretly called themselves 'Friends of Dorothy.' Through all the good times and the rough days, gay men have been my longest and most enduring fans, for which I will be eternally grateful."

Judy had met Kay back in April of 1939 when she'd been a guest, singing "FDR Jones" and "Sweet Sixteen," on CBS's radio show *Time-Up Time*.

Kay had also been on that show, but their life-long friendship did not begin until Judy performed the satirical skit Kay had authored in *Ziegfeld Follies*.

In 1943, Kay had signed with MGM, becoming the studio's top vocal arranger, choral director, and vocal coach, not only for Judy, but as a musical guru to June Allyson, Frank Sinatra, and Lena Horne.

In time, Kay would become the godmother of Liza Minnelli.

In the wake of mostly good reviews, the *Fol-*

Kay Thompson, Judy's long-time guide, protector, mentor, and friend, maintained show-biz ambitions of her own.   In the photo above, she's the featured singer with the Williams Brothers during their Christmas Show of 1945.

UPSTAIRS & DOWNSTAIRS AT THE PLAZA

Kay Thompson was creative, entrepreneurial and multi-talented.

In addition to "steering' crucial aspects of Judy's career, she authored the spectacularly popular **ELOISE** series. Each became required reading for "grown up children" about the ironies of postwar social pretensions.

215

lies took in five and a half million dollars at the box office. Bosley Crowther of *The New York Times* wrote that Judy "shows promise of a talent approaching that of Beatrice Lillie or Gertrude Lawrence."

The *New York Herald Tribune* wasn't as impressed, writing, "Miss Garland has some unpleasant stuff to do."

Newsweek disagreed, claiming that Judy "displayed an unexpected flair for occupational satire. Fred Astaire and Gene Kelly also trade taps and double takes to a photo finish."

[*The Kelly/Astaire routine would mark the last time those two rival dancers co-starred together as a duo...at least until their nostalgic reunion in 1976 when they appeared together in* That's Entertainment Part II.]

The *New York Post* was not impressed with Judy's performance, calling it "flamboyantly dull." In the same city, its rival, the *Daily News,* disagreed, stating their opinion that her skit was a "devastatingly funny burlesque."

Kay Thompson, who had created the skit, told the press, "All Judy had to do was sing and act like a combination of Gertrude Lawrence, Greta Garbo, and five other grand ladies of the screen."

Even though she was a celebrated performer herself, Kay became better known as the author of the *Eloise* series of children's books. They relayed the adventures and antics of a six-year-old girl who lives at the Plaza Hotel in Manhattan. The first of the series, *Eloise,* was published by Simon & Schuster in 1955.

As Kay's biographer, the veteran filmmaker Sam Irvin, wrote: Thompson "went to school with Tennessee Williams, auditioned for Henry Ford, got her first big break from Bing Crosby, later trained Marilyn Monroe, rejected Andy Warhol, rebuffed Federico Fellini, got fired by Howard Hughes, and subdued Donald Trump."

"She also coached Bette Davis and Eleanor Roosevelt, while creating night club acts for Marlene Dietrich and Ginger Rogers. When Lucille Ball had to sing on Broadway, Kay was there to guide her. She also was a member of Frank Sinatra's Rat Pack. The Beatles wanted to hold her hand. Cole Porter hoped to write a musical for her. Danny Kaye impersonated her, and her fans ranged from Queen Elizabeth to Princess Grace Kelly."

One writer interpreted her as "some exotic bird, a multi-colored quetzal perhaps, flying into Culver City to astonish the ordinary seagulls and sparrows."

***

Arthur Freed and Vincente Minnelli teamed once again to offer Judy her first real dramatic star part, and the first star vehicle in which she does not sing. *The Clock* (MGM, 1945), in a nutshell, is a boy-meets-girl story of a romantic pair (a secretary and a soldier) who meet, fall in love, and get married during his two-day leave in New York City. Robert Walker was cast into the role of Corporal Joe Allen, who meets Alice Mayberry (Judy) during his short break in Manhattan before being shipped off to the battlefields of World War II.

In a chance encounter at Pennsylvania Station, Alice trips over his foot and breaks the heel of her shoe. As it's being repaired, they agree to meet later under the clock of the Astor Hotel.

Later, the lovers encounter James Gleason, cast as a milkman, Al Henry. Since Alice has missed her last bus home, he offers them a lift on his milk wagon.

In supporting roles, Keenan Wynn plays a drunk who blackens the eye of the milkman. Lucille Gleason plays the milkman's wife.

Other support is offered by a young star on the rise, Marshall Thompson, with Ruth Brady as Helen.

Fred Zinnemann, who would go on to greater things, was the original director, but Judy—after feuding with him—went to Mayer and bitterly complained, saying, "He gives me nothing as a director. I can't go on working with him."

In response, Mayer said, "So you want your lover boy, Minnelli, instead, don't you?"

"YES!," she answered. Based on her significant star power at the time, her wish was granted.

Long before meeting and working with Judy on *The Clock,* Walker had been type cast as the boy-next-door who becomes a soldier. His most memorable portrayal of a G.I. was in the hit World War II drama, *Since You Went Away* (1944) starring Claudette Colbert and his wife, Jennifer Jones.

Before working with Judy, Walker had recently starred in *Private Hargrove* (1944), in which he had to play love scenes with his estranged wife, Jennifer Jones. *[Before the beginning of filming, she had run away with producer David O. Selznick.]* Walker had also starred in *Thirty Seconds Over Tokyo* (1944), a war film with Van Johnson and Spencer Tracy.

A month before filming started on *The Clock,* Judy had moved out of Minnelli's house and briefly resumed her affair with Joe Mankiewicz. It did not last long, but when it ended, she did not immediately

TICK-TOCK

On the MGM lot for this publicity picture, **Judy** plays out her real-life romance with her troubled and very problematic co-star, "little boy lost," **Robert Walker.**

217

move back in with Minnelli. Although she started to warm to him once again, she stayed independent and began to focus her romantic attentions on Walker.

Around this time, Judy became emotionally disturbed about the direction of her life and kept wondering if she really wanted to marry Minnelli. She didn't actually love him, and her pill-popping had resumed after Mankiewicz deserted her for a second time to return to his long-suffering wife.

In Walker, Judy found "a lost, wandering soul, suffering heartbreak over the desertion by his wife, Jennifer Jones, who wanted a divorce so that she could marry Selznick. With Jones, Walker had produced two sons, Robert, Jr. and Michael.

Judy began to spend evenings with Walker, offering him whatever comfort she could. In his desperation, he responded and reached out to her for support. It eventually led to an affair.

He was drinking heavily, and she spent more time sobering him up in time to face the camera than she spent making love to him. Sometimes, he'd disappear, and Judy, with Kay Thompson, would search the bars of West Hollywood until they found him. Judy would drive him home and put him to bed. Later, she would awaken him and drive him to the studio. On many of those days, he was too hung over to face the camera in a close-up.

Even though New York was the setting, and because a war was on with restrictions, scenes had to be shot in Culver City. There, at a cost of $66,000, Pennsylvania Station was replicated.

"It wasn't the sex—Bob was lousy in bed—but his babyface and his pain-filled soul that lured me to him," Judy told Kay. "He was hard to love and sometimes became jealous, accusing me of screwing young Marshall Thompson, another actor in the cast."

[Mild-mannered Marshall Thompson started his acting career as a gulping juvenile and achieved only minor stardom. In The Clock, *he played the boyfriend who can't get a word in edgewise.*

He did get to play the would-be assassin of Abraham Lincoln in The Tall Target *(1951) before MGM dropped him, forcing him to go to the studios of Poverty Row.*

Like many other hopefuls, Thompson faded into Hollywood history. Contrary to Walker's accusations, there was no affair between Judy and Thompson, although he was very friendly and supportive of Judy and spent a lot of time with her.]

Through their deepening friendship, Walker continued his attacks on Minnelli and resented the attention the director was showing Judy. One night he told her she needed "a real man, not an ugly fag."

"Bob himself wasn't a real man, but a naughty little boy who refused to grow up," Judy claimed, years later. "I've often been called 'Little Girl Lost,' but it was Bob who was 'Little Boy Lost.'"

As expressed by biographer Lee Server, "Robert Walker had a sad vulnerability about him on the screen, and even more so in real life. He was a deeply troubled man, probably schizophrenic, and at the least, a dangerously depressed alcoholic. Metro would eventually force him to undergo psychiatric treatment at the Menninger Clinic in Kansas. He had met his wife [Jennifer Jones] when they were teenagers in college. When she left him for Selznick, Walker plunged into a dark despair from which he would never escape."

According to Judy, "I was sucked into his dark world, although I knew there was no way I would ever replace Jennifer in his life. There was also Vince to think of, as he was still making goo-goo eyes at me."

"Judy certainly caught Robert on the rebound," said his friend, Van Johnson. [Months later, she learned that Johnson himself was having an occasional fling with Walker.]

"I had my pills to rely on," Judy said, "my trusty pills. They never failed me. Bob had something else to knock him out. He would go to a blender and pour in whatever liquor was available—brandy, gin, vodka, bourbon, scotch. He would then drink the entire contents, which usually led to his passing out on the living room floor."

Sometimes, when Judy went to bed with Walker, and he was invariably drunk, he would wake up in the middle of the night weeping uncontrollably, calling out "Jenny! JENNY! PLEASE COME BACK!"

"I also learned a deep, dark secret about him," she revealed. "He wasn't the man he appeared to be on the screen. MGM had created a padded harness for him that made him appear to have bigger arms, a bigger chest, and even bigger shoulders."

"Bob was just a prelude to my running off and later marrying Vince," Judy recalled. "Bob, Joe, Vince—all these men seemed wrong for me. Would I ever meet Mr. Right?"

Jennifer Jones with Gregory Peck in *Duel in the Sun* (1946).

David O. Selznick, the producer, and actress **Jennifer Jones** were photographed in 1949, two days after their wedding.

Her former husband, Robert Walker, never recovered from her desertion, although Judy tried to help him mend his broken heart.

"Bob was on the road to self-destruction," Judy claimed. "He knew it, and I knew it. Perhaps I, too, was on the same road, but I didn't want to tag along with him in his footsteps. Even when I told him goodbye, I believed he'd come back into my world, as he inevitably did. When that happened, and we appeared in another film again, I found his life had become

219

almost unbelievably complicated. I didn't see how he was going to work his way out of the tangled web he had created for himself."

For the most part, *The Clock* generated good reviews and a reasonable profit, but nowhere near the box office bonanzas of Judy's musicals. *Time* magazine found Judy "in unmistakable bloom, and Robert Walker losing his 'shucks-fellows' cuteness he sometimes seems doomed to."

The *New York Daily News* wrote, "The sweetest, most tender comedy-drama yet produced about a soldier and a girl. Judy Garland and Robert Walker are perfectly cast as the modest, sincere girl and the shy, sincere boy."

The New York Times defined *The Clock* as "a tender and refreshing romantic drama. The atmosphere of Big Town has seldom been conveyed more realistically upon the screen, the kind of picture that leaves one with a warm feeling toward his fellow man, especially the young kids of today, who are trying to crowd a lifetime of happiness into a few fleeting hours."

***

As originally conceived, *The Harvey Girls* (1946) was to have been a drama that would reunite Lana Turner with Clark Gable, now back from the war. The two stars had already demonstrated on-and off-screen chemistry together during their co-starring stints together in *Honky Tonk* (1941) and *Somewhere I'll Find You* (1942).

But after musical director Roger Edens saw the Broadway production of *Oklahoma!*, he urged MGM to turn *The Harvey Girls* into a musical.

In a nutshell, *The Harvey Girls* was the saga of a group of young waitresses employed by restaurateur Fred Harvey (1835-1901) to bring tablecloths and civilization as a vehicle for taming the Wild West.

At first, Judy balked at the idea of starring in *The Harvey Girls*, preferring instead to appear with Fred Astaire in *Yolanda and the Thief* (1945), which Minnelli had been signed to direct. But producer Arthur Freed was aware of Judy's upcoming marriage to Minnelli, and he wanted to get another picture out of her before she walked down the aisle.

[Later, she attended a screening of Yolanda and privately delivered her own review: "What a flop! Lucille Bremer got the role I might have done and was far too old for the part. Instead of my sunshine beams, she came off like Mrs. Jack Frost, icy cold in the role. Whereas Vince was depressed for weeks at the picture's failure, The Harvey Girls *became one of the box office champs of the year."]*

In *The Harvey Girls*, Judy got sole star billing, with her name above the title. Roger Edens was named associate producer, and direction was by George Sidney, who had worked with Judy before in *Thousands Cheer*. Songs would be by Johnny Mercer (Judy's former lover) and Harry Warren. As her leading man, John Hodiak was signed.

The film marked her reunion with Ray Bolger, who had starred with her as the Scarecrow in *The Wizard of Oz*. He said, "Judy just worked and worked and worked and then worked some more. She never had a vacation. She had a nervous breakdown."

Judy's competition for Hodiak's affection is Em, an older woman

220

known as "the dance hall harlot." That role originally was slated for Lucille Ball and later, for Ann Sothern. When they did not work out, Angela Lansbury got the part.

Lansbury, of course, would go on to become one of the *grandes dames* of the theater and both the big and little screens. By the time she starred in the Broadway musical, *Mame,* in 1966, Lansbury had become, like Judy herself, a gay icon.

In her eight-decades-long career, she could play almost any role—ingénue to dowager, elegant heroine to depraved villain.

The very talented Preston Foster, cast as the villainous judge in *The Harvey Girls,* could go from playing a snarling, family-deserting criminal in *The People's Enemy* (1935) to the soft-spoken pacifist in *Guadalcanal Diary* (1943).

Other supporting roles would be played by Virginia O'Brien, Marjorie Main, Chill Wills, Cyd Charisse (in her first speaking role on film), and Stephen McNally.

Upper photo: Real-life "tamers" of the Wild West, **Harvey Girls,** prepped and ready to rumble.

Lower photo: **Virginia O'Brien, Judy Garland, and Cyd Charisse** portraying Harvey Girls in Hollywood's 1946 song-and-dance crowd-pleaser.

A bevy of beautiful girls would be cast in this Technicolor spectacular set in the Old West, a fictionalized account of Fred Harvey opening dining rooms at train stops along the rail route West.

Judy had a reunion with Main, who had portrayed the family cook in *Meet Me in St. Louis.* In *The Harvey Girls,* she played Señora Cassidy, the recruiter and trainer of new waitresses. She also appears in some of the group's musical numbers, including "Round and Round" with Judy and Bolger. Main and Judy would appear together one more time in the musical *Summer Stock* (1950).

Joan Crawford had become a friend of Judy's, and she visited her on the set. Crawford surprised Judy when she told her that before Lucille Ball and Ann Sothern were offered the role of Em, the tarty saloon waitress, she was asked by Freed to play her. "I rejected it and went for the star role in *Mildred Pierce* instead—after Bette Davis turned it down."

[That was the right choice for Crawford. She won a Best Actress Oscar for her

performance.]

Sidney had never been one of Judy's favorite directors, although she did admire his recent success with *Anchors Aweigh* (1945), starring Frank Sinatra and Gene Kelly. Her relationship with Sidney became toxic, however, when, in 1949, he cast her in *Annie Get Your Gun.*

According to the story line of *Harvey Girls*, which nine writers had labored over, Judy is lured West seeking a "mail order husband," responding to a series of letters she received, supposedly from a prospective groom. As it turned out, each of them had been written by the owner of the local saloon, as portrayed by Hodiak. Chill Wills, cast as H.H. Hartsey, plays the prospective groom, an old coot. She immediately informs him, "I'm a lousy housekeeper. I'm a terrible cook." Her romantic aspirations soon shift to Hodiak.

Kay Thompson was with Judy throughout most of the shoot, helping her with the vocal arrangements. Their friendship was growing every day, and such a closeness did not go unnoticed. This being Hollywood, rumors began to spread about the nature of their friendship.

Like Betty Grable and Lana Turner, plus countless other female stars, Judy would often be attracted to a virile male associated with either the cast or the crew. She had found Hodiak very attractive ever since she'd seen him play opposite Tallulah Bankhead in Alfred Hitchcock's *Lifeboat* (1944). At the time, however, Hodiak was involved with Anne Baxter and would marry her the following year.

Judy was drawn to Stephen McNally, cast as "Golddust" McClean. Over the course of his career, he would often play a villain in many a Western or action film. But he is mainly remembered today for his performance in *Johnny Belinda* (1948), where he rapes a deaf-mute, Jane Wyman, in her Oscar-winning role.

Judy found McNally "awfully smart" in addition to being sexy. This New Yorker had studied to become a lawyer before abandoning that goal to become an actor.

Van Johnson came onto the set one day to greet her. She told him about her involvement with McNally. "He and I share a mutual love of chocolate. That is what drew me to him. He's a real breast man. He likes to drop chocolate syrup over my breasts and then lick them clean. Very kinky and very messy, but a real turn-on."

An ardent Democrat, Judy broke down and cried and could no longer work when news came over the radio that President Franklin D. Roosevelt had died on April 12, 1945 in Warm Springs, Georgia.

Throughout the shoot, Judy caused endless delays, arriving hours late on the set and sometimes not showing up at all, leaving hundreds of cast and crew members waiting impatiently for her.

One memo dated January 26, 1945 read: "Miss Garland called the assistant director at 3:20 this morning to say that she was not feeling well and would not come to work. We will try to shoot whatever we can without her."

A scene was shot focusing on emotions flitting across Hodiak's face. Instead of getting Judy to emote with, he got a dummy model dressed in one of her gowns.

On another occasion, on February 9, she shut down production because she had two teeth extracted and needed a bridge to fill the gap. Once, she contacted the studio, claiming she'd been up all night and could not face the camera for a close-up.

Later, Judy discussed her condition during filming: "I was a nervous wreck, jumpy and irritable from too little sleep. I couldn't take the tension at the studio. Everything at MGM is competition. Every day I went to work with tears in my eyes. Work gives me no pleasure. The studio has become a haunted house for me. It was all I could do to keep from screaming every time the director looked at me."

After its release, reviews of *The Harvey Girls* were favorable, though not as good as those generated by *Meet Me in St. Louis. Family Circle* described Judy as the "number one exponent of transportation tunes," obviously referencing "The Trolley Song" from *Meet Me in St. Louis,* and also the hit song from *The Harvey Girls,* a best-selling recording of "On the Atchison, Topeka, and Santa Fe," written by Mercer and Warren. *[It generated an Oscar for them as Best Song that year.]*

The *Seattle Post Intelligencer* wrote "Judy Garland is emaciated to a Frank Sinatra degree and needs a few square meals."

Time claimed that "Miss Garland doesn't seem as recklessly happy as she was in *Meet Me in St. Louis,* but she appears to be having a pretty fine time."

Although Bosley Crowther of *The New York Times* was rather subdued in his praise, the *New York Herald Tribune* was most enthusiastic, calling Judy "The film's brightest star, appearing in the glamourized get-ups of the 1890s. Expect pretty girls, great period sets and costumes, lilting songs, and super speedy shuffles."

Judy's most devoted fans, who had seen every one of her movies, perceived that her voice had become more mature and more full-throated.

In spite of all the trouble she generated for MGM, her star power was stronger than ever. A poll placed her as the third most popular female star in America, topped only by Bette Davis and Ingrid Bergman. Male stars topping the list included Bing Crosby, Van Johnson, Humphrey Bogart, Gary Cooper, and Spencer Tracy.

***

In June of 1945, thousands of American G.I.s returned home, following their victory against the Nazis, even though the war against Japan still raged.

Across the country, young women *en masse* were marrying these servicemen. Judy, just turning twenty-three, was about to become a June bride.

Where's Harvey?

Judy, representing America's vision of a "nice girl," finally grabs the prize: A hot, rich business owner portrayed by **John Hodiak**. He runs a brothel, gambling parlor, and saloon in the Wide Open West.

Audiences are left with the impression that Judy, as a Harvey Girl, will be enlisted to run them and make them (and him) "respectable" after they marry.

Whereas **Harvey Girls** referred to wholesome American maidens headed to Western climes as waitresses in Fred Harvey's restaurants, most members of the audience thought the Saloon Girls in the film, as spearheaded by **Angela Lansbury** (center), were a lot more fun.

CHAPTER NINE

VICTORY IN EUROPE
AMERICA CELEBRATES THE END OF WORLD WAR II BY EMBRACING JUDY'S "WORDS & MUSICAL FLUFF"

EXHAUSTED AND PILL-ADDICTED,
SHE LOOKS FOR THE SILVER LINING AS CLOUDS ROLL BY

COMMAND PERFORMANCE
JUDY MARRIES VINCENTE MINNELLI, ENTERTAINS THE TROOPS WITH FRANK SINATRA, & BEGINS AN AFFAIR WITH A "MYSTERIOUS EXOTIC," YUL BRYNNER.

IN AN ATTEMPT TO "STRAIGHTEN OUT JUDY," MGM ENLISTS KATHARINE HEPBURN
TO GIVE THE LASS ADVICE

(FOR JUDY & SPENCER TRACY, IT'S SATURDAY NIGHT AT A PARTY. FOR BISEXUAL, NO-NONSENSE KATE, IT'S THE SOBERING LIGHT OF DAWN ON A BLEAK MONDAY.)

THE PIRATE
IT'S ARTSY AND STYLISH, IT'S RIDDLED WITH SEXUAL TENSIONS, IT'S BRUTALIZING FOR JUDY AND GENE KELLY, & IT DRIVES A WEDGE BETWEEN JUDY AND HER HUSBAND/DIRECTOR

"I was at a dinner party in Hollywood after the news broke that Judy Garland and Vincente Minnelli had been married. All the guests were cynical, claiming Minnelli was an opportunistic director at MGM who wanted to hitch his wagon to the studio's biggest star. But maybe it was a case of two talented, sensitive souls turning to each other for solace."

—Singer Margaret Whiting

"In New York on our honeymoon, I introduced Judy to the most sophisticated people on Broadway, all of whom had their own brand of savage humor. They expected the sugar of her movie image, finding spice instead. She could trade convoluted, high-level sarcasm with the best—and worst—of them."

—Vincente Minnelli

As the year that ended World War II, 1945 will live

forever in world history. It was also marked by Vincente Minnelli's planting a kiss on the moist, succulent lips of Judy Garland. It happened at a gala New Year's Eve party at the home of Jack and Mary Benny.

On June 15 of that year, five days after she turned twenty-three, Judy and Minnelli were wed. Betty Asher, her friend and publicist, was Maid of Honor, and Ira Gershwin was Best Man. A beaming Louis B. Mayer walked the bride down the aisle, at the end of which Minnelli was waiting. The service was officiated by the Rev. William E. Roberts of the Beverly Hills Community Church.

At Ethel's home (near the corner of Ogden Drive and Wilshire Blvd.), just before the wedding, Judy told Minnelli what he already knew: "Ethel is maddeningly meddlesome. She wanted to direct the wedding but I planned it myself. Her days of running my life are over. I won't stand for it."

The chief costume designer at MGM, Irene Gibbons, created Judy's wedding dress, a gun metal gray jersey with pink pearl beading.

Minnelli's mother had previously died of a damaged heart, and his father remained in Florida, too ill to travel to California. Howard Strickling, the keeper of secrets at MGM and the studio's chief publicist, attended, as did Arthur Freed. Yet the ceremony was very intimate, attended by only a few.

When it was over, the pastor held up a wooden staff for the newlyweds. Along with Asher and Gershwin, they grasped it as a symbol of their union. At the last moment, Mayer's hand reached up to latch onto the wooden knob at the top. "We presumably got God's blessings from the heavens above," Minnelli later said, "and from a far greater man than God himself, Mr. Mayer, whom we feared more than the man in the sky, also extended his blessings to our union."

While Judy was changing into her traveling suit in an upstairs bedroom, an urgent call came in from Van Johnson. Picking up the phone, she learned that Robert Walker was threatening suicide and wanted her to come over right away.

She told Van that she was rushing to leave on her honeymoon and begged him to go over and try to comfort and control Walker.

"He says he's gonna kill himself if you don't show," Van answered.

"He's done that a few times already," she said. "Please handle this for me."

Van promised he would and wished her a happy honeymoon, but then said disparagingly about Minnelli: "Personally, if I were ever locked in a room with him, and he was the last man on the planet, he'd be perfectly safe. I prefer John Garfield."

The newlyweds boarded the Super Chief, "The Train of the Stars," for the cross-country trek to Manhattan. En route, Minnelli relayed some devastating news: Betty Asher, Judy's Maid of Honor, was no friend. According to Minnelli: "She works for Strickling and is a spy, indirectly reporting to Mayer details about your every move.

"I trusted the bitch," Judy said. "How dare she!" Her temper flared. From that moment forward, Asher, her former lover and *confidante*, would be banned from her life.

Judy was just five days from her twenty-third birthday when she became the June Bride of **Vincente Minnelli**, who was forty-two.

Hollywood had seen more romantic weddings, but Judy carried it off beautifully and told those gathered, "This time I will make it work. I was just too young when I married David Rose. Vincente will be both a husband for me and a father image as well, all rolled into one talented package. We'll also raise a family together, perhaps five children— three daughters and two sons. At least that is what a fortune teller told me."

Up until then, Judy felt she stood alone in her battle with MGM and Mayer, with Ethel always taking the side of the mogul. She hoped that her groom would become her champion, helping to defend her in her ongoing war with the studio. Although he might be deficient in some areas, "with a figure less than Greek," she was depending on him as her new champion.

To an ever-increasing degree in their future, Judy's anti-MGM stance would place Minnelli in an awkward position. Whereas he desperately needed the good will and support of his studio, as he had told Richard Rodgers, "Judy is self-indulgent, self-deceiving, and in need of constant attention, adoration, and most definitely, approval."

Anne Edwards, a biographer, wrote, "Minnelli needed the admiration of his press more than he did affection from his young wife. He also sought acceptability in the social world more strongly than the bond Judy expected of their union."

Mayer had given the couple a three-month vacation and had arranged for them to live rent-free in one of the most luxurious residences in Manhattan, on high-priced Sutton Place next to the East River. The elegantly furnished home was a triplex penthouse with panoramic views from its plant-filled terraces. The house was fully staffed with a maid and a cook.

From its location, Judy set out with Minnelli as her tour guide. Having lived in New York, the city was familiar turf to him, but not to her. Although she'd visited many times, she was always busy with some commitment and had never explored New York in any depth.

Four days after their arrival, Minnelli and Judy joined some four million New Yorkers as they welcomed home—with a tickertape parade, amid other ceremonies—a conquering hero, General Dwight D. Eisenhower, Supreme Commander of Allied Forces during World War II, the man who had directed the armies which had defeated the Nazis during the world's most devastating war.

Together, the Minnellis explored secret nooks as well as the city's major art museums. He even introduced her to his favorite Italian *trattoria,* a hideaway he'd frequented during his days in Greenwich Village, escorting her there at least once a week.

Occasionally, the couple hosted their own dinner parties, but for the most part they were showered with invitations from his friends.

One night, they entertained the Broadway star Ethel Merman, who was to become a close friend of Judy's. They also attended shows, notably Tennessee Williams' *The Glass Menagerie,* starring the veteran actress Laurette Taylor, a recovering alcoholic.

Judy was so moved by Taylor's portrayal of a Southern matriarch that she shed tears and warmly greeted her backstage, seeing that her face deeply revealed the ravages of her tortured life.

As a collector, Minnelli, with Judy, visited antique stores where he discreetly bought a few treasured items to ship back to their home in California.

Leaving their Sutton Place apartment one night, they walked along the East River. She carried her purse and, at one point, opened it and tossed three bottles of pills into the murky waters. "No more for me," she vowed. "I'm off pills for life. With you at my side, I no longer need them."

Wherever they went, Judy was hounded by autograph seekers, whom she gladly obliged. Sometimes workmen called from a telephone pole or from a taxi, "Hiya, Judy!"

One mother had her eight-year-old son with her and stopped Judy. "Sonny, this is Dorothy from *The Wizard of Oz.*"

"No it ain't!" the bratty kid responded. "More like Dorothy's mother!"

Nick Schenck, from MGM's East Coast office, called and invited the Minnellis to his villa on Long Island. The following Monday afternoon, he asked them to go with him to Tiffany's. Mayer had not given her a wedding present and wanted her to select one for herself.

She was modest in her choice until Schenck urged her to select something far more expensive. She eventually opted for a stunning bracelet of square diamonds and emeralds with a companion gold pin. Minnelli settled for a gold watch.

"I'd like to think that our honeymoon in New York was as perfect for Judy as it was for me," Minnelli said. "If she expressed any slight irritation during our stay, they revolved largely around her child-image, which MGM had held over her head for a decade after she no longer wanted it. She yearned for sleek satins and upswept hairdos but had been held back as the studio forcibly dressed her in blue gingham pinafores and red patent Mary Janes."

"I'll qualify for Social Security before Mayer will let me play my first real love scene," she said.

On July 4, Minnelli escorted Judy to Le Martinique night club to see her sister, Jimmie, sing and dance in a one-woman show. She did not want to capitalize off the Garland name, so she had billed herself as "Miss Dorothy."

[It was assumed by some that she had stolen that name from the Dorothy character in The Wizard of Oz. *Actually, Jimmie's stage name was more legitimate than some witnesses at the time might have understood: Her official birth name was Dorothy Virginia Gumm.]*

Although Judy was not impressed with her sister's act, she greeted her warmly and invited her for dinner at Sutton Place the following week.

At the home of Richard and Dorothy Rodgers, Judy was warmly welcomed. Later in the evening, she stood before his piano as he played the tunes he'd written and that she had sung. She sang them with gusto, and he heartily approved.

Judy was enthusiastically accepted by Minnelli's friends, including Dorothy Parker, whom she had met before in Hollywood. One night, Moss Hart arrived with Kitty Carlisle, and Judy also entertained Mary Martin, Beatrice Lillie, her friend Harold Arlen, S.N. Behrman, and Oscar and Dorothy Hammerstein.

Judy became so enamored with Broadway that she hinted to columnist Dorothy

THE PLAYBILL
FOR THE MARTIN BECK THEATRE

LUNT & FONTANNE

They were so famous that the covers of theater programs didn't even need to list their names: Their profiles in silhouette identified them to theatergoers nationwide

This publicity photo from 1942 promotes **Lynn Fontanne and Alfred Lunt** as the stars of their Broadway production of *The Pirate*. As a stage play, it was daring and avant-garde. Vincente Minnelli adapted it—wisely or not and with uneven success—into a movie for general release.

Judy, Minnelli's new wife, played on screen the role made famous on the stage by Lynn Fontanne.

Kilgallen that she might not renew her MGM contract and desert Hollywood for appearances in an ongoing series of lavish stage musicals.

During their honeymoon, Minnelli began to interest Judy in a possible movie musical in which she might star and which he might direct. In November of 1942, he'd gone to see Alfred Lunt and Lynn Fontanne in the frothy romantic stage comedy, *The Pirate,* which had opened at the Martin Beck Theatre.

Although the leads should have been played by a younger couple, Minnelli found it flamboyant, bizarre, and intriguing. Lunt was around fifty, Fontanne perhaps fifty-five, much too old. Minnelli pictured a movie version that might team Judy opposite Gene Kelly.

During the train ride to New York from California, Judy had brought

This aerial photo shows the effect of **the atomic bomb** that fell on Hiroshima.

Along with the counterpart that detonated on Nagasaki three days later, it was the most terrifying weapon the world had ever seen.

In the postwar aftermath, Judy and the rest of Hollywood struggled to adapt to the changing demands of the American public.

along a black poodle named "Gabo," a gift from Minnelli whose name had been inspired by his lover, Lester Gaba. Judy had fallen in love with the dog and whimsically brought the dog with her to a nightclub. Minnelli, parking his car on the street outside, had foolishly left the dog inside on the back seat, with the windows rolled down for ventilation.

When word spread that the car belonged to Judy Garland, a crowd began to assemble around it. That alarmed the dog, who escaped onto the streets of Manhattan and couldn't be found. Judy became hysterical.

Since she used her star power "to get the entire police department of Manhattan involved in a search for the dog," Gabo was located and returned to her before dawn. From that day forward, Gabo was only allowed outdoors with a leash.

The following night, Lester Gaba attended a dinner hosted by Judy at Sutton Place. As Minnelli remembered it, he treated her politely but with restraint. "He was very, very jealous but tried to conceal it." After that night, he told Minnelli that he wanted to continue to see him, but if possible, secretly and without Judy.

During the summer of 1945, Judy and Minnelli were strolling in Manhattan on August 6 when everybody on the street seemed to be talking about some bomb recently dropped on Japan. They hurried home to learn that Harry S Truman had authorized the dropping of the world's first atomic bomb on the city of Hiroshima. Yet the Japanese stubbornly did not surrender. On August 9, they heard that Nagasaki, another Japanese city, had also been bombed.

"Surely, the Japs realize that Tokyo will be next if they don't give up," Minnelli said. Japan surrendered a few days later, and history's most devastating war came to a sudden, inglorious end.

The newlyweds quickly realized that the end of the war would change their lives and that postwar Hollywood might be vastly different from what it had been during the turbulent war years.

"Old stars will be coming back from the war, trying to re-establish their careers, and new guys released from the service will be all too eager to replace them," Minnelli said. "We'll see the emergence of tomorrow's versions of Clark Gable, Robert Taylor, Tyrone Power, and Errol Flynn—just you wait and see."

Two weeks before their return to the West Coast, Judy woke up with what looked a lot like "morning sickness." She made an appointment with a doctor on Park Avenue, a man recommended by Ethel Merman. He confirmed that she was pregnant.

During the train ride back to California, Judy and Minnelli told no one, but she predicted "It'll be a boy. We'll name the kid Vincente Minnelli, Jr."

Judy was determined not to repeat the abortions she'd had during her involvements with Spencer Tracy, Tyrone Power, and her first husband, David Rose. Before leaving Sutton Place, she placed a defiant call to Ethel. "I'm having a baby, mother dear, and this time you're not having it ripped from my guts." Then she slammed down the phone.

Riding the rails back to California, Judy feared the reaction of both Arthur Freed and Mayer to her pregnancy. She was relieved when both men sent their blessings.

***

At the time, movie studios, especially MGM, were starting to make a series of biopics of composers that had nothing to do with the real artist. Homosexuality could not be depicted on the screen, thus Cary Grant has to play Cole Porter as 100% heterosexual during the filming of *Night and Day* (1946).

Likewise, Lorenz Hart was also reconfigured into a heterosexual in the movie *Words and Music* (1948), which would star Judy.

Before she showed any visible signs of pregnancy, MGM wanted her to appear in an all-star musical *Till the Clouds Roll By*, a fictionalized biopic of the life of the composer, Jerome Kern. *[Kern (1885-1945) had created dozens of Broadway musicals and Hollywood films in a career that lasted for more than four decades.]* Arthur Freed, its producer, had sent Judy a telegram in New York. "Before you start looking like you're giving birth to a watermelon, we want you to perform three or four musical numbers for the Jerome Kern picture," he said.

Robert Walker had been signed to play Kern.

The director of the film was Richard Whorf, but she demanded—and got—approval that Minnelli would direct her sequences in the movie as soon as possible.

***

Back at work at MGM, and with the full understanding she had to finish before she was too obviously pregnant, Judy was rushed through her singing gig in *Till the Clouds Roll By* (1946). Robert Walker, with whom she'd had a brief (disastrous) fling during filming of *The Clock,* was horribly miscast. Blandly and without a lot of flair, he headed an all-star cast, or, as Minnelli put it, "anyone who could carry a tune at Metro," all of them belting out intricately choreographed showcases of Kern's monumental library of evocative showtunes.

Judy, cast as the legendary stage actress, Marilyn Miller (1898-1936), was one of many movie stars showcased in this anthology of song. Freed's lineup included June Allyson, Lucille Bremer, Kathryn Grayson, Van Heflin, Lena Horne, Van Johnson, Tony Martin, Dinah Shore, Frank Sinatra, Angela Lansbury, Gower Champion, Cyd Charisse, Virginia O'Brien, and the Wilde Twins.

Big stardom had been predicted for Bremer, who, as it turned out, was a far better dancer than actress. By 1945, major success in films was looking more doubtful. Judy had worked with her before when she played her sister in *Meet Me in St. Louis* (1944).

After *Till the Clouds Roll By,* MGM lost interest in promoting her, and did not renew her contract. Disillusioned with the entertainment industry, Bremer fell in love with the son of the former president of Mexico, Abelardo Luís Rodríguez and retired from the scene.

Busby Berkeley had been the film's first director, but he was fired and replaced by Richard Whorf, an actor turned director. On the first day of filming, Judy greeted Whorf, who seemed miffed at her for

RAZZMATAZZ & ROLLING CLOUDS

Middle photo: In a kitchen, Judy "devastates" the dishes, all the while producing heart-rending music.

Lower photo: In a performance inspired by the stage star Marilyn Miller (1898-1936), Judy sings and interconnects with a bevy of handsome dancers. Their hearts were young and gay.

leveraging her star power to replace him with Minnelli in the direction of her musical sequences.

Judy knew that she could not dance as well as the vocalist (Marilyn Miller) whose hits she was replicating, but that she could sing better. For publicity, Judy's impersonation was billed as "the wistful, the lovely, the unforgettable Marilyn Miller."

Most of the dance numbers derived from the inspiration of choreographer Robert Alton. George Sidney, who had helmed Judy before, was summoned to direct Sinatra in white tails crooning "Ol' Man River."

The glue that held this song-and-dance extravaganza was Jerome Kern, composer of most of the songs it featured. One of his greatest successes— co-authored with Oscar Hammerstein—had been *Show Boat.* Various versions of it, many of them starring torch singer Helen Morgan, had already captured the imagination of the American public. *[They included the original 1927 stage version; a stage revival in 1932; a "part-talkie" film version released in 1929; and a full-sound version in 1936.]*

In November of 1945, everyone involved in the production of *Till the Clouds Roll By* was thrown into disarray when Kern died midway through its filming. As the central figure in the biopic and the subject on which it was based, his death prompted sudden and immediate rewrites. While he'd been alive, he'd occasionally visited the set to watch Judy sing some of the songs he'd written, especially "Look for the Silver Lining."

Minnelli recalled that he was particularly proud of Judy's rendition of "Sunny," which crammed all aspects of circus life into three and a half minutes of high-octane entertainment. He brought in baby elephants, tigers, and clowns, and dressed Judy in a tutu. Of course, MGM hired a lookalike for the scene where her character jumps on a horse and does all kinds of rider tricks.

Judy ridiculed her immediate situation during her performance of the song "Who?"

"When I shot that damn scene, I thought my kid was going to pop out of my navel at any minute, and I go up and down quizzing a bevy of chorus boys, asking 'Who?,' as in 'Who did this to me?'"

She shared concerns about her interpretation of the sequence with Freed, who responded. "Don't worry, darling, I've seen it. No one in the audience will believe that even one of those boys in the chorus could have fathered a child."

During Judy's involvement in *Till the Clouds Roll By,* Ann Miller visited her on the set. She congratulated her on her marriage and her pregnancy. Yet within a few days, she got catty, telling Freed, "Most of us are still convinced that darling Vince is a fag. If Judy is pregnant, we think it's the newest incarnation of the Immaculate Conception."

After sitting through the final cut, Freed said, "Judy brings a great warmth to every song. It's as if she is singing directly to a person. That's one of the reasons she developed a large cult following."

Although reviews of *Till the Clouds Roll By* were not always good, it became one of MGM's biggest box office successes that year.

Bosley Crowther of *The New York Times* asked, "Why did Metro cook up such a phony yarn about Jerome Kern? Why couldn't it have given us more of such enjoyable things as Judy Garland playing Marilyn Miller, singing her melodious songs?"

Time magazine found Judy charming, but went on to say that Van Johnson looked as if he had a roasted apple in his mouth. Lena Horne was cited for her "careful intensity as if she were expounding existentialism."

New York's *Morning Telegram* wrote: "Judy Garland plays the late Marilyn Miller like she had foreshadowed Garland herself."

Despite the allure of other members of its all-star cast, movie house

Robert Walker, looking romantic, and **Nancy Davis**, looking demure. Peter Lawford was involved in some sort of *ménage à trois* with them.

Years later, Lawford was among the first to aggressively spread the malicious assessment that Nancy—the future First Lady of the United States through her marriage to Ronald Reagan—was "The Fellatio Queen of Hollywood."

managers across the nation put only Judy and Van Johnson on the marquees of their theaters.

***

[After Judy reunited with Robert Walker on the set of Till the Clouds Go By, *she found him more troubled than ever. His sexual entanglements seemed in total disarray, and he still had not recovered from the loss of his former wife, Jennifer Jones, who had deserted him for producer David O. Selznick.*

But Walker's mourning of his lost love hadn't stopped him from pursuing other liaisons. As a bisexual, he had become involved in several affairs. He and Peter Lawford were having an affair which, as Judy was to learn, was complicated because both men were also having sexual relations with the MGM starlet Nancy Davis (later, Mrs. Ronald Reagan).

During the course of her pregnancy, Walker visited Judy on several occasions at her home. In July of 1948, against her advice, he married Barbara Ford, the daughter of Director John Ford. Their union lasted less than five months. Later, he told Judy, "My marriage began to fall apart after only five days."

That same year, Walker was borrowed by Universal to co-star with Ava Gardner in One Touch of Venus *(1948). He also began an affair with her, which was frequently interrupted when she would run off with actor Howard Duff instead of him. Gardner also became involved in an affair with Lawford.*

Hugely pregnant, and from the confines of her home, Judy told Walker, "You've got to be an accountant to keep up with you guys and dolls. All of you seem to be screwing each other in any combination. Since I got pregnant, it seems

I'm missing out on all the action."

When Mickey Rooney dropped in to visit her before Christmas of that year, she filled him in on the many romantic complications of Lawford, Walker, Gardner, and Nancy Davis. "Oh, I still long for Ava," he said. "I can't believe she was my wife."

"And what am I?" she asked. "Chopped liver?"

"You are the most adorable little creature on the face of the earth — that's all."

Judy continued to see Walker on and off during and after her pregnancy, when she gave birth to Liza Minnelli.

As she told Rooney, "I feel some strange link to Bob Walker., I don't know what it is. We're soulmates. He's the only person I know who's worse off than I am."]

***

Even though Judy couldn't work because of her pregnancy, she marked the New Year of 1946 by signing a five-year contract with MGM at an increase in salary to $3,000 a week, which was about twice what the average MGM contract player was granted. The new contract allowed her to appear once a week on radio, and—after paying MGM a percentage—pocketing the rest of the money.

Advertising styles and war efforts of yesteryear- Above is a collage of memorabilia associated with **Judy**'s involvement on Command Performance USA—in this case opposite THE VOICE, **Frank Sinatra.**

[Judy always seemed in demand for gigs on the radio. On September 6, 1945, she committed to a regular delivery of songs and comic skits to Command Performance USA. *It was a radio program inaugurated during the dark war year of 1942, less than three months after the bombing of Pearl Harbor. Broadcasts were typically pre-recorded in Los Angeles and then broadcast through the Armed Forces Radio Network (AFRS) to a weekly audience of as many as 95 million listeners, many of them American troops overseas. Judy was one of dozens of contributors, others of whom included cheerful, morale-building input from Bing Crosby, Jack Benny, Frank Sinatra, Fred Allen, Bob Hope and The Andrew Sisters.* Time *magazine evaluated* Command Performance *as "the best wartime program in America."*

Variety remarked that "sometimes the language on these shows is just a little more robust than is passed by standard broadcasting stations. Jack Benny, as we recall, last Sunday night encouraged our fighting men to 'give 'em hell.'"]

Before their marriage, Minnelli had acquired a pink stucco Mediterranean-style villa [address: 8850 Evanview Drive] with a panoramic view over Beverly Hills. The house needed a $70,000 renovation to make way for Judy, a nursery for their newborn, and a luxurious dressing room with a fur-covered chaise longue and a deluxe bathroom for Judy's personal use. While the house on Evanview Drive was undergoing renovations, the Minnellis rented a villa in Malibu that opened directly onto the beach.

Minnelli later nicknamed Judy "The Lady of the Manor" as she spent a lot of time lying on sofas à la Madame du Barry.

Within weeks after signing her new contract with MGM, Judy had doubts about it, telling Minnelli, "Once again, I have sold myself into bondage."

Then she began to ponder if she had made a mistake in marrying Minnelli, their interests were so different, and he snored so loudly he drove her out of the bed. Even worse, with the intention of protecting her unborn baby, she had to cope with her frailties and illnesses without any pharmaceutical dependence. She began referring to her pills, depending on their function, as "bolts and jolts."

At 7:48AM on March 12, 1946, at the Cedars of Lebanon Hospital, a baby girl came into the world weighing six pounds, ten and a half ounces. Judy had told her doctors she did not think she could endure the agonizing pain of childbirth and requested a Caesarean.

Minnelli and Judy had selected the name "Liza," after the Ira Gershwin song. He requested that that child's middle name be May in honor of his deceased mother.

Thus, a Hollywood princess and a future movie star in her own right was born. Frank Sinatra was the first visitor at the hospital, and, as the little girl grew older, the children of Charlie Chaplin would be her playmates.

Complications set in because of the Caesarean, and that old family friend, Dr. Marc Rabwin, came in to perform corrective surgery.

After Judy's return to her home, June Allyson was one of the first visitors. She recalled, "Judy was absolutely thrilled to be a mother for the first time, having endured all those abortions. She now had a happy home life, or at least it appeared that way. For the first time, she'll be a mom, perhaps with a daughter who adores her, unlike Joan Crawford's adopted children, and a loving caring husband. Of course, knowing Judy, you could never be certain."

In the weeks that followed, Judy— filled with anxiety, tension, and mental anguish—secretly returned to her dependence on pills. One day, she wanted to escape from the house and left Liza in the nursery with her nanny.

Walking along Rodeo Drive in Beverly Hills, she fainted and collapsed on the sidewalk. An ambulance, with red dome lights flashing, rushed her to the hospital, where she was dismissed late the following morning. Bed rest lasting weeks was recommended.

Her last radio appearance had occurred— before giving birth to Liza— on January 28, 1946 on the CBS *Lux Radio Theatre,* for its broadcast adaptation of her movie, *The Clock.* Her co-star in that film had been Robert Walker, but he was not available, so she asked her co-star from *The Harvey*

Girls, John Hodiak, and he went on the air with her. She would not work again until July of 1946, four months after giving birth.

She made a guest appearance at the Hollywood Bowl, honoring Jerome Kern, who had died while she was making his biopic, *Till the Clouds Roll By.* She sang the Kern numbers she'd sung in the movie and also filled in for Lena Horne with her rendition of "Why Was I Born?" and "Can't Help Loving that Man of Mine."

Vincente Minnelli, younger and more handsome here than in many of the later photos in which his looks had faded, was about as *avantgarde* as any film director in America when this portrait was snapped.

In the early years of her marriage, and certainly in its final months, she turned to others for sex. According to Kay Thompson, "Those lovers came and went. When she was through with a man, she cut him off at the ankles."

According to Van Johnson, "When Judy recovered from all that birthin' shit, she and I hit the town, with Minnelli's blessings, of course. Her hubby didn't like to go out on the town, and he hated, absolutely hated, Hollywood parties."

Judy was very candid talking with her close friends about her sex life. As she related to Kay, Van, and others, she did not look forward to resuming sexual relations with Minnelli after giving birth to their daughter.

A look at Minnelli's sexual identity appeared in Emanuel Levy's biography, *Hollywood's Dark Dreamer:* "Minnelli's approach to sex was detached and passive, clearly lacking much heat. He enjoyed foreplay more than actual intercourse, and she [Judy] complained that it took forever for him to get a hard-on, and even longer for him to climax. The easiest way to please her husband was oral sex."

Levy also revealed that on some nights, Judy didn't even make it home by the time Minnelli had to leave to report to work at MGM. "She often crashed at one of the homes of her gay friends, perhaps with a sexual partner," he claimed.

One night in particular was with John Hodiak, whom she had always found sexy during the periods she worked with him. "Anne Baxter's loss, my gain, at least for a night of passion," she told Van the next day. "Now I know why they refer to his endowment as 'the beer can,' a label awarded to him by Tallulah Bankhead."

During her absence, Minnelli visited the home of Lester Gaba for the early part of an evening, eventually rushing home to tuck Liza into bed.

Thus, the married life of Judy Garland and Vincente Minnelli moved on. Sinatra called it "a typical Hollywood marriage."

***

In 1945 and 1946, Kay Thompson worked very closely with Judy, guiding her musical career and her interpretation of songs. In 1937, Kay had married Jack Jenne, a trombonist and bandleader. She divorced him in 1939.

In 1942, she'd wed radio producer William Spier. After Judy settled into married life with Minnelli, Spier and Kay were their guests at the rate of about two nights a week. Judy and Kay were growing closer and closer. Sometimes, Judy, in her anxiety, phoned Kay eight times a day, and she turned to Kay, not Minnelli, during many of her worst depressions.

Reciprocally, Judy offered Kay whatever support she could give her. Kay had a dilemma. She spent all her time trying to make stars out of everybody else, including Frank Sinatra. "I want to be the one in the spotlight too," she confided to Judy.

Judy and Kay were seen everywhere together. In the autumn of 1945, the rumor mill went to work, suggesting that these two married women were engaged in a lesbian affair.

The Hollywood press was more hip than the New York columnist, Walter Winchell, who in a January 1946 column claimed that Spier and Kay were "Hollywood's happiest married couple."

"That's a crock of shit," said actor Jack Carson, who knew both Kay and Spier.

At New York's Stork Club, columnist Dorothy Kilgallen spotted Kay with Danny Kaye. Privately, she claimed," It's purely platonic. Kay has her Judy; Danny has his Laurence Olivier."

Whenever possible, Judy and Kay left their husbands at night and headed for a club called The Hangout. [*Standing across from the MGM gate it was also known as Edwards Bar & Grill.*] On any given night, Judy might be seen there with friends who included Mickey Rooney, June Allyson, and Donald O'Connor, among others. The tavern had a small dance floor on which Gene Kelly could be seen trying out some new dance steps. On some occasions, Judy— because they would soon be co-starring in *The Pirate*—joined him

Leonard Bluett of the musical group, "The Dreamers," said, "Judy and Kay were always seen together. I never saw her with Spier. Maybe he had something else going on. My friends who knew Kay assumed she had the hots for Judy."

Arthur Laurents, who wrote and directed *West Side Story* claimed, "I thought those ladies were dykes—there's nothing wrong with that. Even I have my indiscretions, if that is what to call them."

As the years went by, Judy's second daughter, Lorna Luft, weighed in with her opinion, too: "Kay and my mother were very close. The two might be seen with their arms around each other, offering comfort and support as friends often do. I totally discount any lesbian link, however."

Many biographers have reported on the lesbian affair between the dynamic pair, calling it a fact—and perhaps it was. But so far, most of the evidence is circumstantial.

Certainly, Kay would fit into the stereotype of a glamourous Hollywood lesbian, acting very mannish and wearing pants in the tradition of Katharine Hepburn.

"To me, Kay was quite butch," said Arthur Freed. "If she had a lesbian link to Judy, I think Kay was the man in the relationship. I said 'butch' when I should have said, 'elegant butch.'"

"If Kay, a great help to me, likes the girls, who am I to throw stones?" Sinatra asked. "I like girls myself. But I know she also desired me as time went by. I knew she chased after Howard Duff when he wasn't screwing Ava Gardner. In time, I heard she had an affair with the young singer, Andy Williams—you know, the 'Moon River' guy."

Her business manager, Leonard Grainger, claimed, "I don't think Kay swung both ways."

When Ann Miller heard that, she said, "Hell! Half of Hollywood, maybe three-fourths, swings every which way the wind blows."

Adept at portraying "ethnics and exotics," **Yul Brynner** starred as Tsai-Yong in *Lute Song*

Critic Rex Reed was quoted as saying that he thought Kay Thompson "batted for the other team. She told me she is turned on by whomever is around, be it a duke or a dishwasher."

Michael Feinstein claimed that when Kay was asked if she were a lesbian, she responded, "My dear, we are what we are."

***

"It seemed inevitable that two lusty souls like Vince and Judy would not remain faithful to each other," Freed would recall. "From what I heard, neither of them was sexually fulfilled with each other. Both of them faced tons of opportunities for sex outside marriage, and I'm sure they turned to others for gratification."

Minnelli was out of town when Judy attended the road show version of *Lute Song,* which had opened on Broadway in 1946 starring Mary Martin and a then-unknown Yul Brynner, both of them on the dawn of incredible fame.

The musical encompassed a minor role, that of a "lady-in-waiting" at the Imperial court. Into it had been cast the future First Lady of the United States, Nancy Reagan, then known as starlet Nancy Davis. It was her first (and only) Broadway appearance.

Lute Song had been loosely adapted from a 14th-Century Chinese play, *Tale of the Pipa (Pi-Pa-Ji). Time* magazine called it "the season's loveliest production and most charming failure."

It became significant in theater history because Martin recommended Brynner to her friends, Rogers and Hammerstein, as the actor who should play the Siamese monarch in the classic *The King and I,* which premiered on Broadway in 1951. It was a musical with which Brynner would become forever linked.

Whereas Martin did not go on the road with the *Lute Song*, Brynner did. When it arrived on stage in Los Angeles, Judy, accompanied by Kay Thompson, went to see it. Minnelli, meanwhile, was in New York.

Judy seemed thrilled, telling Kay that *Lute Song*—with her as the female lead, and with Brynner as her leading man—would make a great MGM musical. After that night's performance, both women went backstage to congratulate the cast.

Kay greeted the players and remained with them after an usher escorted Judy to Brynner's dressing room. He had been alerted that Judy Garland had been in the audience, near the front. Still in costume, he greeted her warmly, as she hugged and kissed him. Gushing enthusiastically, she told him that she wanted to co-star with him in a possible MGM musical version of *Lute Song,* and he seemed most intrigued.

Born in Vladivostok in 1920, and speaking little English, **Yul Brynner** and his mother emigrated to the United States after adventure-studded stints in France and China, arriving in San Francisco when he was twenty.

He's depicted here as Pharoah Ramesses II in *The Ten Commandments* (1956).

Prior to that, she had heard very little about him except for an article in *Variety*. This exotic man of mystery seemed to be of Russian and Chinese origin. One story had him being born in Siberia as his mother was riding a horse through a snowstorm, taking time out to give birth.

When she learned that his wife, Virginia Gilmore, like Minnelli, was out of town, she invited him for champagne and caviar at her home. He told her he'd be honored. She volunteered to excuse herself while he changed into street clothes, but he said, "Don't leave....I'm not modest."

Later that night in the bed she shared with her husband, Brynner joined her for a night of lovemaking, marking the beginning of a torrid four-month affair. Each of them promised to be discreet since neither welcomed a scandal. "I don't kiss and tell," he promised, with a vow that wasn't always reliable.

The next day, Kay was perhaps jealous hearing Judy rave about Brynner in bed. "Yul is everything Vince is not—virile, dominant, possessive, willing to satisfy every desire, from throat to ankle. He's the kind of man I should have married, an exotic import from some unknown locale, perhaps the illegitimate son of a Russian prince."

Although Brynner's background was unknown to her, in the years to come, she'd learn some other tantalizing aspects of his past.

Judy would be added to that A-list coven of superstars Brynner had seduced, beginning with an aggressive Tallulah Bankhead, who virtually raped him. His future son, Rock, later wrote a biography of him, in which he claimed that his father seduced virtually every young woman in *Lute Song*, except for Mary Martin herself, who was more inclined to have sex with women. *[At the time Martin was married to her "understanding" husband and manager, Richard Halliday.]*

One of Brunner's seductions, long before Ronald Reagan married her, was Nancy Davis. [*Around the same time, Davis also had an affair with a bisexual male dancer who appeared onstage with them in* Lute Song, *too. Ironically, that young dancer also "serviced" Brynner.*]

While Brynner was appearing in his *Lute Song* gig in Los Angeles, he managed to work in a one-night stand with Joan Crawford, too. She seemed to enjoy being the first to seduce whatever "new boy" was on the rise in Hollywood. But in reference to Crawford, Brynner later complained, "I do not like Hollywood hit-and-run humping. I'm more of a romantic."

Judy never really understood the origins of this exotic man who began visiting her bed almost every night. He confounded reporters by telling different and contradictory stories about himself. "What does it matter?" he asked Judy. "The aim is to sell newspapers. Juicy stories help peddle the news."

One night, Brynner introduced Judy to John Houseman, a close associate of Orson Welles, her former lover. He'd produced *Lute Song* on Broadway. When he was gone, Brynner confessed to her, "I knew he had a homosexual streak in him. When I showed up for *Lute Song's* costume fittings, I invited him to my dressing room. When he came in, I was completely nude. 'You can dress me from my skin outward,' I told him."

Judy became so enthralled with Brynner that had he asked her, she would have divorced Minnelli and married him. Later, she remembered many things he told her. He said, "Girls have an unfair advantage over men. If they can't get what they want by being smart, they play dumb."

Although she always raved about him, she knew that other stars, both male and female, had differing views. At a party, William Holden told her, "Brynner is one of the biggest shits in show business, a real pig."

When Brynner had to fly to Chicago to star at the Studebaker Theatre in *Lute Song*, Judy got to missing him so much that she concocted a scheme that persuaded him to return to Los Angeles for three days and nights. She created the fantasy that MGM wanted to cast him in a film called *Valentino* and asked him to make a screen test. His producer in Chicago was convinced that the idea had merit, and Brynner flew west. Through Judy's influence, he did make that screen test, but it ended up on a shelf in an MGM warehouse.

[*After being "broken in" by Judy and Joan Crawford, Brynner set out in the 1950s to enjoy a series of A-List conquests of his leading ladies. In terms of seductions, his most prolific year was 1956, when he starred in the screen*

Dressed in her trademark color (red), and showing the camera-ready training she learned during her career as a Hollywood starlet, here's **Nancy Davis Reagan** on the occasion of her 50th anniversary to her husband, **Ronald, POTUS.**

version of The King and I, *co-starring Deborah Kerr. She claimed, "Yul is very very handsome and very, very sexy and sensual."*

That same year, he also seduced Ingrid Bergman, his co-star in Anastasia, *and Anne Baxter, with whom he appeared in* The Ten Commandments. *He would go on to seduce Maria Schell during their filming of* The Brothers Karamazov *(1958) and Gina Lollobrigida, his co-star in* Solomon and Sheba *1959).*

Brynner didn't necessarily have to co-star in a movie to seduce a star: Take Yvonne De Carlo, Claire Bloom, and Marilyn Monroe, for example.

His most long-running seduction was with the much older Marlene Dietrich. She was in love with him, but he eventually dumped her. She never got over it. Years later, when informed that he was stricken with cancer, she said, "Goody, goody. He deserves it."

His son, Rock Brynner, was reported to have said, "Of all my father's seductions, he told me that Judy Garland was the love of his life."

Years later, when asked about Brynner, Judy said, "He was every inch a king."]

***

In 1942, Katharine Hepburn was co-starring with Spencer Tracy in *Keeper of the Flame,* directed by their mutual friend George Cukor. Louis B. Mayer was impressed at how she had sobered up Tracy so that the movie was being made without any of his usual alcoholic binges.

Mayer summoned Hepburn to his office to ask if she could "straighten out our troubled singing sensation, Judy Garland. You're her most admired actress. Since she respects you so much, you might at least meet with her."

Hepburn seemed reluctant but agreed to have lunch with Judy

Katharine
The Great

HEPBURN lifetime
A Lifetime
of Secrets
Revealed

Darwin
Porter

In 2004, Blood Moon Productions published Darwin Porter's groundbreaking, then-shocking biography *("everything she desperately wanted to forget')* of **Katharine Hepburn.**

Although many of its never-before-published revelations inspired screams of outrage, and threats of (baseless) litigation, its premises are now considered "standard operating procedure" for her thousands of avid fans.

The filming of **Keeper of the Flame** was a troubled production from the beginning. For reasons known only to herself, **Katharine Hepburn** battled director George Cukor and the scriptwriter, Donald Ogden Stewart.

Even though she'd scored with Tracy as part of a romantic couple in *Woman of the Year* (1942), she wanted the film script to follow more closely I.A.R. Wylie's novel.

In front of the cast, **Spencer Tracy** ridiculed her suggestions: "What are you trying to do? Impotent eunuch? Are you trying to cut off my balls in this film? I thought you liked my balls!"

She walked away, deeply embarrassed.

242

in the commissary. Over their meal, she was touched by the singer's desperation and her admitted dependence on amphetamines and barbiturates. Her immediate advice to Judy was to get rid of "all those sycophants and doctors giving you all those pills."

But Judy refused: "Please understand. I just can't. Even though I'm married to Vince, I get my heart broken almost every day. I love this man. I love that man. But they don't love me back."

Hepburn had long harbored a resentment of both Tracy and Judy for their affair back in the 1930s when he'd taken her virginity and then helped maneuver her into an abortion. It seemed that every player on the MGM lot knew about it.

Hepburn later reported back to Mayer with: "I think Judy requires twenty-four-hour-a-day nurses. She needs so much help. She's sweet. She's adorable. But I already have my hands full with Spencer."

Hepburn's relationship with Judy didn't really unfold until four years later. In 1946, when Minnelli directed her in the murky *film noir, Undercurrent.* It starred Hepburn with Robert Taylor, back from the war, and the rising new star, Robert Mitchum.

Before filming began, producer Pandro S. Berman visited Minnelli and Judy at their home. "Finding a script for Kate is like one man servicing a hundred whores in one night. A possibility, but highly difficult."

After only a week of directing Hepburn, Minnelli came home depressed and raging, telling Judy, "She can't stand me as her director. She says that *Undercurrent* calls for a man like Alfred Hitchcock. She claims that I'm Mayer's joke on her. The god damn part calls for Ingrid Bergman, and he sends me this old dyke," he raged.

Hepburn mocked and raged about Minnelli to her gay friend, George Cukor. "He's got this damn tic. His right eye, as if by clockwork, clicks shut every three minutes, and he constantly purses his lips as if he wants to whistle. The scarlet lipstick, the purple eyeshadow—it's all too much."

One day on the set, Hepburn was surprised when an MGM messenger delivered her a sealed pink envelope. It was from Judy. "Please come by and see me any night next week," the note read. "I'm desperate to see you. Vince won't be home all next week. I want to show you my little baby daughter. Please, please don't disappoint me. It's a matter of life and death.

Robert Taylor, a box office *matinée* idol from the 1930s, returned from World War II to co-star with **Katharine Hepburn** in the *noir* thriller, *Undercurrent* (1946).

It would mark one of the low points of Hepburn's mercurial career, evocative of the time in the 1930s when she was maligned as "box office poison."

Undercurrent was Minnelli's first *film noir,* and Robert Taylor was miscast as a psycho. So was Hepburn as a frail, defenseless woman.

Love, Judy."

It was a Monday evening when Hepburn drove up to the Minnelli house on Evanview Drive. Emerging from her car, she paused to take in the panoramic view of Beverly Hills and Hollywood at night. The lights were just coming on. From the beginning, she was rather awed by their pink stucco, Mediterranean style home.

Judy was no longer Dorothy from *The Wizard of Oz*. Nor was she any longer linked to Mickey Rooney and those *Girl Crazy* pictures. She had blossomed into a beautiful woman with the kind of bright wit that was for the most part lacking in Hepburn herself.

When Mayer had first enlisted her help with Garland, Hepburn had found the prospect of channeling the young Judy too daunting for her. But now, intrigued with the intricacies of another encounter with what she hoped was a more mature Garland, she felt adequate for the challenge.

When Hepburn was ushered into the living room, Judy was curled up on the sofa. It was obvious that she'd been crying. As Hepburn was later to tell her friends, "Judy looked more incredibly alive and more beautiful than I'd remembered."

Fresh faced, and without her usually heavy makeup and lipstick, she had a shy, lonely, and almost pathetic quality to her. Yet, almost in con-tradiction, there was "something demonic about her," as Hepburn remem-bered. "Without meaning to, she appeared incredibly demanding. She was like someone waiting to sweep you away into her own self-created whirlpool. I was captivated, but also a bit afraid of her. I tried to mask it with a certain indifference."

"I wanted to see you," Judy said. "I know you're involved in some way with Spencer—that's your business—but I also know he must be very diffi-cult to live with. I'm finding life with Vince almost impossible, and I'm turning to you for whatever advice you have."

"Spence and I have a most unusual relationship, and I'm aware that in some way it might be compared to you and Minnelli—except that you guys are married. We are not. Spence is entitled to his privacy, and he re-spects my privacy to go off and do whatever on my own."

"Vince has gone off for a week with his true love, Gene Kelly."

"Perhaps they're just good friends," Hepburn said without any real conviction in her voice.

"You don't seem at all surprised by my revelation," Judy said. "I mean, about Vince and Gene."

"You may not know this, but the rumors about Kelly and your hus-band have even made it to the broom closet at MGM. Of course, all of those rumors may be just that—rumors."

"It's not mere gossip," Judy said.

"Do you plan to divorce him?" Hepburn asked pointedly.

"I'm sure that's in our future," Judy said.

To break the tension, Hepburn asked Judy if she'd walk through the garden with her to enjoy the twilight. As the two women strolled, Judy took her hand as if seeking comfort. Later, during Hepburn's account of the enchantment of that night, she recalled that it was one of those incred-ibly beautiful evenings that occurred in the Forties back in Los Angeles when the air was much cleaner. "Suddenly, walking with Judy and holding her hand, I was drawn to her as I never had before. I felt that she was pleading for my friendship."

Hepburn turned to Judy and looked deeply into her eyes. "You're no longer the little girl who met Spence when you were only fifteen. You've been in Hollywood too long. You must have known about Vincente before you married him."

"I turned a deaf ear to all those chorus boys at MGM who told me that he was gay when he was directing me in *Meet Me in St. Louis*," Judy said. "I would turn to them and tell them, 'You're wrong about Vin. You're mistaking artistic flair for gayness.' I should have listened to them."

"Still, you forged ahead."

"Even before my wedding, two chorus boys, Frank Lot and Jimmie Schanker, each insisted that they'd had a regular thing with my future groom. I remembered they called it 'a do.'"

Judy relayed the brief history of her relationship with Minnelli, claiming that he was "very passionate when he directed me in *The Clock*. Some lighting operators up high on the catwalk even spotted me going down on him in the dark shadows during a lunch break."

She went on to confess that when she was dating Minnelli, trying to decide if she wanted to marry him, she was also secretly dating Orson Welles. "Orson told me, 'My dear child, Minnelli doesn't want to create a beautiful image of you on the screen. He sees himself as you! Through you, he's living the illusion of what he passionately wants to be: A screen goddess like my own Rita Hayworth. Of course, all of us have our fantasies, especially me. I once had a dream in which I became Marlene Dietrich.'"

"I know Mayer put a lot of pressure on you to marry Vincente," Hepburn said to her. "He told me that himself. Mayer thinks that marriage to an older man will help stabilize you. But it appears to me that marriage to such a man could drive a weak woman over the edge."

"But it's more than that," Judy said. "In my heart, I knew that Vince is enjoying the sex act more with Gene than he ever did with me. We have rotten sex. He has trouble maintaining an erection. When he does get one, I fear that he's not thinking about the woman under him, but that he's fantasizing about being fucked himself."

"You do believe in telling it like it is," Hepburn said. "I'm amazed that you can talk so openly with me."

"Don't be disturbed," Judy said. "I'm like that with everybody. Now that Garbo's retired, you've become the mystery woman of MGM. Except perhaps for a close pal here and there, you hold in all your secrets."

"If Mayer thought that Vincente would straighten you out," Hepburn said, "who is he going to get to straighten out Kelly and Vincente? He'll find out about them one day. He always does. He's grooming Vincente to be his biggest musical director, and Kelly to be his biggest musical star. He'll want to keep both guys married, lest word get out about what they're really up to."

"There's more," Judy said. "He's also a drag queen. Do you know that Vince sometimes tries to wear my discarded clothing? He gets Irene

Gibbons over at MGM's costume department to alter some of my dresses. I caught him one night in our bedroom wearing my wedding gown. It's this smoky gray number with pink pearl beading. I tried to handle it with a joke. I said, 'Oh, Vin, take it off! It looked better on me.'"

She claimed that even when Minnelli took her to New York, he spent most of his time with his former lover, Lester Gaba. "He invited Gaba for dinner. Wherever we went, Vince paid me no attention at all—he had eyes only for Gaba. The remarkable thing was that the two of them looked so much alike that many people thought they were twins."

"Maybe Vincente isn't homosexual at all, but just a totally out-of-control narcissist," Hepburn said.

"He loves Gaba all right," Judy claimed. "When Gaba came to Grand Central to see us off, Vince was shedding more tears than a school of Greer Garsons."

In this scene of **Gene Kelly** making love to **Judy** in *The Pirate*, **Minnelli** seems to be hovering and handwringing in the background.

But who is he protecting and/or pursuing and/or fretting over? Judy or Gene?

The evening was suddenly growing cold. As Judy led Hepburn back into the living room, she said that whenever Kelly came near him, her husband behaved the same way he did with Gaba.

"They spend hours and hours together sitting like they're in a huddle," Judy said. "Even when I enter the room, they pay me no attention. Those two don't need women to love them, much less wives. They have each other. I should have realized from the beginning what kind of man I was marrying. I've been made love to by men who really like women, and I've been made love to by men who don't. Believe me, Vince falls into the latter category. Kelly can satisfy him in ways I can't."

"Kelly has the equipment, and we don't," Hepburn said. "Damn it, I've been stating the obvious all day."

Over a drink, Judy said that her husband frequently sat in their living room just staring into space and saying nothing to her. "But the moment Gene comes over, those big doe eyes of his light up, and he comes alive for the first time all day."

Hepburn gave her some advice, as she did with everyone she met. "Stick in there a little longer, especially since you've just given birth. You can still be with a man even though he sees other women on the side. Or, men as the case may be. Believe me, you're talking to an experienced person about that. I suggest you launch yourself into another affair." She rose from the sofa. "I really must be going. I'm having dinner with Spencer later. He's got stomach trouble and won't be on the town prowling. But tomorrow, I'll be by to see you promptly at seven a.m. I'm taking you for

246

a long walk in the hills."

"I don't do that," She protested.

"Starting right now, if you want to be my friend, you'll begin by taking long walks with me every morning at seven."

"Is that the price I have to pay for a friendship with you?" Judy asked.

"That and more," Hepburn said, reaching for her coat. "I think we'll be friends. We have more in common that I'd thought at first."

"I just knew you'd become my most important woman friend," Judy said.

"What gave you such self-assurance?" Hepburn asked. "I don't extend friendship easily."

"Because I'm so vulnerable," Judy said. "Just look." In an amazing transformation of her facial muscles, she suddenly became the most pathetic creature in all the world. "How can you resist befriending someone who looks like me? I'm not a strong and independent woman like you. I can't survive alone."

As Judy stood up, a look of agonizing pain slashed across her face like the cut of a sharp razor. She screamed. Hepburn knew at once that her newly acquired friend was not pretending.

Judy fell to the floor where she rolled over several times in agony.

"Call Dr. Marc Rabwin!" she shouted to Kate. "His number's scribbled on the wall. By the phone in the kitchen."

Hepburn rushed into the kitchen, where she spotted the number and immediately dialed the doctor's office. He came on the phone and promised her he'd be at the Minnelli residence in less than half an hour. He assured her that his patient had these attacks frequently. "Don't be unduly alarmed. I know what to do."

She returned to the living room and tried to comfort Judy as much as she could until the doctor came, but there was nothing she could do but lift her back up onto the sofa. At one point, since Judy was sweating profusely, she went into the kitchen and came back with a wet towel which she applied to her forehead.

True to his word, Rabwin arrived and was let in by the nanny. He immediately injected some fluid into Judy's left arm, after which, Judy just seemed to drift off.

Before leaving, the doctor assured Hepburn that his patient would be all right but asked her to remain with her for at least another two hours and call him if there were any change in her condition.

She poured herself a stiff drink, then went and sat down in an armchair to watch over Judy.

Two hours later, when she still hadn't awakened, Hepburn went to rouse the nanny to tell her she was leaving.

Mrs. MacFarlane came into the living room and placed a blanket over Judy and looked down at her protectively.

Before leaving, Hepburn said to her, "Seems to me as if you have two babies to take care of."

***

At seven o'clock the next morning, Hepburn, having returned to the scene of her dialogue with Judy the night before, as promised, had a very difficult time getting a drowsy Judy to arise from her bed. She had to enlist the help of Mrs. MacFarlane, who was engaged mainly with Liza since the child was screaming at the top of her lung capacity.

Driving Judy to a remote spot in the Hollywood Hills, Hepburn came to a stop near a belvedere where she stood holding her hand as they took in the panoramic view.

After all the rapid talk and revelations of the night before, Judy was strangely quiet. Hepburn enjoyed her company and even told her how beautiful she was in the morning light.

Judy said, "Lana Turner is beautiful. Whenever I'm in a room with her, no eyes look at me."

"Until you start to sing," Hepburn assured her. "Then you become the most beautiful woman who ever came into a room." She leaned over and gently kissed Judy on the lips.

Judy looked startled but kept on walking. "I dreamed about Gene Kelly last night," she said.

"I thought you'd dream about me," Hepburn said, pretending that she was offended.

"You'll be the subject of my dreams tonight," Judy assured her. "But first off, I'm seriously pissed at Gene because the only time he invites me to his house is when he wants me to entertain his guests. Imagine getting the great Judy Garland to sing for free at your house."

"That's reality," Hepburn admonished her. "Get to the dream."

"In my dream I was married to Gene and we were embarking from Southampton on the *Titanic*," she said. "Later, when it came time for me to get into a lifeboat and leave Gene aboard the sinking ship, he grabbed Liza from my arms. Amazingly, he had dressed in my ball gown and had disguised himself as a woman. He was going to slip onto the lifeboat with my baby and he did. He left me on the sinking ship as the girl singer for the band. In my dream, I was singing 'Nearer My God to Thee' as the ship went down into the icy waters, and then I woke up screaming."

"A Freudian analyst would have fun with that," Hepburn said, guiding her to a copse of wildflowers covering a hill. Then Hepburn announced that she was enjoying the day so much that she wanted to spend hours in the hills and that they'd return to her car later. "I've packed us the most delicious and nutritious picnic lunch."

"Instead of taking pills in the morning

A VERY ODD COUPLE

Spencer Tracy was teamed for the first time with **Katharine Hepburn** in the highly successful *Woman of the Year* (1942). It would set the style for a string of future "Tracy/Hepburn" collaborations. He always demanded top billing.

Highly touted as one of the great romances of the entertainment industry, the coupling was anything but happy. It was marked by bisexual infidelities, heavy drinking (on his part) and many a violent fight.

and lying in bed lamenting how bad everything is, you should get up and out and live, like we're doing today. I'll bet you haven't breathed fresh air since you left that farm in Kansas."

"You're probably right," Judy said. "I think I'm in Oz right now. Oz is Hollywood."

"We've both known that for a long time," Hepburn said. "Me even more than you."

George Cukor was **Hepburn**'s favorite director. He was also a close friend of Spencer Tracy and was privy to their most intimate secrets.

Both Hepburn and Cukor would have made Hollywood history if he hadn't gotten fired from *Gone With the Wind* and had gone on to make the picture with her as Scarlett O'Hara.

***

It's not known when Judy's friendship with Hepburn turned sexual. She was candid and confidential with George Cukor. Although Hepburn had her own residence, Tracy lived in a cottage on his estate. Cukor know them both extremely well and consistently asserted that their relationship was supportive and platonic, but not sexual. Both stars, he maintained, turned elsewhere for sex. Cukor claimed that Hepburn's affair with Judy began sometime late in 1946 and continued on and off at least through 1948.

Hepburn discussed her relationship with Judy with Laura Harding, the American Express heiress; with actor Kenneth MacKenna; and with Anderson Lawler, the rich tobacco heir who had been an intimate and longtime companion of Gary Cooper.

"Kate provided us with clues about Judy's mental condition at the time," MacKenna later said. "Her daughter, Liza, had been born in March by Cesarean section. Forever after, Judy always claimed that giving birth was one of the most traumatizing experiences of her life."

"Kate met her during one of her most vulnerable periods," MacKenna claimed. "At least in her life up until then. Judy was ripe for seduction when Kate entered her life. I knew that Judy was feeling worthless about herself, especially when she learned that Minnelli had fallen big for Gene Kelly. When he wasn't with Gene, he was with various MGM chorus boys."

The birth of Liza was followed by one of the worst bouts of depression that Judy ever had. "I don't want to get pregnant again," she told Hepburn. "My body was not made for birthin' babies." *[She, of course, was quoting from Butterfly McQueen's famous line in* Gone With the Wind.*]*

Her friend, Mickey Rooney, claimed that "Judy was self-indulgent, self-delusional, and in constant need of attention." Unknown to Rooney at the time, Hepburn was genuinely attempting to minister to Judy's needs.

For Hepburn, it became a losing battle, the way it was with Tracy. In spite of all the times she weaned him from the bottle, he always returned to liquor. Likewise, despite Hepburn's supervision and repeatedly flushing Judy's pills down the toilet, she always managed to procure replacements.

"I could never understand why Kate wanted to mess up her life with yet another emotionally crippled person," actor Kenneth MacKenna said. "Cukor and I knew that there was some sexual attraction between those two. But it was so much more than that. In being the lonely bachelor woman that she was, Kate had had to give up a lot in life."

"It's interesting to note," MacKenna continued, "that as much as Kate loved both Tracy and Judy, she never allowed them to suck her into their own nightmares. She was involved with them, and on the most intimate of terms, but she could always pull back from them at the last minute before being lured into their vortexes."

"For Tracy and Judy, it was always Saturday night at the party. For Kate, it was always the sobering light of dawn on a bleak Monday morning. Kate could be self-delusional, but even so, she was a woman firmly anchored on this earth."

"In contrast, Judy and Tracy would face Monday morning and wonder whether they could get through another day without doing themselves in. Kate would wake up Monday morning and mull over where she was going to find the freshest vegetables for dinner that night," MacKenna concluded.

There is evidence that Hepburn never fully came to terms with the extent of Judy's tendency for self-destruction. According to Cukor, "Kate believed that a few walks in the country and the extension of pure love and affection could pull Judy back from the edge of the cliff."

Rooney was more realistic: "Judy was fighting an addiction to pills and doing everything in her soul to avoid a total nervous breakdown."

Cukor also believed that Judy was forced back to work too soon after the birth of Liza. "She was weakened and traumatized both by the birth of Liza and by her realization that Minnelli loved Kelly a hell of a lot more than he loved her."

Hepburn's worst critics, including Joan Crawford, felt that "Hepburn took advantage of the situation." That was Crawford's first reaction upon hearing rumors of a Garland/Hepburn affair. In fairness, Crawford admitted that Hepburn was not Judy's first lesbian affair. Crawford recalled that she knew that Betty Asher was seducing Judy during the filming of *The Wizard of Oz* in the late Thirties. "Everybody, with the possible exception of Mayer, knew about the Garland/Asher affair. If he had ever found out that his Dorothy in *Oz* was indulging in lesbian sex, his left ball would have collapsed."

Crawford, who knew Judy only casually, said in later years that she felt Judy was basically heterosexual but enjoyed an occasional bout of female-to-female intimacy from time to time. "She was very experimental and very loving in those days," Crawford claimed. "She was in such desperate need of love that anyone—male or female—who got close to her could end up making love to her."

Judy told Hepburn that she was afraid she'd get fat if she gave up the pills. "I can balloon and balloon fast," she said. "Dexedrine keeps me slim."

"But there's a downside," Hepburn ventured to say. "Dexadrine also makes you highly nervous, very irritable, and almost impossible to live with. I've confirmed this with my father. He's a doctor and knows about such things."

"Mayer wants me to look sylphlike on the screen," Judy said.

Hepburn came up with a startling idea. "Why don't you give up the screen and become a concert singer? You could get bookings all over the country. Abandon the pills and eat anything you want. Singers don't have to be thin—in fact, some of the world's best singers are fat. You could become known as 'the little Kate Smith.'" She stopped for a minute. "My God, if I hadn't gotten my husband to change his name, and if I'd followed the conventional patterns of married women, I'd be known today as Kate Smith myself."

"I did give up pills once," Judy claimed. "I was walking with Vin beside the East River in Manhattan on our honeymoon. Like you, he was urging me to stop taking pills. I reached into my handbag, took them out, and tossed them into those murky waters. 'I'll never take them again,' I vowed to him. He became very emotional and even cried with joy. Of course, the next day I found another doctor who prescribed more pills for me."

"Actually, she continued, "I get most of my pills through the dispensary at Metro. There's a doctor there who's very generous with me. He's an addict himself and understands my need for them. When he cracks down on me, I get close friends to get their own doctors to prescribe pills for them, and then they turn their cache over to me."

Hepburn thought this was horrible, and she warned her that she could destroy "a God-given talent."

Sometimes in the middle of the night, Judy would panic, break out in cold sweats, and frantically call Hepburn. Whenever that happened, she would arise from her bed and drive over to Judy's house to help.

"For several months," Lawler said, "Kate tended to Judy even more that she tended to Tracy. After Tracy got back from touring in *The Rugged Path [a 1945 stage play by Robert Sherwood that marked Tracy's return to the stage after a long absence]*, he'd sometimes go for days without actually seeing Kate. They always spoke on the phone. A few affairs with women on the side, plus a supply of boys from Cukor, were keeping Tracy occupied in those days. Kate was carrying on with Judy and with Laura Harding during her occasional visits from the East Coast, so she was kept fairly busy too."

Sometimes Judy would get a crippling migraine that would last for days. Hepburn would try every remedy she knew, often to no avail.

If not a migraine, it was some other ailment plaguing Judy. At least once a week, Hepburn was summoned to her house when her left arm—never her right one—or her left or right leg would become numb. To provide some relief, Hepburn often massaged the limb for more than an hour or so at a time. After that, she'd go into the kitchen and cook some nourishing food for her. Judy would often turn down whatever was offered. "I prefer a diet of pills."

Hepburn told Cukor that Judy would often stand nude looking at herself in the mirror, especially at her breasts. "They each point in a different direction," she said. "Directors, to my embarrassment and humiliation, often point this out to me and order wardrobe to tape them so the nipples don't shoot out east and west."

Hepburn often called her father, Dr. Hepburn, in Connecticut, for long conversations about Judy's condition. She reported to her father that Judy's hands trembled so much that she couldn't apply lipstick or mascara. "It's not because I'm drunk or on medication," Judy said. "All the Gumm women have trembling hands. It's genetic."

Even on the MGM lot, Hepburn would sometimes be summoned by Minnelli himself to help his wife. "I can't do anything with her," he'd say.

In Judy's dressing room, Hepburn often found her huddled in a corner in a fetal position. "I can't face the camera," she said on one such occasion. "It feels like when I go out there, I'm naked! Completely exposed to the world. Without a stitch of clothing!"

"Kate would sometimes comfort Judy in her arms," Minnelli later confessed. "I couldn't do that for Judy. But Kate could."

Lawler felt that eventually, Hepburn began to view Judy more as a daughter than as a female lover. "I think at some point their relationship ceased to be sexual. Judy was back to men again. Later Kate became the most reliable female friend in Judy's life. When she tried to commit suicide in 1950, Kate was the first person at her bedside."

"In 1961, Kate practically held Judy together when we were making *Judgment at Nuremberg*," claimed MacKenna, who was also in the film playing a judge.

"Although Judy would sometimes lash out at Kate, and one time, or so I've heard, actually attacked her physically, there was genuine love between the two women," Cukor claimed. "Kate was the forever scolding but also forgiving mother, and Judy was the always erring, always inconsiderate, but also loving daughter. Judy knew that she could pull any stunt, and Kate would forgive her. And so their relationship went on and on. If Kate didn't really love Judy, she would have walked away from her years before. At least throughout the rest of the Forties, Kate put up with as much from Judy as she did from Spence. Thanks to her self-assumed duties as a nurse, Kate would probably have been brilliant in an on-screen interpretation of Florence Nightingale."

***

Back to work again after giving birth, Judy rode through the gate of MGM to shoot *The Pirate*, directed by Minnelli. Producer Arthur Freed was the first to greet her. He had already given her the songs by Cole Porter, who had been hired for $100,000.

Once again, Judy would be working with Gene Kelly, having already starred with him in *For Me and My Gal* (1942). "He is good, really talented, and I feared that he might walk off with the picture, leaving me in the dust," Judy said.

At around mid-morning of that first day on the set, she had pastries and coffee with him as he told her he was basing his character on the film swashbuckler, Douglas Fairbanks, Sr., and playing the romantic aspect as inspired by John Barrymore. "In one scene, Vince wants me to wear tight black shorts to show off what he calls my 'Betty Grable legs.'"

During her absence and the child-bearing it had entailed, Judy had put on weight. Then, in the weeks before her involvement in *The Pirate,* she had dieted strenuously and looked rail thin, "almost anorexic" She was consuming pills and smoking four packages of cigarettes a day. As it was later revealed, the studio masseuse kept her supplied with pills.

Kay Thompson, who was coaching Judy in her song and dance routines for *The Pirate,* claimed, "She didn't really want to make the picture, but she and Vince had been too extravagant with their money and were in arrears with the IRS, and bills were piling up. She was in horrible shape to face the camera."

Every morning, Minnelli drove her to a psychiatrist for an hour-long session, but in his view, "It didn't do much good."

Sydney Guilaroff, Hollywood's most famous hair stylist, was determined to make Judy come off looking her best ever. "She wasn't a real beauty like my friend, a very young Elizabeth Taylor. But Judy had an aura about her and a great gift as a singing actress, a very, very great talent. A wonderful creature, who felt isolated and alone in the world. When I worked on her, she was candid. 'Oh, Syd,' she said. 'I married the wrong man. I should have married *you.'"*

"You're joking," he responded. "You have the wrong equipment for my taste, but I adore you all the same."

Even though Judy was directed in it by her husband, *The Pirate* marked "the beginning of the end" of her relationships with both Minnelli and MGM. Heavily addicted to pills during the shoot, she had bitter fights with him in full view of the cast and crew. It took four months for him to shoot *The Pirate,* the most controversial of all of Judy's films, MGM's work sheets revealed that she showed up for only 99 days of the 135-day shoot.

The rights for *The Pirate* had been acquired by MGM while it was still running as a Broadway play. At the time, the studio thought it should be reconfigured into a drama—not a musical—starring William Powell and either Hedy Lamarr or Myrna Loy.

From the beginning, Judy warned Minnelli that she felt that this artsy, allegorical, tongue-in-cheek comedy might be too high brow for her fans. "The subtle parts will go over the heads of a lot of my

A stylish, witty, and "artsy" script, **The Pirate,** featured here on the cover of *Screenland* magazine, had been adapted for the screen from the stage play by S.N. Behrman, whom Judy had recently met in New York.

It had flopped, dismally, when Alfred Lunt and Lynn Fontanne had interpreted it on Broadway.

Minnelli, however, was convinced that by morphing it into a movie musical, it would become a box office hit.

audience. The new generation doesn't even know who Fairbanks and Barrymore were. You're confronting me with artistic hoops through which I'll have to jump."

She got more support from Kay Thompson than she did from her husband. Kay had already met everyone in the cast and introduced her to her co-stars, the Viennese Walter Slezak and the London-born actress, Gladys Cooper.

By now, Judy referred to Kay as "my best friend and severest critic."

The film version of *The Pirate* (1948) opens onto the Spanish colonial Caribbean village of Calvados, where the beautiful Manuela (Judy) daydreams of being carried away by the legendary pirate, Mack (a.k.a. "The Black"), who is the terror of the West Indies. Cole Porter (who had composed its music) had borrowed the nickname of one of his African American lovers.

Manuela's stern Aunt Inez (Gladys Cooper) and her Uncle Capucho (Lester Allen) have pledged Manuela's hand in marriage to the town's mayor, Don Pedro (Slezak), who is as hideous as he is round and bullying. Secretly, Manuela despises him.

In the meantime, she is escorted to the neighboring village of Port Sebastian, where she attends the stirring performance of a traveling circus. She is dazzled by its handsome and charismatic master of ceremonies, Serafin (Gene Kelly). He instantly falls in love with her, later learning (through an act of onstage hypnosis) about her deep-seated fantasy of marrying the dashing pirate. Reacting to that, and in an attempt to capture her heart, he (falsely) asserts that he, in fact, is the notorious pirate traveling in disguise.

Later, Serafin recognizes Don Pedro (the town's pompous and aging mayor) as Mack the Black, now retired and obese. The plot grows complicated (and more exaggerated and theatrical) from then on but ends happily as Manuela escapes from her bourgeois confinement and joins Serafin's act.

As the film's master of ceremonies, just before the finale, Kelly calls for a suspension of disbelief and the audience's good will in awarding the young lovers a happy ending. With Judy, in a style that evokes the best of slapstick vaudeville, he performs the very endearing "Be a Clown," the best song Porter wrote for the movie. *[The number was later reprised by Donald O'Connor as "Make 'Em Laugh" in the upcoming MGM musical,* Singin' in the Rain

PIRATES

Even in her weakened condition, **Gene Kelly** found that **Judy** was a fast learner of the dance routines.

"She's quicker than any other girl I ever worked with," he later claimed. "Leslie Caron and Cyd Charisse were far better dancers, but they could not learn dialogue as quickly as Judy could."

254

(1952).*]*

Tensions arose when Kelly and Minnelli began spending nearly all their spare time with each other. Sometimes, they disappeared for hours. Of course, Judy herself was the ultimate disappearing act, in many cases simply not showing up.

She complained to Kay, "Vince practically ignores me whenever Kelly walks onto the set. He moons over him. Like some school cheerleader with a crush on the football captain. When he does come on to direct me, he's more like a drill sergeant."

Whenever she was late on the set, which she invariably was, Minnelli would bang on the door to her dressing room. "Miss Garland, would you god damn please honor us with your presence, regardless of what shape you're in today? Cast and crew have been waiting for you, but only for three hours."

When the movie columnist Hedda Hopper visited the set, she found that Judy was "emotionally disturbed. She was shaking like an aspen leaf and in the frenzy of hysteria, claiming that all those she had once loved had turned against her and that her phone had been tapped."

Kelly was having marital woes, too: In addition to the fallout generated by his indiscretions with Minnelli, his wife, Betsy Blair, had been blacklisted by the House Un-American Activities Committee.

After work, whenever Judy and Minnelli actually returned home together, their evenings would devolve into bitter arguments and accusations. His violent temper competed with her drug-induced hysteria. Friends held out little hope for their marriage, and at times it seemed as if their daughter, Liza, was all that held them together.

On many a night, Judy stormed out of the house to sleep at the home of Lee Gershwin, who was married to Ira. On other nights, she'd continue her affair with Yul Brynner.

On the nights when Minnelli stormed out of their house, he'd head for a rendezvous either with Kelly or to the home of his loyal friend, Lester Gaba, who had moved back to Hollywood after a long sojourn in Manhattan.

Hollywood insiders were aware of Minnelli's crush on Kelly. It was evident even to those who attended parties with the pair. Emmanuel Levy, who wrote the most definitive book on the director, claimed, "The crush Minnelli seemed to have on Kelly was evident from their behavior at parties hosted by Kelly and his actress wife, Betsy Blair. On those occasions, Judy felt that Minnelli was standing too close to Kelly, always embracing him, and looking straight into his eyes."

"I was upset not that he was having an affair—who am I to throw stones?—but I was troubled that he made no attempt to conceal it," Judy said. "After all, he was Liza's father."

"I knew Gene Kelly very, very well, if you get my drift," said dancer Eddie Vale, who was hired as a member of the chorus in many musicals. "He was basically straight, maybe at least eighty-five percent. I'm guessing, but he would allow himself to be serviced. From what I knew about him, he didn't go much farther than that. He was planning to make great pictures, with Vince directing. Actors, especially in their younger days—including John Wayne, Gary Cooper, and Clark Gable—have to perform some career-building seductions. In Hollywood, it's all about succeeding, no matter what you have to do to get there."

One of the few joyous moments for Judy occurred when her nanny brought Liza to the set for her first-ever (but hardly the last) visit to a movie location.

June Allyson also visited the set that day and sat with Judy and Liza in her dressing room. "Look at my baby," Judy said to Allyson. "A lot of gossip is going around that Vince is not the real father. But take in my baby's dark hair, those big brown eyes, those long lashes—it's his kid all right."

During the shoot, the original conceptions for the dance numbers went through many changes: Some were reshot and others ended up on the cutting room floor. Originally, Lena Horne was cast as Manuela's dressmaker and was slated to sing "Love of My Life," but she was dropped.

In 1948, a white dancer appearing on screen with two black dancers was viewed as daring, and such a scene might be cut from a movie's screenings in the Deep South. In spite of that, Kelly insisted on dancing with the highly talented Nicholas Brothers, but their number was indeed cut for screenings in Georgia and Alabama. The brothers were so angered by having been blackballed that they escaped to Europe, not returning until the mid-1960s.

In "accessorizing" a set for the West Indian number, "Voodoo," several carefully controlled fires were lit as centerpieces. When Judy saw them, she became hysterical and ran screaming back to her dressing room. "Vince is trying to burn me to death."

She was finally persuaded to perform near the blazing "accent fires," but the entire number eventually evolved into a futile lost cause. When Mayer watched its rough cut, he denounced it as "too erotic" and ordered that all the negatives be burned.

In *The Pirate's* final cut, Judy sang "Love of My Life," the number that had originally been assigned to Horne. Her numbers also included "Mack the Black," "You Can Do No Wrong," and her slam-bang (and brilliant) finale with Kelly, "Be a Clown."

After Minnelli wrapped the final details associated with the release of *The Pirate,* he stormed into Freed's office and said, "I will never make another film with one Miss Judy Garland."

At around the same time, Kelly approached Freed privately and confessed, "I put out for Vince, thinking he could make the world believe that I was dazzling, brilliant, and clever in *The Pirate,* and that the world would worship me. All I got was Vince on his knees worshipping me."

[Of course, Kelly made that revelation in confidence. But in Hollywood, there are no secrets, especially if it's scandalous.]

At MGM, Kelly sat with Cole Porter to watch the first screening of *The Pirate.* "He seemed to be having a good time, reaching over to feel my basket. He later pissed me off by denouncing it to the press."

Kelly, though, continued his high hopes when *The Pirate* opened in New York City, where it generated a bonanza at the box office. "Then it played across America. Even if you agreed to let people in for free, they stayed away in droves."

In its review, *Life* magazine defined the movie's underlying message as: "It's silly to be serious."

Movieland magazine thought that Judy "looked lovely and sang better than ever."

Freed believed that *The Pirate's* lack of box office success derived from audiences who weren't yet ready to accept Judy as a grown-up sophisticate, and that they failed (in droves) to respond to Minnelli's "artsy ambitions. Personally, I thought it was one of the best things he had ever done. As for Kelly, it seems he can do no wrong—the guy is terrific. I suspect that *The Pirate* was twenty years ahead of its time."

Newsweek asserted, "With Miss Garland and Gene Kelly pitching energetically in the lead roles, *The Pirate* is one of the most delightful musicals to hit the screen in a month of Sundays."

In New York, the *Herald Tribune* stated, "There is more dancing than script, more production pomp than sensible staging. But with Gene Kelly hoofing like a dervish, Judy Garland changing character at the drop of a hat, and resplendent trappings, the show is bouncing and beautiful."

Confusingly (and elliptically) the noted critic James Agee wrote: "*The Pirate* seems to have the death's head, culture cute, mirthful grin of the average Shakespearean comic. Even so, Miss Garland's tense, ardent, straightforward wardness is sometimes striking."

The New York Times defined *The Pirate* as "a fantastic conglomeration of *legerdemain*, dancing, and romance. The momentum is far from steady, and the result is lopsided entertainment that is wonderfully flamboyant in its high spots, bordering on tedium elsewhere. Garland throws herself with verve into a wild slapstick exercise, tossing everything that's not nailed down as the dashing trouper. It's funny, but a mite overdone."

**Lavender Broadway
& *The Avant-Garde***

The music score of *The Pirate* was nominated for an Oscar, but lost to another Judy Garland musical, *Easter Parade.*

Even though he wrote the music for *The Pirate*, **Cole Porter** told the press, "The film is unspeakably wretched. The worst that money can buy."

***

One afternoon near the end of the filming of *The Pirate,* Judy told Minnelli that she'd be dining that night with Kay Thompson and that she wouldn't return home until very late in the evening. As planned, Kay drove her to a restaurant along the Sunset Strip, but Judy soon began complaining of a terrible mi-

He was a notorious homosexual, seducing, in the words of author Mart Martin, "lots of longshoremen, sailors, truck drivers, Hollywood chorus boys, rough trade, and male hustlers supplied by a pimp who ran a male brothel in Harlem staffed with young black men."

graine. She didn't feel she was able to drive her own car, so, as a means of abruptly ending the evening, Kay dropped her off at her house, saying that she hoped she'd feel better in the morning.

Minnelli's car was in the driveway, but the lights were out on their home's ground floor. Judy entered the darkened house and headed for the kitchen. She knew that her husband had had a rough day on the set, so with the belief that he was sleeping, she tried not to make a lot of noise.

Pouring herself a drink, she sat in silence in the living room. [*Under different circumstances, she'd have turned on the record player at very loud volumes.*]

Weeks before, Minnelli had hired a handyman to help around the house and garden. Judy had been stunned by his male beauty. In her words, "Johnny Vente was a blonde-haired, blue-eyed Adonis, built like a brick shithouse and evoking Lex Barker." [*Barker, famous as the movie version of Tarzan, also become widely known as the very good-looking husband of Lana Turner*]. Johnny often worked around the Garland/Minnelli house clad only bathing trunks and sneakers. Judy wasn't surprised when he told her that he posed nude for art classes as a means of earning extra money.

She tiptoed up the stairs and quietly opened the door to the master bedroom. Then, she heard sounds coming from inside. To her surprise, she'd caught her husband "getting plowed" by Vente. In her words, as described later to Kay Thompson, she'd caught the pair *in flagrante delicto.*

Racing back down the stairs, she went into her dressing room, heading for its recently added "state of the art" bathroom. There, she broke a glass holding her toothbrush and sliced her wrist. It was not a deep cut, more of a "theatrical suicide attempt to get attention."

Minnelli soon raced into the bathroom where he found her bleeding, her blood dripping into the white porcelain sink.

Then she heard Vente's voice. Minnelli yelled for him to call an ambulance as he bandaged her wrist. Thirty minutes later, in an ambulance, her husband hovered over her until they were delivered to the Cedars of Lebanon Hospital. Two doctors rushed to attend to her, sterilizing her wound and administering sedatives.

The next morning, Minnelli arranged for her release. She was wheeled out of the hospital and placed onto one of the rear seats of his car. The doctor reassured him that Judy's wound was only a surface cut and suggested that his wife seek a rest cure.

It is not known what was said *en route* back to their house. Two days later, she told Kay, who had come over to check on her, "I'm not moving out of his house immediately until I've found a place of my own for Liza and her nanny. I'm sleeping in the guest room. Vince doesn't give a damn about me."

After wrapping *The Pirate,* Judy—exhausted, pill addicted, and "hysterically nervous"—experienced a total meltdown. Authors sometimes borrow novelist William Styron's description of his own nervous breakdown: "The mind begins to feel aggrieved, stricken, and the muddled thought processes register the distress of an organ in convulsion. It is a storm indeed, but a storm of murk."

Louella Parsons beat out Hedda Hopper in breaking the news of Judy's breakdown: "Judy Garland is a very sick girl and has suffered a complete nervous collapse," the columnist wrote.

In gossipy Hollywood, it wasn't long before the story of her catching her husband in bed with a young man spread like the flames of gasoline thrown on a fire. Soon, it reached the ears of novelist Jacqueline Susann, who in time created a scene similar to Judy's in her best-selling novel, *Valley of the Dolls*.

[Ironically, Judy would be offered a major role in that novel's eventual film adaptation.]

***

Judy was taken to Las Campanas Sanatorium in Compton, southeast of Beverly Hills, and was committed. She was assigned a private bungalow on the well-manicured grounds. When Kay reached her there by phone, Judy admitted, "Vince has put me in a nuthouse."

Kay promised to be her first visitor as soon as she was cleared to receive guests. In the meantime, she was told she could not have "outside stimulation."

In spite of the bucolic look of the place, she quickly realized that she was in an institution that adhered to military discipline. A burly nurse appeared in her room and searched every parcel, every article of clothing, and every nook and cranny of her room, looking for drugs or pills in places one might not expect to find them.

She later learned that she was occupying the same quarters that Margaret Shenberg, the estranged wife of Louis B. Mayer, did during her confinement there in 1944, three years before her divorce from him.

Over the course of her short stay here, Judy was examined by three doctors. One of them, a young intern, asked for her autograph. "You're my favorite singer," he told her. "We've got to get you well so you can sing for us again."

She begged the staff to let her see her daughter. At first, they refused. Finally, Dr. Marc Rabwin, that ever-faithful family friend, arrived with Liza, who at sixteen months was far too young to understand what was happening.

On seeing Liza, Judy hugged her and covered her with kisses. Rabwin later reported, "Liza cried and cried, but they were tears of joy."

Dr. Rabwin determined that the clinic wasn't doing Judy much good, so he arranged for her to be transferred to the Austen Riggs Foundation in the scenic but faraway town of Stockbridge, in the Berkshire Mountains of western Massachusetts.

Her physician in Stockbridge, Dr. Robert Knight, the author of many articles in scientific journals, had one of the best reputations in psychiatry in New England. He'd been a student of Dr. Karl Menninger of the famous Menninger Clinic in Kansas, whom she had met during one of his stints in Los Angeles.

But as hard as he tried, Dr. Knight could not seem to break through to her. He told his staff, "At least I wanted her to see a streak of daylight through the darkness."

Judy quickly evolved into a very difficult and demanding patient. Nothing seemed to satisfy her...neither the food, nor the ambience, nor a host of other realities, too. She complained of "the deadly stillness. I need a record player. I want to hear music played at top volume."

Dr. Knight told her that that would be impossible, since peace, tranquility, and a complete lack of outside noise were some of the chief attributes of the clinic.

Although he urged her to stay at least four months in her capacity as a volunteer patient, she refused. She had the authority to check herself out, and she did.

The clinic alerted Minnelli that she was flying back to Los Angeles. With Johnny Vente, he was waiting for her at the airport. The three of them rode home in silence.

Once again, it was Louella Parsons who broke the news: "Judy Garland, released from a clinic in Massachusetts, has made a remarkable recovery from her nervous breakdown. She is due to report soon to MGM, where she will star in *Easter Parade*. Her co-star will be Gene Kelly." *[As it turned out, Kelly would* not *be her co-star.]*

Although he had vowed never to direct another Judy Garland picture, Minnelli was signed to that task once again by Arthur Freed.

However, after only two days of rehearsing, Minnelli was summoned into Freed's office. Judy had been missing all day, and he didn't know where she was.

"I hate to do this to you, Vince," Freed said. "You're a good man. But you're off the picture. This morning, Judy came to my office and before she bolted from the studio, she told me that she refuses to work with you."

Minnelli froze for a moment in stunned disbelief. An hour later, he told the cast and crew goodbye and departed. There would be a lot of other pictures at MGM waiting for his signature—he'd been assured of that.

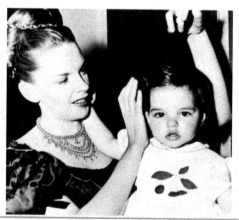

Married and Maternal, Brightly Illuminated for Public Consumption

Even though the marriage was unraveling, here's **Judy with Baby Liza** as part of an MGM publicity campaign associated with the release of *The Pirate*.

CHAPTER TEN

EASTER PARADE

IN A VAUDEVILLE-INSPIRED REMAKE OF *PYGMALION*, JUDY, SOMETIMES WEARING A BONNET, PLAYS A SHOWGIRL GETTING MENTORED BY AN OLDER PRO (FRED ASTAIRE) WITH AN AXE TO GRIND.

WORDS & MUSIC

FLUFFY, ATHLETIC, & FUN, JUDY SHAKES HER WAY THROUGH A SONG & DANCE MEMORIAL TO RODGERS & HART

MARIO LANZA, AMERICA'S CARUSO

LUSTS FOR FOOD, DRINK, AND JUDY

SYLVIA SYDNEY AND CARLETON ALSOP

JUDY STEALS HER BEST FRIEND'S HUSBAND

IN THE GOOD OLD SUMMERTIME

THE STRANGE LOVE OF VAN JOHNSON & KEENAN WYNN, & HOW MGM TRIED TO FIX IT.

ANNIE GET YOUR GUN

JUDY FUCKS IT UP

INTRODUCING MGM'S NEWEST VILLAIN
DORE SCHARY

"The film career of Judy Garland has come to an end."
—Motion Picture Magazine, 1950

"I'm suspended so high, I can't sit down"
> —Judy Garland to Hedda Hopper
> after being fired by MGM

"Every time Judy Garland sings, she dies a little."
> —Frank Sinatra

"From pills to men, I've done everything to excess all my life."
> —Judy Garland

"I believe that if you are lonely sometimes, you should accept it, without feeling that life has treated you badly. There are lonely moments in all our lives. Even if you're in a crowd, a feeling of loneliness can wash over you."
> —Judy Garland

"Pill-popping Judy Garland reported to MGM's recording studio to dub the musical track for the Judy Garland Album for Annie Get Your Gun, a pitiful souvenir of a woman coming apart. In the song, 'I Got Lost in His Arms,' her voice emerges as a terrible moan, drifting off-key dozens of times. "I Got the Sun in the Morning' is virtually unplayable."
> —Peter Harry Brown

Louella Parsons was the first to break the news of Judy Garland's next picture, Irving Berlin's *Easter Parade* (1948), in which she would be reteamed with Gene Kelly. The original dream cast was to have featured Kathryn Grayson, Cyd Charisse, Frank Sinatra, and Red Skelton. But that casting lineup soon collapsed.

In a revised script, some of the previous roles were written out, leaving a leaner supporting cast consisting mainly of Peter Lawford and Charisse. However, Charisse damaged a tendon and had to bow out, eventually being replaced by Ann Miller.

Lyrics and music would be by Irving Berlin, with musical direction by Johnny Green. Producer Arthur Freed was given a budget of $2,750,000 million to make what was to become Judy's most financially successful film.

MGM had come to the end of its long reign over Golden Age Hollywood, and for the 1947-48 season, sixteen of its twenty-five movies had lost money.

With Arthur Freed once again as her producer, music was by Irving Berlin with musical score by Roger Edens and Johnny Green. The original script was by Frances Goodrich and Albert Hackett, although the novelist Sidney Sheldon came in for a vast overhaul as the "script doctor."

On first reading, its director, Charles Walters, had found the script by Goodrich and Hackett "too dark," and he brought in Sheldon to "cheer it up. Give me sunshine and blue skies."

At the time he was hired, Sheldon was known for the Oscar he'd won for his script of *The Bachelor and the Bobby Soxer* (1947), starring Cary Grant and Shirley Temple.

When Kelly read the first draft of the script, he found that in some respects it evoked his own marriage to Betsy Blair—that is, the story of a man who married an unknown woman and tries to convert her into the partner he desires.

THE FRED & JUDY SHOW

As half of a song-and-dance team "hoofing' their way through vaudeville in the early days of the 20th Century, Judy accomplished the nearly impossible: She got star billing over Fred Astaire.

MGM executives were thrilled at the final lineup, thinking it would restore some money to their vastly depleted bank accounts. Movie attendance had dropped drastically in the post-war years. The publicity department got carried away, promoting *Easter Parade* as "The *Gone With the Wind* of musicals, until Mayer ordered them "to cool it."

During the first days of rehearsals with Kelly, Judy approached him. He stood back a bit, perhaps expecting a denunciation from her because of his close association with her husband. But she waved the white flag of truce. "I feel you and Vince have a great thing going with each other. In fact, I think you'll make a fabulous actor/director team, perhaps turning out some of the best musicals of the upcoming '50s."

"Don't get me wrong," he answered. "I'm not in love with your husband. He may be in love with me, but I don't really swing in that direction. Yeah, things happened, but I didn't instigate them. I hope he'll turn elsewhere, and that we can make it 'strictly business' in the future."

"Whatever," she said, turning and heading back to her dressing room.

***

As filming of *Easter Parade* began, a dark cloud hung over Hollywood. The House Un-American Activities Committee was on a witch hunt for suspected communists in the film industry. Careers of writers, directors, actors, and other workers were being destroyed. Many were called to testify, which in some cases led to jail terms.

"Thank god," Judy said. "Unlike Lucille Ball, I never joined the Communist Party, like she did back in the 1930s. Also, I never appeared in a Russian propaganda film [Tender Comrade; 1943] like Ginger Rogers did."

Perhaps to put up a good front in combating rumors, Kelly went with Minnelli and Judy for a political meeting at the home of Ira and Lee Gershwin, a group of elite stars forming the Committee for the First Amendment. In attendance were Humphrey Bogart and his wife, Lauren Bacall, along with such guests as Edward G. Robinson, Danny Kaye, and director Billy Wilder. It was at this party that Burt Lancaster, Judy's future co-star, flirted with her.

That following Sunday, Kelly hosted his weekly volleyball game in his backyard. He'd been rehearsing numbers for *Easter Parade* for more than a month, and he welcomed a diversion.

Along with Van Johnson, he invited athletes from UCLA and USC. Johnson always showed up, hoping to make contacts with one of the handsome, well-built students, many of whom were flattered that a major movie star would take an interest in them.

Kelly's biographer, Alvin Yudkoff, wrote about what happened on the volleyball court that fateful Sunday:

"A giant on the opposite side of the net spiked a shot down on a player on Gene's team. The ball caromed off a hapless hand and was arching up out of reach of everybody, a sure point for the other side. Gene slipped on a patch of wet grass and a foot slid out from under him, simultaneous with a severe twinge of his ankle. The pain was unbearable. He sprawled on the ground."

Taken to the hospital, Kelly was examined carefully and told that he had a broken ankle. He would not be able to film *Easter Parade* with Judy.

Louis K. Sidney, vice president of MGM, phoned Fred Astaire early the next morning. He was in semi-retirement, a time he characterized as "full of ideas and ambition, but no picture to do."

"We've got an emergency," Sidney said. "Gene Kelly broke his ankle in a volleyball game. He's no good to us for months to come. I know that some people consider you two rivals, but he recommended you as his replacement. The film is Irving Berlin's *Easter Parade*. I know you're familiar with it."

"Can't you wait for Gene to recover? Postpone everything?"

"No. Mayer ordered us to move ahead."

"I'll get back to you later today," Astaire said.

Before committing himself, Astaire wanted to confirm that replacing Kelly in the role would be okay with the dancer. When he phoned Kelly, he was told, "Go for it—and have a blast with Judy. I know the two of you will be terrific."

Ironically, at around the same time that *Easter Parade* lost its male lead, it was about to lose its director, too. Judy's psychiatrist had consulted with Freed, telling him that after hours of therapy, he discerned that Judy had come to associate Minnelli with all the problems and exploitation she was feeling from MGM, and from Mayer in particular. "If you want to get *Easter Parade* made without any more of her nervous breakdowns," the psychiatrist recommended, "I suggest you replace Minnelli with another director."

With so much riding on the success of *Easter Parade,* Freed thought it prudent to follow his advice. As its producer, the next day, he summoned Minnelli to his office. After some idle chit-chat, he delivered the blow: "I had a long talk with Judy yesterday. She refuses to work with you. She said she's walking off the picture if you're the director."

"What the hell? I was with her last night. She was quite pleasant. There was absolutely no mention of this."

"It's an ultimatum," Freed said. "We'll find another picture for you. But you're no longer the director. That's it. I'm sorry."

Before leaving Freed's office, Minnelli confessed, "Judy and I may linger on for a few more months, but I know that our marriage is hopeless. She's committed only to those little pills. I think they'll shorten her lifespan, so use her while you can before it's too late."

When he arrived home, he didn't know what her reception would be. At first, he was tempted to aggressively confront her, but decided against it.

She greeted him at the door with a cheery demeanor and a kiss on the cheek. "Welcome home, sweetheart. The cook is preparing all your favorite dishes. I've invited friends of yours over, a surprise. I'm sorry I won't be able to join you guys. I forgot. I already had a dinner date with Kay Thompson. You know how careless I am in confusing dates."

Minnelli later swore, "Judy and I never said one word to each other about her having me fired from the picture."

Chuck Walters, a former dancer, was one of the supervisors of the Freed Unit at MGM. He'd dated Judy once or twice many years before, but it was hardly a serious romance, as his preference was for his fellow male hoofers. He'd been of great help to her, although at times he could be very demanding, leading her to call him "the man with the whip." Metro had been pleased with his helming of June Allyson and Peter Lawford in the collegiate musical, *Good News* (1947). Yet Walters was nonetheless shocked when MGM summoned him as *Easter Parade's* director in lieu of Minnelli.

But it would be *Easter Parade* that would establish him as a major director, especially when it earned more than five million dollars, becoming MGM's biggest hit of the year. It hit the market just as a "little black box" was beginning to appear in some American living rooms, showing fuzzy pictures on its pygmy-sized screen.

[*Walters would re-enter Judy's life when he was hired to direct her once again in* Summer Stock (1950), *after her star was crashing down from MGM's firmament—a skyscape that Mayer had promoted as having "More stars than there are in heaven."*]

Swallowing his pride, and in his capacity as Judy's husband and helpmate, Minnelli called Walters to warn him about his star and to advise him about how she was to be handled: "She can suddenly, without any apparent cause, throw a temper tantrum, as she suffers from paranoia and is plagued with irrational fears. She lives almost constantly in a state of nervous anxiety. It's deep-seated. Her melancholy at times is funereal. She often feels that those around her are plotting against her. She can even suspect someone nearby of planning to kill her and making it look like an accident."

On her first day of working with Walters, Judy confronted him. [What she told him later appeared in the magazine, Films and Filming.] She pranced over to him: "Look, sweetie, I'm no June Allyson, you know. Don't get cute with me. None of that batting-the-eyelids bit, or the fluffing of the hair routine for me, buddy. I'm Judy Garland and don't you forget it."

On the set the following day, Astaire told Walters, "I'm nearly fifty years old, and I fear my joints have stiffened. Can my aging torso take it? If I do a high kick, my leg might leave my body."

"You'll be great," Walters assured him. "Our rehearsals will limber you up once again."

Astaire came in for a (negative) appraisal from his director. "Fred is a real Old Maid, talented but a worry wart, fretting over the most minute detail until he drove me crazy. Perfection. He wanted perfection, knowing there is no such thing."

Pale, wan, suffering from extreme exhaustion, her marriage a sham, Judy proved that she was a real trouper, able to perform intricate dance steps with Astaire, the master himself. Many critics also found her voice in top form.

To her great regret, with hospital and other bills piling up, she was told by her lawyer that the IRS was seizing most of her salary.

Working every day with choreographer Robert Alton, Astaire underwent strenuous rehearsals and in five weeks he was camera-ready for his dances with Ann Miller and Judy.

For her part, Judy was delighted to be teamed with Astaire, viewing

Depicted above are two views of **Judy Garland with Fred Astaire** in *Easter Parade*.

Because of her absences, tantrums, and many delays, Judy had angered many of the stars with whom she'd worked before. Astaire, however, was most patient with her and paid her what she called "the greatest compliment of my life."

He said, "Judy is the greatest artist who ever lived, and probably the greatest who will ever live."

him as the greatest dancer in the history of the cinema. "In white tie and tails, he defined elegance in musicals," she said. "This *bon vivant* was to dance with Audrey Hepburn, Cyd Charisse, even Rita Hayworth, and he ended up with Baby Gumm. Oh, did I leave out Ginger Rogers?"

Judy shocked, but perhaps amused, Astaire one afternoon as they were resting after a difficult routine. "Chuck (Walters) and I have something in common: Both of us have been fucked by my husband *[Vincente Minnelli]*— Chuck back on Broadway and me in Hollywood."

Judy was looking forward to working with Russian-born Irving Berlin, the composer and lyricist, considered one of the greatest songwriters in American history. His first big hit had come in in 1911 when he wrote "Alexander's Ragtime Band."

"It was a mutual admiration society," Berlin said of Judy.

She joined a long line of artists who recorded songs by Berlin. They included Al Jolson, Ethel Merman, Louis Armstrong, Frank Sinatra, Barbra Streisand, Cher, Bing Crosby, Doris Day, Willie Nelson, and Elvis Presley.

Flying into Los Angeles from New York, Berlin showed up for Judy's voice rehearsals of his music. He had told the press, "I'm in awe of her as a singer—that voice, that presence."

When she was rehearsing "I Wish I Were in Michigan," he approached and made three suggestions that he thought

In *Easter Parade*, **Peter Lawford** plays "Just a (very wealthy) fella with an umbrella."

"We were sometimes lovers, but mostly, I was her caretaker," he said.

would sell the song better. She stood her ground: "Listen, buster, you write 'em, I'll sing 'em."

Over lunch with Judy, Berlin discussed his musical, *Annie Get Your Gun*. It had been a big hit on Broadway in 1946. It had starred "The Belter," Ethel Merman. He told her that if plans went through with MGM for its adaptation into a movie, he'd recommend her for its lead role of Annie Oakley.

As musical director of *Easter Parade*, Roger Edens helped Berlin review his dusty inventories of 800 pre-existing songs and to come up with some new ones for inclusion in the movie's anthology of songs and dances. As a result, *Easter Parade* featured sixteen songs, about half of which were original.

In some respects, the plot of *Easter Parade* evokes that of *My Fair Lady*, in which Henry Higgins transforms a Cockney street urchin into the elegant, dignified, and "grammatically correct" Eliza Doolittle.

According to the plot, song-and-dance man Don Hewes (Astaire) is in love with his talented dancing partner, showgirl Nadine Hale (Miller). But she does not love him back, and soon announces that she's breaking up their act to star solo in the *Ziegfeld Follies.*

His best friend, Jonathon Harrow III, nicknamed Johnny (Lawford), arrives on the scene. Nadine is attracted to him, but out of respect for his best friend, Don, Johnny does not move in on her.

Deserted by his star, and depressed, Don boasts that he can pluck "any gal" from a chorus line and make a star out of her. *[By now, you've figured out what will happen next.]*

He yanks the beguiling and unassuming Hannah Brown (Judy) from a lineup of pink-costumed chorus girls and trains her as his dancing partner. At first, she's hopelessly inept at ballroom dancing, but in time, she learns to be his equal partner in dancing and in show biz.

Johnny is also attracted to Hannah, and in his only number with her, "A Fella With an Umbrella," shot in a (simulated) rainstorm, he makes his attraction to her known.

Jointly, Astaire and Judy also sing and dance in "Ragtime Violin," "When the Midnight Coo Choo Leaves for Alabam'," "Beautiful Faces Need Beautiful Clothes," and "Smooky Hookums."

Astaire danced with Miller to "It Only Happens When I Dance With You." Miller's big solo number in *Easter Parade* was "Shakin' the Blues Away."

For her number "Mister Monotony," Judy was given a costume that she would wear in stage performances for the rest of her life. She donned a form-fitting evening jacket over a pair of sheer black stockings, with her legs revealed and her hair concealed under a rakish black Fedora.

SHAKIN' THE BLUES AWAY

Ann Miller told Judy, "I used to fall in love with the best-looking man at a party—and sometimes, I ended up marrying him."

Louis B. Mayer seduced her when she was a teenager.

"We're a Couple of Swells," the song and dance routine originally developed for *Easter Parade*, would be repeated again and again, with different dance partners, for years to come.

The song was riddled with what one critic called *"louche double-enten-dres."*

When Mayer saw it, he ordered that it be cut—"Too erotic for a family movie, and inappropriate for a show set in 1912." *[Fortunately, her stylish and understatedly sexy routine was saved in the MGM archives, restored in the release of the DVD version of* Easter Parade *in 2005, and is usually viewable today as a clip on, among other websites, YouTube.com. She would wear a variation of that same outfit in the finale to her upcoming film,* Summer Stock *(1950).]*

The most beloved number in *Easter Parade* was "We're a Couple of Swells." Elegant (despite the tattered costumes), witty, and inspired by vaudeville acts from the dawn of the 20th Century, it featured Astaire and Judy dressed as hobos. In it, Astaire seemed to poke fun at his own repu-tation for elegance. It was followed by Judy and Astaire as they promenade down a simulated version of New York City's Fifth Avenue in a rousing fi-nale, "Easter Parade."

During the shoot, Judy bonded with tap-dancing Ann Miller, and learned more about this part-Cherokee native of Chireno, a small town in eastern Texas. She usually appeared under a massive bouffant hairdo, wearing heavy makeup with a slash of crimson lipstick, her lithe figure in skimpy costumes that showed off her long dancer's legs.

She told Judy something about her past: At the age of five, she suffered from rickets, and her mother enrolled her in a dancing class, thinking that it would strengthen her legs.

Her mother was deaf and could not find work, so they moved to San Francisco. Miller was only thirteen when she lied about her age and got a job in the chorus line at the Black Cat Club. There, surprisingly, she was discovered one night by Lucille Ball (of all people), who lured her to Los Angeles and got her a screen test at RKO.

In 1936, after a stint at Columbia, she drifted to MGM where she made a big career mark in *Easter Parade*.

Both women agreed that they had made the wrong choice of husbands: Miller revealed that during her first marriage, after she became pregnant, her husband came home drunk one night and threw her down the stairs of their two-story home. She was rushed to the hospital where she went into labor. Her little daughter was born prematurely and survived for only three hours.

When Judy met Miller, she was going out every night with the most impressive list of beaux in Hollywood: Howard Hughes, Conrad Hilton, and Louis B. Mayer himself. Judy dubbed it "mogul fucking."

Years later, Hollywood columnist Norma Lee Browning, wrote: "Today, Ann Miller is still singing, 'Fairy tales can come true. It can happen to you—if you're young at heart.' She's one of those ageless beauties con-stantly besieged by adoring males. Her personal *Who's Who* includes a well-known prince, a shah, an *aperitif* king, a few Maharajas, Spanish bull-fighters, oil millionaires, and international playboys, to name only a few."

During her final days on the set of *Easter Parade*, MGM let reporters in and most of them headed directly for Judy, peppering her with questions. One of them asked, "Do you want Liza to go into show biz?"

"I prefer to wait until she grows up so she can decide for herself," Judy said. "In the meantime, if adoring her spoils her, then I'm guilty."

"I hear rumors there's trouble in your marriage," a writer for the *Hollywood Reporter* asked.

"Mr. Minnelli and I are the happiest couple in Hollywood," Judy claimed. "In fact, it's a match made in heaven. He is my devoted husband, my mentor, the keeper of the flame that keeps my career burning, and the father of my daughter, the world's most adorable little girl."

Ann Miller was standing nearby. When the reporters left, Judy said, "Why tell them the truth? No one tells the truth in Hollywood. We're the dream factory, peddling fantasies."

***

From the moment of its release on June 30, 1948, *Easter Parade* was a big hit. Even negative or tepid reviews did not keep audiences from lining up at the box office.

The New York Times wrote: "Miss Garland is a competent trouper, nimble on her feet and professional-sounding overall, but somehow we feel that Ann Miller pairs better with Astaire."

In that same city, the *Daily News* found Judy "wan and frail, in need of a little more life on her bones to give more verve and bring her up to her old standard as an entertainer."

Another New York publication, the *Herald Tribune,* interpreted Judy's performance as "her best yet."

At the annual Academy Awards ceremony, Roger Edens and Johnny Green carried home Oscars for Best Scoring of a Musical Picture.

***

In the storyline of *Easter Parade,* Peter Lawford's character did not fare well with Judy's character of Hannah on screen. Off screen, however, and after dark, the relationship of Lawford with her heated up.

As she confessed to Kay Thompson and others, including Mickey Rooney, "Peter Lawford and I never really had a love affair. But on and off over the years, we got together to make beautiful music. He and I are very oral and very compatible in bed."

She had begun seeing the bisexual English-born actor in the early 1940s. He was a year younger than her, and, like Elizabeth Taylor, she found him very handsome. Depending on one's requirements in a lover, some of his conquests found him a charming bedmate, whereas others expressed disappointment. Among his critics were the director, George Cukor. "Peter is a lousy lay," he proclaimed to his gay friends. "I suggest you not waste your time with him."

For an actor who may or may not have been a dud in bed, Lawford accumulated one of the greatest rosters of A-list seductions of any Hollywood star. Mart Martin, the chronicler of sexual relationships among the stars, included among his lovers June Allyson, Lucille Ball, Anne Baxter, Noël Coward, Dorothy Dandridge, Tom Drake, Rhonda Fleming, Ava Gardner, Rita Hayworth, Judy Holliday, Van Johnson, Janet Leigh, Marilyn Maxwell,

270

Lee Remick, Sal Mineo, Kim Novak, Elizabeth Taylor, Lana Turner, Robert Walker, Keenan Wynn, and both of the wives of Ronald Reagan: i.e., Jane Wyman and starlet Nancy Davis, who became First Lady of the United States.

In reference to Peter Lawford's sexual profligacies, Martin also added this salacious tidbit to his overview: "Plus lots of college girls, beach bunnies he met while surfing, prostitutes who knew him as a $50 oral trick, call boys, male hustlers, young male extras, and studio messenger boys."

Much of Lawford's childhood had been spent in France, where he was introduced to sex by his thirty-five-year-old nanny when he was only ten years old.

In 1930, at the age of seven, he'd made his film debut in an English production, *Poor Old Bill*. Seven years later, he severely injured his right arm when it crashed through a glass door. Throughout the rest of his life, he managed to conceal his paralyzed arm on camera.

In the late 1930, he arrived in Hollywood, where he was spotted by a talent scout and cast opposite Freddie Bartholomew, Judy's former lover, in *Lord Jeff* (1938).

Because of his arm, he did not go into military service during World War II but stayed in Hollywood making a number of well-received films, none more notable than two he shot with Greer Garson: *Random Harvest* (1942) and *Mrs. Parkington* (1944).

Judy first met him during the dying throes of her marriage to David Rose when he played a student in *Girl Crazy* (1943), in which she co-starred with Mickey Rooney.

"We had a lot of fun together, nothing serious, but Peter and I shacked up on and off for years, even when we were both a member of the Rat Pack in the 1950s," she said.

During Judy's affair with Joe Mankiewicz, Peter often came by her house and drove her over to her psychiatrist, Dr. Samuel. She'd have her hour-long session with him while Peter snoozed in his car outside.

Lawford would later remember that when Judy was co-starring with him in *Easter Parade*, Dr. Samuel died. "She was really traumatized. I didn't understand that. She told me the sessions really didn't do her any good."

Lawford was proud of his work with Irene Dunne in *The White Cliffs of Dover* (1944), and he invited Judy to see it with him. She predicted big stardom for him.

Since Judy and Peter were seen in public so often together, there were rumors in the press that they would soon get married.

Kay Thompson found "Judy and Peter looking very much in love" when they attended her first annual joint birthday bash with Roger Edens. She was thirty-five, and he was thirty-nine, and the date was November 9, 1944 at her Georgian farmhouse at 11580 Bellagio Road in a tony section of Bel Air. Lawford and Judy appeared in outlandish costumes borrowed from the wardrobe department at MGM. *[Judy and Lawford also showed up for Kay and Edens' third annual birthday bash, too.]*

When Kay opened a one-woman show at Ciro's, Judy and Lawford were her most obsessive and devoted fans, showing up night after night, once with Frank Sinatra and his frequent "hot date," Marilyn Maxwell.

[Judy began to see Sinatra quite often years later, when both of them became official members of the notorious Hollywood "Rat Pack."]

***

In the late 1940s, Hollywood succumbed to a craze for fictionalized biopics of famous composers, often as vehicles for the restaging of their music within the context of fast-moving, big-budget song-and-dance extravaganzas.

It was MGM's producer Arthur Freed who devised the concept for *Words and Music* (MGM 1948), an all-star tribute to the showtunes of songwriters Richard Rogers and Lorenz Hart.

Fred Finklehoffe wrote the screenplay, focusing on Mickey Rooney as Hart and Tom Drake—Judy's Boy Next Door—as Rodgers. Judy was hired as the spotlight singer in two of the film's dozens of musical numbers, one of them with Rooney.

The rather weak narrative about the lives and interactions of the two composers would be interrupted by famous stars performing song-and-dance numbers derived from their works. Featured stars included June Allyson, Perry Como, Lena Horne (singing a memorable version of "The Lady Is a Tramp,") Ann Sothern, Cyd Charisse, Betty Garrett, Janet Leigh (as the wife of Rodgers), Marshall Thompson, Mel Tormé, and Gene Kelly with Vera-Ellen. *[Together, Kelly and Vera-Ellen danced an avant-garde, nightmarish interpretation of "Slaughter on Tenth Avenue."]*

Judy and Finklehoffe, whom she affectionately called "Freddie," had known each other for years. He had written the MGM musical, *Strike Up the Band* (1940) in which she had co-starred with Rooney. *[Four years later, Judy celebrated with him after his receipt of an Oscar nomination for Best Adapted Screenplay for* Meet Me in St. Louis *(1944).]*

Finklehoffe was one of three writers who crafted the screenplay for Judy and Kelly of *For Me and My Gal* (1942). He had first discovered Kelly during his stint on Broadway in *Pal Joey*.

A native of Springfield, Massachusetts, Finklehoffe was twelve years older than Judy. At the time, he was married to his second wife, the Scottish actress Ella Logan.

He invited Judy to the Cocoanut Grove to discuss how she was to appear in her number, which was later divided into two separate sequences, one of them with Rooney.

Although she had never expressed a romantic

Uncharacteristically, **Judy** showed up on time to perform a duet with **Rooney** entitled "I Wish I Were in Love Again."

Ironically, the song had been considered "too sophisticated" for insertion into their 1939 hit, *Babes in Arms*, but almost a decade later, it blended perfectly into *Words and Music*.

interest in him before, he re-entered her life when she was feeling vulnerable, lonely, and tormented over her disintegrating marriage. Suddenly, she saw Freddie in a very different light, and she began to flirt with him.

After both of them had had too much to drink, they ended up renting a room in some obscure motel where she stayed in the car while he registered them as man and wife.

It was hardly a love affair—more like a random sexual encounter which was repeated a few times in their future, including when they dated in New York City.

As director of *Words and Music,* Freed briefly considered Vincente Minnelli, but eventually settled on Norman Taurog, who had helmed Judy before.

For a last-minute insertion into *Words and Music,* Freed summoned Judy back again three months later for the filming of her rendition of "Johnny One Note."

Although both of Judy's two numbers were supposed to take place during the same time sequence, they did not appear that way. In the first of them, she looked undernourished and frail, but by the September filming of the second, she had gained weight. This was noted by the critic for *Modern Screen.* "Judy Garland is visually startling, appearing thin as a wraith in her first number and coming back to sing "Johnny One Note" for an encore, looking pounds heavier."

Or, as her manager, Carleton Alsop, phrased it, "She barely casts a shadow in her first number and then comes back minutes later looking like Kate Smith."

Finkelhoffe, as he told Judy, had to camouflage many aspects of the real-life story of Lorenz Hart. Born in New York's Harlem in 1895, and self-defined as "an undesirable freak," he stood just under five feet (Rooney was ideal for the role he was assigned) and was, throughout most of his adult life, wreathed in cigar smoke. He was also an alcoholic and a closeted homosexual who would disappear for weeks at a time, pursuing a secretive and tormented erotic life with a revolving series of male hustlers.

But in Finklehoffe's idealized and sanitized script for *Words and Music,* Hart died at age 48, lamenting his lost love, as portrayed by Betty Garrett cast as Peggy Logan McNeil, "the girl who got away."

Dick Rodgers, in contrast, settles down to a happy home life with children, with Janet Leigh portraying his wife, Dorothy.

[In real life, Rodgers was not the happily married man depicted in the film. An avowed atheist and a notorious serial womanizer, he was prone to depression and alcohol abuse.]

Despite mixed reviews, *Words and Music* grossed $4,500,000, but recorded a loss of nearly $400,000 because of its high production costs.

The New York Times noted that even though it was studded with A-list stars, it was "a patently juvenile specimen of a musical biography."

The New York *Herald Tribune* had praise for the film's music but found the story "both silly and saccharine."

Time magazine noted that "Rooney runs his own narrow gamut between the brash and the maudlin, tottering finally to a ludicrous death on the rain-pelted sidewalk."

Words and Music marked the tenth and final appearance on the screen of Mickey Rooney with Judy Garland.

***

In 1948, as a married couple, Judy and Minnelli bonded with actress Sylvia Sidney and her new husband, Carleton Alsop, whom she'd married the year before. He'd been a film producer, advertising executive, publicist, and radio announcer.

Previously, in 1935, Sidney had married the legendary publisher Bennett Cerf, their union lasting only six months. In 1938, she'd wed actor Luther Adler, divorcing him in 1946.

As a teenager, Judy had watched Sidney on the screen in co-starring roles with actors who included Spencer Tracy, Gary Cooper, Joel McCrea, Henry Fonda, Fredric March, George Raft, and Cary Grant. She'd been directed by everyone from Fritz Lang to Alfred Hitchcock. During her heyday, she was among the highest-paid actresses in Hollywood, taking home $10,000 a week, but by the time Judy met her, she had been labeled "Box Office Poison."

Alsop had grown up in the San Joaquin region of California. As described by biographer Gerold Frank, "He was an urbane W. Somerset Maugham character. He always had the front table at Romanoff's, knew everyone in Hollywood, had a sulfurous eloquence of invective, and a gift for character assassination that kept Judy in raptures."

When Judy could no long stand to live under the same roof with Minnelli, she would go over to the home of the Alsops and spend the night. Usually, she had no appetite, but, because Sylvia was a good cook, she began to put some weight on "my frail bones."

One day, looking out at her backyard, she asked Sidney, "Why did I ever marry a man I did not love?"

The actress pointed out Liza playing in the yard with two other children. "That's why," she answered.

Alsop and Sidney had many opportunities to observe Judy and Minnelli interact with their daughter. "Judy was more restrained, but Vince lavished Liza with kisses and indulged her every whim," Alsop said. "It made me shudder a bit, as it seemed almost incestuous."

"When guests arrived, Liza

Friday, January 24, 1947

They Plan Wedding March

Screen Actress Sylvia Sidney and Carlton Alsop, Hollywood advertising executive, discuss plans in her Hollywood home for their wedding in March. They revealed their engagement recently.

Judy's friend **Sylvia Sidney with her husband, Carleton Alsop.**

Judy's professed friendship with Sylvia didn't prevent her from trying to seduce him.

274

seemed to want to be the center of attention," Sidney said. "If she didn't get it, she'd throw a fit. If that didn't work, she'd faint…anything to get attention. I felt she was definitely going into show business, where, hopefully, she'd would get the adulation she so desperately needed."

In July of 1948, Judy's doctors advised her to move to a separate home from Minnelli, and she obeyed, leasing a house at 10,000 Sunset Boulevard. Here, she could have more privacy for her affairs with various men. Gradually, her health returned, and she gained some much-needed weight. She also withdrew, at least temporarily, from heavy medications.

Having dropped out of the film *The Barkleys of Broadway* (1949), her role going to Ginger Rogers, Judy made very few public appearances. She was heard on ABC's *Philco Radio Time* with Bing Crosby. As always, she was asked to sing her signature "Over the Rainbow," but she also performed two numbers with Crosby—"For Me and My Gal," and "Embraceable You."

In May of 1948, she asked Alsop for help in managing some of her business affairs. Almost immediately, he determined that her finances were "horribly muddled," as were her husband's. Alsop set about trying to put her finances in order, learning that MGM had retained $100,000 of her back pay, since she'd run up production costs during the shooting of *The Pirate.* He met with Mayer, protesting that holding her money was illegal, and he might have to take MGM to court.

He and Mayer worked out a compromise, with the mogul offering her $50,000 to sing one song with Rooney in *Words and Music.* Weeks later, he offered her another $50,000 to sing a solo number in the same picture.

Alsop was twenty-two years older than Judy, but she was attracted to his strong, masculine aura and his ability to take charge of almost any situation. She started calling him at two or three o'clock in the morning, demanding that he come to her home at once. Much to the annoyance of his wife, he would get dressed and drive to her rented home on Sunset Boulevard, where he would stay until she finally fell asleep. She started calling him "Pa," and he referred to her as "my adorable little bitch."

One rainy night, she'd been drinking heavily. Feeling despondent, she phoned him, demanding that he visit her at once. "I'm desperate," she insisted.

When he got there, she was in the living room, nude beneath her flimsy bathrobe. She confronted him, claiming, "You tell me you love me, but you've never made love to me. I want you to show me how much you love me." Then she opened her robe, exposing herself.

From all reports, that marked the beginning of their months-long affair. She would not give herself to him exclusively, but he did come over when she needed him.

Dashing **Ronald Colman** (object of Judy's obsessive fantasy) with **Kathleen Myers** in *His Supreme Moment* (1925)

275

Like all her affairs, this one, too, would run its course. Sidney, long suspicious of the intimacies between Judy and her husband, eventually learned that Alsop had more or less evolved into Judy's lover. She divorced him in 1951 and never married again.

In June of 1948, and to celebrate Judy's twenty-sixth birthday, Alsop asked her what she wanted as a gift. She surprised him by saying, "Ronald Colman," knowing that he was a friend of his. He set about arranging a meeting, checking first with the actor's wife, Benita Hume.

The following night, the doorbell rang, and she answered it to find a messenger from Saks with a delivery. It was Colman, wrapped in cellophane from head to toe, with a red ribbon tied around his neck.

She screamed with delight, throwing her arms around him and kissing him after ripping away some of the cellophane. "This is the greatest present I've ever received."

As she relayed to Alsop, she and Colman spent a delightful evening together, as each of them told each other how much their respective screen appearances had meant.

"It was that voice of his, so cultivated, the best of breeding of the English gentry," she said. "That voice had even survived into a more vulgar age. Unlike some silent screen stars, Colman made a smooth transition to talkies."

"As a teenager, he had delighted me when he starred as Bulldog Drummond. Even when he played a prisoner, he was still suave. I told him that after I saw *Lost Horizon* (1937), I dreamed that night that I was lying beside him in Shangri-La."

Thoughts of Colman soon faded as Mario Lanza, another singing sensation from the Metro stable, entered her life.

***

An American tenor and Hollywood movie star, Mario Lanza (1921-1959) enjoyed wildly popular success in the late 40s and 50s. He was naturally chosen to play *The Great Caruso* in the 1951 film. Professionally, this Philadelphia native could sing like no other American. Privately, he was a mess addicted to food, wine, and women.

In 1942 he studied for six weeks with Leonard Bernstein. "Having his mouth on me week after week sickened me," Lanza later told pals in the Army. "I closed my eyes and pretended it was Betty Grable giving me all those blow-jobs."

Lanza made his operatic debut in Otto Nicolai's *Die lustigen Weiber von Windsor* at Tanglewood in the summer of 1942. But his operatic career was interrupted by World War II when he joined the U.S. Army Air Corps.

It was while still in the Army that Lanza began his life-long career as a womanizer.

Lanza was such a success in the show, he became known as "Caruso of the Air Force." In New York at the end of a nationwide tour, Lanza joined the cast of *Winged Victory*, a big Moss Hart production with many stars, including Karl Malden, Edmond O'Brien, and Red Buttons. One day, after Hart heard Lanza sing "Celeste Aïda" backstage, he came to him with a promise that he could make him into a big-time stage star.

Although he was a closeted homosexual, Moss Hart would go on to marry Kitty Carlisle. Lanza became involved with Hart, but later asked actor O'Brien, "Is everyone in show business a cocksucker?"

"It's called the casting couch," O'Brien told him. "All a good-looking actor like you has to do is lie on it for a few minutes from time to time — and you can end up making millions."

"I want women," Lanza said, "and I resent having to give my seed to all these men. But I was born poor and I want to be rich, so I guess I'll go along with it, but these guys disgust me."

At a Hollywood party in the autumn of 1944, Walter Pidgeon heard Lanza sing in another room and thought it was a recording of Enrico Caruso. Later, Pidgeon introduced Lanza to Frank Sinatra. Lanza sang an aria from *Tosca,* and Sinatra, a devotee of opera, later claimed, "The kid knocked a hole through me."

Lanza quickly discovered that Sinatra was a straight-shooter, even though he admitted to "swooning" whenever he heard Lanza's voice. "When I first met Sinatra, I thought he'd be another cocksucker like all the rest, but he wasn't," Lanza told Pidgeon. "We became great pals."

Lanza and Sinatra began to chase women together. To hell with the wives. Stories still persist that Sinatra asked Lanza to join him on a secret date with Judy Garland at a private hideaway in the San Fernando Valley.

MARIO LANZA

His career was brief, and his output of films very limited, but **Mario Lanza** had one of the greatest voices of the 20th century. He was a trouble-maker as a young boy, and even more of a trouble-maker when he became a star, but no one could deny his talent. His concerts were sold out, as were his box office smash movies. His albums topped the charts. As his professional life soared, his private life collapsed into shambles.

His ego knew no bounds. In Hollywood, he said, "I'm a movie star, and I should live like one. Nobody wants movie stars to be like the guy next door. My major career regret is that I didn't get to co-star in an MGM musical with Judy Garland. I got Kathryn Grayson instead."

The hotel manager later claimed that the trio shared a large bed together. "I wasn't in the bed, writing everything down," Howard Wiess later said, "but when two men and one gal check into a hotel room, and there's only one bed, I can assume only one thing."

Word reached Louis B. Mayer at MGM of the new singing sensation, and the mogul contacted Lanza, signing him to a seven-year contract in 1948. Mayer cast Lanza in *That Midnight Kiss*, starring Kathryn Grayson, who reportedly had the largest bust measurements in Hollywood. In their first love scene together, Lanza instructed Grayson: "You've got to be more sexy. Push up to me. Let me feel your pussy next to my cock." He then stuck his tongue down her throat.

Grayson was horrified. The next day in a huddle with costume designer Helen Rose, Grayson asked that brass knuckles be sewed into her gown. Later, on set, when Lanza plunged his tongue down her throat again, she fisted him in the balls with the brass knuckles. Screaming in pain, he backed away. Future kisses from the tenor were more demure.

Toward the end of filming, Lanza's weight began to balloon. It was a problem he'd have for the rest of his life. Mayer hired Terry Robinson, a physical therapist and "trainer of the stars," to keep his new star in shape. In time, Robinson became Lanza's closest friend.

Years later Robinson recalled how Lanza and he had encountered a drunken Judy Garland leaving a screening room late one night on the nearly deserted MGM lot. Of course, Lanza already

Like Judy, **Lanza** fought a life-long battle with his weight. He constantly attacked the press. "That's all they ever think about—Lanza's fat!"

His wife, the former Betty Hicks, assured him that he didn't have to diet and make himself nervous. "Your voice," she told him, "that's all your public wants from you."

"It's all sex when I'm singing," said Lanza. "That's me. It comes right out of my balls. And the more I lay other women, the better I am as a husband."

In the 1950s, **Mario Lanza** and the beautiful MGM songbird, **Kathryn Grayson**, were the most successful musical team at MGM. In their film together, *The Midnight Kiss* (1949), Lanza was billed as "the singing Clark Gable."

Lanza was always coming on to Grayson, but she detested him and complained to Howard Hughes, who threatened to have Lanza wiped out.

By the time the singing duo filmed *The Toast of New Orleans* together in 1950, they had made up and often worked out at a gym together, with her lifting rather heavy barbells.

In later life, Lanza claimed he repeatedly seduced Grayson, although on several occasions, she denied any sexual involvement with the singer.

Who do you believe?

"knew" Garland as David had "known" Bathsheba.

With Robinson driving, Lanza offered to give Garland a lift, but first they stopped at a liquor store for a bottle of Chivas Regal. Drinking from paper cups in the backseat, Lanza asked Robinson to drive them into the Hollywood Hills.

Coming to a scenic spot an hour later, Robinson got out and left Lanza and Garland in the backseat. After waiting what he thought was a reasonable time, Robinson returned to the car. Though the windows were foggy, he could still see inside. Lanza was mounting Garland, and her legs were up in the air. She was screaming encouragement for him to go to it.

Robinson disappeared for another thirty minutes. Upon his return Lanza and Garland, still half dressed, had resumed their drinking. "Get in!" Lanza commanded Robinson. "Drive Judy home. After all, we promised to give her a lift."

"That he did!" Garland yelled from the backseat.

Judy's affair with Lanza, in her words, was "brief but memorable. Every time we got together, we talked of co-starring in an MGM m u s i - cal. Kathryn Grayson got him instead of me."

***

Variety carried the announcement that Judy Garland's next picture would be *In the Good Old Summertime,* set to be released by MGM in 1949. It was to be produced by Joe Pasternak and directed by Robert Z. Leonard. Van Johnson was their final choice as her leading man, although Frank Sinatra, Gene Kelly, and Robert Walker had also been considered.

The next morning, Judy was summoned to Pasternak's office, where Leonard was waiting for her. He'd last directed her in *Ziegfeld Girl* (1941), co-starring Lana Turner and Hedy Lamarr.

The Hungarian actor, S.Z. Sakall—nicknamed "Cuddles"—would play the third lead. Spring Byington, also in the cast, had last worked with Judy in *Presenting Lily Mars* (1943).

Ironically, Pasternak wanted to "borrow" Liza Minnelli, aged two and a half, for the final reel, in which Judy and Van are no longer hostile toward each other, but have gotten married and had a daughter.

As Veronica Fisher, Judy goes to work in the music shop of Otto Oberkugen (Sakall). She and the shop's senior salesman, Andrew Larkin (Van Johnson) develop an antagonism to each other. Both of them have pen pals to whom they're each writing romantic letters, without knowing that they are working side by side every day. Another romance (a senior citizen version) is percolating between Sakall and Byington.

Of course, at this point the audience knows that love will win out in the end.

To pull off a difficult scene, in which a violin is crushed, Leonard called in Buster Keaton. In silent pictures of the 1920s, he had challenged both Charlie Chaplin and Harold Lloyd as the film industry's chief comedian. Since then, however, he had become an alcoholic and had fallen on bad

279

days. By now, elderly and seriously diminished, Keaton was accepting whatever role was offered, regardless of how small.

For the film, Judy recorded one of her favorite songs, "Last Night When We Were Young," but saw it cut from the picture. However, she performed a rousing "I Don't Care," a song that had already been made famous by vaudevillian Eva Tanguay back in the early 1920s.

Time magazine praised Judy's free-wheeling style calling her "fresh as a daisy."

Despite its weak story line, *In the Good Old Summertime* opened to fairly good reviews and was a hit at the box office. Regardless of Judy's strained relationship with MGM, the studio wanted to hold on to her as long as she could generate revenue. In fact, they were moving ahead to cast her as the female lead in their big musical for 1950, *Annie Get Your Gun.*

***

Judy had seen neither Van Johnson nor his lover, Keenan Wynn, for many months, so she invited them over to dinner. She'd been reading about a divorce and marriage in their lives. They were open and candid about what had happened:

In the previous few years, Van and Keenan had been spending a lot of time with Peter Lawford. One day Lady Lawford, Peter's mother, returned home to find Keenan, his wife Evie, and Van Johnson in her living room. She pointedly exited from the room and ordered one of her servants to fumigate the place when this "threesome" had departed.

"I don't want homosexuals in our drawing room," she told her son. "If you want them here, then notify me and I will leave while they are here."

It was Lady Lawford herself who told Louis B. Mayer that both her son and Van were gay, and the studio honcho was horrified at the news. MGM at that point maintained a huge investment in Van's career.

In the wake of Lady Lawford's betrayal, Mayer summoned Van to his office and demanded that "you are to get married—and I mean sooner than later."

In the Good Old Summertime was the cheerful and upbeat musical remake of a romantically subtle and rather exotic Ernst Lubitsch drama, *The Shop Around the Corner* (1940), starring Margaret Sullavan and James Stewart.

Cast with America's favorite "boy next door," **Van Johnson** and the now wildly popular **Judy Garland**, it would no longer be set in Budapest in the 1930s, but in turn-of-the-century Chicago at a music store.

It will never be known exactly what transpired between Van and his best friend, Keenan. But a deal was reached. Early in 1947, Evie and Van drove to El Paso, Texas, but in separate cars. In El Paso, they checked into a hotel under assumed names. Van wore a straw hat that concealed most of his face, and sunglasses. The next day they drove across the border to Ciudad Juárez in Mexico, where a quickie divorce terminated the marriage of Evie with Keenan.

That same afternoon, on the winter's day of January 25, 1947, Evie became the first and last Mrs. Van Johnson.

In reacting to the news, Lucille Ball later said, "I couldn't believe it. That sweet kid Desi and I knew had become something else. It looked like Van would do anything to protect his star status. But I don't feel sorry for Keenan either. Something about this arrangement stinks. I think Keenan had to agree to it."

After this strange but widely publicized marriage to the wife of his best friend, many young female fans deserted him. Some newspapers called Johnson a "home wrecker." *[The previous year, in 1946, a popularity poll had defined him as number three at the box office, a higher rating than Clark Gable got when he returned home from the war. Now, however, the bobbysoxers weren't screaming any more. Many of his former fans had grown up and were marrying servicemen returning from the war. Few, if any, seemed to have maintained a crush on Van.]*

Gender-Preference Ambiguity in Easy to Wed (1946).

Upper photo, left to right: **Keenan Wynn, Lucille Ball, and Van Johnson** in an amusing and "made for the screen" love triangle.

Lower photo), Van Johnson (right) wrestles with his onscreen rival and offscreen lover, Keenan Wynn

Studio publicist Morgan Hudgins later said, "I think this marriage marked the beginning of the end of Van's career. He would go on for several years and even have a hit or two, but the peak of his popularity was over."

By 1948, *Screen Guide* was asking, "Is Van Johnson dead at the box office?"

America had moved on in its restless search for another male sweetheart.

Despite all that, one segment of Van's fan base remained loyal. Throughout the 1940s Van had received more gay fan mail than any other star at MGM. Young homosexual men throughout America always had their "gaydar" tuned in on Van. Some of the men mailed him candid shots of themselves with full erections.

Van answered most of his fan letters personally. In a few cases, and although recently married, he enclosed his private phone number. On some occasions when he encountered an exceptionally handsome man with a large endowment, he sent an airline ticket to Los Angeles. Throughout his marriage, he maintained a secret hideaway apartment which he kept mainly for sexual liaisons.

On January 6, 1948, a daughter, Schuyler, was born to Van and Evie. Even after he'd fathered a child, however, he continued to sleep around with young men, often aspirant actors. He eventually left California, retreating to an apartment on Manhattan's Upper East Side, immediately next door to Greta Keller, the Viennese *chanteuse*.

As the years went by, Schuyler and her father became alienated. In 2005 she wrote a newspaper *exposé* of her dad for the *Daily Mail* in London.

The book that could not be published — not until after the death of her son Peter Lawford.

with an Introduction by Prince Franz Hohenlohe
As Told To Buddy Galon

MOMMIE, DEAREST

Lady Lawford, Peter Lawford's mother, was probably the most mean-spirited, misguided, and destructive matriarch in Hollywood.

Defiantly, she wrote an autobiography in 1986, perhaps as a means of justifying her cruelty.

***

On August 28, 1951, Van called Judy with more bad news. Robert Walker, her former lover and co-star, was dead. The star's housekeeper found him deeply disturbed emotionally and threatening suicide. She immediately called his psychiatrist, Frederick Hacker, who rushed to his home and administered amorbarbital for a sedation, hoping to put him to bed to sleep it off.

Walker had been drinking heavily for the past two days and nights. Apparently, the combination of the amobarbital and alcohol caused him to stop breathing. Efforts to resuscitate him failed, and he was pronounced dead at the age of thirty-two.

While mourning the loss of their mutual friend, Van told Judy "I had heard that Bob was getting better — now this."

"No way was he getting better, only worse," Van said. "He fell hopelessly in love with that handsome devil, Farley Granger, when Alfred Hitchcock cast them together in *Strangers on a Train* (1951). His love was not reciprocated. Maybe he died from a broken heart."

"Van, dear Van, I hope that is not my own fate, too," Judy said.

***

A week after filming *In the Good Old Summertime,* Judy, in her own words, "started to fall to pieces." So did her marriage to Minnelli.

282

On March 31, 1949, she announced to the press what Hollywood insiders already knew. She and Minnelli had separated and would later file for divorce, which was not granted until 1951. All of her demons—the suicide attempts, the pill popping, the sleepless nights—returned to haunt her.

Her manager and sometimes lover, Carleton Alsop, flew to Boston with her and checked her into the Peter Bent Brigham Hospital. He was aware that she was broke and got Mayer to agree to pay her travel expenses and medical bills.

A week later, Alsop's wife, Sylvia Sidney, flew in to join her husband. Both of them visited Judy every day until they felt, and the doctors agreed, that she was in a good enough condition to fly back to Los Angeles.

In the aftermath of her affair with Alsop, Judy and Sidney became estranged.

***

A trade paper in Hollywood ran the announcement that Judy Garland would head an all-star cast in Irving Berlin's *Annie Get Your Gun*, which had been "packin' 'em in on Broadway" for three full years beginning in 1946 when it starred Ethel Merman.

Set to be released as a film by MGM in 1949, its movie rights had been purchased from Irving Berlin at a cost of $650,000, plus a percentage of the profits. [*It was the highest price ever paid for copyrights. In contrast, the film rights for* Gone With the Wind *had cost only $50,000.*]

Before Berlin signed over the rights, it was with the understanding that Judy would star as Annie Oakley (1860-1926), a sharpshooter in Buffalo Bill's Wild West Show. The plot centered on her romance with her rival sharpshooter, Frank Butler *(1847-1926).*

On Broadway, producer Mike Todd turned down the musical, but the team of Richard Rodgers and Oscar Hammerstein II went for it. Hoping that it might repeat the success of their big hit, *Oklahoma!,* they hired Jerome Kern to compose its music, but he soon collapsed on the street with a cerebral hemorrhage and died on November 11, 1945.

Before she was signed, the producers tapped Mary Martin, who rejected it, later calling it "the mistake of my career." She made up for her error by signing for the post-Broadway tour, which took up the next two years of her life. Her rousing renditions of those super-macho songs affected her voice, which deepened from a normal lyric coloratura soprano to a mezzo-soprano alto.

Irving Berlin was asked to adapt the Broadway musical into a film. At first, he rejected the idea, but eventually was persuaded to work on it. For the film adaptation, many of the original numbers were cut and new ones by Berlin subbed.

During the next few weeks, he created some of his most memorable songs, including "You Can't Get a Man With a Gun," "Doin' What Comes Naturally," and "There's No Business Like Show Business."

Produced by Arthur Freed, the film version of *Annie Get Your Gun* would be directed by Busby Berkeley until he was fired; Chuck Walters until he was fired, and finally, George Sidney, who completed the picture.

Freed hired Roger Edens, Judy's former vocal coach, as one of his assistants. Together, they hired the writer and novelist, Sidney Sheldon, to author a film script, based on the Broadway book by Dorothy Fields and her brother, Herbert. Fields had originally conceived the idea of *Annie Get Your Gun* as a vehicle for her friend, Ethel Merman.

For the film version, the casting of the character of Frank Butler was hotly contested. In the beginning, some thought that Roy Rogers might be cast opposite Judy—"If only he knew how to act." Other names raised included Cary Grant, Bing Crosby, Perry Como, and Dan Dailey, but none was considered appropriate. MGM finally signed the relatively unknown Howard Keel for his film debut. As soon as it was released, he attracted millions of fans, drawn not only to his rich bass baritone, but to his good looks and rugged masculinity.

[Talent scouts for MGM first noticed Keel during his starring role in the 1947 stage production of Oklahoma!, *which he presented before Queen Elizabeth II in London. His performance in* Annie Get Your Gun *led to gigs in such future hits as* Show Boat *(1951),* Seven Brides for Seven Brothers *(1954), and as Wild Bill Hickock opposite Doris Day in* Calamity Jane *(1953). Keel's most wide-ranging exposure to millions of viewers occurred nearly thirty years later in the long-running (1982-1991) hit TV series,* Dallas.*]*

Frank Morgan, Judy's former co-star in *The Wizard of Oz*, was cast

Left: The historic "real life" sharpshooter and carnival attraction, **Annie Oakley**.

Right: **Judy Garland** portraying her before she was fired, in disgrace, from *Annie Get Your Gun.*

According to **Howard Keel,** "Judy became my first friend in Hollywood, and I was thrilled to death to work with her."

"She didn't like Buzz (Berkeley), our director. Nor did I. In my first scene, he had me perform a dangerous stunt on a horse. The poor animal slipped on the slick floor of the set, and I broke my ankle and had to bow out for six weeks. Judy and Buzz went way back and had never gotten along early in her career. He drove her nuts, and she just didn't have the energy for take after take. She tried to give it her all, but her "all" wasn't what it used to be."

284

as Buffalo Bill, but he died and was replaced by Louis Calhern. Other support came from Judy's friend, Keenan Wynn, cast as Charles Davenport; J. Carrol Naish as Chief Sitting Bull; and Edward Arnold as Pawnee Bill.

From the beginning, it was obvious to cast and crew that Judy was not in any physical condition to perform in a high-octane musical requiring great physical dexterity. She was not only going through the trauma of separating from Minnelli but suffering sheer exhaustion from overwork. She often arrived on the set in a drugged state, which made her look wooden in her early rehearsals.

After watching the early footage that Buzz shot of Judy, Freed fired him, replacing him with Chuck Walters, who had helmed her in *Easter Parade.*

Their romantic adventures with each other had long ago faded. He, too, ordered a screening of the footage shot by Buzz, and he demanded that all of it be reshot.

Judy seemed to face one disaster after another. Whereas on many days she was disruptively late, on others she didn't show up at all. Sometimes, she'd alert the assistant director, Al Jennings, at three or four o'clock in the morning, that she was sick. Sometimes, she'd fall asleep at sunrise and arrive at the studio at 11AM or noon.

In 1950, a reporter for *Time* magazine wrote: "**Betty Hutton**, who is not remarkably pretty, by movie standards, nor a remarkably good singer or dancer, has a vividly unique personality in a town that tends to reduce beauty and talent to mass-produced patterns"

"Watching her in action has some of the fascination of waiting for a wildly sputtering fuse to touch off an alarmingly large firecracker... she has a bellicose zeal and a tomboyish winsomeness that suggests a cross between one of the Furies and Little Orphan Annie."

After **Betty Hutton** was hauled in as Judy's replacement, many of her predecessor's friends and fans made it a point not to endorse, applaud, or befriend her.

According to Hutton, "*Annie Get Your Gun* was one of the saddest and loneliest filmmaking experiences I ever had."

Even on days when she showed up, she wasn't camera ready. In the makeup department, one employee referred to her as "a pathetic old drunk." Her heavy medications caused some of her hair to fall out, and makeup had to create a false hairline for her. She mocked herself, walking in and referring to herself as "Baldy."

Her nights—flying skyward with Benzedrine and then falling down below the horizon with Seconal—seemed like long, traumatized journeys into darkness. Her makeup artist at MGM once tallied her drug intake at one-hundred pills or capsules a day.

Whereas Judy managed to finish recording the entire sound track for *Annie Get Your Gun,* on film, she completed only two numbers, "Doin' What Comes Naturally," and "I'm an Indian, Too." They were viewed for the first time on screen in MGM's 1994 documentary, *That's Entertainment III.*

All of her recordings for *Annie Get Your Gun* were released by Rhino Records in 2000 on the film's first remastered soundtrack CD.

In future productions, some of the original songs were considered offensive to Native Americans, including "I'm an Indian, Too" and were altered.

"I'm an Indian Too,"
Top: Judy; Bottom: Betty Hutton:

Two actresses interpreting the same song in their respective versions of *Annie Get Your Gun.*

In the middle of recording all the songs for *Annie,* Judy took time out for six electroshock treatments.

Fearing that her lackluster grasp of the role might damage his own credibility and career at MGM, Walters began to grow disenchanted with Judy.

He told Al Jennings, his assistant, "Judy has never been worse. Her rendition of 'I'm an Indian, Too' is pitiful. She can't decide who she wants to be—Mary Martin, Ethel Merman, or Martha Raye. We didn't want those three old dykes, so we hired Judy. But we're not getting what we paid for."

He met with Judy, who arrived at his office looking nervous and distraught. "Chuck," she said, "It may be too late. I haven't the energy I used to have. I also don't have the nerve to face the camera like I did before."

She freely admitted her fear that she'd been miscast for role of Annie Oakley. "It might have been suitable for a tough old dyke like Barbara Stanwyck back in 1935, but perhaps not for me. It's a big jump to have Judy Garland cast as a gauche, tomboyish, horseback riding, sharp-shooting cowgirl singing 'Moonshine Lullaby.'"

Walters feared that she'd have to be fired. But before he was forced to actually do that, he was dismissed and replaced with George Sidney.

Sidney had previously directed Judy's highly successful *The Harvey Girls* (1946) and was looking forward to working with her again. But on his first day as the film's (new) director, she didn't show up. He listened to all of her recorded sound tracks and concluded that none of them was very good. He, too, deplored the footage that Buzz had shot.

The next day he suffered through a tense meeting with Dore Schary, MGM's vice president in charge of production. If anyone could have been named as the man most instrumental in destroying Judy's career at MGM, it was Schary.

Schary entered the MGM family at a time when the Department of Justice was aggressively fighting Loew's Theatres in an attempt to enforce, through a bruising series of antitrust lawsuits, the division of those theaters from MGM.

MGM's parent company in New York, Loews Incorporated, hoped that Schary might be able to turn the tide. Top executives had lost faith in Mayer.

Almost immediately, Schary and Mayer came into conflict. The new Veep detested Mayer's wholesome family fare, preferring movies that Mayer derided as "dark message pictures." From the beginning, Schary named his least favorite stars, all of whom had been Mayer's favorites: Mickey Rooney, Judy Garland, Van Johnson, Esther Williams, and June Allyson. He also was not impressed with Clark Gable ("too old").

Dore ('the Scary") Schary

A native of Newark, New Jersey, Schary was promoted to MGM's Vice President in charge of production in 1948.

The year before, MGM had recorded its first-ever, end-of-the-year financial loss. Rising labor costs, political turmoil, labor unrest, and the threat of television loomed.

It was a crucial time in the movie industry. Until his forced resignation in 1951, Louis B. Mayer was still more or less in charge at MGM, but the Golden Age of Hollywood over which he'd presided had come to an end.

During Schary's controversial five-year reign, most of the MGM players under contract were let go in a belt-tightening financial squeeze.

Reunited with Sidney again as her new director, Judy learned from him just who Dore Schary was.

He'd written a play in 1932 that impressed film producer Walter Wanger, who wired the New York office of Columbia Pictures. "Hire Dore Schary," he said. "She writes with a lot of vigor...for a woman." He was employed for $100 a week as a writer, but Wanger found out he was a man and dropped him after only three months.

As a writer, Schary drifted from studio to studio: Monogram, back to Columbia briefly, Universal, Warners, 20th Century Fox, and finally, Paramount before landing as a writer at MGM.

His biggest success had been back in 1937 when he won an Oscar nod for Best Screenplay for *Boys Town* (1938), starring Spencer Tracy. He'd also had a success with *Journey for Margaret* (1942), which made a star out of Margaret O'Brien. Working for David O. Selznick, he'd had some hits, notably *The Farmer's Daughter* (1947), which brought an Oscar to Loretta Young. When Howard Hughes took over RKO, he fired Schary, calling him "a shitty Jew."

It was Mayer himself who hired him for MGM, although later defining it as "the mistake of my life."

Schary told the press, "Films must provoke thought in addition to entertainment. They must educate and inform as they amuse. Andy Hardy fantasies are not where it is today. He told Nicholas Schenck, head of Loews, "I did find my job had some fringe benefits. Benny Thau and myself were visited every morning, getting a blow job from starlet Nancy Davis," (later, Mrs. Ronald Reagan). "She's an expert at fellatio—ask Peter Lawford."

Schary cast starlet Davis in *The Next Voice You Hear* 1950), a movie about God speaking on the radio.

As director George Cukor, said, "If I had a nickel for every Jew Nancy Davis went down on, I'd be a rich man."

A year or so after his promotion to president of MGM, Schary became embroiled in the controversy surrounding Judy as the female lead in *Annie Get Your Gun*.

He later said, "I viewed the footage of Judy that had been shot so far. None of it looked or even sounded like her. I felt that if we continued with her, *Annie* would be a disaster. Our costs would soar, and the movie would flop. All of this was occurring when films were not making money. The big studios were in trouble, television was on the way."

He called Schenck at MGM's New York office and explained the situation. Coming down hard on Judy, he blamed the increase in production costs on her endless delays and her indiscriminate consumption of drugs and alcohol. "She's a physical wreck."

His New York boss said, "Dore, do what you have to do, but handle it before we go broke."

***

On May 10, 1949, Carleton Alsop, Judy's manager and sometimes lover, was urgently summoned by phone to the set of *Annie Get Your Gun*. "Your client is going ballistic," Al Jennings, the assistant director advised. "She's freaking out."

Within thirty minutes, Alsop arrived at the scene, where he found Judy shrieking and denouncing both cast and crew. "She was using the most foul language I'd ever heard from her. 'Bastards' and 'sons of bitches' were her mildest terms."

"How dare Mayer treat me like I'm some Saturday night whore?" she sobbed when she saw Alsop, who ran to her and held her in his arms.

She had received a letter from Louis K. Sidney, a vice-president of MGM. In it, he accused her of constantly being late—"that is, when you

288

show up at all. You have seriously run up production costs. We've spent a million dollars and don't have one minute of suitable footage. You have caused considerable damage to our production. We cannot tolerate such outrageous behavior."

With Alsop assisting her, Judy stumbled to her dressing room.

George Sidney, her new director, sent word to Dore Schary and Louis Sidney, "the bitch is freaking out."

Then, MGM fired off another blast, but by the time it arrived on the set, Judy had already left for the day, and that second message was delivered to her home.

"I have been informed that you've walked off the set of *Annie Get Your Gun.* Such behavior, as I've warned you, is not acceptable. This letter is to inform you that you are no longer on the picture. I'm shutting it down for five months until it can be recast. This is also to notify you that your weekly check of $6,000 has been suspended indefinitely.

"I've been fired," she yelled at Alsop. "Those shitheads have fired me. ME, who has made millions for the bastards. May the assholes burn in hell!"

The search for her replacement had already begun.

Betty Garrett, who was under contract to MGM and who could do comic songs very well, was considered as *Annie,* but she demanded too much money, so she was dropped.

Ginger Rogers actively lobbied for the role. She had replaced Judy in *The Barclays of Broadway* (1949). Mayer told her to "stick to those silk stockings and high heels. The part isn't for you, Ginger."

From the beginning, Betty Hutton had lobbied for the role, and had practically begged Paramount to lease her out, which they finally did.

Ever since 1946, when *Annie Get Your Gun* had been a hit on Broadway, Hutton had urged her home studio of Paramount to acquire the screen rights. But executives were unable to negotiate terms with Berlin, so MGM had swooped in and picked up the rights (as mentioned before) for the record-breaking high price of $650,000, plus a percentage of the profits.

Years after Hutton was summoned to replace Judy, she asserted, "Cast and crew were more than indifferent to me. They were downright hostile. And I didn't get along with that stuck-up fart, Howard Keel. He was one hell of a scene-stealer and resented me from the beginning."

The worst was yet to come: One afternoon, Judy had returned, unannounced, to the set for some reason. "She was directly in my pathway to the set, where I was due to shoot a scene," Hutton said. "As I passed by, I called out, "Hiya, Judy! A string of profanities greeted me."

Judy screamed at her replacement, calling her "a son of a bitch. You filthy, untalented whore. How many cocks did you have to suck to take over my role, for which you'll be a joke."

In the early 1950s, Hutton was chosen as the star of two of the decade's biggest box office hits: *Annie Get Your Gun* (1950) and Cecil DeMille's *The Greatest Show on Earth* (1952).

But a few years later, she virtually walked away from her career, storming out when Paramount refused to let her husband at the time, Charles O'Curran, direct her latest picture.

After that, her career collapsed. She ended up bitter and destitute, working as a cook at a Catholic rectory in Rhode Island.

Hutton died in 2007 at the age of 86 as memories of her blonde bombshell heyday in the 1940s grew dimmer, as did her long-ago lovers such as Bing Crosby, Bob Hope, Victor Mature, and Milton Berle.

Years later, Judy was asked what she thought of Betty Hutton as *Annie.* "The crazy blonde overacted, milking every scene dry. She was loud, raucous, a bombastic personality…Really, too much. I'll say this about her. She was one of a kind. And so was I, darling."

MGM was so pleased with George Sidney's direction that he was offered future big-budget musicals that included *Show Boat* (1951), starring Howard Keel and Kathryn Grayson, *Kiss Me Kate* (1953), and *Pal Joey* (1957). In *Show Boat,* Judy was suggested for the role of Julie, but Sidney said, "No way. I want Ava Gardner."

In 1973, *Annie Get Your Gun* was yanked from distribution because Irving Berlin threatened a lawsuit over music rights. The film was shelved for three decades. However, in 2002, on the 50th anniversary of its original premiere, it was put back into distribution.

After her dismissal, Judy told the press, "I don't blame MGM for firing me. Studios are run to make money. I've been a bad girl for not getting to work on time. They can't take chances with careless people like me. I'm sure that Betty Hutton will have the same love of *Annie* that I did."

Within a few days of being fired, she spoke to Minnelli: "I know I'm in for a public beating in the press." Later, she recalled, "I was right. I got attacked with heavy artillery. All the enemies I've made declared war on me."

Encountering Hedda Hopper at the Mocambo, Judy told her, "I don't know when I'm going back to work. I'm suspended so high I can't sit down."

In the summer of 1950, *Motion Picture* magazine informed its readers, "The film career of Judy Garland has come to an end."

Her most devoted fans were sent into a state of shock.

CHAPTER ELEVEN

THOUGH SHE'S WAY
TOO BIG A NAME FOR OFF-BROADWAY, JUDY
—ADDICTED, OVERWEIGHT, AND EXHAUSTED—
DYSFUNCTIONALLY PORTRAYS A FARM GIRL IN

SUMMER STOCK

DEEP DIVING AND CRANKING THINGS UP WITH

SID LUFT

BING! & FRANK!
(MAKING MUSIC & SOMETIMES LOVE WITH CROSBY & SINATRA)

ROYAL WEDDING
FURIOUS, JUDY GETS DISINVITED.
JANE POWELL REPLACES HER AS THE FEMALE LEAD

TOURING THE U.K. AND IN THE MOOD FOR
LONDON'S PALLADIUM
JUDY SPURS, CAJOLES, AND NEEDLES HER NEW
MANAGER/ESCORT TO SET UP A BOOKING

"Any woman who's a real woman wants a man to protect her and love her. Sid Luft is the kind of person you can lean against if you fall down. He's strong and protects me. I like him as much as I love him."
—Judy Garland

"Sid Luft and Judy Garland are a larger-than-life show biz couple. They have a tempestuous relationship, at times loving and true when they aren't off in pursuit of adulterous affairs, a very common occurrence in Hollywood."

—Peter Lawford

"Nobody can be professionally indifferent when Judy Garland is part of the act."

—Bing Crosby

"Love him or hate him (as many do), Luft is a fast-talking, shady dealmaker, a smooth schmoozer, a former boxer, and a smart dresser in silk shirts and suits paid for by Judy Garland."

—Frank Sinatra

"I spent much of my life fucking, fighting, and flying—in that order—before I married Judy. She was hardly the first movie star I ever plugged. She and I flew high in the sky before both of us crash landed."

—Sid Luft

"The novelist, F. Scott Fitzgerald, once wrote, 'There are no second acts in American lives.' He never met Judy Garland."

—Kay Thompson

"He was a gambler, hustler, and con man riding on the coattails of a great but troubled star. The first night Sid Luft met me, he reached into my gown and felt my left breast."

—Ann Miller

"Unlike all of Judy's other husbands, Luft, Mr. Macho personified, was not 'a friend of Dorothy,' which in gay circles is a code to identify other homosexuals. He was the most effective chargé d'affaires she ever had, not counting old Louis B. Mayer. In a moment of pique, Sid told me that Judy couldn't do anything right, except sing a song."

—John Carlyle, actor and sometime lover of Rock Hudson

"Hollywood gossips became aware of the new coupling of Luft and Garland when they showed up at Ciro's one night as ringsiders to see Kay Thompson. They were on a double date with another loving duo, Ronald Reagan and starlet Nancy Davis. He was screwing Doris Day on the side, and Nancy had been dumped by Clark Gable."

—Columnist Mike Connolly

"So Sid Luft is what Judy found at the end of the rainbow. Was it really worth the trip?"

—MGM's Eddie Mannix

292

Judy was often criticized in the press, but she had never responded until a journalist predicted the end of her film career. The profile that made her furious had appeared in the September 1950 edition of *Motion Picture* magazine. With controlled rage, she fired off a response:

"Although I don't believe in answering Hollywood gossip about myself, whether to deny or affirm it, your article in Motion Picture seems to call for some sort of word from me. So I take up the challenge:

First of all, let's talk about the reason I don't act the same way I did when I was 14 years old and 'Skip about the MGM lot like a gay ragamuffin' to quote you. The answer is simple. That was fourteen years ago! I'm quite sure everyone in the world changes rather radically between the ages of 14 and 28 and, if they don't, they should. Certain responsibilities, raising a child, running a home—all add up to changes; very normal ones, but changes nevertheless.

May I emphasize the word normal? You see, I'm so tired of reading articles in newspapers and magazines in which I'm described as neurotic, psychotic, idiotic, or any 'otic' the writer can think of—and also that I am, as I've read too often, a desperately sick woman (Ah, the drama of it all), with everything from falling arches to possessing at least two heads. Allow me to start pulling you writers and columnists down to earth. Whether it makes for good reading or not, I'm sorry to have to tell you I'm hopelessly normal; normal enough to get tired once in a while, normal enough to rest when this happens (No, dear, not in a sanitarium—just some place dull, like Monterey Beach, where I'm writing this), normal enough after I rest, to go back to work and make a hit picture and normal enough to get damn mad at the junk you boys and girls have written about me.

This is my first answer but not my last. I've kept quiet until now because to try to answer seemed to be giving dignity to pure rot. However, enough is enough. So here we go—

Of course I'm not quitting pictures. Are you kidding? I love my work, and I am looking forward with great anticipation to doing my next assignment.

Not doing Annie Get Your Gun was not a tragedy to me. It was a very good part, but there are a lot of good parts. This thing you wrote about my having a doctor or, as you put it, a guard on the set with me, is simply fantastic. My physician (most people have one, you know) wanted to see how pictures were made and asked if he could visit my set. I said 'Of course.' Result—you make it sound as though I was shooting the musical version of The Snake Pit.

And what is the prize remark you quoted as mine? Oh, yes—"The only real happiness in life is found in unhappiness." Wow! That's not only heavy, it doesn't make any sense! If I wanted to convey a Chekhovian philosophy, I'd word it better than that.

If I tried to answer all of the many weird and baffling things that have been said about me, it would fill volumes. Let me tell you how it's affected me. I'm unscathed, unscarred, unembittered and it's left me with a better sense of humor than before.

At first it was uncomfortable having a few people in Hollywood peer at me as though I were either Lon Chaney in full makeup or a walking Charles Addams cartoon. But my good friends laughed long and loud, and I heartily joined them. It's good to be able to laugh at yourself—and I don't think it's considered neurotic!

I have the public, my warm and loving friends, to thank for setting me straight. They seem not even to be aware of all the printed nonsense; they still treat me with deep affection. Their love is constant, mine for them everlasting.

Judy Garland"

But in spite of her letter defending herself, Judy in 1950 continued to be the focus of many a tabloid *exposé*. One magazine labeled her a "pillhead," another called her a "drug addict." A headline read—WHAT HAS HAPPENED TO OUR DEAR DOROTHY?

At one point, she was getting prescription medicine from five different doctors, spread out across the Greater Los Angeles area. Delivery boys on motorcycles arrived throughout the day at her doorstep.

Friends such as Lee Gershwin and Rosalind Russell learned to remove medication from their bathroom cabinets before Judy visited. "She'd loot us of almost any tablet," Russell claimed.

What was to be Judy's last film for MGM, *Summer Stock* (1950), reteamed her with Gene Kelly in spite of their box office failure together in *The Pirate* (1948). Producer Joe Pasternak had originally suggested reteaming Judy with Mickey Rooney, but it was decided that his glory days as a box office champ had long ago faded.

Chuck Walters was tapped to helm a cast that featured Eddie Bracken, Gloria DeHaven, Marjorie Main, Phil Silvers, Ray Collins, Hans Conreid, and Carlton Carpenter.

The plot revolves around Jane Falbury (Judy), who manages an unsuccessful farm in New England. She's assisted by Esme (Marjorie Main), who is called upon to cook, yell, and play nursemaid, evocative of the role she had with Judy in *Meet Me in St. Louis* (1944).

Jane's bucolic life is interrupted by her stage-struck sister Abigail (Gloria DeHaven), who arrives with a troupe of actors, mainly dancers, who want to live with her and convert her barn into a summer theater.

At first, Jane objects until she's won over by Joe Rose (Gene Kelly), who is talented, handsome, and charismatic. She already has a boyfriend (Orville Wingait, played by Eddie Bracken), who is always sneezing because of his allergies. He is dominated by his father, Jaser Wingait (Ray Collins). Hans Conried was cast as a ham actor, Harrison Keath. A talented performer, Carpenter has little to do except serve as an errand boy.

Several critics noted that DeHaven, Bracken, and Silvers were too old for the roles into which they'd been cast. Review after review noted that Pasternak was old-fashioned in producing this show, which would have been more appropriate back in those days when a group of spunky youngsters "put on a show," as represented by those Mickey Rooney/Judy Garland song and dance movies.

As was the custom, Judy began work on the film in the recording studio, turning out such songs as "If You Feel Like Singing, Sing," "Happy Harvest," and "Blue Jean Polka."

Released in August of 1950, **Summer Stock** was a hit at the box office, showing that Judy's movies could still generate revenue.

Critic Pauline Kael wrote, "Judy Garland and Gene Kelly balance each other's talents. She joined her odd and undervalued cakewalker's prance to his large-spirited hoofing, and he joined his odd, light, high voice to her deep one. There was a vulnerability both Gene and Judy brought to each other and which neither one has with any other performer."

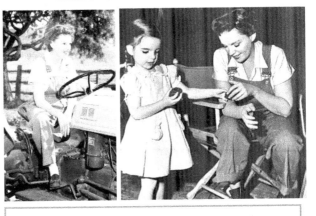

Overweight, puffy, and clad in a farm girl outfit that was anything but chic and certainly not flattering, **Judy,** during the filming of *Summer Stock*, took a break to emote, on the set, with her daughter, **Liza**.

MGM's press and PR cameras rushed to record the moment.

When she showed up for wardrobe fittings, she was twenty pounds overweight, and her dressers did what they could to disguise her gain. Despite their efforts, she looked chubby as if she'd put on all that baby fat she'd lost back in the 1930s.

She continued taking heavy medication for weight loss.

Walters complained to Pasternak, "You hired me as Judy's director, but I'm ending up as her babysitter."

As the troubled production limped along, a desperate Pasternak phoned Mayer and set up an emergency meeting. Facing the MGM chief, he sought his permission to shut down *Summer Stock,* fearing that it would run "hideously over-budget" because of Judy's erratic behavior and her constant failure to show up. He cited at least eighteen major violations.

Left: Judy wheedles concessions from "The Man that (fortunately) Got Away," her character's fiancé, Orville Bracken, as portrayed by **Eddie Bracken.**

Right: Although it took several arduous months of dieting, Judy finally achieved the svelte glamour she conjured for *Summer Stock*'s finale

As an example, he cited a big production number she had sabotaged. She was to have performed a song-and-dance routine with Kelly and Silvers, called "Heavenly Music." That morning, she didn't bother to show up, and didn't even call in.

Although Walters would later attack Mayer for his handling of her, Mayer came to her defense that afternoon with Pasternak: "MGM has made millions off this little girl. Let's give her one more chance. If we shut down the film, it may drive her to suicide. You know, she's tried several times to kill herself."

Although Judy struggled with her demons throughout the shoot, her day was brightened one afternoon when little Liza was brought to the set. There, she was baffled to see her mother dressed as a farmer.

A surprise visitor to the set was Spencer Tracy, the actor who had taken her virginity back in the 1930s. During their subsequent affair, she had had to abort his baby. No mention was made of those days, and they shared talk about the two pictures they were making. He was being directed by Minnelli in *Father of the Bride* (1950), co-starring Elizabeth Taylor and Joan Bennett.

In *Summer Stock,* Kelly also performed one of the most memorable dances of his career, a solo number using as "partners" a discarded newspaper and a creaky floorboard. His "You Wonderful You" was hailed by critics as "one of the breakthrough numbers of his career."

As a team, Judy and Kelly also performed the super-charged "Portland Fancy," a song-and-dance number later hailed as "the best terpsichorean of her career."

Most of the numbers were arranged by Harry Warren (music) and Max Gordon (lyrics).

Two months after thinking that the picture was completed, Judy was summoned back to MGM to film what became the iconic "Get Happy" closing dance sequence. She had been under the supervision of a noted hypnotist—called a "diet guru"—in Santa Barbara and had dropped twenty pounds. A black fedora resting on her head, she appeared in a black dinner jacket, her bare legs encased in sheer black hosiery. She looked stunning. "Get Happy" became one of her most-requested numbers during stage appearances in her future.

Time magazine wrote, "*Summer Stock* is no great shakes as a cinemusical but it serves as a reminder of Judy Garland's unerring way with a song. She is one of Hollywood's triple threat girls."

The *Los Angeles Herald-Examiner* claimed, "The mere flash of her name on the screen creates excitement."

***

Nervous and exhausted, and popping pills like peanuts, Judy was summoned back to MGM from her Malibu beach house after only three weeks of her six-month rest cure.

She was still under contract and producer Arthur Freed wanted to cast her in *Royal Wedding,* a musical starring Fred Astaire slated for release in 1950.

She had failed to show up to star opposite Astaire in *The Barclays of Broadway,* and she'd been replaced by Ginger Rogers, but by now, Freed was willing to take another chance on Judy.

Actually, she was his third choice. His original dream cast was Astaire dancing with Vera-Ellen. When that didn't work out, he awarded the role to June Allyson.

After ten days of dance rehearsals, Allyson became nauseated and dizzy and was driven to her doctor, who informed her that she was pregnant. Months later, she gave birth to Richard Powell, Jr., the son of actor/director Dick Powell.

Judy, therefore, was called in as "emergency casting" in this musical by Burton Lane and Alan Jay Lerner.

Royal Wedding unfolds in London in 1947 during the wedding of Princess Elizabeth to Philip Mountbatten.

A brother and sister act, Tom (Astaire) and Ellen Bowen (Judy), are sailing to England to entertain as part of the festivities. The plot, written by Lerner, was actually based on the real-life careers of Astaire and

Royal Wedding (1951) got made, but without Judy.

In the aftermath of getting fired, Judy attempted suicide.

his sister, Adele.

During their transatlantic crossing, Ellen falls for Lord John Brindale (Peter Lawford) and Tom begins flirting seriously with Anne Ashmond (Sarah Churchill).

Judy's friend, Chuck Walters, was set to direct *Royal Wedding*, but when he heard that Judy was slated to be his star, he bowed out, claiming, "I spent the most horrendous year and a half of my life getting her through *Summer Stock*. I can't do it again."

Freed replaced him with a young and relatively untried director, Stanley Donen. At the time, he was also preparing to direct his off-screen lover, Elizabeth Taylor, in *Love Is Better Than Ever* (1952).

Contrary to Donen's later report to Dore Schary, Judy showed up every day from May 23 to June 13, 1950. She had been ordered to lose weight, and she was on diet pills and Benzedrine.

However, in mid-June, she missed two days in a row. Schary was no forgiving, father-like figure like Mayer could, on occasion, be, and he may have been looking for an excuse to get rid of Judy. On Wednesday, June 21, 1950, he fired off a hand-delivered letter to her, suspending (i.e., "firing") her.

She said, "Goodbye Betsy Booth. Farewell Dorothy. Judy Garland has been kicked out of MGM on her ass."

Under sedation all weekend long, she was able to meet with Carlton Alsop the following Monday morning. Her agent and sometimes lover held her in his arms as she sobbed and clung to him.

She had listened to rampant speculation that from now on, she'd be incapable of finding another movie role in Hollywood. She feared that she'd been blacklisted, but for reasons that were different from what had applied to the dozens of other actors and directors who were being purged by the "commie hunter," Senator Joseph McCarthy.

Her career outlook appeared bleak. Alsop visited every day, showing her letters that were pouring in from her faithful fans all over the country. He gave her a telegram from an NBC executive which read, "We love you

As a social ornament for *Royal Wedding*, and in search of dipthongs suitably British, its producers hired **Lady Sarah Churchill**, the rebellious and sometimes embarrassing daughter of Clementine and Sir Winston. She played Anne Ashmond, the romantic interest of Fred Astaire. It became her best-known role.

In the year it was released (1951), she hosted her own television show. She went on to make two more films, *Fabian of the Yard* (1954) and *Serious Charge* (1959), and appeared in some not-very-successful theatrical productions, too.

By the late 1950s, she had became an alcoholic, and was arrested a few times for making scenes in public, on the street.

Around the same time, she spent a short time in a woman's prison in London (Holloway), which she described candidly in her 1981 autobiography, *Keep on Dancing*.

She died in 1982 at the age of 67.

Judy." He had talked to both Bob Hope and Bing Crosby, who wanted her to sing on their radio shows.

She left Malibu when the weather turned and moved back in with Minnelli, occupying separate bedrooms. Although she still planned to divorce him, she wanted to be near her baby daughter Liza, and he employed two attendants who could look after her whenever they were busy or gone. Also, he was certain that being with her child would hasten her recovery.

One afternoon, she grew morbidly despondent. At three o'clock, she rose from one of the sofas downstairs and headed to the luxurious bathroom that had been installed for her at the beginning of her marriage. Fearing the worst, Minnelli followed her and found that she had bolted the bathroom door. After he called out to her, he was alarmed by her response: "Go away! I want to die!"

After fruitlessly pounding on the door, he took a heavy chair and broke in. To his horror, he found Judy standing at her sink, blood gushing from her throat. "Oh, my God!" he shouted. It seemed that she'd broken her toothbrush glass and had scraped her throat with a jagged piece of it.

When he toweled the blood from her neck and before it started bleeding again, he saw that it was not a deep cut, more of a surface wound. Wrapping her neck to stop the bleeding, he quickly phoned Alsop and told him to come at once with Dr. Francis Ballard. He felt that in lieu of having Judy rushed by ambulance to a hospital, with all the negative publicity that would entail, Ballard could handle, at the site of the injury, whatever measures were needed.

[It is believed that an irate member of Minnelli's household staff, whom Judy had insulted, phoned a reporter with news of Judy's suicide attempt.]

Dr. Ballard arrived and sterilized the wound, bandaged it, sedated her, and put her to bed.

With the hour, news of the incident was broadcast via the wire services around the world. In New York and other East Coast cities, early editions of morning newspapers were being read. The news broke in time for some late afternoon papers, too, depending on the time zone. Headlines blared:

"JUDY GARLAND CUTS THROAT OVER LOST MOVIE JOB,"
"JUDY GARLAND ATTEMPTS SUICIDE AFTER BOOT FROM MGM,"
"SUICIDAL JUDY TRIES TO GO OVER THE RAINBOW."

In the days ahead, story after story appeared in magazines and newspapers everywhere, a sad chronicle of her tormented life. News about her dried up and virtually disappeared on June 25, 1950 when North Korea invaded South Korea. Hedda Hopper was the most empathetic columnist: "Poor Judy, so much talent, so much pressure, so much bad advice."

Kay Thompson became a frequent visitor to her bedside, as did Alsop. Buxom Jane Russell, the sex symbol at RKO, by now a devout Christian, arrived announcing, "I've come to pray for Judy." Minnelli refused to let her enter, so she prayed for a long time on his doorstep before disappearing.

Mayer, shortly before he, too, was kicked out of MGM, arrived for a surprise visit. He had steered and directed her career beginning with her teenage years and continuing throughout her adult life. He spent an hour with her, during which time she told him she was broke and needed a loan from MGM.

Although he no longer had the power to make loans, he put through a call to Nicholas Schenck at Lowe's in New York, then returned to Judy to ask how much she wanted.

She picked up the receiver, preparing to ask Schenck for a loan of $10,000 to tide her over. But before she could make such a request, he cut her off.

"We're not reinstating you, if that's what you want."

"I need a loan from MGM, real bad, sir."

"NO! Schenck shouted into his end of the phone. MGM is not a money-lending agency."

Before Mayer departed from the Minnelli household, someone tipped off the press. Four reporters greeted him outside her home, peppering him with questions about whether MGM had reconsidered firing Judy.

He never addressed that question, but said, "Judy Garland will continue to sing to the world for at least fifty more years. I've adored her ever since I met the little girl with the big voice. In my heart, Dorothy will live forever. For all I know, children will be watching *The Wizard of Oz* two centuries from today."

Judy's exit from MGM marked a massive exodus as movie attendance dwindled.

Clark Gable, once the King of Hollywood, departed, followed by a roster of contract players that included Spencer Tracy and Greer Garson. Tracy told a reporter, "The lion's roar won't be as loud."

***

Judy was not the only luminary thrown out of MGM. In 1951, an even bigger figure also fired was Louis B. Mayer himself. *[In news announcements, MGM politely defined it as his "resignation."]*

During the closing years of the 1940s and into the '50s, MGM had faced dwindling revenues. That's why Dore Schary was brought in, perhaps to turn out a different type of picture that would appeal to a newly emerging post-war generation of Baby Boomers.

Nicholas Schenck from the New York headquarters of Loews had phoned Mayer almost daily with the same budget demands: "Cut! CUT!"

Mayer always had a pat response: "Nick, a picture isn't a salami."

Lillian Burns, MGM's long-standing acting coach and the wife of director George Sidney, visited Mayer after she learned that he had endorsed the hiring of Dore Schary. "Now you've done it," she said. "He'll get rid of our musicals and frothy comedies, certainly our adventure movies. He may even fire most of us—not just me, but you, too. I'm warning you."

Her warning was almost clairvoyant. On a scorching day in August of 1951, Mayer walked out on a red carpet that stagehands had rolled out for his final exit from the Thalberg Building. Current casts and crews applauded him as a recognition of his longtime rule over the studio.

It was an afternoon that was noted in dozens of books about film history and hailed as the end of Hollywood's Golden Age. The Vienna-born actor Turhan Bey defined it like this: "In every meaningful way, Mayer's exit marked the end of Old Hollywood as we knew it."

In the wake of Mayer's dismissal, Mayer raged and ranted, plotting his comeback perhaps as an independent producer. He hoped to make a big splash with a script for *Paint Your Wagon,* but that didn't happen for him. *[Mayer did become Chairman of the Board and the single largest shareholder of Cinerama. He left the administration of that company in 1954 when it was sold.]*

Overcome with leukemia, Mayer died on October 29, 1957. Biographer Scott Eyman evaluated his influence like this: "Louis B. Mayer defined MGM, just as MGM defined Hollywood, and Hollywood defined America. He created Mickey Rooney and Judy Garland, Greta Garbo and Clark Gable—and more stars than there were in heaven."

***

Mayer was not the only major figure to exit from Judy's life. On a hot summer night, after her completion of *Summer Stock,* she got into her most violent argument yet with her mother Ethel. Accusations swirled between them, the resentments having festered since the dysfunctional marriage of Ethel to Judy's father, Frank Gumm.

Judy threw a vase at her. It narrowly missed her before shattering in the hallway. "Get out of my house!" she screamed at her mother. "Never return! Stay away from Liza!"

"But she's my granddaughter!"

"No more! I never want to look in your disgusting face again. You're a devouring tarantula!"

Defeated, Ethel wiped up her affairs in Hollywood and took the train to Dallas, where her older daughter, Jimmie, was living. There, she got a job managing a small movie house like Frank used to do.

***

What finally got a morbidly depressed Judy out of bed and working again was a visit from Katharine Hepburn. Although she had always cared for Judy, there was also a no-nonsense quality to the formidable star. "You're one of the three greatest entertainers on earth," Hepburn told Judy. "So, you've hit rock bottom. Now get your ass out of that bed. When you're down, there's only one place to go—and that's up. Now get up, get dressed, and get the show on the road. What? No film offers? There's always radio."

***

Radio had been a vibrant part of Judy's life since the mid-1930s before practically every household in America got a TV set. "Radio generated a lot of publicity back then, and the shows were treated like Broadway first nights," said Myrna Loy. "So we got all dolled up for an appearance."

Judy's singing voice had reached its greatest audience of untold millions during World War II, when radio stations broadcast songs of hers that included "We're Off to See Herr Hitler" (1943).

She had easily and frequently ad-libbed, live and on the air, with Bob Hope. She had appeared on radio with such stars as Fanny Brice, Jack Benny, Edgar Bergen, Marlene Dietrich, Fredric March, Alan Ladd, Walter Pidgeon, Bette Davis, or Gracie Fields. She and Mickey Rooney had broadcast radio adaptations of some of their movies, including *Strike Up the Band* in 1940 for the Lux Radio Theatre, and *Babes in Arms* in 1941.

In a 1942 radio broadcast, Judy had assumed the role of the character that Katharine Hepburn had portrayed with Douglas Fairbanks, Jr., *Morning Glory* (1933). In the version Judy reformatted for radio, she played opposite "that dreamboat," John Payne.

In an ironic twist, alongside Adolphe Menjou and Walter Pidgeon, Judy was assigned the Janet Gaynor role in a "for radio adaptation" of the 1937 film version of *A Star is Born*. [*This was a straightforward, dramatic, non-musical, audio-only presentation. Judy's more elaborate cinematic reworking of* A Star Is Born *would come later, with James Mason in 1954.*]

She appeared with Bob Hope and Frank Sinatra in *Command Performance*, part of the War Department's entertainment aimed at troops overseas, in March of 1944. Among many other selections, she and Sinatra sang "Embraceable You." She and Sinatra were such a hit, he asked her to star with him on *The Frank Sinatra Show* in May of 1944, in which she sang "Zing! Went the Strings of My

Frank Sinatra, shown here as the focus of thousands of bobbysoxer fans during his early years, had risen to musical success through RADIO.

As Judy's film career collapsed, Kate Hepburn advised Judy to return to the medium that to some degree had made her a household name.

Heart." She also sang and appeared in yet another episode of *Command Performance* in June of 1944 with Sinatra, Crosby, and Hope.

Even after the war ended, Judy continued to star in broadcasts aimed directly at the servicemen who remained in occupied Germany and Japan. While Danny Kaye was away on a USO tour, on October 5, 1945, Judy and Sinatra filled in for him on his radio show. Her memorable song was "How Deep Is the Ocean?".

On December 9, 1945, as part of a 60-minute radio show on CBS, Judy joined Crosby, Sinatra, and Dinah Shore in a broadcast called *Jerome Kern*

Memorial, where she sang "Look for the Silver Lining."

On Christmas Day, 1945, Judy teamed with Shore, Hope, and Crosby for yet another *Command Performance* that was heard by U.S. servicemen around the world. She sang "Have Yourself a Merry Little Christmas," excerpted from *Meet Me in St. Louis.*

On September 29,1946. Judy teamed with Sinatra and Phil Silvers for yet another *Command Performance.* In this show she sang "I Got the Sun in the Morning" from *Annie Get Your Gun,* the musical from which MGM had recently fired her.

For the *Lux Radio Theatre,* a broadcast heard on December 2, 1946, Judy had a reunion with her co-stars of *Meet Me in St. Louis,* Tom Drake and Margaret O'Brien. She sang standards from that classic, including "The Boy Next Door."

MGM may have silenced her voice, but Crosby wasn't going to allow it. On October 11, 1950, she was his guest star on *The Bing Crosby Show.* She sang "Sam's Song," with him and also the soon-to-be-famous "Get Happy."

She went over so big, she was brought back for another Crosby show on October 8, in which Hope was a guest star as well. Her duet with Crosby, "Tzena, Tzena, Tzena," was transcribed by the Voice of America for broadcast overseas.

On November 5, for the *Theatre Guild on the Air,* Judy repeated Katharine Hepburn's film role in *Alice Adams* (1935), with co-star Thomas Mitchell, who had played Scarlett O'Hara's father, Gerald, in *Gone With the Wind.*

To herald the Christmas season, Judy appeared once again on *The Bing Crosby Show* broadcast on December 6, 1950 over CBS. They teamed up to sing "Rudolph, the Red-Nosed Reindeer," and she performed a solo of "Rock-a-Bye Your Baby with a Dixie Melody."

To end the traumatic year of 1950, Judy pulled herself together to appear in a Christmas Day broadcast for the *Lux Radio Theatre.* It was not a typical Christmas show, but a tribute to her by-now-fabled movie, *The Wizard of Oz* (1939). The hit of CBS's show was her performance of "Over the Rainbow," but in a style more mature than what she'd delivered within the movie. She also sang that favorite, "We're Off to See the Wizard."

Judy would always be grateful to Bing Crosby. "I needed a job more than I needed money," she said. "I could always borrow dough from friends. Bing still had faith in me. Thank God I didn't let him down on the shows I did for him."

One critic wrote, "If radio is to be saved and not doomed by television, then Judy Garland is the voice to do it."

In 1955, Crosby gave an interview on CBS in which he said, "Judy is one of the greatest talents, male or female, in Hollywood. She's the perfect illustration of the 100% professional. You can't help being drawn to her magnetism, and it rubs off on you, too. Nobody can be professionally indifferent to Judy Garland's part of the act."

The question often asked in Hollywood was, "Did Bing Crosby get "sexually familiar" with Judy Garland? The question seems valid, since, indeed, Crosby became romantically and/or sexually involved with many of his leading ladies, notably Dorothy Lamour, Betty Hutton, Ingrid Bergman, and Grace Kelly.

The only source claiming they did was Kay Thompson, Judy's close friend. "On many occasions, Bing seduced his leading ladies," Thompson said, "and Judy confessed that several times after a broadcast, he came to her dressing room. But he never took her out on a date."

That same December, Judy separated from Minnelli and re-defined herself as a "bachelor girl." She moved into an apartment at 88509 Westview Drive in West Hollywood that had previously been occupied by Marlene Dietrich.

Here, she was to begin a new life, with a new husband in her immediate future and eventually, new kids, too.

***

Like Judy herself, in April of 1950, Frank Sinatra, too, was fired from MGM. His records weren't selling very well, and many reporters speculated that his once-fabled allure had faded. He was a frequent visitor to Judy's bedroom, offering her support and sympathy.

"It's been a long time since those bobbysoxers lined up during the war to see me in the Times Square area. They all wanted a piece of the 'Kid from Hoboken,' but I can't seem to give it away lately."

One afternoon, he told her he was leaving Hollywood as he had a gig performing at the Copacabana in Manhattan. He urged her to join him back east, where she might generate a number of job offers for herself.

Still her close friend, Kay Thompson was working with Sinatra in New York, and she kept Judy abreast of what was happening. During a strenuous performance, to his horror, he had suffered a vocal hemorrhage. To his relief, he managed a recovery that summer, and was able to go before the cameras for the launch of his TV show that fall.

Kay told Judy that Sinatra was paying regular visits to "Dr. Feelgood" (Max Jacobson), who was injecting him in the throat with what he called "a magic elixir."

"Frankie is taking other medications, too, and is as nervous and irritable as hell," Kay informed Judy. "He's also acting weirdly. He insists on changing his underwear at least twenty times a day, not in his dressing room, but right in front of the cast and crew. It's true he has nothing to be ashamed of. Ava Gardner

Max Jacobson, operating from a base in New York City, became notorious as "Dr. Feelgood."

Judy, along with JFK and many of the most visible movers and shakers in politics and the arts, was also a client.

When celebrities came to him, he injected them with what he called his "magic elixir." Clients rushed to him, since it made them "feel as young as springtime" (Eddie Fisher's words).

But just what was in that elixir?

told me, 'There's only ten pounds of Frank but 100 pounds of cock.'"

Carleton Alsop told Judy that Sinatra's advice was sound, and he agreed to accompany her to New York to scope out what offers might be available. At the time, Alsop's life was in turmoil. He was in the throes of divorcing his wife, Sylvia Sidney, and also changing his profession. Based on his concern that he could longer fulfill his duties as her agent, he was working to sign her with William Morris.

***

After Alsop landed with Judy in New York, he escorted her to the Hotel Carlyle, where he'd rented her a suite and arranged for her to be driven around town in a limousine. Then he hugged and kissed her good-bye and went off to attend to other business.

[Later, during her preparations to exit from the Carlyle on her way back to Los Angeles, when she was presented with the massive bill, Judy handed it back to the hotel staff. "Send it to my agent, Carleton Alsop, who arranged my stay."

Two weeks later, the unpaid bill arrived back at the Carlyle, courtesy of Alsop and the U.S. Mail. "I no longer represent Miss Garland," he wrote in the note that was attached.]

Judy's escort and sometimes boyfriend in Manhattan would be her favorite screenwriter, Fred Finklehoffe, whom she still affectionately called Freddie. He was in the process of divorcing his wife, the actress and singer Ella Logan, whom he'd married in 1942. "Another wartime marriage, another disaster like thousands of others," he said.

[Finklehoffe had showcased Judy favorably in such movies as Strike Up the Band, Babes on Broadway, For Me and My Gal, Girl Crazy, Meet Me in St. Louis, *and* Words and Music.

Throughout the course of her marriage to Minnelli, Judy had used him as a sounding board to air her complaints about what was wrong with her husband. Her major complaint was that, "He always sided with MGM, never with me."]

One night, Finklehoffe invited her to dinner at Billy Reed's popular club on East 55th Street. There had been some vague talk about their "getting hitched," contingent on each of their eventual divorces becoming final, even though she had not yet filed hers in court.

Fred Finkehoffe. If Sid Luft hadn't barged in during his marriage proposal to Judy, he'd probably have become one of her husbands.

[Finklehoffe had been telling her about writing scripts with his partner, John Chery Monks, Jr. In 1936, they had written a play, Brother Rat *(1936), about a group of rowdy cadets at the Virginia Military Institution, a school nicknamed as the West Point of the South. The film adaptation of* Brother Rat, *released in 1938, had starred Ronald Reagan.*

It had been so successful that it had inspired a sequel, Brother Rat and Baby *(1940), that had teamed Reagan once again with his then-wife, Jane*

305

Finklehoffe was on the verge of ordering a bottle of champagne. In his breast pocket, he carried an engagement ring from Tiffany's, and on this special night, he was going to propose marriage to her. Right before he placed the order, Sid Luft approached their table.

His purpose was twofold. He wanted to have a reunion with Freddie, who in Hollywood had been his favorite drinking buddy at Ciro's on the Sunset Strip. On two occasions, the men had roomed together. In those early days, Luft had described Freddie as "Harvard educated, bookish, dressing in a sloppy Ivy League fashion and with a premature balding pate covered by a jauntily worn fedora, giving him a devil-may-care appearance."

Luft, however, wanted to be officially introduced to Judy, whom he had encountered before. He later recorded his impression of Judy that night, referring to her as "a small, voluptuous package, evocative of a ripened cherry."

Without being invited, Luft sat down at their table, and he and Judy began laughing and chattering together, telling each other "wickedly funny stories" about their encounters in Hollywood. "She had a loud, raucous laugh, and she wore her hair short in a kind of bob like a dyke's. Her breasts looked as big as Lana Turner's, and she'd painted her lips a show-stopping scarlet. Incidentally, those lips were far more seductive than those of Hedy Lamarr."

"She devoured me with her eyes," Luft claimed. "She kept stealing furtive glances at my crotch. In those days, men wore baggy pants so there was no bulge for her to see what my second wife, Lynn Bari, had nicknamed 'Daddy Warbucks.'"

Finklehoffe, an escort who was on the verge of proposing marriage to her, was ignored. Growing impatient, he told Luft "to get the hell lost."

Although Judy tried to persuade him to stay, Luft obeyed. But based to some degree on Judy's behavior that night, Finklehoffe abandoned his plan of asking for her hand in marriage.

***

Luft had first met Judy during her filming of *Broadway Melody of 1938.* At the time, he'd been the secretary and lover of Judy's tap-dancing co-star, Eleanor Powell. As he bragged, "I broke her in before her marriage to Glenn Ford."

"Judy at the time was celebrating her fifteenth birthday," Luft recalled. "I found her a bit chubby, not for my taste. I heard she was having an affair with Spencer Tracy, who was older than the hills."

Who was this charismatic man who had re-entered her life, and who remembered her as a chubby teenager in bobbysocks and sandal shoes?

When she returned to her lodgings at the Hotel Carlyle, she phoned several friends, including Kay Thompson, to learn whatever she could about Luft. She was impressed with his imposing physique and charismatic presence. He stood six feet, one inch, with broad shoulders and dark hair. He had a certain swagger to his walk, entering a room as if to say, "I can lick any guy in here."

As it turned out, even without any great credits to his name, he was a well-known personality in Tinseltown.

Seven years older than Judy, Luft had grown up in Bronxville, New York, which in those days had restrictions against Jews. His parents were immigrants from Russia and Germany. His mother, Leonora, was a clothes designer and had a small dress shop. His father, Norbert, was a watch-maker and operated a little jewelry shop.

As a boy growing up in that neighborhood, Luft was frequently beaten up on the way home from school and denounced as "a dirty Jew."

To protect himself from bullies, he enrolled in the Charles Atlas body-building correspondence school. He began building up his physique with dumbbells and weights, which expanded his biceps and muscles. He also enrolled in a local gym where he became an amateur boxer nicknamed "One Punch Luft." He was also a star on the football field, and, in addition, he became a skilled swimmer and diver.

He was also a heavy drinker. As he grew older, he was often at the center of barroom brawls. He was the total opposite of Vincente Minnelli. Luft, as described by Kay, "oozed testosterone from every pore."

In 1940, Luft headed north to Canada, where he joined the Royal Canadian Air Force. [Before the U.S. entered the epic struggle, Canada was already active, involved, and allied with Britain against Nazi aggression during the early years of World War II.]

During his airborne missions with Canadian pilots in Canadian air-craft, Luft was included as part of dangerous mission delivering bombers to both England and the Soviet Union. With each flight, he ran the risk of being shot down by the *Luftwaffe.*

When he left Canada, he headed for Hollywood, using his experience as an aviator to wangle a job as a test pilot for Douglas Aircraft. But when an experimental plane crashed, he was severely burned and dropped out.

His next job in Hollywood was with tap-dancing Eleanor Powell, then a big musical star. He called her "My Pal Powell," since he'd known her when both of them were growing up in Bronxville. She designated him as her "secretary," a polite term for her secret lover.

Since the age of twelve, Luft had regularly carried a revolver with him, allowing him an additional role as Powell's bodyguard.

Once, they flew together to Havana, where, at a night club, the other stage performers retreated and made room for Luft and Powell on the dance floor, where they performed a rhumba. As

The third of Judy Garland's five husbands, **Sid Luft** was largely responsible for her comeback in the Oscar-nominated *A Star Is Born.*

Powell later described the event, "Sid made the cheeks of the *caballeros* blanch with jealousy at his dancing."

In December of 1940, Luft married the aspiring actress Mary Lou Simpson, the union lasting only a few months. By 1942, their divorce was final.

In the meantime, he'd been dating Lynn Bari, known in Hollywood as "The Queen of the B's," playing for the most part, sultry, statuesque, man-killers in the films of the 1930s and '40s.

The couple's first child, a baby girl, was born on August 7, 1945, dying the next day. Two years later, Bari gave birth to a son, John Michael Luft.

During Judy's early involvement with Luft, he and Bari were plotting their divorce.

A gambler, Luft was often seen at the Santa Anita Racetrack, betting on horses. Sometimes, he was written up in the press, especially when he got into one of his frequent brawls. When columnist Jimmie Starr wrote a critical item about him, Luft waited for him to come out of Ciro's. On the sidewalk, as Starr was getting into a cab, Luft punched him in the nose, breaking it.

Luft had once operated a company that sold custom-made automobiles, but introduced himself to everybody as a Hollywood producer. Actually, he'd turned out only two minor films for Monogram on Poverty Row. Both *Kilroy Was Here* (1947) and *French Leave* (1948) co-starred Jackie Coogan and Jackie Cooper, those two fading child stars of yesterday. Both films made a modest profit.

***

Despite Finklehoffe's objections, Judy insisted that they invite Luft the following night to cross the George Washington Bridge from Manhattan to attend a nightclub act by Billy Daniels in New Jersey. Luft gladly accepted. Finklehoffe and Judy picked him up at the Ritz Carlton in her chauffeur-driven limousine and off they went to catch the late show at a joint that had been frequented by Frank Sinatra. En route, Judy directed all her talk—and her laughter—directly at Luft.

After their arrival at the club, where they were seated at a ringside table, Judy and Luft behaved as if they were on a date, excluding Finklehoffe.

When Finklehoffe excused himself to go to the toilet, Judy whispered to Luft, "Freddie told me you were a rotten, no good piece of shit, and that I should wash you right out of my hair. He warned me that you'd use me and then dump me."

"That's what I'd do to a Saturday night piece, not to Judy Garland, a Hollywood goddess."

Luft later recalled, "She was a magnetic personality, casting a spell over me. I could not believe it...me, the tough guy from the streets of New York, letting her crack through my alligator hide. I'd seen dames come and go by the dozens—use 'em, forget 'em. This woman was different."

After Daniels finished his act that night, he joined Judy's table. With Luft and Finklehoffe, she talked with the popular entertainer until well past dawn, even after the club closed down except for one lone bartender.

Manhattan was waking up as Judy's limousine returned, depositing her back at the Carlyle. Freddie turned to her, took her hand, kissed it, and said goodbye: "You and I have done some great pictures together, but the time has come for me to move on. I'm returning to Hollywood. I've got two Martin and Lewis comedies to write."

"Thanks, Freddie," she said. "You've been swell."

"From now on, I'll be looking for a gal who thinks I'm terrific."

"I hope you find her, dear one," she said, giving him a "farewell forever" kiss on the lips.

[Freddie found that woman in the form of fashion model and consultant Carolyn Jo Phillips, marrying her in 1956, rearing a daughter with her, and still married to her when he died in October 1977 at the age of seventy-seven.]

The next day Luft phoned Judy repeatedly at the Carlyle, but the switchboard operator always gave him the same message: "Miss Garland is out."

That evening, not having heard from him *[and by implication, not having received any messages from him]*, Judy dressed in her finery in case there had been some misunderstanding, and with the belief that he might suddenly show up at eight o'clock.

He, too, suspected he had misread her signals. *[Perhaps Judy, presumably as a star with many swains at her disposal, did that with any number of men who attracted her passing fancy. In any event, any date that might have been in the offing that night fell through.]*

A few nights later, Mr. Luft, accompanying a chorus girl from Broadway, attended a party at the apartment of rising comedian Jackie Gleason.

In the corner of the room sat Judy with Martha Raye, perhaps chatting about composer David Rose, whom each of them had married.

Finally, Judy excused herself and approached him. "I thought you'd call. Not a word."

"I called repeatedly after I left you at your hotel," he said. "Always the same answer. You weren't in."

"Like hell I wasn't," she protested. "I was sitting by the god damn phone waiting for you to call."

They finally figured out what had happened. Finklehoffe had bribed the switchboard operator not to put through his calls to her suite.

After dumping their respective dates, they ended up at a "bottle club," the Golden Key, to hear Johnny Mercer sing. The composer had been one of her lovers.

"The management was sure lucky that night," Luft said. "They got Judy Garland to sing for free."

It was five o'clock in the morning when Judy was dropped off at the Carlyle. She invited him to come over around 5PM the following afternoon.

When he got there, right on time, he found out why he'd been invited so early. Judy had brought her four-year-old daughter and two helpers from Hollywood to assist her.

"Liza," Judy said, taking her hand, "I want you to meet your mother's new beau."

The days that followed were punctuated by missed phone calls, club hopping, races at Jamaica Racetrack, appearances at screenings of *Summer*

Stock where autograph mobs awaited her, until finally it happened. She spent her first night with him at the Ritz Carlton.

The next morning, a bubbly Judy was on the phone to Kay Thompson. "We did it," she gushed. "Last night. Sid's been around the block, a very experienced seducer. No David Rose who wouldn't do certain things. No Vince Minnelli who often couldn't get it erect. Sid Luft can satisfy any woman. I'm mad about the guy."

In Manhattan on the evening he took her to the celebrity-frequented Stork Club, he got even more insights into what being Judy Garland's escort meant. She stopped to say hello at a table where Ethel Merman and her friend, J. Edgar Hoover, were seated.

The owner of the Stork Club, Sherman Billingsley, greeted them warmly and seated them at a desirable table. Soon, a waiter arrived with a big bottle of free champagne. Then Billingsley presented Judy with a gift, a big bottle of Chanel No. 5. Luft got a gold cigarette lighter.

Finally, the time had come for her to say goodbye and return to Hollywood. They spent a final night together at the Ritz Carlton before she had to rush off. There were lots of promises to get together after their return to the coast.

"Just in time," Luft recalled. "Among other expenses I could ill afford, I had run up a $700 florist bill, sending all those yellow roses, her favorite flower. Not only that, but she was sinking into debt with the IRS, which was demanding a payment of $80,000. I, too, was being billed by the IRS, but for only $60,000."

***

After Judy's return to Hollywood, she was greeted with Doomsday scenarios from the two leading gossip mavens, Hedda Hopper and Louella Parsons, each of whom suggested that at the age of twenty-eight, her film career was over. "I'll show those two old bitches," she threatened. "Judy Garland is coming back bigger than ever."

It was speculated that no studio wanted to throw away a million dollars on a picture that she might never finish.

"It's three strikes and you're out," suggested the gay columnist Mike Connolly, citing *The Barclays of Broadway, Annie Get Your Gun,* and *Royal Wedding.*

Privately, he suggested that Judy might go to work at Monogram Pictures, the low budget studio on "Poverty Row." It had a policy of hiring stars who were washed up elsewhere.

There was a certain irony in all these predictions that Judy was a has-been in Tinseltown. Her last movie, *Summer Stock,* was still being shown across the country, and had been a box office hit. If, as the saying went in Hollywood, "You're as good as your last picture," she was still making money for MGM in spite of their firing her and in spite of her reputation.

Before their goodbye at the Ritz Carlton in Manhattan, Luft had turned down her invitation to fly west with him. He had plans to make a movie about the champion racehorse, Man o' War.

[Born in 1917, Man o' War, a chestnut-colored stallion, is remembered as the

During Judy's courtship with Sid Luft, when it seemed as if he'd disappeared and was on the verge of becoming another "Man That Got Away," Judy enlisted the help of **J. Edgar Hoover**, the much-feared Director of the FBI.

A closeted homosexual and devoted "Friend of Dorothy," he provided —within just a few hours—the mysterious businessman's whereabouts (at an upscale hotel in Denver) and contact info.

greatest racehorse of the 20th Century. In his heyday, he won all 20 of his 21 races and today's equivalent of $3.2 million in purses. He lived to age 30, dying in 1947 after siring dozens of racewinning offspring. His death was broadcast nationwide on radio stations around the world.]

Luft told Judy that he planned to hunt down Sam Riddle, the multi-millionaire owner of the prize stallion, perhaps finding him in Kentucky. He would have no set address or phone number but promised to keep in touch.

After several days when he didn't call, she began to miss him and grew increasingly desperate to talk to him. One afternoon, summoning her ultimate movie star mode, she picked up the phone and called the F.B.I. "This is Judy Garland calling from Hollywood. I want to speak to Mr. J. Edgar Hoover."

Her call was put through, and she chatted pleasantly with Hoover. Two

Gay men and women have populated the ranks of the entertainment industry since the earliest days of silent filmmaking.

In 2012, Blood Moon, through the authorship of Darwin Porter, revealed how censorship from J. Edgar Hoover and his F.B.I. castrated an accurate perception of what was really happening in Hollywood during its so-called "Golden Age."

This award-winning double biography (**J. Edgar Hoover and his lover, Clyde Tolson**) exposes the obsessive and voyeuristic mania of the era's most powerful man in law enforcement,

It derived from years of in-depth interviews with FBI field workers and actors who suffered through his investigations for information about their sex lives.

It's a unique and chilling, one-of-a-kind overview of the abuse of power on the dark side of the American dream.

Blood Moon Productions: Applying the tabloid standards of today to the hushed-up scandals of America's Entertainment Past.

**IT'S A TOUGH JOB,
BUT SOMEBODY HAD TO DO IT.**

hours later, he returned her call, informing her that Luft had checked into a suite at the famous Brown Palace in Denver, Colorado.

She rang his suite, and he answered the phone. He never told her why he'd flown to Denver but was curious about how she had tracked him down.

"I called J. Edgar Hoover," she informed him, off-handedly. "All I have to do is say, 'I'm Judy Garland,' and I can get through to almost anybody, including the President of the United States."

He relayed that he had business to finish but promised to wing his way back to Los Angeles very soon.

***

No serious movie roles were being offered, only speculated about, and William Morris scouted the studios to determine if a vehicle suitable for Judy Garland might be in the offing Two of her greatest admirers, Bob Hope and Bing Crosby, were eager for her to appear on their radio shows.

On January 9, 1951, she joined a cavalcade of other stars—George Jessel, Louis Armstrong, Amos 'n Andy, and even Hope himself—on a CBS Radio *Salute to Bing Crosby,* honoring his twentieth anniversary in show business. On the air, to an audience of millions, many of them U.S. service personnel, she sang "Rock-a-Bye Your Baby to a Dixie Melody."

On January 23, she returned to the show, singing a duet with Crosby, "You Made Me Love You" along with

Judy's relationship with Bing Crosby was long, creative, highly visible, productive, and sexual. Top photo shows them on a radio broadcast for Oldsmobile in 1952, and (center photo) their likenesses on the cover of LOOK.

That was only two of many. Photos below show cover art for two of the albums they recorded together.

other numbers and a skit. A week later, she starred on *The Bob Hope Show* for NBC, singing "I'm in Love with a Wonderful Guy," backed up with the Les Brown Orchestra.

On February 11, Tallulah Bankhead welcomed Judy to her popular *The Big Show* on NBC. The fading star came up to Judy and startled her by saying, "Give me a wet one, *dah-ling,*" planting her lips on those of Judy. Bankhead told her, "Every vicious thing, every vile rumor, spread about me is the gospel truth. Better watch out for me, I might snatch your snatch."

Other guest artists on the show were the Andrew Sisters, Gordon MacRae (who wanted to date her), Groucho Marx, as well as Dean Martin and Jerry Lewis. The show marked the beginning of Judy's long-enduring friendship with Martin.

On February 15, she was heard on the *Hallmark Playhouse* for CBS, in which she played a writer of fairy tales, each of which "was too much like Cinderella." Her big number was "Wishing Will Make It So."

Crosby hired her for four more shows, singing a duet with him, "You're Just in Love," on his February 23 broadcast.

On February 27, 1951, Judy appeared on television for the first time at a benefit for the Red Cross. She was joined by Hope and Crosby along with a sour-faced Ed Sullivan. The overweight Kate Smith ended the show with a rousing "God Bless America."

After the event, Judy came up to her and jokingly said, "If I don't quit eating so much, I'm gonna look like you."

Also as a guest was President Harry S Truman. He shook her hand, saying, "I've always been more of a Jo Staffard fan, but Bess is crazy about you."

On March 7, again with Crosby, she sang "Mean to Me," followed by a duet with the star, "Just the Way You Are." A week later, she and Crosby did a comedy skit, spoofing "Just the Way You Are," where she was "Bounce-Along Garland" trying to bring law and order to the Wild West. Crosby played the varmint "Singalong Crosby."

March 21 found Judy co-starring with Les Paul and Mary Ford on *The Bing Crosby Show* in which she sang "Carolina in the Morning." She and Crosby did a humorous duet, "How Could You Believe Me When I Said I Loved You When I've Been a Liar All My Life?"

On March 28, before going abroad, she was once again featured as a singer for a final on-the-air songfest with Crosby. It included her rendition of "April Showers" and four duets with him, including "April in Paris."

Crosby remained her biggest fan. In his words, "Judy is one of the greatest talents, male or female, in Hollywood. We've done a great many shows together, and she's the perfect illustration of the 100% professional. You can't help being drawn to her magnetism. And it rubs off on you, too. Nobody can be professionally indifferent when Judy Garland is part of the act."

***

Judy took time out from her singing to do what she had long threatened to do. On March 23, 1951, she appeared before Superior Judge

William R. McCay, wearing a simple black dress, a pillbox hat, and a minimum of makeup that included a light coating of coral lipstick.

In reference to her marriage to Minnelli, her testimony follows:

"When we were first married, we were very happy. We had many interests in common, and many mutual friends. But sometime later, without any explanation, my husband withdrew himself and shut himself out of my life.

"I had to appear in public without him. It was very embarrassing. Finally, I didn't go anywhere myself because it was too difficult to explain his absence.

"I was terribly lonely. I frequently became hysterical. I had to go under a doctor's care. I just couldn't understand his attitude. He lacked interest in me, my career, my friends, everything."

After hearing the case, the judge ruled that the couple would have joint custody of Liza, spending six months with Judy and the other half year with her father. During the time she was with Judy, he was to give her $500 a month in child support. She agreed to pay only $25,000 for their residence at Evansview Drive.

He also agreed to pay all of Liza's medical bills. Judy also got the little villa at Malibu.

"We were virtually broke at the time," Minnelli said. "So we had very little estate to divide. We'd squandered millions with our extravagant lifestyle. Hundreds of thousands had gone to pay for doctors and shrinks for Judy. Once, on an impulse, on Rodeo Drive, she walked in and purchased an $8,000 mink. In one month, she ran up a $12,000 bill for designer gowns at Hattie Carnegie."

"I got the first six months with Liza," Minnelli continued, "because Judy was sailing to England. I must admit that I tried to create a fairytale existence for Liza. I hoped in some way it would make up for the shadowy existence I knew would await her when her mother took custody. I expect she'd experience a nomadic lifestyle, always short of money, always with unpaid bills—in essence, a roller coaster nightmare."

***

Sid Luft flew into Los Angeles and into the arms of Judy, where she moved him into the room recently vacated by Minnelli. He complained of having to sleep in the same bed where her former husband had made love to her—"That is," he said, "if lovemaking were possible from Minnelli."

They were seen everywhere together—Ciro's, Cocoanut Grove, the Trocadero, the Mocambo, and—most definitely—at the Santa Anita Racetrack. He was constantly betting on the horses. What she enjoyed best with him were intimate dinners, followed by a session of lovemaking. "At last," she told Kay Thompson, "I've found a man who can satisfy me."

Abe Lastfogel of the William Morris agency phoned Judy with what he considered the best offer yet—a four-week engagement at London's Palladium, the last great vaudeville theater in the English-speaking world.

She was offered $15,000 a week, but Lastfogel got that fee raised to $20,000.

During the course of their careers, both Danny Kaye and Betty Hutton found their largest and most appreciative audiences at this venue.

Judy began to formulate a show helped by both Roger Edens and her former lover, Oscar Levant. Her teenage lover, Buddy Pepper, signed a contract to appear with her at the piano.

Levant came up with a suggestion that Judy would forevermore use in her concerts: "Since you're often referred to as the female Al Jolson, why not include some of his songs in your repertoire?"

She thought that an excellent idea and incorporated his song "Rock-a-Bye Your Baby to a Dixie Melody," in her London repertoire. Later, she'd add Jolson's "Carolina in the Morning" and "Swanee" to her showcase of songs.

A week later, she was overcome with stage fright, and deeply worried because she'd been overeating and putting on weight, in some instances devouring an entire chocolate cake in a solo session of binge eating. She phoned Lastfogel: "I think it's a great offer, but I fear I'm not up to it. I need work—in fact, I'm desperate to make some money—but with my shattered nerves, I fear I'll fail again and not be able to go on."

He set up a luncheon at the Brown Derby with Fanny Brice, who had worked with Judy before in the late 1930s. She'd been appearing on stage since 1913.

Luft tagged along to the meeting, where Brice virtually ignored him, focusing all of her attention on Judy. Well-wishers approaching the table to greet Judy interrupted them constantly.

Brice, a show biz veteran, lectured Judy: "Honey, don't think you're the only performer who has suffered stage fright. Every time I stand in the wings to go on, butterflies are tap dancing in my stomach. You're a trouper, gal, or else you should be by now. Right now, your ship is sinking where your career is concerned. Do you want to go down on the *Titanic* to the murky waters below, or do you want to sail away in a rowboat to make a triumphant return? We've all known heartbreak, disillusionment, bitterness, betrayal, all facets of life. What you do when we get knocked down is pick yourself up and start all over again. You can do it. I know you can. Now quit moping about, complaining to Abe here—and get your show on the road."

***

Before flying to New York as part of the long transit to England, Judy virtually pleaded with Luft to accompany her, but he didn't want to be the boyfriend standing in the wings, waiting for the star to sing "Over the Rainbow."

So without him, she headed for Manhattan. From the Port of New York, she had booked a suite aboard the *SS Île de France*, accompanied by her secretary, Myrtle Tully, and her makeup artist, Dottie Ponedel.

She used the sea voyage to recuperate and was feeling fine—"but a little afraid"—as the *Île de France* chugged into the English harbor of Plymouth. To welcome her to Britain, ships in the harbor blew their sirens in

315

Morse Code, spelling out the letters J-U-D-Y.

Reporters and photographers had gathered at the dock to welcome her. "It's been a long way to Piccadilly," she said. "But at long last, I'm on England's shore."

Fans waited to greet her, too, some of them with WELCOME JUDY signs. Even though most aspects of her arrival were met with a favorable press, she was called "Tubby," "Chubby," and most often "Plump." A hostile reporter or two referred to her as "Fat Judy."

During her transit into London's inner city, she'd passed entire blocks that had been completely bombed out and hadn't been rebuilt. She was ushered into a flower-bedecked suite at the posh and very deluxe Dorchester Hotel.

One fan, Scott Hatfield, sent her a note and a small bouquet of flowers that touched her heart. His note read, "During the Blitz of London, when we lost our home in the East End when it was destroyed by German bombs, Dorothy's "'Over the Rainbow' gave me hope. I, too, wanted to rise from the ashes and skip along the Yellow Brick Road with you to a better life. In the darkest days of the war, you inspired hope in many of us."

Grand and venerable:
LONDON'S PALLADIUM

After her appearance there, John Barber in the *Daily Express* wrote, "Judy Garland walked into the biggest welcome for a first-time-here Hollywood star. The audience opened eyes wider to drink in the little girl with the big voice that is rangy, metallic, rhythmically lush."

"She bobs her bows, scraping back her hair—brown, not auburn. She melts even the flint-hearted who came to gloat over a star who once fell to earth all screaming nerves and hysteria."

Shown around the Palladium, especially her dressing room, she began dress rehearsals, dreading opening night on April 9, 1951.

She complained to Tully every day about how much she missed Luft. Secretly, Tully phoned him in Los Angeles. He refused to go at first, but finally opted to fly to London to give her support.

On the night before her opening night, she returned to the Dorchester to find Luft waiting in her living room. She screamed with delight at the sight of him and ran to his arms. "Don't ever leave me again. I can't live without you."

On opening night, a stagehand knocked on her door, telling her that the Queen Mother and Sir Winston Churchill would be in the audience. Before going out to face 2,500 people, plus those who had bought standing room tickets, she received a final kiss and a hug from Luft.

Onstage at last, she was greeted with thunderous applause. "Here I am!" she shouted. Impulsively, she signaled the orchestra with a change of plan. She wanted to open the show with "Over the Rainbow," which was greeted with clapping that was deafening.

She sang "Limehouse Blues," "Embraceable You," "Just One of Those Things," "The Trolley Song," "Easter Parade," "Get Happy," "Rock-a-Bye

Your Baby With a Dixie Melody," and concluding, as was inevitable, with another heart-rending rendition of "Over the Rainbow."

Taking her final bow, she tripped and fell. "Right on my fat ass," she later said. Buddy Pepper rushed to her side to help lift her off the floor.

She turned to the audience and, in her self-deprecating way, said, "I have just made the worst exit in the history of show business."

Then she delivered her exit line: "This has been the greatest night of my life. You have made it so."

The audience gave her a standing ovation. Val Parnell, the manager, told Luft that he had never heard such loud applause at the Palladium that then greeted Judy. [Parnell was noted as the impresario who launched the tradition of bringing Hollywood stars for appearances at Britain's number one theatre.]

Backstage, Judy was greeted with a parade of visitors, including Laurence Olivier and Vivien Leigh, who invited Luft and her to their country home, Notley Abbey. Maurice Chevalier had flown in from Paris. Noël Coward was there to greet her, too, whispering in her ear, "I'm a friend of Dorothy," thereby (stylishly) outing himself as a homosexual.

A surprise visitor was Tyrone Power, her long-lost lover, looking much older [some would say "ravaged"] than he had in 1940. Nonetheless, she hugged and kissed him until Luft separated them, ordering them to "break it up, guys." Then, perhaps half-jokingly, he said, "Ty, if you want to kiss someone, kiss me. I've always wanted to fuck you, pretty boy."

Katharine Hepburn and Humphrey Bogart, accompanied by Lauren Bacall, had flown to London from Africa after Bogie's filming of *The African Queen* (1951),, and they greeted her warmly. Judy would later become a member of his Rat Pack.

Leaving the Palladium that night, Judy and Luft still had time to make it to Kay Thompson's opening night at the Café de Paris in the center of London. Instead of teaching others to perform, she was appearing in her own one-woman show. When Judy walked in, the other patrons stood up and cheered. Kay, still her close friend, acknowledged her from the stage.

Judy and Luft were back in their suite at the Dorchester as the early morning editions arrived.

"I doubt if Sarah Bernhardt, Jenny Lind, or Vest Tilley would ever have asked for more from their admirers," wrote a reviewer.

A critic for the *Daily Telegraph* said "She gave a more vital performance than any one I have heard since Sophie Tucker, making me aware that someone I have always thought to be *fortissimo* was merely a force. It was not only with her voice, but with her whole personality."

That afternoon, Beverly Baxter of the *Evening Standard* claimed, "The truth is that Miss Garland is now better than her material. She can command pathos without being maudlin—in fact, she is an artist. We saw a brave woman onstage, but more than that, we saw a woman who has emerged from the shadows and finds the public likes her as she is, even more than what she was."

The schedule called for two shows a night, one at 6:15PM; another at 8:30PM Each time she was preceded by vaudeville acts, and then she came on and sang for thirty-five minutes.

317

A week later, in bed with Luft at the Dorchester, she said, "To hell with fucking movies. From now on, I'm taking a different road—not one of yellow brick. I plan to spend the rest of my life singing for my supper. Whatever town or city wants me, I'll heed the call, all the way to Tipperary. I'll sing until I run out of rainbows."

***

It was during the European extension of her British tour that Luft became more than Judy's live-in lover. She designated him as her business manager at a salary of $500 a week, plus expenses. At first, he was reluctant to take on such responsibility, obviously aware of what a volatile personality she was.

What he really wanted was to become a movie producer. His two films at Monogram meant nothing, but he felt his Man o' War feature about the world's most famous racehorse might put him on the top.

After weighing it over and having too many drinks, he decided to accept her offer, even though— except for a special movie or two with remarkable scripts—her film career might be over. Yet, as her reception at the Palladium had proven, an artist of her caliber could spend the rest of her life in concerts.

Since neither of them had yet finalized their respective divorce, talk of marriage was ruled out. Nonetheless, the *Daily Express* in London wrote, "The American film producer, Sid Luft, is reported about to become Judy Garland's third husband, after she divorces Vincente Minnelli and he dumps Lynn Bari."

The next day, Harry Foster of Foster's Agency, Ltd., a representative of William Morris, came to the Dorchester to meet with Judy and Luft in her suite. He told her he could book her on a two-month tour of England, Scotland, and Ireland as soon as she finished at the Palladium. Included in the tour, as proposed by Foster, would be Manchester, Birmingham, Dublin, Glasgow, and Liverpool.

"Why leave out Edinburgh?" Luft asked.

BING TO JUDY:
(Oops! We meant...)
BING TO JANE:

"THIS IS JUST FOR YOU"

Newspapers were writing that Judy Garland received no film offers after being fired from MGM. That wasn't true.

Bing Crosby's film career was falling notches below his 1940s heyday. But with the blessing of Paramount, he asked Judy to be his leading lady in a picture called *Famous,*

Luft discussed the weak script of *Famous* with her and warned that she'd have to go on a rigid diet, returning to diet pills or whatever. He feared that the strain might harm their burgeoning love affair. She finally agreed with him and cabled Bing with her regrets.

Crosby then changed the film's title to **Just for You** and awarded its female lead to **Jane Wyman,** the ex-Mrs. Ronald Reagan

Released in 1952, it flopped dismally at the box office.

318

"It's a beautiful town. My parents took me there when I was seventeen."

"If you insist, I can arrange that, but I have to warn you, it's not a show town."

The following day, terms were agreed upon. After her triumph in London, On May 21, 1951, Judy set out with Luft for the beginning of the tour. The first stop was at the Empire Theatre in Glasgow. To please locals, Judy added the song "Loch Lomond" to her repertoire. She played there to "standing room only" audiences.

It was in Glasgow, on opening night, that she adopted one of her most famous stage poses, that of hugging herself and cupping her elbows with her delicate hands.

Every night after the show, Luft rounded up stagehands for a game of poker, ordering Chinese take-out for all of them. As one of the players, Judy self-styled herself as "The Shark."

"I cheat," she warned. "In America, it's the custom for everybody to cheat at poker."

A surprise visitor was Freddie Finklehoffe, who had (inadvertently) brought Judy and Luft together on the long-ago night in Manhattan when he planned to propose marriage to her.

He had written some of her most successful movies, and he wanted her to star in his latest script. After sitting and talking to him until four in the morning, Luft and Judy arose at 10AM. After breakfast, each of them read the script. Luft being the first to denounce it as "bullshit. Freddie has lost his touch."

Meeting Freddie for lunch, he was informed of their rejection. Midway through the meal, he stormed out and flew back to New York. He later sent a telegram to Judy. "With Sid in charge of your career, good luck, girl. You'll need it."

***

After Judy's performance in Glasgow, Luft and Judy took the train to Edinburgh for an engagement there that lasted from May 28 to June 1.

After their check-in at one of the old grand hotels, Luft went to the theater to check on advance bookings. To his dismay, he learned that for the first of their shows there, only 500 tickets had been sold for the theater's 3,000 seats. The manager explained, "The sun has been shining all day, and we don't see much of it in all our fog and rain. Edinburghers don't want to go into a dark theater if the sun is shining."

"At the second show, all the seats sold out," Luft said. "Fortunately, it rained during the rest of the run of the show, and it was a triumph for Judy on her final night. The audience rose and sang 'Auld Lang Syne' to her."

In bed that night, before their scheduled departure from Edinburgh the next day, she said to him, "I wouldn't be able to go on living without you in my life. Don't ever leave me."

"I'll always be here for you," he vowed.

With some time off, he took her on a quickie visit to Paris, a city she'd never seen. She recalled, "Vince Minnelli would have taken me to the Louvre for a view of the *Mona Lisa,* but Sid took me to the horse races at

319

Longchamps."

"The following day, we visited Versailles since I wanted to see where Marie Antoinette once romped," Judy said. "I knew all about her, having watched Norma Shearer play her on the screen. Before heading back to England, we spent the final night at the Paris Opera at my request. That afternoon, I'd purchased two designer gowns from Balmain, the couturier to Queen Elizabeth."

On June 10, Judy's 29th birthday, they traveled by train from London to Manchester. As she told Luft, "My birthday is too close to thirty when most starlets in Hollywood are washed up if they haven't made it."

The following night, she opened in Manchester. Something must have gone terribly wrong in their up-to-now-idyllic relationship, a harbinger of things to come. Perhaps the pressure of the grueling tour got to her, or else she heard for the first time that Luft had no intention of marrying her after he divorced actress Lynn Bari.

Whatever transpired between them, she resumed her pill-taking and heavy drinking. All we know is what was reported by Henry Riggs, the representative in the north for EML records. "I noticed her wrist was bandaged. Had she tried to commit suicide again? When I met her, I thought she was intoxicated. In the wings, she suddenly turned to Luft, protesting, 'I can't go on' as she was announced."

He pushed her out onto the stage, barking at her, "Get out there, you drunken bitch."

"Later, three of us took her to the only nightclub in Manchester at that time," Riggs said. "She continued to drink and at one point became belligerent. The manager came to throw her out. Fortunately, Luft came in the door at that time, and he grabbed her and practically dragged her out of the club. That was the last time I saw the great Judy Garland. I was not impressed."

Her last performance in Manchester was on June 17, and the following night she opened in Liverpool at the Empire Theatre in a concert that ran through June 24. On her final night she also starred at the Liverpool Opera House.

In Liverpool, a young writer, Paul Elmer, who later followed the trail of those hometown boys, The Beatles, filed his critique of Judy. "Her voice is formidable. It is backed with the power to infuse whatever she sings with deep, heartfelt emotion. When she steamrolls her way from the favorite songs of her movies, crowds often rise to their feet to applaud. When she laughs, it's boisterous, from the gut. She sings without a safety net."

She interrupted her tour on June 25 to return to the Palladium in London for the *All Star Midnight Matinee*, staged to raise money for the family of Sid Field, a beloved comedian who had died in February of 1950, leaving his family penniless and in debt. [*Some people, including Bob Hope and Laurence Olivier, considered him England's greatest comedian, and a morale-builder in the dark days during and after World War II.*] Noël Coward and Peter Ustinov were there to greet Judy, and the Duchess of Kent later came backstage to congratulate her on her rendition of "Rock-a-Bye Your Baby to a Dixie Melody" and "Over the Rainbow."

That night, Orson Welles, Judy's former lover, appeared on stage, doing his magic tricks. Danny Kaye was also on the bill, and he hugged and kissed her warmly.

She whispered to Luft, "Danny's a busy boy. Two of his lovers are here tonight, Olivier and Princess Margaret."

As Judy sang, a legendary roster of stars were seated in a curved row behind her: Marlene Dietrich, Vivien Leigh, Elizabeth Taylor, John Gielgud, Gloria Swanson, and Douglas Fairbanks, Jr.

The often acerbic British critic, Kenneth Tynan, wrote: "Judy Garland has only to open her throat and send her voice pleading and appealing to the roof, to leave no doubt that talent like hers is independent of age and appearance. The house rose in great crashing waves of applause."

Leaving London, Luft and Judy arrived in Dublin for a booking that lasted from July 2 to 8 at the Royal Theatre. "I'll open with 'Danny Boy,'" she told Luft. "That'll get 'em." [She had first recorded that song for Little Nellie Kelly (1940), but it had not made the final cut of her film.]

One night in bed with Luft, she shared a long-ago dream: In 1937, she'd seen Janet Gaynor and Fredric March in A Star Is Born. In 1942, she'd appeared in the radio adaptation of the drama for the Lux Radio Theatre. She liked the story and characters so much she went to Mayer and asked if she could star in a musical remake for MGM, but he turned her down. "He practically booted me from his office. Why don't you, a producer, Sid, produce it for me?"

"I'll think about it," he said, rolling over in bed.

Next, she and Luft headed for Birmingham, where she was booked for a week-long opening at the Hippodrome, the last scheduled stop on her tour. She hadn't seen her five-year old daughter in three months, and arrangements were made with Minnelli to bring her to Birmingham.

The little girl arrived with her governess, "Cozy," and ran into her mother's arms.

"Judy's relationship with Liza was so loving and filled with tenderness," Luft said. "I was knocked out by her sense of mothering. The two of them had so much fun together, I was almost jealous."

To cap the European tour, Liza went with Judy and Luft to the French Riviera, where they checked into the fabled Hotel Carlton in Cannes. Liza was stashed with her governess as Judy and Luft explored the Riviera. One night, she was seen dancing at Juan-les-Pins with boxer Sugar Ray Robinson.

Noël Coward escorted them to a party at the Hotel du Cap. She also appeared at a benefit in Monte Carlo where she danced with Prince Rainier.

Coward threw a private party at the Carlton in his luxurious suite, which Judy and Luft attended. Luft was a self-admitted homophobe in those days, and Judy was practically the only girl there. According to Luft, "All these guys were kissing each other or whatever. I couldn't take it anymore. I bolted from the party telling Judy that I'd catch her later."

Downstairs in the bar at the Carlton, he met a gorgeous French blonde named "Genevieve," whom he described as a lookalike for Brigitte Bardot. An international playgirl from Rouen, she joined him in touring the hot spots of Cannes, where she was well known. "We drank and drank and then drank some more. She could belt them down as well as myself," Luft said.

"All I remembered was that we ended up on the beach too drunk to go into the water. Both of us passed out on the sands with our clothes on… well, at least most of them."

"The next thing I knew, the sun was in the sky, and someone was pouring a handful of sand in my mouth. It was Judy standing there with Liza."

"Genevieve was asleep beside me with most of her clothes on, too," Luft said. "Seeing it was Judy, she grabbed her stuff and fled from the beach."

Judy looked down at him as he was spitting sand out of his mouth. "Why don't you get up, shit, shower, and shave? We have a luncheon date with Noël at one."

[In his memoirs, Luft admitted to having had sex with Geneviève during the course of that long night. He later found out that someone had "slit her exquisite throat, having gotten caught with the mob. She had fingered thieves who stole a bundle of cash from the Jack Warner villa on the Riviera. They had lifted the entire safe from the house. For all I know, she was part of the ring."]

***

Two days later, Luft flew back to New York, promising to meet her at the Port of New York when her ship, *Queen Elizabeth,* hauled her back to the U.S. after her singing tour of Europe.

Judy had booked passage aboard the ship with Liza and her governess, Cozy. It was a chance to spend extended periods with her daughter and to bond with her. "At times, I felt I was talking with a teenager, not a five-year-old," she recalled.

During the transatlantic crossing aboard the *Queen Elizabeth,* Judy wondered what would await her in America. "What new humiliations will I have to face?" she asked.

She remembered looking at Liza's trusting, big eyes.

CHAPTER TWELVE

Saddled with a Reputation as a
Temperamental, Drug-Addicted Über Diva,
Judy Enters Her

CONCERT YEARS

Zing! Went the Strings of Their Hearts
in L.A., San Francisco, and at The Palace in NYC

The Sid & Judy Show

Fistfights & Brawls with Unlucky Motorists,
Work Colleagues, & with One Another

Hell at Holmby Hills

Sid, Judy, and Their Entourage Battle Suicide Attempts,
Unstable Income, Spontanous Combustions, and the IRS

Ethel Gumm & The Birth of Lorna

Alienated and Embittered, Judy's "Stage Mother from Hell"
Departs Angrily for the Land of Oz.

the Duke and Duchess of Windsor

Invite the Lufts for
Society Gossip & Overspending in Palm Beach

A STAR IS BORN

The Cinematic Celebration of a Man That Got Away

"I may have replaced Judy Garland in Annie Get Your Gun, but her opening night at The Palace was a tough act to follow. If I did four flips in the air, cut my head off and sewed it back on, it wouldn't mean a thing compared to her performance. As the curtain went down, there was bedlam piled on top of bedlam."

— Betty Hutton

"The night she opened at The Palace marked the beginning of the Judy Garland legend."

—Chuck Walters

"I can't go out and face my fans without swallowing some of my wonderful pills."

—Judy Garland

HERE'S HOW A WRITER FOR *HOLIDAY* MAGAZINE EVALUATED JUDY IN 1952:

"Where lay the magic? Why did we grow silent, self-forgetting, our faces lit as with so many candles, our eyes glittering with unregarded tears? Why did we call her back again and again and again, not as if she had been giving a good performance, but as if she had been offering salvation?"

"Some of the effect may be traceable to the extraneous drama of Judy's personal life. After a period of too highly publicized grief and failure and misfortune, this was her comeback. Of course we wanted her to be wonderful, as if her triumphs could somehow help to wipe out our own sorrows and weaknesses. But there was more to it than that."

"Much more. As we listened to her voice, with its unbelievable marriage of volume and control, as we watched her, in her tattered tramp costume, telling the most delicious jokes with arms, legs, head, and eyes, we forgot—and this is the acid test—who she was, and indeed who we were ourselves. As with all true clowns (for Judy Garland is as fine a clown as she is a singer) she seemed to be neither male nor female, young nor old, pretty nor plain. She had no 'glamour,' only magic. She was gaiety itself, yearning itself, fun itself. She expressed a few simple, common feelings so purely that they floated about in the dark theater, bodiless, as if detached from any specific personality. She wasn't being judged or enjoyed, not even watched or heard. She was only being felt, as one feels the quiet run of one's own blood, the shiver of the spine, Housman's prickle of the skin.

And when, looking about eighteen inches high, sitting hunched over the stage apron with only a tiny spotlight, it was as though the bewildered hearts of all the people in the world had moved quietly together and become one, shaking in Judy's throat, and there breaking."

—Clifton Fadman, Holiday (1952)

Judy's engagement in London marked what became

known as her "Concert Years." She'd go on to make a hundred or so different stage appearances, some lasting several weeks, others only a one-night stand. Her last concert would be in Copenhagen in 1969 right before she died.

Her voice rang out across America, the British Isles, and in the far reaches of Canada and Australia.

Her most devoted fans stayed loyal to her after her heyday had long passed and her reliability came under question, fans never knowing if she'd actually show up at her own widely advertised concerts.

Her reputation as a "living legend" stems from those years, as did the formation of the Judy Garland Cult. In the beginning, MGM intensely cultivated her image as the girl next door. Her fans were drawn to her partly for her portrayal of Dorothy in *The Wizard of Oz,* which immortalized her. But that was back in the late 1930s and '40s.

Of course, as her fans grew older, so did she. But as the years passed, that old image went the way of the jitterbug. Fans still flocked to see the more mature Judy, who became known for her self-deprecating wit, which was sharp, though not as cynical as that of Frank Sinatra. To every song, even though her voice changed over the years, she still brought a "vocal electricity."

Her performances and vocal renditions of her classics often varied, even though she sang from a familiar repertoire, not just "Over the Rainbow, " but "The Trolley Song" and "Zing! Went the Strings of My Heart."

"Judy virtually brought back vaudeville," said George Jessel.

In time, her concerts became "love fests," attracting an audience familiar with her past but curious about how she looked and performed today.

Her legions of devotees were eventually joined by a younger generation, often gay men in cities such as New York, Los Angeles, San Francisco, and London.

In her later years, a critic for *Time* magazine suggested that audiences went to her concerts to watch her fail. Judy found that assertion particularly hurtful. Of course, there would always be people like that, but for the most part, her fans were very forgiving, wanting her to go "Over the Rainbow" with them.

One thing is certain: No one who ever attended a Judy Garland concert was likely to forget it.

***

Judy's muted arrival in New York was in marked contrast to the fanfare that greeted her when she sailed into Plymouth, England, aboard the *Queen Elizabeth* to great ceremony and pomp. No reporters, no fans showed up. Only Sid Luft was there to welcome them, taking Judy, Liza, and her governess, Cozy, back to the St. Regis Hotel. It was one of the hottest days that year in New York City, and everybody was sweating.

At the hotel, the air conditioning system was broken, and Judy retreated to the bathroom to soak in a cold bath. In the wake of her triumph in Britain, she had expected her agents at William Morris to have arranged a major debut for her at Carnegie Hall. When Luft left to "scope out" William Morris, she remained in her bra and panties in front of a fan.

To his disappointment, he learned that there were no offers for stage or screen, only six radio shows that would pay her $1,500 each, hardly enough to cover their hotel bill and expenses. He tried to reach Judy at the hotel, but she had gone to Grand Central Station to put her daughter and Cozy on the Super Chief, as they set out on the long cross-country trip by rail to Los Angeles.

Feeling he'd failed Judy, Luft headed back to the St. Regis in the sweltering heat. He loosened his tie and took off his jacket. Along the way, he stopped in front of the 1,610-seat Palace Theatre.

From 1913 and throughout the Roaring Twenties, The Palace had booked some of the biggest vaudeville and theatrical acts in America, featuring every performer from Sarah Bernhardt and Ethel Barrymore to Mae West. The roster also included Al Jolson, Caruso, Eddie Cantor, Bob Hope, Sophie Tucker, George Jessel, Vernon and Irene Castle, Burns & Allen, Kate Smith, Ethel Merman, Bing Crosby, Jack Benny, and Rudolph Valentino dancing the tango with his second wife, Natacha Rambova. During the Depression, it was retrofitted as a movie theater.

In 1949, under the direction of RKO's vice president, Sol Schwartz, there was an attempt to bring back vaudeville with Frank Sinatra, Jerry Lewis, Danny Kaye, and Harry Belafonte.

Luft purchased a $1.25 ticket at the box office from an overweight man smoking a cigar and went into the lobby, which he found dirty and depressing. Someone had dropped a bag of popcorn, and no usher had swept it up. The carpets were worn and dirty, and a neglected sense of musty decay hung over the place. He had to go and take a leak and found the men's room littered with paper and the toilets soiled.

The auditorium was mostly empty, showing a John Wayne movie. In the rear seats were three drunks passing a bottle among themselves.

In such a dour environment, the showman in him bubbled to the surface, and he devised what was to be the best idea he'd ever had in his lackluster career. Why not use The Palace as a venue for the spectacular American comeback of Miss Judy Garland?

Outside on the street, he went over to Whelan's Drugstore, where he called RKO's Vice President, Sol Schwartz, whom he knew slightly from Los Angeles, at his office in Manhattan. Schwartz, who was aware of Judy's spectacular recent success in the British Isles, agreed to meet him at the theater in thirty minutes. When he got there, he escorted Luft on a tour of the theater's faded grandeur. Downstairs, they saw a rat "the size of the torch on the Statue of Liberty" dart across the floor.

Luft pitched the idea of a Judy Garland concert backed up by some vaudeville acts. The showman in Schwartz envisioned the possibility right away. He agreed to restore the theater, putting in new carpeting and re-upholstering the frayed seats. "We own a theater up in Harlem with spectacular chandeliers. I'll have them moved and installed here to glamourize the lobby. Of course, I'll have to get an okay from the big boys in Hollywood."

Schwartz recalled the Rooney/Garland movie, *Babes in Arms,* in which the would-be troupers dreamed of playing The Palace in New York City. "We might make that dream come true for her."

Back at the St. Regis, Luft encountered Judy still in front of the fan. When he relayed the news, she bolted out of her chair and ran toward him,

Built in 1913 as the flagship of the Keith-Albee theatrical chain, **The Palace** was the most desired booking venue for vaudeville artists of the Jazz Age.

Performers who revered it included Judy Garland's father, Frank Gumm. Some performers wanted to play here so badly they agreed to pay cuts as a means of increasing their theatrical prestige.

Beginning in 1949, its owner, Sol Schwartz, tried to revive the charms of vaudeville by prefacing feature films with as many as a half-dozen live acts.

In October of 1951, one of them (Judy Garland) appeared for a five-month "comeback," following it with additional appearances in 1956 and 1967.

Rumor has it that the theater is haunted, perhaps with the traumatized souls of performers whose hopes and dreams were thwarted after failed debuts at The Palace.

taking him in her arms. He warned her, "It's not definite yet."

Word soon reached them that RKO in Hollywood had endorsed the renovation of The Palace as a showcase for Judy's New York City "debut and comeback." Luft packed up their things and headed west by train, because Judy had a deep-seated terror of flying. *[In contrast, he found train travel a bore.]*

In Hollywood, two reporters and a photographer greeted them along with Liza and Cozy. Liza introduced Judy to her pet poodle, "John Cook."

The next day, she put through a call to Dore Schary at MGM, not knowing if he'd take her call, but he did. As if he feared that she'd be calling to beg for a job, he immediately said, "Welcome back, Judy. I heard your trip was a triumph. But, sorry to say, we don't have any musical in production, or going into production, that would be suitable for you."

"That's not what I was calling about, Mr. Schary," she said. "I'm opening at The Palace in New York, and I need to borrow your arrangers, my dear friends, Chuck Walters and Roger Edens."

He promised to get back to her, and she viewed that as a rejection. However, Edens phoned two days later and said, "Dore has agreed to give you Chuck and me on a temporary leave of absence. Both of us are excited to be working with you again."

Rehearsals began at Nico Charisse Studio on La Cienega Boulevard, where Ethel had taken a very young Liza for dancing lessons.

Edens and Walters choreographed a dramatic opening where Judy would be preceded by eight "Dancing Boyfriends" who would rhythmically escort her to a spotlit point, center stage. Her costume—a tuxedo jacket and black silk stockings—would be inspired by what she'd worn in *Summer Stock* during her "Get Happy" number.

The next day, Luft went to RKO to get payroll approval for the dancers. "The RKO vice president I met there was even more of a homophobe than I was. He told me, 'Don't hire any swishes.' I reminded him that finding a coven of dancing boys in New York or in Hollywood who are not homosexual is like moving the Rock of Gibraltar to Los Angeles."

Before returning to New York, Judy, Edens, and Walters agreed on her numbers, and that they'd run for fifty minutes on the stage. Luft approved of their sketches, songs, and skits. Many of the songs would come from her more popular movies.

Wherever they went, reporters asked the same question: "When are you two lovebirds gonna get married?"

"Later, later, guys," she would say, fending them off.

Actually, their divorces had not become final. Luft had divorced Lynn Bari in 1950, and she had custody of their son, John. However, during rehearsals for Judy's upcoming appearance, Luft was served with papers, Bari accusing him of falling behind in his $500-a-month child support.

In her brief, Bari charged that her former husband was "half a millionaire," an assertion that was false. At their divorce hearing, Judy had been named as "the other woman." There was a certain irony here, as in film after film, it was Bari who had portrayed "the other woman."

At the divorce hearing, Judy had been served a subpoena, but she failed to show up. Under threat of arrest, she answered the second subpoena. On the witness stand, she told the judge that she had failed to make an appearance because she was suffering from "psychic trauma."

One dark secret occurred during rehearsals that the press never found out about. At 7PM, after a long day of vigorous rehearsals in Los Angeles, Luft picked Judy up while she was still wearing her rehearsal clothes of silk trousers and Capezio shoes. He noticed traces of gray at the edge of her brownish hair, which could have easily been handled by a hairdresser in New York.

Over dinner at the Cock 'n Bull, she ordered Welsh rarebit as he devoured a rare Texas steak. He was drinking Kentucky bourbon that night, and he signaled the waiter for a refill just before she told him she wanted to make a major announcement that would change their lives.

As he settled back to hear the news, she informed him that she had seen a doctor that afternoon. "He told me I'm going to have a baby. Our first together. The beginning of our family."

He later admitted that his reaction was insensitive, as he immediately understood that they'd have to cancel their engagement at The Palace.

Back at their home, it was a night he remembered as filled with "tears and accusations." Before dawn came, she agreed to have an abortion at the time and place of her own choosing. She did not want him to get involved. He later told Walters, "Judy is a familiar body at secret abortion clinics."

He consistently pointed out that their having a baby out of wedlock might destroy her career in the way it had when the married Ingrid Bergman became pregnant with the child of the Italian director Roberto Rossellini.

"America has a strict moral code, and your public won't stand for you having a child out of wedlock, even if your name is Judy Garland," he said.

Abandoning rehearsals for five days and nights, she just disappeared, and he called around, even contacting Minnelli, but no one knew where Judy had gone. Suddenly, she re-appeared for rehearsals, making it obvious to everyone that she wasn't speaking to him. "I knew she'd gone through with the abortion and was mad as hell."

Luft came to rehearsals every afternoon, hoping she'd speak to him again. He tried to break through to her, but she resisted him. One afternoon, he called to her that he was going to the Ready Room Bar next door, if she'd like to join him after rehearsals.

There in the bar, beset with troubles, he began to drink Kentucky bourbon, finishing off half a bottle. Then he went next door and looked in on her, finding her still rehearsing. He decided he'd better not drink anymore or else he might not be able to drive home.

Intoxicated, he got behind the wheel of his car and drove out onto La Cienega Boulevard, immediately ramming into the side of an automobile driven by a male student.

The sound of the crash brought Judy, Edens, and Walters rushing out of the studio to investigate. She found the student and a drunken Luft fist fighting. Judy rushed over to the student, striking him in the face with the Coca-Cola bottle she'd carried. When his glasses fell to the street, she stomped on them.

In the meantime, a tuxedo-clad Dr. Larson, a Beverly Hills dentist, stopped to see if he could help. Luft immediately attacked him, bashing in his nose, causing it to bleed.

A police squad car arrived on the scene to make arrests. In the rear of Luft's car they found a .38-caliber revolver. It was later revealed to have been stolen from Douglas Aircraft during the days when he was an employee there.

Amazingly, at the Wilshire police precinct, Luft was released after posting a $100 bail on a drunk driving charge.

A reporter was tipped off, and news of the incident made the wire services. Judy awoke late the following morning to face headlines—JUDY GARLAND ATTACKS STUDENT DRIVER. POLICE ARREST DRUNK DRIVER SID LUFT.

The following day, the student driver sued for $10,000 for assault and battery, and the dentist also filed a suit, asking for $15,000 on the same charge.

[Judy was already appearing on stage at The Palace when Luft had to return to Los Angeles for a court hearing. Astonishingly, he had to pay only $150 on the DWI charge. All the other charges were dropped, including possession of the stolen gun and the assault-and-battery charges. Paying the fine, he flew back to New York and Judy.]

A few days later, Judy bid a tearful goodbye to Liza at the Minnelli home. With Luft, her musical directors, and the dancers, she boarded the Super Chief for New York. There, they checked into the St. Regis again as the October winds were blowing down from Canada.

The next day, Luft took the troupe to a decaying old studio on Broadway that had once been used for rehearsals by Mary Martin and Ethel Merman.

Meanwhile finishing touches were being applied to the renovations at The Palace. On the evening of their first night back in New York, Judy and Walters made a sneaky visit to Times Square, standing across the street from The Palace, where the words JUDY were on the marquee in letters twelve feet high.

On opening night, October 16, 1951, Luft went early to the theater to check on the final arrangements. It seemed that every florist in central Manhattan had been stripped of flowers and that all of them had been sent to Judy.

Walters went by to escort Judy to the theater, but their taxi could proceed only to a point about a block from the theater because of the massive crowd assembled outside.

A reporter for *The New York Times* suggested he hadn't seen such a mob since the celebration of the Allied vic-

Voluptuous, Curvaceous, and Zaftig: IT'S JUDY!!

One reporter dared to ask her about her increased poundage: "I know I'm awfully fat, but I haven't felt so good in years."

330

tory at the end of World War II.

Luft learned that celebrities had flown in from Los Angeles, Chicago, and London to attend her show. To a packed audience, it opened with a series of vaudeville acts that included acrobats and a dancing duo billed as "Vernon and Irene Castle of London." Doodles and Spider mimed popular songs.

At Judy's request, an English comedian, Max Bygraves, who had worked with her at the Palladium, had also flown in from London. The Nicholas Brothers followed. For the sake of nostalgia, Smith & Dale performed their "cross-talk duet," an act they'd perfected in 1922.

On the second bill, "The Boyfriends" went through a number, then stood aside to make way for the spotlight to shine on Judy. The ovation was thundering.

Tears came to the eyes of Sophie Tucker when Judy performed her signature song, "Some of These Days." She also sang "My Man," made famous by Fanny Brice. Among her solos, Judy chose "You Made Me Love You," "For Me and My Gal," "The Boy Next Door," "The Trolley Song," and "Liza."

When she exited from the stage to prepare for her next number, the "Dancing Boyfriends" performed gallantly. Then she emerged from the wings dressed as a hobo, her cheeks smudged with clown makeup. Together with Walters, they performed "We're a Couple of Swells," which Judy and Fred Astaire had made famous in *Easter Parade.*

For her concluding number, and still in her hobo costume, she moved to the front of the stage. Illuminated with a single spotlight, she delivered her rendition of "Over the Rainbow," which many of her fans considered the finest version ever of her signature song.

Her curtain call roared on for ten minutes (some source claimed twelve). Backstage, telegrams arrived. Enough to fill a mail bag, they were mainly from California.

After a quick shower, she emerged from her dressing room in a silk robe to receive a roster of celebrities backstage.

Marlene Dietrich, Jack Benny, Irving Berlin, Gloria Swanson, Jimmy Durante, Joan Crawford, Tallulah Bankhead, Martha Raye, Samuel Goldwyn, singer Jane Froman, Moss Hart, Billy Rose, Blossom Seeley, and the theatrical impresario Lee Shubert congratulated her. Honored guests included the Duke and Duchess of Windsor, marking the beginning of her unlikely friendship with them. In the next few days, she and Luft were seen all over town with this fabled couple, dancing at the Stork Club. A few nights later even General Douglas MacArthur came backstage to greet her.

Years later, Liza reflected on that period in her mother's life: "There was in Judy a very deep wound, somewhere far down, which she could never close up because she had to use it when she sang and when she acted. She needed the pain there because it was part of her work."

When the other stars departed, Luft came into her dressing room and took her in his arms. "Sweetheart, I am going to produce *A Star Is Born* for you."

After supper at "21," Luft took Judy back to the St. Regis to wait for the reviews of her appearance at The Palace in the morning papers.

Variety wrote: "The Palace is back to a two-a-day vaudeville rebirth and if it ever takes hold permanently, Judy Garland gets credit for birthing it. Hers was a *tour-de-force* of no small caliber."

In *The New York Times,* a critic said, "Full of zip and electric excitement, Judy Garland gave plenty of evidence that she knows her way over the boards."

John Chapman of the *Daily News* wrote, "I spotted an elderly juvenile named Montgomery Clift sitting with a nice-looking and well-behaved girl named Taylor or something." [*Of course, he was artfully referring to Elizabeth Taylor.*]

Even a reporter for *Life* magazine covered the event: "At the end of the concert, almost everyone in the theater was crying and for days afterward, people around Broadway talked of it as if they had beheld a miracle. What they had beheld was Judy Garland making her debut at the old Palace, which was having a comeback to straight two-a-day vaudeville."

"But the real comeback was Judy's," the reporter for *Life* continued. "The girl with the voice meant equally for lullabies, love songs with plain whooping and hollering, deserved the most overworked word in her profession—great. And the long, unhappy years of illness, divorce, and declining stardom were over."

Her overweight figure didn't go unnoticed. One critic wrote, "Our little girl, Miss Judy Garland, has the face of Judy but the body of a middle-aged housewife."

***

At first unknown to Luft, Judy had resumed her pill popping. She was being visited almost daily by a mysterious "Dr. Samuel," who wore a black cape like Dracula's.

Although she was appearing increasingly agitated, in a matter of weeks, she'd gone from a size fourteen to a size ten.

Luft was growing more and more suspicious of this doctor. Judy resented his snooping around, saying, "What are you in training for? To become some sort of flatfoot?"

One afternoon, when Dr. Samuel arrived at their hotel suite, Luft confronted him. "Doctor, if indeed you are one. If you dare to come to this suite again, I'll kill you."

"I demand to see my patient," he responded.

"Shall I repeat my threat?"

Apparently, Luft looked so menacing, the doctor swirled his cape and disappeared.

Three weeks into the engagement, as Judy on stage was singing "Rock-a-Bye My Baby to a Dixie Melody," she stumbled and collapsed just before the curtain went down.

She was rushed to the LeRoy Sanitarium, where she was hospitalized for several days, suffering from nervous exhaustion. Luft was not in town, having flown to Los Angeles to face another lawsuit from Lynn Bari.

Judy ended her historic engagement at The Palace on February 24, 1952, after 184 shows. The box office had grossed $800,000.

On her final night at The Palace, many of the celebrities who attended her opening also showed up for her finale, which many considered even more spectacular, and certainly more practiced, than the first night. Unexpectedly, the great opera tenor, Lauritz Melchior—the next big star slated for an engagement at The Palace—walked onto the stage.

The Windsors: A late-in-life, semi-official portrait.

The British press referred to their marriage as "The Love Affair of the Century."

What was left out was the fact that both of them were bisexuals, and according to some witnesses, they secretly hated each other.

"Judy has been singing her heart out for us," he addressed the audience. "Now let's sing for her." Then he led hundreds of people in a community singalong of "Auld Lang Syne."

The RKO chief in New York, Sol Schwartz, waited backstage for Judy. "From now, little girl," he said. "The Palace will be your home."

***

During her run at The Palace, Judy and Luft had been introduced to the Duke and Duchess of Windsor. She'd read about their fabled life, especially how, as King Edward VIII, he abdicated the British crown "to marry the woman I love."

Judy considered Wallis Warfield Simpson as the most mysterious and fascinating woman of the century. At the end of the war, during which they had been accused of Nazi sympathies, the pair had emerged as the dazzling monarchs of international society.

The Duchess invited Judy and Luft to join them for a holiday in Palm Beach. They accepted, although he felt edgy about hanging out with "such high-falutin' royals."

The Duke had declared himself as Judy's most ardent fan, claiming that he had memorized most of her songs. He proved that during society parties in Florida, when he frequently joined her and a pianist in joint performances of her famous songs in front of millionaire and/or A-list guests.

Charles Cushing, the Duke's best friend and business manager, came along, too. During daylight hours, when many of the men were on the golf course, Judy was the center of attention, dazzling women and those who hated golf with her "naughty tales about the handsome leading men of Hollywood."

During her London gig at the Palladium, Luft had spent lots of Judy's money at tailors on Savile Row, amassing a $75,000 wardrobe of tailor-made suits in elegant fabrics, and twenty-eight pairs of shoes crafted from "exotic skins."

In Palm Beach, Luft showed up every night in his new wardrobe. The local newspapers designated him as the best-dressed man of the season.

Around the same time, Judy's Los Angeles attorney notified her that her divorce from Minnelli had become final, and, if she wished, she was free to marry Luft.

[Throughout the rest of their lives, Judy and Minnelli, unlike many other Hollywood couples, continued their friendship and often socialized. There was no fight over who would get custody of Liza, who came and went more or less as she — or they — liked between the two households.]

Judy summed up her holiday: "We were the toast of Palm Beach, even taking some of the aura away from the Duke and Duchess. At one party, I learned that each hostess paid the Duke and Duchess to attend their gatherings."

Eventually, their holiday ended. When it was over, Judy and Luft traveled by rail back to Los Angeles and the fate awaiting them there.

***

When Judy returned after her gig at The Palace and her holiday with the Windsors, there were no massive crowds to welcome her back. During her absence, Luft had negotiated with Charles K. Feldman, considered the best theatrical agent in Hollywood, to line up some possible film deals for her.

He had no firm movie offers for her, but the backers of the upcom-

"But can you play it British, dahling?

Flushed with the fame generated by her gig at The Palace, Judy considered a brief but fleeting offer to star as Liza Doolittle in the Broadway production of *My Fair Lady*.

The photo above shows **Julie Andrews and Rex Harrison** in 1956 in this publicity still from the stage version for which Judy was almost hired.

"Or perhaps you might play it with a brogue, dahling?"

Photo above depicts **Gene Kelly and Cyd Charisse** in the 1954 "frock flick," *Brigadoon*, for which Judy, riding on the crest of her success at The Palace, was considered and later formally announced by MGM.

Like the mythical pot of gold spirited off by the Leprechauns, the offer disappeared.

ing stage version of *My Fair Lady,* eager for a splashy opening on Broadway, were debating whether to offer Judy the lead female role of Eliza Doolittle.

Around the same time, George Jessel hinted that he might want her to co-star in *Bloodhounds of Broadway.*

Also, even though Dore Schary did not admire her, he did discuss bringing her back for a role in *Brigadoon* (1954) with Gene Kelly and Van Johnson. At one point, he went so far as to announce that Judy would co-star in the picture directed by Vincente Minnelli, but eventually, that deal fell through.

Feldman suggested that she might consider the then-novel medium of television, following in the footsteps of Frank Sinatra, Perry Como, Bob Hope, Eddie Cantor, Burns & Allen, Jack Benny, Groucho Marx, Ethel Waters, and Dinah Shore.

Eventually, a decision was made to bring her show at The Palace to the Philharmonic Auditorium in Los Angeles for an opening on April 21, 1952. Whereas she'd been paid $15,000 per week in New York, here on the West Coast, she would make $25,000 a week.

For her opening, *tout* Hollywood turned out, a glittering array of celebrities and stars. Henry Ford II chartered a plane to fly in from Detroit with some close friends. Even Judy's flamboyant rival, Lana Turner, showed up. *[When Judy was told that Lana was in the audience, Judy said to her assistant, "I bet she's here tonight to watch me fall on my ass."]*

Most of the reviews were raves. One headline read: RAINBOW GIRL FINDS POT O' GOLD. The *Herald Express* wrote, "Within ten minutes of Judy's arrival on stage, the audience found itself on a trolley ride. It was a night of nights for star and audience alike—the great big audience cried."

A critic from *The New York Times* gushed, "The throng of motion picture personalities packed the auditorium for the sentimental occasion. There was scarcely a dry eye when Miss Garland, in a tramp costume, sat on the rim of the stage and sang 'Over the Rainbow.'"

Lee Zhito in *Billboard* claimed, "Judy sang as this reporter has never heard her sing before."

After the show, a private party was held at Romanoff's, where Judy greeted, hugged, and kissed Joan Crawford, Humphrey Bogart, Lauren Bacall, George Burns, Gracie Allen, Esther Williams, and June Allyson. The surprise guest of the evening was Louis B. Mayer.

One woman who came backstage to see Judy was definitely not welcome. It was the now-single Ethel Gumm Gilmore, who had lost both of her husbands and was now struggling to survive on her $61 weekly paycheck from Douglas Aircraft. *[It was the same company where Luft himself had worked when he first arrived in Los Angeles.]*

She wanted to see Judy, but her daughter refused. Ethel then asked Luft for a $200 loan to keep her car from being repossessed, but he refused. She then pleaded with him for a monthly check to pay for her insurance, and he agreed to send her $25 a week.

Newly embittered, and in retaliation, Ethel went to columnist Sheila Graham, telling her, "My daughter has been selfish all her life, beginning when she was a little girl. She was far more demanding than her sisters, and always wanted to be the center of attention. She had one desire, and that was to be famous, regardless of the cost. I struggled and sacrificed most of my life to please her, and now she refuses to see her own mother, although I am in ill health. I have diabetes, a heart condition, and high blood pressure."

Judy fought back, claiming, that her mother and her former husband, Will Gilmore, had spent or squandered all of her earnings from MGM in the 1940s. "When I had to go to the bank to support myself, I found my account had only $56.11 in it."

Still seeking support from Judy, Ethel filed court action, but the judge refused to hear the case.

It was during her Los Angeles gig at the Philharmonic Auditorium that Judy began her dependence on morphine, as later reported by Harry J. Anslinger, who headed the Bureau of Narcotics.

A policeman found out that her supplier was none other than a doctor who was himself an addict. Pressure was put on the doctor to stop supplying her, but Judy was clever enough to find another source. She later admitted to Anslinger that she took a shot of morphine before going out onto the stage.

***

The next big offer came in from the large Curran Theatre in San Francisco, which hired Judy to replicate for the City on the Bay the show that had been such a hit in New York. It was said that the largest concentration of her fans, hundreds of them gay, were centered here, so the manager of the Curran was anticipating lines at the box office. From May 26 till June 22, 1952, she played to audiences there, receiving thunderous applause after most of her numbers.

William Hogan in the *San Francisco Chronicle* wrote, "Judy Garland brought a touch of The Palace and a touch of the Palladium to the Curran stage. The headline act is warm and gay, and Judy's songs may bring legitimate lumps to an audience's throat. It is just that the legend of her comeback gets in the way of the act."

Luft informed his honored guests that he found inspiration for Judy's comeback in the career of Joan Crawford. [*After Louis B. Mayer had fired her from MGM, Crawford signed a contract with Warners that extended her career and led to some of her greatest movies, eventually winning an Oscar for her performance in* Mildred Pierce *(1945) after Bette Davis rejected that role.*]

During Judy's gig at the Curran in San Francisco, Luft had nothing but praise for Louis Lurie, the owner of that theater. "He paved the streets of San Francisco with gold for us. After the show, and to wind down, Judy and I walked the streets, exploring San Francisco, usually ending up in Chinatown for a late-night supper. She discovered a dress shop called Gump's, where she ordered custom-made outfits made of Japanese silk."

One night at a little out-of-the-way bistro, she delivered some news that almost sent Luft into cardiac arrest: "I'm pregnant again, and this time there will be no abortion."

He decided there, on the spot, that the time had come for him to stop postponing marriage. His exact words to her, as he later revealed, were, "Darling, will you marry me?"

She reached for his hand and held it for a long time. "Since I've received no better offers today, I'll accept. When you take my virginity on my wedding night, I suspect you'll be a tiger in bed."

He was putting up a good front, pretending joy at the announcement of their first child together. Actually, he was devastated. Unknown to her, he had been organizing, in collaboration with her agents, a road show through the major cities of America, a year-long series of bookings with performances in Chicago, Boston, Detroit, Miami, Washington D.C., Dallas, Atlanta, Philadelphia, and more.

Since Judy was already three months pregnant with their child, neither of them wanted to alert the press to their upcoming nuptials. Luft put through a call to the oil millionaire Ted Ward, a close friend and business associate, asking him to be his best man. Ted not only accepted but promised to stage the wedding at the home of his brother, Bob. Bob and his wife owned a beautiful, sprawling ranch on the outskirts of the hamlet of Hollister, ninety miles south of San Francisco.

On June 8, 1952, two days before Judy's 30th birthday, she and Luft were married in a quiet ceremony. Their honeymoon night transpired within in a small cottage scenically located on the grounds of the Ward estate in Hollister.

After thanking the Ward brothers, Judy and Luft departed by car the next morning for San Francisco. En route, they were listening to the radio when news of their marriage was revealed, nationwide, by Louella Parsons. Obviously, someone at the Ward Ranch had phoned the gossip maven with the story. Liza was watching television with her father when the news bulletin flashed across the TV screen.

Judy's 1952 concert in San Francisco was celebrated, gossiped about, and mobbed by her armies of fans.

Many were gay men who roared with laughter at the jokes she delivered about (lower photo) **Jeanette MacDonald.**, the cinematic "patron saint' of the city because of her starring role in the 1936 classic film, *San Francisco*.

Everyone in the audience, especially the drag queens, remembered the fluttery way MacDonald belted out the film's namesake song as an earthquake demolished the city around her.

When Judy arrived at their hotel in San Francisco, Judy phoned Liza: "You'll be so happy," she assured her daughter. "Papa Sid will dote on you, no doubt spoiling you. I can't wait to welcome you to our new home. Sid's

337

son, Johnny, will come and live with us, too. You'll have the brother you always wanted."

"Okay, mother," Liza said. "If you say so." When she hung up the phone, she didn't appear to be too happy.

Back in southern California, from her new home on Mapleton Drive in Holmby Hills, Judy postponed Liza's visit for a week and set out to meet her new neighbors. They included Bing Crosby, who wanted her to keep singing on his radio show. [*Crosby had forgiven her for rejecting the co-starring role in his latest movie,* Just For You *(1952). "During its filming, something good came out of it," he said. "Jane Wyman, my co-star, and I had a torrid affair."*]

The Bogarts, Humphrey and Lauren, called on her for tea, Bogie preferring vodka. Lana Turner also called and invited Judy and Luft for drinks around her pool one late afternoon. She was married at the time to the well-muscled actor, Lex Barker, who had recently been voted "Hollywood's Sexiest Movie Star."

Since Luft had not returned home, Judy went alone to the Turner household. A maid let her in, informing her that "Miss Turner is due at any minute" and suggested that she "go out to the pool and have a drink with Mr. Barker."

Judy walked outside and saw the former screen Tarzan swimming a lap. Spotting her, he swam over to the edge and climbed out of the water. He was stark naked and took his time going over and reaching for a towel to wrap around himself. As he turned to Judy, he said, "I believe that if you've got it, flaunt it."

As she later relayed to Kay Thompson, "There was meat there for the poor."

***

On June 29, 1952, Judy became the second woman ever "roasted" at the Friars Club at the Biltmore Bowl in Los Angeles. [*Sophie Tucker had been the first.*]

At Judy's *fête*, Olivia de Havilland, Marie Wilson, and Rosalind Russell gave humorous speeches, pretending to mock Judy. They were followed by Ronald Reagan and George Burns, with George Jessel serving as master of ceremonies. Judy ended the roast singing "Palace Medley" and "Over the Rainbow."

In the weeks leading up to the birth of her second child, Judy began to

EDGAR RICE BURROUGHS'

TARZAN AND THE SHE-DEVIL

LEX BARKER
JOYCE MacKENZIE

RAYMOND BURR · MONIQUE VAN VOOREN
TOM CONWAY

GRAPEVINE GOSSIP FROM SUNNY L.A.

Who did Judy meet, nude, at the edge of Lana Turner's swimming pool?

Lex Barker, Lana's then-husband, one of the sexiest men of the 1950s.

He's depicted in the upper photo with **Joyce MacKenzie** in this shot from *Tarzan & the She-Devil* (1953).

338

put on weight, her doctor calling it "water retention." For about a week, she lost the power in her right arm, which became so numb she could stick a pin into it and not feel any pain.

Before the birth of Liza, Judy had given up drugs, but she was in such a state of high anxiety before giving another birth that she began to take Seconal and Dexedrine again. Her doctor had warned her that drugs might impair her infant in some way, either physically or mentally, but she persisted nonetheless.

Aware of that, Luft would come home in the evening and search the house for her stash, but he never found any medication. She had become skilled at concealing her pills.

To welcome their many friends and associates, Judy and Luft hosted a party for 150 guests within their new home in Holmby Hills. It had three purposes: To belatedly celebrate Judy's 30th birthday and to announce her pregnancy, but mainly to reveal a new picture deal that Luft had signed with Jack Warner.

Tout Hollywood showed up, none more notable than Gary Cooper and his wife, Rocky, and her neighbors, Bogie and Bacall. Many of her former co-stars attended, too, and Mickey Rooney entertained the guests in duets with Judy, replicating hits such as "Strike Up the Band" and "Heaven Will Protect the Working Girl" from bygone films.

At the party, Luft addressed his guests, telling them that he'd concluded a deal with Jack Warner; that he'd formed a new production company, Transcona Enterprises; and that he intended to produce nine films, three of which would star Judy. The new company would launch itself with Judy starring in a musical remake of *A Star Is Born. [An earlier version, released in 1937, had starred Janet Gaynor and Fredric March.]*

He didn't announce it, but Judy would be given $100,000 for the musical remake, and the production company run by Luft and herself would take home fifty percent of the profits—it was widely acknowledged as a "sweetheart deal" for both Luft and Judy.

Arthur Freed was at the party. On the way out the door with Rooney, he whispered to him, "I can't believe those two alleycats are making a musical."

Yet Judy had more on her mind than filming a new musical. In the first week of December, she concluded a deal with her agent, William Morris, to sign a contract with a top publisher like Random House for her autobiography. It was to be a 90,000-word manuscript to be submitted on or before August 25, 1953.

The agency hired a ghost writer, Cameron Shipp, and a $25,000 advance was proposed. But during their first meetings, Judy said, "I can't tell my true story, beginning with my childhood as Frances Gumm. It's all too painful." With that in mind, the project, and the book it would have entailed, collapsed.

***

At 4:17PM on November 21, 1952, Lorna Luft entered the world, weighing six pounds, four ounces. The birth was by Caesarean, as had been

Liza's. At first, she was named Nora, a designation that was later changed to Amanda before Lorna was agreed upon. Judy took the name from the heroine of Clifford Odets' *The Golden Boy*, one of her favorite plays. It was adapted into a screenplay and filmed in 1939 with Barbara Stanwyck and William Holden.

Ethel showed up at St. John's Hospital in Los Angeles to see her granddaughter, but Judy ordered that she be sent away.

***

After the birth of Lorna, Judy entered a deep postpartum depression, and Luft feared—considering her previous history— that she might become suicidal. He hired a butler to look after her. "Check on her at least every thirty minutes. If she locks herself away in the bathroom and won't answer you, then beat the damn door in."

Three days later, at Luft's office nearby, he received a frantic phone call from the butler. "Miss Garland has locked herself in her bathroom and won't respond to my pounding."

"Call Dr. Fred Pobirs at once. I'm on my way." [*Pobirs' office, too, was in the general vicinity, and he, too, had been warned to expect a phone call at any hour, with the understanding that Judy was on a "suicide watch." Both Luft and the doctor arrived at the Luft-Garland home at the same time.*]

Once they were inside, Luft rushed immediately to her bathroom. He pounded on the door but she didn't respond. He beat down the door and stepped inside to confirm his worst fear. He later wrote, "Blood, bright red, in contrast to the whiteness of her skin, was pouring out of her neck. She had cut her throat with a razor blade. The doctor took charge to stop the bleeding, finding that she'd made a deep gash.

"The doc managed to stop the bleeding, sort of, and I carried her to the bed," Luft said. "By this time, his assistant arrived, and I left the room. I could not bear to look at what was going on. Some equipment was delivered from the hospital, and I let two guys in. By the time I was summoned back to her bedroom, Judy had been sedated, and was lying there with her neck bandaged, seemingly sleeping peacefully.

"At least five people now knew of her throat slashing, and I didn't know if I could trust all of them. One might call the press. If word gets out about yet another suicide attempt, *A Star Is Born* might never be made."

"She emerged from her bed days later in a shaky mood," he claimed. "She would plunge into a crying jag, and I couldn't bring her out of it. Her mood could alter in a second, even in the middle of a sentence. She would start out almost giddy but plunge into darkness sometime before the words ended."

He feared bringing it up, but he felt he had to get some explanation from her about why she'd tried to kill herself. "Why did you do it, dear?" he asked one afternoon during an otherwise calm moment together. "You're back on track. A whole new world, a marriage, an enlarged family, a grand career contract, everything seems to be going your way."

She sat up and looked at him with total sincerity. "I swear, Sid, I have no memory whatsoever of cutting my throat."

"Everything was going right for Judy except for one thing," Luft claimed, "and that was her hunger for self-destruction."

Luft later came up with what he thought might have driven Judy to the point of suicide. Two nights before she slashed her throat, they had gone to see a restored version of *Meet Me in St. Louis.* By the time he drove her back home from the screening, she was crying. As soon as they were inside their home, she collapsed on the floor, sobbing, "I'm not beautiful anymore."

A sleepless night was followed by her sitting in front of her vanity table for most of the next day, examining her face closely in the mirror. "Oh, Sid, what am I going to do? How can I fight the ravages of time?"

"Cut the theatrics, girl," he said. "You're one of the most beautiful and desirable women in Tinseltown."

For a change of pace for Judy, and to appease his new boss, Jack Warner, Luft agreed to bring Judy to New York to sing at the coming out party of Warner's daughter, Barbara. At first, Luft thought that Judy would resist, but she seemed eager to get involved. She would wear a dress with a high collar to conceal the bandage around her neck.

Although Judy arranged for Liza to spend Christmas with her father, she wanted to take Lorna with her, along with her nurse. Together, they boarded the Manhattan Limited, heading east from Los Angeles on Christmas Day.

When the train arrived in Manhattan, a limousine was waiting to haul them off to a lavish suite at the Waldorf Astoria, compliments of Jack Warner.

For New Year's Eve, Charlie Cushing invited them to a private party for the Duke and Duchess of Windsor at the Sherry Netherland. Before midnight, guests gathered around the piano to hear Judy and the former King of England harmonize. At the stroke of midnight, Judy was in Luft's arms, hugging and kissing him as the Duke led the crowd in a rendition of "Auld Lang Syne."

By January 3, Judy was at a the private "coming out" party hosted by Elsa Maxwell, the reigning hostess *duenna* in America, in honor of Barbara Warner, whose powerful father had spared no expense. To the delight of the A-list guests, Judy went through a medley of her songs. Onlookers included several major Broadway stars and a scattering of movie idols in town for the New Year.

Two days later, Judy, from within her bedroom at the Waldorf Astoria, received devastating news: Her mother, Ethel Gumm Gilmore, had been found dead of a heart attack in the parking lot of Douglas Aircraft that morning just before reporting to work. She was fifty-nine years old.

Here's a Warner Brothers' publicity photo of studio chief **Jack Warner with his daughter, Barbara,** at the opening of Elia Kazan's *East of Eden* in 1955.

***

Although she'd been alienated from her two sisters, Judy phoned each of them from the Waldorf. It was agreed that Jimmie and Suzanne would meet at Judy's home in Holmby Hills the following afternoon to formulate the funeral arrangements. In preparation for this, Judy agreed, despite her fears of flying, to take a plane with Luft back to Los Angeles.

According to Luft, in reference to their flight to the Coast, "Judy huddled in a fetal position, warning me that the plane was likely to crash somewhere over Kansas. We arrived safely, but her nerves were completely shattered."

It was a tense reunion with her sisters, as there was no love lost. Privately, both Jimmie and Suzanne blamed Judy for their mother's premature death. Solemnly, the three sisters with their husbands migrated from Judy's home to Forest Lawn, where it was agreed that services would be held at the Little Church of the Flowers, followed by a burial at the Forest Lawn Memorial Park.

Luft rented two limousines to take the family to the funeral. The sisters could be heard sobbing as the minister spoke kind words against a backdrop of mournful organ music. All three were dressed in black, and Judy's face, framed under a pillbox hat, was for the most part obscured with a large pair of very dark sunglasses.

After the funeral, Judy told her sisters goodbye and announced that she would go into seclusion. "I wish to see no one."

She had come under fire from the press, one attack following another. Except for a few newspapers, most of the reporters depicted Judy as an ungrateful daughter, citing the fact that Ethel was working for $1.25 an hour while her daughter had pulled in $25,000 a week for her recent gig at the Philharmonic Auditorium.

Luft did not mourn his mother-in-law. When Ethel heard that Judy had married him, she told a reporter from the *Mirror* "The big lug is a *no-goodnik*. When will Judy ever learn when it comes to picking husbands? When will she grow up?"

Three days after the funeral, a letter arrived for Judy from her mother. It had been written just before she died. In it, she asked, "Where did I go wrong? I sacrificed everything to make you a star! How can you treat me like this? Not letting me see my own granddaughter? Not letting me be part of your life? How can you hate me so?"

Judy allowed Luft back into her bedroom for the first time since the funeral. He had deliberately chosen not to even mention Ethel, so it was she who brought up the subject. She poured out a string of abuses she'd suffered since she was Baby Frances Gumm, and she blamed Ethel for her drug addiction. Throughout the rest of her life, she would vilify Ethel.

One of her revelations genuinely shocked Luft: "I've never told anyone this, other than my dear father, Frank. At one time, Ethel wanted me committed to this clinic for a lobotomy. She told me that there was something wrong with my brain, and that it would put me at peace, and that I could go on with my musical career without suffering such anguish."

342

Early one evening, exhausted after a day at the office, Luft returned to his home, had a small supper, and retired. He paid Judy almost no attention, which infuriated her.

Upstairs and in bed, he fell into a sound sleep until 2AM the following morning. Then he was brutally awakened by Judy, who was pounding her high heels into his face. He rose up and slugged her, knocking her down on the floor and leaving her with a bloody nose. Then he locked himself in the bathroom and slept in the bathtub till morning.

It was only later in the day that he deciphered the reason for her fury. A neighbor must have told her that he had been seen leaving the nearby Holmby Hills home of one of their neighbors, actress Gloria Grahame.

Grahame had only recently won a Best Supporting Actress Oscar for her performance in *The Bad and the Beautiful* (1952), starring Lana Turner and directed by Vincente Minnelli. It may have been the director himself who tipped off Judy to Luft's clandestine affair. Perhaps he'd retained some lingering jealousy.

Three years younger than Judy, the blonde goddess Grahame was Los Angeles born and bred. As described by author Barry Monush, "With her pouting upper lip and an arched brow that could speak volumes, Grahame was about the sexiest thing to emerge from the 1940s. She also happened to be a terrific actress who could play sweet, cunning, dumb, brash, or pathetic with equal aplomb."

Because of her checkered past, she was the most notorious resident of their neighborhood. She was once married to director Nicholas Ray, who had returned early one afternoon from the studio and found his twenty-eight-year-old wife in bed with Tony, her thirteen-year-old stepson.

Ray kicked both of them out of his house, but when Tony grew up, Gloria married him, and the couple produced two sons.

Reporters liked her, since she was always good for a quote. "It's not the way I look at a man, it's the thought behind it."

When asked about a possible affair with Luft, Grahame said, "No comment." Then she went on to say, "Of course, let it be known that I prefer men to women."

WOMEN WE LOVE

Gloria Grahame was an Oscar-winning supporting actress in *The Bad and the Beautiful* (1952) and the subject of the 2017 biopic starring Annette Bening, *Film Stars Don't Die in Liverpool.*

Spectacularly notorious for several major-league sex scandals, she became the subject of Judy Garland's fury for events associated with the philandering of her errant husband, Sid.

***

Judy might have attacked Luft for his extramarital fling, but she was indulging in her own affairs on the side, too—in fact, a series of them. Her

343

best friend, Kay Thompson, admitted, "Judy doesn't have any qualms about having an affair with a servant. In fact, if she's drunk enough, she might demand it."

Harry Rubin, a well-built young man with unruly black hair and a super masculine aura, was an electrician. Luft had hired him to rewire a part of their home. Before he learned his craft, he'd been a hoodlum in Brooklyn, where he had served time in jail for petty theft.

One afternoon, while working, he smelled smoke coming from the eastern side of Judy and Sid's house. The children were in the west wing. He rushed to trace the origin of the smoke, discovering it was coming from under the door leading into Judy's bedroom.

Fortunately, she had not locked the door. He discovered her nude and unconscious on the floor about five feet from her bedroom's thick draperies, all of which were ablaze. He opted not to try to put out the fire, as it was too far advanced. Instead he dragged her away, phoned the fire department, wrapped a sheet around Judy's nude body, and carried her out by the pool at the far end of the garden. Laying her down there, he escorted the kids to safety. The nurse had already run out of the house with baby Lorna in her arms.

The press had been alerted, and two reporters were told it had been an electric fire sparked during remodeling. Rubin lied and asserted that Judy had already fled from the scene after rescuing her children.

It took a long time to extinguish the flames, and the west wing was burnt to the ground. Luft moved Judy and their children into the Bel Air Hotel that night.

After her life was saved from a fiery death, Judy began to think of Rubin as "my knight in shining armor."

When Luft arrived on the scene and was told how heroic Rubin had been, he made him his general *factotum* with a large raise in salary.

After the damaged part of the house was reconstructed, the Lufts moved back in. Within a week, Judy launched a clandestine affair with Rubin that lasted until the end of the 1950s as an on-and-off event. She told Kay, "He excels in both oral and anal sex."

During rehearsals and filming of *A Star Is Born*, Rubin was assigned the thankless task of getting Judy up, dressed, and delivered to the studio on time, regardless of her condition. Often, he carried her into a cold shower, stripping off his clothes and joining her in his attempts to revive her.

When she needed pills, he could supply them for her, as he maintained contacts with a dealer who owned a sporting goods store. When she had to travel out of town on a singing engagement, he went with her, sharing her hotel room. He became a familiar figure at concerts, standing in the wings with a Thermos bottle filled with vodka, another with ice cubes.

Judy was often in no condition to drive her own car. Even so, at one point, Luft purchased a new Chrysler for her. However, the next day she presented it as a gift for Rubin.

Judy's monopoly of Rubin's time threatened his marriage. At one point, his wife threatened to divorce him, naming Judy as "the other woman."

Finally, in 1959, Rubin resigned with the admission, "I've had it, and I can't take any more."

During one of her live performances, Judy had brought Rubin up onto the stage with the intention of introducing him. "This is the man who holds my head over the toilet bowl when I throw up."

***

A Star Is Born, a 1954 remake of a 1937 movie, is sometimes hailed as the finest hour in the history of Warner Brothers. Janet Gaynor and Fredric March had made the first version, and its 1954 reformatting into a musical would star Judy Garland as the focal point of Sid Luft's newly formed production company, Transcona, which operated in partnership with its financial backer, Warner Brothers.

In 1932, Cukor had directed a similar story, *What Price Hollywood?* starring Constance Bennett and Lowell Sherman. When he was offered the directorship of the 1937 version of *A Star Is Born,* he rejected it because its story line too closely followed the plot of *What Price Hollywood?*

The plot of the 1954 version deals with a boozing screen star named Norman Maine, an actor on

Judy Garland's 1954 interpretation of **A Star Is Born** has been praised as director George Cukor's greatest film, with some of Moss Hart's best dialogue.

Even before he began, Hart had a lot to work with. A three-member team that included Dorothy Parker had written the screenplay for the film's earlier (1937) version, and for the 1954 update, the ideas of at least six other writers, many of them uncredited, were included.

Its other technicians were among the best in their fields: Music was by Harold Arlen, who had written the melody for "Over the Rainbow."

Its cinematographer, Sam Leavitt, had previously worked as Judy's camera operator at MGM. The new-fangled CinemaScope had come into vogue the year before—it had been used in the filming of Richard Burton's *The Robe* (1953)—and he was struggling to master it.

his last legs. At a nightclub, he hears a young singer, Esther Blodgett (Judy). He's so impressed with her talent that he arranges a screen test for her at his studio. Of course, her name has to go, so the studio changes it to the more marquee-friendly "Vicki Lester." As her star rises, his fades into the Hollywood sunset.

Norman Maine falls in love with the newly christened Vicki and marries her. Theirs is an ill-fated union as his heavy drinking continues, causing her major public embarrassments, but she sticks it out, trying to save her marriage.

When it appears that all is doomed, and with deceptive cheeriness, he tells her he's going for a swim in the Pacific. He never comes back, deliberately and suicidally swimming out so far that he drowns.

Judy was surprised when Sinatra called, telling her, "I'm Norman

Maine. I drink too much, and I'm a has-been, unless my role as a supporting player in *From Here to Eternity* can give me a push upward. I've also been known to take a drink or two. I'd be ideal playing that drunk, Norman Maine."

"Oh, Frank," she said. "I think I'd love to make a movie with you. But I'll have to get an okay from Jack Warner...and from Sid, too."

Mostly, Sinatra did favors for Judy, even, on occasion, saving her life. "The only time I ever asked her to do a favor for me, she didn't come through," he told Burt Lancaster. "I wanted to play her has-been husband, Norman Maine, in *A Star Is Born*, but she really wanted Cary Grant. Marlon Brando and Laurence Olivier each rejected the role. I found myself competing against Humphrey Bogart — yes, Bogie himself — for the role, but I lost."

Why is **Judy** "framing" her face with this unusual configuration of her hands?

Her character, showbiz neophyte Esther Blodgett, is satirizing the "eye of a movie camera" and how it captures nuances of human expression.

It's a parody that amuses her jaded and world-weary (alcoholic) husband, Norman Maine, as portrayed by **James Mason**.

In their attempts to woo Grant, Judy and Luft entertained him and his wife, actress Betsy Drake, at least two or three times a week. They tried to overcome his reluctance to portray a drunken has-been. That offer ended when Grant's agent delivered an ultimatum: To hire Grant, Warners would have to pay him $300,000 up front, plus ten percent of the gross.

The idea of casting Sinatra or Bogie was submitted to Jack Warner, who reacted with: "Sinatra is finished in this business, and Bogie, even with a hairpiece, is too old. I hear he's in rotten shape. He might die midway through the shoot."

Judy had to phone Sinatra with the news that Warner had rejected him. Sinatra flew into a rage and got drunk that night, lashing out at anyone who would listen, defining Judy as "the worst singer in the business, rivaled only in horror by Ella Fitzgerald. Judy forgets she's telling a story in a lyric. Fitzgerald makes the same mistake. Peggy Lee is great with a lyric. Jo Stafford is even better. She can hold a note for sixteen bars if she has to."

"I didn't speak to Judy for three weeks, until I decided it hadn't been her decision to deny me the part. One night, she called me very late and sang 'Over the Rainbow' to me. After that, I could forgive her for anything. I did hold out, though, with one more request: I asked her to describe in graphic detail what it was like to get penetrated by John F. Kennedy. I figured I should know in case some chorus gal asked me about it one night. I wasn't going to find out personally, so I needed a second-hand report, and Judy was in a position to tell me."

"It's funny. Judy and I loved each other when we first met in the '40s, but we could also become furious with each other. She said she thought of me whenever she sang that song about the man that got away."

Sinatra's dismissal was followed by Cary Grant's final rejection of the male lead in *A Star Is Born:* "I just can't see myself in this downbeat role. It's not for me. Get Ray Milland. He was terrific as the alcoholic in *The Lost Weekend."*

Many months later, Grant said, "Career wise, it was one of the three biggest mistakes of my life. I also turned down starring with Audrey Hepburn in *Roman Holiday* (1953) and *Sabrina* (1954)."

Stewart Granger was next in line. To show his qualifications for the part, he agreed to submit to three separate readings at Cukor's home, including one with Judy. On the final reading, he was alone in the house with Cukor.

"It was a very hot day, and he suggested I go for a swim in his pool," Granger said. "He told me that no one wears bathing trunks in his pool. I knew then that he was more interested in sucking my cock than he was in letting me play Norman Maine."

Word arrived from London that Olivier didn't want the role. Other contenders included Gregory Peck, Robert Taylor, Robert Young, Glenn Ford, Henry Fonda, and Richard Burton, who bowed out to make another film. Judy's former lover, Tyrone Power, was also a contender, as his own star was sinking.

Granger called Luft a week later to recommend his fellow Brit, James Mason. A son of Yorkshire, England, Mason had been Britain's leading male star in 1944 and '45.

"I needed a hit at that time," he said, "and I jumped as fast as a jackrabbit when Cukor asked me to star. It was a real meaty part, but I was reluctant to work with Garland. I'd heard all sorts of tall tales about

Any member of the audience with any experience onstage or on camera reacted to this scene with acute embarassment.

It portrayed how the (drunken) actor, Norman Maine, portrayed by **James Mason**, accidentally slugged his (sober) wife, Esther, (**Judy**) at the moment of her greatest triumph.

EVERYONE flinched at this, the film's most excruciating scene, a lesson about what not do at an Academy Awards ceremony.

Photo shows Esther's (Judy's) press agent, portrayed by **Jack Carson**, set against a blown-up photo of the star **(Esther/Judy)** he helped discover.

Carson's admiration for Esther is matched only by his contempt for the decadence and perceived egomania of her husband (also Carson's client), Norman Maine.

how she sabotaged every film role she was offered."

At Warners, Jack Carson had played the male lead in many movies, but this time, he was cast in the third lead of Matt Libby, the publicity agent for the studio. For years, he's covered up for the tantrums and sins of Norman Maine and has grown to despise him. When Norman has fallen to the point where he's been fired and Libby no longer has to protect him, he cruelly mocks and taunts him.

In the fourth lead as studio chief Oliver Miles, Charles Bickford, once Garbo's leading man, believes that Vicki is just a passing fancy for Maine, and—mostly as a means of indulging him—casts her in a small role. She performs in it so brilliantly that he decides to morph her into a star and she becomes a roaring success.

Reporting to Warners on her first day at their studio, Judy, as Esther Blodgett, learns that she's been assigned the dressing room formerly occupied by Bette Davis when she was hailed as "Queen of Warner Brothers." [It was here that Davis made her last film for the studio, Beyond the Forest (1949), in which she delivered her most iconic and campy line: "What a dump!"]

At first, Cukor and Mason conflicted over the British actor's interpretation of the role, Cukor wanting him to model his performance on John Barrymore during the drunken, fading years of that actor's once-fabled career. Mason, however, wanted to play the role "drawing more on my own personality."

They eventually settled their differences and worked smoothly together. Mason's greatest scene is when he crashes Vicki Lester's acceptance of an Oscar. Extravagantly bombastic and drunk, he takes over. At one point, he whirls around, arm outstretched, and accidentally knocks her in the face.

Judy was deeply invested in this movie's success. Whereas an upfront fee of $100,000 had been negotiated for her involvement, it was understood that if the film were a hit, she might collect millions because of her status as a stockholder in Transcona.

Her erratic habit of showing up very late on the set—or calling in sick—immediately evoked memories of her bad behavior on the set of Annie Get Your Gun, which had led to her firing from MGM.

When she did show up, cast and crew, especially Cukor, noted a bizarre habit she had. "Many members of my crew were seen coming and going from her dressing room, spending at least thirty minutes there. Only the best-looking and well-built guys."

Author Christopher Finch expressed it this way: "As tension grew on the set, Judy added a voracious sexual appetite, to her usual array of hungers for food and drugs and reassurance. A steady stream of men found their way into her dressing room. Nothing could provide her with relief, however. Under pressure, her needs became inhuman."

Cukor said, "Judy did her worst in her dressing room before doing her best on camera. Once before the camera, she became almost superhuman as she, in scene after scene, delivered her greatest performance on film. She could play anger, madness, disappointment, tenderness, whatever I asked. She seemed to draw from reserves deep within herself. She became Vicki Lester."

Bob Thomas, the Hollywood correspondent for Associated Press, claimed "Judy Garland's behavior at times seemed to border on dementia. She borrowed expensive designer clothes to attend parties and premieres and returned them in tatters. When she wanted to own a white gown for the Academy Award sequence, she staged a scene in front of Jack Warner. 'Look at this thing! How can you expect me to wear this? It makes me look like the great white whale.' Warner ordered a designer to come up with a new gown. In the weeks ahead, Judy wore that white gown to at least three different galas, showing it off."

Judy's most dramatic onscreen moment occurs when, heavily veiled, she attends Maine's funeral as masses of screaming fans have formed a mob outside the church. As she leaves the service, the surging crowd breaks through a police barricade and malevolently surrounds her. As Judy struggles to pass through them and into a waiting limousine, a woman rips off her black veil. Vicki releases a resounding scream of primal terror.

"Cukor had finished work on the film," Luft said, "He was on his way to St.-Tropez to pick up French hustlers when Jack Warner called, demanding a big number to emphasize what a great star Vicki Lester was. I called Roger Edens. He had once written a song about a star born in a trunk in Pocatello, Idaho, who climbs to the top of the show biz ladder."

That "postscript" performance ultimately added fifteen minutes to the already overly long movie and cost $300,000.

Including a rousing rendition of "Swanee," it illustrated with music various scenes from Vicki Lester's (or Judy's) life—as a teenager making her debut in "I'll Get By," followed by such songs as "You Took Advantage of Me," "The Black Bottom," (her days as a chorus girl); "The Peanut Vendor" (her vision of herself as a chanteuse); and at the end, "My Melancholy Baby."

As a partner in a dysfunctional marriage, why was Esther's (Judy's) star rising?

It's because she knows how to put on a show, as **Judy** had demonstrated many times in her early films with Mickey Rooney.

Here, in A Star Is Born, she struts her stuff in a musically wonderful "scene within a scene"

Although "Born in a Trunk" has emerged as one of the iconic moments in film musicals, Noël Coward expressed a negative view of it when *A Star Is Born* opened in London. "By the time we have endured montage after montage and repetition after repetition after repetition in the 'Born in a Trunk' sequence, I found myself wishing that enchanting Judy was at the bottom of the sea."

In London's *New Statesman*, critic William Whitehall disagreed. "The 'Born in a Trunk' number, as far as I am concerned, could go on forever in the splendid knowledge that it's something as good as Fred Astaire or Gene Kelly did at their best."

The song, "The Man That Got Away," would forever be linked to Judy in each of her upcoming concerts. "It reflected the story of my life," she said. She had to perform it twenty-seven times before Cukor approved.

Not only did production of the film fall days, then weeks, behind, but its production costs began to soar.

Cukor complained to Luft, asking him to exert more control. "Luft was a producer in name only, spending more time at the race track than on the set."

One morning, Judy was so late that Cukor violated his usual rule and visited her in her dressing room. There, he found her sitting in almost paralyzed despair in front of her makeup mirror. "I had to get down on bended nylon and beg her to come to the set. I've never had to humiliate myself in front of a star like that before."

Throughout the shoot, Luft also endured attacks from Jack Warner, who constantly complained of Judy's temper tantrums and her unreliable and unprofessional habit of showing up late—or not at all.

When Warner wrote his autobiography, he said, "Sid Luft is one of the guys who promised he'd never work a day in his life—and he kept his promise."

By now, Luft had painfully learned that he could not control Judy's addiction to drugs. She would go for two or three days without food, even when he tempted her with her favorite dish, a hamburger heavily coated with peanut butter.

One afternoon, Pamela Mason *[the British actress formerly known as Pamela Kellino]*, showed up on the set and met Judy. The air between them was not just chilly, but icy. Pamela had heard rumors that her husband was spending a lot of time between set-ups in Judy's dressing room.

That was true, as Mason and Judy exchanged frequent confidences. Judy had learned that Mason was a virgin until he turned twenty-six. He also confessed, "There have been ups and downs in my life, more downs than ups."

Jane Greer, who had recently starred with Mason in *The Prisoner of Zenda* (1952), also vis-

Jane Greer—saucily depicted in this press photo accessorized only with a cigarette and a bedsheet—had previously starred with Mason in *Prisoner of Zenda*.

ited the set one day and met Judy. Greer recalled, "There was no doubt that Judy had fallen in love with James. She doted on him. She had slimmed down and seemed desperate to please him. I was told he was very patient with her, even on days when she showed up very late on the set. He kind of nursed her through the film, Cukor told me."

Greer's statement was confirmed by Verne Alves, Luft's production assistant. "I found that my main job was as a nursemaid to Judy. I had to drive her home at night and often stayed with her until Luft got home. I was driving her home after a night shoot when she made a confession to me: 'I always fall in love with my leading man, except Gene Kelly. Vince Minnelli staked him out before me. Right now, I'm in love with James Mason, but it won't last.'"

Mason had had love affairs with

Ann Todd with James Mason in *The Seventh Veil* (1947). She plays a suicidal mental patient under hynosis.

Mason plays the American musician who rescues her.

some of his leading ladies before, including with Ann Todd when they had co-starred in the British melodrama, *The Seventh Veil* (1945).

Todd later said, "There was something electric and at the same time very dangerous about James, which had nothing at all to do with conventional screen stardom. He was one of the few people who could really frighten me, and yet at the same time, he was the most gentle and courteous of men. There was really no end to our love for each other."

Judy tried to explain to some of her close women friends, including June Allyson and Kay Thompson, about her philandering so soon after her wedding to Sid Luft. "Our honeymoon didn't last long. It soon became obvious that we weren't compatible. When I wasn't working, I got tired of playing nursemaid to kids. I was bored as a housewife. I needed outside stimulation, and I could never resist temptation. Sometimes I ran off when Sid got violent. At times, he'd haul off and slap me halfway across the room. He was a very violent man."

***

For Luft, *A Star is Born* marked the end of his dream of becoming a bigtime movie producer. "It all went up in smoke," he said. "The film made millions, but it also cost millions to make. Jack Warner pulled the plug."

The Actor Whose Suicide Inspired
A Star Is Born

It has long been debated which real life movie star was the inspiration for the alcoholic has-been in *A Star Is Born*. A forgotten name today, John Bowers, a son of Indiana born in 1885, tops the list of contenders.

He had been a major star in silent pictures, appearing in some one-hundred flickers, including as the love interest of Mary Pickford in the 1916 silent film, *Hulda of Holland*.

Bowers gained his greatest fame starring opposite Marguerite De La Motte in *Desire* (1923). Sparkling both on and off the screen, they were married in real life after the film was crafted and finished. They would go on to make a dozen other movies together.

A Minnesota-born belle, De La Motte had made her screen debut opposite Douglas Fairbanks, Sr. when she was only sixteen. She was his leading lady in such classics as *The Mark of Zorro* (1920) and *The Three Musketeers* (1921). Both of their careers faded with the advent of the talkies.

As silent films evolved into Talkies, and as he aged, Bowers' allure as a romantic lead faded. At the age of fifty, he made one last attempt to get a role in *Souls at Sea,* a picture with dialogue released in 1937 under the direction of his friend, Henry Hathaway. To his distress, he learned that the male lead had already been awarded to the younger, hotter, fast-rising new star, Gary Cooper.

Deeply depressed, Bowers rented a small sailboat at Santa Monica, and on November 17, 1936, aimed it into the sunset and headed out into the Pacific. His body was later found washed up on a beach.

The last that was heard of De La Motte was when she was discovered working at a factory job in a war plant in the 1940s. She died at the age of 47 in March of 1950.

The only actress who came anywhere close to impersonating her on the screen was Janet Gaynor in 1937—not Judy Garland, not Barbra Streisand, and not Lady Gaga in any of the later adaptations of *A Star Is Born*.

Left photo: **John Bowers**; center photo, a poster for *Lorna Doone* (1922), a silent movie starring John Bowers and **Madge Bellamy**, and (right photo) Bowers' beautiful wife, **Marguerite De La Motte**.

CHAPTER THIRTEEN

GETTING AWAY FROM IT ALL
SID & JUDY'S BROUHAHAS ON THE CÔTE D'AZUR

"IT'S A SNAKE PIT"
JUDY'S REVIEW OF THE FRENCH "REST CLINIC" TO WHICH SHE'S TEMPORARILY COMMITTED

20,000 SCREAMING FANS
ATTEND THE OPENING OF *A STAR IS BORN*
THE END OF AN ERA, IT'S THE LAST GREAT STAR-STUDDED PREMIERE IN TINSELTOWN

JUDY GOES BALLISTIC
THE CONVOLUTED ACADEMY AWARDS OF 1954

PACKING IT IN WITH THE RAT PACK
VERY COOL, VERY HIP, VERY VEGAS

JUDY'S AFFAIR WITH PRINCE ALY KHAN
COSMOPOLITAN, SPECTACULARLY PROMISCUOUS, AND UNIMAGINABLY RICH, HE'S A DIRECT DESCENDENT OF THE PROPHET MOHAMMED

PAUL NEWMAN, *THE HELEN MORGAN STORY*, &

THE THREE FACES OF EVE
JUDY: "It's a tacky little *film noir* that no one will see." JOANNE WOODWARD MAKES IT HER OWN AND LATER, WINS AN OSCAR.

"I tackled Judy once. She came at me. She was out of control. She snapped. She was screaming at me, 'You don't love me! You don't love me!' She was hitting me. I was nude, having emerged from the shower at her house in Brentwood. I struggled with her right in front of the fireplace. You had to stand up to Judy, or she would walk all over you. I tackled her, and when we realized what was happening, we just started to laugh."

—John Carlyle

"I was back on stage again, regaining my confidence about how to handle an audience once more. What I didn't know how to do was manage Sid Luft, the big lug."

—Judy Garland

"Maybe Judy Garland won't make another picture, but this is one triumph they can't take away from her."

—Picturegoer Magazine

One afternoon, Jack Warner summoned Sid Luft to his office and handed him a telegram from Samuel Goldwyn. He'd seen the final cut of *A Star Is Born* and had predicted that it would gross $25 million.

The studio mogul was so pleased with Goldwyn's prediction that he offered Judy and him a vacation in the South of France, where he would pay for their airfare and hotel bill.

Luft was almost broke—so was Judy—and he asked Warner for a loan of $30,000 to cover his household expenses, including a nanny for his two daughters and any costs they might incur in advance of and during their trip.

At first, Judy didn't want to go until Luft persuaded her. Two days later, they boarded a chartered plane owned by aviator/film producer Howard Hughes and winged their way to Paris.

"There, Sid did all the things rich tourists do—an elegant dinner in *belle époque* splendor at Maxim's; onion soup in the pre-dawn hours at Les Halles; the Eiffel Tower; the *Mona Lisa* at the Louvre; the races at Longchamps; a designer gown from Jean Louis; scarves and leather goods at Hermès; and all-night jazz sessions with musicians at Montseigneur

Club."

After Paris, they boarded a train that took them south to Nice, capital of the French Riviera. Warners arranged for a chauffeured Rolls Royce to transport them west to the elegant Hotel du Cap in Cap d'Antibes.

"During our stay there that August, it was like Hollywood on the Côte d'Azur," Luft claimed. "Everybody we didn't want to see from Tinseltown was on vacation: a fat Elsa Maxwell arranging parties where she wanted Judy to sing for free; a cigar-chomping, whore-mongering Darryl F. Zanuck; wheeler-dealers Sam Spiegel and that shifty agent, Swifty Lazar; the sultry French sex kitten Corinne Calvet, who couldn't keep her hands off me until I plugged her—you know…the usual."

During their stay, they were invited to a chic charity event in Monte Carlo, where Judy had a reunion with Marlene Dietrich who sang, "Lili Marleen" and "Falling in Love Again."

Judy danced with Prince Rainier. Later, she would, perhaps jokingly, say, "He should have married me rather than Grace Kelly. Except I would have demanded that his status after that would be elevated to king, not a mere prince. My title then would have been Queen of Monaco."

The Azure Coast of southern France (i.e., "the Riviera") was in vogue, big-time, among successful "Hollywoodiens" like Sid and Judy.

The only trouble was, once anyone got there, he or she couldn't help but run into everyone they'd wanted to leave behind.

She danced with another prince that night, Aly Khan, who had been married (1949-53) to the love goddess Rita Hayworth. He and Luft were devotees of horse racing, and the prince invited Luft—and Judy, too—to his stud farm in Deauville, a resort that was the second major gathering place for *tout Paris* in August.

Judy didn't want to go, preferring a side trip to London instead. Luft left without her. During his absence, Vern Alves, Luft's personal assistant, was assigned the daunting task of looking after her.

"By now, I had been around Judy long enough to know that her moods could change faster than you could spend a nickel," Alves said. "She had been fine the night before, only demanding that I go to bed with her. But by 10AM the next day, she received a call from California. She never told me what was said to her. But after about ten minutes, she slammed down the phone and became hysterical."

"She had a sleepless night, pacing the floor. I knew she was pill popping again. She seemed on the verge of a nervous breakdown. By noon, she was sobbing hysterically, her body shaking all over. She tore at her hair and seemed almost suicidal. I went into a panic and phoned Luft in Deauville."

He recommended that Alves take her to a clinic at Grasse.

"It's not really a psycho ward, just a tranquil retreat where skilled doctors and psychiatrists will know what to do," Luft said.

Alves had to be very forceful to get her to go, but Judy finally relented. "I was never sure what happened there—perhaps she exaggerated—but she was allowed to call me after three days. During the call, she demanded that he come and retrieve her at once.

She said, "This joint is the Snake Pit. I've been strapped down, beaten, and injected with something. I think this burly nurse has been ordered to kill me. I've got to escape."

When Alves arrived to retrieve her from the clinic, the staff seemed only too relieved to get rid of her. "A nurse who looked like the character actress, Hope Emerson, told me she was glad to release Judy—and so was her doctor."

"She drove me crazy," the nurse said.

Back at Hotel du Cap, Judy gorged herself, claiming that she hadn't eaten in three days. She surprised the waiter by wanting only a plate of mashed potatoes with creamy butter, followed by a big, juicy steak and an entire chocolate cake.

The next day, Luft called to announce that he was returning to Paris, where he'd booked a suite at the Hotel de Crillon. By train, Alves and Judy, from the South of France, headed north to Paris, where Luft was waiting at the hotel. They had scheduled only one night there, retiring early in preparation for their morning departure for London.

There, they stayed at the Savoy Hotel, with dinner and dancing at Les Ambassadeurs, a favorite of Princess Margaret.

That night, Judy informed both men that once again, she was pregnant.

By the time they arrived back in Los Angeles for a long-overdue reunion with her daughters, she had to prepare herself for the spectacular Hollywood premiere of *A Star Is Born*.

***

Before its gala celebration, she had a chance to see a final cut of *A Star Is Born* at a preview outside Los Angeles. Whereas Louis B. Mayer—not Jack Warner—and Luft attended an advance screening at Encino, Judy and Vern Alves drove to a theater in Huntingdon, a suburb of Los Angeles.

As Alves remembered it, "She squirmed and moved about all through the showing, at one point cowering down in her seat. At the end, the audience applauded wildly, delivering a standing ovation. She fled from the theater, so as not to be recognized. En route back to Holmby Hills, Alves assured her mile after mile that she was great.

The premiere in Hollywood, on September 29, 1954 at the Pantages Theatre went down in Hollywood history as the last great star-studded premiere that Tinseltown ever held. A mass of 20,000 fans, including the A-list elite of America's entertainment industry, gathered at the theater, most of them awaiting the arrival of Judy. George Cukor called the premiere "the end of an era."

Arriving there by limousine, Marlene Dietrich, escorted by Elia Kazan, made one of the most glamourous entrances. She was followed by stars who included Gary Cooper, Edward G. Robinson, Kim Novak, Rock Hudson, and Ann Miller. Then came Elizabeth Taylor and her husband, the British actor, Michael Wilding. Judy's arrival, as she waved to the crowd, received the loudest screams of approval.

The gala event was followed by an invitation-only party at the Cocoanut Grove, where *tout* Hollywood turned out to applaud Judy for the release of her greatest movie.

Although the film garnered both popular and critical acclaim, it was running too long. For its New York premiere two weeks later, on October 11, Cukor cut down its original 196-minutes to 182 minutes.

The Manhattan premiere was actually held in two different theaters in Midtown, the Victoria and the Capitol. By now, Judy was four months pregnant.

Unlike the relatively calm crowd in Hollywood, the mob assembled in Manhattan went wild and broke through police barricades to get at Judy. In her condition, she feared she'd be faced with physical harm, but Luft and four police officers held back the crowd, allowing her to enter the lobby of one of the theaters, where well-wishers greeted her.

Later that night, she attended a party at the Waldorf Astoria, where she had a reunion with Senator John F. Kennedy, who, as part of an arrangement organized by Robert Stack,

Tennessee Williams, clad in Edwardian finery, introduced Judy to the Italian actress, **Anna Magnani.** She was in America to film the movie adaptation of his hit Broadway play, *The Rose Tattoo*. Her co-star would be Burt Lancaster, who in the future, would also make a film with Judy.

She was surprised to discover that Magnani knew her popular songs. As the drunken evening wore on, Magnani, at a piano with Judy, singing some of her staples, entertained the glamour-soaked guests.

Wanna know more about how three of the the era's starring show-biz writers conducted their feuds?

Released by Blood Moon in 2015, this triple biography reveals how **Tennessee Williams, Gore Vidal, and Truman Capote** remained competitively and defiantly provocative.

Initially hailed by critics as the darlings of the gods, each of them would, in time, be attacked for his contributions to film, the theater, and publishing. Some of their works would be widely reviewed as obscene rantings from perverted sociopaths, nursing betrayals that evolved into lawsuits, stolen lovers, public insults, and the most famous and flamboyant rivalries in America's literary history.

How did they review the big-wigs of Hollywood? The private opinions of these authors about their celebrity acquaintances usually left scar tissue.

had seduced her in 1940. JFK greeted her warmly with a kiss. Standing beside him was Peter Lawford, who introduced Judy to his wife, Patricia Kennedy.

For the most part, reviews were excellent, the best of her life.

Bosley Crowther, of *The New York Times,* hailed *A Star Is Born* as "one of the grandest heartbreak dramas that has drenched the screen in years. George Cukor gets performances from Judy Garland and James Mason that make the heart flutter and bleed."

Time claimed that "Judy Garland delivers what is about the great-

Grace Kelly (depicted above, right, with her co-star, **William Holden**) was no country girl.

Biographer Wendy Leigh wrote: "Both Paramount, for whom Grace Kelly made *The Country Girl*, and MGM, where she was under contract, campaigned heavily for her to win the Best Actress Oscar.

"In contrast, Warner Brothers, for whom Judy Garland made *A Star Is Born*, perhaps because of her volatile temperament , drug use, and repeated absences from the set—hardly campaigned much for her at all."

est one-woman show in modern movie history." *Time's* rival, *Newsweek,* labeled it "a personal triumph for Judy Garland. In more ways than one, the picture is hers."

Variety came out with praise, too. "*A Star Is Born* is a *socko* candidate for anyone's must-see list, scoring on all counts as fine entertainment."

Saturday Review claimed that "her singing strikes straight to the heart."

Douglas McVay in *Musical Films* defined *A Star Is Born* as "the greatest musical picture I have ever seen. This film is a tragic masterpiece."

Film in Review asked, "What picture ever again will give Judy Garland such scope?"

Arriving in Chicago in mid-October for its premiere there, Judy and Luft checked into a suite at the Ambassador East Hotel. Entering the Pump Room later that night, fellow guests rose and gave her a standing ovation. The Chicago premiere was a grand success. Trouble arose the next morning when it came time to pay the bill.

Jack Warner had already received Judy's extravagant bills from her stay in New York and found them "outrageous." He immediately called the hotel manager in Chicago and cut off credit, telling him, "Warners isn't going to pay these ridiculous charges. Tell Luft that he's got to cough up the dough himself."

That depressing news hung over them until their return to Los Angeles. *Picturegoer* magazine voted Judy "Best Actress of the Year," followed by Doris Day in second place for *Love Me or Leave Me* (1955), in which she played the torch singer Ruth Etting opposite James Cagney as her mobster boyfriend. Grace Kelly came in sixth in that magazine's ratings for her performance in *The Country Girl* (1955).

Before *A Star Is Born* went nationwide, theater owners objected to the running time even of its recently truncated version. They made it loudly clear to Warners that, if the film were cut drastically, they could fit another daily screening into theaters around the country, thereby increasing their box office revenues.

Consequently, and pointedly without Cukor's approval, another round of cuts, these more drastic than the first, were made to the film, leaving it with a running length of 154 minutes.

"When I sat through it, I cried," Cukor confessed. "They turned it into a vandalized masterpiece. Entire musical scenes were cut along with some dramatic scenes, especially those defining the Vicki Lester/Norman Maine relationship that I considered vital."

Most critics across the country saw only the final, radically truncated version, so some of their reviews weren't the raves of viewers in Hollywood and New York.

With a production cost of $5 million, *A Star Is Born* became one of the most expensive films ever made. Even though it grossed $6.1 million after its initial release, it showed little profit after all the advertising and final costs were tallied. *[Of course, although it eventually generated additional income, most of that wouldn't come in until years later.]*

***

In Hollywood, Judy and Luft eagerly awaited the news of the Oscar nominations. Most insiders were predicting that Judy would win an Academy Award for *A Star Is Born*. She quickly evolved into the odds-on favorite in the gambling dens of Las Vegas.

When the news was announced, they weren't disappointed. For her

In addition to Judy for *A Star Is Born* and Grace Kelly for *The Country Girl*, the other artists competing for best actress of the year were formidable indeed: They included **Jane Wyman, Dorothy Dandridge, and Audrey Hepburn.**

performance as Vicki Lester, she received a nomination for Best Actress.

Her main competitor was Grace Kelly for *The Country Girl.* In it, she had portrayed the long-suffering wife of an alcoholic singer, Bing Crosby, who co-starred in the film with William Holden. In real life, Kelly was sustaining affairs with both of them.

Also competing for the gold that year was Jane Wyman for *Magnificent Obsession;* Dorothy Dandridge for *Carmen Jones;* and Audrey Hepburn for *Sabrina.*

For his role as Norman Maine in *A Star Is Born,* James Mason was nominated for Best Actor. He faced formidable competition from Marlon Brando for his performance [*"I could have been a contender!]* in *On the Waterfront.* [*Ironically, Mason and Brando had recently appeared together in Julius Caesar.*]

Also in the race was Bing Crosby for *The Country Girl,* although Humphrey Bogart was strong competition for his role in *The Caine Mutiny.* Bogie had already beaten out Brando when he starred in *The African Queen,* winning in 1951 when Brando lost for *A Streetcar Named Desire.*

Grace Kelly graces the cover of the November 1954 issue of *Redbook.*

Soon to be Her Serene Highness, the Princess of Monaco, Kelly's cool beauty has never been eclipsed in Hollywood.

Not expected to win was Dan O'Herlihy for *Adventures of Robinson Crusoe.*

Mason would go down in film history as a three-time nominee but also as a three-time loser, not only for *A Star Is Born,* but also for *Georgy Girl* (1966) and *The Verdict* (1992).

***

In consultation with Dr. Morton, her obstetrician, Judy was told that it was likely that she'd give birth two weeks after the Academy Awards presentation. It had been scheduled for March 30, 1955 at the Pantages Theatre in Hollywood.

He warned her that under the right circumstances, she might be able to attend the ceremony, but precautions had to be taken. It was agreed that she'd discreetly enter the theater through its back entrance and not face the hundreds of fans assembled outside. It was also decided that, like the birth of her other two children, it would be a Caesarean birth, and that during that procedure, her Fallopian tubes would be tied. "Sid and I agree on one thing," she said. "No more kids."

Hoping to attend the ceremony "for one of the most memorable moments of my life," she had already ordered a chic maternity gown that would de-emphasize her swollen midsection.

However, at 11PM on March 28, two days before the Oscar ceremonies, she began to experience premature labor pains. Luft summoned an ambulance, and rode with her in the rear, holding her hand as it raced through the streets, with dome lights flashing, to the Cedars of Lebanon Hospital. After a quick examination by Dr. Morton, she was rushed into emergency surgery.

In the stately lobby of the hospital, Frank Sinatra and Lauren Bacall—later to become lovers—arrived to await the birth, joining Luft and his assistant, Vern Alves.

Not knowing how long they'd be waiting, Sinatra disappeared and returned with a delivery man who wheeled in a cart laden with bottles of wine and food, including pizza. At around 1:30AM Luft disappeared. Hot and sweating, he returned about half an hour later. "It's a boy! Judy's doing fine."

The premature infant weighed five pounds, eight ounces. He was named Joseph Wiley Luft and nicknamed "Joey."

Plans were made for the following evening: Bacall would appear at the Pantages Theatre as a surrogate to receive Judy's Oscar, in the event she won it.

Then Luft left the hospital to check on their daughters at home. He did not inform them that Judy had given birth, leaving that for her to do. Perhaps under sedation, she slept through the night, having convinced herself that "Our son is going to live."

Dr. Morton waited until noon before giving Luft and Judy the bad news: The infant's left lung had not opened, and he had been immediately placed in an incubator. In an attempt to prepare them for the worst, he warned them that Joey had only a fifty-fifty chance of surviving.

Judy burst into tears as Luft held her in his arms, offering what comfort he could.

By four that afternoon, Dr. Morton met again with Judy and Luft to deliver the good news. In the incubator, the infant's left lung had opened, and he was breathing, although a bit irregularly.

For a very brief three minutes, the boy was brought in, allowing Judy to hold him in her arms. "He looked so vulnerable, almost pathetic, but he was my bundle of joy."

After the nurse carried the baby away, Judy put through a call to Liza, informing her that she and Lorna had a baby brother. "Oh, mama," Liza said. "That is what you wanted so much—a dream come true."

In her 1998 memoir, Lorna Luft raised the possibility that her mother's intake of Benzedrine and other barbiturates during her pregnancy with Joey might have cause his birth defect.

She wrote, "Joey still struggles with the long-term effects of our mother's intake of drugs during pregnancy. She lost the Oscar, but Joe's recovery was the best consolation prize she could have gotten."

In fairness to Judy, the conclusion of most doctors at the time was that an unborn fetus was mostly protected from chemicals in the bloodstream of its mother. That theory, after lots of research, was later discounted.

***

Whereas Joan Crawford's Oscar had been awarded to her a decade before Judy's, hers would be presented in the age of television. Luft wanted to import a TV crew to a location beside her hospital bed so that Judy could be photographed in a discussion with Bob Hope, who had already been designated as that year's Master of Ceremonies.

To disrupt a hospital like Cedars of Lebanon, Luft had to pass out several bribes, but finally got permission. A TV camera crew would be brought in so that Judy, from her hospital bed, could be interviewed, live and on the air in front of millions of people. To catalyze a party mood, he also sneaked in two cases of champagne.

The night of the Oscars finally arrived, and Bacall visited Judy at the hospital en route to the ceremony. The motive for their meeting involved coordinating their respective statements and speeches.

Watching the Oscars on TV, Judy was disappointed when the award for Best Song was announced, fully expecting that it would embellish her rendition of "The Man That Got Away." Instead, regretfully, she looked on as it went to "Three Coins in the Fountain."

After what seemed an eternity, the moment came to announce the Best Actress Oscar. There was a murmur across the audience at a surprise upset that horrified Judy and her fans: Grace Kelly was announced as the winner for her performance in *The Country Girl*.

In an interview with reporter Joe Hyams for *Photoplay*, Judy described what happened next: "Just picture this," she said. "There I was in bed, weak and exhausted. The TV men with all their equipment had invaded my room, and I was wired up. A platform had been erected outside my window. I was told that I would be able to talk back and forth to Bob Hope. Believe it or not, these guys had built a four-story high tower outside my window. The camera was pointing at me in my bed. There were people standing on that tower, and there was much excitement. All this activity got me all

For the uncertainties associated with Judy's upcoming Oscar night, Luft was inspired by the experience of **Joan Crawford**.

When she had won her Best Actress Oscar for *Mildred Pierce* (1945), she was in bed with a cold, but a camera crew arrived to photograph her at her home. There, from her bed, she officially accepted the Oscar that the Academy had designated as hers only an hour before.

Oscar winners **Grace Kelly** (*The Country Girl*) and **Marlon Brando** (*On the Waterfront*) walked off with the gold that memorable night.

He later had a prize for her, too, presenting her with what he termed "My noble tool."

worked up, and I was positive I was going to win—and there I was, trying to look cute. Then the guys found out that something was wrong with the sound. So they strung wires all over the room and put a microphone under my bedjacket. I was gearing up to give a performance of acceptance when Hope opened the envelope and called out Grace Kelly's name. I said, 'WHAAAAAT?' I'll never forget it to my dying day. The technicians in my room all said, 'Kelly! Ah!.' Then they started lugging all that equipment out of my hospital room. You should have seen the look on their faces. I really thought I'd go into hysterics."

When she delivered that statement, she was putting up a brave front, with self-deprecating humor. What actually happened when the winner was announced was that she burst into uncontrollable sobbing.

On the verge of a major depression, she directly addressed the television set: "Okay, Kelly, you've got your god damn Oscar, but I've got little Joey, and he's more important than some stupid award. A hundred actresses in Hollywood—maybe thousands—could have played your part just as well or better. And off screen you fucked both Bing Crosby and William Holden."

Luft said, "Kelly gave a cockamamie performance looking dowdy in a sweater and horn-rimmed glasses. Big fucking deal. I never liked her. Too stuck up."

Lauren Bacall gave her own version: "Judy carried it off beautifully, saying that her son Joey was more important than the Oscar. But she was deeply disappointed—and it hurt her greatly. It confirmed her belief that the industry was against her. She knew that it was then or never. Instinctively, all her friends knew the same. She wasn't like any other performer. There was so much emotion involved in her career—in her life—and it was always all or nothing. And although she put on a hell of a front, this was one more slap in the face. She was bitter about it, and for that matter, all those closest to her were, too."

The night she lost the Oscar, hundreds of telegrams were delivered to the hospital. The most famous message of condolence arrived from Groucho Marx. "This is the biggest robbery since Brink's."

There was a footnote to the Academy Awards that year: Grace Kelly disappeared into the night with her fellow Oscar winner, Marlon Brando, for a brief romantic fling.

Someone must have tipped Judy off that Kelly had been seen arriving at Brando's home later that evening. Judy had his phone number, as she had seen him casually at three or four parties, and he had once visited the Lufts at their home.

Henry Willson, the notoriously predatory gay talent agent, dances with a grown-up **Shirley Temple** at a party honoring Judy Garland.

Temple complained to Willson that David O. Selznick, her producer, "wants me to keep my breasts strapped down, but they are my pride and joy."

363

Carlo Fiore, Brando's best friend, answered the phone, and Judy insisted that it was a matter of life and death, and that she must, absolutely MUST, speak to Kelly.

If for no other reason other than curiosity, Kelly accepted Judy's call. "This is Judy Garland," Kelly heard her say. "Judy FUCKING Garland. YOU BITCH! You took what was rightfully mine. Tonight was my last chance for an Oscar. You'll have many chances in your future. This was it for me. I'll never forgive you!" Then she slammed down the phone.

Brando was vastly amused, and he spread the word around Hollywood.

Some people, including columnist Liz Smith, disputed Brando's story, citing the fact that Judy was in the hospital, which would not have allowed her either to be served alcohol or to place late-night calls. [Smith was unaware that Luft had gone to great lengths to arrange both the champagne and the late-night phone service for Judy.]

In fact, when the nurse came in to check on Judy the following morning, she was already deep into an animated conversation with someone on the phone.

Despite the rave reviews and her character's Oscar nomination, *A Star Is Born* did not re-establish Judy as a superstar. Her movie career ground to a virtual standstill except for some minor pictures and a supporting role in another (major) film.

As Gregory Peck recalled, "Judy told me this was her one and only chance to win an Oscar. She deserved that damn honor. After *A Star Is Born*, she'd be off the screen for seven years."

[Although Judy Garland fans would be perpetually devoted to her version, A Star Is Born was remade less successfully in 1976 with Barbra Streisand and Kris Kristofferson, and then remade again in 2018 with Lady Gaga and Bradley Cooper.

POSTSCRIPT: On July 19, 1983, twenty-nine years after its premiere, A Star Is Born had its second premiere, this time with those jarring cuts restored—displayed in the full-length form that George Cukor and Judy Garland had originally crafted. The elite of Hollywood showed up, including Judy's three children, to witness the 're-premiere' of this cinematic masterpiece.

At the end of the showing, pandemonium broke out in the auditorium, with wild clapping and shouts of "BRAVO!"

It was one of Judy's greatest ovations, albeit post-

On the set of *A Star Is Born*, a handsome young actor, **John Carlyle,** met Judy Garland, his goddess.

He became involved with her, remaining inside her orbit even during her desperate years, often coming to her assistance during the very late hours of her (tormented) nights.

She often turned to him for support, eventually pressering him to marry her.

There was a problem: He was gay.

The lower photo illustrates the cover of the memoir he wrote about it .

mortem.

Today, Judy's reissued full-length version of A Star Is Born *is regarded as one of the great musical classics of cinematic history, ranking in the same sublime category as* Casablanca, Gone With the Wind, *and* Citizen Kane.*]*

***

Although the gay (and predatory) talent agent, Henry Willson, is sometimes credited with the invention of "the casting couch," that overused piece of furniture had existed since the creation of Hollywood. Frequently, however, Willson often (some said "always") maneuvered, persuaded, or coerced one of his male clients into having sex.

Although Willson specialized in promoting the "pretty boy movie stars" of the 1950s, he was not personally blessed with good looks himself—far from it. His personality was bitchy, his pear-shaped body was flabby, and he had frizzy hair and a pudgy chin. He was known for a voracious sexual appetite, preying upon well-built young men who were willing to have sex with him with the hope that he could help them break into movies.

For reasons known only to herself, Margaret Truman, daughter of President Harry S Truman, dated Willson for several months, despite her father's harsh protests.

In addition to sexually compromising many young actors, Willson also become well known for renaming them, evaluating their original names as "not worthy of a marquee." Thus, Arthur Gellen became Tab Hunter; Robert Moseley became Guy Madison; Francis Durgin became Rory Calhoun; Carmen Orrico became John Saxon; Nicholas Adamschock became Nick Adams; Merle Johnson morphed into Troy Donahue; and perhaps the most laughable of all, Elmore Rual Torn was re-christened as Rip Torn.

A remarkably handsome young actor, John Carlyle, more than passed Henry Willson's "audi-

Rock Hudson Erotic Fire

Darwin Porter & Danforth Prince

Rock Hudson (dancing with Judy at the Cocoanut Grove in 1958) "was the man of my dreams," she told Kay Thompson. "He took me home from a party hosted by Van Johnson, and he spent the night."

"As far as I was concerned, he could have spent every night of his life in my bed. But alas, as is so often the case, many of the really interesting dreamboats of Hollywood turn out to be gay."

In the dying days of Hollywood's Golden Age, a post office worker, Navy vet, and truck driver named Roy Fitzgerald **(Rock Hudson)** became the most celebrated phallic symbol and lust object in America.

In 2017, Blood Moon described his rise and fall, the inside story of the entertainment industry that created him, and the multiple instances of casting couch persuasions he endured and/or enjoyed.

It applied the tabloid standards of today to the ironies of sexuality during Hollywood's heyday, and the lengths that newsmaking celebrities like Rock took to conceal them.

It's was a tough job, but somebody had to do it.

tion." Before Carlyle , Rock Hudson had "graduated" with flying colors and in time, became Willson's greatest creation, changing his name from Roy Fitzgerald. Hudson eventually emerged as one of the entertainment industry's biggest box office stars in the late 1950s and '60s.

Robert Osborne, long the host of *Turner Movie Classics*, wrote: "Stories about John and Judy Garland on Norma Place (the site of Carlyle's residence) were legendary at the time. 'Madame Gumm,' as he called her, was a perfect playmate for 'the Black Star,' her nickname for Carlyle. During the period they partied together and pilled together, he was mad about her, as he had been for years, and she adored him and his razor-sharp wit. A dangerous combination those two, but for the most part, their relationship seemed to be as much about laughter, pranks, mischievousness, and affection as it was about all the wine and roses that were also part of it."

Many of Carlyle's recollections were can be read in his autobiography *Under the Rainbow; an Intimate Memoir of Judy Garland, Rock Hudson, & My Life in Old Hollywood."* Regrettably, Carlyle died in 2003 and didn't live to see its publication. *[A photo of him with Judy seated on a banquette in a nightclub graced its front cover.]*

His publisher promoted the book with this: "Carlyle takes us on a rare, behind-the-scenes tour of gay Hollywood. He sleeps with Marlon Brando and James Dean, rubs shoulders with another gay actor, Raymond Burr, double dates with Rock Hudson, and watches Montgomery Clift spiral out of control. He befriends Lana Turner, Joan Fontaine, and Hedy Lamarr, 'dances' with Fred Astaire, and is granted a private audience with Mae West."

Regrettably, that advertising material had been distributed in advance of the book's publication, and at the last minute, some of its more risqué details were removed. Some of the items killed within the book's manuscript before publication spun around a one-night sleepover between Rock and Judy. It appeared in its full, original form in Blood Moon's 2017 biography, *Rock Hudson Erotic Fire* based on later revelations by Henry Willson.

***

In the 1950s, Van Johnson invited Rock Hudson to his first A-list Hollywood party. Unfamiliar with how such parties went, Rock was unaware that the hosts usually hired valet parkers to attend to the cars. He parked two blocks away, where he positioned his car in the first available space, and arrived on foot, much to the surprise of the attendants.

As he entered, he heard the sound of Judy Garland's voice, and just assumed it was a recording. But as soon as he was inside the living room, he spotted Oscar Levant playing the piano and Judy herself performing beside him. She had kicked off her shoes and was going through her repertoire. In the far corner of the room, he spotted Elizabeth Taylor seemingly having a tense moment with her new husband, Nicky Hilton.

Rock looked around the room and didn't know anyone. Van Johnson caught his eye and beckoned him to join them. When Johnson introduced Rock to his wife Evie, she looked at him a bit skeptically. "What movies

366

might I have seen you in?" she asked.

"Oh, I'm just getting started. I've done *Fighter Squadron* (1948) and *Undertow* (1949), but I wasn't on the screen for very long in either of them."

Rock told Johnson, "Judy Garland is my favorite female singer. I can't believe I'm getting to see and hear her in person."

"Judy's having a rough time," Johnson answered. "We're filming a movie together called *In the Good Old Summertime,* but nobody is having much fun making it. Judy is unhappy and shows up late for work. And sometimes she doesn't show up at all."

"I'm very sympathetic to her and know the strain she's under," Johnson continued. "She's a real pro. She can read a script and get it right away. Her problem is in the love department—or should I say the lack of love department? Men don't do her right. She's actually the loneliest person I know."

Then Evie said, "Mr. Hudson, I'm glad you like Judy. I just adore her. But she's drunk tonight. Since you arrived stag, I'm going to ask you to take her home. She's all alone."

"I'd like to," he said. "My buddies back in Illinois will never believe this."

"Suddenly, another Hollywood legend, Lana Turner, joined their group. Rock had seen all of her movies, including multiple viewings

Judy perceived herself to be not particularly alluring or glamourous, not at all like the sensual movie goddess, **Lana Turner.**

The lower photo shows Lana getting to know Clark Gable in *Honky Tonk* (1941)

367

of *The Postman Always Rings Twice* (1946).

When he was introduced to Lana by Johnson, who had co-starred with her in *Week-End at the Waldorf* (1945), Rock was shocked. She was not the screen goddess he had envisioned.

As he later told his lover, Bob Preble, "Lana can curse like a sailor. From those succulent lips emerge a torrent of vulgar words."

Lana was in a foul mood that night. Ignoring Rock, she let Evie and Johnson know the cause of her troubles. "Look at him over there," she said, pointing to her husband, the tin plate heir, Bob Topping. "The fucker started drinking at ten this morning. By midnight, I'll need to call for an ambulance. I married him for security, but I'm paying the bills. He's going through every penny he's inherited. Just throwing it away on gambling and in bad investments. Shit! Shit! SHIT! I'm going to dump the asshole. Another failed marriage."

"Perhaps you can make it work," Evie said, sympathetically.

"Like hell I can," Lana said. "The son of a bitch is lousy in bed. His dick's not big enough. As you know, I've been fucked by the best of them. Where is Victor Mature now that I need the big lug? I need another drink." Then she rose abruptly from her chair and staggered off.

As Rock watched Lana leave, he saw Garland approaching.

"Here comes another drunk," Evie said. "Welcome to Hollywood, Mr. Hudson. We're the sweetest, dearest people on earth."

When Evie finally got around to introducing Rock to Judy Garland, she stood on her tiptoes and kissed him on the lips. "What a big, strong, handsome man with a kind, loving face," she said. "The type of man I always fail to attract."

"I'm honored to meet you, Miss Garland. "You're my favorite sinner." She laughed at his mistake. "I mean 'singer.' I've been designated to drive you home tonight."

"We'll see the dawn come up," she answered.

After midnight, he left Garland standing in front of the Johnson home during the time it took to retrieve his car two blocks away. When he returned, he found her laughing and talking to the two valet attendants.

Once he got her into his car, she directed him to Marlene Dietrich's former apartment on Sweetzer Avenue, off Sunset Strip. She explained that she'd recently moved there, leaving her daughter, Liza, with her father, the director Vincente Minnelli, whom she planned to divorce. "He was always more in love with Gene Kelly than with me."

Inside her apartment, she made for the bar, inviting him to get comfortable if he wanted to. "Strip down to your underwear, or whatever. We're very casual around here." Between bouts of drinking, she would disappear into the bathroom, where he suspected she was downing pills.

Although a lot of his manuscript was expunged, actor John Carlyle gave us a preview of the burgeoning Garland/Hudson friendship when he published *Under the Rainbow: An Intimate Memoir of Judy Garland, Rock Hudson, and My Life in Old Hollywood* (2006). Many of the passages in his original manuscript were removed by his editor at Carroll & Graf.

Carlyle remembered driving with his lover, actor Craig Hill, and Rock to a weekend cabin near Lake Arrowhead.

There, according to Carlyle's unexpurgated manuscript, Rock told the two men about his first night with Judy Garland, which marked the beginning of a long friendship and "an occasional fuck," as Rock ungallantly phrased it.

"In good humor, Rock was high camp," Carlyle wrote in his memoir, "a laughing lunatic, but he was a glowering bore when he wasn't. He kept his closet door shut, which he said was hell. His towering melancholy and inherent unhappiness could empty a room, and his buck-toothed haw-haw could convulse the same. The lighter side of him usually prevailed."

"In Judy, Rock found a new friend who could lovingly accept both sides of his personality," Carlyle claimed.

On their first night together, in the early dawn of a Wednesday morning, Judy found a kindred spirit in Rock, and they talked for hours. As Rock later said, "We ripped open each other's insides."

Although he'd been a total stranger, she seemed desperate to talk to someone. "She spoke to me with an openness and candor that I'd never known before. I'd always kept things bottled up. She spoke of her failed marriage to Minnelli and her love for her daughter. 'At times, my husband wore more lipstick than I did,' she said."

"Before Vincente, there was a first marriage to the musician, David Rose," Judy said. "Why did that marriage fail? He told me he was repulsed when I demanded that he perform cunnilingus on me. For that, I have to turn to Hollywood's lesbians. Ethel Merman is very good at it, men usually aren't. I hope you don't have an aversion to it."

"I rarely have any aversion to any kind of sex," he confessed.

"When one of my dark spells comes, it follows with uncontrollable weeping," she said. "I'm not able to sleep, pacing the floor, drinking, and pill popping. I become so tired it's like climbing Mount Everest to perform the simplest task. Even if I go to bed, I just lie there staring at the ceiling."

"When a depression comes over me," he responded, "it's because I get tired of living a lie, not being allowed to be myself. Living a life of pretense can be very exhausting, very demoralizing."

"I can't be myself either," she claimed. "Ever since I was a little girl, I've tried to do what other people wanted me to do. But at times I can't even do that. Something inside me clicks, and I rebel. Even as a kid, I was a born trouper, come hell or high water. Today, I'm known for not showing up and leaving cast and crew standing around waiting for me. I don't know how long Louis B. Mayer is going to put up with my shit. But I can't help myself."

"My reputation in Hollywood was de-

According to **Joan Blondell,** who's depicted above with **Douglas Fairbanks, Jr.:**

"All of us—Tallulah Bankhead, Marlene Dietrich, Noel Coward, and (Sir) Laurence Olivier—had the hots for Doug."

stroyed a long time ago," she continued. "Perhaps you spend too much time worrying about your reputation before you've even begun to build one. People will believe anything, good or bad, about movie stars. I should know. You get used to it. Of course, lies have shock value, and they can still hurt."

When the first streaks of dawn began breaking through the windows, she invited him to come out and enjoy the sunrise. He stood with his arm around her, watching the sun rise in the east.

"I fear every morning when the sun comes up," she said, "and I have to go out in the world and be Judy Garland."

Then she turned to him. "Now take me to the bedroom and fuck hell out of me."

When he woke up the next morning, it was after eleven o'clock. As he stumbled toward the bathroom, he found a note, hastily scribbled, "You're welcome to put your shoes under my bed any night. Love, Judy."

***

John Carlyle also recalled, "I only went to bed with Henry Willson to advance my career. I thought he was repulsive. He did get me a small part in *A Star Is Born,* which led to a sort of 'death-until-we-part' relationship with Judy."

"Naturally, that jerk, Willson, had me go over to George Cukor's house for one of his notorious all-male pool parties," Carlyle said. "I had to do this on two occasions, each time submitting to a blow job from Cukor, who was even more repulsive than Willson."

It wasn't much of a part. Carlyle would appear as an assistant director "in a movie within a movie." His segment depicted a film being made that starred Norman Maine (James Mason). It was one of those Errol Flynn swashbuckler movies, depicting the star as too intoxicated to pull off the scene, showing how his career was falling apart.

At the time Judy met Carlyle, he was appearing as a secondary character alongside Natalie Wood and Carleton Carpenter in General Electric's made-for-TV movie *Feathertop* (1954). Willson was billing him as "the new

Although **Frank Sinatra** never offered to marry **Judy Garland**, he was always protective of her, the way he had been with Marilyn Monroe. He spoke frequently about Judy to his fourth and final wife, Barbara Marx.

One night, he arranged for them to meet: "She was so enormous and puffy-faced," Barbara said. "It was sad to see her like that."

Frank was such a loyal friend that he opted to be with Judy the night Liza Minnelli was born. "I ordered pizzas for the waiting group of Judy loyalists," he said. "When I first heard cries from Lisa's throat, I knew a star had been born."

370

Montgomery Clift," and was organizing dates for him with Natalie Wood for publicity purposes. "She was gorgeous, very melancholy, and horny, with *horny* being the operative word," Carlyle said. "It was not unusual for Natalie to be at some party and go off into the bedroom and make out with some guy. You could walk into a dark room and there was Natalie going at it."

One day on the set of *A Star Is Born*, he noticed that Judy was sitting nearby "staring at me with an appreciative eye. I was playing the make-believe assistant director in the film when the real-life assistant director of the film, Mecca Graham, took me over to meet Miss Garland in the flesh. She was trying to light a cigarette. As it turned out, we both liked menthol-laced Spud cigarettes, and I held out my lighter. That simple gesture marked the beginning of a tumultuous relationship that would stretch over years until I placed that fateful call to her London flat to discover that she was dead."

"Frank and **Sid** shared one thing in common," said Lana Turner. "Both men were a volcano and might erupt at any minute. Poor Judy. I knew she'd end up with many a black eye from Sid. He was known by his prizefighter name, 'One-Punch Luft.'"

"I was born angry," he told Judy on their honeymoon."

"Let's understand each other right from the beginning," she said. "You like the boys, don't you? Or did I misread you?"

"Who doesn't like boys?" he answered.

She laughed. "I think we'll get along just fine."

Her prediction was correct.

***

[POSTSCRIPT: *When Carlyle attended his first screening of* A Star Is Born, *he was devastated to discover that his scene had ended up on the cutting room floor. "I had to prostitute myself for that," he lamented.*]

***

When Dolly Sinatra went with her son, Frank, to see Judy Garland as Dorothy in *The Wizard of Oz* (1939), he told her after the show, "I'm gonna marry that gal one day."

As life turned out, she would propose marriage to him, not the other way around.

Their romance blossomed in 1949 when both were in New York and secretly headed for a house in the Hamptons which belonged to a mob friend of Frank's.

Judy was on the verge of a nervous breakdown, as her marriage to her gay husband, Vincente Minnelli, was all but over. Their divorce would be finalized in 1951.

In the Hamptons, walking along the beaches, Judy shared many memories of Hollywood in the late 1930s before Frank arrived. She remembered at the age of thirteen when Louis B. Mayer would routinely summon her to his office, where he would "grope my adolescent breasts, which were more perky then than full."

According to all reports, Judy and Frank turned out to be very compatible sexually, but he found personality problems he'd never encountered before. She suffered from insomnia and often paced the floor at night, haunted by demons.

She also was in need of constant self-assurance. He liked to be alone to read and to talk to friends on the phone, but she seemed to resent his attention being diverted elsewhere.

"I like Judy a lot, and, except for me, she's the most popular singer in America," he told Ava Gardner. "But she can be suffocating. I don't like it when you bang a chick, and she wakes up the next morning thinking you're going to marry her."

He later told Peter Lawford, "I broke with Judy because neurotic women are not my *cuppa*."

One night, back in Hollywood, Judy called Joan Blondell at around 10PM. She contacted Joan only when something major was going on in her life. Both actresses identified with each other, having grown up in vaudeville and having had nothing but trouble from the men they loved. years later, Blondell repeated much of the information relayed in this chapter directly to the senior co-author of this book, Darwin Porter, during many visits to his home, Magnolia House, on Staten Island.

Judy begged her to come over for dinner, and Joan told her she'd already eaten. But after listening to her protests, Joan finally gave in. When she arrived at Judy's home, she found an elegantly set table, still under the glow of candlelight.

Judy confided in her, "Frank was due here for supper. He stood me up."

An hour later she disappeared into her bathroom and emerged looking drugged. Whatever she'd taken seemed to have loosened her tongue. "I'm in love with Frank. He's going to marry me. It's all set. He's definitely going to be my next husband."

"But he stood you up tonight," Joan said, trying to bring reality into the conversation.

"He was just too busy to call," Judy said. Joan feared Judy was heading for major heartbreak. It became four o'clock in the morning, but Judy still wanted her to stay. She insisted that Joan go into Liza's room where the little girl was sleeping.

Judy picked her up tenderly and began to sing "Over the Rainbow" to Liza in a cracked voice. "Tears were running

The Montana Mule (Gary Cooper) with **Helen Hayes** in *A Farewell to Arms* (1932).

down Judy's face," Joan said. "She crooned the song so gently, so softly, embracing the baby with her eyes, her voice, her arms, seeing perhaps her own youth."

Later Judy collapsed on the floor of her living room, and Joan covered her with a fur rug and quietly left the house.

"I will remember that night forever," Joan said. "And where was Frank? Probably fucking some Las Vegas showgal."

Judy's relationship with Minnelli had reached the screaming stage, and Frank would not accept her phone calls any more, especially her desperate pleas at four o'clock in the morning. She was plagued with migraine headaches and insomnia, and there was more. Her hair had begun to fall out in clumps.

Judy's contract with MGM was suspended as of May 10, 1949.

From her home, Judy placed an urgent call to Frank, although his career also seemed in a hopeless slump. This time, he took her call, hoping to cheer her up. He didn't want to marry her, but he sure as hell didn't want her to commit suicide. "We'll come back," he told her. "We'll show the bastards. One day in the near future we'll come back bigger than before." His golden voice had a hollow ring.

The next time he heard from Judy was on May 29, 1949. She had checked into the Peter Bent Brigham Hospital in Boston. She was deep into a nervous breakdown, but still had hopes of getting back with Frank. She still fantasized about a possible marriage. Even in her drugged condition, those hopes grew slimmer every day, Frank claiming, "Let's just be friends."

In spite of their occasional rifts, Frank was always there for Judy when she faced her latest crisis. During her stay in the Boston hospital, he did more than send flowers every day. He even flew in a planeload of friends from Hollywood to cheer her up.

When Judy married Sid Luft in 1952, Frank breathed a sigh of relief. "Now I can bed her from time to time, without her asking me if she can become the next Mrs. Frank Sinatra," he told Lawford. "Of course, Luft is one prick son-of-a-bitch. Poor Judy. She doesn't know how to pick her men. She went from the bed of that faggot Minnelli into the bed of a whore-chaser."

Even during the course of her marriage to Luft, Judy's affair with Frank continued on an on-again, off-again basis.

Judy learned the hard way not to cross Frank. In Las Vegas, he had made the Copa Room at the Sands Resort a platform from which he was doing it "My Way," and expecting his friends to perform at the Sands exclusively. When Judy accepted an engagement at another hotel, he called her and denounced her as a "broken down, drunken old bag, and fat to boot."

"My playing the New Frontier was strictly a showbiz deal," Judy said. "But Frank took it as a personal insult to him. He became really repulsive to me and started making fun of me in his act."

One time on stage he said, "Judy Garland tried to fly Over the Rainbow but was too fat and fell on her ass." The audience didn't laugh.

Yet by December of 1954, Frank had forgiven her for her "disloyalty."

373

He invited her to join him to hear her friend Mel Tormé at the Crescendo on Sunset Boulevard in Hollywood. On the way out, Jim Byron, Tormé's publicist, saw Frank leaving but didn't recognize Judy, who was pregnant. As he was leaving, Frank heard Byron call out to someone, "Who's that broad with Sinatra tonight?"

Byron entered a phone booth to call a newspaper with a late deadline. He wanted to get a plug in a column for his client, Tormé.

Frank rushed back and headed for the phone booth, yelling at Byron, whom he had mistaken for a newspaper reporter. "Take off your glasses, you leech. I'm gonna beat the shit out of you. I'm tired of you fuckers who spend your lives sucking off other people."

Frank slammed his fist into Byron's face, bloodying his nose. Byron struck back but a hotel attendant separated them. As Kitty Kelley quoted in her biography of Frank, the next day he gave his own version. "Byron was trying to make it seem like an illicit date or something. Me, with a star six months pregnant. I told him I resented him calling Judy a broad, and I told him if he didn't know who Judy Garland was, he must have been living under a rock. Suddenly two guys held my arms and Byron tried to knee me. He dented my shin bone and clawed my hand. I broke loose. It ended when I gave him a left hook and dumped him on his ass."

***

The Holmby Hills Rat Pack was formed in 1955, with Frank Sinatra as pack master and Judy as first vice-president. Lauren Bacall was den mother, and her husband, Humphrey Bogart, was named rat-in-charge-of-public relations. It was Judy who eventually brought in President John F. Kennedy, making him an honorary Rat Packer.

374

Whenever the Rat Pack—(left to right) **Frank Sinatra, Dean Martin, Sammy Davis Jr., Peter Lawford, and Joey Bishop**—appeared at The Sands in Las Vegas, the box office quickly sold out of tickets. "We never knew what these guys were going to do," said a former manager. "Strip down to their underwear,? Maybe rape Angie Dickinson on stage? Tell the audience that July Garland was a secret dyke?"

Whenever he wasn't performing and wanted to see a show, such as the rare appearance of Noël Coward in Vegas, Frank flew the extended members of the Rat Pack in to stay free at the Sands. "Some of us weren't really into the scene," said David Niven, the English actor. "Gamblers and mobsters, all very *déclassé.*"

That former Sands manager also made a startling revelation—at least startling for that time. After endless repetitions, including the appearance of his story within *Variety*, it's not so revelatory any more:

"Once, Frank arrived with Katharine Hepburn and Spencer Tracy. Privately, he arranged sexual trysts for them—a beautiful showgal for Hepburn ('absolutely no skin blemishes whatsoever,' she demanded) and a virile young male dancer for that dear old closeted faggot, Spencer Tracy."

Vincente Minnelli, who had long since divorced Judy, signed to direct Frank in *Some Came Running* (1958). He suggested that Judy might be ideal for one of the female leads. "There's no way in hell I'm gonna do a picture with her," Frank said. "Life's too short for that." The role eventually went to Frank's pal, Shirley MacLaine.

The other male co-star of the film, Dean Martin, read the script and asked, "Why not Judy? After all, the plot calls for a luckless floozie stuck on Sinatra."

Judy and Frank shared violent and suicidal episodes in each other's lives. In the late 1950s, Judy went with him and Peter Lawford to a dinner party at the home of Gary Cooper. Even for the Rat Pack, it was a heavy drinking night. The talk grew more raucous as the evening progressed. Judy seemed to down more liquor than anyone.

In a huddle in the corner with Lawford and Cooper, Judy became quite provocative. She was on drugs that night. "Where I go," she said to Cooper, "my size queens ask me who's got the biggest one—you, Mr. Montana Mule, or Frankie. You should really go into the bathroom with me and put on an exhibition so I can judge for myself. Men are not to be trusted when it comes to giving the exact measurements of their dicks."

"You'll never find out, Judy," Cooper replied. "Ask Marlene Dietrich. She's gone to bed with both Frank and me."

At that point, Cooper jumped up at the sound of breaking glass. Frank had thrown a blonde bimbo through a plate glass window. Blood was everywhere. Judy screamed, and Cooper rushed to the woman's rescue. It was later discovered that the young woman's arm was nearly severed.

Aided by Frank's friend, Jimmy Van Heusen, Cooper called an ambulance to come to his home at once.

Judy had rushed to Frank's aid. His white shirt was covered in blood. Somehow he'd cut himself on the jagged glass. Lawford and Judy helped him into the kitchen where they cleaned him up. His injury was only a flesh wound, and he didn't need to go to the hospital.

Lawford and Judy stumbled out Cooper's front door, where he stood waiting for the ambulance. "No one told Coop what a good time we'd had," said Lawford. "There had been just too much liquor and too many drugs that night. We were a mess. We really put on a horror show for Coop. Frank never told us what that gal said to him that made him react so violently. Another Hollywood night, another Hollywood party. I found out later that the girl was paid off, and it never got in the papers."

Many intimates knew how much Judy still wanted to marry Frank, including his valet, George Jacobs, who witnessed the relationship up close and personal.

***

"The Rat Pack consists of two Dago singers, a kike comic, a limey swell, a hot puta with red pussy hair, and a slightly off-color entertainer."
[His reference was to Frank Sinatra, Dean Martin, Joey Bishop, Peter Lawford, Shirley MacLaine, and himself.]

—**Sammy Davis, Jr.**

"During the heyday of the Rat Pack, of which I was a notorious member, Frank in the wee hours of the morning seemed to be in a marathon race with loneliness chasing on his heels. I know that feeling."

—Judy Garland

"When he gets to heaven, Frank's gonna give God a hard time for making him bald."

—Marlon Brando

Singer Eddie Fisher claimed that he was present at the "beginning of the end of the Rat Pack."

He performed at the Desert Inn in Las Vegas in 1961. That was followed by an engagement at the Cocoanut Grove in Los Angeles. *Le tout Hollywood* showed up for his opening, including Frank and his fellow Rat Packers, the tribe that he was still calling "The Summit." Their partying had begun long before Fisher's appearance onstage.

Fisher viewed his opening at the Grove as a sort of comeback after eighteen months out of work except for that Vegas gig. As he started to sing, Frank, Sammy, and Peter started heckling him. On wobbly legs, this trio of Rat Packers climbed onto the stage to take over Fisher's performance.

Hopelessly giving up, Fisher took a seat while Frank and his cronies went into a drunken routine, a sloppy rehash of what had been well-received a few months before in Vegas. The audience shouted down the Rat Packers, including Frank. The boos became so strong that management sent two burly waiters to remove the drunks from the stage.

With them out of the way, Fisher mounted the stage again and asked his fans, "Join me in singing 'God Bless America' to show President Kennedy we're behind him." That brought loud clapping.

Fisher was a bit too hasty in predicting the demise of the Rat Pack, but the peak of their popularity certainly faded that night at the Cocoanut Grove.

Frank went on to develop *Sergeants 3* (1962), with his Rat Pack buddies, Dean Martin, Sammy Davis Jr., Joey Bishop, and Peter Lawford. It was an updating of *Gunga Din*, based on the Rudyard Kipling poem that had first been made at RKO in 1939. From India, the setting moved to the American West of the early 1870s, where hard-drinking, lusty calvary officers (each played by a Rat Packer) play anti-heroic jokes on each other while rescuing the U.S. Army from an Indian ambush.

It was less successful than *Ocean's 11*, *Variety* calling it "warmed over *Gunga Din*, with American-style Indians and Vegas-style soldiers of fortune."

"Of course, these are not great movies," Frank said. "But you know what's great about them? They make money, and isn't that the name of the game?"

***

Before and after he married Elizabeth Taylor, Eddie Fisher had been an occasional presence in the life of Judy Garland. Their first seduction of each other had actually occurred when he was married to Debbie Reynolds. He told Judy, "Debbie just can't satisfy me sexually. She won't do all the things you do."

Two views of **Eddie Fisher**—the first, doing what he did best, singing in front of a mike.

In the lower photo, he's doing what he did worst, being a husband to **Debbie Reynolds.**

Fisher and Reynolds often showed up at Sinatra's house for an all-night party. According to Eddie Fisher, "We were regulars on Frankie's A-list. Debbie often didn't want to go. Judy filled in for her on those nights, if you get my drift. Frankie also had a bedroom free for some action. Judy and I often entertained around his piano, later disappearing upstairs."

Fisher and Judy could be quite confidential with each other. After Reynolds co-starred with Bette Davis in *The Catered Affair* (1956) by Gore Vidal, Davis sometimes showed up at the gatherings. "I couldn't wait for her to leave," Fisher confided to Judy. "Davis was no longer the great screen diva I'd seen in Philadelphia growing up. She was a washed-out ugly drunk, who sat on the sofa making drool eyes at me. If she thought I was going to slip around and hop her, she was sadly mistaken. Judy, yes, Davis, no."

In 1966, when Judy appeared at The Palace, Fisher was booked in to follow her. "She almost burned down the joint," he said. "She was fighting with Sid Luft, and she started a fire in her dressing room. It was a big fire and could have put her in jail. I had to dress in her 'charcoal room,' which still hadn't been restored after she set it on fire."

"I loved Judy," he wrote in his memoirs. "Figuratively and literally. Back during my marriage to Debbie, Judy and I fell in love. I was going to divorce Debbie and marry Judy. She could satisfy me sexually. And Debbie

377

could not. Then along came Elizabeth Taylor, and, for Judy, I became another of those men that got away."

Thus, Judy always appears on the list of Eddie Fisher's high-profile seductions, in such good company as Marlene Dietrich, Edie Adams, Pier Angeli, Ann-Margret, Mia Farrow, Hope Lange, Merle Oberon, Stephanie Powers, Juliet Prowse (shared with Sinatra), Maria Schell, Mamie Van Doren, and dozens of hookers (a different one every night) from coast to coast. An oddity on the list is Judith Campbell Exner, who divided her duties among President John F. Kennedy, mobster Sam Giancana, and Fisher himself.

In *Gilda* (1946), **Rita Hayworth** starred in her most famous role as a seductive temptress in love with Glenn Ford, both on and off the screen.

Released after World War II, *Gilda* became a major hit, applauded by hundreds of thousands of U.S. soldiers returning in droves from wartime service overseas.

In it, their favorite pinup (Hayworth) was blown up on the screen and acting out one erotically charged scene after another.

***

Judy Garland's on-again, off-again love affair with the "playboy prince," Aly Khan, has escaped the attention of all but a few biographers. In its day, it was more whispered about than written about.

Once a tabloid headliner, with dozens of *exposés* devoted to him, Aly Khan came to the attention of most Americans during his widely publicized marriage (1949-1953) to the love goddess of the film industry in the 1940s, Rita Hayworth.

As Hayworth famously said, "He fell in love with *Gilda* and woke up with me."

Aly was the son of Sultan Mahommed Shah (aka Aga Khan III), the spectacularly wealthy leader of the Nizari Ismaili Muslims. As a prerequisite for marrying him, Rita, a Roman Catholic, gave up her film career.

Party giver Elsa Maxwell, the world's most famous hostess, was privy to the romance between Aly and Judy. She once said, "He had thousands of mistresses, and made love to more women than he could count. Often, he seduced big names, not only Rita but Gene Tierney, who wanted to marry him after John F. Kennedy turned her down. There were many more: Kim Novak, Marilyn Monroe, Zsa Zsa Gabor, Merle Oberon, Joan Fontaine, Yvonne De Carlo, and last, but certainly not least, Judy Garland."

One of his lovers, the French singer, Juliette Greco, said, "I don't know who hasn't gone to bed with Aly."

Edith Piaf, the great French singer, once said, "Aly had a perverse streak in him. He told me that during the course of a week in an Egyptian boy bordello, he seduced twenty-eight comely boys."

The fashion designer, Oleg Cassini, was a friend of Aly's. He was once married to Tierney, but "we were too sophisticated to allow any jealousy

ALY KHAN
The Playboy Prince; 1911-1960

A priapic and deeply obsessed womanizer, Aly Khan was a tabloid staple of the 1940s and 50s. He was the widely celebrated only son of an aristocratic Italian mother and the Aga Khan III (1877-1957), the third-generation descendent of a tribal prince who had provided military assistance to the British durng the First Anglo-Afghan War (1841–1842).

Aly Khan's youth was spent in opulent settings in cities thoughout the Middle East and Europe, especially the U.K. He had been reared and educated with the understanding that he would one day shoulder the responsibilities of his lineage, that of a counselor, advisor, and sustainer of the Nizari Ismailian sect of Muslims. They did not occupy a clearly delineated land mass, but were instead scattered widely in close-knit communties across the Middle East, South Asia, and Africa (especially Kenya).

Prince Aly, alas, did not live up to the conservative standards of his well-educated forebears, showing instead a taste for opulence, celebrity flashbulbs, wanton promiscuity, and overspending. As a slap in his face, his father deliberately bypassed him in the rites of succession in favor of Aly's son (i.e, the Aga Khan III's grandson.) Today the Aga Khan IV (born in 1936) bears the title and controls the wealth that might otherwise have gone to the Playboy Prince.

The Playboy Prince died in 1960 at the age of forty-eight after a fatal automobile smash-up in a suburb of Paris, He was buried on the grounds of Château de l'Horizon in the south of France. In 1972, they were moved to a mausoleum in Syria.

To many of the survivors who remember him today, he's interpreted as a bizarre, flamboyantly decadent failure, a cosmopolitan blip on the radar screen of the postwar landscape.

Three views of
PRINCE ALY KHAN

Upper photo: Clad in formal attire, he's at the horse races at Longchamps, outside Paris.

Middle photo: On the French Riviera in May of 1949, he's with **Rita Hayworth**, love goddess of the American film world. When they married (she was already pregnant), it created an international tabloid frenzy. At the reception, guests consumed 600 bottles of champagne and fifty pounds of caviar. During the first months of their marriage, a daughter, Yasmin, was born.

Lower photo: He's with **Elsa Maxwell,** the flamboyant American gossip columnist and "professional hostess." According to Maxwell, "Whenever Aly fell in love with a woman, it was madly and deeply, if only for the night. But In Judy Garland's case, it survived at infrequent intervals over a period of years. It was destined for heartbreak...one of thousands of mistakes she made."

to come into our relationship. He once told me that he was famed in certain circles for his skill at cunnilingus, sometimes demonstrating his skill on three different women in a day. He drove Judy Garland up the wall."

Judy confided to Kay Thompson, Ann Miller, and June Allyson that Aly had a "Herculean staying power. He could go for hours. He kept a large bucket of ice beside the bed during intercourse. If he neared a climax, he would thrust his arms into the bucket of ice water to prevent ejaculation. Then he'd start all over again, giving a woman multiple orgasms."

"Aly and I both made love to Judy Garland," said Orson Welles, the ex-husband of Rita Hayworth. "He was far better at sex than I was. He told me that as a teenager in Egypt, he had learned the Arabic sexual technique known as *Imsaik*. One mastered, a man could go for hours in intercourse, taking time out for a cigarette while still imbedded."

Louella Parsons once asked Aly about his affair with Judy. He gave her an enigmatic answer. "I must have women around me. Life means nothing without them."

Luft and Judy flew to the French Riviera after the filming of *A Star Is Born*, staying in a suite at the very posh Hotel du Cap, near Antibes. Prince Aly had booked a suite there, too. According to the staff, when Luft went off on one of his gambling binges in Nice, Judy was spotted slipping in and out of Aly's suite.

Later, the prince invited both Luft and Judy to his stud farm in Normandy. Whereas Luft accepted, Judy remained behind.

In a memoir, Luft wrote that he and Prince Aly "had a mutual passion for horses, women, and fast cars." From his base in Deauville, Aly once drove Luft at 130 MPH along the roads of the Norman coast. Luft later claimed, "I'm not making this up, but Aly had three mistresses stationed at various inns *en route*. Before the sun set, he stopped at three different inns for sex with each of them, while I cooled my heels downstairs with a bottle of wine."

He also wrote that Aly lavished expensive gifts on them, a diamond and ruby brooch for Judy, a pair of sapphire and diamond cufflinks for Luft.

At one point, Judy told Hedda Hopper that, "For the first time, I'm in love." The gossip columnist spoke to her assistants, "She was married to Luft, but I knew she meant Prince Aly. She was seen coming and going from his bungalow on the grounds of the Beverly Hills Hotel."

There were various sighting over the years. On October 16, 1957, at the Savoy Grill in London, they were seen having lunch together. She was in the British capital to give a concert at the Dominion Theatre. After lunch, according to the staff, she disappeared into his suite until it was time to go to the theater.

In mid-March of 1958, Judy, Lorna, Liza, and Joey arrived in Manhattan, checking into the Drake Hotel. Aly was also in town, occupying a suite at the Waldorf Astoria.

Judy needed not only his love making, but his advice, even his financial assistance. "I'm in deep trouble," she confessed. "The IRS and the income tax authorities of the State of New York are threatening me."

Before leaving Hollywood, she had hired attorney Jerry Geisler to represent her in what she envisioned as an upcoming divorce from Luft. [*Later, for a while, at least, the couple reconciled.*] She visited the prince at the Waldorf, and he aided her financially.

Two days later, Elsa Maxwell phoned Judy at the Drake. Beset by personal and financial woes, Judy had been crying all day. Maxwell was throwing a party for Prince Aly, and she invited Judy as a guest of honor. At first, she refused to attend "because I look awful," but she finally accepted, pulling herself together as best she could.

At the party, where the elite of New York was gathered, including columnist Dorothy Kilgallen, Aly paid little attention to Judy, although he had only recently been loving and kind. All his attention was focused instead on a blonde beauty from Denmark, who a year or two before had held the beauty title of "Miss Denmark."

"It was painfully obvious that Aly had moved on," Judy said. "We had reached the stage in our relationship of 'let's be friends.' I left the party early. File Prince Aly into the category of men that got away."

[*POSTSCRIPT: In Hollywood, Rita Hayworth, Aly's divorced wife, had been studying with Kay Thompson to improve her dancing and vocal techniques.*

One day, Judy visited her at her studio as Rita was leaving. The two women had been longtime rivals when Harry Cohn at Columbia had billed Rita as his studio's answer to MGM's Judy and Fox's Betty Grable.

Running into Judy in the hallway, Rita said, "I see we have the same taste in men." No doubt she was referring to Orson Welles and Prince Aly.

On May 12, 1960, while Judy was in bed, resting, Luft phoned her. "It's just come over the radio from Paris. Aly is dead."

Two years after his appointment as Pakistan's ambassador to the United Nations, Aly had sustained massive head injuries in an automobile accident in a suburb of Paris after his speeding car collided with another vehicle. In the car with him was his pregnant fiancée, Bettina Graziani, a fashion model who survived with only minor injuries.

His Royal Highness died shortly after he was rushed to a local hospital. His remains were later reinterred from France and shipped to a monumental grave in Syria.]

***

Jack Warner decided to take another chance and to risk casting Judy in the namesake role of *The Helen Morgan Story* (1957), the saga of the torch singer of the 1920s and '30, who descended into alcoholism. He'd have to make sure that she was physically and emotionally capable, since her delays and various illnesses had massively increased the costs of *A Star Is Born*.

He selected Michael Curtiz as its director and called him in for a conference. When Warner pitched the plot line of the Morgan story to him, Curtiz said, "It sounds like the life story of Garland herself. Personally, I think she's so unreliable these days that she won't be able to finish this or any other picture. Why not Peggy Lee?"

"I want an actress, not a nightclub singer," Warner replied.

"Well, you've got Doris Day under contract," Curtiz said.

"Been there, done that," Warner said. "She turned it down. Said she found the life of Helen Morgan too sordid for her. I want to cast Paul Newman as her gangster lover."

"Sounds like a role for James Cagney, not pretty boy Newman."

"Cagney these days would be up for grandfather parts," Warner said. "If Judy doesn't work out, perhaps Susan Hayward. She delivered a brilliant performance with a dubbed voice as Jane Forman in *With a Song in My Heart* (1951)."

The idea was pitched to Newman and, "to break the ice," Curtiz asked him to deliver the script to Judy. An appointment was set up for him to bring it to her the following afternoon.

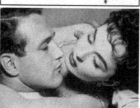

The **Helen Morgan Story** derived from the biography of a torch singer whose intensity rivaled that of Judy herself.

Paul Newman, its male star, lobbied unsuccessfully for its producers to hire Judy as the film's female lead. In the photo, Newman is shown romancing actress **Ann Blyth,** who was awarded the the role of the doomed Helen Morgan instead.

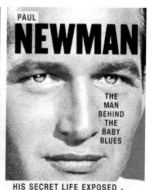

HOW MUCH DO YOU REALLY KNOW ABOUT "THE MAN BEHIND THE BABY BLUES?

Here's the front cover of Blood Moon's 2009 "insider's overview" of the ambisexual and "impossibly handsome" Navy veteran **(Paul Newman)** who steadily climbed the rungs of the Hollywood ladder—rung by seductive bisexual rung.

Arriving at Judy's house, Newman found her alone and a bit intoxicated. Did all screen legends drink in the afternoon? She no longer looked like Dorothy in *The Wizard of Oz,* but she still possessed a certain allure and a charm that he found mesmerizing. He didn't know if he were looking at the real Judy or the reel Judy. Instead of actually seeing what she looked like today, he envisioned her in all those Technicolor MGM movies from the 1940s.

"I once met Helen Morgan," she said. "Of course, I was a mere babe at the time, part of an act called The Gumm Sisters. Don't you love it?"

As the afternoon deepened, and as he and Judy talked, he realized how very different she was from Susan Hayward, who had absolutely no sense of humor. Judy, in contrast, had a quick wit and a gift for self-satirization. She was, in fact, the single most fascinating woman he'd ever encountered.

"I'm sure you've read all about me," she said. "Who in hell hasn't? The pills, the booze, the failed marriages. My being broke all the time. My being temperamental on the set or not showing up for work at all. My getting fired from gigs like *Annie Get Your Gun.*"

"I don't believe what I read in the papers."

She giggled. "In my case, it's all true, but don't hold that against me.

Clouds always get in my way." She moved over and joined him on the sofa. "But I'll change for this picture with that psycho bastard, Curtiz. I want to play Helen Morgan opposite you. I like you, kid. You and I can pull off this picture. Make it a big hit. I don't know you, but I feel there's a definite chemistry between us." She gently ran her hand across his cheek. "You like a woman on occasion, don't you?"

"Are you kidding?" he asked in astonishment. "I don't know what rumors you've heard, but I adore women, on all occasions. I adore you."

She kissed him gently on the lips. "If you do—and I think you're telling the truth—I want you to take me dancing tonight. I love to go dancing."

***

Five hours and five drinks later at the Cocoanut Grove, Paul sat with Judy at a secluded table. She seriously discussed why she wanted to do *The Helen Morgan Story*. "It gives me a chance to sing and be a dramatic actress." She clutched her throat. "My voice is my curse. I got cast in all those frothy musicals, but what I really wanted to be was a dramatic actress. Play Laurette Taylor's part in *The Glass Menagerie*. I could do that. Makeup could age me a bit." She uttered a little laugh that sounded like suppressed hysteria. "Of course, these days it wouldn't take much makeup to age me."

"Judy, you can do anything," he assured her. "Musicals, drama."

"You bet your left nut I can," she said. "Mickey Rooney and I are the most talented performers ever to walk through the gates of MGM. Hell, I could have become the most dramatic actress in the world, if those fucking bastards like Louis B. Mayer had given me a chance." She looked at her empty glass and then gazed into his blue eyes. "Order me another drink, sugar. The night's still young."

It was at that moment that a strikingly handsome man with a beautiful blonde danced by their table. He looked vaguely familiar. Suddenly, Paul realized he was staring into the eyes of Robert Stack, whom he hadn't seen since his days in the Navy.

Stack came to an abrupt stop. "Paul? Paul Newman? I can't believe it. And out with my favorite gal, Judy herself. Hi, Judy." He bent over and kissed her on the lips, as he let go of the blonde beauty. The blonde leaned over and kissed Judy on the cheek.

"Paul Newman, meet the one and only Lana Turner," Judy said. "And, Robert, why did you stop calling?" She faked a mock jealousy as she eyed Lana. She turned to Paul. "This sultry goddess here steals all my men."

"Nice to meet you, Paul," Lana said, "and, Judy, you know I don't take your

Robert Stack in 1960 as Eliot Ness, leading a group of Federal agents against the Chicago Mob in *The Untouchables*, a hit TV series

383

men. It was you who shacked up with one of my husbands." She was referring to the musician Artie Shaw.

Switching from Judy to Paul, Lana extended her hand. "You almost got to make love to me."

"Have I lost my chance forever?" he asked smugly, taking in her beauty. He glanced furtively at Stack, also taking in his beauty. He felt awkward, not knowing what to say to him. He managed a "Long time, no see, buddy." Then it was back to Lana. "Exactly what did you mean about that making love thing?"

"You may not know this, but I was originally thought of for the Virginia Mayo part in *The Silver Chalice.*"

"Maybe you could have saved that turkey," he said.

[A "sword and sandal" saga released in 1954, The Silver Chalice *was the film that Paul Newman famously and frequently cited as his worst movie and his worst movie-making experience.]*

Stack joined Judy at table, while Paul asked Lana for a dance. On the floor, he whispered to her, "Wait until the gang back in Shaker Heights hears I danced with the glamorous Lana Turner."

"Someday maybe you'll be my leading man," she whispered back. "With all the privileges that entails."

"That would be a dream come true," he said. "After all, Tinseltown *is* the Dream Factory."

Stack and Judy joined them on the dance floor. Judy broke from Robert and cut in on Lana, who was immediately swept away in Stack's arms.

Now it was Judy whispering into Paul's ear. "Way back when dinosaurs roamed the Earth, Ida Koverman at MGM arranged for Robert to date me. She thought we made a lovely couple for photographers. But after a few fucks, he drifted away. When I sing about the man that got away, I think of Robert. I didn't know you knew him too."

"From our Navy days," he said. "He was my instructor."

"Knowing Robert's reputation, I can just imagine what he instructed you to do." She laughed as he whirled her around the dance floor. When the orchestra played a slow number, she snuggled up close to him. To his surprise, he felt a deft hand unzipping him. Before he knew what was happening, Judy was inside, expertly feeling the family jewels. She performed this stunt with any number of handsome young men over the years, as Robert Vaughn related in his 2008 memoir, *A Fortunate Life.*

"Don't mind me," she said, noting his embarrassment. "I like to check out what I'm getting. That way, there will be no unpleasant surprises when your pants come off later in my bedroom."

***

Five days later, Curtiz was summoned to the office of Jack Warner. "Would you believe it, Judy Garland turned down Helen Morgan. She told me that after *A Star Is Born,* she doesn't plan to make any more movies with sad endings. I've given the role to Ann Blyth, a woman well known to you. You got a brilliant performance out of her as Joan Crawford's daughter in *Mildred Pierce* (1945). Of course, we'll have to dub Ann's singing voice. I'm getting Gogi Grant for that. She sounds like Judy."

***

Nunnally Johnson was getting ready to film his next movie, *The Three Faces of Eve* (1957). He thought the role might be ideal for Judy, since she'd once told him she wanted one day to play a strong, dramatic part. "I know it's against type. But so was Grace Kelly in *The Country Girl,* and she won an Oscar."

He sent her a copy of the script, and Judy phoned him for a conference that following afternoon. She said she would like to do it if he could get Paul Newman to play opposite her.

The idea was pitched to Newman, and he agreed to phone Judy. He called her several times, but she didn't pick up the phone until 9PM that evening.

"Why haven't I heard from you?" asked one of the world's most famous voices. It was Judy. "I'm not a leper you know. I'm fucked up but it's not contagious."

She wanted to talk for half the night. After an hour, she was only getting started. Hoping to end her long, rambling, drunken monologue, he agreed to slip away the following afternoon and see her.

"Good," she said, before ringing off. "I'll make sure we have the house to ourselves."

The next afternoon when Paul drove up to Judy's house, he hoped that Sid Luft was in New York, or shacked up in some motel in Palm Springs with one of his prostitutes. He also hoped Judy didn't have any children running around the house.

She answered the door and ushered Paul into her foyer, where he met Nunnally Johnson, a writer-producer-director for 20th Century Fox, and his wife, Dorris. After a handshake and pleasantries, the Johnsons were out the door. Judy, wearing slacks and a man's white shirt, ushered Paul into her living room.

"Before we get down to commando tactics, I want to share a script with you," she said. "It's called *The Three Faces of Eve.* It's based on a book written by two shrinks. It's about this dame from Georgia who's got not two but three multiple personalities. I know that the *Helen Morgan* thing didn't work out, but there's a great role in *Eve* for you, the part of her husband. Warners makes plenty of dough renting out your hide. Those bastards will gladly lend you to Fox."

They spent the next hour and a half reading the script.

When they finished, he told her, "It's a fabulous part for an actress. My role's not so great but not bad either. But I see Oscar on it for a woman who can tackle the role of Eve."

"That's amazing," she said, her face lighting up. "Orson Welles, God knows why, read the script and said the same thing. You know, of course, that Orson was an old fuck buddy of mine?"

"Actually I didn't know that," he said, smiling. "But I'm sure I can sell the news to *Confidential.*"

Standing over him, she reached for his hand. "I can't go dancing with

385

you tonight. The kids are going to arrive around eight o'clock." She checked the clock. "That gives us at least two hours alone. Sid's in New York trying to arrange a booking for me at The Palace. We're all alone. You lucky boy."

"We are indeed," he said, "and I know how lucky I am. I've got a confession to make. I got a hard-on watching you in *Meet Me in St. Louis*. I wanted to be the guy, not that wimpy Tom Drake, who took your virginity."

"Honey, I lost that a long time ago to Spencer Tracy when I was fifteen, give or take a year," she said. "Now come along upstairs."

***

Paul borrowed the script from Judy but did not rush to show it to Joanne Woodward. She was in negotiations to do a low-brow version of John Steinbeck's *The Wayward Bus* (1957) so he didn't bother her with it.

He wanted Gore Vidal to read it first, since he respected his literary opinion. He was also hoping Gore would write some pages to beef up his character as Eve's husband, in case he got the part. He could take the revisions to the director.

Reportedly, Gore approved the script, but also suggested that it should be a star vehicle for Joanne.

When she was presented with the script, Joanne claimed that her mother had already read the book and had called her, urging her to go for it. "I told mother I didn't have a chance at a star part like that. Fox will want a big name. The most obvious candidate Fox can come up with is Susan Hayward."

"Would you believe Judy Garland?" Paul said. "She's been offered the role."

"She could probably do it if she can hold herself together," Joanne said. "But if Judy does it, Fox will have to call it *The Five Faces of Eve*."

A week later, back at Judy's house, Paul encountered a very different actress from the one who had endorsed the desirability of her involvement in *The Three Faces of Eve*. She informed him that she'd talked it over with Sid Luft, and that he was

After Paul Newman saw the rushes of *The Three Faces of Eve*, he told his best friend, Gore Vidal, "**Joanne (Woodward)** breathes life into all three of the characters she portrays.

"Each has a distinct personality. My favorite is Eva Black, which Joanne interprets as a whore. If Oscars are awarded on merit, she'll win one."

adamantly opposed to her appearing in "that tacky little *film noir* that no one will see. He told me I could break records in Vegas. Make tons of money."

Over a drink, Judy talked more candidly about why she was turning down the role of Eve, an ordinary Southern housewife, given to splitting headaches and fainting spells as she switched between radically different personalities.

"I fear I have all of Eve's characteristics in myself," she confessed. "I think playing this gal could tip me over the deep edge. The role terrifies me. I identify too strongly with the character. There are no songs to sing. They want me to lose thirty pounds. I don't know if I can do that. I'm not going to do it, even though I'll put in a good word for you if you still want to play Eve's husband."

"We'll see," he said, not wanting to commit himself. He was eager to rush out of her house and inform Joanne that the part had become available, but he thought better of it. She might become suspicious as to why he knew so much about what was going on in the life of Judy Garland.

"Actually I've decided to do another movie, and there's a great part in it for you," she said. "The Gentleman Caller."

"You mean Tennessee Williams' *The Glass Menagerie*?" he asked.

"No silly, I've been asked by General Teleradio—you know, Howard Hughes' old RKO—to do a remake of *Alice Adams*. I'll take the Katharine Hepburn role, of course, and you can be Fred MacMurray."

"I don't know," he said. "Tampering with a classic…"

"I'm sure that before the night ends, I will have convinced you," she said, moving closer to him on the sofa.

Later, Paul would share a confidence with Frank Sinatra, perhaps seeking his affirmation. He found the story amusing and passed it along the grapevine.

"Newman told me," Sinatra said to Peter Lawford, "that he was learning something about seducing movie legends. There is no foreplay. They spend most of the night talking about their beauty or how wonderful they looked in their latest picture. Then, when they're ready to get plugged, they demand it. A man is virtually ordered to rise to the occasion whether he's in the mood or not."

Nunnally Johnson told a reporter that, "As so often happens, dear, dear Judy is obviously not going to do *Eve*. She won't even return my calls. Once again, clouds got in her way. She'd rather get laryngitis in the dry desert air of Vegas than play Eve. I've offered the part to Susan Hayward."

***

Five days later, Susan Hayward phoned, claiming that she was "much too fragile" to take on a challenging, intensely dramatic role like *The Three Faces of Eve*.

With Susan off the picture, the pathway was cleared for Joanne Woodward. But Nunnally Johnson had other plans. He sent the script to three different stars—Jennifer Jones, June Allyson, and Doris Day.

"Shit, piss, and hell!" Paul said.

One by one, each of these screen legends turned down "the little film." In desperation, Johnson sent the script to Carroll Baker. She, too, turned it down. Johnson finally placed a call to Joanne herself. "Would you consider the role?" he asked.

"You've found your gal," she said. "I won't even have to fake a Georgia accent. I'm from Georgia. Pot likker talk comes naturally to me. Would I take the part? I'd cut off my mother's tit for a chance to play Eve."

The next day, Joanne gladly surrendered her role in *The Wayward Bus* to Joan Collins, the British bombshell.

At the time relatively unknown in Hollywood, Woodward would go on to win the Best Actress Oscar for her performance in *The Three Faces of Eve.*

***

In the spring of 1955, Judy and Sid Luft were flat broke, living on a loan from a business associate.

The deputy sheriff had paid two afternoon visits, ringing the doorbell several times before pounding on their front door. Each time he'd delivered a dire warning that the bank was ready to foreclose because of overdue mortgage payments.

Not only that, but Luft's ex-wife, Lynn Bari, kept hauling him into court, too. He had not kept up with his $500-a-month payment of child support for their son, John. He had also failed to keep up the monthly payment for his son's college education fund.

As the latter half of the 1950s loomed before her, Judy no longer expected any big movie role, certainly not a hit Broadway musical of the kind that Ethel Merman excelled at.

It seemed that concert tours were the most hopeful road for her to travel.

When Ann Miller dropped in one afternoon, Judy told her, "I expect to be singing for my supper until the last days of my miserable life. City after city for the 'Born in a Trunk' dame. I've got to put food on the table not only for myself, but for Sid, too, and for Liza, Lorna, and Joey. There are many, many bills that are only six months late."

"What's on the horizon?" Miller asked.

"Sid is working on a 'Seven City' tour in the West followed by a 'Thirteen-City' tour in the East."

"Good luck, girl," Miller said. "Judy Garland needs some god damn luck for a change."

"I hope I don't collapse on stage somewhere,"

"Hang in there, you'll make it," Miller said. "Hollywood will never know another dame like Judy Garland."

CHAPTER FOURTEEN

BITTER AND BROKE, JUDY

RECORDS ALBUMS &
ENTERTAINS SOME RANDOM BEAUX,

BEGINS A "DAZZLING" SEVEN-CITY TOUR BUT
SOURS IT BY CUTTING THE ENDING SHORT,

CRAFTS TV SPECIALS FOR FORD MOTOR CO. &
RONALD REAGAN'S GENERAL ELECTRIC THEATER,

COMPLAINS ABOUT HER FAILING MARRIAGE,

"DOES VEGAS,"

HIRES ALAN KING AS HER "WARM-UP" ACT,

MOVES SID AND HER CHILDREN TO SCARSDALE
Liza: "I didn't fit in"

ATTEMPTS MULTIPLE SUICIDES &
SELF-MUTILATIONS

PROFOUNDLY ALIENATES THE OWNERS OF A
MAJOR NIGHTCLUB IN BROOKLYN,

AND OPENS ANOTHER ACT AT
THE DOMINION THEATRE IN LONDON.

"Liza, take your mother's advice.
Follow me as the best example of what not to do."
—Judy Garland

"My mother made all those suicide attempts without any real resolve to kill herself. She craved attention. She would not have done herself in in a million years. As a little girl, I had to cope with a living legend with millions of fans and some ominous detractors."

—Liza Minnelli

"I had stability with my father and lived under a roof over my head that I felt would not be stripped off the following day. With Mother, it would be a series of ducking out on hotel bills and running away from process servers. Even at her home, we had to be on the lookout for men coming to repossess our furnishings."

—Liza Minnelli

"I think my dear daughter, Liza, and my former wife, Judy Garland, were in a kind of competition to become the American version of the great Edith Piaf. Both Judy and Liza, too, wanted to be that blue bird flying over the rainbow."

—Vincente Minnelli

"I am what I am, and I'll never change. So get used to it, Sid Luft!"
—Judy Garland

Judy as she appeared on April 8, 1956, in a broadcast of Ronald Reagan's *General Electric Theater*

After the successful launch of *A Star Is Born*, movie exhibitors were shocked to learn that Jack Warner had "pulled the plug" on Transcona Enterprises, the film company jointly owned by Judy and Luft. Warner Brothers announced, in effect, that there would be no further collaboration between themselves and productions from Garland and Luft.

"There went our dream," Judy said. "The news broke Sid's heart. As for me, my heart had already been broken in so many pieces that it was almost immune to pain and disappointment."

For the next few nights, Harry Rubin, their *factotum,* reported, "Sid and Judy never sobered up. Heavy drinking, charges, counter-charges, accusations of infidelity. Luft would disappear, sometimes for weeks at a time, and then suddenly show up. He never told Judy where he'd been or what he'd done. Later on, a number of women in Hollywood claimed affairs with him."

Gerald Clarke, another of Judy's biographers, claimed that Judy was also indulging in extramarital affairs. "Judy got frisky, including almost certainly at least two or three affairs with women, about which she remained mute."

Rubin, who still remained her lover, once asked her about the charges of lesbianism, which were spreading along the Hollywood grapevine.

She told him, "Whenever you've eaten everything in the world there is to eat, you've got to find new things."

***

During the winter of 1955, Marilyn Monroe was a frequent visitor at the home of Judy and Luft. "She seemed heavily medicated and was very unhappy, but also quite sweet," Luft said. "She'd chat with us and play with the kids. Sometimes, she became quite confidential about her private life. After she divorced Joe DiMaggio, the playwright, Arthur Miller, became the new man in her life."

"She told us she was in love with him—not his body, but his mind. I have to go down on him and work hard to bring him to orgasm."

"Sid doesn't have that problem," Judy chimed in. "Perhaps I'll have to rent him out one night for stud duty. Just kidding..."

According to Luft, "Long after I went to bed, Judy and Marilyn would often stay up till dawn, talking, talking, spilling secrets. Judy wanted to know all about her involvement with the Kennedys, dating back to old Joe Kennedy himself. Marilyn said that she was introduced to Papa Joe in 1950 when she was filming *The Asphalt Jungle.*"

In a 1967 article that ran in the *Ladies' Home Journal,* Judy wrote of her friendship with Marilyn, whose mysterious death occurred in August of 1962.

DiMaggio and Monroe—their photo snapped for the passport they needed for their 1954 trip to Japan.

"I knew Marilyn Monroe and loved her dearly. She asked me for help. Me! I didn't know what to tell her. One night, at a party

at Clifton Webb's house, Marilyn followed me from room to room.

"I don't want to get too far away from you," she said. "I'm scared!

"I told her, 'We're all scared. I'm scared too.'"

"If we could just talk," she said. "I know you'd understand."

I said, 'Maybe I would. If you're scared, call me and come on over. We'll talk about it.'"

"That beautiful girl was frightened of aloneness — the same thing I've been afraid of. Like me, she was just trying to do her job — to garnish some delightful whipped cream onto some people's lives. But Marilyn and I never got the chance to talk. I had to leave for England, and I never saw that sweet, dear girl again. I wish I had been able to talk to her the night she died."

"I don't think Marilyn really meant to harm herself. It was partly because she had too many pills available, then was deserted by her friends. You shouldn't be told you're completely irresponsible and be left alone with too much medication. It's too easy to forget. You take a couple of sleeping pills, and you wake up in 20 minutes and forget you've taken them. So you take a couple more, and the next thing you know you've taken too many. It's happened to all of us; it happened to me. Luckily, someone found me and saved my life."

When Luft, Rubin, and others read Judy's assertion that she hadn't had any serious conversations with Marilyn, as phrased during in interview with *McCall's*, they were surprised, but not really. Marilyn had had dozens of conversations during long evenings with Judy. The two troubled stars had, in fact, become both confidential and confessional with each other.

According to Rubin, "Throughout her life — or at least during the time I knew her — Judy, for reasons of her own, would deny knowing someone even though they had been intimate friends. In later life, she said she had never met Ethel Merman, even though she'd appeared on television with her."

***

In attempts to slim down, Judy indulged in a lot of pill-popping, and then frequently became very aggressive toward Luft, at times demanding that he "get the fuck out."

During intervals when there was peace between them, they sometimes migrated to the Santa Monica Beach villa owned by Peter Lawford and his wife, Patricia Kennedy. It had once belonged to Louis B. Mayer.

On rare occasions, Senator John F. Kennedy was there. According to Luft, "I knew that Judy had had a fling with him before the war, and they were still the greatest of friends. Whenever JFK was in town, Peter [Lawford] the Pimp always arranged a bevy of beautiful starlets for him to fuck."

Once, when Luft was out of town, Judy attended a party at the Lawford house in honor of Bobby Kennedy.

A week later, when Luft was back in town, he and Judy were invited once again to the Lawfords. He recalled the venue: "Pat and I sat on the terrace overlooking the ocean. She'd been drinking heavily and very indiscreetly told me that Judy had come to the party because of Bobby and

392

that she'd been seen going into one of the upstairs bedrooms with him and that she'd remained there with him for two hours."

"Perhaps they were playing chess," Luft said, seeming to take the revelation in stride. [*Considering his numerous adulterous affairs, he was in no position to point fingers at his errant wife.*]

On yet another occasion, Luft met Bobby and the two men seemingly got along. RFK told him that his brother was considering running for President in 1960 against Richard Nixon.

Luft advised Bobby to tell his brother to forget it. "I'm a Jew, he's a Catholic. No Jew or Catholic is ever going to be elected President of the United States."

***

In August of 1955, Judy signed a five-year contract with Capitol Records and soon began recording songs for a twelve-inch LP being marketed as *Miss Show Business.*

Alan Livingstone, president of Capitol, said, "We want to record Judy's greatest songs for posterity. The audio tracks of her early recordings are flawed and scratchy. Since then, the technology in the recording industry has vastly improved. Nelson Riddle will lead the orchestra on her album."

A native of New Jersey, and a year older than Judy, Riddle was an arranger, composer, bandleader, and orchestrator. He rose to prominence in the late 1940s and played a major role in the career of Judy's friend, Frank Sinatra. Their first song they recorded together, "I've Got the World on a String," became a runaway hit and is credited with re-launching Sinatra's career after a long slump.

Riddle also played a major role not only in Judy's career, but with other singers such as Dean Martin, Peggy Lee, Nat King Cole, ("Mona Lisa"), Ella Fitzgerald, and Johnny Mathis.

In 1957, Riddle and his orchestra were featured on *The Rosemary Clooney Show,* a thirty-minute syndicated broadcast. Although married to Doreen Moran at the time, Riddle and Clooney had a clandestine affair. Judy later admitted she sometimes served as their "beard," spotted in public with them as a means of disguising their affair.

At Capitol, Judy joined a roster of other recording stars who included Sinatra, Nat King Cole, Gordon MacCrae, and Jo Stafford (aka "GI Joe" because of her success at entertaining U.S. troops during World War II.)

After a photographer arrived to snap Judy's picture for the cover of her album, he retreated to Livingston's office to complain about how she looked: "She weighs a thousand pounds. The cover of this album isn't large enough to take in the bulge!"

In lieu of a more recent likeness of her, Livingston finally agreed to use a framed blowup of Judy that had been snapped during one of her deliveries of "My Melancholy Baby" in *A Star Is Born.*

When *Miss Show Business* was released on October 10, 1957, it won almost universal praise, with "Come Rain Or Come Shine" hailed as one of its best numbers. Some critics cited her singing as "electrifying." The *New Yorker* hailed it as a triumph.

For five weeks, it remained among the Top 40, peaking at seventeen. The album also featured some of her less familiar numbers, including, "I Feel a Song Coming On" and "Dirty Hands, Dirty Face."

***

After all the agony attached to the filming of *A Star Is Born,* Judy and Luft ended up broke. In spite of that, they still maintained a staff of servants and faced annual expenses of $100,000 for the running of their home in Holmby Hills, a chunk of that going to child care for their children.

Desperate for cash, Luft announced a Seven City Tour, *The Judy Garland Show.* Beginning in California, it would continue, it was believed, through the Pacific Northwest. *[It was rehearsed and crafted with the intention of continuing it with bookings in an additional thirteen cities in the Middle West and points East, including Chicago, New York, and Washington, D.C.]*

Jules Stein of MCA was in charge of arrangements for the concert tours, and Charles Feldman, still involved in an on-again, off-again affair with Marilyn Monroe, would deal with any film offers.

Judy was in rehearsal for the tour when, on June 10, she turned thirty-three. Celebrating her birthday were Luft, Lorna, Joey, and Liza, whom Judy collectively called "my beloved ones."

On July 5, 1955, her tour opened in San Diego with an introduction that featured a series of vaudeville acts. Then—to the sound of wild applause—Judy made a grand entrance and went through a repertoire of songs, most of which had first been introduced through her movies of the 1940s. They included "The Boy Next Door," "The Trolley Song," and the inevitable "Over the Rainbow."

Variety appraised her San Diego show as "dazzling. She's added a magnetic maturity to the old *gamin* quality."

Heading north from San Diego to Long Beach, she opened on July 9 at the Municipal Auditorium there as part of a non-profit charity event benefitting developmentally disabled children.

For the event, Frank Sinatra rented a bus with a well-stocked bar to transport her friends to see the show, where they occupied front-row seats. Sinatra, Dean Martin, Humphrey Bogart, and Sammy Davis, Jr. joined her on stage. Davis brought down the house with his impersonation of Jerry Lewis, Martin's former stage partner. Cheering them on were Lauren Bacall, Peter Lawford, Van Johnson, Eddie Fisher, David Wayne, and Leslie Caron.

Abruptly, the remainder of her Seven City Tour had to be canceled because Luft had signed a deal with CBS-TV for Judy's television debut. Box office refunds were issued in cities that included Eugene and Portland, Oregon; Spokane and Seattle, Washington; and Vancouver in British Columbia.

During three weeks in September, Judy went into rehearsals for her TV special, *The Ford Star Jubilee.* It would be aired to an audience of forty million viewers on the evening of September 14.

The night before filming, Luft, fearing Judy's nervous unpredictability, hired a nurse to guard her, with instructions not to let her out of her sight.

Then he went to sleep in the adjoining bedroom.

When he woke up at 6AM to prepare her for the final rehearsals at CBS, he found the nurse gone and Judy in a deep coma-like sleep.

He could not awaken her, and he rushed downstairs to find the nurse brewing a pot of coffee. He lashed into her for disobeying his instructions.

Back in Judy's bedroom, Luft stripped off all her clothes and his, too, forcing her under a cold shower. That did little to revive her, and she still remained groggy. Then he tried to walk her around the room, but he almost had to carry her as dead weight. It was painfully obvious that she'd ingested Seconal.

She must have been awake when the nurse left the bedroom to retreat downstairs. During that brief interval, she'd accessed her secret stash, swallowed the pills, and returned to bed.

Luft phoned Dr. Fred Pobirs with a request to meet him at the local drugstore when it opened at 8AM, and to write out a prescription for Benzedrine, the amphetamine-based stimulant. As deeply as he opposed giving them to her, he felt he had no choice.

The doctor agreed to drive with them to CBS's studio and spend the rest of the day supervising her health. Luft did not want to alert the cast and crew that his wife was under a doctor's care, so as a means of avoiding that, Pobirs was introduced as her "assistant."

Jack Carthart, Judy's brother-in-law, was in charge of the orchestra, and he promised Luft that he'd do anything in his power to get her through the show.

Finally, it was show time, and she went on the air at 6:30PM in Los Angeles [aka 9:30PM Eastern Standard Time]. She was a bit slurred in her opening number, "You Made Me Love You," but seemed to pull herself together during her next number in which she lip-synched "Swanee." Finally, by the time she went into her standards such as "Get Happy" and "Over the Rainbow," she was in full-throated voice.

Immediately after the show, Luft rushed to her dressing room. To his shock, he discovered her standing in front of the mirror, one wrist bleeding. Had she attempted a razor blade suicide again? She quickly explained that she had been so nervous that she had dug into her wrist with her sharp fingernails, causing it to bleed.

"Oh, Judy, Judy, Judy," he said.

"You sound like one of those Cary Grant impersonators, using those exact words," she said.

"Whatever, babe... you wowed them tonight."

It had cost $300,000 to produce the TV special, and she was given $100,000. *Variety* hailed her for still having "that old Black Magic and magnetism." Weeks later, she was nominated for an Emmy as Best Singer of the Year, losing to Dinah Shore.

The TV show was such a hit that CBS-TV signed her to a five-year deal in which she'd star in five annual "specials" priced at a collective total of $450,000.

***

Early in 1956, Judy became known for complaining to friends such as Kay Thompson that her marriage to Sid Luft had been a disappointment.

"I had hoped that he would put a firecracker under my ass and sky-rocket me to the moon," she told Thompson. "I wanted him to do for me what David O. Selznick did for Jennifer Jones. I wanted him to set career goals that one day will immortalize me like Sophie Tucker and Fanny Brice."

As she moved deeper into her marriage, she became more disillu-sioned with Luft, especially his long, mystery-shrouded absences from home. He would sometimes lose $10,000 in one day at the horse races or at a poker game with his cronies. With money set aside for household ex-penses, he visited an automobile showroom in Beverly Hills that catered to movie stars and bought a Mercedes Benz.

A friend and fellow Rat Packer, Humphrey Bogart, claimed, "The Luft home at times was like the front lines of a war zone."

One night, Judy and Luft dined with Bogie and Bacall at Chasen's, the most exclusive and celebrity-soaked restaurant in Los Angeles. There, as part of an ultra-glamourous quartet, Judy began to drink heavily until she became quite intoxicated. She suddenly turned on Luft, verbally attacking him, outlining in detail sins that included heavy drinking, heavy gambling, adulterous affairs, being a spendthrift of their dwindling resources, and his violence toward her.

Her voice grew so loud that the *maître d'hotel* approached their table and asked Luft and Judy to leave the restaurant. He told them he hoped it would not be necessary to call the police to escort them out. Both of them said goodbye to the Bogarts and left peacefully.

Bogie had insisted on remaining behind, with Bacall, to finish his meal. When he and his wife were finished, the *maître d'hotel* approached their table to apologize once again for the eviction of their guests, telling him that there would be no bill for their food and drink.

That same evening, after their incident at Chasen's, Judy did not make up with Luft. He left the house without telling her where he was going. When Lorna and Joey wanted their daddy, Judy told them he was away on a business trip.

Had he resumed his affair with Gloria Grahame? Or was it some other starlet?

Adding to her rage was the fact that Luft had a friend, Kenny Morgan, who was married at the time to Lucille Ball's cousin. Morgan had previ-ously introduced Luft to Ball, and they had struck up a friendship. He began to call on her when Desi Arnaz, her husband, was out of town. [Arnaz himself was known for numerous affairs outside his home.]

Judy had met Ball one day when she was visiting George Cukor on the set of *A Star Is Born*. When a stagehand brought her over to meet Judy. Judy looked her up and down before saying, in jest, "I hate this whore."

[Actually, Judy had great respect for Ball, her business sense, and her vast talent as an actress.]

In a memoir, Luft wrote:

"After fifteen minutes or so, Judy was informed that Lucy was upstairs in a *bathroom and would not come out. Judy raced up the steps to see her. Through the door, Lucy told her, that she had taken Judy's jest seriously. Judy, astonished, apologized. Then, Lucy let her in, and Judy hugged and kissed Lucy, explaining that the remark had been meant as a tease. Incidents such as that never deterred Judy's sense of humor and style."*

On February 3, 1956, Judy and Luft descended into in one of their most scorchingly violent fights. She'd heard of his affair with Ball. In their kitchen, she broke a glass and lunged at him waving one of its sharp-edged shards. As she lurched toward him, "One-Punch Luft" knocked her out cold, and she fell to the kitchen floor unconscious.

Without checking on her, he left the house for the night. She regained consciousness and wandered upstairs for more pills.

Awakening groggy the next day, she headed for a lawyer to file a bill of divorcement against Luft, charging physical violence and mental cruelty and demanding custody of both Lorna and Joey.

He heard what she'd done and returned to their house that afternoon. As he later confessed, "I made love to her all night, and the next day, she dropped her plan to divorce me."

Their peace treaty lasted for only four days. Late one afternoon she heard him on the downstairs phone. He said, "Lucy, Lucy, c'mon, don't be like that. I'll be right over. I'll explain everything."

A few minutes later, he told Judy he'd been invited to a game of poker with the boys of the Rat Pack and headed out the door. Feeling abandoned and unloved, Judy drifted in and out of sleep until around 3AM. She didn't know how many pills she'd swallowed. Weakly, she placed a call to the home of Peter Lawford.

Picking up the receiver, he was awakened, as was the African American singer, Dorothy Dandridge, who was in bed with him. His wife, Patricia, was in Hyannis Port for a reunion with the Kennedy clan.

He registered the panic in Judy's voice: "If you don't come here at once, I'm going to cut my throat. Little Joey is sleeping in the bed with me. I'm going to cut his throat, too." Then she put down the receiver and didn't answer the phone when he called back.

Making apologies to Dandridge, he dressed hurriedly and speeded over. There, he pounded on the door and rang the bell until he aroused a maid from her sleep.

He hadn't known whether to take Judy's threat seriously, so he ran up the

Dorothy Dandridge with Harry Belafonte in *Carmen Jones* (1954).

"Some people kill themselves with drink or hurl themselves in front of a train," Dandridge said.

"I hurl myself in front of another white man like Otto Preminger who directed me in *Carmen Jones*. And, of course, Peter Lawford."

steps and into her bedroom. She was calmly lying in bed stroking the hair of a sleeping Joey. Everything was tranquil.

Quietly, so as not to disturb the boy, he asked her, "What the hell!"

She directed him out onto the terrace, and the two of them talked until dawn. She apologized for alarming him, saying that it was just a desperate ploy to get his attention.

On another of Judy's desperate nights, weeks after her original alarm, she placed yet another frantic call to Lawford. This time she claimed that Luft had slashed her face with a razor blade, and that she was bleeding.

Again to the rescue he arrived. The maid let him in, pointing the way to the downstairs bathroom. There, he found her, and indeed, her face was bleeding. Like a nurse, he washed her face and managed to stop the bleeding, discovering her wounds were only very minor cuts, requiring—after stopping the bleeding and applying iodine—only Band Aids. He didn't feel it was necessary to call a doctor.

Sitting with her and comforting her, he talked with her until dawn broke over California. At one point, she confessed that she'd turned the razor blade on herself, blaming it on Luft.

During the final months of Bogart's life, Judy was a frequent visitor at the home he shared with Bacall. One night, Judy and Luft were introduced to Richard Burton, with whom she shared memories of their first pictures in CinemaScope: *The Robe* (for Burton), and *A Star Is Born*.

As Judy and Luft became more intoxicated, they began to share tales of their marital strife with Bogie. At one point, when he could take it no more, Bogie stood up and confronted Luft with, "Get the hell out of my house and take your dull, drunken wife with you."

"I don't have to take crap like that from anybody," Luft shouted at him. "If you weren't such a decrepit, dying old bastard, I'd bash your nose into your head."

Bogie smiled at him, "You won't lay a hand on me."

"How in hell do you know I won't?" Luft asked.

"Because you love me," Bogie said. "Now come over here, give me a bear hug, and plant a wet, sloppy kiss on my lips. That will mean we're making up."

"Okay, I'll kiss you, but I won't fuck you," Luft said.

"Thank God for that."

Burton looked on at this scene in amazement. "Americans!" he told Bacall. "I will never understand the fuckers."

Bacall, a close friend of Judy's, wrote her own assessment:

"She (Judy) was a complicated woman of tremendous wit and intelligence who had survived a distorted childhood and distorted marriages which had left their mark. But she and I became good friends. She was fun and, when we'd sit quietly on an afternoon or evening, great company. It was hard for her to think beyond herself—it had been that way too long. But A Star Is Born was made in spite of the cynics' predictions, and it was Sid who helped her get through."

Bacall was hardly the only person who wrote about Judy. Literally dozens of people shared their memories with the public, including Ned Wynn, the son of actor Keenan Wynn. Judy had befriended his father back in the 1940s when he was deep into a torrid romance with Van Johnson.

According to Ned, "By the late 1950s, Judy's drinking and pill popping had become the stuff of legend. At every party, she was always out of control, a real bad mama when liquored up. She was always bitching Luft, calling him that sonofabitch, the whoremonger and gambler. Hollywood royalty is forgiven everything. People loved Judy in spite of her excesses. I think they loved her because of them."

In the 1964 edition of *McCall's*, Judy looked back on that time in her life:

> *"The birth of our daughter, Lorna, was the only bright spot in the first year of our marriage. From the beginning, Sid and I weren't happy. I don't know why. I really don't. For me it was work, work, work, and I didn't see much of Sid. He was always dashing off to places, lining up my appearances. I wasn't made any happier looking into mirrors, seeing myself balloon out of shape from liquids trapped in my body. The doctors said it was caused by metabolic imbalance, brought on by all those crash diets and nervous strain."*

***

Judy returned to Capitol Records for another recording session of March 10. It was for her second album, one simply entitled *Judy*. Once again, she worked with the Nelson Riddle Orchestra, although before their working relationship, she had requested Leonard Bernstein.

On that day, she was in good form to record four songs, including "Maybe I'll Come Back." A week later, she recorded more songs, such as "Memories of You." But the following day, she had swallowed too many pills, wasn't feeling well, and managed to get through recording only one song, "Lucky Day."

On the final day of March, she finished the recordings, including her best-ever version of "Come Rain Or Come Shine." Her most evocative song was "Last Night When We Were Young."

Riddle pronounced her "the female Frank Sinatra."

Released on October 10, the *Judy* album made the Top 40 list for five weeks. *Variety* proclaimed, "Thrush is in top voice on this set and shows a maturity and song-selling savvy that makes her one of the standout belters in the business."

SWEAT, BLOOD, & MUSIC

Judy's erratic moods and bad health anxiously delayed some of her scheduled recording sessions, but when the album named **Judy** was released, *Variety* called it "a socko album," and *The New Yorker* wrote that "Judy Garland is at the top of her form."

***

One night an unhappily married couple drove over to the house of a happily married couple, Ronald and Nancy Reagan. The former MGM starlet—gossiped about at the studio as "The Queen of Fellatio"—was his second wife.

Reagan had been previously married to an A-list star, Jane Wyman. She had won an Oscar for playing a deaf and mute rape victim in *Johnny Belinda* (1949). During the shoot, she had fallen in love with her leading man, Lew Ayres, and divorced Reagan.

Actually, Reagan—who had been seeing Nancy on the side—had wanted to marry Doris Day. But when Nancy announced that she was pregnant, he did the honorable thing. She gave birth to daughter Patti, explaining the timing of her birth as "a premature delivery."

After dinner, Reagan and Luft disappeared into his library to talk over a business deal. Nancy and Judy remained in the living room, giggling and indulging in "girl talk," especially about their lives before marriage.

As it turned out, both of them, at least on

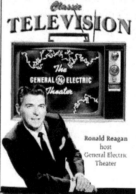

Ronald Reagan
host
General Electric
Theater

Upper photo: **the Reagans** in *Hellcats of the Navy* (1957). It took some time, but Reagan, a former "horndog" like Kirk Douglas, eventually settled down with his overly protective second wife.

Lower photo: As a then-out-of-work actor, Reagan managed to re-invent himself as a TV personality (1954-1961) and later, a politician though his role as host of the **General Electric Theater.**

The gig was arranged by the media tycoon and philanthropist Walter Annenberg, who persuaded him to shift his allegiance from the Democrats to the Republicans.

LOVE TRIANGLE

Here's the best overview ever published about the *Love Triangle* whose combatants included a star (**Jane Wyman**), a starlet (**Nancy Davis**), and the **future President of the United States**.

Produced by Blood Moon in 2014, it's a rare, award-winning treasure that appeals to both the devotees and the detractors of **Ronald Reagan**. Monumentally researched. with points of view from EVERYONE who mattered, it has all the dish here from the (bad) good old days of Classic Tinseltown.

As Lauren Bacall ruefully exclaimed on the eve of Ronald Reagan's Presidential inauguration:

"This would never have happened if Hollywood had given him better scripts."

400

occasion, had the same taste in men. Each admitted that she was in love with Frank Sinatra. They shared other equivalent experiences, too. Spencer Tracy was the man who had taken their respective virginities, and each had had a sexual fling with Yul Brynner.

When Luft and Reagan meandered back into the living room, Judy learned of her new gig. His film career fading, Reagan had turned to hosting *The General Electric Theater* for CBS-TV. He wanted Judy to star in one of their 30-minute broadcasts on April 8. *[In most cases, the series focused on dramas, but hers would be a musical program.]*

She told him she'd be thrilled.

Before the show, she had tried to slim down, but still was a bit overweight. Nervous and filled with anxiety the day before the taping, she had popped a few too many pills and appeared a bit groggy. Earlier that morning, she had complained to Luft about a sore throat.

To calm her nerves, it was agreed that she would lip-synch her first two songs, "I Will Come Back" and "I Feel a Song Coming On." She followed them with a silly little dance number with a cane. By the time she sang "Last Night When We Were Young," she was back performing at her usual peak level. Again, she lip-synched "Dirty Hands, Dirty Face." She nearly fell down during her closing number, "April Showers," when she had to walk backwards up a winding staircase.

[Luft had been the producer of that night's TV broadcast, with Richard Avedon directing. Peter Gennaro and Leonard Pennario had appeared on the show as her guests. Actually, it was not so much a General Electric Theater production, but a special for CBS.]

Following the show, she invited old friends to a private party at her home, notably the ever-faithful Kay Thompson. Also arriving were Roger Edens and his assistant, Leonard Gershe, who, among other accomplishments, had created her "Born in a Trunk" number.

As the drunken evening wore on, Judy had not gotten out of her last costume. She excused herself to go upstairs and change into something more comfortable. She was gone a long time, before she returned, making her way down the steps. As she reached the last three steps, she stumbled and fell. Her guests rushed to pick her up, discovering to their relief that she was not injured. Edens and Gershe carried her back up the steps and put her to bed. Luft had not come home. The party was over.

The next day, Judy told Luft what had happened. "I should name my memoirs, *The Party's Over.*"

Often her reviews were raves, but not this time. Coyne Steven Sanders wrote, "Rarely did Judy Garland's instincts err in performing a song, but for General Electric Theater, she was overwrought to an uncomfortable degree."

In the *New York World Telegram*, Harriet Von Horne wrote: "The notes that tremble so gloriously in that rich throat tremble a little too long. There was too much anguish in the songs, and there was too much wild glee. At one point, Garland ruffled the hair of the boys in the band. Every gesture, every emotion, was a little bigger than life."

Variety found that "Her voice had a rough quality, especially in the higher registers. In one of the early numbers, her voice broke and her showmanlike flair couldn't quite cover it up."

Despite the criticism, her show was among the top dozen watched that night across America.

Luft and Judy would not see the Reagans again until the couple attended her show at The Greek Theatre in Los Angeles in the summer of 1957.

Her performance was followed by a party at Romanoff's. Judy was standing in a corner, chatting with Nancy when an aging Clark Gable approached them, kissing both of them on the lips. He talked pleasantly for a while before being summoned away by Gary Cooper.

"I didn't know you knew Gable," Judy said.

"I dated him a few years ago and wanted to marry him, but he turned me down," Nancy said. "I ended up with Ronnie."

Luft remembered the party, recalling, "Reagan stood out in a sea of black and navy blue suits. What man wears a brown suit? Reagan does."

***

It seemed inevitable that the casino owners of Las Vegas would view Judy as "possible dynamite" if she'd take her act to Nevada and book into one of its showrooms.

In the spring of 1956, Luft was fully aware of this potential. He received three or four offers for engagements before deciding that the best bet—and the most profitable—would be at the New Frontier Hotel. Judy would be paid $55,000 a week, the highest salary ever offered to a performer in Las Vegas at that time.

After closing the deal, he was overjoyed and rushed home to share their good fortune with Judy. Inside the house, he found, to his regret, that she'd gone on another bender. She didn't seem filled with glee at all, and, at one point, as the dreadful evening wore on, denounced him: "Like hell, I'm going to play Vegas in front of a lot of drunken gamblers!"

It took a lot of work and even more persuasion, but finally, he got her in better physical shape, and she went with him to Vegas to begin rehearsals. That's what she was doing on June 10 when she turned thirty-four.

She'd brought along her brood—Liza, Lorna, and Joey—installing them at the New Frontier Hotel in a suite, separate from her own, with a nanny. Also in her party was Jack Carthart, her brother-in-law, who would be her conductor.

Luft lined up a number of vaudeville acts to open her show, including "The Boyfriends," whom Luft held in a certain contempt. He told Dean Martin, who was in town, "If you want a really good blow job, I can set you up with one of those prancing boys." Other acts included the Amin Brothers and the Risley Acrobatic Team.

Kay Thompson arrived in town and found Judy filled with complaints. At least some of them stemmed from the air conditioning in her suite, others from the dry desert air, which she claimed "parched my throat."

During her wardrobe fittings, she complained that her gowns were too tight, "like suits of armor." Truth was, she'd put on weight and was desperately trying to slim down before her act's opening night of July 16.

Before the show, David Niven paid her a visit. Sitting with her in her dressing room, she shared a secret about what kept her going. "She showed me something that was the size of a horse pill and told me that it was filled with little nuggets of energy that went off every half hour, "making me feel like Little Bo Peep, hopping along through a field of wildflowers."

That night finally came, and the demand for seats was almost unheard of, the casino having to turn away 7,000 potential customers. Her performance met with thunderous applause, much of it derived from her delivery of such songs as "Come Rain Or Come Shine," "Happiness Is Just a Thing Called Joe," "Rock-a-Bye Your Baby to a Dixie Melody," and ending with "Over the Rainbow."

Newspapers compared her opening night to a gala premiere on Broadway. Movie stars flew in from Hollywood to catch her act. She was greeted backstage with some of the biggest names in show business, all of whom seemed to agree that "Judy Garland caught fire."

Daily Variety cited her as "a singer's singer, her voice and delivery the pride of her profession." *Variety* noted, "Late in making her start on the saloon belt, Judy Garland nevertheless belted across an unmistakable message that not only is the tops in her field, but also the likely champ entertainer for as long and as often as she desires to play the bistro circuit."

Midway through the run of her act, Judy needed money for shopping and approached the casino's cashier to cash a check for $500. She knew that her weekly paycheck was routinely deposited into a joint account she maintained with Luft. The teller told her, "Miss Garland, your account doesn't have enough money in it to cover this check."

She was stunned, but soon realized that Luft had spent every dollar of her earnings at the gaming tables. Later, she agreed to add an extra week to her engagement to cover his debts.

One night, as it always seemed to happen, Judy developed laryngitis. Luft notified management, who had already sold all the seats.

An agreement was worked out. Jerry Lewis was in town, and available. The casino maneuvered Judy into going onstage to exchange a few words with him as a foil for his madcappery act. He had broken from his longtime partner, Dean Martin, and was eager to prove that his *schtick* could thrive alone as a solo.

Although the audience had paid to see Judy, they got Lewis instead. He faced a few boos when he was announced as her replacement, but won over the crowd with a burlesque of Judy's most celebrated songs.

Lewis later said:

"People now know the troubles Judy has been through. Who among us isn't plagued with troubles too? So people of all kinds, with worries and problems and heartaches, go to see her; and they identify with her. And when she sings, she is communicating for them all the emotions they can't communicate themselves because they don't have a stage and a microphone and talent. The stout women in the audience loudly identify with her; and the people who remember their own unhappy childhoods identify with her. All the people whose insides have been torn out by misery identify with her, and she is singing for all of

them. In a way, she's singing with a hundred voices."

It was in Las Vegas that Luft and Judy began to plot what they hoped would be a triumphant return to The Palace in Manhattan.

***

In Las Vegas, near the end of her booking, Sol Schwarz, the RKO vice president, phoned Luft. He wanted to book Judy for a return engagement at The Palace.

Luft flew to New York to make the arrangements for a two-month gig set for a premiere on September 26, 1956.

As agreed, her repertoire would be similar to her Vegas act, but with a difference. Roger Edens migrated to New York to arrange a city-specific opening, beginning with "New York, New York," which her daughter Liza would, years later, make more famous. That was to be followed by "Take Me Back to Manhattan" and "Give My Regards to Broadway." Of course, it was almost mandatory to feature "The Trolley Song" and to end with "Over the Rainbow."

Before the finale, Judy would perform a highly skilled number, "Be a Clown," evocative of the version that

Alan King during one of the fifty appearances he made on the **Ed Sullivan** show. Sullivan interpreted his first appearance (December 30, 1956) as "bold and raw," and kept inviting him back.

Audiences fell in love with his comedic monologues about marriage, suburbia, and everyday life.

Judy was drawn to his comedy, and he became one of her best opening acts.

had appeared in her movie, *The Pirate* (1948), in which she had co-starred with Gene Kelly.

Installed at Manhattan's Park Lane Hotel, Judy would draw $4,000 a week. Since she would be in Manhattan for such a prolonged period, she had some of her favorite items shipped in from Holmby Hills. She also brought her family with her.

On opening night, as before in 1951, masses of people formed outside the theater and the police had to erect barricades. Her show opened with vaudeville acts which included "The Boyfriends."

One noted difference between now and her earlier appearance at The Palace was the stand-up comedian, Alan King, beginning his long theatrical association with Judy.

A New Yorker, he had grown up on the Lower East Side of Manhattan, the son of Jewish immigrants. As a comedian, he became known for his biting wit and angry but humorous rants.

He was so successful with Judy that he also became an opening act for

Nat King Cole, Patti Page, Tony Martin, and Lena Horne.

Liza Minnelli, age ten, was lifted out of her front row seat by Rock Hudson and placed directly onto the stage. To wild applause, she danced around as her mother sang "Swanee."

On November 3, Liza would gain a far greater audience when she and Burt Lahr, the Cowardly Lion from *The Wizard of Oz,* hosted the first telecast of that film, a prime time event watched by millions of families.

Since the lights in most of the theaters on Broadway went dark every Sunday night, other stage stars, many visiting from Hollywood, came to see Judy on their night off. Showing up were the likes of everybody from Helen Hayes to Julie Andrews, who was appearing at the time in the stage production of *My Fair Lady.* Andrews came backstage to thank Judy for not competing with her for the role of Eliza Doolittle.

Judy's longtime co-star, Bing Crosby, was there on opening night to greet her and embrace her. George Jessel came to see the show on one of her worst nights. When he went backstage, she told him, "I know I was not my best tonight."

He warmly embraced her. "Honey, it's like sex. Even when it's bad, it's not really that bad."

As with any show starring Judy, there were problems. Trouble began when RKO informed Luft that Judy was not insurable, and that he would have to take out a policy protecting them in the event that Judy didn't show up. To pay for it, he had to borrow the cash.

She had many bad nights. In advance of some scheduled performances, she'd refuse to go on, complaining that she was coming down with stomach flu. "I've got this splitting migraine," she told Luft some nights.

She often demanded that he send for Dr. Pobirs, who probably gave her Benzedrine or a placebo.

One night as he was leaving their suite, she turned to Luft to ask, "Why in hell did you marry Judy Garland?"

"Every morning when I wake up, and she's not in her bed, a panic overcomes me," Luft said. "Was this going to be another morning of self-mutilation?"

On opening night of her second (1956) gig at The Palace, a star-studded array of celebrities was seated in the audience. Many of them migrated backstage to greet her after the show. Cary Grant hugged and kissed her, telling her, "I'll always regret turning down your Norman Maine."

Frank Sinatra was there, assuring her, "I'll always be there for you, babe."

Even her long-time rival, Lana Turner, showed up on the arm of her gangster boyfriend, Johnny Stompanato, a henchman of Mickey Cohen. *[Stom-*

Lana Turner, Johnny Stompanato, and Lana's "take the blame" daughter, **Cheryl Crane** in 1958.

Death by stabbing lay in Stompanoto's near future.

panato would not survive the end of the decade. On April 4, 1958, he would be stabbed to death in Lana's home in Beverly Hills. Was it Lana who did it, or her daughter, Cheryl Crane? The debate continues to this day. For more on this, refer to Darwin Porter's biography of Lana Turner, published in 2017.]

Reviews of Judy's "return" were raves. *The New York Times* claimed, "A song has not really been sung until Judy Garland pulls herself together and belts it out through the theater." *Variety* called her "the prime singer of our times. She could sing a Toots Shor menu and have 'em hungry for more. She takes command of the rostrum as no one does."

Walter Kerr in the *New York Herald* wrote, "It was perfect. Her barrel-house voice can bend the back walls into cyclotrons. The glorious steam-whistle that can shatter the chandeliers with a single sustained note flung recklessly skyward is in great shape."

The most popular columnist of the day, Walter Winchell, claimed, "For the second time around, Judy Garland owns Broadway."

Shortly before Christmas of 1956, Judy experienced a total physical collapse, and The Palace grew dark until she recovered. She complained to Luft that all those shows every week was more than her frail body could take. However, by Christmas, she had recovered and attended a party hosted by Gilbert Miller, a well-known theatrical impresario. There, she met the handsome British actor, Dirk Bogarde, who in time would become not only her future co-star, but her lover, despite his sexual preference for men.

The following day, she returned to the stage at The Palace to complete her gig, much to the delight of RKO executives. Her show closed on January 8, 1957.

In her final moments on stage, Judy addressed the audience: "This was the house where I was reborn."

***

Liza faced an almost nomadic existence when her mother had custody of her in the years that followed the release of *A Star Is Born*. In a span of five years, she would be enrolled in more than a dozen different schools. The disruptions prevented her from making friends and anything approaching a normal girlhood.

With her parents separated, and/or busy elsewhere, Liza went through periods of terrible loneliness and feelings of being neglected. Her father, Vincente Minnelli, would always be there for her in moments of genuine crisis, even if Judy were not. Whereas at times, Liza felt she was Judy's mother on a "suicide watch" over her unstable daughter, she knew she could rely on Minnelli as a father figure.

Minnelli himself once said, "It was a mother-daughter relationship, with Judy being the daughter, and Liza the mother."

In an interview with *McCall's* magazine, Judy confessed that she always checked into the best hotel in whatever city she happened to be in, "I did so even if I were broke. After three or four weeks, the manager would present me with a big bill. I would put him off, telling him I'd phone my business manager and have a check in the mail that very day."

"One afternoon at the Beverly Hills Hotel, I left three relatively empty pieces of luggage in my suite, telling the desk that I'd be back in four days and to keep my suite and baggage left behind."

"Then I'd travel to New York with the kids and pull the same stunt at the St. Regis. Of course, after getting away with that, I could not go back to the same hotel."

"When that ploy didn't work, I would have Lorna, Liza, and Joey dress up in at least three layers of clothing, leaving the rest of our things behind, and walk rapidly through the lobby, hoping not to attract attention."

Years later, Liza would recall those turbulent days of growing up with Judy and her stepfather. "I was bounced back and forth between the two of them. By the time I was thirteen, I knew that life was not a bowl of cherries. At times, when I needed love and sympathy, it was not there for me. I might long for happiness, living with some loving man in a cottage behind a white picket fence. I don't like picket fences. They're not comfortable to sit on. At times when I arrived at their house in Holmby Hills, I would find Judy and Papa Sid in an epic battle."

Even on a school night, Judy would often enter Liza's bedroom at 3AM. She'd wake Liza up just to have somebody to talk to. Luft was wherever he went in the pre-dawn hours.

"She would pour out her woes, and often talk most unfavorably about her mother, Ethel," Liza said. "Sometimes, she blamed her for ruining her life."

When Liza had to get up to prepare for school, Judy would wander off into her own bedroom. A few hours later, Liza would fall asleep in the classroom.

"When she was with me, I spoiled Liza outrageously," Vincente Minnelli confessed. "I did so in the clumsy belief that I could be a proper balance in her life, creating a sound, stable, and loving relationship during her time with me, unlike the environment generated over at the Luft household. I asked nothing from Liza but love. We shared many carefree happy moments."

In contrast, the Luft household was a forum for everything from slugfests to lawsuits.

But life with Judy was not always bleak. Liza recalled happy times, too.

She remembered sitting with Lorna in the kitchen watching her mother bake a cake. "It was so domestic. I felt I was part of a family. The only problem with the cake was that she had forgotten the sugar."

The very next day, this cozy domestic scene was replaced with something more terrifying:

One otherwise quiet afternoon, while the girls were in the living room listening to

Liza, aged twelve in 1958.

In her early days as a teenager, Liza referred to herself as "Princess Ugly," to some degree because she wore braces.

The bullies at school mocked her looks and frequently referred to Judy, her mother, as "a big fat pig."

407

records, Judy, clad only in her underwear, came down the stairs in a rage. She called out, "I'm gonna kill myself" before rushing into the bathroom of the downstairs study and locking herself inside. In a panic, Liza summoned the butler, who fetched the key to the locked door.

When the sisters, with the butler, rushed in, they found Judy standing above the toilet bowl, trying to flush the contents of a container of Bayer aspirin. "My mother just wanted to be noticed, I guess," Liza concluded.

As Liza matured, Judy, unlike most mothers of her era, was direct and frank in their discussions of sex, explaining menstruation as "a wonderful time in a girl's life."

"We had many loving talks, but she never went too long before popping some pills. Her mood varied dramatically from one hour to the next."

At times, when Judy was inoperative and confined to her bed, a very young Liza had to be like a mother to Joey and Lorna.

Liza and her (biological) father enjoyed their closest relationship with each other following his divorce from Judy in 1951. In February of 1954, he married Georgette Magnani, and in the following year (1955) they had a child, Christiane Nina Minnelli. The marriage took place during the filming of *Brigadoon*, a fantasy romance directed by Minnelli and released in 1954. Cyd Charisse, one of the stars of film, was the bride's matron of honor, and Claude Dauphin was Minnelli's best man.

The couple divorced in 1958.

Minnelli waited four years before marrying again, this time to Denise Gigante, a beauty from Yugoslavia. At the time, he was preparing a remake of *The Four Horsemen of the Apocalypse* (1962). An earlier silent version had propelled Rudolph Valentino into stardom. The male lead of Minnelli's remake was Glenn Ford, who, ironically, was having an affair with Judy.

Minnelli divorced Gigante in 1971 and spent most of the rest of that decade as a bachelor, conducting a series of affairs with young (male) actors hoping to break into movies.

His fourth and final marriage, in April of 1980, was to Margarette Lee Anderson. A very attractive English publicist, she had been married twice before—to a Parisian millionaire, Eugène Suter, and later to a cattle rancher, Marion Getz.

Minnelli and Anderson remained married until Minnelli's death in 1986, when he was 83. He suffered from Alzheimer's disease. His wife survived, eventually dying at the age of 100.

Liza must have found all these fast-evolving relationships confusing, especially when Judy divorced Luft and went on to marry again, twice. "There were a lot of 'steps' (stepfathers and stepmothers) and half-brothers and half-sisters to get used to in this menagerie. I was often ignored, drifting off on my own."

***

Unlike Judy's film career, Minnelli went on to make an array of Hollywood classic melodramas and musicals. Both *An American in Paris* (1951) starring Gene Kelly, and *Gigi* (1958) with Leslie Caron would win Oscars for Best Picture, and for *Gigi*, Minnelli carried home the gold as Best Director. Other much-lauded musicals directed by Minnelli included *The Band Wagon* (1953) with Fred Astaire and Cyd Charisse.

He also excelled at directing dramas. One of the best that he directed was *Lust for Life* (1956) starring Kirk Douglas impersonating Vincent Van Gogh.

Minnelli also tackled the directing of *Some Came Running* (1958) starring Frank Sinatra, Dean Martin, and Shirley MacLaine. *[Derived from a novel by James Jones and set three years after the end of World War II, it's about an emotionally tormented Army veteran who returns to his childhood home in the Midwest and his disastrous encounters with the bourgeois brother he left behind.]*

Vincente Minnelli did not sit idle after his divorce from Judy Garland. He married three more times, and in 1956, he directed a genuinely superb biopic (*Lust for Life*) of the Impressionistic painter, **Vincent Van Gogh.**

In it, superstar **Kirk Douglas** (right photo) portrayed the tormented Dutch painter (left photo) in ways remarkably evocative of the era. Their physical resemblance, it was said at the time, was almost mystical.

It was Gene Kelly who discovered Liza's singing talent. Liza was thirteen when he and Minnelli invited her to join them at a party at the home of Ira and Lee Gershwin. *[There was a rumor that Judy might be there, too, but she didn't show up.]*

Lee asked Liza to sing a song.

Gamely, Liza belted out a rendition of "Swanee." Kelly was impressed and approached her, asking if she would perform a duet with him from *For Me and My Gal,* the 1942 film in which he had co-starred with her mother. Halfway through the song, he stopped singing so that he could listen to Liza's rendition. He liked it so much that he invited her to appear with him in an upcoming TV special.

In its edition of April 24, 1959, *Variety* defined Liza as "a physical and vocal ringer for her mother, Judy Garland."

Throughout the rest of her life, Liza would be compared to her mother.

***

Judy was in Los Angeles in January of 1957, preparing for an upcoming "special" on CBS-TV. She didn't like the proposal sent over by the network, feeling that the songs it featured were duplicates of what she'd already presented either on TV or at The Palace.

Also, the special called for her to lead a big production number, maybe two. She informed CBS that she preferred a more intimate show, an event suitably geared for presentation in family-friendly living rooms across the country. She seemed on the verge of locking herself into a battle station.

Around this time, a story appeared that sent her into a screaming rage: The *Herald Tribune* published an article by Marie Torre quoting an unnamed CBS executive who claimed, "Judy Garland is known for a highly developed inferiority complex. She often doesn't want to work because she's always complaining that something is bothering her."

Torre speculated that what might be bothering her is "that she thinks she is terribly fat."

In the same article, CBS was quoted as having stated, "Miss Garland is not going to treat CBS like she so horribly did with MGM in her younger days."

Already infuriated by all this damaging press and indiscreet leaks to reporters, Judy filed a million-dollar lawsuit, alongside another $400,000 suit for damages after CBS notified her that her five-year deal for those annual TV special concerts had been canceled.

In an attempt to get her to reveal her sources at CBS, Torre was summoned to court during pre-trial hearings She refused to reveal them, and the incident evolved into a *cause célèbre*. The *Journal American* hailed Torre as "the Joan of Arc of Journalism."

The judge sentenced Torre to thirty days in jail. *[It was later reduced to ten days in jail.]* The case generated lots of bad publicity for Judy as Torre was depicted as a mother torn from the arms of her children.

The case dragged on until 1961, when it was officially settled. Judy won nothing and ended up with a bad reputation in show business. It was an aftermath which probably scared off studios and casino showrooms considering whether or not to hire her.

***

At least her contract with Capitol Records was being honored. On February 6, she showed up at the studio on time for a recording session for *Alone,* the title of her next album, a celebration of blues with a theme of loneliness. *[In an earlier era, the songs might have been ideal for Helen Morgan.]*

Gordon Jenkins, its conductor, guided her through such numbers as "By Myself" and "How About Me?" She excelled in Harold Arlen's "I've Got a Right

A theme of existential loneliness as an inevitability of the human condition was alive and thriving in 1957.

The sad implications of being **Alone** were echoed by such writers and philosophers as Jean-Paul Sartre, Albert Camus, and even by Judy Garland.

The cover of her album, *Alone,* is replicated here. It shows her on a lonely beach, glamourously clad in high heels, long gloves, and a tailored coat straight from the pages of Sputnik-era *Vogue.*

410

to Sing the Blues" and also in "Me and My Shadow."

Jenkins said, "Judy is my doll, and I love her madly. Like all great stars, she is inclined to moodiness, which to me is as natural as rain. An artist without temperament is likely to end up a plumber."

Variety wrote: "*Alone* marks a definite departure in the fashioning of Judy Garland for the market. And it should bring big returns. Instead of being big voiced, blasting-grooved technique, applied to her previous packages, she's toned down to a tender and touchy mood that's tremendously affective."

The album was released on May 6 and spent three weeks on the Top 40, though never rising higher than the No. 17 slot.

***

May of 1957 found Judy and Luft back in Las Vegas for a three-week run at the Flamingo Hotel. Her brother-in-law, Jack Carthart, would be her conductor.

The songs she featured as part of her act (they included "Come Rain Or Come Shine" and—you guessed it—"Over the Rainbow") were already familiar to her fans.

"The Man That Got Away" is the story of my life," she said. "I almost cry when I have to sing 'The road gets rougher, lonelier and tougher... There's just no let up...the live-long night and day'"

The African American singer, Pearl Bailey, had just completed her engagement in Vegas, but remained behind to hear Judy sing. She came onstage to greet Judy and embrace her, a gesture that brought wild applause. Bailey said, "My heart drips with tears when I hear Judy sing 'How About Me?' She sings it like she's afraid for her own life."

Judy summoned Liza onto the stage to sing "In Between" and "Swanee." Even Lorna, not quite five, came on to sing "Jingle Bells," the song Judy sang during her first appearance on a stage in 1924 at the age of only two and a half.

The *Hollywood Reporter* noted, "To explain Judy Garland's artistry is like trying to take into parts a globule of mercury."

Variety wrote, "The Strip headliners and the local VIPs were there, and they gave Garland a standing ovation for her efforts. Her act is dramatic yet punctuated with down-to-earth casualness. It is nostalgic yet holds its own in the

Judy would forever sing Harold Arlen's "The Man That Got Away."

**The night is bitter
The stars have lost their glitter
The winds grow colder
Suddenly you're older.**

freshness department. It is fulfilling in that it warmly presents—with intimacy—a living legend."

***

For May and June of 1957, Luft had Judy booked for appearances in Detroit and Dallas. On the last day of May, she began a week-long engagement at the Riviera Theatre in the motor city of Detroit. She performed the same act she'd presented in Las Vegas. On June 2, she was carried onstage because she had injured her ankle.

She completed that engagement and showed up in Dallas in June 19 to entertain at the Dallas State Fair that seemed to bring out half the state of Texas. She had a long-overdue reunion with her sister, Jimmie, who lived there.

Booked for a week, she performed well until Saturday night. She managed to complete only four numbers before bringing the show to an unexpected halt. She announced that she was too emotionally disturbed to go on singing because just before that night's show, she had learned that her long-time dance director, Robert Alton, had died. "I can't sing any more."

She had just passed her 35th birthday. Alton had staged her act at the New Frontier in Las Vegas; her second appearance at The Palace in Manhattan; and most recently, her act at The Flamingo in Vegas.

As they headed back to Los Angeles, Luft told their staff that he feared Judy would not make it through the year. Then another disaster struck. His fears were well grounded.

The final stop on her nine-week tour ended at The Greek Theatre in Los Angeles. She had not played in her "hometown" in five years, and advance ticket sales for her upcoming show there had broken all of the theatre's previous records.

The *Hollywood Reporter* wrote, "The terrific hand she got upon her entrance was nothing when compared to the way she proceeded to put the crowd into the palm of it."

The *Mirror News* claimed, "The capacity audience was mesmerized by her clean, full voice, ringing on the soft summer evening like a mockingbird serenading the moon."

She got through the gig without a hitch. Then, devastating news arrived in her dressing room on the final night of her gig. Her agents at MCA confiscated $38,000 of her fees as "unpaid commissions" to which, according to her contract with them, they were entitled.

She insisted in front of Luft that she needed to make money—and quick. The IRS was hounding her for back taxes, and household expenses, including her mortgage payments, were going unpaid. She told her agents at MCA that she was "bored and fed up" with playing American cities, and that she wanted them to set up a return engagement for her at the Palladium in London.

The next day, she was informed that although the Palladium was not available, the large Dominion Theatre, was.

Luft began to calculate the math of what it would cost to transport Judy, the kids, and "The Boyfriends" to England. He simply did not have enough cash, so—managing her protests and setting her hopes for a return to England into the middle-term future—he arranged gigs for her in Washington, D.C. and in Philadelphia, instead.

***

In Washington, they checked into the Sheraton. Almost immediately, Judy announced that she felt a case of the flu coming on, and that she was running a temperature.

The hotel doctor was summoned and she insisted on seeing him only when Luft wasn't present in the room. When the doctor emerged from her bedroom, he assured Luft that he had given her a mild sedative so that she could sleep peacefully.

The next morning, Luft grew suspicious that he'd given her doses of more powerful medications, perhaps Seconal and/or Dexedrine. But although she was quite hoarse, she was determined to go on on opening night, September 16.

She more or less "pulled off" the show, although one critic claimed, "No one gets a frog in her throat or misses a note with more grace and enthusiasm than Judy Garland."

After the show, Luft escorted her to the home of Perle Mesta, the most famous and celebrated hostess in Washington and the former ambassador (for four years beginning in 1949 during the administration of Harry S Truman) to Luxembourg. Mesta had invited the elite of Washington to meet and greet Judy.

The next morning, *Variety* wrote: "This is a different kind of theatrical arrangement. It's a love affair between Judy Garland and the folks who are paying up to $6.60 for a ticket. Miss Garland makes a quick rapport with her audience, and you can feel the affection they have for her from the time she opens up with her big, deep voice."

For the Saturday matinee, she brought both Lorna and Joey up on the stage. To Lorna, she sang "Rock-a-Bye My Baby to a Dixie Melody," and Joey sat on her lap as she sang "Happiness Is a Thing Called Joe."

On the morning of her final performance in Washington, she slept until 11AM and woke up as her breakfast was being prepared. Luft was already awake and greeted her as she headed for the bathroom, where she was gone for about ten minutes. When she emerged she held up both of her wrists to him. She had slashed each with a razor, and blood was pouring out.

Shouting for the maid, he ordered her to bring him two of his neckties and managed to stop the flow of blood by applying a tight tourniquet to each of her lower arms.

Then he called the hotel's doctor but was told that he never worked on Sunday. A substitute doctor, who was available for emergencies every Sunday, was summoned from across the state line in Virginia. Luft got him on the phone and explained the situation, urging discretion. All he needed now was more publicity about another of Judy's suicide attempts. The doctor promised to cooperate and informed Luft that he had a small operating room attached to his home.

413

Luft and his assistant, Harry Rubin (Judy's secret lover), drove her to Virginia where the doctor was waiting. He gave her an injection of Sodium Pentathol, which rendered her unconscious. The then sutured and bandaged her wrists.

Judy slept for three hours. When she opened her eyes, Luft was there at her bedside, looking down at her. "Why did you do it, darling?"

She stared at him blankly. "Sid, in all honesty, I don't know. I don't recall doing it."

Then he had to call the theater and listen to the abusive fury of its manager after he canceled her final show. Seat holders who had gathered were given a refund.

Back with Judy alone in their lodgings at the Sheraton, he dreaded having to ask the next question: "Do I cancel Philadelphia, too?"

"No," she said. "I think I can make it—with a little help from you. I have these bracelets to cover the bandages on my wrists."

***

On September 26, Judy appeared for her opening night at the Manhattan Theatre in Philadelphia. *[It had been the largest in America until the opening, in 1932, of Radio City in Manhattan.]* She had recently changed her hair style, now wearing it long and with a ponytail.

Comedian Alan King, her opening act, was followed by two vaudeville performances. Then Judy came onstage to sing the familiar songs, plus two she had performed less frequently in the past, including "Mean to Me" and "By Myself," concluding with "Over the Rainbow."

The *Philadelphia Enquirer* wrote: "If the audience had its way, Judy Garland would still be singing."

Trouble seemed to be her middle name. The Asian flu came back to attack her, and her two last performances scheduled as part of the gig in Philadelphia had to be canceled.

***

After the cancellation of shows in both Washington, D.C. and Philadelphia, Judy and Luft ended up with no profit for the two-week engagements. "She was making my life miserable," Luft protested. "Still demanding that I take her to London with the kids and those dancing boys. I felt she might be better off in a clinic."

He flew to New York, checking into the elegant Hotel Pierre. He must have called a dozen business associates before Peter Lawford agreed to extend a small loan. There was a certain irony in that: *[In his declining years, it was Lawford who hit Luft up for a loan, as he did to several others of his friends, including Elizabeth Taylor.]*

In desperation, Luft sold his racehorse, Sienna II, a baby mare. Shortly after that, he received an unexpected visitor, Freddie Finklehoffe, who had once written film scripts for Judy and—until the arrival on the scene of Sid Luft—had seriously considered marrying her.

According to Luft, "I met him (Finkelhoffe) in the bar at the Pierre, and he sashayed over to me and ordered a double martini. He had news for me, telling me that Roman II had broken his leg.

[Roman II was a racehorse that Luft jointly owned with Charlie Whittingham. The horse was insured for $30,000. Luft's 50% of the insurance payout would, several weeks later, be sent to him in England.]

The following evening, Judy, along with Lorna and Joey, arrived in New York from Los Angeles. As Luft remembered it, she was "wearing a trillion pearl bracelets to cover her bandaged wrists after that razor blade slicing."

"I was in dire straits, and I needed money immediately," Luft said. "I had written checks to everybody, including Judy's dancing boys, and I had no money in my bank account."

He met with Ben Maksik, owner of the Town and Country night club in Brooklyn, where he had signed a contract for Judy to appear there in March of 1958.

As an advance payment for Judy's impending appearance at the Town and Country, Maksik promised he'd bring $15,000 in a brown paper bag to the S.S. United States. Built in 1950-51, and retired from transatlantic passenger service in 1969, it was waiting in port and about to sail to England. Fifteen minutes before departure, Maksik had not arrived, and Luft was in a state of panic. But at the last minute, he showed up with the money.

The Luft family departed for the U.K. aboard the S.S. United States on October 4, and many of the passengers were excited by the possibility that they might get to meet Judy Garland.

"Judy and I had sex en route to England," Luft told his assistant, Harry Rubin. "But the love, the passion, was gone. I'd have to find that in other women. I'm sure Judy had her fellows on the side."

[Luft may have been aware that Rubin himself was one of "her fellows," although the two of them never had a confrontation over Judy.]

"I know my days as Judy's husband are coming to an end, although I may hang out as her manager for a few more years. I have to find a new source of money making. She's too much for me. I'd get her jobs and then she wouldn't show up, or else show up drunk and drugged. She turned me into her whipping boy. She would sabotage me with her sliced wrists, her pill taking, he constant physical breakdowns, I loved Lorna and Joey, however, and they kept me hanging in there for far too long a time."

***

The S.S. United States pulled into England's port of Southampton on October 9, and the Lufts boarded a train to London's Waterloo Station, arriving at 4:30AM. From there, they took taxis to the Savoy Hotel [two were required to transport their entourage and their luggage] and checked into two separate suites.

The desk handed Judy a note from Prince Aly Khan, who was staying at the Savoy, too. He urged her to call him for a rendezvous.

After sleeping for most of the day, Judy put on her most elegant gown and went with Luft to Londonderry House [a posh 18th-Century townhouse on Park Lane in Mayfair] where a reception had been arranged in her honor from 6:30 to 8:30PM.

During the night that followed, two members of the Savoy staff spotted Judy coming and going from Aly Khan's suite. In spite of his secret affair with Judy, Khan still maintained his friendship with Luft, which was based on their shared devotion to horse racing.

Two days later, Judy arrived at the studio of Capitol-EMI to record "It's So Lovely To Be Back in England," a song written for her by Roger Edens specifically for her opening night at the Dominion Theatre. Posters and handbills distributed throughout London alerted locals that Judy was set to open *The Judy Garland Show* at the Dominion on October 16, 1957. Clearly understood was that her engagement would run for four and a half weeks, causing Luft to wonder how many performances Judy would miss.

[The Dominion had already enjoyed great success with other bookings of American talent. Previous headliners there had included Judy's friend, Sophie Tucker, as well as Louis Armstrong, and Bill Haley and the Comets. The Rank Organization, owner of the theater, had been so pleased with the idea of booking Judy that they had already spent $180,000 on its restoration.]

On opening night, the 3,000-seat theater was filled to capacity.

Buddy Bragman, Judy's music arranger, devised a musical package that he later designated as "The Garland Overture," a medley of her most crowd-pleasing songs: "The Trolley Song" and "The Man That Got Away." The style of that "package" would open Judy's shows for the rest of her life.

She ended her opening night with "Over the Rainbow," and was then called back for two encores, "Me and My Shadow," and "Swanee."

Richard Finlater of the *Observer* filed the most evocative report of the many that reviewed her return to London:

> "Judy Garland turns the Dominion into a place of pilgrimage for all nostalgists who sigh for the splendours of the old-time music hall. Carefully rationed, atrociously dressed, and brilliantly reinforced, she presents at first the melancholy sight of a star who has outgrown her myth. In the quick turn of her head, the upward glance of her eyes, one sees for a moment the little girl lost, trapped in someone else's body by time's practical joke. And then, as she warms up to the audience, one hears the sound of trumpets: the approach of the new Garland, lifting up her voice and making what Archie Rice calls 'a great big beautiful noise' that cannonades around the theater.*
>
> *Although `A Couple of Swells' has been fussed-up since she first danced it with Astaire on the screens, it is in the girl-tramp's patched and baggy trousers, with muck face and golliwog wig, that Miss Garland gets her freedom, and demonstrates that heart-warming strength and energy and exuberance in which our own songstresses are so sadly lacking, however tasteful their wardrobes, however slim their waists."*

Some members of the British press were rather blunt in commenting on her weight. In the *Daily Express*, John Barber wrote: "At her current 165 pounds, it is easy to see why Judy Garland can't fly over the rainbow." Other comments called her "square-faced, homely, a bang-it-out Garland,"

and compared her to the heavyweight Sophie Tucker.   Another wrote, "Today, Dorothy is a heavy matron."

In the *Daily Mirror,* Clifford Davis wrote, "Judy Garland came back to London last night—and London loved her for it. There will never be another like her."

The New Chronicle wrote: "The spotlight picked up the dirty little gamin's face as she sang 'Over the Rainbow,' squatting on the stage by the footlights. We wondered at the strange guise in which genius can appear."

During three nights of the gig, Judy developed a sore throat. On some of these occasions, Luft brought her onstage in her dressing robe to show the audience that she was neither drunk nor drugged, but genuinely ill. On one such night, she said, "What the hell! I'll sing 'em all anyway, even in my froggy voice." Then, after some flawed renditions, she quipped, "I sounded like Sophie Tucker's grandmother."

During the run of Judy's gig, Prince Aly Khan and Luft went to Newcastle for three days to bid on a filly. To help her get through those nights, Judy summoned Alan King to her suite, keeping him away from his wife, Jeanette. She continued talking and drinking until the break of dawn.

DOMINION TOTTENHAM COURT ROAD — THEATRE

OPENING
WED 16th OCTOBER
(inc. SAT 19th NOV.)
NIGHTLY AT **8.0 p.m.**
MATINEES WEDS & SATS at 2.30

ON THE STAGE

Incomparable!
Delightful!
The one and only!

MISS SHOW BUSINESS

JUDY GARLAND

in Person and her own **ALL STAR VARIETY SHOW**

with **ALAN KING** WARNER BROTHERS NEW COMEDY STAR

BOOK NOW!
ALL SEATS BOOKABLE PHONE: MUS 2176
& AT ALL TICKET AGENCIES
COACH AND PARTY BOOKINGS ACCEPTED

One British critic wrote, "After keeping a star-studded and critical audience waiting at the newly and expensively decorated Dominion on Tottenham Court Rd., where she is appearing for a 4 1/2 week booking, the diminutive, dumpy figure, clad in a dress which did nothing to help, and a most extraordinary hair style, came on to be greeted with roar after roar of welcome..."

"Afterward, Petula Clark, Vera Lynn, Donna Reed, and Alma Cogan presented her with baskets of flowers."

"There was no hanky-panky," King said. "She needed someone at her side to get her through the night. One time at 2AM, she demanded that I take her to Petticoat Lane to see the hookers."

"We picked up three of them and brought them back to her suite. Judy just wanted to talk to them and hear their stories about the tricks they'd made it with. When dawn came, she had me pay the girls what they might have earned for a night's work. I became the only man in England who spent the night with a coven of whores—and didn't get laid."

***

On November 18, Judy took time out to join the all-star cast at the *Royal Command Performance Variety Show* at the Palladium, the scene of her earlier triumph. Guests of honor included Queen Elizabeth II; Elizabeth, the

Queen Mother; and Prince Philip.

Judy sang three songs, including "Over the Rainbow." Also on the bill were Gracie Fields, Count Basie, and Tommy Steele.

Mario Lanza (Judy referred to him as "My fling from yesterday") had been hired to fly in for a guest appearance. He was overweight and in poor health.

Onstage, he was not in good voice, and many in the audience jeered and mocked him. He sang only two songs before hastily exiting from the stage. Luft followed him to his dressing room and found him bent over the toilet bowl "vomiting his guts out."

Judy was still loyal to Lanza, and asked Luft if he'd manage his career. Luft rejected the idea. As he told Alan King, "Trying to manage one walking disaster is more than I can handle."

Backstage, Judy joined the performers lined up to greet Queen Elizabeth and her entourage. The Queen Mother told her, "I had tears in my eyes when I heard you sing 'Over the Rainbow.'"

Queen Elizabeth told her, "You've long been a favorite of mine, and I've seen many of your movies. Come back to England more often."

Standing apart from his wife, who was otherwise engaged, Philip was rather flirtatious. "When I saw you in *Easter Parade,* I wanted to skip out on Liz and rush off to Hollywood to track you down."

"I wish you had," she answered.

***

On November 21, 1957, Judy, with Luft and the kids, sailed back to New York. There, with virtually no time to settle in, they boarded a train to Chicago for a brief stopover, then transferred to the Super Chief for the ongoing railway transit to Los Angeles.

November 30 found them settled once again in their home in Holmby Hills, where months of unpaid bills had piled up. "Talk about coming home to face a dose of reality," Luft quipped.

The trip to London had been a critical success but a financial failure. Luft was left with only $1,400 in the bank, with urgently overdue bills totaling $50,000, and massive additional debts owed to the IRS.

Their financial adviser, Morgan Maree, arrived with two boxes filled with their important documents, returning them before resigning. As he headed out the door, he gave them some final advice: "File for bankruptcy."

Luft rejected that idea, fearing an avalanche of unwanted publicity that would further damage Judy's career and "bankability.'".

Although she didn't want to talk about it, Luft demanded that she listen to him. "I've got to find gigs for you or soon you, me, and our offspring will be out on the street."

"I know how I'm going to handle this crisis," she said. "Time for me to get a razor blade and slash my wrists."

The next morning when Luft awakened, he headed immediately to her bedroom. There, he found her in a deep, trance-like sleep. Obviously, she had sedated herself. Luft decided to let her continue sleeping...for the rest of the day if she could.

On her night table, he picked up a note she'd written. He was relieved that it was not a suicide letter, as he had first anticipated.

It read:

"Dear God. I am asking for help. I need help. I need strength and some kind of courage that has left me. My soul needs healing. My needs are many. Give me the strength to crush my fear and cowardice. Let me face life and the fun it must hold. Help me with my bad nerves and illness until the whiskey is out of my body. Let me see the loveliness awaiting me. Help me find You. Help me make the most of my splendid life. I have lost my way—Please God—let me find it. Let me find dignity and health."

Perhaps her parents' invitations to join them in adult settings were their way of increasing her social skills, self-confidence and poise. In any event, beginning early, **Liza** was positioned on a fast track to adulthood, whether she fully understood it (or wanted it) or not.

On the left, **Liza appears onstage with her mother** at the Cocoanut Grove in 1958.

On the right, at around the same time, **she dances with her (adoring) father** at a Hollywood party.

A Proud and Loving Parent: Judy with her children **(Liza, Lorna, and Joey)** appeared in this press photo taken at NYC's Idlewild Airport in 1962, prior to its renaming after JFK's death

COMEBACK CONCERTS
LATE NIGHTS, FAST LIVING, TOO MANY PILLS, & HIGH-JINX RAZZMATAZZ RISK DAMAGING HER VOCAL CORDS

THE LONG ARM OF UNCLE SAM
TAX AUDITS AND PENALTIES FROM THE IRS

JUDY FIELDS ISSUES WITH BOBBY VAN, CAPITOL RECORDS, & DRUNKS WHO HECKLE HER ONSTAGE IN VEGAS.

FIGHTS & FANCY FINANCING FROM SID LUFT.

LIZA DROPS OUT OF COLLEGE FOR A CAREER IN SHOW BIZ

JUDY GOES HIGHBROW
HER OPERA TOUR BRINGS OUT A MORE DIGNIFIED DIVA AND ELICITS A CITATION FROM HIZZONER, THE MAYOR OF NYC

BENNETT CERF, PRESIDENT OF RANDOM HOUSE, COMMISSIONS JUDY'S AUTOBIOGRAPHY, WHICH SHE FAILS TO PRODUCE

JUDY PROMOTES THE DEMOCRATS
JFK, ADLAI STEVENSON, AND ELEANOR ROOSEVELT WELCOME HER TO THEIR PARTY

SAPPHIC SUSPICIONS FROM ETHEL MERMAN

"Life with Judy Garland is like trying to climb Mount Everest in high heels."

—Sid Luft

"Liza Minnelli's voice makes me think of her mother, although I'm sure she doesn't want to be compared all the time. But she can't escape it. She's got the same kind of pathos as Judy. Liza is sweet and charming, with a lot of her mother's qualities."

—Gene Kelly

"I often think of all my god damn, marvelous, failed, successful but hopelessly tragic and sorrowful years I have survived."

—Judy Garland

To rescue his family financially, Luft hurriedly negotiated a deal for Judy's return to Las Vegas. Judy and kids arrived in Nevada on Christmas Day, 1957, and checked into the Flamingo, where she would open the following night for a three-week engagement. The booking carried with it a hefty paycheck of $40,000 a week in an era when some "name" entertainers were drawing $3,000 to $4,000 a week.

Alan King was not available to appear with her, so Luft hired bouncy Bobby Van instead. Born to Jewish vaudeville parents in the Bronx, he was six years her junior. From the 1950s to the '70s, he had a career in films and TV. Judy had seen him in *The Affairs of Dobie Gillis* (1953) in which he'd co-starred with Debbie Reynolds. He had achieved a dubious kind of fame that same year when he'd made like a human pogo stick during an expansive musical production, *Small Town Girl*. In the 1960s, he would do comedy work in films and television with Mickey Rooney.

Judy asked him about the origin of his name, Van. Bobby answered, "I stole if from Van Johnson. It's really Stein."

Although as her gig progressed, Judy would usually open her show with *The Garland Overture*. On this, its opening night, she sang numbers from *My Fair Lady,* and a duet with Van, "You're Just in Love."

If a singer wants rapt attention, Las Vegas is not the place to perform during a national holiday. Its showrooms were packed with revelers. Eating and drinking, they seemed to prefer talking and dancing to paying rapt attention to a performer — even one with a *schtick* as celebrated as Judy's. She certainly didn't wow her audiences with a trim physique, as she looked bloated and her voice was fading, no longer with any of its former power.

As she moved through more and more of her numbers in ways that even she considered lackluster, she stopped singing altogether. Liza had been waiting in the wings, watching as her mother struggled through her act. "Ladies and gentlemen," Judy suddenly announced. "I give you Liza Minnelli."

Bobbie Van with Debbie Reynolds in The *Affairs of Dobie Gillis* (1953).

One critic wrote, "An exuberantly gawky,. ever-smiling dancer with something of a passing resemblance to Ray Bolger, it was Bobby Van's bad luck to come along just when his sort of showcase was riding off into the sunset."

Whereas die-hard Garland fans knew who the eleven-year-old was, many members of the audience that night didn't keep up with daughters of movie stars.

A bewildered little girl was virtually yanked onto the stage to perform before a tough, hard-drinking crowd. Although she had not been rehearsed, and had no agreement about what to sing, she knew most of her mother's songs, and signaled the band what they should play. In this baptism of fire, she struggled on like a brave trouper, even enduring catcalls and jeers from the audience. Finally, her act ended with only scattered applause.

The next day, the Vegas press wanted to know why Judy dragged Liza on when the audience had obviously paid to see her.

Judy replied:

> *"I don't want to bring my children up as performers. I want to bring them up as human beings. But because I make a living in show business, I want them to know what it is I do, to understand completely that there are many other people involved, both backstage and in the audience. I think it would be a mistake to keep them from meeting the wonderful people I come in contact with. In addition, I want them to be unself-conscious in public, and to have a completely natural feeling about the fact that their mother is a public figure."*

For the next four nights, Judy complained of damaged vocal cords and insisted that she could not go onstage at the Flamingo. That meant a salary loss of a desperately needed $160,000.

423

In a subterfuge, with the intention of rustling up some cash, Luft went to the casino's cashier on one of the building's lower floors and asked for $5,000 in gambling chips, with instructions to deduct their value from Judy's salary. Then, as part of his plan, he migrated upstairs to one of the gaming tables and—perhaps intentionally—lost $300.

Then, when a crony, as pre-arranged, summoned him to a phone call, he left the table, waited until a new cashier came on duty, presented the $4,700 in chips as if he'd won them at the gaming tables, and exchanged them for cash.

In Vegas, during the final days of 1957, the tension between Judy and Luft became so raw and toxic that he opted to be absent most of the time. On virtually any occasion they came together, there was a fight. Then he was reported to have been seen at the Sands going up the elevator with two showgirls.

When he did return on December 31, she told him she wanted to attempt a star performance at the Flamingo's New Year's Eve show.

That night, as Vegas was ringing out the old and bringing in the new, Judy faced the rowdiest, rudest audience of her entire career. The room was jam-packed and smoke-filled, the revelers, as before, preferring to eat, drink, dance, and be merry rather than listen to a singer, even a big name like Judy Garland.

She struggled on with her songs, facing catcalls and jeers. A large man in a booming voice yelled, "Get off the stage, fatso!" There were calls of "has-been," even charges that she was drunk and drugged. Finally, she burst into tears and ran off the stage.

She came back on at midnight to sing "Auld Lang Syne" with Van.

***

After Judy's return to Holmby Hills with her children, she bolted herself in her bedroom and would not see Luft. He checked into a motel.

To meet emergency expenses, he borrowed another $25,000 from the Town and Country night club in Brooklyn. [He'd already borrowed $15,000 from the club as an advance against Judy's upcoming booking there in March.]

Liza, in retrospect, recalled this "perilous" time in her life. "My childhood was an interesting period for me, except it had nothing to do with being a child."

"I was not quite twelve when I was pushed out on that Vegas stage before that crowd of revelers. Some people found it odd that a girl of my age put so much emotion into 'The Man That Got Away.'"

***

As the first days of 1958 unfolded, Judy relentlessly wandered from room to room of her house in Holmby Hills, wondering what to do next with her life.

She had grown increasingly disillusioned with her marriage to Luft and felt she had to come to a decision. "It had degenerated into one big quarrel. I knew what a sexual animal he was, but he wasn't getting it at home—that's for damn sure."

"When I did come home, which was rare," Luft confessed, "it was mainly to see Joey and Lorna. If I encountered Judy, I never knew what mood she'd be in. She had never stopped pill popping, and on some days, she swallowed more than the usual dosage. You couldn't be in the room for more than five minutes before she started raging about something, picking a fight. It got so I had nothing to come home to. At times, as she became more and more withdrawn, Liza, as the older child, assumed the duties of getting the kids off to school and seeing that they were fed."

"Judy was not only heavily drugged but had taken to boozing to excess. I kept the liquor cabinet locked. One night when I slipped in, I headed for it since I needed a triple before facing her. To my amazement, I found all the bottles full. That didn't make sense. I had lowered the liquor in some, and we'd had guests in. I decided to test a bottle of bourbon. My suspicions were confirmed: It was filled with colored water."

"So now, flowing through her blood stream, I could add booze to the barbiturates. Hell broke loose one night in late January. She found me packing two suitcases and accused me of running out on the children without providing enough money to feed them. I told her I had placed $25,000, a loan, in our joint account for groceries and to provide for their expenses. She rushed over to assault me, and I sort of spun her around, shoving her back on the bad. She hit rolling over, reminding me of Raggedy Ann."

"Hearing her screams, I left the house with my baggage and checked into a small hotel on Wilshire Boulevard. Peace at least."

In one of her most outrageous claims, Judy charged that she came upon Luft having sex with the very young Liza. "That was outrageous," Luft said. "Didn't she know how explosive a charge that was? Perhaps she did."

One afternoon, Frank Sinatra dropped by, having not seen her for a long time. She poured out her bitter feelings about Luft. "I need to work but going on stage to perform in my condition frightens me. It's all been too much, and I don't know if I can go on singing."

"In the past, Luft sometimes literally had to push me onto the stage. Trouble follows me around. I could rattle off the disasters—a doomed marriage, bad health, weight gain, a pill addiction, too many boozy nights, unpaid taxes, bad press, endless pressure. But most of all, lost illusions."

"Welcome to the club, baby," Sinatra said.

In late February, she phoned Jerry Giesler, hailed as the best lawyer in Tinseltown. Word was out that if you committed murder, "call Giesler." He had defended Errol Flynn on charges of statutory rape, and Marilyn Monroe during her divorce from Joe DiMaggio. Others he'd represented included Cheryl Crane, daughter of Lana Turner, when she was charged with fatally stabbing her mother's gangster lover, Johnny Stompanato. Giesler's clients had also included Joan Crawford, the gangster, Bugsy Siegel, Zsa Zsa Gabor, and Charlie Chaplin.

On March 1, Judy had Giesler officially file for divorce, charging Luft with physical violence and mental cruelty. She claimed that at their home, he had tried to strangle her. "He wanted to cut off the beautiful songs that came from my throat," she told Giesler.

After Luft deposited that loan of $25,000 into their joint account, she withdrew $9,000. Five thousand of it went to pay Giesler, an advance on his fee.

She also got him to hire Fred Otash—the most famous private investigator in Hollywood— for security services on their home, specifically to prevent Luft from entering it. *[Forever associated with the problems and cover-ups associated with the death of Marilyn Monroe, Otash was the inspiration for the character portrayed by Jack Nicholson in Roman Polanski's* Chinatown *(1974).]*

After filing for divorce, Judy gathered up her children, including Liza, and boarded a train for New York in advance of her appearance at the Town and Country nightclub in Brooklyn. *En route,* Judy staged a small birthday party for Liza, who had turned twelve.

In Manhattan, her engagement would mark her first opening night without Luft since 1951. She was overweight and in poor physical condition, but she was determined to pull it off.

Before that could happen, she was visited by an agent from the State Collector's office in Albany, demanding that she pay $8,000 for back taxes stemming from income earned from her 1951 performance at The Palace in New York City.

An agreement was forged whereby the tax authorities would deduct $3,000 a week from her $25,000 weekly paycheck from the Town and Country. She knew she had to pull off that gig in Brooklyn...or else.

She'd made a deal with Ben Maksik, owner of the Town and Country, to rent her (without charge) a beach house and to supply two Pinkerton guards who would prevent Luft from entering it. Maksik's "rental" was in the sea-fronting neighborhood of Neponsit, in Far Rockaway, Queens.

During her stay there, Liza became what Judy dubbed, "My Girl Friday." She ran errands, answered mail, handled phone calls, and nursed and massaged her mother. She even offered counseling during Judy's sleepless nights. With braces and a ponytail, the twelve-year-old became almost essential to her mother's survival.

On the morning of her opening on March 20, a ferocious 24-hour blizzard descended on New York City. In a chauffeured limousine, she made it from her rented house in Neponsit to the Town and Country Theater, a 20-mile trek through the blinding snow. She wondered if any fans would show up for her opening.

She need not have worried, since 1,700 fans filled up all the seats. She was supposed to go on at 10:30PM but went on at 11, following Bobby Van's opening act. Luft had flown to New York and was staying in Manhattan at the Warwick. Van phoned him every night to report on Judy and the show.

She opened with the song "Brooklyn," which brought loud cheers from the audience. Otherwise, she performed songs well known to the audience, many of which she had made famous. With Bobby Van, she sang two duets, concluding the show with "Swanee" and "Over the Rainbow."

Although Maksik had been generous in the weeks leading up to the gig, giving her a free home, hiring security guards, arranging a chauffeur, and loaning her money, trouble set in right away. As had been agreed, she was to perform two shows a night, but belligerently, she insisted that she was going to do only one. An agreement was subsequently negotiated and sealed. Her fee was revised to payment of only $12,500 per week, reduced from her original fee of $25,000 per week.

More trouble set in on her second night, when her performance did not rise to the level it had reached on opening night. She was not in top form, and the applause generated was lukewarm. She also had a big, somewhat demented argument with Maksik, accusing him of plotting with Luft to kidnap her children.

Her condition worsened by the day, with many emergency trips to the bathroom. She'd developed colitis, a painful inflammation of the colon.

Then she phoned the club owner, demanding that he pay her entire fee in advance, which he refused. "Then I'll not go on tonight," she said, before slamming down the phone.

The audience had already started to fill the room, and he was forced to inform them from the stage that Judy would not be performing, and that the box office would refund the cost of their tickets.

Just after he made that announcement, word reached him that Judy had appeared and was almost ready to go on. She'd also phoned Luft at the Warwick, asking him to come back to her, He was *en route* to the theater.

Defying the owner, whom she'd thrown into chaos, Judy went on, singing (probably with a sense of irony) "Life Is Just a Bowl of Cherries." But she broke off before finishing, explaining to the audience that she had laryngitis and couldn't continue. Furious, Maksik ordered the control room to switch off her microphone, but not before she said, "What does it matter anyway? I've been fired!" The news stunned the audience.

Just after she left the stage, she en-

THE WORLD'S MOST MAGNIFICENT NIGHT CLUB

VOICE OF BROADWAY—

Round-The-Clock Guards Protecting Judy Garland

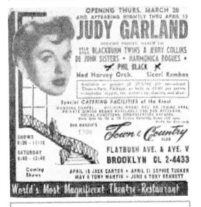

HOW NOT TO BE A POPULAR SUCCESS IN BROOKLYN

Judy's gig there was embarrassing, badly managed, ruinously expensive, socially awkward, and regrettable in almost every way.

Completely fed up, Town & Country's owner finally shouted at Luft: "Get that bitch out of my club!"

countered Luft, who was feuding with Maksik, who had moved Judy's jewelry into his safe and was refusing to give it back.

Maksik told Luft, "I didn't want your wife to go on tonight. Each performance has gotten worse and worse. I owe it to my customers to dump her."

In front of Judy, Maksik ordered Luft to "get that bitch out of my club. She's a fucking lunatic. **Out! OUT!** I've had it with her."

Judy finally got her jewelry back, but he evicted her from the beach house. Luft arranged to move her and the kids into a pair of suites at the Drake Hotel in Manhattan.

That night at the Drake, Judy and Luft had a reconciliation. He slept in the same bed with her. As he later claimed, "She told me, 'Take care of your Little Girl Lost. She needs you, baby. Don't ever leave me.'"

On April 1, Judy and Luft called a press conference. As reported in New York's *Daily News,* he announced that the Town and Country had already advanced them $25,000.

In front of reporters, Judy turned to him and asked, "What happened to the money?"

He answered, "Just ask Uncle Sam." He also claimed that in the previous three years, Judy had earned "a cool million."

Once again in front of reporters, she asked him, "But what happened to the money?"

He answered, "You'll find out, dear."

That afternoon, Deputy Sheriff John Brennan arrived at the Drake with a warrant. Two policemen barged in after him and confiscated Judy's jewelry and costumes with the intention of holding them as "ransom" until she paid her taxes.

She was ordered to get dressed, after which she was escorted by squad car to the courthouse. In the meantime, Luft phoned attorney Maurice Greenbaum to meet Judy at the courthouse, where a judge ruled that she could not leave the State of New York until the taxes were paid.

Luft desperately phoned around, trying to raise money. Peter Lawford sent a check for only $1,500. Then Luft managed to get through to Frank Day, one of his business associates in Detroit, who wired $9,000.

It was Judy who saved the day when she heard that Prince Aly Khan was in town. They met that afternoon, and he agreed to settle her back taxes with New York. She was seen dancing with him, cheek to cheek, that night at Harwin's, a chic night club. Her overweight did not seem to bother him.

In Brooklyn, Town and Country quickly booked Betty Hutton as Judy's replacement. She had previously replaced her in *Annie Get Your Gun* and was now doing it again.

On Hutton's opening night, she rather quirkily chastised the audience for being rude to Judy, describing her as "one of the great entertainers of our time." [Alas, the problem with that was that the audience being criticized were not the patrons who had witnessed Judy' previous debacle onstage.]

It wasn't until mid-April, when California was in blossom, that Judy, Luft, and the kids migrated by train back to Los Angeles to face an uncertain future.

Before her next gig, Judy had lunch with June Allyson, telling her, "The wolf is at my door. Kids cost so much money, as do husbands. Fortunately, you're married to a provider."

Judy went on to describe her upcoming performance at the Minnesota State Ceremonial Celebration. "I'm from Minnesota. For my opening number, I think I'll steal from the song that goes, 'California, here I come, right back where I started from.' I'll switch to 'Minnesota, here I come.'"

On May 7, 1958, she appeared before a crowd of 20,000, opening with a specialty number, "At Long Last, Here I Am." She also publicly shared memories of her girlhood growing up in Minnesota, but only the good ones.

During her time in Minnesota, Judy and Luft held a press conference, announcing that in the autumn he'd produce a big Broadway musical, *Born in Wedlock,* whose cast would include "a big name yet to be cast."

He then revealed that he would make the film version, too, and that it would star "my own little canary, Miss Judy Garland, otherwise known forever as Mrs. Sid Luft." Then he planted a big wet one on her lips.

***

Back in Hollywood, Capitol Records still had faith in Judy. Her previous records had sold well, each making the Top 40. She returned to their studio on May 19 to begin recording her latest album, *Judy in Love,* as arranged by Nelson Riddle.

There would be no more songs about loneliness in this album. It would be devoted to happy times and happy tunes.

Three numbers from Cole Porter were included: "I Concentrate on You," "Do I Love You?," and "I Am Loved." On the flip side, she sang such numbers as Johnny Mercer's "Day In, Day Out."

"Do I Love You?" had been introduced on Broadway by Ethel Merman in 1939 in the stage production of *Du Barry Was a Lady.* "This Is It" was also introduced on Broadway by Merman the same year. "I Can't Give You Anything But Love" was the first big hit of Dorothy Fields and Jimmy McHugh back in 1928.

When her **Judy in Love** album was released, *High Fidelity* wrote that it was grateful that she had opted NOT to include "Over the Rainbow."

"She tackles songs somewhat removed from her regular repertoire," their critic wrote.

"She gives an exuberant and exciting performance. In some numbers, she still manages to suggest the wide-eyed wonder that endeared her to the public twenty years ago. The album is a must for Garland fans."

On June 10, Judy took time out from recording to celebrate her 36th birthday.

***

Judy's most glamourous booking in 1958 was for a return to the exclusive Hollywood nightclub, the Cocoanut Grove at the Ambassador Hotel, where, in June of 1968, Robert F. Kennedy would be assassinated.

Although the venue itself was elegant, the star being featured there claimed, "My ankles were swollen and so was my face. I looked like I'd been pumped up with a bicycle pump."

Freddy Martin conducted the orchestra, with staging by Chuck Walters and special material by Roger Edens.

Judy's two-week engagement opened on July 23. There were no vaudeville acts or comedian opening acts to precede her appearance. All it involved was an hour's worth of songs, a one-star, low-key presentation. Once again, as she had in other concerts, she opened with the "Garland Overture," before entertaining the audience with renditions of "Day In, Day Out," "After You've Gone," "Over the Rainbow," (of course), and one novelty song that had become a big hit earlier in the 1950s, "Purple People Eater." *[Frank Sinatra also had a crack at that hit.]* Edens had written special material for her to sing. His satirical renditions provided a platform from which she could gracefully poke fun at her overweight body and her recent tangles with the New York State Tax Authorities.

The Cocoanut Grove was loaded with stars who arrived to welcome and acknowledge her, including Rock Hudson, who had once had a fling with her. One of her most faithful supporters, Sinatra himself, showed up, although their romance had disappeared with the summer wind.

Marlon Brando, whom she knew only casually, came backstage. As he later told his best friend, Carlo Fiore, "When I went to kiss her on the cheek, she gave me a lip lock and felt my crotch."

Lauren Bacall welcomed her, as did Lana Turner, Don Murray, Jerry Lewis, and singer Pat Boone, whom she referred to as "Goodie Two Shoes."

Reviews of her performance, for the most part, were raves. Critic Wylie Williams wrote, "The audience wanted to bring her back for more. There was foot stamping on the floor, plus cries of 'Bravo,' most unusual for a Grove audience."

Hollywood's reigning gossip maven, Louella Parsons, gushed, "In all the years I've been covering this town, I've never seen such a turnout of stars, nor have I felt under one roof such an outpouring of affection and love as greeted Judy, the home town girl, when she appeared at the top of the stairs in her cute 'lady tuxedo' garb. What a show—what a night! She gave back all that affection by singing her heart out. I think we all realized we were enjoying an event that has seldom been equaled and will hardly ever be topped."

The Hollywood Reporter gave her one of her greatest reviews: "What words fit Niagara Falls and the Grand Canyon, tornadoes and volcanos, sunset and dawns, and Judy Garland at the top of her form? At the top of her gold-lined lungs, shoulders back, elbows out, fists clenched, she pelted our ears with the magic of that voice—an earthquake, a battering ram, a holocaust."

At her last performance, technicians from Capitol Records arrived to record it live. She lamented, "The gods had it in for me. I developed laryngitis but went on anyway. "

As could be predicted, the album remains one of her least impressive. The strain in her voice is clearly evident. Critics were unkind, but her fans were forgiving.

As could be predicted, the album, *Garland at the Grove,* was her least popular.

***

Judy arrived in Chicago for an appearance at Orchestra Hall, starring in a concert produced by Sid Luft. He hired comedian Alan King as her opening act and Nelson Riddle as its music director. Staging was by her ever-faithful Chuck Walters and her musical mentor Roger Edens.

The concert became the biggest and most successful in the history of the hall, attracting an audience of 17,500, although 6,000 had to be turned away at the box office.

She went through her familiar repertoire, saving "Over the Rainbow" for her next-to-last song. As a crowd pleaser, she ended the concert singing "Chicago."

Bently Stegner in the *Chicago Tribune* weighed in with this review:

"A little girl who was born in a trunk stretched a rainbow from wall to wall of the cavernous Chicago Opera House Monday night. The personality of Judy Garland ranged from the tiara-crowned operagoer she impersonated in her first number to the waif in tattered tramp's clothes in her last. But from the beginning to the end, from dowager to hobo, she carried the crowd over the rainbow on the strains of her soaring, throbbing voice.

"She was weighted down with bouquets, but she set them aside for a go at 'Chicago.' The spectators sat in their seats and cheered until the asbestos curtain finally convinced them that Miss Show Business was really through for the night."

The *Chicago Sun Times* summed it up like this: *"Judy Garland received the kind of audience reaction usually reserved for the World Series. The crowd came running down the aisle to shake the hand of Miss Show Business."*

The week's gross was $80,000.

***

On October 1, after hopping from city to city, Judy was once again in Las Vegas for a two-week engagement at the Sands. Backed up by the Antonio Morelli Orchestra, she went through her usual repertoire. Her most memorable rendition was "The Man That Got Away," before ending with a tear-soaked "Over the Rainbow."

Attending opening night were Gary Cooper, Shirley MacLaine, and Debbie Reynolds, among others. Even Betty Hutton was in town and showed up, coming backstage to greet Judy.

"I have to ask," Hutton said. "It wasn't my fault that I replaced you in *Annie Get Your Gun*. But I gotta ask: What did you think of my performance?"

"I don't know," was Judy's chilly response. "I was too busy to go and see it." Then she turned her back on Hutton and stalked toward her dressing room.

Privately, Luft gave his own review, describing his wife as "Helium faced and stuffed with Ritalin."

"Our *schtick* had a handsome man, **Deano** (Martin), and a monkey, namely me," **Jerry Lewis** said.

"Sex and slapstick. That's what we were. Deano made it with Judy. I didn't dare ask for the same favor, since I didn't want her to laugh in my face."

Variety claimed, "The act is pure Judy Garland, and on opening night it was Judy Garland at her best."

Her best review came from critic Ralph Pearl. "*You sit there completely awed as your spine turns to jelly, and the roots of your thinning hair ache and stand straight up in the air.*"

On her closing night, the audience got a rare treat as Sinatra and Dean Martin appeared on stage to perform with her. Collectively, they were awarded with thunderous applause.

Later that night, Martin visited Judy in her suite and was seen leaving at 4AM.

Where was Luft, one might ask? Before Judy's engagement ended, he had disappeared, headed off to Reno, more than 440 miles to the northwest with a showgirl, justifying it (perhaps accurately) with the assertion that he was setting up another night club engagement.

Although she was married, June Allyson had been having a torrid affair with Martin herself. When some gossip told her about Judy's involvement with Martin, she dismissed it. "It was a mere fling. Dean is madly in love with me. He was just getting his rocks off—that's Dean."

[*Martin was also having affairs with Lana Turner and Marilyn Monroe.*]

Jerry Lewis, Martin's former stage partner, was a friend of Judy's. After hearing that she had spent most of a night with Martin, he dismissed it. "I love both of them dearly, but let's face it—they're druggies. It was a case of Percodan (Deano) meeting Ritalin. That's our Rainbow Gal, Judy."

***

The year of 1959 got off to a rousing start as a re-edited and restored version of *A Star Is Born* opened at 500 theaters across the country. Thousands of people who had seen the badly chopped original release got to see it in all its full-length glory, in an expanded format that fitted its original aspirations. Thousands more were seeing it for the first time. Judy was overjoyed at its re-release

By January 16, she was back in a recording studio at Capitol Records, belting out songs for inclusion in her latest album, *The Letter*. Its contents were arranged by Gordon Jenkins and narrated by actor John Ireland. Judy was backed up not only by the Jenkins Orchestra, but by the Ralph Brewster Singers, too.

Variety wrote: "As in Jenkins' earlier work, *Manhattan Tower*, the platter presents a romantic story in song and narrative. The songs far outshine the narrative here, and Miss Garland is at the top of her form through close to ten Jenkins creations."

High Fidelity claimed, "Miss Garland is her usual taut emotional self."

As Judy told Jenkins, "John's reputation in Hollywood has preceded him. I want to find out for myself if he has the biggest dick in town."

Ireland (1914-1992), coming out of Vancouver, brought his angst-ridden features to Hollywood. He made a few good pictures such as *Darling Clementine* (1944) before shooting to wider fame with Broderick Crawford in *All the King's Men* (1949). It won an Oscar for Best Picture of the Year, and Ireland got an Oscar nod for Best Supporting Actor.

His career after that fell into a long, slow descent.

Ireland had recently (in 1957) divorced his actress wife, Joanne Drew, and he was living in a hotel in downtown Los Angeles.

[Judy had first seen John Ireland in Red River *(1948), in which he co-starred with John Wayne and Montgomery Clift. There was an infamous scene that escaped the attention of the censors, but hip Hollywood knew what it was about. The two actors were ostensibly comparing the size of their guns, Ireland winning the prize.*

Offscreen, when Ireland made Queen Bee *(1955) with Joan Crawford, she praised his en-*

Even to ardent fans, **The Letter** is one of Judy's lesser-known albums, yet one critic called her performance "a socko."

The LP was released on May 4, 1959.

It would be reissued with the title changed to **Our Love Letter** almost four years later.

A Canadian, **John Ireland**, depicted here in *The Bushwackers* (1952), got his start as a swimmer in water carnivals, wearing a bikini so brief it left little for the imagination.

As such, he developed a coterie of loyal fans, many of them gay. He eventually made it to Hollywood, where he was signed by 20th Century Fox.

dowment, claiming "It's the biggest in Hollywood. I should know."

After one night with Ireland, Judy told Jenkins, "Joan didn't exaggerate. I felt a tree trunk was going up inside me."]

***

Still beset with a fear of flying, Judy insisted that Luft join her during the train ride to Miami for her next engagement. He gave in, finally traveling by train with her to New York, where they changed trains for Miami. When they got there, he checked her into the deluxe Fontainebleau Hotel on Miami Beach, where she was set to star from February 17 to March 5, 1959. It was her first big appearance that year, and the club was filled to capacity. Each of its 800 seats had been booked for opening night.

She admitted, "I looked puffy, my once-trim physique bloated, and I was taking pills around the clock."

George Bourke, the entertainment columnist for *The Miami Herald*, wrote: "I was a well-wishing Doubtful Thomas at the start, and a completely 'sold out' and devoted Boswell eager to sing deserved praise at the finish."

During her time on Miami Beach, Judy visited the home of her longtime friend, Sophie Tucker, who noted her expanding waistline. "If I keep this up," she told Tucker, "I'll be your equal. We can appear on stage as twins. Actually, I'm fattening up for my debut at The Met in New York. Fat ladies have always been welcome at the opera."

***

Almost as a rehearsal for The Met, Judy was booked into the Stanley Opera House in Baltimore from April 25 to May 3 for a gig that paid $65,000. [*Also known as the Stanley Theater, and built in 1927, it was Baltimore's largest show-biz venue, outfitted, one critic said, like an overdecorated railway station. It was closed and demolished in 1965.*] On opening night, each of its 2,800 seats were filled. Otherwise, throughout the remainder of her gig there, Judy attracted large audiences on most nights, except when terrible rainstorms struck Baltimore.

For the most part, reviews were favorable, and she thanked patrons for extending such a welcome. As the audience clapped loudly, she called out, "I love all of you back!"

Once again, Alan King was her warmup act. The only glitch came when she sang "I Happen to Like New York." She received scattered boos, but quickly tried to explain that she was just trying out the song for her debut at the Met in Manhattan.

A critic for Maryland's *Evening Sun* wrote, "Nobody, but nobody, can belt out a song like Judy Garland. At its best, her voice is piercing, trumpet-like and packed with amplified emotion that can fairly tear your heart out of its sockets."

The *Baltimore Sun* claimed, "It may be that Roger Edens, who put together most of the scenes, is depending too much on Miss Garland to make a show sorely lacking in originality seem fresh and new. It's a rich, exciting

434

voice capable—when its owner really lets loose—of shooting prickles up the spine of even the most prosaic reviewer."

***

The dream of many opera stars was (and is) to sing at the Metropolitan Opera in New York City. Even though she was a pop singer, that was true of Judy, too.

From May 11 to the 17th, she enchanted audiences for the most part, all for the benefit of the Children's Asthma Research Institute in Denver. The show grossed $190,000 which in those days was a spectacular revenue flow.

Produced by Luft, her show contained special music and lyrics by Roger Edens, with Alan King once again functioning as her opening act. Among other numbers, Judy performed her "Born In a Trunk" sequence from *A Star Is Born,* and she and King sang a duet, "A Couple of Swells" like she'd done with Fred Astaire in *Easter Parade.*

Her songs included *The Garland Overture,* which included "The Man That Got Away," and "I'm In Love With a Wonderful Guy." Unlike the audience in Baltimore, the people gathered to hear her applauded wildly for her rendition of "I Happen To Like New York."

Reviews were good, *The New York Times* writing, "From the roars and bravos that echoed through the house, it was evident that long hair or short, the Metropolitan was still the haven of good company. The magnetism that she always had managed to exert upon an audience is as powerful as ever. The smooth voice that comes from deep down continues to stir the emotions and set an audience on the edge of its seat."

After the show closed, a review from the often notoriously trenchant Kenneth Tynan appeared in the *New Yorker* magazine. "The engagement, which is now over, was limited: The pleasure it gave was not. When the voice pours out, as rich and

"During the first act of the show at the Met," said actress **Ruth Warrick,** "I felt I was watching the end of Judy Garland. I had a front row seat, and her ankles looked swollen and thick. Even worse, her face was puffy, and her body was all out of shape, a sad caricature of the Judy Garland of yore. I admire her courage for daring to come on in her condition."

"But in the second half of the show, she seemed to undergo a mercurial change for the better. She dazzled us with that same talent we'd fallen in love with in those movie musicals of the 1940s when I, too, was a movie star."

Ruth Warrick, one of the stars of *Citizen Kane* (1941), appearing here as Phoebe Tyler from *All My Children.*

435

pleasing as ever, we know where, and how moved, we are—in the presence of a star and embarrassed by tears."

A critic for the *Journal-America* wrote: "Her full, thrilling, throbbing voice welled up in the vast cathedral of vocal culture, filling every bit of space above the orchestra, the boxes, and family circle. Not even Maria Callas got a better reception."

The famous New York critic, Judith Crist, gave her impression of Judy's debut at The Met:

"She must have weighed about 200 pounds. And someone in his great wisdom had put her into a red velvet dress that flowed; and boy, it flowed all over that stage. Now there was no air conditioning in the old Metropolitan Opera House, and I remember having a girdle on that night and thinking what a fool I was to come to the Opera House in anything like this! The perspiration was just pouring off us; it was one of those grand nights in New York. The place was crowded, and the seats were velvety and hot. It was just horrible. And there was this obese woman on the stage with some back-up that was not very good. And the show went on and on, and you thought: I have come to see the end of everything.

And then, by George. After the interval, she came out. And she had on that old tuxedo outfit, with the top hat, and the legs that were simply fabulous in the black stockings. She went into 'We're a Couple of Swells' and wound up all smudgey, sitting on the edge of that stage. Well, hitherto, we'd all been a little damp, but now it was the eyes. I then knew what 'there wasn't a dry eye in the house' meant. It was fantastic."

New York City's Mayor, Robert Wagner, presented Judy with a citation for "distinguished and exceptional work for charity."

Although it had been a smashing success with the public, financially, the opera tour had been disastrous for Judy and Luft. Their bill at Manhattan's very posh Plaza Hotel was $10,000. Producing the show cost $150,000. To cover their mounting debt, he borrowed money from both Prince Aly Khan and Chuck Walters, and even re-mortgaged their Holmby Hills home for $95,000. There were endless salaries to pay, including the musicians in the orchestra, press agents, and lawyers. He and Judy had also hosted three parties at the Plaza, inviting three hundred guests.

***

In the continuation of her Opera House Tour, Judy stopped next at the Chicago Opera House, where she was booked for a week (June 1 to 7) performing seven shows for a top ticket price of ten dollars. She told a reporter for the *Chicago Daily News*, "I've been singing since I can remember. That's what I love and what I want to keep on doing."

On June 10, she celebrated her thirty-seventh birthday, later saying, "It wasn't much of a celebration. No gal in Hollywood wants to celebrate getting that close to forty. That's when all the minor female movie stars are sent out to graze in the pasture until they die of a heart attack, wrinkles, or cancer."

The Chicago critic, Richard Christian, attended her performance: "(It's) something for which theaters were built—a constant outpouring of the best a performer has to give— that makes an audience roar with excitement and joy. That is Judy Garland."

As California melted into the hot summer of 1957, Judy opened at the San Francisco War Memorial Opera house, a ten-day gig. Roger Edens arranged a revised version of that standard, "San Francisco," which Judy performed until the end of her life. *[In fact, she sang it as part of the last concert she ever gave.]*

Before she launched into a tribute to its charms, Judy elicited a lot of laughter when she said, "I'm sure all of you remember the movie *San Francisco*? It starred Jeanette MacDonald, Spencer Tracy, and Clark Gable. It was about the 1906 earthquake.

"To think of her, it gives my heart a pang,
I never will forget
How that brave Jeanette
Stood there in the ruins and saaaaaang and sang,
A powerful rendition of "San Francisco."

The *San Francisco Chronicle* wrote: *"Judy Garland opened to a deliriously happy audience, consisting in part of a lot of young men, who clapped and shouted their approval throughout the performance. They finally ended by giving her a standing ovation."*

A critic for another paper claimed, *"Judy Garland had her audience in a state akin to the fever that matched the Oklahoma land rush. If they had taken out their uppers, removed their toupées, and tossed same over the footlights, it would not have surprised me."*

For this latest gig, she received about $45,000.

During her time in San Francisco, ASCAP (The American Society of Composers, Authors, and Publishers), slapped her with a lawsuit, alleging that Luft had not paid them for the rights to "A Couple of Swells," "This Can't Be Love," and "A Wonderful Guy." He counter-claimed that he had paid for performing rights. The case was settled.

***

Back in Los Angeles, Judy was in a car driven by Bobby Van *en route* to lunch for a discussion of future gigs where he'd continue as her opening act. His wife, Diana Garrett, was in the front passenger seat, with Judy sitting by herself in the back.

Suddenly, their car was rear-ended by another vehicle. Judy was badly shaken but suffered no injuries. Diana, however, claimed a back injury, asserting that she'd been unable to move for three weeks. Bobby also cited a severe back injury and migraines sustained when his head was thrown against the steering wheel.

During a court trial, Judy was called upon to testify in a case for which the couple sought compensation of $107,000. *[As a settlement, Van got $1,500, Diana got $5,000.]*

After the accident, she spent most of the day rehearsing for her next big gig. This one would be from July 11 to 18 on her home turf of Los Angeles at the Shrine Auditorium.

Her loyal fans turned out in droves to hear her sing songs they knew from her movies, records, and concerts. Once again, the highlights were those two old standards, "The Man That Got Away" and "Over the Rainbow."

The next morning in its review, the *Los Angeles Times* noted: "The Shrine Auditorium echoed and trembled with applause, stomping, and shouting. The best of all the Garland acts on the program were 'Born In a Trunk' and 'A Couple of Swells.'"

On closing night, Vincente Minnelli showed up at her concert with his daughter. Together, after the show, they both went backstage to congratulate Judy. That night, driving home with Liza, he told her, "I think Judy is in dire shape. She could have a heart attack at any moment. I've never seen her this bloated. She should be in a clinic or a hospital, certainly at least under a doctor's care. Perhaps you can persuade Luft to do something or take the matter into your own hands. She might listen to you."

Judy described her own condition at this dreadful time:

"I had so many fears, so many anxieties. I'd had them as a child and I guess they just grow worse as you get older and more self-centered. The fear of failure. The fear of ridicule. I hated the way I looked. I cried for no reason, laughed hysterically, made stupid decisions, couldn't tell a kind word from an insult. All the brain boilers gave me up. I staggered along in a nightmare, knowing something was vitally wrong, but what? It got to the point where I was a virtual automaton—with no memory! I played some very big dates in 1958 and 1959. I don't remember any of it. I didn't know what I was doing."

***

In November of 1959, Judy worried that she wouldn't live to see the end of the decade. Her physical condition seemed to worsen daily as her weight ballooned to 180 pounds.

Luft finally convinced her to fly to New York for treatment at Doctors Hospital. It is not clear why she chose a medical venue in New York when she could have received excellent medical care in Los Angeles.

One of the reasons might have derived from issues not associated with her medical condition: She had been designated as the guest of honor at a shindig that Elsa Maxwell had organized for Prince Aly Khan at the Drake Hotel. Soon after she got there, she was surrounded by well-wishers, each of whom told her different versions of "the big lie' so often heard at showbiz parties: "You look wonderful!"

The next day, Luft checked her into Doctors Hospital, where doctors made a remarkable discovery: After years of indiscriminate pills and liquor, it was determined that her overburdened liver had swollen to four times its normal size, and her body had retained an extra twenty quarts of liquid.

An early diagnosis tentatively suggested that she'd contracted one of the most severe cases of hepatitis her doctors had ever seen, and that she might lapse into a hepatomic coma at any moment. It was later determined, however, that she was suffering from cirrhosis of the liver.

According to Luft, in a *tour de force* of misguided bravado, before departing for the hospital on the day of her appointment, Judy had insisted on downing a triple vodka.

During her treatment, day after day, liquids drained from her body, drip by drip. Her weight dropped to 120 pounds. Doctors suggested (but didn't insist) that she should try to lose another twenty pounds for a return to the weight they defined as appropriate for her small frame.

After years of damage derived from Judy's extreme highs and bottomless pits, Luft was warned by her doctors, "Your wife might die at any minute. We'll do everything we can to save her life. Even if we succeed, we expect her to be a semi-invalid for the rest of her life. She should give up her career. She'll never sing again."

On January 5, 1960, after seven weeks of pain and discomfort, Judy was released from the hospital. Luft had already transmitted her doctors' theories that she should abandon her performance career as a means of sidestepping a fatal heart attack. One of them had suggested, "In retirement, you might find a new and satisfying career, perhaps devoted to being a good wife and mother."

The 1960s started with that as its first bombshell. She was facing a new decade, one seemed to hold very little promise for her.

***

Back on home turf in Los Angeles, still in recovery and very weak, Judy wandered aimlessly through the empty rooms of her expensive and very large house in Holmby Hills. She began to overeat, favoring juicy steaks, creamy mashed potatoes, and comfort foods containing chocolate. Her weight slowly rose to 150 pounds, an increase of thirty pounds since she left the hospital. The only pills she took were Ritalin.

Afraid that she had only a year or two to live, she had agreed with Luft to write her "tell-all" memoirs. To that effect, before leaving New York, Luft had met with Bennett Cerf of Random House. Together, they persuaded Judy to sign a contract to deliver a manuscript that fall. In return, Cerf gave Luft an advance payment of $35,000.

Selected as her ghostwriter was Freddie Finklehoffe, the former beau who had written some of her screenplays in the 1940s. For three weeks, he listened intently to tales from her early life, detailing her love for her father, her hatred of her mother, and her development as a vaudeville entertainer with the Gumm Sisters.

But as the autumn approached, no publishable manuscript was ever produced. Cerf demanded copies of the work in progress but received only 65 pages detailing only her early days. *[In them, she admitted to an abortion during her teen years but never named Spencer Tracy as her partner at the time.]*

Eventually, Luft was forced to admit to Cerf that Judy's pain in dredging up the agonies of her past had been debilitating. There would be no manuscript. Not only that, but he was unable to return the $35,000 advance because he'd already spent it.

[Eventually, Cerf salvaged some of his investment by revising the raw pages of the unfinished manuscript into feature articles that were eventually sold to (and published by) McCall's magazine.]

***

In June, Judy returned to Capitol Records, singing the first of her songs for her latest album, *Judy: That's Entertainment.* It featured such songs as "How Long Has This Been Going On?" and "If I Love Again."

She celebrated her thirty-eighth birthday on the same day she recorded two final songs for that album: "Old Devil Moon" and "That's Entertainment."

New Musical Express defined the album as *"a tour de force.* Judy's qualities of heart and conviction speak loud and clear."

John Mitchell in the *Nottingham Evening Post* predicted, "Her voice will never lose its warmth or its power to hold an audience."

***

The Democratic Convention of 1960 was sited in Los Angeles. During its run, Judy shared a reunion with the leading contender for President of the United States, Massachusetts Senator John F. Kennedy, who was running against Richard M. Nixon of California. Nixon had been Dwight Eisenhower's Vice President for the previous eight years.

At a fund-raising event, JFK invited Judy to sit at the head table next to Adlai Stevenson, who had run unsuccessfully against Eisenhower in both 1952 and 1956.

Nearby was Eleanor Roosevelt, who warmly greeted Judy. "I'm so happy you're a member of our party. Franklin and I enjoyed those Andy Hardy movies at the White House during the war. They cheered us up in some of our darkest days."

That night, Judy attended a party for Democratic donors, and went around the room telling anybody she met, "Jack is charming and smart, witty and clever. He'll

In 1960, at a fund-raising event for the Democratic Party, **Judy** was in distinguished company, seated between **Adlai Stevenson** (who was seeking the Democratic nomination for the presidential elections of 1960), and **Eleanor Roosevelt.**

But whereas Judy was an ardent supporter of John F. Kennedy, the former First Lady wanted Stevenson to run instead, even though he had already been defeated twice in previous elections by Eisenhower.

Judy had always been a great admirer of the former First Lady, referring to her as "The Greatest Woman of the 20th Century."

make a great President." Columnist Earl Wilson reported, "Judy Garland was the life of the party."

Before JFK said goodbye, she told him she was going to London, having "overcome my fear of flying."

"I want to ask you one big favor," he said. "My staff will make all the arrangements if you'll fly to Wiesbaden in Germany to entertain our troops stationed there. And I want you to urge our soldiers to vote for me…You know…absentee ballots."

She willingly agreed, and flew there in October of 1960, right before the U.S. Presidential elections in November. Soldiers greeted her with wild approval, and she ended her concert with both "Over the Rainbow" and "The Battle Hymn of the Republic."

The morning after the presidential election results were announced, she put through a call to the Kennedy compound in Hyannis Port. She later recalled, "I think everybody in the world was phoning Jack. But amazingly, he took my call and I congratulated him as President."

"Thanks," he said to her, "Madame Ambassador, I'm appointing you as my new Ambassador to England. My dad used to have that job, but he fucked it up."

[JFK's quip about Judy as "Madame Ambassador" appears not to have been serious. He never inaugurated any steps to elevate her to that position.]

***

As a young singer, Judy had found inspiration in the singing voice of Ethel Merman. She was nicknamed "The Belter," because of her distinctive, powerful voice in Broadway hits that had included *Girl Crazy, Panama Hattie, Annie Get Your Gun, Call Me Madam,* and *Gypsy.*

On Broadway, she introduced such hits as "I Got Rhythm," "It's De-Lovely," "I Get a Kick Out of You," and "You're the Top." Irving Berlin's "There's No Business Like Show Business" became her signature song. And although Judy recorded these same numbers, Merman never viewed her as a rival. A deep friendship between the two singers evolved.

Judy tried to catch Merman's performances, telling the press, "Ethel makes a song an expression of her own distinctive personality."

Merman regularly hung out with Jimmy Durante, Mary Martin, director Joshua Logan (who nicknamed her "Sarah Bernhardt, Jr."), as well as Stephen Sondheim, and producer Mike Todd. She was often seen with Tallulah Bankhead: "We used to bump pussies, *dah-ling.*"

Unexpectedly, the Duke and Duchess of Windsor were also Merman's friends, as they were to Judy.

One night on Broadway, when Merman was performing as Annie Oakley, General Dwight D. Eisenhower went backstage to congratulate her. "I haven't seen a Broadway play in thirty years, but you have lured me back."

Cole Porter said, "I'd rather write songs for Merman than for any other singer in the world, and that includes Judy Garland."

Bosley Crowther of *The New York Times* wrote, "Merman is too hot for Fahrenheit to measure."

The critic for the *Daily Express* in London claimed, "Seeing Ethel Merman on the stage is rather like being clobbered by boxer Sonny Liston."

Of course, Merman wasn't always wise in choosing her roles. She viewed turning down the namesake role in *Hello, Dolly!* as the career mistake of her life. After six years, she finally starred as the scheming matchmaker, joining the cast in 1970, six years after the musical's premiere on Broadway. At many of her performances, she received prolonged standing ovations. It marked her last appearance on Broadway.

Judy's friendship with Merman dated from the 1940s. They were often seen together in both Hollywood and New York. Rumors about a possible lesbian link didn't go public, however, until 1960.

Judy had to be in London in the August of 1960 to make some recordings for EMI, the English affiliate of Capitol Records.

She phoned Merman and suggested she fly with her. Her friend, Kay Thompson, wanted to go, too, as did Benny (*sometimes spelled Benay*) Venuta, an actress, singer, and dancer, and a well-known lesbian.

She and Merman had been intimate for years, ever since she replaced Merman in the lead role of Reno Sweeney in Cole Porter's *Anything Goes* in 1935. The singing pair also co-starred in the revival of *Annie Get Your Gun* in 1966.

A native New Yorker, **Ethel Merman** went from being the secretary at a vacuum booster brake manufacturer to the biggest star on Broadway.

Some of the most famous people in the world became her friends, none more notable than J. Edgar Hoover, long-time Director of the F.B.I.

He was a cross dresser, and she often bought dresses and gowns for him, or else presented him with some of her hand-me-downs.

Merman's biographer, Geoffrey Mark, wrote: "Hadn't Kay Thompson taught a young Judy the joys of Sappho-hood? Wasn't Benny Venuta a lover of men as well as women? What were these four women doing together in London? Hmmmmm???"

Flying into London's Heathrow Airport, the coven of women arrived on July 14. Judy put up a brave front for the press, claiming, "I feel just great, and my husband and children are terrific."

In spite of her troubles with Luft, Judy pronounced their marriage "perfect," even though they were having adulterous affairs on the side.

Since all the women at one time or another had been accused of lesbianism, one Fleet Street tabloid dared refer to them as being on a "Sapphic vacation."

After their arrival, the women seemed to disappear, perhaps staying at a secret address in Surrey. Judy did turn up on August 2 at EMI Studios in London to make the first of a two-record set for an eventual album. Released in 1962, it was known as *The Garland Touch*.

[Rumors of Merman's lesbianism resurfaced again in 1967 when Broadway buzzed with the affair of Merman and the married Jacqueline Susann. Venuta privately claimed, "At the time that Ethel met Susann, she was disillusioned with men, having been hurt or betrayed by her husbands. When Susann made a pass at her, Ethel intercepted it."

In 1966, Merman got an early copy of Susann's best-seller, Valley of the Dolls. *After reading it, and to her horror, she knew she was the inspiration behind the creation of the diva, Helen Lawson, a most unappetizing betrayal. She never spoke to Susann again.*

As Sid Luft said, "Venuta was Merman's best friend or else her worst enemy."

After Merman's death in 1984, Venuta outed her as a lesbian to Cindy Adams, the gossip columnist for the New York Post.

In her final years, Ethel, like Judy herself, was surrounded by gay men," Mark claimed. "The older she got, her pals were replaced by these fawning gay men who were happy to worship at the hem of her skirts."

Merman became a heavy drinker, and Mark admitted that she was "fed up with men, their cheating, and their using her for notoriety and money." In 1964, she married her fourth husband, actor Ernest Borgnine. As she told Carroll O'-Connor when she toured with him one summer, "My marriage hardly lasted through our honeymoon night."

When she wrote her 1978 autobiography, she devoted Chapter XXVIII to her final husband. The entire chapter had only a single page, and it contained only five words: "My Marriage to Ernest Borgnine." The rest of the chapter was blank.]

***

In reference to this period of her life, Judy recalled, "For the first time, I was learning to do things for myself without having someone look after me."

She changed planes in London and flew onward to Rome, where the handsome Italian actor Rossano Brazzi had given her the use of his villa. She shared the home with Ethel Merman and Kay Thompson.

Later, she flew back to England, where she hoped to hook up with Liza before the end of the summer. Liza had migrated to France with some of her fellow students and was being chaperoned by one of their mothers.

At the London airport, some reporters were alerted to Judy's presence, and she granted them an *impromptu* press conference. "I'm so damn calm these days, really quite dull. I go along the same old line all day long—no more highs, no more lows. I never lose my temper anymore, and I don't throw one of my legendary tantrums. When something happens that annoys me, I just walk away and forget it."

Then she added a tantalizing followup: "For all I know, I may be moving with my happy family to live in England forever, even though I've been called a 'Black Irish Bitch.' California is a ghost town. They're not making movies like they used to in the heyday of Louis B. Mayer and the moguls."

Suddenly, at the airport, she was interrupted by the arrival of a newly minted friend, the English actor, Dirk Bogarde, who warmly hugged and kissed her. He steered her away from the clutches of the reporters and drove her to his home in the country for a much-needed rest.

As she later told Kay Thompson, "I was looking forward to having an affair with this handsome, dashing actor. There was a problem to overcome, however. He was ninety-eight percent gay."

It was no surprise that **Liza** grew up to become a musical star. After all, she was the supremely talented daughter of "The Musical King and Queen of MGM."

In the dying years of the studio system, she emerged into a vast fantasy land dedicated to the business of creating illusions.

Judy Tells Hollywood Filmmakers
"I COULD GO ON SINGING"
But After Her Wretched Behavior,
a Lot of Them Don't Really Want Her Anymore.

Introducing **DIRK BOGARDE**
Gay but Cooperative, He's a Man with a Talent for
Soothing the Wild Beast, One Suicide Attempt at a Time

CUTTING RECORDS AS A RELIGIOUS RITE
Variety defines Judy as "The High Priestess of Pop."

FALLING IN LOVE AGAIN, & AGAIN, & AGAIN
Eddie Fisher, Douglas Fairbanks, Jr., Glenn Ford

PARIS: LE PALAIS DE CHAILLOT
How do you say "Judy" in French?

IS THIS ANY WAY TO RUN A MARRIAGE?
Management Changes: Luft is Out; Begelman In

She's an Emotionally Damaged Wreck
But Critics Insist "Her Pipes Are Better Than Ever"

PARTIES AT THE WHITE HOUSE
Jack! Jackie! Bobby! Ethel!

JUDGMENT AT NUREMBERG
Crimes Against Humanity

CARNEGIE HALL
"Judy! Judy! Judy! becomes a Mantra
for Thousands of her fans

"My marriage to Sid Luft is finished. It lasted eleven years, and it will take another eleven years to tell you what went wrong."

—Judy Garland

"You are probably the greatest singer of songs alive."

—Noel Coward

"Judy Garland is like a piano. You touch any key and a pure note of emotion comes out."

—Director Stanley Kramer

"I'm living the best year of my life, 1961"

—Judy Garland

"Judy Garland refuses to fade into oblivion. She haunts us because we can't figure her out. And what we can't figure out is that standoff between talent and doom."

—Elizabeth Kendall

"You know, I can't really sing, I holler, really. Oh sure, I'm no Deanna Durbin, now she really can't sing, that silly horse Jeanette MacDonald, yakking away at wooden-peg Nelson Eddy with all that glycerine running down her Max Factor! I have a voice that hurts people where they think they want to be hurt—that's all."

—Judy Garland

446

"Judy Garland is the only enchanting woman in the world."

—Dirk Bogarde

In England, *en route* **to his country home** with actor Dirk Bogarde, Judy was both physically and mentally in a better state than when he'd last seen her in Hollywood. Back then, as he remembered it, "She was fat, ill, and moved in a trance. Those wide brown eyes of hers were buried in a white puffy face."

Behind the driver's wheel, he kept glancing over at her, finding her almost playful, laughing and giggling like a little girl. "She was no longer fat, but a bit plump."

"I've lost a lot of poundage, the biggest load to dump being Sid Luft. I needed time away from him, time even to escape from my family. I love each of my brats dearly. But let's face it: I'm not that much different from most stars. We are self-centered. I need to escape from this mother-wife gig to breathe the fresh air. Get acquainted with myself and cement my relationship with you. You're rapidly on the way of becoming my new best friend. Mickey Rooney was yesterday. This is the 1960s, not the '40s."

She revealed that whereas Luft was still in Hollywood with Lorna and Joey, Liza was in Annecy, France, with a group of kids from her school, with one of the mothers acting as chaperone.

"Girls of Liza's age

Serious and Sophisticated. Two views of **Dirk Bogarde**

Right: Handsome, conventional-looking, reliable, and mainstream, and

Left: As the desperately lovesick, suicidal and gay protagonist in *Death in Venice* (1971)

are a horny bunch. I sure was at her age. No teenage boy, or older man, for that manner, was safe from me in the late 1930s when I had to endure Louis B. Mayer feeling me up."

Bogarde had become the new man of interest in her life. A famous British actor in his day, he had been born in London a year before Judy. His mother named him Derek Jules Gaspard Ulrich Niven van de Bogaerde.

He'd begun his screen career in 1939 shortly before England declared war on Germany. When war came, he joined the British Army, serving in both the European and Pacific theaters. At the age of twenty-two, in 1943, he was commissioned in the Queen's Royal Regiment as a second lieutenant.

After the war, known for his good looks and charm, he was put under contract by the Rank Organization, which turned him into a matinee idol. Often, he competed with Stewart Granger, another matinee idol, for roles.

His early fame derived from his portrayal of a medical student in the British film, *Doctor in the House* (1954), a movie that spawned six sequels and a television series based on books by Richard Gordon. His second doctor film, *Doctor at Sea* (1955), starred the French sex kitten, Brigitte Bardot.

Some of his greatest acting lay "post-Judy" in his future. They included notable leading roles in such films as *The Servant* (1963), *Darling* (1965), and the film adaptation of Thomas Mann's *Death in Venice* (1971). In 1992, Queen Elizabeth II designated him as a Knight Bachelor of the Order of the British Empire for his achievements in the entertainment industry.

As he pulled into his driveway, his lover and manager, Anthony Forwood, rushed out to embrace him before Bogarde introduced him to Judy.

As she settled in with the two men, she found them "the happiest couple I'd ever seen, better than any straights I knew." She'd been told that "Tony," as he was called, had been married to the actress Glynis Johns until he left her for Bogarde.

The next day, the men took her on a tour of the Cotswolds, a scenic district northwest of London with grazing sheep, rolling hills, thousands of intriguing "Olde English" buildings and market towns crafted from honey-colored stone. They drove through villages with names like Stow-on-the-Wold that seemed left over from the Middle Ages, lunching there at a small inn, the Red Lion.

She enjoyed the camaraderie of the two men and relaxed in their flower-filled summer garden where the sun spent a long time going down after casting a pink glow over the sky.

As his friend Eric Braun described Bogarde during this era:

"Dirk was a paradox. Adored by teenagers during those Rank years, he was increasingly outrageous in his choice of film roles. He was also fiercely closed regarding the truth about his sexuality."

One night in the garden over a bottle of wine, he discussed the trauma he still suffered from his war experiences.

Bogarde, portraying a diagnostic surgeon, evaluates Judy in much the same way that he did as her real-life friend and—on rare occasions and not for long—lover: With respect, admiration, and a kind of clinical and very realistic detachment.

In April of 1945, during the slow-motion collapse of the Third Reich, he had been one of the first Allied officers to reach the Bergen-Belsen Concentration Camp. "I looked into Dante's Inferno," he claimed. "There were mountains of rotting flesh underneath a pile of dead bodies. I heard moans, sounds of life that had to be dug out. I still have nightmares about it."

As the hours and days in the English countryside went by, Judy felt she was falling in love, which she had done so many times before, deeply and impulsively. As long as Forwood was in residence, Bogarde felt safe from her advances.

One day, Forwood announced he was driving to London, where, for business matters, he'd stay for a few days. Judy and Bogarde would remain behind.

She seized the opportunity to make her intentions clear: "When we first became friends, you assured me one night that you'd be there for me. Now I'm putting you to the test. I desperately need you to make love to me, to hold me in your arms and to tell me you love me—and that you'll never leave me."

He was surprised that she'd demand such a commitment. Not really in the mood, he responded to her need anyway. An hour later found her in his bedroom, where he was able to perform, sexually, for her, although, as he later admitted, "My heart was not in it."

The next morning, she told him, "I have Sid, sort of, and my little darlings, but other than that, I'm alone in the world. That is, until I met you. Outside my family, you are the single person in this god damn stinking world that I care for, and who cares for me."

He knew that was not true, but he listened patiently. "I can be there for you, but only within reason," he cautioned her. "As you know, Tony comes first in my life, and I'll never leave him."

"I know that, darling," she said. "I'm prepared to live with that. I've made compromises all my life."

***

Back in London that June, and with the goal of recovering her health, Judy rented a three-story Georgian townhouse on King's Road in Chelsea. It was one of the most unusual structures in the neighborhood in that its two-level living room ran the length of the house and was lined with shelves of books. As such, it could easily have been mistaken for a library. Former tenants had included the novelist W. Somerset Maugham and Ellen Terry (1847-1928), hailed as England's greatest actress.

Her landlord was Carol Reed, the film director and Knight of the Realm who is remembered mainly for his direction of *The Third Man* (1949), the *film noir* starring Orson Welles and Joseph Cotten in a cinematic *tour de force* set in postwar Vienna.

Judy claimed that it was in the steamy shower of her bathroom that "I found my voice again. I could sing just as powerfully as ever. Those damn quacks told me I couldn't and that I'd end up in a wheelchair. They pictured me as a female Lionel Barrymore in the last years of his life."

Once she'd settled into the rented house, she sent for Luft, Lorna, Joey, and—at the end of her studies in Annecy—Liza.

Judy's fondest memories included when all of them gathered together in the leafy garden behind the house as her recuperative summer was coming to an end.

***

When Luft and her daughters agreed that Judy's voice had fully recovered, she kept the first of five appointments with EMI Studios, an affiliate of Capitol Records, for the production of another album. Her musical director was Norrie Paramor, whom she dubbed "Noilly Prat." In awe of her, and

Her album, **Judy in London,** was recorded in the summer of 1960.

For a number of reasons, it was put into storage until after her death.

It was at last released and distributed in 1972.

450

perhaps intimidated, Paramor never really pushed her to do her best. Where was Roger Edens now that she needed him?

Drawing from her familiar repertoire, it would take five recording sessions to produce the two-disc set. Songs included "Swanee," "The Man That Got Away," and (of course) "Over the Rainbow," as well as lesser-known works such as "Lucky Day." Judy seemed to improve with each session, and when the project was wrapped, she felt she'd regained her full vocal power.

One night at around 3AM, she awakened Luft to express her powerful desire to appear again in London for another concert at the Palladium, this time without any distracting comic or vaudeville acts. "I just want to stand up there on stage and sing my heart out. None of the dancing boys you ungallantly refer to as 'my flaming fairies.'"

The very next day, he set out to stage her "comeback" at the Palladium, devising its name as *An Evening with Judy Garland.* Its premiere was at 8PM on August 28, 1960. Almost as soon as it was announced, all the tickets disappeared. *[The impresario, Harold Davison, decided to stage a repeat performance featuring her on September 4.]*

Oscar Hammerstein had died five nights before the opening of her show, and, in tribute to him, she sang "You'll Never Walk Alone." She also sang "Stormy Weather," despite its long association with Lena Horne as the song that had made her famous.

She looked out at the first row of the audience, where she saw Liza seated next to the Duke of Windsor, who sort of hummed, throughout the course of her concert, most of her songs as she performed them.

At one point, Judy summoned a reluctant Dirk Bogarde out from his seat in the audience to appear on the stage with her as she sang "It Never Was You."

The audience virtually demanded "San Francisco" and "Chicago." At some of the requests, she responded, "Oh, no, not that one! I've been singing that song for the last century and eight years!"

In *The Record Mirror,* Isadore Green wrote: "At the conclusion of every number, there was an outburst of applause of tornado-like dimensions, at the end, a standing ovation. People just went crazy with exhilaration."

Peter Evans in the *Daily Express* claimed, "Judy Garland, who has probably made more comebacks than a Cape Canaveral rocket, returned to the stage for the first time in a year last night. It was a triumph."

Columnist Angus Hall pronounced Judy "The High Priestess of Pop." Critic Jack Hutton found it "incredible to see so many stars wallowing in unashamed admiration for another."

After making another of her many "comebacks" at the Palladium, Judy looked back on the experience in an interview she gave to Shana Alexander for *Life* magazine.

"You stand there in the wings, and sometimes you want to yell because the band sounds so good, Then you walk out and if it's a really great audience, a very strange set of emotions can come over you. You don't know what to do. It's a combination of feeling like Queen Victoria and an absolute ass. Sometimes a great reception — though God knows I've had some great receptions and I ought to be prepared for it by now — can really throw you. It kind of shatters you so that you can lose control of your voice and it takes two or three numbers to get back into your stride. I lift my hand in a big gesture in the middle of my first number and if I see it's not trembling, then I know I haven't lost my control.

"A really great reception makes me feel like I have a great big warm heating pad all over me. People en masse *have always been wonderful to me. I truly have a great love for an audience, and I used to want to prove it to them by giving them blood. But I have a funny new thing now, a real determination to make people enjoy the show, I want to give them two hours of just* pow!*"*

Wherever she went in London, she was well-received. When she attended a West End play written by Noel Coward, the patrons rose and applauded her arrival. She got the same treatment at certain chic restaurants such as the Savoy Grill. She told Luft, "The British people seem to adore me, but those damn bastards on Fleet Street still write that I am 'matronly' or 'plump.' FUCK 'EM!"

At her rented house in Chelsea, Judy, reunited with her family, resumed some semblance of a private life. They began to entertain, their first guests being Elizabeth Taylor and her husband, Eddie Fisher, with whom Judy had once had a fling.

Fisher told them that he had once come close to renting the Carol Reed house until he discovered it had no central heating, and tenants had to rely on fireplaces or portable electric heaters in every room.

Before leaving, Fisher called Luft aside, asking if he could see him tomorrow in the bar at the Dorchester where he and Elizabeth were staying.

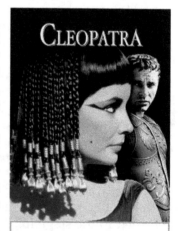

Burton and Taylor: They were a worldwide sensation at the time, stealing thunder from every other entertainer in the world, including Judy

Luft arrived there at five o'-clock to face a very distraught singer on the verge of tears. During their time together, Fisher broke down and confessed that Elizabeth had been having a fling with Richard Burton, her co-star in *Cleopatra* then being filmed in Rome. "That Welsh bastard is screwing her. Not only that, but the drunken devil overpowered me one night at our villa in Rome and raped me just to humiliate me."

Fisher and Luft bonded, each sharing stories of what it was like "to be a footman" to a star goddess.

It was at this time that Douglas Fairbanks, Jr. entered the lives of Judy and Luft. He was the son of Fairbanks Senior, the former husband of Mary Pickford, who had become world famous in silent films as a roguish swashbuckler.

Handsome, elegant, and well mannered, Fairbanks, Jr. was the opposite of Luft, who referred to himself as "a diamond in the rough."

At the time that Fairbanks, Jr. came together with Luft as friends, he was married to Mary Lee, although having a secret affair with Marlene Dietrich.

Sid Luft's growing friendship with **Douglas Fairbanks, Jr.** (upper photo), was about as close to Hollywood Royalty as he ever got.

The lower photo shows Fairbanks, Jr. in the early 1930s with this then-wiife, **Joan Crawford** (left) and his spectacularly famous stepmother, **Mary Pickford**.

Perhaps as two Americans from the worlds of show biz isolated in the U.K. at the time, the men became close. Consistently, Luft had been drinking heavily, and had gained some weight. Fairbanks took him for a consultation with a doctor he knew in Battersea. The doctor injected Luft with the urine of a pregnant woman and he returned regularly for more. According to Luft, "as unbelievable as it sounds, my extra pounds faded away."

Fairbanks and his wife were often entertained by Queen Elizabeth and Prince Philip. One night Fairbanks astonished Luft with a revelation: "Philip has plenty of affairs on the side, and Her Majesty must know about them. He keeps me abreast but swears me to secrecy. Not only that, but I think Elizabeth is falling in love with me."

On several occasions when Luft was away, Fairbanks paid late-night visits to Judy's house in London. He was seen doing so, and rumors spread, although not through the tabloids.

As he told personal friends, "I'm not the kind of man to fall seriously for any pretty young ship that passes by in the middle of the night. But when legends like Dietrich and Garland call, what's a man to do but answer their siren wail?"

***

Before her opening night (October 5, 1960) in Paris, Judy had been billed as "The American Piaf" and "The Volcano of Broadway."

To Sid Luft's fury, advance ticket sales had been so poor that he had to fill the house by giving away free tickets.

During her studies in Annecy in Eastern France, Liza had become quite adept at speaking French. In contrast, her mother spoke no French, but decided, during the early autumn of 1960, to test her allure to Parisians anyway. She appealed to Luft to secure a booking for her at the 2,700-seat Théâtre du Palais de Chaillot. *[Built in 1937 in the Art Deco "modern" style, it was the site where the United Nations General Assembly adopted the Universal Declaration of Human Rights in 1948.]*

Garland musicals had not always gone over well in France, so her appearance there was commercially risky. *[Mickey Rooney/Judy Garland musicals and Andy Hardy films had not been shown in Occupied France during World War II. When some of them were released there in the years that immediately followed, they didn't do very well at the box office.]*

A critic for *L'Ecran française* wrote, somewhat snarkily: "Mickey Rooney and Judy Garland represent all that is reprehensible in the youth of the United States."

Critics noted that Judy's great voice overcame the horrible acoustics of that "big barn," at the Palais de Chaillot. *Variety* claimed that "Judy Garland killed them by her sheer talent, one of the first standing ovations since the war." Word spread, and the second night was a sell-out at the box office.

[In 1973, the interior of the renamed Théâtre National du Palais de Chaillot was radically renovated, acoustics were improved, and the space was subdivided into three separate performance spaces.]

After the show, a party in Judy's honor was hosted by one of the U.K's "Beer Barons," Jonathan Guinness, 3rd Baron Moyne, at his penthouse in Paris. Luft had to meet with the management of the theater and therefore couldn't attend, but asked Glenn Ford, who had been seated near the front of the audience, to escort Judy to the event in his place.

The American actor had been married to tap-dancing Eleanor Powell, one of Judy's early co-stars, but they had divorced in 1959. At the time, Ford was a very eligible bachelor-at-large.

Judy was thrilled to meet him. She had once confessed to Mickey Rooney that the only time she'd been seriously tempted to have a three-way was when she went to see Ford and his best friend, William Holden, star together in *Texas,* a western released in 1941.

She found Glenn Ford masculine, handsome, and charming. That night marked the beginning of their torrid romance.

On her concert's opening night, Maurice Chevalier, with a group of friends, sat in the theater's front row, cheering Judy on. That night at the party, he invited her for lunch at his home the following day.

Also in attendance were director Anatole Litvak and two of his stars, Ingrid Bergman and Anthony Perkins. They were filming *Goodbye Again* (1961), a romantic drama based on a novel by Françoise Sagan. Yves Montand was one of the leads. Later that night, Perkins talked privately to Judy: "What am I to do? Ingrid is all over me, and I don't go that route."

A native of Ukraine, Litvak had a long talk with Judy, telling her how much he'd like to star her in a movie. Formerly married to actress Miriam Hopkins, he had returned Bergman to a state of favor with American audiences in 1956 by directing her in *Anastasia. [She won a Best Ac-*

Throughout her concert tour years, **Judy Garland** appeared at some of the great theaters of Europe and America. These included the Olympia in Paris.

At the time, excerpts from her concert there were broadcast on French radio, but the concert's soundtrack wasn't distributed as an album until 1992.

455

tress Oscar for her performance in it.] Before that, he'd directed Olivia de Havilland in *The Snake Pit* (1948) which brought her an Oscar, too.

At the party, Judy had a reunion with the Duke and Duchess of Windsor, who invited her to dinner. She also met Soraya, former wife and consort to the Shah of Iran, who attended the party with film director Terence Young.

***

From Paris, Judy and Luft returned to England so that she could perform in front of audiences at sold-out concerts in Leeds and Birmingham. Then they returned to Paris for a concert Luft had booked her into at the Olympia Theatre where she opened on October 29. Portions of this event were recorded and released as *Judy Garland: Paris.*

The Olympia was the theater where the French songbird, Edith Piaf, had scored some of her biggest triumphs, and Judy, too, went over big with audiences for whom a performance in English was not a problem.

Leaving France once again, she headed for Manchester for a performance at the Free Trade Hall on November 5.

Souvenirs from **Judy's Amsterdam concert** in 1960.

It was rumored that every gay bar in Amsterdam closed for the night so their staff and patrons could attend.

Regrettably, Lorna, followed by Judy and then Luft, all came down with food poisoning, and the concert had to be rescheduled until December 4. Liza appeared on stage with her mother singing "After You've Gone."

But before she gave that rescheduled concert, she migrated by train to London for an appearance on December 1 at the Royal Variety Show at the Palladium. The Queen Mother was among the honored guests who showed up backstage to congratulate Judy.

On Friday, December 9, she and Luft flew to Amsterdam and checked into the Doelen Hotel.

The next day (Saturday, December 10), she presented a "Midnight Concert" broadcast live from the Art Deco Tuschinski Theater. Her performance, which continued until 3AM, was recorded. Its soundtrack was released in 1979, almost twenty years later, as a three-disc LP called *Judy Garland in Holland.*

According to Judy, "Amsterdam that night was overflowing with Friends of Dorothy, and, for a while, facing so many of my camp followers, I felt I was back in San Francisco. The guys seemed to love me, and I loved them back."

The leader of a local gay organization told the press, "The song that really got me was 'The Man That Got Away,' the story of my life, except that in my case it was ten men that got away."

***

On the last day of 1960, Judy, with Luft and their children, returned to New York and checked into the Carlyle Hotel. The press had announced her arrival. A major change would soon affect the course of Judy's career, and Luft was gone for the day.

At around 11AM, a call came in from a suite at the Plaza Hotel, inviting her to lunch and to spend the afternoon.

It was from Glenn Ford.

***

"My father, Glenn Ford, always needed to be 'in love' with someone—he was lost without a lover. He relished having a beautiful young woman on his arm. Raven-haired, blonde, redhead, or brunette, it didn't matter who or what type—he loved all beautiful women. Women defined his very existence."

—Peter Ford

Glenn Ford had first met Judy when she was Frances Gumm, and the Gumm Sisters were appearing at the Wilshire Theater in Santa Monica. Ford was a "horny eighteen" (his words) and worked there as an assistant stage manager.

They became quite friendly, since, even at that age, she had an interest in boys, particularly one as charming, handsome, and compelling as Ford. With Ethel Gumm's permission, Judy was allowed to go with Ford to the movies and to visit his home, where his mother cooked dinner for them. With Mom in the next room, they often sat around his living room listening to records. It was a harmless flirtation, ending with a chaste good night kiss.

Ford and Judy did not really resume their romance until the early 1960s, when they met again in Paris. Their actual sexual involvement began in New York, after they each (separately) returned from France. At the time, Judy was in the throes of dumping Sid Luft, and Ford had recently divorced Eleanor Powell.

In 1959, Ford was Hollywood's most desirable and sought-after "bachelor-at-large" and a reigning box office champion. In 1958, he'd been named the top male box office star in the film industry, beating out both Duke Wayne and Rock Hudson.

Over the years, Judy had followed Ford's film career. One of her all-time favorite pictures was *Gilda* (1946) in which he'd co-starred with Rita Hayworth in this seething cauldron of perverse eroticism and social aberration. Its stars launched one of

Rita Hayworth and Glenn Ford appear in this publicity picture for their most famous film, *Gilda* (1946).

Although he was Rita's love interest both on and off the screen, Ford later confessed, "My co-star, George MacReady, and I knew from the beginning that we were playing homosexuals. Rita got me first, but Judy more than picked up the pieces of my broken heart."

the most torrid romances of the 1940s. It eventually evolved into a lasting friendship.

"Judy fell too quickly for Ford, wanting to consume him," Kay Thompson said. "He loved her back but feared that she was far too possessive. Since he often had an early morning call onto a sound stage, he didn't like being phoned at 3 or 4AM but she desperately needed to talk to him and the conversation would usually continue until dawn, at least. She was in love with him, and he cared very much for her. That's quite a difference."

Her real desire was to marry him. She told several sources, "Glenn is the best sex I've ever had. What a man! When he leaves my bed, I'm completely satisfied."

"Judy wanted to get more deeply involved," Ford admitted. "I cared too much for her to marry her. I just knew that it would have been wrong. I didn't feel that marriage would work out for either of us. I saw only problems ahead, and I was having enough problems of my own. I didn't want to compound them with Judy's."

What Judy didn't know was that after his marriage broke up, he plunged into a series of seductions, during which he fell in love with the actress Hope Lange, his charming co-star in *Pocketful of Miracles* (1961). In that film, Bette Davis plays an old, drunken hag who manages to transform herself into a *grande dame*.

During filming of *Pocketful of Miracles*, Ford fell "hopelessly" in love with Lange, the winsome blonde star of *Payton Place* (1957) and *The Best of Everything* (1959). At the time she took up with Ford, she was divorcing Don Murray, who had appeared with her in *Bus Stop* (1956), starring Marilyn Monroe.

According to Ford's son, Peter, "When Lange put some distance between Ford and herself, it wounded my father's ego. He was hurt that he could not have someone he wanted so much."

Ford, however, found plenty of other women who wanted him to seduce them. It had begun with Joan Crawford, who made it a badge of honor to seduce every good-looking male newcomer in town. Crawford had begun an affair with young Ford in 1942 when she was filming *They All Kissed the Bride,* having replaced Carole Lombard when she died in a plane crash.

"Joan was the most dazzling, the most glamourous woman I've ever met, and she had a voracious sexual appetite."

Crawford must have extolled Ford's bedtime virtues to her close friend and occasional lover, Barbara Stanwyck. When Stanwyck's husband, Robert Taylor, walked out on her, the first man she phoned was Glenn Ford. She greeted him at the door dressed in a pink "Baby Doll" *négligée*, holding out a glass of champagne. She said, "Come on in, Glenn. I want you to take me to my bedroom and make me a woman again."

Soon after his divorce, Ford had an affair with the Austrian actress Maria Schell. She had co-starred with him in the western, *Cimarron* (1960). "The mo-

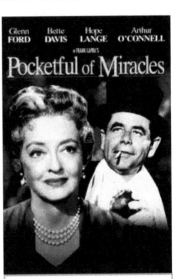

Glenn Ford had been instrumental in getting **Bette Davis** cast in *Pocketful of Miracles* (1961), the last movie made by Frank Capra.

When he asserted to the press that he had helped her get her role, Davis—who herself had fallen for Ford and been rebuffed when they'd starred together in the drama *A Stolen Life* (1946)—was outraged and less than gracious:

"Who is that son of a bitch that he should say he helped me have a comeback? That shithead wouldn't have helped me out of a sewer."

ment I met her, she was a shining beacon in my life," Ford said. He found her very passionate. She told him, "Without love, I cannot glow."

He even managed to work in a one-night stand with Marilyn Monroe in 1962, the year she died. He met her at a party for Abraham Ribicoff, JFK's Secretary of Health, Education, and Welfare. She asked him to drive her home, but after they set out in his car, she changed her mind and wanted to go to his home instead.

"Once we got there, she asked me to hold her, and I did. I did a lot more than that, but after that night, I never saw her again."

After his father's death, son Peter sold the sofa on which Ford had made love to Monroe for $1,750.

That same year, Ford also dated singer/actress Connie Stevens, who before the decade's end would marry singer Eddie Fisher, Debbie Reynolds' ex. Stevens was also dating Elvis Presley at the time. She'd become famous when cast as Cricket Blade in the hit TV detective series *Hawaiian Eye* (1959-1963).

Along came Carol Lynley, a former child model, who shot to fame appearing in James Leo Herlihy's *Blue Denim* (1959), for which she was nominated as "Most Promising Newcomer of the Year."

By 1965, Lynley was posing nude for Hugh Hefner's *Playboy*. That was the year that Judy was slated to play "Mama Jean," Jean Harlow's mother in the film called *Harlow*. Lynley was cast as Harlow, but soon after getting the part, Judy bowed out. Ginger Rogers grabbed up the role instead.

Musician Mel Tormé, who worked with Judy on her ill-fated television series, was privy to the burgeoning affair between Judy and Ford. She told him, "Glenn is good and strong, a real man, just what a red-blooded dame needs. He was one of the actors considered for the role of Norman Maine in *A Star Is Born*. I knew him years ago when I was a girl."

Tormé was also around when her affair with Ford ended. One afternoon, he found Judy in her dressing room sobbing. "It's all over," she said. *"Kaput!"* There was no argument, no fight, no re-criminations. I became painfully aware that he had moved on to other conquests. It was, 'let's not be lovers but friends forever.'"

When it was clear that the affair had ended, before she left on one of her trips to New York, she stopped at Ford's home to deliver to a servant a large photograph of herself to present to him. On its back, she'd written, "Glenn, dear one, now I can look forward and see the beauty of the sun and the moon and the love you give me. You have my heart, and I adore you. Judy."

***

As 1961 roared in, Judy and Luft were on the verge of being evicted from their home in Holmby Hills. He'd taken out yet another mortgage (they now totaled three) and was between three to five months behind in payments to all of them. Every day, threatening calls came in from bankers.

Judy was told that film offers, even concert bookings, were getting more and more difficult because of her un-dependable record of not showing up at performances during the previous months. For that, she'd recently gener-ated some of the worst press of her ca-reer.

She blamed much of their financial failure on Luft himself: "The more I work, the more I go into debt. Where does all the money go?"

She was aware that she had to re-vitalize herself, yet she didn't know how to do it. She wanted to publicize a new Judy Garland, in top form with a reliable voice, as an entertainer who fulfilled every engagement—"rain or shine"—in spite of her dismal atten-dance record.

She decided to hire Arthur P. Ja-cobs as her publicist, and to work with his assistant, John Springer, who would soon have his own agency.

Sardonically, she told Jacobs, "I'm ready for my 187th comeback."

Judy's new press agent, **Arthur Jacobs.**

A native of California, Jacobs had worked as a publicist for both MGM and Warners before branching off to form his own PR agency in 1956.

His roster of clients was "small but choice," and included such super-stars as Gregory Peck, James Stewart and—until she died—Mar-ilyn Monroe, whom he replaced with Shirley MacLaine.

When Jacobs teamed with Judy, he was on the dawn of his greatest success. It was generated by his own production company, APJAC, which struck box office gold with *Planet of the Apes* in 1968 and spawned a franchise with four sequels and a television series, comic books, and more.

[Jacobs biggest mistake involved his acquisition of the film rights to a novel, Midnight Cowboy, *about a male hustler. He decided not to make a picture that wasn't "family friendly," and turned over the rights—without charge—to his associate, Jerome Hellman. The film version of* Midnight Cowboy *won an Oscar for Best Picture in 1969, and its stars, Dustin Hoffman and Jon Voight, each received Best Actor nominations.]*

Springer would soon break away to form his own agency, and became known as the best publicist in New York and Hollywood with special skills as "the Guardian of the Stars," famous for sometimes keeping the names of his clients out of the papers instead of in them. A notable example of that was when he represented both Elizabeth Taylor and Richard Burton. His list of clients was strictly A-list Hollywood: Ginger Rogers, Joan Crawford, Bette Davis, Myrna Loy, and Grace Kelly. The men he represented included Henry Fonda, Montgomery Clift, Gary Cooper, Dirk Bogarde, and Warren Beatty.

None of his clients equaled the fame of Marilyn Monroe and Judy Garland.

[The co-author of this book, Darwin Porter, was introduced to Springer by Lucille Lortel, the Queen of Off-Broadway.

Darwin spent many a night listening to Springer's stories about Hollywood, some of them dating back to the era of Mary Pickford. He always protected the secrets of the stars, at least in public, but Darwin found him only too willing to speak privately.

Springer provided much of the insider information for Darwin's biographies of Lana Turner, Marilyn Monroe, and Elizabeth Taylor, but demanded that none of the revelations be attributed directly to him.

He had compiled the largest catalogue of frontal nude pictures of the stars, snapped in various situations and various settings, as stars frequently had to get dressed and be fitted for costumes. He was proud of his nudes of Yul Brynner, Marlon Brando, Steve McQueen, Johnny (Tarzan) Weissmuller, Tyrone Power, Gary Cooper, Tab Hunter, Warren Beatty, Rock Hudson, Tony Curtis, and James Dean, plus dozens more.

He also had frontal nudes of Lucille Ball, Joan Crawford, Jane Russell, Esther Williams, Hedy Lamarr, Ava Gardner, Carole Landis, and Kim Novak, among others.

It is not known if his catalogue of (nude) celebrities exists today, or if he destroyed it before his death, as it was rumored at the time.]

It was Springer who suggested that Judy, then alienated from

Luft, drop him as her manager. "All he did with all your earnings was leave you heavily in debt."

Springer phoned MCA to speak to an agent there, who told him that the company was "fed up" with Judy for having missed too many performances. "Bookings for her are drying up. No one wants to hire her and then have to tell an audience to line up at the box office for a refund. She's washed up."

A break in what seemed like an impenetrable wall came when Springer was told that Freddie Fields, one of MCA's vice presidents, was breaking away to form his own agency. He wanted only a special few clients that he would personally manage, beginning with his wife, actress Polly Bergen. His list also included Phil Silvers, Ethel Merman, and Peter Sellers.

In time, after he formed a partnership with David Begelman, their client list would also include Jack Carter, Woody Allen, Henry Fonda, Marilyn Monroe, Robert Redford, Steve McQueen, George Lucas, Richard Gere, Mel Gibson, and Steven Spielberg. Later, Fields would become president of both MGM and United Artists.

***

Fields flew to London, where he signed Judy to a contract, naming him as her representative. She had made up with Luft but then had separated from him. He could not keep up with whether Luft was in or out of her life.

After Fields' return to New York, he immediately settled Judy's long-standing lawsuit with CBS, since he wanted to negotiate a very lucrative future deal with that studio.

She left England soon thereafter, flying to Miami, where a limousine was waiting to take her to a suite at the Deauville Hotel on Miami Beach. There, she fulfilled an obligation she'd made in December, but had to cancel because of illness. On the night of January 9, 1961, she sang to a packed house, concluding with–what else?– "Over the Rainbow." For the one-night engagement, she was paid $10,000.

She left Florida immediately after her engagement, landing in New York. She was driven to the Carlyle Hotel, where a suite filled with flowers awaited her. That night over dinner, Fields introduced her to his new partner, David Begelman. Before the evening ended, the men proposed forming a company called Kingsrow Enterprises, each of them having one third of the stock.

As the evening came to an end, since they knew Judy was tired, they departed, but not before Begelman had given her a rather passionate kiss on the lips. He promised he'd return at seven the following night to take her to dinner.

She seemed amazed at how he'd just entered her life and had become immediately possessive. In the late morning and afternoon, she phoned around, contacting friends who knew Begelman. From what she learned he was an aggressive agent always making deals for his clients.

That night, Begelman arrived in Judy's suite, and he took her in his arms and gave her another of his passionate kisses. As she later told John Springer, he overpowered her with his masculinity, "a real take-charge man of the type some women dream about."

David Begelman was born in Manhattan to a Jewish family. He had been a pilot for the Army Air Forces during World War II. When it was over, he became one of the vice presidents of MCA. A year prior to meeting Judy, he co-founded Creative Management Associates (CMA) with Freddie Fields.

Over dinner, he revealed a surprise: "I've been talking with Stanley Kramer. It's almost certain that he's going to assign you a small but pivotal role in his upcoming courtroom drama, *Judgment at Nuremberg,* a movie about the trial in the late 1940s of Nazi judges.

His client list was impressive: Barbra Streisand, Fred Astaire, Woody Allen, Gregory Peck, Steve McQueen, Jackie Gleason, and, in time, Liza Minnelli.

As their drunken evening progressed, he was very blunt about what he included as his services: "I not only want to be your agent, but your 24-hour-a-day lover, too. It's a package deal just for you." Then he rose from the table and walked over to her, taking her hand and pressing it against his half-erect penis. "It's a big one and it's all for you."

CMA became known in Hollywood circles for putting together package deals—that is, an arrangement that included the collaboration and shared vision of a star, his or her director, and a scriptwriter for an as-yet-unmade movie.

He spent that night with her and many nights to come. The next morning, after a joint shower and a room service breakfast, he drove to The Dakota, the most famous apartment building in Manhattan. There, she learned that he'd made arrangements for her to have her own apartment.

[The elaborate and elegant building stood on the northwest corner of 72ⁿᵈ Street at Central Park West. Built in 1884, the structure looked like something from the German Renaissance, with high gables and deep roofs, dormer, hidden niches, balconies, spandrels, and balustrades.

Over the years its tenants would include Lauren Bacall, José Ferrer, Lillian Gish, Boris Karloff, and ultimately, John Lennon, who would be as-

sassinated in front of the building in 1973.

Judy had been approved by the committee who ruled on tenants. Over the years, they rejected Antonio Banderas, Melanie Griffith, Gene Simmons, Billy Joel, and Carly Simon, among others.

The Dakota was used as a backdrop in Roman Polanski's film, Rosemary's Baby *(1968).]*

Before the debut of filming for *Judgment at Nuremberg*, Fields and Begelman booked Judy into two concert gigs in Texas, one in Dallas, another in Houston.

For these tours, she stripped away the dancing boys, the vaudeville acts, the lavish costumes, and the nostalgia-inducing sets. "The audience is going to get just me," she told Begelman.

"Baby, that's plenty to offer," he assured her.

***

Her concert tour of 1961 became part of the Judy Garland legend as she won new "converts" across the country.

Stanley Kramer flew to the State Fair Auditorium in Dallas to see her perform. Up until then, he had been considering casting Julie Harris in *Judgment*. He did not go backstage but left the city and later phoned Begelman. "I'm convinced. Garland is perfect for the role."

In Dallas, she had a reunion with one of its residents, her sister Jimmie. During Judy's preparations for her concert, Jimmie found her agitated, confused, and sweating in ways she interpreted as paranoid. Aware that Judy's medication of choice was Ritalin, she worried about her health, as she was ingesting, every day, between 20 and 100mg of it, often with Benzedrine capsules on the side.

Judy might have been a nervous wreck, but *Variety*, the day after her opening, proclaimed "Her pipes were never better." In two hours, she had sung thirty songs.

The next day, the critic for a local newspaper hailed her performance as "The greatest show ever given in Dallas."

After that, she moved on to appear in Houston at the City Auditorium. "I saw some of our most staid citizens acting like teenagers at an Elvis Presley concert," wrote Gene Harper, a California writer who flew to Texas just to see her. "She was overweight, but what in hell did that matter when she brought tears to my eyes singing 'Over the Rainbow?'"

Judy was back in Los Angeles in time for the beginning of filming for *Judgment at Nuremberg*, which in 1959 had originated as a television play starring Claude Rains.

***

Judgment at Nuremberg was shot on the Universal lot in Los Angeles in March of 1961. Stanley Kramer had assembled an all-star cast with Spencer Tracy, Burt Lancaster, Richard Widmark, Maximilian Schell, Marlene Dietrich, Montgomery Clift, and William Shatner.

With a screenplay by Abby Mann, it was a fictional depiction of the infamous "Nazi Judges' Trial" of 1947 in the heavily bombed-out city of Nuremberg, scene of Hitler's greatest Nazi rallies. On trial were judges accused of crimes against humanity for their involvement in atrocities committed by the Third Reich.

The film in part depicted actual footage shot by American and British soldiers during the liberation of the concentration camps. The mammoth pile of naked and rotting corpses laid out were so graphic that some shocked members of audiences in America walked out of the movie houses.

Kramer's reputation was well known to Judy, as he'd become famous for his "message pictures," which included High Noon (1952) starring Gary Cooper and Grace Kelly, and The Caine Mutiny (1954) with Humphrey Bogart.

For Judy's supporting role of Irene Hoffman, Kramer paid her $50,000. As the star, Tracy drew $400,000.

Lancaster was the biggest money earner at $750,000.

On the set, Judy had a friendly reunion with Tracy, who'd been

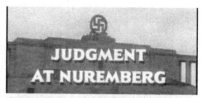

ACADEMY ★ AWARD WINNER!
BEST ACTOR! BEST SCREENPLAY!

In **Judgment at Nuremberg**, an overweight Irene Hoffman (**Judy**, lower photo) is summoned to court to testify.

She made a most creditable witness, providing details about the death of a former friend, an elderly Jew. He was falsely accused of having a sexual relationship, which had led to his execution for "polluting the Aryan race."

Maximilian Schell (on the left in the upper photo, where he appears with an aging **Burt Lancaster**), comes down hard on her, accusing her of distorting the truth.

In a well-performed reaction, she almost breaks into hysteria.

cast as Chief Judge Dan Haywood. No mention was made of his early seduction of her, which led to her having an abortion. All that was buried with the scandals of yesterday.

He asked Judy, "Still married to Luft the lug?"

"On and off," she answered. "Now it's off."

"I never thought the bum was right for you. I don't like men who exploit women stars, and Hollywood is riddled with them. Actually, I have only one thing in common with Luft, or two if you want to be more precise. We've both fucked Hedy Lamarr and Gene Tierney."

That was news to Judy.

She met and had several long talks with Montgomery Clift, concluding with, "He was even more messed up than I am."

Kramer offered him the role of the prosecuting attorney, Col Tad Lawson, but Clift rejected it, agreeing to work for nothing in the smaller role of Rudolph Peterson, a feeble-minded Jew who is sterilized by the Nazis for being "abnormal."

"Spence was a great help to Monty," Judy said. "He was in such bad shape he flubbed his lines and had to do take after take. Finally, Spence came over to him, telling him, 'fuck the lines—just play to me. You know the character.'"

"When his own words poured out of Monty's mouth, they were shattering," Judy said. "The whole cast and crew were mesmerized.

It was one of the first film roles for the Canadian-born **William Shatner**, who would become a cultural icon for his portrayal of Captain James T. Kirk of the USS Enterprise in the *Star Trek* franchise.

He appears here with an aging **Spencer Tracy.**

Despite the vulnerability and tremulous emotions Judy brought to her role in *Judgment at Nuremberg*, moviegoers tended to view her (relatively small) contribution to the film as less riveting than the performances of at least a half-dozen other vintage, golden-age pros.

They included **Spencer Tracy** and the divine **Marlene Dietrich,** who appear stylishly together on the cover of *Films and Filmmaking*

467

Would that I could be so great as Irene Hoffman."

For his efforts, Clift received an Oscar nomination for Best Supporting Actor of the Year.

Judy met Lancaster but didn't spend much time with him. That would come later when they co-starred in a movie, *A Child is Waiting.*

Dietrich and Judy had known each other for years, and Judy shared her dressing room. Dietrich had been cast as "a good German" in the role of Frau Bertholt, the widow of a Nazi general who had been executed on orders from Hitler, who suspected him of disloyalty to the Third Reich.

When she re-encountered Judy, Dietrich held her in her arms for a long time before giving her a passionate kiss on the lips. Each of them reflected on the ravages of time. Dietrich told her, "Don't whisper this to a soul, but I'm going on sixty. Life is far too short. It was only yesterday that a former Navy lieutenant on the Côte d'Azur made love to me and raced across the sands with me. Now he's the President of the United States."

"Another beautiful man," Dietrich continued, "Gary Cooper, is dead. He and I crossed the Sahara in *Morocco* (1930). My beloved Ernest Hemingway has put a shotgun to his head. In the once enchanting city of Berlin, the Soviets are putting up a wall. And I'm off to Switzerland to have myself injected with the cells of an unborn lamb."

After their work was finished, Judy and Dietrich embraced for a final time, unsure of when their paths would cross again. "We should have been lovers," Dietrich whispered in her ear.

"Kramer gave me the respect I deserved as an actress," Judy claimed. "If he ever summons me again to take the role of a leper in Molokai, I'm his gal."

The premiere of *Judgment at Nuremberg* was held in West Berlin.

But Did He Fit Into Hollywood?

Fascinating, cosmopolitan, sharp-tongued, and *Mitteleuropean*:

Maximilian Schell

Judy flew there with Maximilian Schell and Kramer. Tracy showed up with Katharine Hepburn. The setting was the Kongresshalle on December 14, 1961. Berliners dubbed the building "the pregnant oyster."

Some three hundred journalists from 22 countries attended. At the end of the film, many of the perhaps embarrassed Berliners sat in stony silence. The city's mayor, Willy Brandt, honored the stars and their director with a welcoming speech.

At the time of the film's premiere in New York, emotions and public sentiment about Nazi atrocities were running high. Adolf Eichmann, the Nazi sadist, was going on trial in Israel.

Judgment at Nuremberg was a courtroom drama weighing universal issues associated with brutalities, war crimes, and the rights of humankind.

Depicted above is **Burt Lancaster,** cast as defendant Dr. Ernst Janning, who breaks his silence and testifies to his Nazi guilt, which gets him sentenced to life in prison.

Critics hailed *Judgment at Nuremberg* as one of the best of the year. Bosley Crowther at *The New York Times* wrote: "As a young *Hausfrau,* Judy Garland is amazingly real, telling a horrifying tale of a trumped-up charge of racial contamination against an elderly Jew."

Variety claimed, "Both Montgomery Clift and Judy Garland bring great emotional force and conviction to their roles." Brendan Gill of *The New Yorker* cited the film as "so overloaded with stars that it occasionally threatens to turn it into a judicial *Grand Hotel.* Imagine Judy Garland and Marlene Dietrich in the same film."

Gavin Lambert also looked carefully at the cast, claiming, "It's an All-Star concentration camp drama with special guest victim appearances."

The *Monthly Film Bulletin* critic was not impressed, viewing it as "hackneyed courtroom hysteria."

Most of the stars, including Judy, were praised, but Dietrich came in for rebuke, some reviewers citing her performance as "glassy" and "wooden."

Competing with Spencer Tracy in the same movie, Schell won the Best Actor Oscar. Judy was nominated for Best Supporting Actress, losing to Rita Moreno for her performance in *West Side Story.* However, Judy did win the Cecil B. DeMille Award in 1962 for her contribution to the entertainment industry.

***

On March 29, Judy and Luft met for a celebration of Joey's sixth birthday. The tension between them was obvious, as he was very skeptical, and certainly jealous, of the takeover of her career by David Begelman.

Luft nicknamed Freddie Fields and David Begelman "Leopold and Loeb," after the notorious thrill killers of the 1920s. Judy's husband, using racetrack vernacular, felt he was "being put out to pasture" as her new managers seized control of her life.

A gleeful **Greg Bautzer** (center) in a rare bare-chested photo, is seen with **Ginger Rogers** accepting the Pimm's Cup for mixed doubles.

It was presented in Palm Springs by that fading star of yesterday, **Charles Farrell,** in August of 1960.

In 1961, Judy and Luft underwent a staggering number of separations— some of them lasting no more than three or four days—and reconciliations, Their children were often left wondering, "Is Dad in or out the door?"

Lorna, in a 1998 memoir, revealed her feelings at seeing her family torn apart: "My Dad was helpless to prevent our family from breaking up. He loved my mother as much as ever, but he knew her well, and he was terrified of what would happen to us without him there to take care of us. The world as I knew it was about to topple off my father's shoulders. When it fell, it made a crash that still reverberates."

Early in the summer, Judy and Luft had an almost volcanic eruption about Begelman. She kicked him out of the house and headed East with Liza, Lorna, and Joey.

"I'm going to divorce the bastard," she told Begelman, who recommended that she consult attorney Greg Bautzer.

Bautzer was the most famous divorce lawyer in Hollywood. As a sideline, he was having a long-term affair with Joan Crawford. Hailed as "Movieland's Don Juan," he seduced a string of other leading ladies, too: Ginger Rogers, Lana Turner, Ava Gardner, Rita Hayworth, Peggy Lee, and lots and lots more.

"Maybe if I put out for him, he'll give me a discount on his fees," Judy said.

Judy signed a power of attorney, giving Begelman complete control of her finances and future earnings.

By now, Begelman was the controlling force in Judy's life, collecting all her money and paying what bills he could. After the sale of the house in Holmby Hills [*most of the proceeds went to IRS],* he told Judy to put all future real estate in her own name and to exclude Luft. "In our new deal, Luft is just another hired hand," he told her.

Begelman made one concession, agreeing to put Luft on Judy's payroll, a dubious concession since Begelman retained the ability to determine how much that monthly payout might or might not be: If funds were low, perhaps it might be nothing at all.

***

In April of 1961, Judy and Luft, with their children, flew to Washington, D.C. and checked into the Mayflower Hotel. On the following night, she gave a concert at Constitution Hall, attended by Robert and Ethel Kennedy. JFK was in Key West, meeting with the British Prime Minister, Harold Macmillan.

President **John F. Kennedy** and his brother, Attorney General **Robert F. Kennedy.**

Are they whispering secrets about Judy? We doubt it.

Once, Judy was invited to the White House to an event that at the last minute, her long-ago lover and ongoing friend, JFK, could not attend.

The dinner at the White House proceeded anyway, with the understanding that the president's brother, Bobby Kennedy, his long-suffering wife, Ethel, and Jackie Kennedy would serve as hosts during JFK's absence.

Depicted above are **Ethel and RFK**.

The following evening, Robert and Ethel invited Luft and Judy to the White House for a dinner party, at which she would sing. [*Whereas JFK would not be there, Jacqueline and Bobbie and Ethel would preside.*] Judy was impressed with Ethel, who seemed very level-headed and "so down to Earth," whereas Jacqueline seemed like "more of a princess descended to earth."

The next day, JFK (who had not attended the party at the White House the night before) flew back to Washington from Florida. At 9AM, the White House put through a call to Judy and Luft at the Mayflower, awakening them.

His call extended another invitation to the White House. JFK wanted to thank her for entertaining the U.S. troops stationed in West Germany. Judy became almost hysterical getting dressed and prepped for the event, even having Vern Alves, Luft's assistant, shave her legs.

At the appointed time, Luft and Judy showed up at the White House. She claimed, "This was the first time in my life I was ever on time."

JFK welcomed them into the Oval Office, hugging and kissing Judy. "You don't mind, do you, Sid?" he asked. "After all, I saw her before you did."

"Mr. President," Luft answered, "All I have is yours."

JFK did not have a lot of time, since he was soon due for a public appearance, but he walked Judy around the Oval Office, taking her behind his desk to show her holes in the floor.

"You have termites, too?" she observed.

"It's not that," he said. "Those holes were made by Ike's [*Dwight D. Eisenhower's*] spiked golfing shoes." Both of them laughed. He hugged and kissed her goodbye and saw them off.

During his short term as president, JFK would often call her on "some of my darkest days." He wanted to hear her voice once again, singing the last eight bars of "Over the Rainbow."

***

Judy had to put aside, for the moment at least, her marital woes, her financial distress, and even the welfare of her kids. She faced a grueling agenda with upcoming concert bookings in various American cities, and she had to plot her debut at Carnegie Hall. It loomed ominously on April 23, 1961.

She flew to Birmingham, Alabama, for a concert at the Municipal Auditorium. She addressed the audience, "Any state that could produce the formidable Tallulah Bankhead must be doing something right." She sang to thunderous applause "Swanee" and "Rock-a-Bye My Baby to a Dixie Melody."

It was on to Atlanta, where she recalled, "It must be the gay capital of the Deep South. I never knew my boys were so plentiful down there in the land of cotton and molasses."

She opened at Atlanta's Municipal Auditorium on April 13, telling the audience how she almost got cast as Scarlett O'Hara's younger sister in *Gone With the Wind* (1939).

Fueled by Ritalin, she kept her traveling companion, Vern Alves, up and awake for most of the night, talking over everything from the horrors of her life from her mother, Ethel, to her dysfunctional marriage to Sid Luft. She also talked openly about Vincente Minnelli's homosexuality.

On another night, she met up with some good ol' Southern boys, members of a country band from Nashville called the Pot Likkers, staying up until 5AM playing poker with them.

Before returning to New York, she fulfilled two obligations in North Carolina. In Greensboro, she had booked into the Coliseum on April 13. She told Vern Alves to tell the stage manager to cancel the concert because she was ill. Fortunately, David Begelman had finished his business and flew in during the afternoon. He spent several hours alone with Judy in her suite. He later notified Alves that she had decided to go on after all.

"All she needed was for a man to plug her and regenerate her. I did that and lubricated her throat, too. She'll be fine tonight."

Indeed, she was. A local critic found her voice as "clear as a North Carolina mountain spring."

Trouble began before she opened on April 17 in Charlotte, NC, at the Coliseum. She had been difficult and demanding all morning, and again after lunch, which she refused to eat. She ordered Begelman to fly in Lorna and Joey. He pleaded with her to be reasonable. They were nearing the end of their term at school, and she would be joining them soon in New York.

She refused to listen and became more and more belligerent. "I can't see my children? Is that what you're saying to me, you god damn son of a bitch? I work my ass off making money for you slugs, and I'm denied just one simple request?"

He urged her to calm down, but she lashed out, clawing the right side of his face, drawing blood with her razor-sharp nails.

Bleeding, he rushed into the bathroom. When he came out, she had passed out on the sofa. He picked her up and carried her to the bed, leaving the door open to his adjoining room.

When she awakened the next morning, she called out to him. Then she sat up in bed, claiming, "I feel like I haven't eaten in days. This morning I'm going to have sausage, grits, lots of hashed browns, and at least three eggs."

There was no mention of the previous night, only a passing reference to Begelman's bandaged face. "Cut yourself shaving, huh?'

The show was a success, one local critic claiming, "Judy Garland last night looked so fresh and was so fine a voice that she appeared to have emerged from the set of *Easter Parade*. But when she sang 'Over the Rainbow,' she became our beloved Dorothy all over again. She's almost forty but the wistful sound of a teenager came across."

After North Carolina, she returned to Manhattan, where Carnegie Hall was waiting for her.

***

At 8:40PM on the night of April 23, 1961, Judy Garland stood in the wings of Carnegie Hall, listening to the Mort Lindsey Orchestra play *The Garland Overture*. She emerged to the wildest applause of her career, a standing ovation. She was about to become the star of what became known as "the greatest night in the history of show business."

Whereas the dynamics of Judy's April, 1961, concert at Carnegie have long faded, millions of Americans commemorated it with the purchase of the record album it generated. **JUDY! JUDY! JUDY!** became something of a lifelong mantra for many of them.

She was already a legend when she went onstage that night, and by the time the curtain fell, she was even more of one. "At least for that one night, Judy buried her demons long enough to give the performance of a lifetime," said Vern Alves. "At the age of thirty-nine, most artists have reached their peak—not Judy. I witnessed her that night. After Carnegie, it would be downhill. The boys from Capitol were there to record it for posterity. So was the cream of show business in both New York and Hollywood."

Celebrities had flown in from the Coast, including her old MGM boss, Dore Schary. In the front row sat her beaming kids, proud of their mother.

What the audience didn't know was that fifteen minutes before her entrance, Luft was holding Judy as she vomited into the toilet bowl of her dressing room.

When David Begelman and Freddie Fields entered the room, Luft warned them that she might not be able to go on. Begelman looked like he was going to have a heart attack. Although the theater was at the point of having to sell only "standing room," there were still about a thousand people waiting outside, hoping to buy tickets.

At the last possible minute, Judy rallied, and walked onstage. "I think if she had stood up that audience, she would never get a booking again—maybe in a saloon in Kansas City, Missouri," Fields said.

It was rumored that some of the celebrities from California who arrived late paid as much as $500 a ticket from scalpers assembled outside like vultures.

Some of Judy's dearest friends were out front that night: Harold

Arlen, Chuck Walters, Roger Edens, and Kay Thompson. Celebrities included Henry Fonda, Carol Channing, Ethel Merman, Merv Griffin, Henny Youngman, Adolph Green, Betty Comden, Maurice Chevalier, Hedda Hopper, Leonard Bernstein, Spencer Tracy, Myrna Loy, Anthony Perkins, Anne Jackson, Eli Wallach, Julie Andrews, Phil Silvers, Richard Burton, and Mike Nichols.

Rock Hudson claimed that "Every gay bar in Manhattan emptied out that night as her most loyal fans flocked to Carnegie Hall."

For her repertoire, she mixed the old with the new, appearing first on stage with slim legs and a big bosom in a black sheath with a blue-jeweled Mandarin jacket. After intermission, she did a quick change into black toreador pants and a top studded with sequins.

A singer himself, Merv Griffin predicted, "No act will ever top Judy's."

After singing Arlen's "Come Rain Or Come Shine," she introduced its composer from where he was sitting in the audience.

After two dozen songs, she was breathless, claiming, "I don't think I have much more." But the screams of "encore" were so persuasive that she managed "Chicago" and "After You've Gone." Fans even demanded "Over the Rainbow" in both the first and second act of that night's performance.

Her performance was both a marathon and a *tour-de-force.*

In the pre-dawn hours, critics were writing some of the greatest reviews of her life. Cecil Smith in the *Los Angeles Times* wrote: "There was a winning simplicity to the show. She did none of the routines she had leaned upon in recent years—there was no clown make-up, no tramp outfit. She stood up there and sang."

Variety noted, "The tones are clear, the phrasing meaningful, and the vocal passion is catching. It is virtually impossible to remain casual and uninvolved. The audience couldn't resist anything she did. Capitol Records' engineers were on hand to put *Judy at Carnegie Hall* into the groove, even pruned to the limitations of an LP's running time, it should be a socko platter."

Bill Roberts reported for the *Houston Post* what happened at the end of the concert: "Hundreds began crowding the aisles. Some of these creatures were actually in a transport of ecstasy and did not know what they were doing. They stared only at Judy with a fantastic light in their eyes."

Judith Crist in the *New York Herald Tribune* wrote: "Judy Garland's ingenuous warmth dominated the evening, but there is neither coyness or girly-girlishness in her approach. Well, I can't give you anything but raves, Miss Garland."

Judy's favorite review was by Burt Boyar in *The Long Island Daily Express:*

"The condition in which Miss Garland left her audience is totally indescribable. Never before have I seen hundreds of people fill the aisles and move toward the stage where they stood in a mass with their hands outstretched, just trying to touch her. She might have been a great faith healer endowed with magical powers, so urgent was their need to get closer to her. The bravos roared from the back of the great concert hall like a massive tidal wave. When she had sung every song for which the orchestra had music, the people shouted, `Just stand there.' If she had remained there for an hour, they would have applauded that. If the building had caught fire, I think they'd have perished on the spot rather than leave her. Within thirty seconds of her entrance, the audience was on its feet greeting her with a standing ovation, the first of at least a dozen that were to follow. People were on their feet so often, it seemed a shame to have had them pay for seats. God knows what has happened to her, but it should happen to everyone. She is completely relaxed, she danced around like a happy kid between and during her songs and her voice is rich and loaded with her unique Garland sound…She is full of fun and absolutely lovable. When she bends back and pulls those big notes up from her toes—well, forget about it— there is no other woman in show business."

Her glittering career high was followed with a private disaster. At P.J. Clarke's, the most famous bar in Manhattan at the time, she and Luft kept the owner up until 4AM as he talked about horse racing, a subject that bored her.

On the way back to The Dakota, she informed Luft that she and Begelman had agreed that they owed Luft only $400 for his contribution, as associate producer, to the production.

Luft exploded in fury. "You're making $100,000 a week on this concert tour, and you're giving what I'd give a groom in a horse stable! Hell, I pay $200 to $300 a night to take you out for dinner and dancing. I'm being treated like a god damn butler or servant."

She slapped his face, followed by his telling her, "Shove that $400 up your ass."

When Freddie Fields phoned him following morning, Luft told him: "I got your paycheck—how generous! You and Begelman are busting my balls!" Then he slammed down the phone and walked out on Judy—their most serious separation—after another bruising fight.

***

That May, Judy was profiled in *Life* magazine by Shana Alexander: "Judy Garland is the most electrifying entertainer to watch on stage since Al Jolson. She has moved beyond talent and beyond fame to become the rarest phenomenon in all of show business—part bluebird, part phoenix. She is a legend in her own time."

The double album, *Judy at Carnegie Hall,* became an immediate best-seller, squatting for seventy-three weeks on the *Billboard* chart, including thirteen weeks as Number One. That made it certified gold.

It also won four Grammy Awards: Album of the Year; Best Female Vocal Performance; Best Engineered Album; and Best Album Cover. The artwork on the album's jacket became famous, a black sketch of her face over a solid red background emblazoned with the words "JUDY! JUDY! JUDY!" for Album of the Year, Judy beat out Henry Mancini and Nat King Cole, becoming the first woman singer so honored.

Cary O'Dell wrote:

"Judy at Carnegie Hall represented a phoenix-like re-ascension of an individual's power—personal and professional. It was a victory of the human spirit fueled by sheer will power and audience adoration. That Garland overcame all her previous troubles in order to give this one flawless concert was something not missed by anyone."

***

At the invitation of the Kennedys, Judy decided to spend the rest of the summer of 1961 at Hyannis Port on Cape Cod. Luft was definitely not invited, but she took along Liza, Lorna, and Joey.

For a while, Vern Alves would be a fixture in the Luft family, but months later, he could take it no more and departed to start life anew elsewhere.

On Cape Cod, she poured out her heart to Alves one night, telling him that she feared that Luft was plotting to kidnap Joey and Lorna. "But I figure with all these security guards here at Hyannis Port, we'll be safe."

Luft flew to the Cape to see her and checked into a nearby motel. When he managed to get her on the phone, she said, "Sid, my man, I guess I'm going to divorce you. But when? I'll let you know. You've made your trip here in vain. Now leave!" Then she put down the phone.

Later, she told Alves: "I want Liza to get to know the Kennedy clan. Maybe she'll marry one of the grandsons."

From the Kennedy compound at Hyannis Port, Judy got Liza a job painting scenery at $15 a week at the Cape Cod Melody Tent. "If you want to get into show business, start at the bottom."

Judy's brood bonded with the Kennedys. At first because Joey was a bit frail, he had a hard time bonding with these athletic children, but in time, he developed a friendship with Chris Lawford, son of Peter and Patricia.

Lorna later claimed that of all the Kennedy family, her favorite was First Lady Jacqueline. "Her voice was soft and gentle, and I loved to listen to her speak."

She also found JFK fascinating because he had more hair than any man she'd ever seen. Once he escaped from the Secret Service and took her and some of the Kennedy kids on a wild ride in a golf cart. Their high-adrenaline, high speed ride, with agents from the Secret Service in hot pursuit, was evocative of the Keystone Cops.

At summer's end, Judy and her kids returned to Manhattan and set up residence at The Dakota, where fellow resident Lauren Bacall was almost a daily visitor.

Suddenly, without any warning, Luft returned into Judy's life.

"The Battling Duo made up once again," Alves said. "Luft was allowed to return to her bed, and it was 'honey' and 'baby,' which replaced 'bastard' and 'shithead' in Judy's vocabulary. I predicted it might last three days, maybe four, before the tug-of-war began once more."

There was an intensity to Judy's style in the finale of *I Could Go On Singing* that some of her fans considered overblown, and perhaps unnervingly representative of her fragile emotional state during its filming.

For more about **Judy, Judy, Judy** and how, against the odds, she went on singing, please move on to the next chapters.

CHAPTER SEVENTEEN

Why Did Judy Define 1961 as Her Best Year?
READ ABOUT IT HERE

AMERICAN PIE
Judy Tours the U.S.

Stevie Phillips
As the Suicidal Diva's Handler, She Asks,
"What's a Nice Girl Like Me Doing in a Place Like This?"

GAY PURR-EE!
In an Animated Cartoon, Judy Talks Like a French Pussy.
Robert Goulet ("Sir Lancelot") Plays a Horny Tomcat
& Hermione Gingold Stars as "Mme Rubens-Chatte"

TV MAGIC
with Frank (Sinatra) & Dean (Martin)

Liza Gets Cast as Anne Frank in a High School Play

GAY MEN ADORE HER
Judy Reinforces Her Status as a Quasi-Religious Icon

With the Collaboration of Bonny Burt (Lancaster),
who plays a Child Therapist and Hospital Administrator
A CHILD IS WAITING
and Waiting, and Waiting, and Waiting

"She never came across as a 'star,' making an appearance and impressed with her own status and abilities. She was an entertainer who earnestly wanted to entertain her audience. She carried to the concert stage the traits with which she had imbued her film characters, a general good-naturedness and a self-deprecating sense of humor, which could be sharp but never cynical."

—Emily Coleman

"Even songs that were not written especially for her become hers by right of interpretation. She is an original."

—Seymour Raven

"My concerts were lovefests between my loyal fans, my audience, and me."

—Judy Garland

"A Judy Garland concert combines old-time revivalism with the ancient rite of Dionysus."

—Bacchanale

"When the voice pours out, as rich and pleading as ever, we know where and how moved we are—in the presence of a star—and embarrassed by tears."

—Kenneth Tynan

"When all is said and done, it is Garland's singing, acting, and even her dancing that make her unforgettable. She could not save herself off the stage, but on it, she kept honing her craft, infusing whole movies and concerts with her own restless and transcendent vitality."

—Elizabeth Kendall

"I have served as musical director for a number of artists. It would be demeaning or belittling to state that Judy Garland was head and shoulders above them all. She was as warm and generous as she was talented. Her sense of humor was fantastic. In short, it was an honor, a virtual experience, and a privilege to make music with her. In all her concerts, TV shows—no matter where and how often—I always had goose bumps when she sang."

—Mort Lindsey

"Judy wanted romance around the clock. She was starving for it. The love she got from her audience was never enough. Not even close. The minute she was not in front of the footlights, she craved male attention. She could not feel attractive or beautiful without being told so by a man. When he was present, Judy sublimated so it could be all about him. He was everything as long as he adored her. Without a man, fifty percent of her was missing. And this was David Begelman's moment."

—Stevie Phillips

F. Scott Fitzgerald once wrote: "There are no second acts in American lives." But in 1961, Judy Garland set out to prove the novelist wrong.

Because no film offers were on the horizon other than the promise of, "You're being considered," her managers, Freddie Fields and David Begelman, knew they had to come up with a new and profitable gig. An idea was spawned: Why not replicate her 1951 success at the London Palladium with a U.S. equivalent in perhaps forty-five cities stretching from New York to Miami, from Chicago to San Francisco via Texas.

Begelman calculated—and then promised her—that she might earn as much as $375,000, the equivalent of $3.2 million in 2020 currency.

During her months-long "pilgrimage," she would face many mishaps, including—if she were in an outdoor area—the weather. Such was the case one night when she starred at the Hollywood Bowl and a rainstorm with thunder and lightning descended over Los Angeles. She went on singing, which led to a headline in the *Los Angeles Times*—JUDY DOESN'T FRIZZLE IN A DRIZZLE.

On the road, various friends dropped in as members of the audience and then migrated backstage to see her. Many of them were faded Hollywood stars, past their own cinematic box office prime, appearing at the time in roadshow productions at sites along her concert trail. One night in Manhattan, Montgomery Clift showed up at one of her performances, telling her, backstage, that he was on the verge of suicide.

481

"Suicide!" she said. "Hey, that's my gig. Get a different act for yourself!"

Ironically, most of her earnings during this tour would eventually be confiscated for back taxes by the Internal Revenue Service. Unlike many of her contemporaries, she, with Luft, had not managed to wangle any successful tax shelters.

As regards her spending patterns, and to her credit, Judy was not extravagant in her tastes for clothing and jewelry, unlike other stars like Lana Turner or Joan Crawford. Around the house, she wore ski pants and had only a few gowns—some designed by herself. On stage, she often wore off-the-rack toreador pants.

In contrast, Luft, who sheltered an (unrequited) dream of being designated "Best Dressed Man in America," spent lavishly on wardrobe. And whereas Judy usually had less that twenty-five dollars in her purse, "Bigshot" Luft often carried around thousands of dollars, usually in cash, which he'd take with him to the horse races.

During this year on the road, beginning in February of 1961, Judy labored frequently and intensely with Mort Lindsey. She had first worked with him on a one-night stand at the Concord Hotel along the "Borscht Belt" of the Catskills, a 2 ½-hour drive north of Manhattan.

Lindsey became her regular conductor for concerts and later, during the production of two films, more than thirty hours of TV.

"I used to come out onto the stage after some other performers' vaudeville acts," she claimed. "Then, for a while, at least, I used a stand-up comedian like Alan King to warm up the audience. But in time, the audience got only me, flawed but enchanting."

"I became my own chorus line, minus all the dancing boyfriends. That was just as well. When some handsome stud came back to congratulate me, someone always managed to 'waylay' him *en route* to my dressing room. I'm sure I missed out on some prize meat."

Her concert gigs were legion: From 1951 until the year of her death (1969), Judy would star in more than a hundred one-woman concerts, ranging from one-night stands to weeks-long engagements in cities across the world As might have been anticipated, her voice wasn't what it used to be in her heyday, but she could still move an audience with the force of her personality. In time, she'd break through the generation gap, winning new fans, especially young gay men.

These concert tours became part of her enduring legend, positioning Judy Garland as the greatest entertainer of all time.

***

Here begins a rundown of "Judy's Greatest Year" (1961) a concert schedule interspersed with high drama, applause, and inordinate amounts of pain.

PHILADELPHIA: A critic for *Variety* was in Philadelphia on April 19 and made it a point to attend Judy's concert at the Academy of Music on

April 19. Their review? "It's virtually impossible to remain casual and un-involved when Judy Garland is at work. She demands as much from the audience as she does from herself, but everyone seems to enjoy participating. In fact, the audience couldn't resist anything she did."

NEWARK, NEW JERSEY: Begelman drove her to the Mosque Theatre in Newark, where she appeared on stage on May 2. That was the day Hedda Hopper broke the news that Chuck Walters had been hired to direct Judy in the film adaptation of the Dorothy Fields musical, *By the Beautiful Sea*. She would have played the owner of a boarding house on Coney Island, circa 1900, a role that Shirley Booth had developed on Broadway, but the deal fell through.

Her presentation in Newark generated raves. *Time* wrote: "There are not many good girl singers these days, although there are plenty of echo chamber yowlers, and there is no one who can come within miles of Judy. She has, in addition to lungs, clarity, drive, and rhythm, an incredible amount of pizzaz, a quality of bad repute because it is so unpleasant when it's faked. Garland is the best belter in the business."

CHICAGO: Because she was still nervous about getting into an airplane, any airplane, Begelman held her hand *en route* to Chicago in time for her May 6 opening at the Civic Opera House. With verve, she thrilled the audience, opening her repertoire of songs with "Chicago."

DALLAS: Judy showed up at the Music Hall there for a concert on May 8. "The Yellow Rose of Texas" was part of her act. As she was checking into her hotel, the manager appeared to present her with an unpaid bill from 1957. Deeply embarrassed, she later said, "I hated owing money. It's humiliating, especially since with my earning power, I should never be in debt."

Her sister Jimmie sat in the front row. After the show, the two sisters talked until deep into the night, mostly about Judy's troubled relationship with Sid Luft.

Earlier, Judy had complained that she never saw any of the money she earned. Begelman made a deal with the box office and put all the night's receipts into a paper bag and carried it to Judy's suite. She opened it and, seeing all that cash, she picked up wads of it and tossed it into the air, not stopping until every banknote had been airborne. Begelman spent the next hour retrieving and organizing the bills and putting them back into the paper bag.

HOUSTON: Only two night later, Judy was in Houston, appearing before some 10,000 concertgoers at the Sam Houston Coliseum. At the Shamrock Hilton, Conrad Hilton himself was on hand to welcome her. With humor and irony, she said to him, "I'm in Houston to replace Zsa Zsa in your life."

[Built by oil-industry wildcatter Glenn McCarthy, one of the most famous "bad boys" in the history of Texas, The Shamrock was the largest hotel in the United States during the 1940s. Its opening in 1949 is still cited as one of the biggest (and most disastrous) social events ever held in Houston. The Houston Chronicle's society editor described the event as "bedlam in diamonds."

Sold to Conrad Hilton in 1955 and operated till 1985 as the Shamrock Hilton, *the facility was acquired by the Texas Medical Center before it was demolished in 1987.]*

Later, from Houston, Judy sent a vindictive telegram to Luft: "Sid, my darling. I don't give a damn about you."

DETROIT: She flew into Detroit a day before her May 12 concert at the Masonic Auditorium. From her hotel suite, she called the headquarters of Ford, Inc., and asked to speak to the president. She got a vice president instead. She informed him that Henry Ford had promised her a new Ford in January of every year, but no cars had ever arrived. *[Henry Ford II (1917-1987) was the eldest son of Edsel Ford and the eldest grandson of Henry Ford, founder of the Ford Motor Corporation.]*

"I'm afraid I can't honor such a request," the executive told her.

"Just like a man. They promise you the world and can't even deliver Rhode Island."

CLEVELAND: Two nights later found Judy in Cleveland appearing on stage at the Music Hall. Since it was Mother's Day, Begelman flew in Lorna and Joey. Introducing her children to the audience, Judy hugged Lorna and sang "Rock-a-Bye My Baby to a Dixie Melody" to Joey.

MANHATTAN: Moving on to New York City, she was in top form as she performed there on May 21, once again at Carnegie Hall. Although the *frissons* it generated didn't match those of her star-studded opening night performance there the previous month (April 23, 1961), she delivered a stellar performance, this time with a difference: Liza appeared onstage with her for a duet of "Swanee."

After the concert, Begelman promised he'd bring her brood together to celebrate her 39th birthday on June 10.

She didn't want to deliver any concerts in June, as she needed time off. She used that break to reunite her family, including Luft, in a rented home at 1 Cornell Street in Scarsdale, New York.

She told a reporter from *Show Business Illustrated,* "I've been reborn. The old Judy Garland is dead." Luft wondered if that were true. She was tired and weary from the first part of the tour, and he wondered if she'd be able to finish without some mishap. He referred to that year's concert tour (the first that he'd ever been involved in) as "a real ball-buster."

When Luft was absent, away in Manhattan on business, Begelman and a lawyer drove to Scarsdale to have her sign her Last Will and Testament. The document specified that all of her assets would be moved into a trust which, upon her death, would be divided three ways among her children. Begelman and Freddie Fields were named as trustees. Begelman told her that if she purchased any real estate in the future, it should be in her name and not in joint ownership with Luft.

Judy had chosen the affluent New York suburb of Scarsdale as her family's temporary home because of its superior school system, among the best in the nation at the time. The town itself was the second-wealthiest in the United States. The local newspaper, *The Scarsdale Inquirer,* splashed her arrival there across its front page.

Biographer George Mair wrote, "Liza was the classic new kid on the block. Though she was rather chubby, many people were impressed that she was the daughter of a movie star. However, some faulted her for being among "show business people."

In July of 1961, Judy said, "I'm ready to go back on the road. My fans at times seem to want to eat me alive. I feed them by giving them a quart of my blood at every performance."

BOROUGH OF QUEENS, NEW YORK CITY: When the second leg of that year's tour began, she faced an audience of 14,672 fans at the Forest Hill Stadium in Queens on July 1. In the audience that night sat a future president of the United States, Donald Trump.

After the show, she attended a party that lasted till dawn.

In reference to her open-air concert, *Good Housekeeping* wrote: "Judy Garland sat beside the piano and gave a poignant new meaning to long forgotten show tunes. Her voice soothed the stadium like a gentle hand on a silken coverlet, while she crooned intimate love lyrics. When she belted out torch songs, her ringing tones overpowered the sound of a thirty-piece orchestra behind her. Between songs, she told stories on herself and kidded with the musicians and stagehands. She was like a middle-aged imp cavorting in front of a mirror, unaware that she was being watched."

NEWPORT, RHODE ISLAND: After some severe mood swings prior to her July 3 appearance at the Newport Jazz Festival, Judy refused to go on before a matinée audience. Overly medicated, and among other objections, she claimed that the microphone was "too phallic. I'll look like I'm going down on it." A stagehand broke the escalating tension by stretching a condom that he carried in his pocket over its tip. It remained there temporarily.

Eventually, Judy relented and went on to wild acclaim among the hip and youthful audience.

For her appearance, she wore a gown she'd designed herself. She told Begelman that as a girl, she had wanted to be a fashion designer.

[During future appearances, she'd sometimes wear a dress or a gown of her own design, as when she appeared on The Michael Douglas Show. "Do you think I'll become known as the American Chanel?" she asked the TV host.]

MANHATTAN: In mid-July, Judy left her children with a nanny and drove with Begelman to Manhattan in time for a July 20 appearance at Carnegie Hall.

[During her sojourn in Manhattan, Capitol Records invited Judy as its guest of honor for a celebration of the release of one of her albums recorded back in April. A critic for Melody Maker magazine reviewed the album like this: "I've always been a fan of Judy Garland without getting to the fever stage. But, brother, I am converted now after hearing her album. Let me confess I've never sat through such recorded emotion in my life."]

BOROUGH OF QUEENS, NEW YORK CITY: Both Freddie Fields and Begelman were on hand to witness Judy's return engagement at the Forest Hills Stadium in Queens, New York, on July 30. To her familiar repertoire of songs, she added "Just In Time." The concert was a hit. It was followed by a late-night supper with her agents. Their drinking and talking continued until around 3AM. Finally, a wobbly Judy stood up and asked, "Freddie, when in hell are you going to move your ass out of here? I want you to leave David and me alone so he can fuck me until the rooster crows."

ATLANTIC CITY, NEW JERSEY: On August 3, Judy checked into the Claridge Hotel in Atlantic City, New Jersey, for a concert the following night at the Convention Hall Ballroom. A lot of New Yorkers were at the resort, taking advantage of the beach during the hottest month of the year. The concert she delivered was a smash hit, both artistically and financially.

Critic Dumont Howard later described what it was like seeing Judy in the flesh: "So potent are film images that they begin to challenge and intermingle with our perceptions of reality. How, for instance, does one envision a cowboy and the 'Wild West' without conjuring up 20th Century actor John Wayne? And so, Judy Garland, as a woman of forty, never quite lost, in the public eye, the aura of an innocent girl. She seemed to co-exist with the young Judy who helped stage countless shoestring musicals in the barn, pined after Andy Hardy, and set off down the Yellow Brick Road on her way to Emerald City."

Judy was so successful in Atlantic City that the managers of the Convention Hall invited her for a return engagement on September 3. As the summer began its sultry decline, Labor Day vacationers flocked to see her perform.

***

Even as a young actress in Hollywood, Judy had cultivated a coven of gay friends, and often went to gay bars with them. Chief among them were Chuck Walters, director George Cukor, Van Johnson, Keenan Wynn, and Roger Edens.

SAN FRANCISCO: On September 13, she flew back to her beloved San Francisco to deliver a memorable concert at the Civic Auditorium. It was attended by 8,700 people, many of them devoted fans from the gay colony of the City on the Bay. The concert, which grossed an impressive $45,000, was recorded as an event that immediately reinforced her status as a deeply entrenched gay icon.

After Judy's performance that night in San Francisco, the nation's leading gay newspaper, *The Advocate,* defined her as "the Elvis of homosexuals. In many ways, the life-long struggles of Judy paralleled the torments of gay men and women."

Another critic commented on "a claque of young men in attendance who seemed to be homosexual. They rolled their eyes, tore at their hair, and practically levitated from their seats."

In reference to Judy, writer William Goldman said, "Homosexuals tend to identify with suffering. They are a persecuted group and they understand it. So does Garland. She's been through fire and lived—all the drinking and divorcing, all the pills and all the men, all the poundage come and gone—brothers and sisters, *she knows.* If homosexuals have an enemy, it is age. And Garland is youth perennially over the rainbow."

Comedian Bob Smith, in what became a popular ditty, imagined Elvis as King and Judy as his Queen:

486

*"Elvis had a drinking problem.
Judy could drink Elvis under the table.
Elvis gained more weight.
Judy lost more weight.
Elvis was addicted to painkillers.
No pill could stop Judy's pain."*

Richard Dyer, a gay film scholar, defined Judy as a camp figure, and went on to define "camp" as:

"A characteristic way of handling the values, images, and products of the dominant culture through irony, exaggeration, trivialization, theatricalization, and an ambivalent making fun of and out of the serious and respectable. Garland is camp because she is imitable, her appearance and gestures copiable in drag acts. Her ordinariness in the early MGM Andy Hardy films are camp in their failed seriousness and her late style in concerts were wonderfully over the top."

LGBT people have long identified themselves under the code words of "Friends of Dorothy," a reference to Dorothy Gale, the character Judy played in *The Wizard of Oz*.

One observer wrote:

"Dorothy's journey from Kansas to Oz mirrored many gay men's desire to escape the black-and-white limitations of small town life for big, colorful cities filled with quirky, gender-bending characters who would welcome them. In the film, Dorothy immediately accepts those who are different, including the Cowardly Lion (a very camp performance by Bert Lahr). The Lion identifies himself through song as a sissy and exhibits stereotypically gay (or at least effeminate) mannerisms. The Lion is seen as a coded example of Garland meeting and accepting a gay man without ques-

Drag queens often impersonated Judy, acting their way, sometimes brilliantly, through exaggerated caricatures of her.

Craig Russell, a female impersonator from Toronto, depicted above as Judy Garland, was one of the best. His lifestyle resonated with hers, as he lived in an "overmedicated" world of booze and men that got away.

After developing an international fan base of his own, reinforced with well-reviewed, spectacularly popular performances at gay bars and cabarets throughout North America and Europe, he, too, arrived in New York to perform at Carnegie Hall.

His drunken performance weirdly emulated some of the worst of Judy Garland's. After screwing up long segments of his *schtick*, his fans began to walk out. Although in tears from the stage, he begged them to come back, his career never recovered.

Like Judy herself, he suffered an early death in 1990 from a stroke complicated by AIDS and drug abuse. He was only 42 years old.

tion."

Even the Baltimore-born cult film director, John Waters, famous for "transgressive" films that include *Pink Flamingos* (1972); *Female Trouble* (1974); *Hairspray* (1988); and *Polyester* (1981), said:

> *"I was the only child in the audience that always wondered why Dorothy ever wanted to go back to Kansas. Why would she want to go back to Kansas, to this dreary black-and-white farm with an aunt who dressed badly and seemed mean to her, when she could live with magic shoes, winged monkeys, and gay lions? I never understood it."*

***

LOS ANGELES: In mid-September, in Los Angeles on September 16, as arranged by Begelman, Judy performed at the Hollywood Bowl in front of 17,800 people, many of them avid fans. She planned to deliver more or less the same repertoire of songs she had showcased at Carnegie Hall.

Strung out and exhausted on the afternoon before that night's show, she took too many pills and threw a tantrum, defiantly telling Freddie Fields, "I will not go on." He rushed to her side, as did Begelman. Even Stanley Kramer, her director in *Judgment at Nuremberg*, came to her home. United as a front, this trio of deferential supporters maneuvered her into agreeing to go on with the show. Her performance that night grossed $75,000, a record high at the time.

Weather reports had warned of a major rainstorm, so many fans arrived with umbrellas and raincoats. They would need them. Although it poured on the audience in that open-to-the-skies venue that night, most of the fans remained in place, despite the rain and the battering winds that ruffled her hair during her performance and brought a sudden chill to the air. She risked slipping on the glistening wet runway. At one point, a moth flew into her mouth as she was inhaling air during her rendition of "Swanee," but with a flick of her tongue, it lodged in her cheek and she went on singing.

The next morning, a critic for the *Los Angeles Examiner* wrote, "Perhaps last night as Judy Garland sang at the rainswept Hollywood Bowl was perhaps the most enjoyable night in show business history."

***

DENVER: Four days later, September 20, found Judy singing at The Coliseum in Denver before a crowd of some 7,500 fans, for which she was paid $12,500.

Local critics raved, one of them claiming, "She came out on that stage and covered us with the glitter of her stardust. This former MGM super star has truly found her calling; and that is as a concert artist who zips with excitement and has a voice that can shout, sob, and caress with a rainbow

488

of emotions."

WESTCHESTER COUNTY, NEW YORK: After Colorado, she performed at the Westchester Country Club in White Plains, New York. The audience was mostly white, upper class, and unflappable, so there was not any particularly feverish and/or hysterical response, only dignified, respectable clapping. She was a success there, although she admitted backstage, "The crowd out front was a little more restrained than my wilder fans."

HARTFORD, CONNECTICUT: In early October, Judy was in Hartford, Connecticut, the historic capital of that state. *[Founded in 1635, it's the former home of the fabled author, Mark Twain (1835-1910), who wrote some of his most celebrated works here.]*

Judy performed at the Bushnell Center, the state's premier venue for the performing arts. Filling all of its 2,800 seats, she zapped the audience with her show. A newspaper critic wrote: "Judy Garland's vocal efforts are incomparable. Never has Hartford experienced such a rich and spirited singer from a woman who, from all reports, has led a tormented life."

Liza Minnelli was spotted in the audience.

NEWARK, NEW JERSEY: So many fans had shown up for Judy's one-night concert at the Mosque Theatre in Newark, New Jersey, that management invited her back for another hit concert on October 7. As Buddy Watson said, "I was a Peggy Lee devotee until I attended this event. Judy stole my heart away. The song that won my heart forever was 'What Now, My Love?'"

A RECORD STUDIO IN MANHATTAN: Capitol Records at its Manhattan studio welcomed Judy on October 13 for a recording session. She sang two songs from Broadway musicals, "Sweet Danger" and "Comes Once in a Lifetime." Mort Lindsey, who had become her favorite conductor, headed the orchestra.

A review in the *New Musical Express* read, "With Judy Garland so hot on LPs at the moment, the single could easily be a big smash for her—something I would like to see, as there are not many artists of her caliber in the singles field."

ROCHESTER & PITTSBURGH: *Variety* reviewed both Judy's Rochester and Pittsburgh appearances in the same article. *[On October 17, she had starred at the Memorial in Rochester and on October 19, she'd been at the Civic Auditorium in Pittsburgh.]* "Judy Garland had half the audiences in both cities pressing against the stage, begging for more at the end of her two-and-a-half-hour show. In Rochester, she drew an audience of 4,500; in Pittsburgh, 12,500."

***

HADDONFIELD, NEW JERSEY: After Judy's performances in Rochester and Pittsburgh, she and Stevie Phillips drove east into New Jersey for an October 21 performance at the Arena in Haddonfield, just across the New Jersey state line from Philadelphia.

There, Phillips and Judy experienced the worse venue on her concert tour.

Phillips later described the Arena in a memoir, featuring it in a chapter called "Have You Heard of Haddonfield?"

Phillips, who worked for Begelman and Fields at MCA, had been recruited as Judy's assistant at the time. She described the Arena at Haddonfield as a "shit hole, old and dirty, the dressing room filled with doors falling off, decaying jockstraps, broken furniture, and windows of grime and mold."

Phillips was maneuvered into a role as a one-woman cleaning brigade before Judy would enter. There was no bathroom attached to her dressing area, so Phillips bought a chamber pot. Even after her cleaning, Judy sobbed after entering it. "Year after year, I work my butt off, and this is where I end up, in a fucking rat hole. I'm gonna kill Freddie fucking Fields and that cocksucker Begelman."

After Phillips assured her it would be over soon, Judy turned on her: "What exactly is it that will be over? My fucking life?"

She was late that night as 10,000 patrons clapped and stomped their feet in impatience.

After that disaster, Phillips drove Judy northeast into New England all the way to

BOSTON: After checking into the Ritz Carlton, the first thing both women did was to take a much-needed bath, a luxury denied them in Haddonfield.

Judy went on stage on October 27 at the Boston Garden before a capacity audience of 13,909. *[The best seats in the house had sold for $6.50.]* The press later proclaimed that Judy made Boston history that night by filling up the Garden.

There was high drama unfolding behind the scenes, as later relayed by Phillips: In Boston, sitting at her makeup table, with Phillips helping her to get ready for her entrance, Judy suddenly grabbed a razor and slashed deeply into her wrist, all the while still smiling at Phillips. Blood spurted out, staining Phillips' white dress a shade of dark crimson.

Richard M. Nixon, making a speech and ready for fisticuffs, appears above.

Knowing what an avid supporter of JFK Judy had been, he met her by chance in an elevator at the Beverly Hilton.

Later, he would use his connections with the California State Tax Authorities to have her investigated.

Phillips immediately applied a tourniquet fashioned from a towel and a hairbrush and summoned the house doctor.

At that moment, Begelman entered, having flown to Boston from New York City to attend the concert. He rushed to Judy's side to survey the damage. Suddenly, the doctor arrived, and after sterilizing the wound, he wrapped it in bandages. Before the doctor completed his work, Begelman ordered

Phillips to fetch a rack of bracelets for Judy's wrist in an attempt to hide the bandages.

As it turned out, Judy's motivation for this suicide attempt had derived from learning that Begelman had taken his wife, Lee, with him on a recent business trip to London.

Horrified and distraught, both Begelman and Phillips stood in the wings, offstage, during Judy's concert as she summoned resolve and strength to complete that night's venue.

MONTRÉAL: Crossing the border into Canada, Judy, on October 29, opened at the Montréal Forum, sited on Cabot Square in the center of the most populated city of the province of Québec. Every seat had been sold within an arena best known for sporting events, especially ice hockey. *[In later years, it would feature Bob Marley and the Wailers from Jamaica; The Beatles from Liverpool; David Bowie, and Madonna.]*

"Never in my long life have I heard a singer with the voice of our visitor from south of the border," wrote critic Glenn Harper. "But it was a night of terror before it even began. Would she appear or not? She was running late, and we'd heard all those rumors of how she suddenly canceled an appearance at the last minute. We need not have worried. The orchestra began playing 'Over the Rainbow,' as the lights in the Forum dimmed."

"Out she came like a tiny robin in a mammoth cage but singing with the lungs of a lion's roar. She sent one on an emotional binge, as I relived all sorts of memories she evoked in my own life: Lost love, despair, hope, joy, sadness, defeat, triumph, tragedy. My heart went out to her until at long last, exhausted, she told us she had no more songs to sing. She bid us *adieu* and told us to leave with love in our hearts, sent not only from her, but from America itself."

LOS ANGELES: The elite of Hollywood showed up on the night of November 20 to see Judy perform her solo concert at the Beverly Hilton, site of the annual Golden Globes. Later owned by Merv Griffith, the hotel had been (and became) the site of some of the most notorious scandals and tragedies in Hollywood history.

At the Hilton, Stevie Phillips got on the elevator with Judy at the 12th floor. From there, it descended to the tenth floor, where Richard M. Nixon got on with, presumably, a Secret Service agent. Knowing what an avid supporter of JFK Judy was, he kept his back to her until they reached the fourth floor. Then he turned around to face her: "And you must be Judy Garland," he said.

She answered, "And you're Richard Nixon."

Without another word, he turned his back on her once again and exited from the elevator.

[It was in this same hotel, in 1962, that Nixon delivered his so-called "last press conference" after losing that year's California governor's race to Democrat Pat Brown. During that press conference, he attacked the press, telling them they wouldn't have Dick Nixon to kick around anymore. Of course, thanks to his election to the U.S. presidency in 1968, that was a promise he did not keep.]

After her concert, *Variety* claimed:

"Zing! That Fascinating Rhythm girl tells us she's always chasing rainbows.

She still has that old Judy Magic, still lamenting The Man That Got Away. She takes a ride on that Trolley predicting a forecast of Stormy Weather. She suggests that our love could be just One of Those Things. She's in Los Angeles but seems to have left her heart in Chicago or San Francisco. This is one Melancholy Baby who Made Us Love Her. Yet she wonders if This Could Be Love or Is It Like Being in Love? In spite of the weather report, she predicts she'll face tomorrow Come Rain Or Come Shine. She ends with a promise that she'll be fine As Long As He Needs Me."

MIAMI: Dating from 1958, the Miami Beach Convention Center has seen it all, taking place in its four exhibition halls, two ballrooms, and its concert stage. It also hosted *The Jackie Gleason Show* on TV when it wasn't hosting Miss America contests, listening to Martin Luther King, Jr., or (in 1964) watching a Muhammed Ali vs. Sonny Liston boxing match. The Center also hosted conventions for both the Republicans and Democrats. On November 25, 1961 it gave Southern Floridians Judy Garland.

The critic for *The Miami News* said that "seasoned performer Judy Garland conducts a love affair with her audience. She sets off fireworks and makes the audience a part of her act. Call it if you wish a near-holy alliance between herself and her fans. She belts out the old show tunes better than Ethel Merman. She croons love songs better than Peggy Lee. Last night, she urged us to 'Get Happy' and 'lo and behold, we did. *Viva* Judy Garland.

JERSEY CITY: "New Jersey people are the toughest audience in America," Judy said as she headed back to that state for an appearance on November 28. "In the land of Frank Sinatra, they want only the best—no bullshit, no fluff."

Since 1928, The Stanley Theater in Jersey City had been a center for popular culture, a showcase for The Three Stooges, Jimmy Durante, Tony Bennett, Janis Joplin, The Grateful Dead, and Dolly Parton. In time, the theater fell into disrepair and was taken over by Jehovah's Witnesses. But that came later.

In the meantime, Judy came onto the stage to announce, "It's great to be back in New Jersey. But I ask myself, 'What is this little girl who milked cows in Minnesota doing in New Jersey, land of macho studs and sexy women? I'll tell you why I'm here. It's to belt out songs and entertain you. Why in the fuck do you think I'm here?"

That was the first but not the only time Judy used the word "fuck" on stage. The Jersey audience cheered her wildly.

TORONTO: Judy returned to Canada for standing room only audiences in Toronto at the 3,211-seat O'Keefe Center (aka Meridian Hall) on December 3 and 5. She was greeted with the same affection she found in most of her U.S. appearances.

One critic pondered as to how, "in this great, big, crowded, noisy house, Judy Garland can find you out and sing directly to you."

Another critic noted that, "She is one star who never takes ovations for granted, or the affection that greets her. Her discovery of it was as spontaneous as her singing. The house vibrated with the wonder of her limitless power."

The *Telegram* wrote: "How do you record that the massive pile of the Center shook, that the air inside stirred and shuddered strangely, and that a host of citizens seemed supernaturally shocked with pleasure? How do you explain that it is due to the uncanny powers of one tiny woman singing songs? How do you measure miracles?"

[Meridian Hall opened in Toronto in 1960 and is the greatest center for entertainers in Canada. In time, it would be a venue not only for Liza Minnelli, but for Liberace, Mickey Rooney, Julie Andrews, Carol Channing, Katharine Hepburn, Bob Dylan, Danny Kaye, Marlene Dietrich, and Sammy Davis, Jr. It was at this venue in 1974 that a young ballet dancer, Mikhail Baryshnikov, Liza's future lover, bolted from the center's stage door and fled away in a waiting getaway car.]

WASHINGTON, D.C.: On December 9, Judy, exhausted, drained, and troubled, ended her massive concert tour on a successful note as she entertained at the 10,000-seat Armory in Washington, D.C. She sang to standing-room-only audiences including a lot of senators and their wives, on the same stage where other entertainers would include (or had included) Harry Belafonte, Nat King Cole, Ella Fitzgerald, Gene Kelly, Ethel Merman, and Leonard Bernstein.

[The Armory is also the setting for presidential inauguration balls, ranging from Harry S Truman to Barack Obama. Its most famous inaugural was when Frank Sinatra produced an inaugural ball one wintry night, January 19, 1961, for John F. Kennedy.]

***

Before her epic year of 1961 came to an end, Judy would be named "Show Business Personality of the Year" and "Best Female Vocalist of the Year," and her album, recorded at Carnegie Hall, was cited as "Best Popular Album of the Year" by *Show Business Illustrated* magazine

Her conclusion: "The bastards practically pronounced me dead, but I've come back, stronger than ever. Let the word go out: Judy Garland is back in town."

***

Judy took time out from her hysterically busy schedule to star in *Gay Purr—ee,* a film eventually released in 1962. Even though she got star billing above the title, she never appeared on the screen. Only her voice is heard in this feature-length musical cartoon released by Warner Brothers. To craft it, in November of 1961, she spent three weeks in a Los Angeles studio, recording voice overs and songs.

For years, Judy admired the wry and sometimes trenchant humor of the English actress **Hermione Gingold.**

Indiscreetly, Judy once told her, "When I'm your age, I plan to take over movie roles that might have been assigned to you."

Tartly, Gingold replied, "You'll wait a long time, dearie, since I plan to live forever."

At the studio, she was reunited with old friends, including Kay Thompson, its musical advisor. Mort Lindsey conducted the orchestra, and songs were by her favorites, Harold Arlen and Yip Harburg. Around the time of the film's release, at a concert in 1962, Judy presented a whimsical overview of its plot:

"The cartoon is about French pussy. Ooops, a slip of the tongue. What I mean to say was it is about French pussycats. I play Mewsette, a beautiful white Turkish Angora cat, kind and demure but very naïve. Type casting, darlings.

I leave the farm and head for the bright lights of Paris where I fall under the spell of Hermione Gingold. She's cast as Madame Rubens-Chatte, a crafty Persian cat, a fat, horrible pink feline who runs a cat house. She tried to transform me into a glamourous courtesan like she did to Leslie Caron in Gigi (1958), pimping her out to Louis Jourdan.

Oh, I look beautiful in this film, never so beautiful, not even in my heyday. I find she is fattening me up to sell me as a mail order bride to a cat in Pittsburgh known as The Money Cat. I escape and run through the streets of Paris. I decide to jump in the Seine, but before I do, I take time out to sing a song. I guess that's the usual thing to do before one jumps into the river to drown."

Others in the cast included Robert Goulet as the handsome orange Tabby Cat. He arrives in Paris to search for

Her detractors defined it as the ultimate crash—promoting the sale of cat food with her likeness—when Judy's involvement as the voice-over of an amorous cat in **Gay Purr-ee** morphed into an incentive for the sale of Friskies food for felines.

The film never really hit any mass market, and the kids whose parents bought their tickets couldn't have cared less about the (unseen) movie star mouthing the plot developments of the animated comedy.

494

Mewsette. He's accompanied by his sidekick, Robespierre, a young black cat played by Red Buttons, the comedian who'd won an Oscar for his supporting role opposite Marlon Brando in *Sayonara* (1957).

An unusual feature of the animated film involved artistic parodies of artists who included Manet, Toulouse-Lautrec, Cézanne, Gauguin, Van Gogh, Modigliani, Degas, Renoir, and Picasso. Perhaps, as was suggested, these beautiful graphics and backgrounds were a bit too "artsy" for the kids who went to see the cartoon.

Gay Purr-ee got passable reviews. *Time* magazine proclaimed, "Judy Garland yowls enchantingly."

The *Chicago Daily News* critic wrote: "Always ready to belt out a song or squeeze the last heart-throb out of a lyric, Judy gives the full treatment to her numbers. One expects her to sweep aside the feline creatures, step downstage front, and talk it over with the audience. It's just too much Judy for this kind of cartoon feature."

Its rival newspaper, the *Chicago Tribune,* praised Judy's "warm voice, singing some pleasant songs from Harold Arlen."

At the box office, *Gay Purr—ee* flopped.

Of the other members of the cast, Judy found Gingold and her drawling, deep voice especially fascinating. Gingold told her, "I started out in the late 1920s when my voice was a Shakespearean soprano. But I developed nodules in my vocal cords, which brought on a drastic drop in pitch. One morning, it was Mozart, the next morning 'Old Man River.' My voice has been called 'powdered glass in deep syrup.'"

Kay Thompson later claimed that Judy "fell hard" for the handsome singer, Robert Goulet, a native of Massachusetts of French and Canadian ancestry. He had become famous when cast as Sir Lancelot in the 1960 Broadway musical *Camelot*. Forever after, at all future appearances, he would be asked to sing "If Ever I Would Leave You."

Before the release of *Gay Purr—ee,* he and Judy were asked to go on a promotion tour

Two views of
Robert Goulet

The lower photo depicts him a part of the astonishingly famous trio of actors cast, in 1960, as the leads of the Broadway production of *Camelot*. Adapted by Rodgers & Hart from the King Arthur legend, it cast Goulet as "Knight of the Round Table" Lancelot, who falls destructively in love with Queen Guinevere, as interpreted by **Julie Andrews,** the unfaithful but remorseful wife of King Arthur, portrayed by a "pre-Elizabeth Taylor" **Richard Burton.**

Astonishingly successful, *Camelot* ran for 873 performances, spawned a rash of sequels and remakes, and eventually evolved into a paradigm for the presidential administration of John and Jacqueline Kennedy.

together. "Judy set out to seduce this handsome hunk and she got her man," Thompson said. "But I don't think he was really into it. They remained friends and would appear together on TV. He was falling in love with Carol Lawrence at the time and would marry her in 1963.

***

In Scarsdale, several of her classmates, especially the boys, reported that Liza Minnelli wasn't exactly what they expected when they were told that Judy Garland's daughter was going to attend their school. Perhaps they were expecting a more glamourous creature than Liza, who showed up on the first day looking rather plain.

She was not necessarily enthralled with them, either. She didn't seem to fit in. As she explained, "I couldn't find anyone as bright as I was. I grew up with adults, and my school chums weren't interested in adult conversation. If I started to talk about art and literature, I bombed."

Nonetheless, Liza was cast in the title role of a high school production of *The Diary of Anne Frank.* For its opening on December 8, Judy took time off from her concert tour for a detour to Scarsdale to see her daughter onstage. She found Liza brilliant throughout the performance, admitting, "I sobbed many times."

She even promoted a plan wherein Liza and her fellow players would spend a month in Israel the following summer (1962) to replicate their performances for a deeply sympathetic audience.

After having experienced the suburban charms of Scarsdale from within her rented house there, Judy decided to uproot and transport herself and her brood back to Hollywood. "My kids are very portable," she told the press. "I constantly uproot them. Once they settle into a school, I yank them out again. I want them with me whenever possible. I don't like leaving them in the care of servants. Liza is growing up real fast. It won't be long before she sets out on her own."

Luft was left to close down the Scarsdale house and to ship their possessions back to Los Angeles. In early 1962, he joined Judy and the children at a rented house on 924 Bel Air Road in Bel Air. Whereas Judy had signed to appear as the centerpiece of a TV special for CBS, Luft was trying to launch a foothold in Aerophonics, *[in his case, the artificial and cost-effective generation of sounds produced by woodwind and brass musical instruments, then in its early development].*

He claimed that Judy was impressed with his startup ideas, and that she had shopped it to Freddie Fields and David Begelman. They were not impressed. As Luft claimed, "Those jokers couldn't afford for me to be successful. Not at that point. They needed Judy to pay their rent."

***

Stevie Phillips, employed by Fields and Begelman at their company, MCA, continued with her tasks of handling Judy. "I became Judy's shadow," she said, "putting out fires—figurative and literal—to get her to

496

the next town."

In time, she would work for Liza Minnelli, plus clients who included Robert Redford, Henry Fonda, Paul Newman, David Bowie, Cat Stevens, and Bob Fosse. In 2015, she published a tell-all memoir, *Judy & Liza & Robert & Freddie & David & Sue & Me. [The reference to "Sue" was to the powerful talent agent, Sue Mengers.]*

In one part of her memoir, Phillips described what working with Judy Garland was like on a "typical" day.

"I'm in the bedroom of Judy Garland's suite in New York's Plaza Hotel. It's just past four thirty in the afternoon on a cold November Day, and Judy is still in bed, late for the four o'clock meeting in my office with her business manager. 'Get her here' David Begelman has ordered.

'What do you want to wear' I ask Judy sweetly. She doesn't answer me. I stand there, like the dummy I was at twenty-five, staring at her. She takes the Salems off the nightstand, removes a cigarette, and puts it in her mouth. She takes a pack of matches, strikes one, and sets her night gown on fire 'Please God...not now!' I grab the blankets and smother the flame. Judy offers no resistance and no help. Done. It is over. Another catastrophe averted. Her leg is slightly burnt. She puts her hand on it, examines it and gets out of bed. Not a word from her about it. She heads to the bathroom. 'I better wear tights' she tells me."

"Should Judy Garland have been put in an institution?" Phillips asked. "Get the help she needs? That's the scream that was raging in me. It never came out of my mouth. Could anyone have institutionalized Judy without her permission? Maybe, but it didn't matter, since there were no candidates. Everyone was too busy exploiting her."

On the road, Phillips traveled thousands of miles with Judy, a series of airports, hotels, rides in limousines, each heading to the next gig. One day on one motor trip she described what happened:

stevie phillips

This photo of **Stevie Phillips**, Judy's tormented personal assistant, was snapped around the time she was struggling to do the best she could under traumatic circumstances.

Lower photo: Front cover of her memoir.

"Her hand began a trip from my knee, where she had placed it when the car lurched, to my crotch. As it slowly crept no more than an inch every two or three minutes, I started to panic. Her move was not inadvertent. For me, it was

497

a close encounter of the unwanted kind. Her hand was now fully in my crotch, as she was staring ahead. The idea of being intimate with her revolted me. I loved her talent but didn't like her. Fearing I'd lose my job as her assistant, I took her hand and put it back in her lap."

Phillips worked for Begelman but didn't approve of him, claiming he was "toxic" for Judy. She even denounced him as a flamboyant psychopathic personality in his Savile Row suits and Italian-made leather shoes. She viewed him as witty, intelligent, and charming to women, but a complete fraud willing to prove himself to Judy in bed.

On many an occasion, Judy told Phillips that Begelman was going to divorce his wife, Lee, as a precursor to marrying her (Judy).

But when confronted, Begelman said, "Judy means nothing to me. A ragpicker wouldn't throw a hook into her."

Phillips clearly understood that his relationship with Judy was doomed.

The worst was yet to come.

***

Frank Sinatra did not take his occasional sexual flings with Judy very seriously, as they mostly involved random sex acts here and there. His biographer, J. Randy Toraborelli, claimed that "Judy was just another dame to him" like Marilyn Maxwell or Angie Dickinson.

"Frankie toyed with Judy's feelings," said fellow Rat Packer Sammy Davis, Jr. "He treated her like a dog. Poor Judy. She was just his chow toy."

Two views of **Judy, Dean Martin, and Frank Sinatra** in promotional photos for her 1962 stand-alone TV special, *The Judy Garland Show.*

The success of this one-time program contributed to the studio's belief that JUDY, a.k.a., MISS SHOW BUSINESS, could successfully "carry" a weekly variety show named after her.

That weekly venue was (disastrously) inaugurated in 1963.

Sometimes when he made a date with her and stood her up, she denounced him, calling his behavior "repulsive."

Her close friend, Lauren Bacall became intimately involved with Sinatra after the death of her husband, Humphrey Bogart. She told Judy she fully expected that he would marry her. But when word of that leaked to the press, he unceremoniously dumped her.

Sinatra, or so it was said, treated Marilyn Monroe much the same way he behaved toward Judy. Ava Gardner, whom he did marry, had his heart and broke it, but none of his other girlfriends achieved the hold on him that Ava did.

When Judy began to view her relationship with Sinatra unrealistically, and told his fellow Rat Packers that she was certain he was going to marry her, he phoned her with a rebuttal: "Listen, I don't go for broads who are too much into the sauce like you. Get clean and we'll see what we will see. In the meantime, cool it with this marriage crap. You have as much chance of bagging me as I do of getting Jacqueline Kennedy to divorce Jack to marry me!"

He told Dean Martin and others that "both Marilyn and Judy have one thing in common: They're self-destructive. They abuse their bodies with drugs. You can't take dames like that seriously. You never know what condition they'll be in from night to night. At times, I hold most of them in contempt."

Despite his having said that, he almost always showed up at whatever hospital Judy was in whenever she was in one, and brought her flowers, kisses, and good wishes for a speedy recovery.

In the first days of January (1962), Judy came together with Frank Sinatra and Dean Martin, each of them a former lover of hers. The passion and energy of her affairs with them had disappeared with the summer wind that Sinatra was always singing about.

A friendship had emerged, however, and each seemed delighted to be guests on CBS's *Miss Show Business* (later changed to *The Judy Garland Show*). The videotaping of this special broadcast took place on January 8 and 9, 1962. It was the first time Judy had filmed a TV special in six years.

When the program aired nationwide, its ratings surpassed those generated by *Bonanza* and reached an audience of some fifty million viewers.

TV Guide asserted that "No performer can match Judy Garland." The *Los Angeles Times* called the show "A beautiful hour with moments as memorable as any that television has to offer."

At that time, the special was the highest rated in terms of the numbers of its viewers in the history of CBS.

It was nominated for four Emmys: Best Program of the Year; Outstanding Variety or Musical Program; Outstanding Performance in a Variety or Music Program; and Best Art Direction. Judy and her special lost in each of those categories.

After it was taped, Stanley Kramer—who continued to express his delight with Judy's performance in *Judgment at Nuremberg*—phoned her for a luncheon date. He wanted to give her star billing in an upcoming movie that would co-star Burt Lancaster.

***

Judy later defined her next film, *A Child Is Waiting [eventually released in 1963]*, as "an ambitious failure." Its plot had originated in 1957 as a nine-minute television short written by Abby Mann, who had also penned *Judgment at Nuremberg*. Dr. Matthew Clark (Burt Lancaster) portrays the director of a state institution for mentally handicapped or emotionally disturbed children. Jean Hansen (Judy), a Julliard graduate, joins the staff at the Crawthorne State Mental Hospital and almost immediately clashes with the director over his strict training methods.

The film's director was a New Yorker, John Cassavetes, who was younger than either of his two stars. He was a pioneer of American independent filmmaking, eventually writing and directing more than a dozen movies. He was also a well-known actor, acclaimed for such films as *The Dirty Dozen* (1967) and *Rosemary's Baby* (1968).

He was married to Gena Rowlands, whom he'd cast in the film as Sophie Widdicombe Benham, the mother of a disturbed child, Reuben (Bruce Ritchey). In her capacity as a health care worker, Judy hovers over him protectively like the mother he should have had. The other children who surround him are each disabled in some way.

Rowlands, whose acting career would span six decades, would, in time, become known for her role in a total of at least ten films, some of them collaborations with her husband. They included *A Woman Under the Influence* (1974) and *Gloria* (1980). Each of those would earn her an Academy Award nomination.

Another character in the film was portrayed by character actor Paul Stewart. A friend of Orson Welles, he'd made his film debut in *Citizen Kane* (1941).

Like Judy, Burt Lancaster was a much written-about figure in Hollywood. This blurb was written by Minty Clint:

The names of mega-stars **Burt Lancaster and Judy Garland** were billed above the title in publicity for *A Child is Waiting.*

Judy had met him, but only briefly, when he starred with her in *Judgment at Nuremberg*. She got to know him much better on location at the Pacific State Hospital in Pomona, California.

She, of course, had already read most the hype about him.

"At age thirty-two, Burt Lancaster left behind a career as a struggling acrobat and shot straight to the top in Hollywood—on his own terms. His magnificent physique and brooding good looks were perfect for film roles. He was often cast as a swashbuckler, but in time, could play sensitive roles in such movies as Birdman of Alcatraz *(1962). He*

played the title role in John Cheever's classic, The Swimmer *(1968) and won an Academy Award as a conman/evangelist in* Elmer Gantry *(1960). He is the man on the beach with Deborah Kerr in From* Here to Eternity *(1953)."*

In Hollywood, Lancaster was known for his sexual conquests. *[Judy wondered if she'd be next.]* He'd already seduced every actress from Shelley Winters to Marlene Dietrich. Columnist Sheilah Graham proclaimed that he "oozed" masculinity from every pore."

According to Lancaster, as confessed to starlet Liz Renay, "I guess I'm the guy who went to bed with every girl—even if it were after the movie was shot."

He also had a lingering reputation as a bisexual. After their sexual encounter during the filming of *From Here to Eternity*, Montgomery Clift did not give Lancaster a good report: "He's a bag of wind and the most unctuous man I've ever met."

Kate Burford, the best biographer of Burt Lancaster, summed up the tense atmosphere on the set of *A Child Is Waiting*:

"Lancaster, having spent two months at the hospital, observing, started coaching Garland on the side. Kramer, reviewing the rushes, joined with Lancaster in opposing Cassavetes, often scene by scene. When the director insisted that Lancaster erupt furiously at Garland in one of the takes, ordering him to 'tear her to pieces, tell her she's a fucking idiot,' Lancaster objected, claiming that, as a doctor, he would never overreact in such an unprofessional manner.

When Kramer saw the scene, he thought, according to Lancaster's retelling, that the male star indeed looked 'ridiculous' and it was reshot. During the editing process, Kramer yanked the movie away from Cassavetes and finished it himself. Cassavetes disowned it."

After the release of *A Child is Waiting*, **Bruce Ritchey** evolved into a footnote of film history. A total unknown, he almost stole the picture from Lancaster and Judy.

He portrayed an abandoned, mentally challenged boy searching for the love of a parent and finding it in Judy.

Even though Ritchey generated rave reviews, he disappeared from the radar screen after the film's release.

Years later, a blog site asked: "What happened to you, Bruce? Are you alive today? Let the world hear from you."

In *A Child Is Waiting*, Judy sang only one song, "Snowflake," aiming directly at the disabled children. She consistently relied on pills to get her through the shoot. Acting and reacting within such emotionally charged scenes brought back some of the more nightmarish moments from her own childhood.

She was devastated when she learned that as an actress, she had been

Kramer's fourth casting choice. He had originally envisioned it with Ingrid Bergman in Judy's role. After Bergman dropped out, it was offered to (and rejected by) both Elizabeth Taylor and Katharine Hepburn.

During filming, Liza sometimes showed up on the set to help her mother, often rehearsing her lines with her. Judy told her daughter, "At times, I want to kill Cassavetes."

Although Judy missed several days of shooting, the film still came in on time, and Kramer had only praise for her:

"Judy Garland was a gem as a person. Top drawer. Wonderful. Beautiful. Touched everybody. She really did have it all. MGM only touched what she could do. She was a magnificent 'classic' actress—emotionally and spiritually. She gave it a frame. She could make it a rectangle or a big square: Any way you wanted it. She felt it inside. Her on-screen emotions came from deep within her soul."

A Child Is Waiting recorded a loss of $2 million and more or less propelled Judy to "The Twilight Zone" of her once-fabled acting career. When a reporter asked Sid Luft what he thought of her performance, he answered, "I didn't bother to see it."

As published by *The New York Times*, Bosley Crowther posted one of the film's most sensitive and thoughtfully restrained reviews:

"Don't go to see it expecting to be agreeably entertained or, for that matter, really uplifted by examples of man's nobility. This drama of social service, written by Abby Mann to convey a general illustration of the philosophy and kind of work done in modern institutions for retarded children, is presented in such conventional terms that it has no more impact or validity than an average television-doctor show. Miss Garland's misty-eyed compassion and Mr. Lancaster's crisp authority as the all-seeing, all-knowing doctor who patiently runs the home are of a standard dramatic order. Gena Rowlands and Steven Hill are a bit more erratic and thus convincing as the highly emotional parents of the boy. But top honors go to Bruce Ritchey, who plays the latter role, and to the group of actual retarded children who appear uninhibitedly in this film. To them and to John Cassavetes, who directed them with notable control, we must be thankful that what might have been harrowing and even distasteful beyond words to behold comes out as a forthright, moving documentation of most unfortunate but hopeful youngsters in a school. From the graphic accounts of how their teachers treat them and train them, how the rule of firm, realistic and unemotional discipline is preserved, and from the simplifications of theory that appear in the dialogue, one should learn a great deal from this picture—all of which should be helpful and give hope."

Richard Brody, a critic for *The New Yorker*, wrote: "Garland gives banal and histrionic dialogue the same frenzied, self-searching lilt that she gives to song lyrics, playing a woman whose musical life is behind her and whose artistic soul is buried deep. She lends the drama an extra element of psychodramatic pathos."

Variety defined the film as "a poignant, provocative, revealing dramatization" and added, "Burt Lancaster delivers a firm, sincere, persuasive and unaffected performance as the professionally objective but understanding psychologist who heads the institution. Judy Garland gives a sympathetic portrayal of an overly involved teacher who comes to see the error of her obsession with the plight of one child."

Time Out London said, "Cassavetes elicits magnificent performances from his cast, making especially fine use of Garland's tremulous emotionalism, although the occasional drifts into didacticism entail the sort of special pleading Cassavetes was keen to avoid. Flawed but fascinating."

Brendon Gill wrote: "It is almost unbearable to be made to observe and admire the delicacy of the acting skill of Lancaster and Garland as they—

the charming, the successful, the famously gifted ones—move among the lot of pitiful children."

***

Sexually, Judy was still alive, as was evident on the set of *A Child Is Waiting*. She later told Kay Thompson, "I must be the only leading lady in history who Burt Lancaster did not seduce, although I sent out signals."

However, she did find a cast member interested in seducing her. Cast into the minor role of Douglas Benham was one of the most extroverted of Hollywood's "Bad Boys," Lawrence Tierney. "He came on to me, I didn't come on to him," Judy said. "He overpowered me with his raw sexuality. Anne Bancroft had an affair with his more famous brother, actor Scott Brady, and she told me what Brady was like in bed. Naturally, I just assumed that Larry, his older brother, might also be top rated."

Vintage actress Barbara Pepper also had a small role in *A Child Is Waiting*. Her reign as a Hollywood Venus lasted from 1937 to 1943, during which she appeared in forty-three movies. But she became

Blood Moon's tribute to Hollywood Bad Boy **Lawrence Tierney**, participant in many fights, blood lettings, and psychotic moments, behind the scenes, in *film noir* Hollywood.

In the upper photo, he's shown as a terrified crewman in *Ghost Ship* (1943). The lower photo shows how low-cost studios marketed his rough-and-tumble self in this poster for *Dillinger*, a macho blood-and-guts thriller from 1945.

By the time Judy got down for peek-a-boo and party games with him in the early 60s, he was way, way, WAY past his glory days and still, in the eyes of many, a bit scary.

an alcoholic, put on a lot of jowly weight, and lost her sexy look. She and Judy became friends during the shoot, and Pepper became privy to Judy's affair with Tierney.

Lucille Ball had briefly considered Pepper for the role of Ethel Mertz in *I Love Lucy*, but, prompted by her associates, eventually changed her mind.

In reference to Tierney, Judy told Pepper, "Larry doesn't make love to a woman. He has to feel he's raping her to get off. I pretended to resist, but I loved it."

Onscreen, the Brooklyn-born actor usually played tough guys and mobsters. Offscreen, he often battled cops in barroom brawls, getting arrested many times. Critic David Kehr wrote, "The hulking Tierney was not so much an actor as a frightening force of nature."

The first time Tierney took Judy to bed, he told her, "I want to do to you what I did to Jayne Mansfield in *Female Jungle* (1956)." Judy also told Pepper that Tierney had proposed a three-way with him and his younger brother, Brady. *[Judy didn't reveal if she eventually accepted that invitation or not.]*

Barbara Pepper, in her later years, on a bad day.

She told Judy, "In the late 1930s and even into the war years, I was considered one *hot tamale* in Hollywood, far sexier than Marilyn Monroe. Every straight guy in Tinseltown was after my snatch."

After their filming of *A Child Is Waiting*, Tierney ended his affair with Judy, telling her that he was fed up with America and that he was moving to France.

That did not work out, so he returned to New York, but found no acting roles. He went to work as a bartender and construction worker, and later ended up driving a horse-drawn carriage in Central Park.

Eventually, an acting job appeared through Andy Warhol, who hired him for a role in *Bad. [Warhol later referred to hiring him as "a terrible experience."]* Then John Cassavetes re-entered Tierney's life and cast him in two of his films, *Gloria* (1980) and *The Prowler* (1981).

The last time Tierney saw Judy he told her, "I'm one of those 'live fast, die young' kind of guys. You know, like James Dean."

But as time went by, that turned out not to be true. Tierney died in a nursing home in Los Angeles at the age of eighty-two. He never married, but had a daughter, Elizabeth Tierney, of Park City, Utah.

CHAPTER EIGHTEEN

THE SLAMMING OF DOORS & THE GNASHING OF TEETH
As a Business Team and as a Marriage, "Sid and Judy" Become Unglued

JUDY KIDNAPS HER CHILDREN,
Sid Pursues Them in the U.S. & British Courts

THE LONELY STAGE
It's the Only Place Where Judy Can Go On Singing

SLUGFEST AT THE SAVOY
Miss Garland vs. Mrs. Begelman

HANDLING JUDY
Sexually Liberated, Sardonic, & Sophisticated, Dirk Bogarde Has Greatness Thrust Upon Him.

CRASH DIETS & TOO MANY PILLS
Judy Collapses at Lake Tahoe, Then Rallies in Chicago

TWO JACKS
(Paar and Kennedy) and a JUDY
Enigmatic, thin-skinned, and mercurial, Jack Paar, as a TV Host, is like "Little Lord Fauntleroy with a Switchblade."

JOURNEY BACK TO OZ
Liza Puts Her Best Foot Forward

"She sings a number of songs in I Could Go On Singing, *but singing isn't really what she does anymore. Acting is not exactly what she does, either. And glamour surely isn't what she's selling: Edith Head's costumes, especially one unflattering red number, make her look downright potty. But she's, well, Judy Garland. And we love her. We have to love her. It's part of our way of life, like cookie jars, and baseball, and oral hygiene, and the call of the open spaces. And for people who like this kind of thing, this is the kind of thing they'll like."*
—Newsweek

"More than the love of his life, Judy Garland was Sid Luft's passion, and their tempestuous relationship was one of the great untold stories of the 20ᵗʰ Century. Garland left him, returned, and left him again, but Luft thought of Garland every day from when they met until the day he died."
—Producer Lawrence Schulman

"On signing the biggest television deal of my life, I trust I'm doing away with my public image up to now. People seem to think I'm either a breakable Dresden doll or a wide-eyed Kansas teenager named Dorothy. I haven't been a teenager for a long time. And if I were breakable, as sure as hell I wouldn't be around today."
—Judy Garland

After Judy's return to Hollywood from her engagement in Washington, D.C., at the end of her road tours, the tension between Sid Luft and her boiled over on their first night together. Their children heard, but did not witness, one of their most bitter fights.

The next morning, after her husband left the house for an appointment, Judy packed suitcases for Liza and herself and moved into the Beverly Hills Hotel for a two-week stay. Lorna and Joey were left with their father in the Bel Air house, under the supervision of a governess.

Then, she phoned Luft, telling him to close down their Bel Air home and fly Joey and Lorna to Manhattan, where she'd meet them.

What she didn't tell him was that she'd been offered another movie deal, this one to be shot outside London—the final destination of the trip she was about to embark on. She didn't want him to try to cash in on, or interfere in, a complicated deal that Freddie Fields and David Begelman had set up for her.

The film's working title was *The Lonely Stage,* and Begelman told her that her co-star would be either Peter Sellers or Laurence Olivier. Then, still in New York and before flying to England, she was informed that neither of those actors wanted the role, and it had been offered instead to her friend and former lover, Dirk Bogarde.

The script excited her, since she could sing in it, something she hadn't done in a film since *A Star Is Born.*

In Manhattan, Judy resumed her affair with Eddie Fisher, who was still married to Elizabeth Taylor. Like Judy, he was called "a druggie" too.

"I later heard the runt was shacked up with Judy," Luft said. "In case you didn't know, that creep was an utter asshole. Ask Debbie Reynolds."

Judy was taking 200 mg. of Ritalin a day, plus nighttime doses of Valium and Seconal, even though various doctors kept warning her that she was committing suicide through damage to her kidneys and liver. She experienced rapid mood swings, going from giggly highs to the bottomless pits of despair.

Often, she would rant against "atrocities," raging against Luft, MGM, Dore Schary, even Artie Shaw and Tyrone Power for deserting her.

After shutting down their Bel Air house and laying off the servants, Luft, Joey, and Lorna flew to New York. Judy had arranged for them to stay in a suite on another floor at The Stanhope on Fifth Avenue.

She didn't want to see him and forbade him from coming to her suite. But she was determined, through a devious plot that later became apparent, to fly Joey and Lorna with her to London.

Liza was not at The Stanhope with her mother. Instead, she was staying with a friend of Judy's, Dr. Lester Coleman and his wife. Coleman visited her at The Stanhope every other day. On his first visit to her suite, he found a drugged Eddie Fisher emerging into the living room in his jockey shorts. Coleman later told Luft that "your wife is a very sick woman. She can't take care of Lorna and Joey in England. She can't even look after herself. It's a good idea, though, for Liza to go with her to England. At least she's old enough to take care of her mother."

***

On April 26, Judy, as had been arranged, showed up for a late-night recording session, with Capitol Records, in front of a live audience for what was later released as *Judy Takes Broadway.* Regrettably, she had not recovered from a case of laryngitis, so this would not be her best album. In fact, it was not released until 1989, and then recommended only to Judy's most loyal fans, the ones who bought every album she recorded.

From midnight to 1:30AM, Judy sang to a live audience that included nineteen-year-old Barbra Streisand, who was starring on Broadway at the time in *I Can Get It For You Wholesale.* Also attending was Marilyn Monroe, who would remain with Judy for the rest of the night.

Because of her throat, Judy apologized to the audience, which was mostly comprised of Broadway show people. "I wanted to sing beautifully to you. But we'll get there. That is, if you stay with me. You usually do, and that is what keeps me alive."

When the session was over, a few hours before dawn, Judy invited Monroe to return with her to her suite at The Stanhope. There, they talked until eight that morning. Monroe always maintained that Judy was her favorite singer, and both of them shared many of the same troubles, mostly a pursuit of all the wrong men and pill addiction.

Monroe told Judy, as she later recalled, "I picked up some bug when I sang to servicemen in Korea, and I can't seem to shake it. I'm exhausted day and night. I can't remember when I've had a full night's sleep."

"Tell me about it," Judy said. "You're ripping a page from my own life."

"Fox, I'm sure," said Monroe, "is going to fire me from my latest picture, [i.e., George Cukor's unfinished 1962 movie, *Something's Got to Give*]. Most days, I don't show up, but when I do, I can't remember my lines."

"I had the same experience when I tried to make *Annie Get Your Gun,*" Judy said. "Goodbye, MGM contract. I always turn to my pills. Although they offer temporary relief, they never really solve my problems, which each mount by the day. In fact, they make it worse. But I'm addicted to them."

"The same with me," Monroe lamented. "I feel I'm a hopeless addict."

As the sun came up over Manhattan, both women began talking about Frank Sinatra.

"You may not feel the same way, but I think he's more paternal than romantic these days," Monroe said. "I won him over by praising his singing and his sexual skills."

"Sometimes, I feel that Frankie is hovering over me like a guardian angel," Judy said. "I know that in a dire emergency, he'll be there for me."

It was obvious that both women wanted Sinatra to play a far greater role in each of their lives than he did. He told Sammy Davis, Jr., "Marilyn and Judy are great stars, but hopelessly neurotic and as

Judy and **Marilyn Monroe** bonded as they identified with their mutual sorrows. On a lighter note, they shared intimacies about lovers they had shared in common.

Displayed above is Marilyn in 1961 posing at the Actors Studio in NYC as part of a feature article that appeared in the May, 1961 issue of the since-bankrupted *Radio TV Mirror.*

needy as a starving child in a snow blizzard. I can't be their guardian, watching after them day and night."

"I never know, though, when Frank is going to explode," Monroe said. "He's a dangerous man, even brutal whenever the mood hits. Once or twice, he's slapped me across the room, perhaps to knock some sense into me."

"Been there, done that," Judy said. "The only thing I've managed to avoid, and perhaps you should, too, is getting involved with those gangsters he hangs out with. Sam Giancana is a mob kingpin killer."

"I know," Monroe said. "And I've already become involved. One day, Giancana might have me wiped out. I know too much."

After Monroe stood up on wobbly legs after their night of drinking, she embraced Judy, kissing her passionately. "Oh, Judy, what is to come of us?"

"I shouldn't say this, but terrible things are probably gonna happen to us unless we change. We should have married a postman, had kids, and lived in a cottage behind a picket fence with a rose garden."

"Perhaps," Monroe said. "It's a *cliché,* I know, but no one ever promised us a rose garden."

Judy, as she admitted later, was overcome with a strange foreboding as she watched Monroe depart.

She would never see her again.

Before the end of August 1962, Monroe would be dead. Her legend, already begun, would continue for decades.

***

From The Stanhope, Judy scheduled her flight to London, booking seats for Liza, Lorna, and Joey. Liza was still living with Dr. Coleman and his wife, but Luft, from within his suite on a different floor of the same hotel, was holding "my two little darlings prisoner" (Judy's words).

After several mishaps, and seemingly endless charges and counter-charges, Judy felt she had to take desperate measures to free her two children from Luft. As such, she hired two private detectives to come to The Stanhope to help her organize an assault on his suite.

A scheme was devised which she put into effect the afternoon of her departure for London.

She phoned the police, deriving maximum effect from the magic words, "Hello, this is Judy Garland." Pouring out a tale of horror and stating that Luft had kidnapped her son and daughter, she persuaded the chief at a nearby police headquarters to send over two cops.

Flanked on either side with her security force, Judy approached Luft's suite and pounded on the door. At first, he refused to let her in until she assured him that she was alone. Inside, after discreetly unlatching the door lock from the inside, she began to scream through the closed door, "Help! He's beating me! He's going to kill me!"

At that, four men, two of them police officers, rushed in. Luft later referred to them as "Judy's goons."

As an ex-boxer, Luft was a difficult man to subdue, and he fought back until the police officers put him in a chokehold. During the struggle, Judy rushed about, throwing some clothes into a suitcase for Lorna and Joey. Then the three of them followed a bellhop to a pair of limousines (one of them contained Liza) waiting on the street in front of the hotel. Judy, Joey, and Lorna joined Liza in her limousine. As a quartet, they then headed off to Idlewild Airport. The second limousine, carrying Judy's luggage, followed close behind.

Back amid the wreckage of his suite, Luft was held at gunpoint until the phone rang. After one of the detectives answered, he was notified that Judy and the three children were airborne.

***

Headlines greeted Judy's arrival in London:

JUDY GARLAND FLEES AMERICA.
"I'LL GUARD MY CHILDREN WITH MY LIFE,"
CLAIMS JUDY GARLAND.
JUDY FLIES IN AS HUSBAND STORMS.

Joey and Lorna were placed under 24-hour guard in their rented residence at 33 Hyde Park Gate. David Begelman, who also flew to London, announced to the press that a guard at the film studio where shooting was to begin would refuse entry to Luft.

Luft flew to London a week later, only to learn that Judy, Lorna, and Joey had been made wards of a British court. In England, he also learned that because Liza had flown to Paris to study French at the Sorbonne, he could no longer rely on any help from her.

***

When newsman were sent this publicity picture, they thought it was Marilyn Monroe. Actually, it was the English actress **Diana Dors** trying to look like Monroe.

Throughout her tumultuous life, the words "sexpot" and "bombshell" were often applied to Dors.

In London, Luft attended her notorious "sex parties."

Three days after her arrival in London, Judy held a press conference where she told reporters from Fleet Street: "My marriage to Sid Luft is finished. He says I'm an unfit mother, but my kids love me. I've heard that he'll fly in from New York in a few days. He claims he's coming for Joey and Lorna, but he'll never take them away from me. There is no chance for a reconciliation."

Begelman was with her at the press conference, informing the press that Judy's residence would be under 24-hour guard, and that Luft would be barred from Shepperton Studios out-

510

side London, where most of the film would be shot. *[Other scenes would be filmed at the London Palladium, the venue of one of Judy's greatest triumphs.]*

Begelman arranged for her to live with her children in a rented house at 33 Hyde Park Gate. Then, after checking that Judy was settled in, he flew back to New York to join his wife, Lee.

At that point, fearing that his romantic involvement with her was nearing its end, Judy began writing to Begelman, sending passionate letters, many of them composed through the filter of her "medicated" state.

In one letter, she wrote: "After you, I will never love again. You are my last love, and I gave and gave and then gave some more, until I could not give another thing. I gave you all that was left. There is no more to give to any other man. You must be quite a guy to have a woman like me fall so deeply in love with you, needing and wanting you day and night."

When she reported for filming at Shepperton Studios, Dirk Bogarde, her co-star, was the first to greet her, coming to her dressing room. She clung to him, kissing him passionately, almost wanting to have sex on the spot.

He withdrew. "I'm your friend, but friendship has a limitation. All my future loving belongs strictly to my lover. I've made an iron-bound commitment to him to be faithful. I can't break my vow."

When she heard that, she abruptly changed moods and ordered him out of her dressing room.

"Director **Ronald Neame** survived the mood swings of **Judy Garland** during the making of her last film, *I Could Go On Singing* (1963), which was almost a parody of her own life, but still captured the frenetic feel of her stage performances,"wrote critic Matthew Sweet.

Neame, depicted with Judy in this photo, recalled that, in one sequence: 'Suddenly, she became the real Judy. It was no longer acting, and it was absolutely wonderful. She bared her heart. Whilst we were shooting, I thought. 'My God, what am I going to do?' because this was a one-time thing. So I kept the camera running right through the whole six minutes, and everybody on the set was in tears when I said 'Cut! That's it! We'll never ever get that again.'"

In the meantime, still in London, Luft began a legal battle for custody of Lorna and Joey. To his rage, he found the British judge sympathetic to Judy's cause. In a hearing, she charged that her husband had never contributed "one penny piece" for the children. She retained custody, and the two kids remained as temporary wards of the court.

Luft decided to stay in London for a while, and he took a flat six blocks down the road from Judy and his children.

During his residence there, Diana Dors, England's answer to Marilyn Monroe, was seen coming and going late at night from his apartment. The quintessential blonde bombshell, she was, in her own words, "The only sex symbol England has produced since Lady Godiva. Who's my competition? Deborah Kerr? Julie Andrews? HA!"

The press noted that Dors' remark omitted any mention of Elizabeth Taylor.

When she wasn't battling Luft, Judy turned to filmmaking, meeting her director Ronald Neame. He would live to be ninety-nine years old. His position in the history of cinema was summed up by film historian Ronald Bergan:

"The producer, director, writer, and cinematographer, Ronald Neame, played an important role in British cinema for more than half a century. The critic Matthew Sweet once called him 'a living embodiment of cinema, a sort of one-man World Heritage site.' Neame was assistant director to Alfred Hitchcock on Blackmail *(1929), the first British talkie; he was the cinematographer on* In Which We Serve *(1942), Noel Coward's moving tribute to the Royal Navy during the second world war; he co-produced and co-wrote David Lean's* Brief Encounter *(1945) and* Great Expectations *(1946); and he directed Alec Guinness in two of his best roles, in* The Horse's Mouth *(1958) and* Tunes of Glory *(1960). As if this weren't enough, Neame also conquered Hollywood with one of the first and most successful disaster movies,* The Poseidon Adventure *(1972)."*

In her farewell to the screen, **Judy** starred with **Dirk Bogarde** in *I Could Go On Singing.*

In the words of author Joe Morella, "The picture manages to capture the excitement of her concert appearances, although the story line is rather trite."

The first day of Judy's shoot had been scheduled at the London Palladium, with the strict understanding that cast and crew had to clear out by 4PM so that preparations could get underway for that night's show.

Judy was in marvelous voice, singing her first big number, "Hello, Bluebird."

To make up with her, Bogarde had given her a bluebird brooch set with sapphires.

She told the press, "I've learned that everything, especially men, are

512

passers in life. Even your children leave and sometimes you can't stop it. You can only rely on yourself."

Vocal arrangements for *I Could Go On Singing* had been crafted by Saul Chaplin, who had last worked with her on *Summer Stock* at MGM. When they encountered each other in London, it evoked a homecoming. They discussed the day Louis B. Mayer had fired her. Once again, her favorite conductor, Mort Lindsey, provided the orchestration.

Cast as the movie's third lead as George Kogan, Jack Klugman played Judy's sidekick

In this scene from *I Could Go On Singing*, **Judy**, impersonating an actress whose character was crafted from her own (i.e., Judy's) life, in a flood of rapture, prepares to go on stage to deliver a song in the style of Judy Garland.

Jack Klugman, playing her sidekick and enabler, appears in the center.

and soulmate. In one scene, he tells her, "Singing is your job, and you do it better than anybody else in the world."

[Klugman, starring opposite prissy Tony Randall, would become a household word when he appeared as Oscar Madison in The Odd Couple *which ran as a TV series for 114 episodes.]*

Later, back in the States, Luft encountered Klugman, who said, "Sid, I just wish you two had been together when I co-starred with Judy. It was really difficult working with her. She tried to cooperate, but she was much too heavily medicated—it was obvious to the crew. Dirk Bogarde, her former friend, told me, 'I never want to see that diva as long as I live.'"

According to Klugman, Judy had told him bitterly, "Chalk Dirk up as another man that got away. I didn't have the right equipment for him."

In years to come, Bogarde claimed, "Making *I Could Go On Singing* with Judy was a case of ricketing and racketing. Judy was a monster, and she knew she was monstrous. But she was magic on camera."

A young English actor, Gregory Phillips, had been cast as Judy's abandoned son, Matt, in *I Could Go On Singing*. Enamored, he'd seen *The Wizard of Oz* five times and was more or less expecting to work with Dorothy. Instead, he encountered Judy. "She wasn't at all what I thought she'd be. But she helped me through all my scenes and was very kind to me. I was very nervous meeting her, but she put me at ease."

Film historian Foster Hirsch claimed that the plot of *I Could Go On Singing* was a "tabloid-level exploitation of the real life of Judy Garland."

Perhaps that is why, when she first read the script, she believed that she understood Jenny Bowman, the concert singer she portrayed, better than either of the film's scriptwriters, Robert Dozier and Mayo Simon.

One day, in a rage and in front of Bogarde, she tossed the script onto the floor. "This is just plain crap. One fucking script if I've ever seen one."

To the rescue, Bogarde said, "Let's set about reworking it and improving the dialogue. We can make something great from it because you know your character of Jenny Bowman to your toenails, since you've lived it."

"You've got yourself a deal, pretty boy."

Described by the script's authors as "a *femme* version of Al Jolson," Jenny Bowman, a concert singer, has toured the world and been adored by legions of fans. She

A young British actor, **Gregory Phillips**, portrayed Judy's long lost son in *I Could Go On Singing*.

According to Judy, "I think my scenes with this darling young man came off so well because during the shoot, I imagined him as my own boy, Joey, whom Luft was trying to kidnap."

has returned to England after more than a decade. Before her self-exile, she had conceived a child, a boy with David Donne (Bogarde), an E.N.T. [*Ear, Nose, & Throat*] surgeon, but she had abandoned him and the child she had borne.

According to the plot, now that she's back in England, she wants to see her son, but Bogarde resists, until she promises not to reveal her identity to the boy. As it turns out, Jenny (i.e., Judy) gets along fabulously with her (secret) son, and she maneuvers to take him on tour. Of course, Donne (Bogarde) objects, and the plot thickens. Who will win?

After about a week of shooting, Judy was rushed to a local hospital, where her stomach was pumped. She had attempted suicide with an overdose of sleeping pills.

When she was able to return to the set, she demanded that United Artists fire Neame. He had gone, in her estimation, from "pussy cat" to "son of a bitch."

"Who in hell does he think he is?" she asked. "Otto Preminger?"

According to Neame: "She absolutely refused to do some pivotal scenes. They were necessary for the picture, but we had to work around them."

On July 5, she was rushed to the hospital once again after yet another failed suicide attempt. This must have been the most painful attempt yet to kill herself. She ran bath water into her tub, and then started banging her head against the steel fixtures, time and time again until her forehead started to bleed. It was amazing that she didn't knock herself unconscious.

Suspecting that something was wrong, and alarmed by the noise, a maid rushed into the bathroom, discovering Judy's face down in the water, which had turned blood red. She yanked Judy from drowning, tended to her, and, as soon as she could, called for an ambulance. In the meantime, she administered to Judy's bleeding head wound.

"Before the end of filming, Judy tried two more suicide attempts," Neame claimed. "Every morning when I showed up to direct, I asked my assistant, 'Did Judy try to kill herself last night?'"

"Judy antagonized my cast and crew" Neame continued. "She kept us waiting for hours and hours on end. My crew really had a wallop of her. But when she did show up, she was brilliant on camera. With her, it was all about 'me, me, me.' No one else seemed to matter to her. She was so unlike her living image."

As one critic claimed, "Judy gives more love than anyone but takes more love than anyone could possibly give."

She defended herself: "It's not me. It's those damn pills. They turn me into a bitch from hell."

For a one-day shoot in the cathedral city of Canterbury, in southwest England, Judy was driven there by limousine, and the local press turned out to greet her. Even the Archbishop of Canterbury invited her to the cathedral, where he greeted her warmly. "Aren't you the guy who crowned the head of Queen Elizabeth?"

Judy, portraying a stage star, Jenny Bowman, a fictional character modeled on the life and persona of (GUESS WHO?) Judy Garland. The setting of this scene is from *I Could Go on Singing?*

It was filmed at the London Palladium, site of many of the REAL Judy Garland's greatest triumphs.

"By tradition, that's what the Archbishop does, among other tasks."

The scene was set up and ready for her before noon, and the cast and crew began waiting for Judy to appear. Suddenly, her wardrobe mistress ran out from her dressing trailer to confront Neame. "I quit!" she said. "The bitch is a raging lunatic. Calling me the worst names I've ever heard. Names a drunken sailor wouldn't use. I'll not work with her. I quit."

Neame sent Bogarde in to try to tame Judy. He brusquely entered her dressing trailer without knocking. "What's up, pussycat?" he asked.

"You!...You're what's wrong. I'm furious at you. I wanted you to spend the weekend at Folkestone with me and the kids. I've already reserved rooms for us. Then an hour ago, I got your note. You're not available!"

"As I said in my note, I have another engagement in London tonight," Bogarde told her. "At eight o'clock, and I can't go with you."

"Who are you going with?" she asked. "Some hustler you picked up at Piccadilly Circus?"

She had been served a luncheon tray of salmon, and it rested nearby. From it, she picked up a knife which had been dipped in mayonnaise and lunged at him, screaming, "I hate you! I HATE YOU!"

Before she could stab him with the knife, he grabbed her arm and twisted it until she screamed in pain. The knife fell to the floor.

Not ready to give up, she picked up a fork from the tray and aimed it at his eyes. Once again, he blocked her action before she could stab him in the face.

Impulsively, he reached for her, holding her tight in his arms and planting kisses on her sobbing face. "Baby, it's going to be okay. All okay. Trust me."

She stood amid the wreckage of her lunch tray with flowers scattered about. The contents of an entire florist's shop had greeted her arrival on the set.

"Her nose was running, and I used my index fingers to wipe the snot dangling down," Bogarde recalled. With a wry smile, he told her, "You're completely putrid."

At first, she looked ready for more combat, but suddenly broke into laughter. She hugged him as he held her and kissed her. Before leaving, he said, "Thirty minutes on the set...or else..."

"Else what?" she asked.

"I'll become a raging maniac and will come at you—not with a fork—but with a switchblade and carve up your face."

Jenny Bowman (i.e., Judy) in a state of semi-hysteria (*à la Judy*) belting out a song.

It was a LOT of Judy at her most demanding and most intense.

Question: Who probably suffered the most?

Answer: Her co-stars, who came to refer to her as "It."

"Well, if you put it that way, I'll be ready in half an hour."

Back on the set, Bogarde told Neame, "She's coming out...It was no trouble at all."

***

As regards the plot of the movie Judy was filming during these interpersonal horrors, a major scene occurred at its end. The male lead (Bogarde) visits the film's female lead (Judy, playing a diva) in her dressing room when—in a fit of pique and nursing a broken ankle— she refuses to go on stage at the Palladium.

"But you're keeping the audience waiting." Bogarde informs her.

"I don't care if they're fasting," she said. "You just give them their money back and tell them to come back next fall. I can't be spread so thin. I'm just one person. I don't want to be rolled out like pastry so everybody can get a bite of me. I'm just me. I belong to myself. I can do whatever I damn well please with myself."

"It was a moment of truth caught on film," Bogarde said. "That was not in the script. That was Judy speaking for herself."

Neame later said, "Call that speech 'Judy's farewell to the movies.'"

Judy unleashes the film's title song ("I Could Go On Singing") after her character arrives late for her appearance in front of a capacity crowd at the Palladium. Just before going on, she blithely tosses aside her furs to a stagehand, telling him, "I just shot 'em."

On stage, she's greeted with thunderous applause. She has lost both her son and her former lover, but she's back where she belongs... on *The Lonely Stage,* the original title of the film.

On the final day of the film's shooting, Neame was hovering on the verge of a nervous breakdown. At long last, he expressed what he'd longed to say during the making of this difficult film: "That's it, Judy. It's a wrap."

Judy answered: "You'll miss me when I've gone," before turning her back to him and brusquely walking off the set.

***

In 1978, Dirk Bogarde published a memoir, *Snakes and Ladders,* in which he relayed his experience of working with Judy on the set of *I Could Go On Singing.* He had to leave the set a week before the end of shooting because he had already signed to report to work on a new movie by Basil Dearden, one of the youngest and brightest of England's crop of promising young directors.

Here is an excerpt from Bogarde's memoir:

In 1957, **Dirk Bogarde** published a memoir entitled *Snakes and Ladders,* in which he was rather candid about his tumultuous relationship with Judy Garland.

In her farewell to him, she said, "You were such a bastard to me all the time...so mean!

"How could you have been so mean when I love you so much? You'd better be sweet to me next time around, Buster!!"

"Judy gave me the week in order that I could go off to do my 'damned movie' as she called it, knowing full well that she would then be on her own to finish off the film which she so detested. The following week only a few seconds were shot, and she behaved unkindly and uncontrolledly, falling, in one instance, in a bathroom, cracking her head badly, necessitating, yet again, hospital treatment, Finally, on Black Friday, the 13th of July she walked off the film. I still had one or two small pick-up shots to do with her, and was forced to do them with a double, wigged, and dressed in her clothes.

"I could no longer stay at her side, and she felt completely rejected. In a hostile atmosphere, untrusting and by now quite unloved, she was unable to contain her terror and her unhappiness; her private life lay about her like a pillaged room, there were court cases, and a bitter struggle to retain her children whom she adored above all things, but I could no longer heed her urgent summonses by telephone, nor could I make her understand that my duty, if one dared use such a word, now lay with Dearden and a new, extremely involving film.

'You are walking away from me,' she cried in anguish. 'You are walking away, like they all do . . . walking away backwards, smiling.'

"Useless to try to explain; there was no way now that I knew to help her. All I did know was that being with her, working with her, loving her as I did, had

517

made me the most privileged of men."

Upon its release, *I Could Go On Singing* got many raves, but that did not stop it from being a box office dud. Judith Crist in *The New York Herald Tribune* filed the most sensitive review:

"Either you are or you aren't a Judy Garland fan... And if you aren't, forget about her new movie, I Could Go On Singing, *and leave the discussion to us devotees. You'll see her in close-up...in beautiful, glowing Technicolor and striking staging in a vibrant, vital performance that gets to the essence of her mystique as a superb entertainer. Miss Garland is—as always—real, the voice throbbing, the eyes aglow, the delicate features yielding to the demands of the years, the legs still long and lovely. Certainly the role of a top-rank singer beset by the loneliness and emotional hungers of her personal life is not an alien one to her."*

Dorothy Masters in *The New York Daily News* gave the movie three stars: *"Judy Garland is back on screen in a role that might have been custom-tailored for her particular talents. A new song, 'I Could Go On Singing,' provides her with a little clowning, a chance to 'be gay,' a time for wistfulness, an occasion for tears. She and Dirk Bogarde play wonderfully well together, even though the script itself insists on their being mismatched."*

Bosley Crowther in *The New York Times* wrote: *"Considering what Judy Garland has done in movies over the years and how many of her fans still love her, no matter what she does, it is sad to have to say that the little lady is not at the top of her form."*

Newsweek wrote: *"The Magna Carta was signed in 1215. Shortly thereafter, Judy Garland sang 'Over the Rainbow,' and ever since, she has had her special place in the hearts of millions."*

Variety noted, *"A soulful performance is etched by Miss Garland, who gives more than she gets from the script."*

The *Miami Herald* claimed, *"Judy hits a new high...a peak and then some. Her portrayal will be remembered at Oscar-nominating time. Oh, such potent entertainment."*

The critic for *Good Housekeeping* posted this observation: *"Judy proves she is still one of the movie greats. No matter...an improbable plot. No matter, too, that Judy is now middle-aged and plump. As she belts out song after song or reveals what show business*

Then and now, **The Savoy** in London is a spectacularly posh, rigorously traditional hotel that prides itself on its restraint and British decorum

Presented above is a staff member from around the time Judy Garland was part of a catfight with the wife (Lee) of her manager (David Begelman) in one of the upper corridors.

Loudly destructive, and profoundly embarrassing to everyone who witnessed it, it ranks today as yet another of the gossipy anecdotes still circulating there about "show-biz Judy" and the hotel's "Hollywood on the Thames" era.

has given her—and what it has taken away—you know you're in the presence of a topflight performer."

Films & Filming wrote: "I Could Go On Singing, *without Garland, is un-thinkable. With her, for all its faults and they are many, it has moments of infinite richness and variety. She can work effortlessly from comedy to drama, as she does here in her long final scene with Dirk Bogarde; she can bring a glimmer of tragedy to her role, as she does here in one last telephone conversation with her son; she can sustain the longest and most searching of close-ups without faltering."*

***

Months later, David Begelman and Stevie Phillips, Judy's assistant, flew from Los Angeles to London with her for the British premiere, on March 6, 1963, of *I Could Go On Singing*. Heathrow was fogged in, so their plane landed in Manchester. Judy and her entourage had to take the train to London, where she checked into the Savoy, familiar turf to her.

Lee Begelman, David's wife, as the by-product of a sustained and on-going rage, flew into London and—unknown to him and while he was away—moved into her husband's room at the Savoy. After settling in, she called the front desk to learn that Judy was lodged directly across the hall from the Begelman's suite.

Enraged and clad in her nightgown, Lee knocked on Judy's door. Perhaps thinking it was room service (she'd placed a call), Judy, also in her nightgown, opened the door.

As Phillips later recorded in a memoir, "Clearly, they hated each other. I couldn't see who landed the first punch from where I was sitting in the living room. By the time I realized what was happening, a ferocious fight was underway, and I couldn't stop it."

"The women were trying to kill each other, kicking and clawing, pulling hair and clothes," Phillips claimed. "Both were bleeding, gowns torn, now almost naked in the fifth-floor corridor. Guests on the floor came out of their rooms. A crowd started forming."

Within minutes, the manager of the hotel was summoned, but he, too, could not break up this "catfight," as he termed it. By now, Begelman had returned to the hotel and was alerted of the altercation. He rushed to the fifth floor and put an immediate stop to it, ordering Lee back into her room as he tended to Judy before returning to his suite and his wife.

Shouts could be heard coming from Begelman's suite. Within the hour, Lee was on her way to Heathrow for a return to New York. After that, Begelman was back in Judy's suite, "spreading black confetti like so much fairy dust," in Phillips' colorful phraseology.

***

Back in Los Angeles, Judy checked into the Beverly Hills Hotel for two weeks, not wanting to see Luft. However, her children were brought to her.

After her stay, she flew immediately to Lake Tahoe, Nevada, for much-needed rest and to file for divorce once again from Luft. While there, she went on the most rigid diet of her life, slimming down to only one-hundred pounds. When a reporter asked how she'd done that, she answered, "I did nothing but drink tea."

But her rigid diet came with a price. On the morning of September 15, a maid discovered her lying unconscious in her suite at her hotel. An ambulance was summoned, and she was dispatched to the Carson-Tahoe Hospital.

After she was hauled in, Dr. Richard Grundy worked to save her life. After he made a complete examination, he determined that she was suffering from acute pyelonephritis [kidney infection] of her right kidney. The press was alerted. Confronted with a slew of misinformation, and buttressed by her previous attempts to kill herself, many of them assumed it was just a continuation of her already-established self-destructive pattern.

Even though her doctor urged her to remain in the hospital, but horrified by the negative publicity, Judy checked out after forty-eight hours because she had to be in Las Vegas for her big opening at the Sahara Hotel on September 18, 1962. Begelman had booked her for a month-long concert gig for which she'd be paid $40,000 a week.

She was accompanied by her favorite conductor, Mort Lindsey and his twenty-seven musicians.

Although tickets to each of her upcoming performances had sold out, they remained in such high demand that they were supplemented with a unique 2:30AM show, and those, too, sold out quickly.

Variety reviewed the show, writing, "Judy Garland is more dramatically electric than ever, giving her stylized tones a vibrancy as she sobs, shouts, and caresses her songs."

Accompanying her to Vegas was Stevie Phillips, her personal assistant, still referred to as "Judy's Shadow." Almost every night after her performance (s), Judy demanded that Phillips—despite her irritation and exhaustion— go with her on a nightly prowl of the Las Vegas Strip. Very often, usually after devouring a huge breakfast that included a juicy steak and a three-egg omelette, Judy didn't get to bed until around 8:30AM.

Almost always at her side, Phillips was horrified by the number of pills Judy consumed, likening it to "swallowing a drugstore." Pills came in tutti-frutti colors of red, green yellow, purple, blue, and white, even tri-color, and washed down with Blue Nun. [An "easy drinking" semi-sweet German wine, it's said to have been the first wine marketed to an international mass market. In the early 60s, for a while at least, it was Judy's favorite "chaser."]

After one of her all-night binges, Judy suffered a serious accident, an event later reported by Phillips. In the living room of her suite, she stumbled and fell, hitting her head against a coffee table made of steel and glass. The fall opened a gash on her forehead, the blood running out onto the ivory-colored carpet.

At first, Phillips thought Judy was dead. Deeply alarmed, she called for help. Within twenty minutes, a doctor arrived and found Judy bleeding and still unconscious.

After an examination and some bandaging, the doctor determined that the wound was superficial and that the patient was "dead asleep." He instructed an assistant to carry her into the next room and put her to bed. Then he advised Phillips to move into the second bedroom in Judy's suite,

520

but otherwise not to awaken her, predicting that she'd be asleep for several hours.

Phillips followed his instructions, and then retreated to her (new and improvised) lodgings and immediately fell asleep. About an hour later, she was awakened by Judy, who was standing at the foot of her bed.

She looked a fright, having ripped off her bandage, exposing the dried blood caked around the gash on her forehead. Her face was riddled with bruises, by now very visible and alarming. In a memoir, Phillips asserted, "The swelling on her face was so severe she looked like the Elephant Man."

Furiously, Judy was searching everywhere for her pills, and viciously denouncing Phillips for hiding them. Actually, the departing doctor had gathered up the trove of pills from their location on the (broken) coffee table and had hauled them away in his black bag.

Phillips relayed that information to Judy, who denounced her as a liar. Then the tension between them reached a boiling point. Phillips had never seen Judy—who even called her "a fucking cunt"—behave so viciously.

Suddenly, Judy ran toward the suite's kitchenette and emerged like a raging maniac holding a large butcher knife with a black handle. She lunged toward Phillips, who fled back to the suite's second bedroom—the one the doctor had advised her to move into. To her horror, she found that there was no lock on the bedroom's door, so she used her weight to try to block her aggressor's entry. But the frail but determined Judy overpowered her and—still wielding the knife—barreled her way inside.

As Judy stumbled forward, and before she regained her balance, Phillips rushed out, first from the bedroom and then out from the suite and into the corridor, locking herself into her own room. Exhausted, overwhelmed, and discouraged, she fell into a coma-like sleep.

She was awakened six hours later by a pounding on her door.

Fearing that it was Judy, she didn't open the door until David Begelman called out. Once inside her room, he told her that Judy had settled down, wanted to apologize, and wanted her back.

At first, Phillips refused to return until Begelman offered her a $200-a-week raise.

When she re-entered Judy's suite, the star rushed to her and embraced her, promising, "It'll never happen again."

Days later, Judy appraised her health and her looks—her face was less swollen and the bruises that remained could be concealed with makeup—and pronounced herself ready to go on with the show.

In the interim, Judy had had many conversations with Begelman, some of them overheard by Phillips. They discussed everything from Begelman divorcing his wife, Lee, to visions about a big future for Judy in TV specials—perhaps even a weekly series. At one point, Begelman suggested that she team her act with Elvis Presley's for the filming of what she predicted would be "the most watched show in TV history."

***

The only real concert Judy gave in 1962 was in Chicago at the Arie Crown Theater. Regrettably, she was suffering from laryngitis but went on anyway and wooed the sold-out audience. It applauded wildly after she opened her act with "Chicago."

The *Chicago Tribune* hailed her appearance as a "comeback." That infuriated her. "I can't even go to the crapper and emerge without some jerk claiming I've made a comeback. Surely, I hold the world's record on comebacks. In fact, I've been dubbed 'The Queen of Comebacks.'"

"I had a few falls from grace," she admitted. "If life knocks you down eight times, get up nine. It's not how you get hit by life, but about getting up again."

***

December 2, 1962 marked a turning point in the turbulent life of Judy Garland. That was the night she taped an appearance on *The Jack Paar Show* for NBC-TV at Rockefeller Center in Manhattan. It was set to be aired on December 7, the anniversary of the 1941 Japanese attack on Pearl Harbor.

"Everyone knew what a great singer Judy was," Paar said. "But on television, I discovered what a wit she was, a great storyteller. On her first appearance on my show, we talked more than she sang. She was hilarious both on camera and off."

During **Jack Paar's** struggling days as a young actor, he played alongside Marilyn Monroe as a wolfish lawyer in the 1951 *Love Nest*.

"I had the hots for this *tamale* both on and off the screen," he claimed.

She often told tales of her early days at MGM. "People said I was under the thumb of Louis B. Mayer," she said. "I was under more than his thumb."

Although she expressed praise for Mickey Rooney, she didn't like her fellow schoolmate, Elizabeth Taylor. "She has a terrible speaking voice. Richard Burton told me it reminded him of a fishmonger's wife."

Long before the reign of Johnny Carson, Jack Paar was the king of late-night network TV. He liked to take credit for "putting sparkplugs" into the flickering career of Judy Garland. By booking her on his show, she played to millions of Americans, many couples watching Paar from their beds.

He was on five nights a week, and for five years in a row, entertained Americans before bedtime, often ruffling censors.

He'd first tried to make it as a leading man in Hollywood, appearing with Marilyn Monroe in Fox's *Love Nest* (1951). "I screwed Marilyn but so did everybody else. I played a wolfish lawyer. Marilyn did things to me no woman had ever done before. I never knew gals did *that*."

It was as a TV interviewer that Paar became a household name: He interviewed "saints and sinners" (his words), everyone from Albert Schweitzer to Tallulah Bankhead, from Robert Kennedy to Richard Nixon. "Chemically and biologically, I'm allergic to bullshit," Paar said. "That's why I liked to bring on Judy."

The other guest appearing with her on Paar's show that night was Robert Goulet. She performed a duet with him, "Musette," lifted from *Gay Purr—ee* (1962), the animated film they'd made together about a year before. As solos, she also sang "Paris is a Lonely Town," and "Little Drops of Rain."

After the taping, as reported by musical producer Saul Chaplin, she said to Goulet, "Come back with me to my hotel suite and do your duty."

Judy had long been a fan of Paar, finding him "enigmatic and mercurial." At any moment, he might get up and storm off the set of his own show as it was being broadcast in front of a live audience.

In February of 1964, McCalls ran a bio feature on Judy entitled "There'll Always Be an Encore":

"**Judy**'s dazzling appearance on **Jack Paar**'s Show solidified her viability as a television personality. Not only did she look slim and radiant, she was sharp-witted and exhibited an energy and warmth that communicated effectually through the broadcast medium. Whether truthful or tall tales exaggerated for effect, Judy's anecdotes were hysterical and well received by both studio and home audiences. 'I liked myself for the first time on television,' she later recalled. 'I thought I was kind of funny...Jack made me show off.'"

She was amused at the descriptions of him coursing through medialand in those days: "*Little Lord Fauntleroy with a switchblade knife,*" "*The world's tallest elf,*" "*A bull in his own china shop,*" "*The most exciting personality in television,*" "*A minister after four martinis.*" Paar himself published these quotes on the back cover of his 1983 memoir, P.S. Jack Paar, *but he did not attribute them to any one source.*

Paar claimed, "Judy could be the most difficult talented person in show business. Many TV shows would not touch her because of her unreliability. She would always refuse to come out of her dressing room. You had to beg her. She would not come to rehearsal. But that was only when shows were taped, and she knew she could get away with it. But why? When shows were live, she would appear seconds before her time to go on and give everybody a mild cardiac attack. To this day, I cannot figure the reason for it."

Variety reviewed Judy's late-night TV appearance, evaluating her as "a picture of mental and physical health. Her appearance with Jack Paar was a highly rewarding and gratifying display."

One night, Judy told Paar, "I haven't reached the stage in my career where people come up and ask me, 'Didn't you used to be Judy Garland?'"

"If my career falters, I can always get a job selling hemorrhoid suppositories. I'd bet I'd be terrific at that."

"A lot of my former enemies and detractors have gone to that great restroom in the sky, where they've been assigned latrine duty," Judy facetiously claimed. "If anyone asks me if I used to be Frances Gumm of the Gumm Sisters in vaudeville, I deny it. I tell them I'm a direct descendant of Adam and Eve.'

Judy's appearance on late-night TV was such a hit with viewers that Freddie Fields and David Begelman went to work immediately to create the biggest deal of her entire career.

***

Four days after the taping of her appearance on the Jack Paar show, Judy flew to Washington, D.C. to sing for President John F. Kennedy at the White House. She sang his two favorite songs, "The Trolley Song," and, inevitably, "Over the Rainbow."

In a private chat with him, she told him she was staying in a suite at the Mayflower. "I remember when you once had Suite 812 there," she said. "I recall the night you threw that big party for Frank Sinatra and me—what fun we had."

"Yes, and I remember the following night when I had that intimate dinner for just the two of us."

"I'll never forget it either," she said. At that point, Jacqueline Kennedy appeared, and they changed the subject.

Later, Judy told Begelman, "Audrey Hepburn and that statuesque stripper, Tempest Storm, were also staying at the Mayflower. On different nights, they, too, were invited for an intimate dinner. What a contrast! I don't know how Audrey with her boyish figure managed to compete with Tempest, who was known for her gyrating vagina."

Throughout her life, Judy was a Democrat, and in time became of member of the Hollywood Democratic Committee. She also was a financial and moral supporter of various causes, including the struggle for civil rights.

Even as a starlet, she contributed to the campaign of President Franklin D. Roosevelt and, in time, to the campaigns of Adlai Stevenson and later to both John and Robert Kennedy.

When he was president, and regardless of how busy he was, JFK always accepted Judy's calls to the White House.

***

During Judy's filming of *I Could Go On Singing* in London, she enrolled Liza at the Sorbonne in Paris. As her older daughter later recalled, "I didn't get much schooling there, but I did improve my French, which helped later in my concerts."

One night while walking along the Seine, Liza made a life-changing decision: No more regular schools, only those which taught acting techniques and dancing. "I wanted to strike out on my own and become an independent woman even though I was only a teenager. My dream was Broadway, where I hoped to audition for parts as a singer and dancer."

Without informing Judy, she abandoned her classes and flew from Paris to New York, where her father, Vincente Minnelli, was waiting for her.

That night, she met with him and his third wife (her stepmother), Denise. *[Formally known as Danica ("Denise") Radosavljević Gay Giulianelli de Gigante, her marriage to Minnelli began in 1962 and ended in divorce in 1971.]* Liza sensed in advance that he was going to object to her decision to drop out of the Sorbonne.

When she informed him of the new plan for her life, she was pleasantly surprised at how supportive he was. "You're a bundle of energy and a runaway talent. I can't wait for the day when you're a sensation on the Broadway stage, as I know you will be."

Even her stepmother encouraged her goal. "You should take both acting and dancing lessons instead of learning Latin and algebra."

"I'll take Manhattan over Tinseltown," Liza told them. "I want to be a star on Broadway, not in the movies. I'd like a career more like Ethel Merman's or Mary Martin's instead of Ann Miller's and June Allyson's."

Before Liza settled into New York City, her father presented her with a round-trip ticket to Las Vegas where her mother was appearing at the Sahara. The purpose of the trip was to let Judy know that her daughter was no longer enrolled at the Sorbonne but in New York pursuing dreams of stardom on Broadway.

In contrast to Minnelli, Judy opposed Liza's decision to drop out of school, unleashing a litany of reasons why Liza should continue her studies. Soon, however, Judy, in her words, realized that her daughter was "one very determined young lady who had made up her mind, hell be damned."

Their reunion turned sharper when Liza could stand Judy's objections no more. "You fucked up—and are fucking up—your own life. That hardly qualifies you to give me advice on my own life."

In 1970, Liza gave an interview about what happened when she confronted her mother with her decision:

"She got that cold, dispassionate look in her eyes that told me she knew, though she was against it, that there was nothing she could do about it. 'All right,' she said. 'You do as you please. I can't stop you. I won't try. But you're going to have to make it on your own. I know it's been bothering you for a long time. I hope you make it, baby, I really hope you do. But you might as well know something else now, so you won't expect it later. There will be no money from me. When you leave, you leave me and everything I have. It's got to be that way. You can't have me to fall back on every time you fail or you'll do nothing but fail, knowing I'm waiting. Do you understand what I mean?'"

"I don't think I did. I was sure she'd soften up sooner or later. That time I was wrong."

Later, in an interview in Las Vegas, Judy put a different face on what had transpired. "My sixteen-year-old daughter, Liza Minnelli, is a brilliant performer, both as a singer and a dancer. She'll be living in New York taking voice and acting lessons from some old pros. I predict she will in a short time be wowing them on Broadway, something I never did."

"My daughter Lorna is still in school, and, from what I hear from the drama department, is on her way to becoming a teenage Gertrude Lawrence, even though at the moment, she's only nine years old, but aging fast. As for my darling little Joey, light of my life, he can't decide what he wants to be, but has narrowed the choice down to two professions: an orchestra conductor or an auto mechanic."

Liza had arrived in Manhattan with only a hundred dollars, hardly enough to live on while searching for a job in the theater. *[It is not known why Vincente Minnelli didn't give her a check for basic living expenses after learning that Judy had cut her off financially. He could have afforded it at the time.]*

In Manhattan, Liza avoided paying rent by rooming with friends—an aspiring actress, Tanya Everitt, and her brother, Tracy Everitt. *[At the time, Tracy was in the cast of the Broadway production of* How to Succeed in Business Without Really Trying.*]*

Liza didn't want to overstay her welcome and soon moved out and into the Barbizon Hotel for women. As the weeks passed, she postponed payment of her bill, giving excuses, eventually prompting the manager to evict her from the building, holding her luggage as "hostage."

The teenage wannabe spent that night sleeping on a bench in Central Park.

When Frank Sinatra learned about her plight, he sent her a check for $500, but she had too much pride to cash it and returned it with her thanks.

Gradually, after Liza didn't find any acting gigs, she began posing as a teenaged model, hawking new fashions. Her work paid the rent, fed her, and handled the fees of her vocal coach and acting teachers. Fortunately, the "pixie look" had roared into vogue as a fashion statement. *TV Guide* even went so far as to label this innovation in fashion modeling as "The Liza Minnelli Look."

Liza Minnelli was an obvious choice to craft a voice-over for the troubled animated spinoff, *Journey Back to Oz*, of the 1939 classic film

Which character did she, with her voice, portray?

It was Dorothy Gale, a role her mother had perfected and immortalized in *The Wizard of Oz*.

***

At last, Liza got a bizarre film offer as the star in the voice-over of an "animated adventure musical fantasy" entitled *Journey Back to Oz*. It was loosely based on Frank

Baum's classic novel *The Marvelous Land of Oz*. *[Published in 1904, it was the sequel to* The Wonderful Wizard of Oz *(1900) from which Judy's 1939 film was derived.]*

The backers of the new animated film, at least in private, were candid about why Liza's voice was selected for the voice-over: She not only sounded like Judy did in *The Wizard of Oz*, but as the daughter of the original movie's iconic star, she might become a draw at the box office.

The film went into production in 1962 but was not finished and released until a decade later because the producers ran out of money.

The voices of the various characters in the film all emanated from stars. Mickey Rooney was cast as the Scarecrow and Ethel Merman was the Wicked Witch of the West.

Margaret Hamilton, the original witch in the 1939 film, was also hired for her voice, playing Dorothy's dowdy Kansas-born Auntie Em. Essaying other voice-over roles were Danny Thomas as the Tin Man; Milton Berle as The Cowardly Lion; and Rise Stevens in the Billie Burke role of the Good Witch Glinda (of the North). The voice of Pumpkinhead was assigned to prissy Paul Lynde.

First released in England in 1972 *[and in the U.S. two years later]*, *Journey Back to Oz* faced harsh criticism. One reviewer claimed, "All is not well in Oz, certainly not in this unimaginative and repetitive animated feature. However, Liza Minnelli's intelligent reading of Dorothy strikes just the right note."

***

To prep for a Broadway, or even an Off-Broadway musical, Liza had

A pixie-looking **Liza Minnelli** found early success as a young fashion model. In fact, she became so popular that fashion columnists began describing her pysical style as "The Liza Minnelli Look."

In the center figure, Liza is one of the pivotal figures in the Off-Broadway musical, *Best Foot Forward*.

spent her early years watching some of moviedom's greatest entertainers rehearse—and not just Judy. She'd studied Fred Astaire, Gene Kelly, and Cyd Charisse, among many others, go through their paces. Her big, intense, and dark eyes took in all their movements and was inspired by them.

By 1963, she was tapped to appear Off-Broadway in a revival of the musical *Best Foot Forward*.

[In 1941, George Abbott had produced the original version of Best Foot Forward *on Broadway, with choreography by a young Gene Kelly. It had starred Rosemary Lane, with Nancy Walker making her Broadway debut. The musical also launched June Allyson, Judy's close friend, into stardom. Two years later, it was made into a film, starring Lucille Ball, Allyson, Walker.]*

The revival that co-starred Liza was presented at Stage 73, a seedy, 100-seat theater adjacent to a bar. Liza was hired for $45 a week, although the producers claimed, "She's worth a million dollars in publicity," and the press agent for the show asserted, "With Liza in it, we'll get more publicity than any show in the history of Off-Broadway."

Liza did not play the lead, but was cast in the secondary role of Ethel Hofflinger, the role that Walker had crafted so brilliantly in the original production. Liza lacked her toughness, but substituted vulnerability instead, with grace notes evocative of Judy herself. *[Her mother had always claimed, "When I appear I always get the sympathy vote...well, in most cases I do."]*

During rehearsals, Liza formed a life-long bond with Danny Daniels, the show's director and choreographer. Years later, in 1991, he would direct her in *Stepping Out*.

In *Best Foot Forward*, Liza performed a solo, "You Are For Loving," written by Hugh Martin and Ralph Blane. The two writers had also composed "The Trolley Song" and "The Boy Next Door" for Judy's *Meet Me in St. Louis* (1944).

During rehearsals, Liza did indeed put her *Best Foot Forward* but broke her ankle when she tripped over a loose wooden board on stage. The producers could have easily replaced her but opted not to, fearing they'd lose the publicity she'd generate.

Liza celebrated her seventeenth birthday in the hospital. Although the producers had considered postponing the opening of their show to accommodate her recuperation, when it was learned that her healing

These are early publicity photos from 1963, widely distributed at the launch of **Liza Minnelli**'s stage career in New York.

Many in the news media thought her emerging facial features evoked her father, Vincente Minnelli, more thatn they did the look of her mother, Judy Garland.

528

would take many weeks, they decided that she'd return to her role wearing a cast. She would sing her numbers, but walk, with a noticeable limp, through the dance numbers. As far as it is known, that had never been done in the history of stage musicals in New York.

Liza's Off-Broadway revival of *Best Foot Forward* opened on April 2, 1963, and the premiere was mobbed, as several hundred people, restrained behind police barricades, showed up for the opening. Many of them hoped to catch a glimpse of Judy Garland, but were disappointed. Even though at the time, she was lodged at the nearby Plaza Hotel, she did not appear that night.

This publicity shot from the Off Broadway production of *Best Foot Forward* depict an unidentified young actor and **Liza** looking befuddled and bewildered.

Liza was shocked, having reserved three seats in the front row for Joey, Lorna, and "my mama."

She phoned Judy at the Plaza after the first act to ask what had happened. "Oh, Darling," she said. "I thought it was tomorrow night. I'll bring your brother and sister and show up then."

[Actually, Judy fully understood the date of the premiere, but later confessed that she didn't want "to steal the show from Liza," which she knew she'd do if she put in an appearance for the reporters and photographers waiting, like a mob, to descend.]

One headline the next morning read: JUDY FOREGOES LIZA'S TRIUMPH.

The next night, Judy and her two kids showed up, later telling the press, "I was so moved for my baby I cried and cried throughout her performance. I'm so happy for her."

Although **Liza** broke her ankle, the producers decided that she had to go on anyway.

She opened the show in spite of her injury, singing but not having to fake her dance steps.

After the show, Judy invited friends to her suite at the Plaza. She reflected on the mother-daughter rivalry: "It's a virtual law in Hollywood that as one star rises, another must fall. Isn't that, dear ones, the plot for *A Star Is Born*? Liza's rise might be matched by my own spectacular decline. Do you think Liza one day will usurp the spotlight of the great Judy Garland?"

Her friends rushed to reassure her: "No one, absolutely no one, including Liza, will ever take the place of Judy Garland."

Women's Wear Daily wrote: "About five minutes before the final curtain, Liza Minnelli stands alone on the stage, singing a new song, 'You Are for Loving.' If you close your eyes, you would swear it was a young Judy Garland. If you keep your eyes open, you will still have chills running through you. Nothing else in the show can match those few minutes for sheer intensity of talent."

Liza braced herself for a lifetime of comparisons with her mother. "There is no escaping it," she said. "I am who I am, the daughter of two of the most talented people in Hollywood, Judy Garland and Vincente Minnelli. I do sound like my mother when I

Critic Walter Kerr reviewed **Best Foot Forward**, writing: "Liza Minnelli is certainly appealing, and would be even if she weren't Judy Garland' daughter, with something of her mother's faintly scratchy tremolo clinging to her—and with a fading half-laugh that trickles away after lines. She is easy and confident and accomplished and winning and, also, I would think, a person."

sing, but that's me, that's who I am. I'm not like some female impersonator imitating my mother. When I hear myself on a recording, it's sort of spooky, like the voice of Judy Garland implanted in my throat."

Look magazine proclaimed, "A new star was born last night. Liza brought down the house."

In *Newsday,* George Oppenheimer wrote: "Young Miss Minnelli, barely out of school, cannot belt out a song the way her mother does, but I feel fairly competent it will come, too. In other respects, Liza resembles Judy, not only in appearance and mannerisms, but in that intangible quality of vulnerability. You want to get up on the stage, take her in your arms, and tell her how good she is."

A critic from the *Daily News* wrote: "*Best Foot Forward* is worth seeing, if only to remember some day to having witnessed a Broadway star in her professional debut."

In the *New York Mirror,* Robert Coleman claimed, "Liza is great! Liza sparkles!"

When Liza left the show in September, she was replaced by Marcia Levant, the daughter of Oscar Levant, Judy's former lover. As attendance began to drop off, the producer brought in Veronica Lake, the fading movie star of the 1940s who had been famous for her peek-a-boo hairdo. She was hired in the flush of publicity generated after news had broken that the legendary star was working as a cocktail waitress in a Manhattan bar. But her allure belonged to another day that had faded after World War II. She was no longer the sexy, sultry, and enigmatic star of those movies with

Alan Ladd.

The Off-Broadway revival of *Best Foot Forward* closed in October after 244 performances.

***

Although Judy had promised not to interfere in any way in Liza's career, she didn't keep her vow. She arranged for her to appear on *The Jack Paar Show.* As a gimmick, he introduced her as "Dyju Langard," a jumbled acronym of "Judy Garland."

Since her leg was still in a cast, Paar introduced her as a crippled singer from Armenia. At the end of her song, he revealed to the audience that she was really Liza Minnelli, the daughter of Judy Garland.

Paar later proclaimed, "On my show, a starlet was born. Liza was a charmer and looked like a wet sparrow. If she weighed one-hundred pounds, at least ten pounds were in those eyes of hers. She had her hair done by the North Wind and was a sixteen-year-old darling. She could really sing."

After all this publicity, Liza was swamped with non-paying offers, such as TV appearances. She even showed up on *The Ed Sullivan Show.* "I had no money," she said. It was widely reported at the time that she spent a night sleeping on the steps of the fountain in front of the Plaza Hotel.

Although she'd gotten tons of publicity, she had no immediate "second act." She knew that if she didn't get another gig soon, she'd soon be forgotten in the fickle world of show business.

"I might end up as a six-month wonder," she said, "like some other progeny of Hollywood greats. Take Gary Crosby or John Barrymore, Jr., for instance."

By November of 1962, Dorothy Kilgallen, in her column, even referred to Liza as a "has-been."

***

Ignoring how unreliable Judy was as a performer, Freddie Fields and David Begelman proposed that she star in a weekly series, *The Judy Garland Show* for CBS-TV. They were asking that the studio pay her $25,000 to $30,000 per week. Both ABC and NBC were intrigued with the proposal, but only CBS was willing to meet Begelman's financial demands.

The long-range package deal, with renewals, might stretch over four to five years. The entire deal was expected to bring her $24 million, which could have provided her with security for life if managed properly. Not only that, but Begelman wanted another $4 million when the series went into syndication.

Judy met with James Aubrey, president of CBS, and their confab went well. Fields claimed, "Judy did a charm number on him."

Later, meeting with CBS executives, she signed an agreement at the St. Regis Hotel in Manhattan. At the time, she said, "I'm going to be a female Perry Como."

For the 1963-64 season, Judy would be joining the CBS roster of TV entertainers that included Carol Burnett, Danny Kaye, Phil Silvers, and George C. Scott, who was starring at the time in a gritty TV drama series, *East Side, West Side.*

Variety called her contract, "The greatest ever issued to a TV performer."

On March 31, 1963, Judy spoke to Margaret McManus, a syndicated columnist, about her upcoming weekly television show:

> *"It was a big decision, but a wonderful decision. I don't think of it as so formidable. I'm going to take it easy, and have wonderful guests, and share the spotlight. I'm not going to try to carry the show every week all by myself. A weekly show isn't anything like a 'special.' On a 'special' you feel so pushed, so responsible. You only have one chance. It's concentrated chaos. Everything depends on it. If you're on every week, you can relax. If you are not absolutely great one Sunday, there's another Sunday coming right up. I want to keep the show very simple. In television, you are in a room, not on a stage, so you don't get too fancy."*

"At long last, I've found that pot of gold at the end of the rainbow," she said.

How wrong she was.

The CBS "Eye"

CHAPTER NINETEEN

CBS-TV, THE SMILING COBRA &
THE JUDY GARLAND SHOW

SPECTACULARLY DYSFUNCTIONAL,
& DESPITE MORE OF JUDY'S WIDELY PUBLICIZED
SUICIDE ATTEMPTS,
26 EPISODES OF HER PRIME-TIME TV SHOW GET STRESSFULLY BROADCAST.

EXPLOITED AGAIN. WAS IT SABOTAGE?
AGAIN AND AGAIN, CBS DENIES JUDY THE CHANCE TO CONFIGURE HER SHOW THE WAY SHE WANTS.

"I wanted Noel Coward as a guest on my show, but instead they give me a Hillbilly Banjo Troupe and all the wrong advisors."

JUDY IS PRESENTED WITH EVIDENCE OF
MAJOR EMBEZZLEMENTS FROM HER MANAGERS.
VIEWING BOTH OF THEM AS VITAL TO THE LAUNCH OF HER TV SERIES, SHE REFUSES TO CONFRONT THEM

"Okay, so Freddie and David took $300,000 from me. I stand to make $24 million. I can deal with these crooks after the show gets successfully launched"

LIZA DANCES UP A STORM, HELPS HOLD HER MOTHER TOGETHER, AND BECOMES A THEATRICAL PERSONALITY IN HER OWN RIGHT.

PLUS GOSSIP ABOUT BARBRA! PEGGY LEE! LENA! PHIL SILVERS! ROBERT GOULET! VIC DAMONE! STEVE & EYDIE! BOBBY DARIN! GEORGE MAHARIS! & SOME OF THE OTHER GUESTS ON HER SHOW!

"Sid Luft was the nearest Judy Garland came to the man that didn't get away. By the end, the nights were bitter, and the star had lost her glitter, but he was hanging in there. The longest-lasting of her five husbands, he played Mr. Judy Garland from 1952 to 1965, or half her adult life. Unlike his predecessor, he was not 'musical,' in either the artistic or the euphemistic sense. He was not voraciously gay, and he wasn't a 'friend of Dorothy.'"

—Mark Sten

"Judy was not even five feet tall—just a shrimp of a gal, really—but she had a very sensuous body and, up close, her skin was like porcelain, pure white. I was crazy about her. She had incredibly kissable lips. You don't fall out of love with somebody like Judy."

—Sid Luft

"CBS hired Judy Garland as a star, but they would not let her be one."

—Chicago Sun-Times

"By the time the 1960s roared in, I had become a cult goddess, at least to my loyal gay followers. Obviously, they have the best taste in America. My God, when I die, all the flags on Fire Island will be at half-mast. My boys will be standing by the 'Meat Rack,' singing 'Over the Rainbow.'"

—Judy Garland

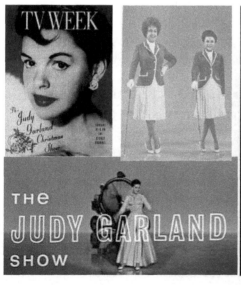

"The Judy Garland Show is the Cleopatra of television."

—Norman Jewison, in reference to the very expensive 1963 film that almost bankrupted 20th Century Fox.

"This year (1963) is going to be the most challenging of my life," Judy told Liza and Sid Luft. "I'll be so busy I won't even have time to slit my wrists, much less set myself on fire."

Even so, she took time out to fly to Washington, D.C., for the first-year anniversary of the inauguration of President John F. Kennedy and his Vice President, Lyndon B. Johnson. "I adore Jack," she told press secretary Pierre Salinger, "but I'm uneasy around LBJ. I fear he'd like to put his Texas paw up my dress."

Each of her two previous specials for CBS had garnered high ratings, and Aubrey, head honcho there, was now willing to build a full-blown TV series around her. It eventually morphed into *The Judy Garland Show*. Back in Hollywood, Freddie Fields and David Begelman kept her up to date as its pre-production, now scheduled for the autumn, gained momentum.

Fields called for a strategy session— pointedly without Judy—with his staff and the CBS crew. "This is a life-or-death trial for Judy. If she fucks up this TV series, her career will probably end. She narrowly survived a firing from MGM after the *Annie Get Your Gun* crisis, and she rebounded. But if she's fired by CBS, her show-biz games will end, forever. Frankly, she's a post-forty-year-old 'damsel in distress.' To back her up, and to get her though this project, all of us have to be as strong as U.S. Steel. She's one hell of a load to carry, but she's amazingly talented and, with our help, she'll pull it off."

Eventually, and with many mishaps, *The Judy Garland Show* became a CBS-TV variety series that aired on Sunday night during the 1963-64 season. She had long feuded with CBS, even taking them to court, but in the light of the new circumstances, she and James Aubrey, the studio's president, had "buried the tomahawk" (Judy's words).

Judy herself claimed her new contract "was the deal of my life," and she hoped it

One of the many posters issued by CBS as publicity for her much-discussed, very controversial TV show. The one inserted above promoted her on-the-air nostalgia-soaked reunion with **Donald O'Connor**.

535

would secure her financial future and rescue her from her mountains of debt.

Her contract was for a duration of four years. For the 1963-64 season, she agreed to perform in twenty-six shows. Her corporation would be paid $140,000 per episode. The belief at the time was that after expenses, she'd receive about $25,000 to $30,000 per episode.

Kingsrow Enterprises, the company she'd established with Fields and Begelman, would retain ownership of the tapes. Fields told her that syndication alone would be worth "perhaps four million big bucks."

When *Variety* announced her show, a reporter "nailed" her with this question: "In 1955, you said you would never do a weekly TV series. What made you change your mind?"

"That was then and this is now," she said. "It's like being in love. Just because you were in love with a man in 1955 doesn't mean that you'll be in love with him in 1963. For God's sake, boy…Welcome to Hollywood."

Judy had already been the centerpiece of two previous CBS specials. The first, *Miss Show Business*, had been videotaped during the first week of January, 1962, and had included two of Judy's fellow "Rat Packers," **Frank Sinatra** (right) **and Dean Martin.**

During its taping, she'd been nervous and uncertain about whether she could "pull it off." As the cameras rolled, in a way that some observers found unsettling, she kept fondling, touching, and hugging Martin and Sinatra, as if seeking reassurance. After the taping, and right in front of Martin, she begged Sinatra to return with her to her hotel and "make love to me."

He bowed out, pleading other commitments.

In contrast and in response, hearing her pleas, Martin said, "But *I'm* free!" Then, looking a Sinatra with a mock sneer, he said to anyone within earshot, "The gals tell me I'm better in the sack than Ol' Blue Eyes, here." Then, in his good-natured way, Martin turned to Sinatra and said, "Can you still get it up, daddy?"

An hour later, Martin left the studio with Judy "to do my duty," as he later recalled.

The night that *Miss Show Business* was aired on national TV, Judy, without an invitation, arrived on Sinatra's doorstep. He had scheduled the evening around watching the show with Bill Colleran, the TV producer.

"Judy was obviously high when she arrived that night," Colleran claimed. "Frank was sitting in his lounge chair reading a book, and he didn't really want to entertain Judy."

"But within an hour, she was down on her knees in front of him, unzipping his pants and reaching in. She tried to get him at full staff, but he didn't seem interested. Then, brusquely, he stood up, stuffing himself back into his trousers."

"I'm not in the mood," he told her. "Besides, I'm married."

"I couldn't believe I heard that," Colleran said. "Since when did Frankie let marriage interfere with his sex life?"

Infuriated, Judy rose to her feet and stormed out the door. She paused only briefly to shout back, "No one wants to fuck the legend."

In its review of *Miss Show Business*, *The New York Times* claimed, "Judy Garland held television in the palm of her hand last night in her first video appearance in six years. The singer carried on the music hall tradition of Al Jolson."

"Nobody can match her," hailed *TV Guide*.

The *Los Angeles Times* defined it as "a beautiful hour with moments as memorable as any that television has ever given us."

[In her final years, when Judy faced entertainment venues not worthy of her, she'd sometimes say, "Would Frank Sinatra perform in this crapper?"

"No, Judy," a manager would say to her. "But you're not Frank Sinatra, and he's not in hock to Uncle Sam for about half a million dollars."

Judy once told Ava Gardner, when they were discussing Sinatra, "When I sing about the man that got away, I always think of him."

Potty-mouthed Ava didn't respond like a jealous former wife. "Whenever a small dick goes in me, I always ask myself, 'Where's Frankie now that I need him?'"]

The second "stand alone" TV special that Judy had crafted for CBS—awkwardly named *Judy Garland and Her Guests Phil Silvers and Robert Goulet*—was aired in March, 1963. It went over big and was even nominated for an Emmy.

Robert Goulet later told Norman Jewison, "I thought I'd have to perform stud duty for Judy again, but fortunately, Glenn Ford was doing the honors, and I could keep Carol Lawrence satisfied instead."

JUDY GARLAND AND HER GUESTS, PHIL SILVERS AND ROBERT GOULET
Fast, funny Phil, romantic Robert and enchanting Judy, Judy, Judy!

7:30-8:30 P.M.

Variety wrote, "Taking her special as a sample of what may be in store when Judy Garland has her own weekly CBS-TV series next fall, it's going to be welcome fare indeed. Her singing last night projected over the footlights, with an immediacy and an impact that is rarely achieved on video. The series will have a star who is steeped in the know-how and who vocally is far from past her prime. If this performance doesn't bring in the final sponsors for next season's series, probably nothing will."

537

Wearing gowns designed by Edith Head, the most famous designer in Hollywood at the time, Judy, with Goulet and Silvers, went on the air during prime time on March 19. She sang a medley of Garland standards and performed duets with each of her co-stars. Goulet, alone, also sang his standard, "If Ever I Would Leave You," from *Camelot* before she joined him for a rendition of "Love Is a Lovely Thing."

The TV special with Goulet and Silvers also had Judy impersonating such characters—as expressed by journalist Scott Schechter—"as a Park Avenue matron; a lady wrestler; a terrible singer auditioning for a big Broadway producer; a thick New York-accented woman just attacked by a 'masher' in Central Park; one of the 'Three Musketeers'; a beatnik folk singer; an inept ballet dancer destroying *Swan Lake*; and even a fall-off-your-chair funny spoof of Judy Garland."

Despite the popularity of the show, critic Jack Gould, writing for *The New York Times,* was less than flattering: "Miss Garland and Robert Goulet indulged in a protracted duet of standard tunes that were distressingly overranged and oversung. And the meaning of the lyrics was made subordinate to the awkward direction which required the two principals to look into each other's eyes for an interminable period."

The *Philadelphia Inquirer* noted, "Miss Garland, looking youthful, vibrant, and strikingly slender, opened strong and closed the same way."

***

Before the launch of the first episode of her TV series, Freddie Fields spoke to a reporter from *Variety:* "For once in her life, this little dynamo is going to be financially secure. And it's about time. Judy is forty-one. She's done everything there is to do in show business, from vaudeville to one-night stands. She's earned fortunes for other people, but she's been victimized over and over again. Before we made this deal with CBS, she was practically broke. But television is going to give her what it's given others much less talented than she—security. These shows are going to bring in money so that she doesn't have to sing her guts out in concerts night after night to support her kids."

Luft was in Los Angeles, trying to launch a new business deal, when he read Fields' comments. That day, he'd checked into the Beverly Rodeo Hotel.

Later, he recalled, "Judy must have used Irish witchcraft, but she tracked me down."

A call came in for him at 4AM, waking him up. Judy was in Miami. "Hi, darling," she cooed. "Do you believe in second chances?"

"You know I do," he answered. "And you must also know I still love you even after all the crap we've gone through."

"Maybe we'd better get together and have a long talk," she said.

"I agree, but where?"

For the thrill and novelty of it, they decided to rendezvous at the airport in New Orleans.

On the agreed-upon day, her plane arrived there first. After landing, she maneuvered her way to meet him at his arrivals gate with a chilled bottle of champagne and a paper bag of confetti.

En route to New Orleans' Prince Conti Hotel, they drank the champagne out of paper cups. At the hotel's check-in desk, he was surprised that she'd booked them in separate rooms on different floors.

That night, after a Cajun dinner, he took her dancing at a jazz dive in the French Quarter. For two days and nights, they explored the city, enjoying the local cuisine, went shopping for her, and listened to a lot of jazz. There was a lot of talk about Lorna and Joey, with hopes for their future.

What they didn't do was sleep together. Fortunately, his libido was handled by a young Cajun girl from the Bayou, working as a maid. Their brief fling was discovered by the hotel's night clerk, Bill Broyhill, who was also dating the same woman. The item was hinted at in a local paper that revealed that Judy Garland was in town with her estranged husband. On the morning of their third day together, Luft woke up to find a letter slipped under his door.

THE GREAT GARLAND GAMBLE

"Dearest Sid,
No matter what way or what manner you handle what's ahead for us in our divorce—your children need love and want you. You're their father and always will be! Our marriage failed—but I'll be your friend forever.
With deep sincerity,
From J."

***

No one was ignoring Judy's status as an "against the odds" risk. The executives at CBS were clearly aware of her reputation for being late for rehearsals, for missing performances, for suicide scares, and for collapsing on stage. If the TV series were to remain viable and on schedule, they knew it would have to be videotaped, as they could not depend on her performing live and on schedule.

Variety was blunt in its appraisal. "It's hardly betraying a secret that the multi-million-dol-

RISKY BUSINESS
(Her Name Was Judy)

Many key players at CBS-TV, including its president, considered Judy a bad risk.

Would she show? Would she get sick? Would she try to kill herself? Would her success in concert halls translate to the mass media and the "small screen" of television?

Most worrisome of all? As a performer, would she survive the changing tastes and social unrest of the revolutionary 1960s?

lar investment in Judy Garland is a calculated risk, since there's no guarantee of a lock-in of her full services. Depending on a number of reasons, Miss Garland, some feel, might suddenly decide to blow the whole thing."

To fulfill an obligation made months before, Judy arrived on February 7 at Harrah's Resort at Lake Tahoe for a three-week engagement. With Mort Lindsey conducting, she ran through some of her old favorites, adding "Hello, Bluebird," perhaps with the intention of promoting her recent movie, *I Could Go on Singing.*

However, on February 11, because she'd had another of her many attacks of the flu, she told her handlers that she could not appear onstage. Feeling better on February 12, she waited in the wings to go onstage. Right before she was announced for her entrance, she collapsed and was rushed to a nearby hospital in Carson City.

Although she insisted that she was fine and that she could return to work in a day or so, management relieved her of her obligation and hired Mickey Rooney to fill in for her.

From Los Angeles, Luft flew to Lake Tahoe for another reconciliation. On his first night in her bedroom, she assured him that he was a better lover than her current beau, Glenn Ford. "You don't have Glenn's male beauty, but you make up for it in other ways," she told him.

[She had long been aware that Luft, in the late 1930s, had been the lover of Eleanor Powell before she became Mrs. Glenn Ford.]

Leaving Lake Tahoe, Luft drove Judy to Las Vegas for a two-night stay at The Sahara, where "we tried to cram in as many shows as possible."

After that, they headed to San Francisco and were seen checking into a suite at the Fairmont. When confronted by a reporter, Judy announced, "We're having a reconciliation honeymoon."

It wasn't to his taste, but Judy insisted that Luft escort her to three of the most popular and crowded gay bars in San Francisco. At each of them, she was surrounded by mobs of adoring young men.

"I was pushed aside for the most part, until I went to the men's room in one joint," Luft said. "Then I got some attention at the urinal. I used to be a real homophile, and I still was, but to a much lesser degree. I could never understand why a guy would turn to a guy for sexual satisfaction when women are so delectable."

After San Francisco, Luft and Judy made a leisurely drive south to Los Angeles, where they stopped in any town that caught their interest. Back home again, she was planning for another "assault" on London.

He escorted her to the Los Angeles Airport and saw her off, later telling *The Hollywood Reporter,* "I love Judy...still! I want to protect her from the trauma she's known for most of her life. I don't want her to be bewildered or hurt again. I want her to find happiness with me...*again.*"

Arriving in London on March 5, 1963, she checked into the Savoy once again and gave a press conference that rambled on for about two hours.

The following night, she made a glamourous entrance at the Plaza Theatre for the premiere of *I Could Go On Singing,* that movie she'd made with Dirk Bogarde. Posters outside heralded—*IT'S JUDY LIGHTING UP THE LONELY STAGE.*

A TV crew was on hand to record her arrival. Its footage would later be broadcast on *The Ed Sullivan Show*.

On March 10, she returned to what she called "my home in London," The Palladium, scene of her legendary success in 1951. She did her rendition of "Smile," which she was trying to make a permanent part of her repertoire. She also introduced the song, "It's Almost Like Being in Love."

The Sullivan crew would also film part of her show. Its footage would also be aired (on April 14) on *The Ed Sullivan Show*.

The next day, she flew back to New York, where she checked into the St. Regis Hotel, despite a dispute with the manager over what he claimed were charges never paid from her previous sojourn there.

On March 12, she hosted a party for Liza that celebrated her seventeenth birthday. Each of her guests commented on "The New Judy," who was laughing, talking, joking, and praising "My very talented daughter, Miss Liza Minnelli" and "the dreamboat of the man I married, Mr. Sid Luft."

That's why New Yorkers were shocked two days later when columnist Earl Wilson revealed that she had attempted suicide after an overdose of sleeping pills.

Although ebullient at Liza's party, when it was over, Judy became despondent and depressed. She didn't want to turn into what her own mother, Ethel, had been—a stage mother overseeing her daughter's career. She also had grave fears about her marriage to Luft. She didn't know how long their tenuous reconciliation would last. She spent sleepless nights fretting over the direction of her career and became demoralized after learning about the box office failure of *I Could Go On Singing*.

She admitted to Luft and others that she was "hysterically nervous" about her upcoming TV series: "If I fuck this up, my career is more or less over, except maybe for some late-night gigs at gay bars in Greenwich Village and San Francisco."

Since her previous engagement at the Sahara in Las Vegas, Judy had employed Orval Paine, a hairdresser, as her "Girl Friday." In addition to answering Judy's phone, Paine tended, every day, to a mountain of details associated with her private life.

From her bedroom at the St. Regis one night, Paine heard Judy sobbing in the next room. As her sobs grew louder, she went to investigate. Judy had been acting strangely all afternoon, and she feared the worst.

When she entered without knocking, she found Judy sitting up in bed, her face ravaged with a kind of tremulous agony. "I'm sleepy, very very sleepy," her voice drifted off. "Sleepy…going for a long, long nap." Then she collapsed on the bed. As she did, she began to vomit.

On her nightstand rested an empty plastic bottle that until recently, had been

JUDY GARLAND RECOVERS

Sleep Pills Fell Singer

BY EARL WILSON

As it appeared on March 14, 1963, in the **Los Angeles Times**, here is Earl Wilson's syndicated show-biz column referencing Judy's suicide attempt at the St. Regis Hotel in NYC.

541

full of sleeping pills. It was obvious that she'd swallowed all of them. Judy had not eaten all day but had been drinking heavily since 2PM that afternoon. Violently, her stomach was rejecting the combination of liquor and pills.

Paine immediately phoned the hotel doctor, waking him up. Within twenty minutes, he was in the room, administering to Judy, deciding not to send her to the hospital. Paine and the doctor half dragged her, half carried her, to the clean sheets of the spare bedroom, where she appeared to drift into a deep sleep that in some ways resembled a coma. The doctor agreed to remain for two hours to make sure she was sleeping peacefully, and Paine called the night maid to change the soiled sheets.

Luft was out of town when the news of her attempted suicide broke in Earl Wilson's column, and he flew into New York before the end of the following day.

By now, Freddie Fields and Begelman were also aware of her condition. They'd each been counting on "making millions" from Judy's upcoming TV series, and they were enormously alarmed, especially because they knew that the executives at CBS had been alerted, too. "It wasn't that Freddie and I were worried about Judy's physical stability," said Begelman. "We were concerned with her sanity."

During the final two weeks of March, Luft "escaped" with Judy, Lorna, and Joey to Cat Island in The Bahamas, hoping that she'd get some much-needed recuperation before her upcoming television ordeal.

"She didn't' get all that much rest," Luft told one of his backers, Ted Law. "She demanded it two or three times a day. I had to tell her that men reach their sexual peak at the age of nineteen, and I had celebrated that birthday a long time ago. She informed me, without a lot of good evidence, that women don't reach their sexual peak until they hit forty."

"Surely, Mother Nature didn't plan it that way," Luft told her.

***

In May, Judy was curtly informed that her television series would be filmed in Hollywood instead of in New York, as had been previously agreed. That meant she had to find a home for herself, her children, and possibly for Luft, too. For a while, all four of them, including Lorna and Joey, lived in a rather ramshackle villa on Malibu Beach.

But eventually, she located a home to her liking at 126 Rockingham Drive in Westwood, south of Sunset Boulevard. She took out the mortgage in her own name, excluding Luft, as she'd been advised by Begelman and Fields.

It was rumored that the move back to California marked the beginning of Aubrey's disfavor with both Judy and her series. As president of CBS, on the eve of the launch of her TV series, he knew that he could make her life miserable.

Unknown to Luft at the time, Begelman had instructed Judy to reconcile with Luft because that is what Aubrey had demanded. CBS was horrified by the possibility that she might decide to inaugurate a messy divorce during the run of her TV series. "It would damage your image and reputation, and, as everyone knows, you don't need any more damage," he'd told her.

Meanwhile, Luft was increasingly suspicious of Fields and Begelman, fearing that they were stealing thousands and thousands of dollars from her.

"Begelman was fucking Judy in more ways than one," Luft charged. "I didn't trust him in my sight, much less out of my sight. The same goes for Fields." He had long suspected that they were embezzling from Judy, and one afternoon, he set out to prove it to her.

He persuaded Judy to hire Oscar Steinberg, the best-known accountant in Beverly Hills, an expert who often handled the complicated business affairs of movie stars. Steinberg launched an audit of Judy's books for the fiscal period of January 1961 to April 1963. It appeared that in most cases, Judy was collecting the fee that would have gone to her agents, and that they had consistently banked her much larger salary as a performer.

**THAT'S SHOW-BIZ
(i.e., Betrayals & Larceny)**

Even when Judy learned that her managers, David Begelman and Freddie Fields, were embezzling her hard-earned money, she gave them a pass, at least in the beginning.

She would later sue them. "Both Freddie and David promised me the world but didn't even deliver Rhode Island."

Checks ranging in size from $6,000 to $10,000 had been cashed at the casinos of Las Vegas to pay for Begelman's losses at the gaming tables.

One check had been made out for the partial construction of an apartment building in Manhattan, a structure which would later provide a spacious apartment for occupancy by Begelman and his wife, Lee.

Another check for $125,000 had been defined as an expense for Judy's "protection." Another (for $50,000) had gone "to pay off a blackmailer." [A nurse—who was threatening to sell it to the tabloids— had allegedly taken a snapshot of a nude and comatose Judy during one of her hospitalizations.]

There were many other discrepancies: Jack Paar had given Judy a 1963 Cadillac as a gift after her appearance on his show, but Begelman had seized it for himself, thereby forcing Judy to buy a new vehicle for her use in Los Angeles.

All in all, it appeared that Fields and Begelman had stolen more than $300,000 that would otherwise have gone to Judy. Her lawyer, Grant Cooper, personally surveyed Steinberg's audit, eventually pronouncing the theft and laundering of Judy's money as "criminal."

When Luft presented her with the evidence, she was devastated. Then came the surprise: She refused to confront them, because she viewed both of them as vital to the launch of her TV series. "Okay, so Freddie and David took $300,000 from me. I stand to make $24 million. I can deal with these crooks after the show gets successfully launched."

According to Luft, "After my disappointment in hearing that, and not really believing it, all hell broke loose when we were together under one roof. In the meantime, those two crooks continued to rob her. It's like guards robbing the bank they worked for."

"How did Judy respond legally to this wholesale fraud?" Luft asked. "She fired her lawyer, Grant Cooper. She was a fucking goner *whoop-de-do* on her little pills."

***

For Judy's forty-first birthday on June 10, and also to celebrate a house-warming for (her) new house at 126 Rockingham Drive in Westwood, Luft threw a big bash, inviting lots of friends and fellow actors.

At the party, George Schlatter, who was set to direct Judy's TV series, managed to corner some of the big- name guests and sign them for appearances on Judy's television show. They included both Donald O'Connor and June Allyson.

According O'Connor at the time, Judy and Luft seemed like the most happily married couple in Hollywood. "I heard they were constantly feudin' and fightin', but not at the party. I felt their marital troubles were behind them, and that they had settled down like a loving, middle-aged couple."

As predicted, a few days after the party, Luft and Judy resumed their feud, always over money, but also over charges of adultery on both sides. He decided to "take a break from my life" over the weekend and check into a small hotel on Newport Beach. In his sexual frustration, he called an escort agency, ordering two prostitutes. "Make sure they're young."

Late Monday morning, he returned to Judy's new house on Rockingham Drive, only to discover that Judy, Lorna, and Joey had moved. A servant didn't know where they'd gone, but he was allowed to come in and remove his possessions. That same day, he moved into a $100-a-month apartment on Manning Avenue in Los Angeles.

For all practical purposes, those events marked the end of their marriage. All that remained were future arguments, often legal, over finances, and an ongoing war for custody of Lorna and Joey.

***

Judy's first videotaping of her new TV series, *The Judy Garland Show,* took place at 8:10PM on the night of June 24 at Studio 43 at CBS's Television City in Los Angeles. She emerged from her mammoth dressing room to walk down a "Yellow Brick Road" (painted specifically for her) before facing an audience studded with the *glitterati* of Hollywood.

Lucille Ball was seated in front. Also in the audience were Hedda Hopper and Louella Parson, each seated as far from each

Judy Garland fans gathered *en masse* for admittance to the taping of the first episode of her TV show.

The venue was **CBS's Television City** in Hollywood, and it was publicized around the country.

544

other as possible—along with Jack Benny, Natalie Wood, Clint Eastwood, Carl Reiner, Dick Van Dyck, and a host of other stars then in their prime.

CBS's producer, George Schlatter, had assembled a winning cast and crew, hiring Edith Head to design Judy's wardrobe. Mort Lindsey had been imported to direct a thirty-three piece orchestra. Gary Smith was art director, Danny Daniels the choreographer. Jerry Van Dyke, the brother of the more famous Dick Van Dyke, had been hired as "the second banana;" show-biz lingo for a co-entertainer in tandem with Judy.

Mel Tormé with Judy on her TV show singing the most popular song he ever wrote, "The Christmas Song ("*Chestnuts Roasting on an Open Fire*').

It was all very "Christmasy."

Unlike some of her directors, Schlatter worked well with Judy. "I framed her as someone very special, with a background of elegance and incomparable talent. I framed her every performance as a major event, because I think it was."

Schlatter was best known for his hit TV series, *Rowan and Martin's Laugh-In*. [*Inaugurated in 1968, and wildly popular with the "counterculture" in an era of rapid social change, it eventually ran for 140 episodes on NBC.*] A son of Alabama who wandered West, he had first met Judy when he was running Ciro's on Sunset Strip.

Years later, he would produce *The Ultimate Event* (1989), a TV special starring Liza Minnelli, who appeared on it with Frank Sinatra and Sammy Davis, Jr. Schlatter would also produce prime-time shows for Dinah Shore and Shirley MacLaine.

Schlatter phoned Mel Tormé and invited him to join the series' talented staff as a writer of special musical material for Judy and perhaps to join her for an occasional performance beside her. At first, Tormé resisted, but he relented when Schlatter predicted, "We're going to send *Bonanza* wandering down that lonesome trail into the setting sunset. Mel, Judy wants you. I know you won't let her down."

Nicknamed "The Velvet Fog," Tormé was a musician, singer, composer, drummer, arranger, actor, and author. Singer Ethel Waters once said, "Mel Tormé is the only white man who sings with the soul of a black man."

[*One of his alltime successes as a singer and composer, with Robert Welles, was his holiday hit, "The Christmas Song (Chestnuts Roasting on an Open Fire)," first published in 1945.*]

Born to Russian Jewish parents, Tormé was a child prodigy, like Judy herself, except that he waited until he was four years old before performing professionally.

In Hollywood in 1943, he made his movie debut in Frank Sinatra's first film, *Higher and Higher*. By 1947, he was a teen idol in the musical, *Good News*.

He would later write a memoir, *The Other Side of the Rainbow*, in which

Judy does not appear in a flattering light. The small book traces Tormé's roller-coaster ride through the triumphs and disasters of her short-lived CBS-TV career. On looking back, he reflected on his months with the show:

"I wish I had known then as much as we all know today about the pervasive effects that alcohol and drugs have on the human condition. Judy's chemical dependency certainly played a large part in triggering her sometimes aberrant behavior. I was ignorant of how the long-time use of uppers and downers and liquor had come to affect her by 1963. She was not perfect. She was human, and I became impatient with her human frailties. I am rather ashamed of that."

Jerry Van Dyke, irrepressible and sometimes abrasive, vamping with Judy on her show.

He was her "Second Banana," but he wasn't always funny.

As the show continued to shakily look for its footings, Jerry Van Dyke was brought in to add a "family friendly" feeling to the lineup, but he often came across as a "cornball" and didn't blend well with Judy's image. Schlatter recalled his first meeting with Van Dyke, whose casting he had opposed. His first words to the comic were, "I don't know what I'm going to do with you."

[Months later, after he was booted from the show, Van Dyke went on to play attorney David Crabtree in My Mother, the Car *(1965), the worst TV sitcom of all time.]*

According to Judy, "Say what you will about Jerry, he was one of the best poker players I ever faced off against. We often played a late-night game after the show. We were joined by others until dawn. The only way I could win was by cheating."

Still friends after all these years, Mickey Rooney and Judy sat, when the camera was rolling, on director's chairs, viewing stills from their former heydays. Images that flashed across the background included scenes from MGM's *Girl Crazy* (1943). "Such moments between them came off beautifully as they reminisced about their long-ago careers," Schlatter said.

"Contrary to many press reports, Judy and I never had that grand romance," Rooney said. "Since we were kids, both of us had enough lovers to fill a phone book." When I appeared on TV with her, she was involved with André Phillipe, a French actor and singer who sang duets with her in her dressing room—and did other things, too. When she wasn't with him, she was getting plugged by Glenn Ford."

"Depending on her mood," Rooney continued, "Judy could be quite loving with André, but at other times, when she was too overly medicated, she would be hostile to him. Sometimes, she treated him like a servant. He was always there by her side when she wasn't needed on camera. I noticed one time, he lit a cigarette for her, and she accepted it. But when he went to kiss her on the cheek, she pushed him away. Everyone was watching

Judy, wondering what she was going to do next. Her mood swings went from Alaska to Florida, always in the extreme. But don't get me wrong. I loved the girl dearly."

"In spite of all the tension backstage, Judy on camera was magnificent," Rooney said, "When she sang 'Old Man River,' something usually sung by a man, there was bedlam in the studio. The crew had witnessed one of the most memorable moments in show business, later to be heard by millions across the land."

"Cast and crew got used to Judy ringing them up at four in the morning, inviting them over for a drink. Those who accepted her invitation became known as 'the Dawn Patrol,'" Rooney said. "But she knew better than to pull that shit with me."

The CBS brass wanted Judy to end the episode with her rendition of "Over the Rainbow," but she refused. "I've got rainbows coming out of my ass."

Judy on a Bad Day

She insisted on ending the show with a vaudeville number, "Maybe I'll Come Back" from 1911. Frank Gumm had taught it to her as a little girl. During her rendition, she spoofed her own image:

I will come back when the elephants roost in the trees.
I will come back when the birds make love to the bees
I will come back when the sun refuses to shine
And President Coolidge* is a cousin of mine.
I will come back when the fish walk around on two feet
And promenade up and down Washington Street
When the snow has turned from white to blue,
Then maybe I'll come back to you."

*[At subsequent performances, she substituted the phrase "President Coolidge" with the name of a person more current.]

A critic for the *Los Angeles Times* reviewed the videotaping, although the fully tweaked and edited footage would not be aired until December 8, almost six months later.

"Judy Garland, almost paper thin, stood on her spike heels, feet wide apart in that way of hers, rolled those wide, haunted eyes at the lights above, and sang her heart out. The audience was with her all the way. She seemed so self-assured, so self-possessed, so happy in her work, that it sounds good for the shows."

Hollywood critic Tom Mackin was not so optimistic. "The talk of the TV industry is *The Judy Garland Show*. Stars, producers, directors at NBC and ABC as well as CBS, are betting the controversial, troubled star will not make it through the entire season."

Edith Head, her dress and gown designer, told the press, "I'm designing a wardrobe for Miss Garland that will not overwhelm her. I want the audience to remember Judy's performance, not my costume designs."

Four days after Head made that statement to the press, CBS fired her.

***

After Head's dismissal, fashion designer Ray Aghayan took over, creating a wardrobe that made Judy look more glamourous than she'd ever been before on TV. "Her bosom was not big, but her saving grace, at least from a designer's viewpoint, were her long legs. After modeling my clothes, she stared at herself in a full-length mirror. She turned to me, pretending to be terrorized. 'If I look this good, I'm afraid to face the crew. They'll rip off my gown and gang bang me.'"

In their attempts to attract a younger audience, CBS brought in singer Judy Hensky, a "Joan Baez imitator" (Judy's words). After hearing her sing, Judy reviewed her, informally, as "Easily forgettable, heading for oblivion."

Mel Tormé suggested that Judy sing "Birds Won't Bud," which she had previously recorded for Decca. "No, not that one," she protested. "It makes me fart."

Beginning with slight disagreements, Judy's tiffs with Tormé grew more and more heated as the series progressed. According to Tormé, "I joined the rest of the crew in calling her 'The Concrete Canary.'"

"Appearing with Count Basie was like having a shotgun at your back," Judy claimed. She joined with him for a rendition of his hit song, "April in Paris." Another of her numbers, "As Long as He Needs Me," stood out among the rest—at least in the view of some of her critics.

According to Tormé, "In the beginning, we had high hopes for the series and continued to talk about beating out *Bonanza*. But we were running blindly toward the cliff, poor unsuspecting lemmings."

"Liza had far to go as a performer," George Schlatter claimed.

"At first, she seemed nervous going on with her mother, since she didn't want to mess up the series. But she only added to its allure, and mother-daughter singing together was one hell of an act."

***

On July 16, 1963, Judy began

videotaping the third episode of her TV series, this one a novelty in which she co-starred with Liza Minnelli. Also on the show were Soupy Sales, the Brothers Castro, and Jerry Van Dyke, who was becoming more and more her "regular," and in the opinion of some of Judy's fans, increasingly abrasive and distracting.

Tormé later claimed, "When I worked with Judy alone, something seemed wrong with her. In her first rendition of 'Come Rain Or Come Shine,' she slurred the words, the 'ne' in 'shine completely lost. Her eyes looked glazed. But two days later, she was back in full voice—in fact, the show turned out to be a blockbuster."

Judy opened the show with the Gershwin song, "Liza," which she rendered with tender emotion. As she sang, blown-up images of her daughter from infancy to the present day were flashed across the background.

Their duets were memorable, including "We Could Make Such Beautiful Music Together," (which was true in reality), and "The Best Is Yet to Come." They finished with a soft shoe rendition of "Bye, Bye Baby." Singing "Two Lost Souls" from the hit Broadway show, *Damn Yankees,* they each wore a tramp costume designed by Aghayan.

The Brothers Castro were most often compared to the singing group, "The Lettermen," with castanets singing "Malagueña." Soupy Sales did a comic sketch, playing a fanatical Garland fan interacting with Van Dyke.

In the control room on the last day of taping was Vincente Minnelli, an observer, not a director. He gave the show five stars, his highest rating, but admitted, "I'm prejudiced."

***

In the early 1960s and beyond, as TV variety shows become more and more popular, a race developed for the booking and showcasing of celebrity guest stars. Schlatter asked Judy to compile a list—"with comments"—about actors or singers she wanted to invite onto her show.

Frank Sinatra topped her list. When Schlatter phoned him, he said, "Sure, I'll go on, but Judy has to ask me personally." [*As it happened, Sinatra never appeared because Aubrey intervened, nixing it because he had already seen a TV special populated with Judy, Sinatra, and Dean Martin.*]

Then Carol Channing was approached. She and Judy were each well known for their deadly impersonations of the other, so Judy thought it would be a "hoot" to replicate some of them on the same TV episode: According to Judy, "Carol could sing 'Over the Rainbow,' and I could be Lorelei Lee belting out 'Diamonds Are a Girl's Best Friend.'"

Betty Grable and Dan Dailey (Judy's former lover) were considered as temporary stage mates for Judy, replicating some of their numbers from musicals made at Fox in the late 1940s.

Carol Lawrence, now married to Robert Goulet (another of Judy's former lovers) was envisioned singing two solos, plus a duet with Judy.

Van Johnson, who had worked smoothly with Judy during the filming of *In the Good Old Summertime* (1949), was also considered as a possible guest on the show.

Judy then began lobbying for an appearance on her show by the husband-and-wife team, Tony Martin and Cyd Charisse, perhaps an updated rendition of the "Slaughter on Tenth Avenue," the musical ballet by Richard Rodgers and choreography (for its original 1936 production) by Georges Balanchine.

On another occasion, as part of her "wish list" for visiting guests, Judy said, "What about Fred Astaire? He's still got some fancy steps in him, and we could reprise some of the dance routines from 'Easter Parade.'"

She went on to suggest, "Bobby Darin would be a natural singing 'Mack the Knife,' and I could impersonate Lotte Lenya," Judy suggested. "Incidentally, Liza might get involved, too. I heard she once had a crush on him."

After that her other suggestions for guests she wanted on her show grew rather erratic and bizarre. She wanted to bring on Marlon Brando for a comic restaging—almost a burlesque—of Tennessee Williams' *A Streetcar Named Desire*. "I could be Blanche DuBois with a difference: Instead of him raping Blanche, I'd forcefully pursue *him*."

She also suggested Rock Hudson, with whom she'd had a brief fling. She cited his brilliant and stunning appearance in 1958 with Mae West at the Academy Awards, where their shared presentation of "Baby It's Cold Outside" had been the highlight of the show. "I could dress in Mae West drag," Judy said.

Her most provocative suggestion involved Charlton Heston as part of a comic sketch. She'd heard that years before he became famous, he'd worked as a nude model for art students in Manhattan. "I'd play an art student more interested in enjoying his body than in painting it. Of course, we'd let him wear a loincloth."

For reasons not entirely clear, none of Judy's recommendations about guests she wanted, except for Darin, were ever used.

***

Before the fourth episode of Judy's TV series was videotaped, Hunt Stromberg, Jr., the son of the legendary film producer, Hunt Stromberg, Sr., intruded into Judy's universe, muscling in on the territory previously staked out by George Schlatter.

He had long been known as a "CBS hot shot," the young *protégé* of James Aubrey, the studio chief himself. At the age of twenty-three, Stromberg Jr. became one of the youngest theatrical producers in the entertainment industry when he revived, on Broadway in 1945, Victor Herbert's operetta, *The Red Mill*.

Eventually, as a rising star at CBS, he was designated as the executive producer of such long-running TV classics as *The Beverly Hillbillies, Hogan's Heroes, Green Acres,* and *Gilligan's Island*.

With Aubrey's blessing, Stromberg moved in to take charge, aggressively maneuvering Schlatter into a radically altered "new vision" for Judy's TV series: "I want her to be more like the girl next door, not some glamourous super star."

When Judy heard that, she quipped, "If the bastards want the girl next door, why not hire Jane Powell?"

[Singing star Powell had worked on musicals when she and Judy were both ingénues at MGM. She had a sweet, wholesome image, so different from Judy's. In fact, long after her memory had faded from the consciousness of many younger consumers, she entitled her memoir, The Girl Next Door.*]*

Simultaneous with the other whirlwinds he was unleashing, Aubrey voiced strong objections to Judy's propensity, on camera, to get "touchy-feely" with her TV guests, citing her onscreen behavior with Robert Goulet, Frank Sinatra, and Dean Martin. "What in hell is she trying to do? Give them a hard-on on screen?"

When she was made aware of his objections, she exploded in fury: "Who do these jerks think I am? They don't understand my allure, which I perfected on stage during my concerts."

In an interview with Howard Tucker of *Newsweek,* Judy said, "I've always touched people. It's a habit, not nervousness, but pure affection. I'm a woman who needs to reach out and take forty million people into my arms. But CBS has warned me to watch myself."

She later told Edgar Penton of *Show Time,* "I tackled this series because I wanted to be a whole, total person. I wanted to sing anything I wanted to, including *Old Man River,* an oddity for a woman. And I want to talk, just talk, to my guests. Not just come out and say, 'I'm Judy Garland and that's that and now I'm going to sing a song.' I want to carry on a conversation with someone. You know, I bet before the series went on the air that a lot of people had no idea I could talk without someone writing a script for me."

When Stromberg relayed Judy's objections to Aubrey, he fired off a memo to Schlatter: "Unscripted touching is not allowed on national TV. It is also up to you to humanize Judy."

When she was informed of that new corporate mandate, "Judy was more pissed off than I'd ever seen her," Schlatter said. "'What in hell does 'humanize' mean?,' she said in a rage. 'Does Aubrey think I'm a damn robot? I

URGENT
To: Judy Garland

From: CBS-TV

Re: Offending your viewers

Dear Judy:

PLEASE DO NOT TOUCH YOUR GUESTS

There was deep anxiety from studio brass that Judy—always a hit on late-night TV—was too touchy-feely with her guests in this "family-friendly" timeslot.

Here's **Judy with Robert Goulet** having a sophisticated and intimate conversation that was distributed nationwide and judged as unacceptably relaxed, even permissive.

Other menfolk that raised the anxiety of CBS in reference to her "touchy-feely tendencies" included Frank Sinatra and Dean Martin, both of whom she'd already had affairs with.

don't even know what de-glamourizing or humanizing me is—I don't feel I'm glamourous or inhuman.'"

***

For the fourth episode in her TV series, Lena Horne was designated as Judy's guest of honor. They had long been friends, perhaps more than that. Frank Sinatra told his fellow Rat Packers that he suspected "a tinge of lesbianism there."

The gap-toothed British comedian, Terry Thomas, was also brought in for that episode—in his case, for comic relief. With his handlebar mustache, he was often cast as a hissing British ninny.

Horne and Judy bonded over dinner and, since they had not seen each other in some time, talked over this current stage of their lives. Like Judy, Horne had suffered a rough chapter in her life after leaving MGM. She'd been saddled with a public image as a "race agitator."

She told Judy, "I've fought a lot of battles just to be me. My identity is clear. I am a black woman. If somebody doesn't like that, to hell with them. I no longer have to be a mere 'credit' in films like I was at MGM, where all the footage and music I made was cut from the roles they screened in the South. I no longer have to be a 'dark-skinned imitation of a white woman' that Hollywood wanted me to be. *I am me!* I am nobody else."

[Horne found more acceptance on TV than she'd ever derived from her work in films, especially when she appeared on Your Show of Shows, a 90-minute weekly variety show broadcast live from 1950 to 1954. As her career progressed, her success came more from nightclubs and from record sales.

Ironically, years later, Horne would play Glinda, the Good Witch of the North, in the 1978 film adaption of the all-black stage musical, The Wiz, the Broadway adaption of Judy's 1939 classic film, The Wizard of Oz.]

After the warmth of their dialogue at dinner the night before, Horne was puzzled when Judy didn't show up for rehearsals the next day

Lena Horne told Judy, "I'm tired of being offered only small singing parts in all-white musicals. Like, for example, the tiny appearance I slaved over in *Words and Music* with you and Gene Kelly.

I want a chance to do dramatic roles and have the story spin around me for a change— perhaps with Harry Belafonte as my leading man."

The chief honcho at CBS was **James Aubrey**, also known as "the Smiling Cobra."

Jacqueline Susann used him as inspiration for the brutalizing media mogul she inserted into one of her novels, *The Love Machine.*

He and Judy feuded bitterly over her TV series. "He wants to turn me into Betty Crocker," she lamented.

and again, the day after that, and beyond. Finally, from afar, she got angry at Judy for her lack of consideration. Tormé described her frustration:

"Her celebrated dimples deepened, her eyes widened, as if she were watching a horror movie. She was hopping mad, and her target was Judy."

"Who in hell does she thing she is?" Horne shouted at Tormé.

Their performances, and the episode itself, went off reasonably well, but suffered from a lack of coordination. With Lena, Judy sang "Day In, Day Out" as a novelty. One segment of the final cut showed them performing each other's hits, Judy singing "Honeysuckle Rose" and Lena rejoining with "Meet Me in St. Louis." In contrast, Judy's, Lena's, and Terry Thomas's song-and-dance rendition of Noël Coward's "Mad Dogs and Englishmen," should have been rehearsed more.

Judy's "Born in a Trunk" segment included some amusing banter about losing the Oscar to Grace Kelly in 1954.

Then, at one point, as the cameras rolled, Judy referred to Horne and herself as "two rejects from MGM," a reference that made every insider on the set wince. The line was cut before the show was aired by the network.

When Schlatter showed up for work on July 30, he didn't know that he'd be directing his final episode, one that wouldn't be aired until December 15. Judy co-starred with the very talented Tony Bennett and with comedian Jack Carter.

Although Bennett was in top form, Judy was not. She seemed distracted. Tormé later defined her *schtick* that night as "a study in mediocrity."

On August 2, Tormé showed up at Television City. There, he encountered Schlatter, who told him that after six weeks of creative input and the directing of five episodes, he'd been fired. "Maybe Aubrey will fire you next," he warned Tormé.

Ominously, production on the remainder of the series was then suspended for four weeks.

In the aftermath of Schlatter's firing, and after that, the dismissal of the show's choreographer (Danny Daniels) and several of its writers, Judy would be hurled into a CBS cyclone. As one writer predicted, "Even Dorothy Gale in *Wizard* could not have survived the coming storm."

***

Buffeted by the shifting and difficult-to-define stresses associated with her show, Judy submitted to a five-week shutdown of production. Rehearsals and videotapings of *The Judy Garland Show* were suspended until a different creative staff could be hired.

Lena Horne as "Glinda the Good Witch" in *The Wiz*, Sidney Lumet's 1978 Motown adaptation of Judy's 1939 classic, *The Wizard of Oz*.

Judy flew from Los Angeles to New York with André Phillipe, her lover, the French singer. But once installed there at the St. Regis, she dumped him, telling him "goodbye forever." He flew back to Paris the next day.

During the next few weeks, she was seen around Manhattan at all the "hot spots," often with a different man every night. Many of these were gay dancers from Broadway shows, who seemed to worship her. "I love New York, and New York loves Judy Garland," she told columnist Dorothy Kilgallen.

Frank Sinatra was in town, and phoned to invite her to his favorite bistro, Jilly's. "My affair with him was long ago," she said. "But he remained my steadfast friend."

He was drinking heavily and often spoke in blunt terms. "I hear you and Eddie Fisher get together on occasion to bump pussies. After Ol' Blue Eyes, sweet little Eddie boy must be a disappointment."

At Jilly's one night, Judy met Bobby Cole, a New Yorker who was known for his jazz singing and piano playing. Sinatra praised him as "my favorite saloon entertainer."

A decade younger than Judy, Cole played in other New York venues, including at some dives in Greenwich Village. He also entertained in Miami Beach at the Fontainebleau Hotel and in Las Vegas at Caesar's Palace and at The Sands.

Judy met him and reportedly was entranced by him, little knowing at the time that he would loom large in her future.

In the dying days of August, she flew back to Los Angeles, where she experienced both a real-live heat wave and also a symbolic one heating up everything associated with CBS. "There was a damn purge going on ordered by the big enchilada, James Aubrey," she said. "Heads were rolling. I feared that little Miss Judy Garland was about to become the Marie Antoinette of 1963. I was stunned and bewildered."

She learned that a ready-to-roll script for the filming of her next episode, a program that would have co-starred her with Nat King Cole singing together such hits as "Mona Lisa," had been scrapped by Aubrey himself.

Cole told the press, "I was dismissed because I'm black."

That was probably not the case, as major upheavals were exploding throughout CBS. Cole was not the only artist who'd been dismissed. Judy learned that an armada of her future guests had also been dropped. The hit list included Betty Grable, Dan Dailey, and Eydie Gormé, the wife of singer Steve Lawrence. Also notified that their services would not be needed were Phil Harris and his wife, Alice Faye.

Judy had barely settled in after her return from New York City when she was summoned into Aubrey's West Coast office at CBS's Television City. Aubrey was blunt in his assessment of her: "I've sat through your first shows for the series, and I was terribly disappointed. You've got to do better...or else!"

She was horrified by his assessment, and that night, after lots of pills and some heavy boozing, she slit her wrists in yet another attempted suicide.

On August 26, a nurse who doubled as a paid informer to the press, tipped them off that patient #63-11859 (i.e., Judy Garland) had been committed to Cedars of Lebanon Hospital in Los Angeles after yet another of her suicide attempts. A spokesperson for CBS denied it, claiming that she had checked in only for a "routine yearly check-up." Within a few days, she was released and sent home.

A Hollywood executive, Sherry Lansing, one of Aubrey's best friends, heard about his treatment of Judy and remarked, "Jim is different. He does his own dirty work. He's one of those guys who dares to say, 'I didn't like your movie or performance.' Directness is disarming to performers like Judy, who is accustomed to hearing sugar-coated praise whether it's deserved or not. It's tough on people like her who need constant approval, even if it isn't deserved. At the time of her show, Judy was a star enveloped in myth and legend. She might have come to believe the image her most devoted fans projected of her."

Judy was outspoken, too, and she had her own appraisal of Aubrey, which she freely shared and which was probably reported back to him. "I know now why he's nicknamed 'The Smiling Cobra,'" she said. "He's also 'The Hustler's Hustler.' He's said to have a 'smell' for programs that appeal to blue-collar viewers. He 'smells' all right."

[As time went by, Aubrey became known for his support of shows that appealed to the widest public, including The Beverly Hillbillies, *even though he expressed contempt for "those ignorant bastards who watch I Love Lucy."*

"The jerks who watch that stupid show are dumb and dumber," he said. "The only civilized places in America are Hollywood and New York. The rest of the country is strictly fly over, except for Las Vegas."

Aubrey had another reputation and that was his "addiction to broads." He resented that, claiming, "I don't like broads. I go for sexy dolls. Garland is a broad, Marilyn Monroe is a sexy doll, although she fell apart. It's rumored that I screwed Garland in the beginning before turning on her, and I'll not admit to that one way or the other. Frankly, Julie Newmar and Rhonda Fleming are more to my taste, especially the tall and sultry Julie."]

Then, Judy was informed by letter from Aubrey's office that her new producer would be Norman Jewison, who was a Protestant in spite of his name. Since he had been her original choice as her show's producer, she expressed no objection, even at this late stage of her show's development. Actually, she had worked smoothly with Jewison during his production of her "comeback" TV special in 1962, in which she'd co-starred with Sinatra and Dean Martin.

In 1958, Jewison was recruited by NBC in New York City and assigned to *Your Hit Parade* and *The Andy Williams Show.* He also helmed TV specials for Jackie Gleason, Danny Kaye, and Harry Belafonte.

His success with those entertainers led to his involvement with Judy's TV show at CBS, where he would direct episodes six to thirteen.

"Judy is a sophisticated performer," he said, "appealing to intelligent and literate people. She is definitely not the girl next door. She will never attract the meat-and-potatoes mass audience drawn to *Bonanza.* It is foolish to even let her try."

According to Jewison, "Judy is a bit of Sammy Davis, Jr., combined with a spoonful or two of the evangelist Aimee Semple McPherson, and a *soupçon* of Greta Garbo. CBS wanted to turn her into a combination of Perry

Como, Dinah Shore, and Bing Crosby. But what's wrong with her just being Judy Garland?"

He didn't agree with those attempts "to make the sacred cow less sacred. We can't let her be subjected to Van Dyke's stupid jokes that denigrate her weight, her reputation for unreliability, and the lows and highs of her career. I also want a new feature called 'Be My Guest,' with Mel Tormé's writing tailored material for the guest of the week to perform with Judy near the top of every show."

Jewison opted to hire Steve Lawrence and June Allyson for the first episode (#6) he directed. It was videotaped on September 13, although not aired until October 27. Jerry Van Dyke, who had a contract, was reluctantly kept on the payroll, at least for a while.

A native of Toronto, **Norman Jewison** was an actor, film director, producer, and the founder of the Canadian Film Centre.

After directing some of the episodes of Judy's shows for CBS, he moved on —with relief—to other venues.

He eventually received Oscar nominations as Best Director for three of his films: *In the Heat of the Night* (1967); *Fiddler on the Roof* (1971); and *Moonstruck* (1987).

***

James Aubrey arranged for Norman Jewison to receive a fee of $100,000 for his direction of eight episodes of *The Judy Garland Show*. "After that, I'm out of here," Jewison said. "The question is, will Judy believe the adage that the show must go on?"

With expenses mounting, the cost to CBS of Judy's show had ballooned to $200,000 per episode in an era when that amount of money could have financed a full-length motion picture.

"James Aubrey, when he was in Los Angeles, never let up on the pressure," Jewison said. "He'd come down from his ivory tower to the set, put his arm around her, and paint 'The Yellow Brick Road' for her. Then he'd summon me to his office later that afternoon and stab her in the back."

Judy was on to him, privately calling him "Turd Blossom," that lovely flower that blooms from cowshit.

"Before rehearsals for our first episode began, I sat Judy down for a come-to-Jesus 'Heads Up,'" Jewison said. "In spite my last name, I was a Canadian Christian."

"Here's the deal, Judy," he told her. "We've got a weekly show to do, and we can't do it from your bedroom, showing your bandaged wrists, as you recover from another of your god damn suicide attempts. And we can't do it if you do show up but then refuse to come out of your dressing room. If you pull that shit with me, I'll come at you and force you out. We're going to do it my way before Aubrey shows you the highway."

"I'll be there," she promised. "You can count on me. I'll wow them so much I'll knock off their jockey shorts exposing their tiny dicks."

"I don't think I ever heard a star make such a commitment before," he said, later.

"I had to keep Jerry Van Dyck because of some contract," Jewison lamented. "But I didn't want him. In the role of Judy's second banana, he was wrong, completely wrong." Actually, my dream choice would have been Jonathan Winters, but, alas, you don't get what you want in life. I learned that the day I found out there was no such thing as the Tooth Fairy."

"I was also stuck with Mel Tormé, about the only one who had survived Aubrey's massacres," Jewison confessed. "The person I really wanted was Kay Thompson, Judy's longtime girlfriend. She would have been terrific. I took a chance and phoned her, but she turned me down for reasons of her own, all the while reassuring me that 'I still adore that little girl with all my heart.'"

Jewison eventually met with Tormé, assuring him, "I'll handle Judy. She'll be no problem for me."

"Don't be so sure," Tormé warned. "At the beginning of all this, she arrived on the set with George Schlatter, and for a while, the two of them did the *do-si-doe* together, but then, one morning, and for several mornings to come, she was a no-show."

"During one of my conversations with Judy in her dressing room, an emergency call came in from Sid Luft," Jewison claimed, "She wandered off to take it in her bathroom, where she turned on the running water as a means of drowning her voice. But as she continued talking, through the closed door, I heard cuss words that only an American, never a Canadian, might utter. Finally, she opened the door and I distinctly heard her farewell line to Luft: 'I'm still going to divorce you, but I want you to know that I think you're a hell of a son of a bitch.'"

News that Aubrey was planning to drop Judy and was searching for her replacement spread to the press, perhaps a leak from someone who worked in his office. The *Hollywood Reporter* was the first to claim that Aubrey was faithfully watching Vic Damone sing every Thursday night on *The Lively Ones*. [The Lively Ones *was a musical TV variety show configured from 1962-1963 as a 16-episode summer replacement by NBC for "Hazel."*]

The *Hollywood Reporter* went on to write, "We hear that

A Playboy and His Mates

Vic Damone in a publicity photo for the recordings of his performance on the then-popular variety show, *The Lively Ones*. Its mood and setup evokes the "Playmates and Bunnies" being publicized at the time—with resounding success—by *Playboy's* Hugh Hefner.

To Judy, it appeared that the addition of Damone as a regular feature on her show, was CBS's attempt to upstage her.

the handsome, charming Italian singer is the number one choice to replace, in mid-season, a certain CBS live show series that features a fabled musical star of yesterday."

More reports about Damone appeared in the press, one paper going so far as to claim that Aubrey would rather hear him sing "On the Street Where You Live" from *My Fair Lady* than listen to Judy warbling, for the fiftieth time, "Over the Rainbow."

Another trade paper noted, "Judy Garland has not yet had the premiere of her projected TV series, but current speculation is that either Vic Damone or Robert Goulet is going to replace her at least by November. James Aubrey, so we are told, is very disappointed at what he has seen so far on videotape."

Aubrey was also spotted in Los Angeles at The Greek Theatre, attending a sold-out performance of Harry Belafonte. Later, he was reported to have visited the singer backstage, in his dressing room, perhaps with the intention of having him replace Judy Garland. "Velvet-voiced Belafonte, who was raised in Jamaica, could open the show with 'Yellow Bird,'" wrote one columnist, but any association of Belafonte with CBS's variety show never materialized. Before that, CBS had struck out with another black singer, too: Nat King Cole.

To top it off, in a way that probably terrorized poor Judy, a London tabloid reported that "someone—not Dirk Bogarde—is writing a book about Judy's 'unprofessional' behavior on the set of her last film, *I Could Go on Singing*."

Jewison told Judy that her next two celebrity guests would be June Allyson, her longtime friend from their days at MGM, and Steve Lawrence.

She was well aware that Lawrence was being weighed as her replacement in case her ratings tanked, but she put up a brave front and made no mention to him of the circulating rumors.

Lawrence came off very well in his solo numbers. "Time After Time" and "I've Got You Under My Skin," and he and Judy also blended well in "Be My Guest." Judy, Allyson, and Lawrence also performed well as a trio in a "Salute to MGM," singing such numbers as Lawrence performing "Look for the Silver Lining," and Judy's solo rendition of "Till the Clouds Roll By."

It was widely rumored that the husband-and-wife singing team, **Steve Lawrence and Eydie Gourmé** ("The Queen of Sophisticated Pop") would be reconfigured as Judy Garland's replacement if James Aubrey decided to fire "the undependable, always late Miss Garland" from her TV series.

[Eydie Gormé was announced for a September 11 taping with Judy, but at the last minute, the engagement with her was mysteriously canceled.

Judy may have gotten some "sweet satisfaction" in 1965 when Lawrence was chosen by Aubrey to headline a weekly variety show for CBS, with the very gay Charles Nelson Reilly as his second banana. The series was not a hit and was can-

558

celed after four months.]

As its musical arranger, Tormé pronounced Lawrence "a thing of beauty, professional and prepared to his fingertips. Now if Sadie (his pet name for Judy) could only stay in control of her *Liebfraumilch.*"

Since Allyson had arrived on the set, she and Judy had been celebrating their reunion with bottles of that brand of wine [i.e. *Liebfraumilch*, distributed by Blue Nun wines]. Apparently, Allyson was matching Judy glass for glass.

Tormé went to Judy's dressing room to summon them. He found the "*Liebfraumilch* Girls" tipsy—more than tipsy, actually—like a pair of giggly, girlish Bobbsey Twins. "I came upon them as they were discussing dick sizes of lovers they'd shared in common. They included John F. Kennedy and Dean Martin, with a harsh appraisal of David Rose, Judy's first husband."

But once on camera, both performers proved to be troupers, bantering with each other and making jokes. Allyson claimed that she and Judy "were so short because Louis B. Mayer kept beating us down."

Judy was greeted with wild applause for her rendition of "San Francisco" and "Born in a Trunk."

At the end of that episode's taping, and as a surprise, CBS had ordered a mammoth, many-tiered cake brought onto the set to celebrate Tormé's thirty-eighth birthday.

As it was wheeled in, Allyson stumbled and fell into the cake. She emerged laughing and coated with icing. Then she began throwing pieces of it at the cast and crew. The incident became notorious and received some press coverage the next morning. That brought a denial from Judy, who claimed (falsely) that "June and I were not intoxicated on the day of the taping, a completely false report. On occasion, we might have a glass of wine, but that is all."

***

On September 5, and despite Sid Luft's strident objections, a Los Angeles judge granted custody of Lorna and Joey to Judy. Their father was allowed visitation rights every other Wednesday and on weekends.

The next day, Luft phoned Judy and asked if he could dine with his kids at their home, since he was going to be away for some time on business. She agreed, promising that her housekeeper would welcome him and prepare and serve them dinner.

That night with Luft, his children, Joey and Lorna, learned their family's new setup and rules: He was

June Allyson with Judy in a comedy number built on the seductive legend of Cleopatra. Each is wearing a cobra headdress satirically inspired by the Serpent of the Nile.

Judy recalled, "Darling June was a serial seducer, and at times we often bedded the same men."

559

still committed to his role as their father, despite his new status as a short-term visitor.

As he was about to leave, Judy barged into the living room. The nanny was on the verge of ushering her children to bed. Judy kissed them good night before confronting Luft.

She poured herself a drink and offered him one, too. "Are you broke?" she bluntly asked.

"I've got ten dollars, so I can't take you out."

She walked over to her desk in the corner and wrote him a check for $10,000. "There's more where that came from, as I'm making the big ones."

"I hope some of it will go to pay off back taxes," he said. "We filed joint returns, which showed we owed them money. We haven't filed a tax return in three years. The IRS, I fear, will be cracking down on us soon."

"How dare you bring up tax problems with me now, when you know I'm under unbearable stress this month, making the debut of my show. You have no concern for my feelings!"

He started to apologize, but she burst into fury, tossing her drink in his face.

Although he desperately needed the money, he tore up the check and threw the pieces in her face.

In the hall, before he stalked away, he called back to her: "This time, I'm really walking out. This officially ends our husband-and-wife gig. From now on, I'll see you, maybe, when I visit my kids. And I'll definitely see you in the divorce courts."

Despondent, he returned to his seedy hotel room in downtown Los Angeles. A blinking pink neon sign outside his hotel window illuminated the dark street. He tried to sleep but woke up in a cold sweat within less than an hour. Dawn had not yet come.

He went to the dresser and removed his revolver. He stood for about an hour contemplating his next move. Her seriously thought about putting its barrel to his temple and pulling the trigger. "It would be real and not another Judy Garland stunt."

Finally, he took the revolver and fired into his mattress. To him, the shot seemed so loud it would wake up the hotel. But no one came. He assumed his fellow tenants, a coven of druggies, had been too stoned to notice.

He was leaving town on some ill-planned scheme to earn money in Las Vegas and would not see his children for months.

He later recalled, "Whatever bad things happened, you don't fall out of love with a Judy Garland. All I know is that I tried to save a woman who was breaking apart. I did the best I could. It just wasn't enough."

***

James Aubrey told Mel Tormé and Norman Jewison that the premiere of *The Judy Garland Show* would be a "make-or-break" rite of passage for its star. When they relayed that to Judy, she increased her intake of pills, perhaps as a means of easing her nervous obsessions.

She also learned that Aubrey didn't want to lead off the series with the episode that had nostalgically co-starred her with Mickey Rooney.

Instead, he preferred an all-new show that would pair Judy with Donald O'Connor, her limber-legged friend and co-star.

Tormé, the series' music director, and the writers were told that a radically reconfigured script had to be rehearsed and ready for taping on September 20, in time for the series' on-the-air premiere nine days later. Millions of Americans—or so it was believed—would be watching her either triumph "or fall on her ass," in the view of "The Smiling Cobra."

Several weeks had passed since she had last seen Liza, who was living in Manhattan and reported to be indulging in "heavy dating" with Tracy Everitt, her dancer boyfriend. She'd met him during her rehearsals for *Best Foot Forward*. He was appearing in a show on Broadway, *How to Succeed in Business Without Really Trying*.

Judy persuaded Jewison to have Everitt cast in her TV series. Soon, Liza and her boyfriend were flying into Los Angeles from New York for a reunion with her mother. Although Liza was only a teenager, Judy reportedly was happy to see her "so in love."

At CBS, Judy met up again with Donald O'Connor. *[Judy, at the age of 2½, and O'Connor, at 39 months, had each been pushed out onto a vaudeville stage.]*

She told him that *Singin' in the Rain* (1952), in which he had co-starred with Debbie Reynolds and Gene Kelly, had been her alltime favorite musical: "better than any musical I ever made for Mayer and MGM. Of course, your all-time masterpiece in that film was 'Be a Clown.'"

She also told him that he'd best showed off his dancing in *Call Me Madam* (1953), with Ethel Merman.

They both laughed and joked about his hit low-end movie series in which he'd co-starred with "Francis the Talking Mule," beginning in 1949.

He also brought her up to date on his private life: In 1956, he'd married Gloria Noble, with whom he produced three children. She noted that he was as nervous as she was, each of them smoking four packages of cigarettes a day. O'Connor also revealed that early in his career, Universal had hired actress Peggy Ryan and him to portray that studio's version of Mickey Rooney and Judy Garland in an All-American "Puppy Love, Next Door" *schtick*. "In that, we did not succeed," he confessed.

Jewison said that Judy and O'Connor on camera were the perfect troupers, having spent all of their lives in show business. Both of them shone brilliantly in a "Be My Guest" medley of songs, including "Inka Dinka Do." Another of their medleys evoked the days of Old Vaudeville, highlighted by a "soft shoe" number.

On the night of her show's premiere, Judy learned that Aubrey had negotiated with both Eddie Fisher and Robert Goulet to take it over if she faltered, and probably viewed it as yet another corporate betrayal.

When that episode went on the air, it competed in the same high-stakes time slot as NBC's *Bonanza,* challenging it for ratings. The Western series would in time become the longest-running series in the history of NBC. Launched in 1959, it didn't ride off into the sunset until 1973.

Its plot revolved around the saga of the Cartwright family, who lived in Virginia City, bordering Lake Tahoe, in Nevada in the 1860s. The family's Ponderosa Ranch became a household name across America. Lorne Green and Michael Landon headed its cast of players. [*Coincidentally, one of the musical composers associated with the show was David Rose, Judy's first husband.*]

O'Connor visited Judy the day after the reviews came out. CBS had imported newspapers from across the country, and on the day of O'Connor's visit, he found dozens of them scattered across the room.

Variety's opinion was that "Judy Garland, youthful and sprightly at forty, was in fine fettle. She's in a position to whittle on and perhaps even surpass the Nielsen numbers scored by *Bonanza.*

The Judy Garland Show's competitor, sharing the same prime-time slot, was **Bonanza** one of the most spectacular TV successes in the history of media.

Lorne Green, his TV sons, and the passion among TV viewers for all things western and cowboy-related, were fierce competition, indeed.

However, it's not a perfect show, being long on nostalgia and short on bounce and zip."

The *Los Angeles Herald-Examiner* wrote: "For the plain truth of it, Judy Garland can do no wrong. When she is nervous, the audience doesn't fidget. The crowd "feels" for her and goes right along with the tension. She captured us within five minutes."

The critic for *The New York Herald Tribune* noted, "Never looking better, Judy Garland worked a wizard's sell in her big variety numbers and was sparkling and magnetic. For expert showmanship, and simple human appeal, there's no one to compare to her."

Coming in for the most criticism were the comic antics of Jerry Van Dyke and the scriptwriters themselves for "weak material in the sketches."

Judy showed O'Connor her favorite review. It was from President John F. Kennedy, sent directly from the White House: "Congratulations on a wonderful show last night. I know it will be a bit hit in the coming season."

Jack Gould, writing in *The New York Times,* said, "What should never happen to Judy Garland did last evening at the CBS premiere of her weekly program. The busybodies got so in the way that the singer never had a chance to sing out as only she can. To call the hour a grievous disappointment would be to miss the point. It was an absolute mystery. The thinking of CBS executives was to develop a 'new' Judy, one who would indulge in light banter and make way for suitable guests to share the weekly tasks. Those telephones on the twentieth floor of CBS's home should buzz this morning with but one directive to Hollywood—*Free* Judy."

On the Nielsen rating, her opening got a 33.9 score and a 44.0 share of the viewing audience. But in just a short time, it fell below the ratings for *Bonanza* and would never top the ratings for that series. Judy begged Aubrey to reassign her to a new time slot, but he refused.

Michael Dann, the talent chief for CBS, privately delivered his own assessment to the cast and crew: "In our views, Miss Garland should no longer appear in comic sketches. Nor should she be cast as other characters. In the future, she should be no one but herself."

Behind Tormé's back, Judy began demanding a new musical arranger.

***

For Judy's next taping, on September 27, two days before the premiere of her series, she was given an odd cast. It was spearheaded by heartthrob George Maharis, an actor famous for starring for three seasons (1960-1963) of the four-season hit TV series, *Route 66*. At the height of his fame at the time, he recorded several pop music albums. He told Judy that he'd had to leave the series for health reasons, including hepatitis.

"If I kept going at the grueling pace I was going, I might have ended up dead. Even if you have four million in the bank, you can't buy another liver."

"Been there, done that, except for the mil in the bank," she answered.

Maharis and Judy bonded. She found him handsome, charming, and sexy, though her inner radar signaled that she was not his type.

"She was as friendly to me as she was open," he recalled.

In a joint decision, they selected the song, "Side by Side" as their duet. She had been criticized for her excessive touching of her guests, but as the cameras rolled, it was Maharis who kept hugging and kissing her.

Judy was cast in one episode as part of an "odd couple," teamed as she was with the fabled baseball coach, Leo Durocher. Together, they sang "Take Me Out to the Ball Game." Incorrectly, she referred to his team as the Brooklyn Dodgers, although that team had long ago relocated to Los Angeles.

In reference to Durocher, Judy lamented to Maharis, "I requested as my guest Bing Crosby, Noël Coward, or Gene Kelly. You sure don't get what you want in life, especially when it comes to husbands."

Judy appeared with The Dillards, a rustic "clawfoot banjo, porchboard, vocalist, and guitar group" that later in their lives defined themselves as "grounded in the values of Andy Griffith's Mayberry."

According to Judy, one of the most sophisticated women in the world, "They were hillbillies. I was forced to sing 'Y'all.'"

Her best solo and most tender moment came later, during her on-camera delivery of "I Wish You Love."

That episode with Maharis received her rock-bottom worst reviews so far. Some critics called her guests "second rate." Van Dyke's comedy routines were defined as "poorly written." Maharis himself came under fire for being "nonmusical." Even so, one reviewer referred to Judy as "shining brightly as the star."

Maharis later said, "Judy is a honeypot who draws bees."

She told Mel Tormé, "If only I had a dick, I could make out like a bandit in this town."

[After Judy's death in 1973, Maharis became one of the first celebrities to pose nude for Playgirl. *As Johnny Carson said, "It takes guts for a man to pose nude in a stable with a horse."*

Judy buried that episode, moving on to face the videotaping of what came to be the most celebrated show of the entire series. Norman Jewison told the *Los Angeles Times*, "By appearing in this TV series, Judy Garland has destroyed her reputation as a legend."

When she read that, she responded, "Like hell I have."

***

Judy was notified that she would be teamed with the new singing sensation, Barbra Streisand, for Episode Nine, scheduled for videotaping on October 4 and set for airing two nights later.

Ethel Merman had agreed to a brief guest appearance, and a relatively new act, The Smothers Brothers, had been signed for a two-episode deal.

"Cast and crew were alerted to get ready for "The Battle of the Century" when "two belters" *[Streisand and Garland]* were united on the same stage.

Before rehearsing with her, Judy invited David Begelman and Liza Minnelli to hear Streisand in her one-woman show at the Cocoanut Grove. At one point, from the stage, Streisand introduced Judy to the rest of the audience, crediting her as "the world's greatest singer and the world's greatest actress."

Backstage, as she embraced

George Maharis (left) and **Martin Milner** in a publicity photo for their TV series, Route 66.

"I wanted Noel Coward, and CBS gave me **The Dillards**," Judy said, a reference to the hillbilly banjo band assigned as an anchor to one of her shows.

Evocative of moonshine stills, mountain twangs, and long-standing associations with Andy Griffith's *Andy of Mayberry*, the Dillards were not a good fit for Judy Garland, one of the most sophisticated and savvy entertainers in the world. ,

Streisand, Judy said, "There's one thing about you I love—you really sing out. You know how to belt out a song. There are very few of us left these days."

Later, Judy told Begelman, "After hearing that girl sing, I'll never open my mouth again."

Mel Tormé was having enough problems with Judy, so he didn't welcome another diva—even an aspirant one—joining her on her show. "I'd heard that Streisand was foul-mouthed, VERY Brooklynese, and a nut job, but a helluva singer. Yet the Doomsday that was predicted didn't come off, as she and Judy seemed to form a mutual admiration society."

Judy could easily have viewed Streisand as a rival on the dawn of worldwide fame. She'd already been scheduled to appear on Broadway in *Funny Girl*, based on the life of Fanny Brice. Judy had previously been considered for the role.

Throughout the few remaining years of her short life, Judy always resented being compared to Streisand. "She has her way of singing, and I have mine. She is splendid indeed. There is room for both of us."

On *The Tonight Show*, Johnny Carson asked Judy to name her favorite singer—and she did. "No doubt about it. Barbra Streisand." Then she paused, adding, "and Liza Minnelli."

As was the case for the filming of most of the episodes of her TV series, tickets to Judy's episode with Streisand and Merman became the hottest show-biz venue in Hollywood.

"To get in, you have to go down on both Aubrey and Bill Paley," said Tormé, in reference to William Paley, head of CBS.

Another person said, "Breaking into Fort Knox would have been easier than getting a ticket to hear those two divas."

During the episode's filming, Streisand got the most applause when she sang "Bewitched, Bothered, and Bewildered" and "Down With Love," which struck the audience, according to Tormé, "like a bombshell. It started down here, built up to here, and ended way up

Whereas **Judy** already had a massive gay following, **Barbra Streisand** was on the verge of developing one.

She'd gotten launched by winning a singing contest at a gay bar in Manhattan, The Lion, as a result of which she won fifty dollars. Later, she generated huge attention by appearing at New York City's gay Continental Baths.

When asked about what she thought of her gay following, Streisand said, "I could not have done it without 'em."

there at the top of the excitement range."

"Judy's 'Just in Time' broke our hearts," said Herbie Key, a member of her fan club. "She caressed the lyrics like my fantasy 'studly lover' caresses me at night. Mort Lindsey, on the piano, wasn't bad, either."

Two classic moments from that episode, never to happen again, occurred when Judy sang "Happy Days Are Here Again" (a staple from Streisand's repertoire), and when Streisand sang "Get Happy" (one of Judy's standards). Together, their renditions became interwoven and harmonized into one magnificent opus. Tormé concluded that "Judy gave more to Streisand than she gave back."

Another electrifying moment was when Ethel Merman rose from the audience and joined Streisand and Judy on stage. The trio of "belters" sang "There's No Business Like Show Business," a bravura performance later hailed as one of the great moments in the history of show business.

Discontent from backstage came not from Judy or from Streisand, but from Jerry Van Dyke and the Smothers Brothers. Tormé had from time to time found Van Dyke drinking in his dressing room at 8AM. As Van Dyke told Tormé, "Judy got it right. The road gets rougher, lonelier and tougher. My marriage is breaking up, and I feel my days on this series are numbered. The critics are lynching me."

As Streisand left to fly out of Los Angeles, Judy hugged and kissed her as she set off on a spectacular upcoming career. The forty-one-year-old Judy gave the twenty-one-year-old some motherly advice. *"DON'T LET THE FUCKERS DO TO YOU WHAT THEY DID TO ME."*

Back in the early '60s, it would have been almost unbelievable that Streisand would reprise Judy's role in a 1976 remake of **A Star is Born**, appearing opposite Kris Kristofferson in what many viewed as a mistake.

One critic retitled the adaptation of that classic romance as, "A Bore is Starred."

Of course, Judy had long turned to dust when Lady Gaga took over the role for yet another remake in 2018.

***

In reference to Judy, Lloyd Shearer, writing for *Parade,* said: "One night each week at 9:30, a little left-handed lady with large luminous brown eyes and a throaty, vibrant voice, larger than life, slithers onto the Stage 43 at CBS-TV Studios. For an hour and a half, she sings, reminisces, sips tea, chats slightly, and cavorts with such guest stars as Lena Horne, Count Basie, Mickey Rooney, Mel Tormé, and Barbra Streisand."

Along with Danny Kaye, Judy had become the most highly paid personality on television.

But as the series ground on, and as *Bonanza* continued to beat her in ratings for every episode of her shows, Judy faced the depressing possibility that she'd never see that $24 million at the end of the rainbow. Her lack of success with the show had destroyed her hopes of bringing financial stability to her life. As she told Kay Thompson, "I ain't getting' any younger, *honey chile.*"

Her Nielsen rating of 18 meant that about nine million families watched her, as opposed to the 35 million viewing *Bonanza* in the same time slot.

The tenth episode, filmed on October 11, 1963, would not be aired until March 1, 1964. Her co-stars included Ray Bolger, Jane Powell, and—once again, to her regret—Jerry Van Dyck.

During its taping, Judy was reunited with the multi-talented Ray Bolger, the Scarecrow from *The Wizard of Oz.* As the cameras rolled, Bolger and Judy, who had always admired each other, performed "If I Only Had a Brain" and "We're Off to See the Wizard" from that 1939 film classic.

A number called "The Jitterbug" had been cut from the original release of *The Wizard of Oz,* and Judy had always liked it, so it was resuscitated in a number where her co-stars included Bolger, Powell, and the dancers.

For this episode in particular, Tormé thought it would be a natural for Judy to end it with "Over the Rainbow," but she adamantly refused. "Haven't I told you? I'm sick and tired of too many damn rainbows!"

Likewise, Bolger also refused to sing his big hit, "Once in Love with Amy."

"I'm tired of that crap," he told Tormé.

Unlike Judy, Powell was truly The Girl Next Door and so described herself that way in the title she assigned to her memoirs, *The Girl Next Door,* released in 1988.

After the taping, Powell had nothing but compliments for Judy. "She really was unique. There was nobody like her, and there never will be again."

During the rehearsals, Powell had been startled by Bolger's antics. "He liked to take his clothes off, a real exhibitionist. He didn't go all the way, but he liked to tease me. Back then, I was far more prudish than I

Judy was not impressed with the comedic talents of **The Smothers Brothers**, Tom and Dick. Tom carried an acoustic guitar, Dick wielded a string bass, and their occasional music was interrupted with long-winded arguments between the siblings.

The brothers had signed a deal to appear on two episodes of Judy's show. After they were axed after the first one, they threatened a lawsuit.

In a way they got their "sweet revenge." After Judy's show was canceled, CBS hired the brothers to replace her in her former time slot.

am today. I found him to be a kind of dirty old man. I don't mean to sound so terrible. I mean it endearingly. I don't know if he pulled that stunt on Judy, too."

Powell was given high praise for her lavish production of "Dear Friend."

Judy borrowed "I Remember It Well" from Vincente Minnelli's *Gigi*. In this rendition, she played the Hermione Gingold role, with Van Dyck impersonating Maurice Chevalier.

After Judy performed her last number with Van Dyke, she hugged and kissed him as a final farewell. She knew he'd been fired.

On camera, he held up a stack of newspapers, announcing, "Reviews don't mean anything. Oh, by the way, this is my last show with Miss Garland."

***

On October 5, Judy taped Episode 11, which would launch the new year of 1964 when it was aired on CBS on January 5. Guests stars included the then-popular TV talk show host Steve Allen and his actress wife, Jayne Meadows. Mel Tormé also devised an appearance for himself.

"Our show was in transition at the time," Judy said. "People were coming and going, as heads rolled. Every morning when I woke up, I checked my own head to make sure it hadn't been cut off."

Judy bonded with Steve Allen and Meadows, becoming good friends with both of them, especially Meadows. "For a short time, I was Judy's best friend, at least that's what she called me. She even discussed her love life, claiming that her 'thing' with Glenn Ford was near its end. She also confessed that she was in love with David Begelman, even though she knew he was looting her treasury."

"Trouble is," Judy admitted, "He doesn't love me. So in the meantime, I go after every pretty boy who drifts into my orbit."

Freddie Fields was also Allen's agent, and he phoned him to report on his latest huddle with Judy. Allen—in addition to his role as a TV host—was also a songwriter. Fields suspected (and claimed) that Judy wanted to introduce some of his songs on her upcoming show.

One of the highlights of Episode Eleven was a splendidly choreographed number "There's That Rainy Day," which Judy sang with empathy and style. She wore a

OLD ACQUAINTANCES
Jane Powell on
The Judy Garland Show

Judy graciously welcomed Jane—star of such musicals as *Seven Brides for Seven Brothers* (1954)—as a guest on her show, concealing her resentment that she had replaced her in *Royal Wedding* (1951).

Judy and Jane had been on-again, off-again frenemies since their early days together at MGM.

Humphrey Bogart-style trench coat and carried an umbrella. She was backed up by a bevy of high fashion-styled women, each of them provocatively seated astride motorcycles.

Tormé—himself a self-styled motorcycle freak—positioned Judy on a white motorcycle for their number, "The Party's Over."

"For a brief time, I became a glamourous motorcycle mama, unlike those big, fat, butch girls seen riding around Los Angeles on cycles."

In the middle of taping, an unflattering article about Judy appeared in the *Saturday Evening Post*. It suggested that she often showed up drunk before her performances.

"I never saw that," Meadows stated. "She was always on time, always knowing her material and songs, a true professional. I think she was libeled."

Judy's chat with Meadows during the "Tea for Two" segment was later reviewed as one of the highlights of Episode Eleven. Judy also joined Allen in a "Sophie Medley" dedicated to Sophie Tucker, The Last of the Red Hot Mommas. She sang "I Love You Today" and "When I'm in Love."

In another "Songwriter Medley," Judy, Steve Allen, and Tormé sang old favorites that included "Makin' Whoopee."

Midway through rehearsals, Judy invited Steve Allen and his wife, Jayne Meadows, to her home for a small Sunday night dinner with some of her other friends. Meadows recalled her first time there, at a social event that also included Roger Edens, who flamboyantly arrived carrying Roddy McDowall over the threshold as a celebration of their just-defined status as "a newly married couple." At one point in the evening, Mickie Rooney serenaded them with love songs.

When Episode Eleven aired, Allen pronounced it a success: "Forgive me for sounding immodest."

Judy was too distracted to take much notice herself. She had been curtly instructed to fly at once to New York for a meeting with James Aubrey at CBS's headquarters.

Before departing, she told Allen, "I think I'll return jobless and homeless. Woe is me."

***

In New York, Aubrey did not fire Judy, but launched into a dialogue with her that was very tense. It began with a gloomy outlook about the

Jane Powell's appearance on Judy's TV show in 1963 was not the first time she'd followed in her shadow.

The left-hand photo shows **Judy with Tom Drake** as sweethearts in the 1944 original of *Meet Me in St. Louis.*

The right-hand photo depicts **Jane Powell with Tab Hunter,** emulating those roles in a television remake in 1959, more than a dozen years later.

sale of advertisements associated with her show. In the beginning, CBS was earning $36,000 a minute from sponsors for their ads. With the fall in the show's ratings and audience share, he feared that the rate per minute would be reduced to $20,000. "Your audience continues to decline, and we've got to make big changes. Vic Damone is really hot. Let's bring him on for three shows. And what about two old pros like Peggy Lee and Ethel Merman?"

"I'd prefer to work with Noël Coward," she said.

"No. He's too high brow, and too gay."

Nonetheless, she dined that night with Coward, who was in Manhattan for a visit. He told her

Some historians interpret the "lesser" skits on *The Judy Garland Show* as insights into the social mores of their era..

Here, comedienne **Jayne Meadows**, shares a gossipy "Tea for Two" with **Judy Garland.**

he'd be glad to appear with her in her "Tea for Two" segment. "The two of us will have a gay old time. Who should we dish? Perhaps my fellow Brits, Burton and Taylor?"

Any hope of an on-the-air collaboration with Coward was nixed by CBS. Judy suspected it was Aubrey who rejected him. "He'd rather I appear with Andy Griffith and Don Knotts."

As Judy was leaving Manhattan, a reporter confronted her, asking if her show might be taken off the air. With a kind of bitter humor, she shot back, "I used to watch *Bonanza* before I got this gig for CBS. If my show doesn't get better, I'll go back to watching *Bonanza.*"

She also told the reporter, "I'm thinking of teaming up with my daughter, Liza, since she's so talented—in fact, I think she's being considered as my replacement on TV."

That same day, Aubrey met with his executives at CBS and told them, "Let's face it: Judy Garland, THE LEGEND, is an expendable multi-million dollar mistake."

Judy had told Aubrey that she wanted to bring back George Schlatter, who had helmed her TV show's first episodes. Aubrey briefly considered it but decided to bring in "a member of his team," eventually hiring Bill Colleran.

[Unknown to Judy, and perhaps treacherously, David Begelman may have played a role in Aubrey's decision: Colleran was a client of his, and he might have been "playing him off" against Judy.]

Begelman met with Colleran and told him, "Judy is a god damn mess. Impossible to work with, crazy as a cuckoo bird. It's a *helluva* deal for you, and I'm begging you on bended nylon. Frankly, if it's played right, this can be a feather in your cap. You'll be the man who can stand up to her and knock some sense into the bitch. Pump some fresh blood into a dying corpse on the air."

Colleran then met with Aubrey, finding him abrasive. "So how do you plan to deal with the fucking cunt?" he asked.

"I'm going to ditch the third-rate entertainers and let her do what she does best…sing. I want to drop the vaudeville acts. Get some first-rate talent like the show she did with Streisand."

"People were coming and going on my show so fast I didn't know who would be there when I showed up," Judy said. *"A small army of wannabe producers, directors, and writers had already lined up at the studio's door."*

Gary Smith, one of the best scenic designers in Hollywood, lasted for twenty-one shows, claiming, "Everybody was afraid of Judy—me, too. She gobbles up people emotionally and wears everybody out, calling them in pre-dawn hours."

"Yet, she's a hell of a performer. As a singing artist, she experiences her mountain peaks and low valleys, and is often drunk or drugged during rehearsals. I called her a red-light performer—no, that's not a whorish reference. When the red light is blinked on, the camera ready, she is an awesome personality. But in time, she also got me fired. Thanks, Judy."

Judy's oft-repeated request for **Noel Coward** to appear on her show was repeatedly rejected by CBS management.

One of the most sophisticated playwrights in the world, and one of Judy's first choices for the kind of guest she really wanted on her show, he was judged as "too highbrow and too sophisticated for mainstream audiences" by the brass at CBS.

The photo above, as it appears in the *Encyclopedia Britannica*, shows him as a channel of what he might call "divine inspiration" in 1963.

Whatever would he have thought of the hillbilly banjo players from Mayberry, "The Dillards," who did make it onto her show?

***

Back in Hollywood, Judy had a "heart-warming catchup" (her words) with her children, Lorna and Joey. "Liza was somewhere over the rainbow," she said.

Judy was keenly aware that CBS executives, notably James Aubrey, would be tuned in to her next show, an event scheduled for airing on November 3. "I had to be good…or else…," she lamented.

She was delighted when she learned that Vic Damone would be her main guest. After Sinatra, he was her favorite singer, and she praised his "vocal instrument."

She had met him during her final days at MGM, when she happened to arrive at the studio as he was arriving for a screen test. She quickly ascertained that the inexperienced crew was inept, and then begin choreo-

571

graphing the screen test herself, directing the camera angles and supervising his deliveries.

Damone recalled, "She know how to present me, and I got hired. I was always grateful for that."

She reportedly found him "handsome, sexy, and appealing, with a certain boyish charm." But any hopes of getting involved with him romantically were dashed when another MGM star, Elizabeth Taylor, arrived to retrieve him.

The Taylor/Damone affair was reported in Hedda Hopper's column: "Fickle Elizabeth Taylor has fallen in love again, this time with a handsome crooner, Vic Damone, who is giving Frank Sinatra's career a push to oblivion."

Their affair ended when Damone was drafted to serve (from 1951 to 1953) in the U.S. Army. Taylor told the press, "Vic is adorable, but he was drafted and I'm not the type of woman to wait around."

After he returned to Hollywood from the Army, he made two movies, *Deep in My Heart* (1954) and *Athena* (also 1954), but by then, Judy was no longer working at MGM.

Damone began an affair with the Italian actress, Pier Angeli, and married her in 1954. Their romance led to the breakup of her affair with James Dean, who had only months to live. *[Dean died in a car crash in 1955.]*

[The details associated with Vic Damone's competition with James Dean for the heart and hand of the very temperamental and very complicated Pier Angeli is documented in Blood Moon's 2016 biography, James Dean, Tomorrow Never Comes.*]*

It didn't make the press at the time, but Judy's affair with Damone began in early 1963 after she attended one of his nightclub performances. She'd heard rumors of his violent relationship with Angeli. After the couple's divorce in 1958, they launched immediately into a custody battle over their son, Perry, born in 1955.

After not seeing him for several months, Damone came back into Judy's life when he "kidnapped" his nine-year-old son, Perry, from

Judy soon learned more about the man CBS had hired, against her wishes, as her director, **Bill Colleran.**

A native of Wisconsin, he had begun his career in the story department of 20th Century Fox, taking time off to serve in the Navy during World War II. He became known in Hollywood as an assistant director to Louis de Rochemont, turning out such hits as *13 rue Madeleine* (1947) and *Boomerang* (also 1947).

In the early 1950s, Colleran became an associate director of *Your Hit Parade* on TV and helmed specials for Frank Sinatra, Debbie Reynolds, and Bing Crosby.

For a while, he'd been married to the actress, Lee Remick, a union that ended in divorce.

the custody of his mother in New York, bringing the child to Los Angeles. Judy quietly arranged, through attorney Greg Bautzer, to house the father and son at a secret location. Damone, however, was eventually arrested as a fugitive from a kidnapping charge.

[Eventually, Damone—through Bautzer—was cleared of the kidnapping charge and ultimately regained (temporary) custody of his son. Angeli, after long and expensive wrangling in the U.S. courts, got him back and emigrated with him to Italy. Following Angeli's suicide in 1971, Perry moved back to California to live with his father.]

Reunited with Damone at CBS's studio, Judy found him "as adorable as ever. I didn't believe all those charges that he abused women. He was always loving, tender, and kind to me, a real 'dream boat.'"

Bill Colleran reported, "The two of them acted like love birds. On their first day of working together, I saw them leave the studio in his Cobra sports car. They returned the next morning like two enchanted lovers."

The marriage of **Vic Damone** to the 1950s "perpetual ingenue" **Pier Angeli** was one of the most widely publicized tabloid weddings of its era.

The marriage failed miserably, and eventually, the bride, broke and desperately searching for movie roles that never materialized, committed suicide.

Mel Tormé, often critical of Judy, found her in top form during her rendition of "Moon River," which Andy Williams had made famous. She joined Damone in a rendition of excerpts from *Porgy and Bess,* including a medley that featured "You Is My Woman." One of the highlights for her was singing "From This Moment On." Damone was at his best singing "On the Street Where You Live."

When the press asked Damone about working with Judy, he said, "She lived life to the fullest, more than any woman I've ever known. I admired her as a person and a singer. She lived every word of the music she sang."

One night in Las Vegas, according to Sammy Davis, Jr., he and Damone talked about their love lives with three of their friends. Davis mentioned his two greatest conquests: Ava Gardner and Marilyn Monroe.

Damone said that his favorite bedtime partner had been Judy Garland: "She'd do all the things to me that my prudish ex-wife, Pier Angeli, refused to do."

Davis was cynical about Damone's motivation for his affair with Judy: "I love Judy dearly, but she was looking her age. I suspected that Vic was messing around with her for only one reason—and that was because she was Judy Garland."

***

It has been said that if some sculptor wanted to create a Mount Rushmore of American Pop, the figures would include the faces of Frank Sinatra, Louis Armstrong, Bing Crosby, and Peggy Lee, each carved into the side of a mountain.

Miss Lee herself, a well-read and well-liked eccentric, claimed, "I learned courage from Buddha, Jesus Christ, Abraham Lincoln, and Mr. Cary Grant."

Biographer Peter Richmond wrote, "With her platinum cool and inimitable whisper, she sold twenty million records and presided over music's greatest generation along with pals Frank Sinatra and Bing Crosby. Albert Einstein adored her, and Duke Ellington dubbed her "The Queen.""

Judy maintained that Peggy Lee was her favorite female vocalist. Yet despite her admiration, her competitive insecurities were aroused when she learned that CBS wanted to conjoin them as a work-together team on the next episode of *The Judy Garland Show*. Taped on November 8 and aired on December 1, it marked Jewison's final episode as the series' producer. Co-stars would include Jack Carter doing a comedic monologue, and Carl Reiner bantering with her in a "Tea for Two" segment.

The highlight of that episode was Lee and Judy performing a duet with bits from "It's a Good Day," followed by Judy going "Over the Rainbow" and Lee sitting "Under the Bamboo Tree." For many, the most touching segment was when Lee sang "When the World Was Young."

Judy and Lee also performed a medley, "I Like Men," singing "Fever" (Lee's hit song), and "It's So Nice to Have a Man Around the House."

Judy and Lee got along splendidly on the show, one great artist coming together with an equally great artist and respecting each other's talent.

Actually, Judy had known Lee since 1945 and, though they saw each other on occasion, they were never close friends. Each, however, tried to attend one another's performance whenever they were in the same town.

Another bonding had occurred in 1959, when Judy attended performances of Lee's fabled one-month-long engagement at Basin Street East in Manhattan. One night, Judy arrived with Sammy Davis, Jr., followed by Jackie Gleason and Art Carney. On another occasion, Lee spotted Judy in the audience sitting with Marlene Dietrich, and on the following night sandwiched between Tallulah Bankhead and Joan Crawford. "I knew all three women swung in all directions and wanted to get in Judy's pants, but I never make value judgments about such liaisons."

When Lee was living in the Waldorf Towers, she invited some special guests back to her apartment for a late-night supper. Martha Raye and Cary Grant were also invited, and each guest was served hot dogs or else raw onion sandwiches with champagne. "It's a refreshing change from caviar," Grant said. On other nights, she invited Tony Bennett, Elizabeth Taylor, Jack Lemmon, Louis Armstrong, and Lauren Bacall.

Anthony Quinn cabled from Italy, "Your records keep me sane." When he arrived in New York, he was Lee's only guest, and seen leaving at ten the following morning.

One night, Martha Raye, Judy, and Lee talked about men, with Raye and Judy sharing their experiences when each of them had wed David Rose. Lee spoke of her ill-fated marriage to Dewey Martin, a handsome young actor and former Navy pilot.

"We were married in April of 1956, and things started to go wrong on our honeymoon night," Lee said. "In my suite, in Palm Springs, I ordered champagne and appetizers. While I was changing into something more appropriate, he switched on a movie starring Robert Preston. Apparently, he'd heard that I'd once had an affair with Robert. He jumped to his feet, turning over the champagne and food, and struck me several times until I fled down the hall and booked into another suite. Our honeymoon night didn't go too well, wouldn't you say?"

"After I dump Luft, I'll never marry again," Judy vowed. "Never! Never!"

"That means you will," Lee predicted.

***

In Dallas, Texas, on November 22, 1963, all television programs were pre-empted as news flashed across the screens of the nation. President John F. Kennedy had been shot in a motorcade as it moved through the city.

Judy had slept until eleven that morning. When she arose, she flipped on her bedroom TV set as she headed to the bathroom, leaving the door open.

The duets sung on *The Judy Garland Show* by her and in tandem with other guests are collectively considered works of art in their own right.

So well-done were Judy's duets with **Peggy Lee** that repackagers of reruns of the show opted to publicize them front-and-center on the cover.

There, she heard the latest bulletin coming out of Dallas. Rushed to the hospital, the President was dead. Vice President Lyndon B. Johnson would soon be sworn in as President aboard Air Force One before flying back to Washington. Pictures of Jacqueline Kennedy in a blood-soaked dress were flashed across the screen.

Judy started to scream hysterically, throwing herself onto the floor, kicking and screaming. Staying with her at the time, Liza rushed into her bedroom and tried to comfort her, but Judy jumped up and started to bang her head against the wall.

Finally, Liza was able to restrain her, cuddling her into her arms like a baby. Her sobs became hysterical shrieks.

As her daughter mopped her mother's tear-soaked face, Judy looked up into Liza's big eyes. "What are we going to do? He always took my calls. When I complained that my ratings were falling off against *Bonanza's,* he said, 'Fine art is not for the masses.'"

For three days and nights, Judy was a vision of sustained grief and at times, uncontrolled hysteria. Finally, on the fourth day, she pulled herself together and set up a meeting with her director, Bill Colleran. She proposed to him that the next episode of *The Judy Garland Show* should be dedicated to the slain president. Colleran thought that was a splendid idea and shot the proposal to James Aubrey in New York.

Within the hour, his rejection of the plan was relayed to her: "What a dumb idea! The news coverage is dying down. The public will move on and forget about this whoremonger."

575

When Judy heard that, she exploded and began throwing things against the walls of her dressing room, wrecking it.

Nevertheless, in spite of objections from CBS, she managed to give a "blood curdling" rendition of "The Battle Hymn of the Republic" as her final tribute to him. Before launching into the show on the night that it aired, January 12, 1964, she simply said, "This is for you, Jack."

She didn't speak publicly about JFK until September of 1967 when she gave an interview to Dale Remington on NBC's radio show, *Monitor:*

"I can honestly say that I was very honored to be friends with President Kennedy. I was allowed to call him on the phone because I'd get a bit confused about my television shows, and it seemed to me an awful lot of slipshod business was going on. And if I got into wondering about state income tax or government tax, well, I thought it was all right to call the President of the United States. And he always took time to talk to me. He took the calls. I think he probably took lots of calls. Not just mine. But he was a very good friend, a very fine president, and a very fine man.

"Mrs. Lincoln was President Kennedy's private secretary, and it always used to be kind of funny. I'd say, 'This is Judy Garland calling President Kennedy at the White House in Washington,' and there'd be a bit of confusion. I'd say, 'If you can't get through, ask for Mrs. Lincoln,' and the operator would always say, 'Whoa. This is ... really ... She's really gone now! It's Judy Garland. She thinks Abraham Lincoln is still in the White House and she's asking to talk to Mrs. Lincoln!'"

Judy wanted Episode #14 scrapped, but CBS executives insisted that it be rehearsed and videotaped. Bobby Darin and Bob Newhardt had arrived in Los Angeles around the time of the assassination in Dallas, and the taping of the show was delayed until November 30 to be shown at the end of December.

Judy performed a "Train Medley" with Darin, featuring *"Sentimental Journey"* (*"better than Doris Day,"* claimed Judy) and "I've Been Working on the Railroad."

Newhardt delivered a solo comedic monologue, and with him, Judy taped a funny sketch showing her and Newhardt watching *The Judy Garland Show.* Just three years before, the comedian had released an album of comedic monologues that reached #1 on the *Billboard* chart.

Offscreen and informally, Judy had several talks with Darin and felt great sympathy for him. In Los Angeles, he'd seen a specialist, who told him his life would be short, estimating it at no more than five more years. As a boy, Darin had suffered several bouts of rheumatic fever, which left him with a weak heart.

The doctor's gloomy forecast came true. At the age of thirty-seven, right before Christmas of 1972, Darin died after unsuccessful heart surgery in Los Angeles.

***

What became Judy's favorite episode of the entire series was the taping of *The Christmas Special* with all three of her children, Liza, Lorna, and Joey.

Fearing that she might not show up because of a pill-popping night, Mel Tormé was relieved when she walked through the door in time for its taping. She greeted her fellow guests, singer Jack Jones and dancer, Tracy Everitt, Liza's boyfriend. She warned him, "Don't get my daughter pregnant!"

She told Jones that his father, Alan Jones, had starred in one of her first films, *Everybody Sing*. "That was so long ago. Deanna and I kept our pet dinosaur in the backyard."

The handsome young pop singer, Jack Jones, was Hollywood born and bred. When he met Judy, he had just won a Grammy for his recording of "Lollipops and Roses" and would soon win another for "Wives and Lovers."

For an opener, Judy sang "Have Yourself a Merry Little Christmas." Off camera, she asked, "Where is that damn Margaret O'Brien?" referring to her co-star in *Meet Me in St. Louis*. "What am I saying? I sang it to my beloved kids, Lorna and Joey."

Judy and all three of her brood joined to sing "Consider Yourself" from the stage musical, *Oliver*.

Liza's big moment came when she sang "Alice Blue Gown," written long ago by Roger Edens for a young Judy to sing on radio. When he saw the show, Edens said, "It was like listening to Judy reborn."

Lorna's rendition of "Santa Claus Is Coming to Town" was one of the highlights of the show. Judy claimed, "Lorna has the best voice of all of us, and she's not even out of the gate yet."

Liza and her boyfriend, Tracy Everitt, did a song-and-dance number, "Steam Heat." Judy, Jones, and Liza also performed a medley that included "Jingle Bells," the first song Judy had ever sung on stage, age two and a half.

To end the show, Judy sat on a sofa in a replication of her own living room and sang "Over the Rainbow" to Joey and Lorna.

***

The multi-talented **Bobby Darin,** a son of East Harlem in New York City, was married to Sandra Dee, the perky blonde who, in the late 1950s, became the symbol of the bygone era of "virginal" teen romances on the screen.

Her movies with Darin, including *Come September* (1961), were labeled cock-teasing and "bubble-headed" by critics.

Darin himself was a charismatic pop singer, turning out such hits as "Dream Lover" and topping the billboards with "Mack the Knife."

Darrin appears on her show here with **Judy.** Her fashionable pillbox hat evokes the one Jacqueline Kennedy was wearing in a Dallas motorcade on the day of her husband's assassination a few months later.

Episode Sixteen would inaugurate Judy's 1964 season when it went on the air on January 12. It had been taped on December 20 before a live audience, uniting her with her longtime friend, Ethel Merman, backed up by comedian Shelley Berman and dancer Peter Gennaro.

At the time, word coming out of Aubrey's office in New York didn't sound good for the fate of the show. The entire crew agreed with Judy and Bill Colleran that the show should be rescheduled to Monday night at 10PM.

But Aubrey was insistent that it remain in its present slot, continuing to (unsuccessfully) compete against *Bonanza*. At the time, there were some eighty regular shows on national television and *The Judy Garland Show* ranked 66th.

The Garland/Merman show was the one in which Judy sang her rousing tribute to the slain President Kennedy. Colleran and Judy had to slip in the number secretly so that Aubrey would not find out and perhaps kill it. On hearing it, Tormé said, "I found myself crying. I was not alone."

"As for those damn ratings, I felt Aubrey was deliberately sabotaging me for reasons known only to himself," Judy charged. "He seemed determined to watch me sink into a quicksand."

Both Judy and Merman belted out songs that included "I Get a Kick Out of You." They performed a duet, a medley wherein "Two belters belted out each other" in such numbers as "It's De-Lovely" and "Together (Wherever We Go")."

Berman had never worked with Judy before, although he'd long admired her. One of his comedy sketches with Judy had to be dropped because she appeared intoxicated. He performed a telephone sketch.

"When I encountered Judy, I thought she was very ill," Berman said. "She looked like she was on the edge of a nervous breakdown. She said she feared this would be the last show in the series."

"There will be no more *A Star*

Judy's Christmas Special, 1963, was widely promoted, endearing, and very charming.

Upper photo: All hands on deck, as (left to right) **Liza, Judy, Lorna, and Joey** make a vaudevillian "soft shoe" staple a family event.

Lower photo: **Liza and** her beau, **Tracy Everitt,** demonstrate a jazzy version of *The Pajama Game's* "Steam Heat."

Is Born for The Legend," she told him.

Berman was both a genuinely funny comedian and a serious actor. By 1959, he'd made three gold records and won a Grammy for spoken comedy.

After working with Judy on her show, he'd appear in the 1964 screen adaptation of Gore Vidal's 1961 stage play *The Best Man* (1964), alongside Cliff Robertson and Henry Fonda.

Regardless of Judy's tabloid scandals, Merman always defended her. "There was a lot of melodrama in Judy's life, what saved her was always looking on the funny side of her troubles. There was a wide streak of the clown in her. Of course, her marriages all went wrong. But who am I to judge? Me, who married Ernest Borgnine."

***

For the last taping (Episode 17) of the year, Judy reteamed with Vic Damone. The show was taped on December 20 and aired on January 19, 1964.

She had hoped to rekindle her brief fling with Damone, particularly after she was dropped by Glenn Ford. She was eager to find a replacement for him, and she had been disappointed to learn that Damone, in 1963, had married Judith Rawlins, with whom he eventually produced three daughters.

On the set, she found him considerate and loving, hugging and kissing her, yet not responding to her very obvious invitations to visit her in her dressing room.

Damone told Bill Colleran, "Judy is like a little canary. You want to hold her and protect her from the world. She only becomes a giant when she sings."

An often critical Mel Tormé found them both at the zenith of their vocal powers, especially when they joined in a medley from *West Side Story*, singing such numbers as "Maria," "Somewhere," and "Tonight."

Chita Rivera, an actress, singer, and dancer, was also booked on the show. She'd been in show business since 1950. In time, she would become the first Hispanic woman and the first Latina American to receive the Kennedy Center Honors Awards (2002) and the Presidential Medal of Freedom (2009). Backed up by "The Dancers," she sang, "I Got Plenty of Nothin'."

Louis Nye had became known on *The Steve Allen Show,* and he provided comic relief for Judy. Ken Murry also appeared on the show and showed his home movies of film stars caught off camera. As he exhibited his clips, Judy made whimsical comments.

Then, in a reversal of his former indifference, a few days before Christmas, Damone made an unannounced visit to Judy's home. After he entered into her living room, he told her that he'd come over to give her her Christmas present.

Since he was empty-handed, she asked him if he'd left it in his car.

"Not at all," he said. "I brought it with me. If you'll invite me upstairs to your bedroom, I'll present you with it. I'm calling my gift to you, 'Take

All of Me.'"

She laughed, saying, "That's the most original come-on I've ever received. You're on, Big Boy."

***

As she moved deeper into the 1960s, the last decade of her life, Judy's saga was summed up by author James Spada:

In this "portrait" from Episode 17, Judy replicated the razzmatazz showbiz motifs of her 1940s heyday.

"For Judy, John F. Kennedy's death was another blow to a woman who was approaching her final round. Her life, beginning late in 1963, would contain too many desperate comeback attempts, soaring triumphs followed by canceled concerts or poor performances, failed marriages, ugly, hurtful actions against her servants, her friends, and her family. Before long, Judy Garland would drive away almost everyone who cared about her — including the one person who loved her the most, Liza."

Perhaps it was the timing, in 1963, of *The Judy Garland Show* that doomed it from the start.

Free love, LSD, social unrest, and *The Beverly Hillbillies* were about to sweep over the land.

In a climate like that, the emotionally fragile allure of Judy's edgy nostalgia, plus her notorious unreliability and instability, contributed to her "corporate doom."

Her widely repeated negative comments about James Aubrey ("The Smiling Cobra') the director of CBS-TV, didn't help matters, either.

CHAPTER TWENTY

How CBS-TV's

THE JUDY SHOW

STAGGERED DYSFUNCTIONALLY ONWARD

"I've met The Devil, and his name is James Aubry"
—Judy's reference to the director of CBS

LEGALESE, SEX, & CONTRACT DISPUTES
BETWEEN THE SHEETS WITH HOLLYWOOD'S SUPER LAWYER, GREG BAUTZER

FRENCH AIRS WITH LOUIS JOURDAN,
A "FART FEST" WITH MARTHA RAYE, AND
ONGOING CONFLICTS (*CARNIVAL!*) WITH LIZA

MORE ABOUT MEL TORMÉ (*HINT: IT ENDED BADLY*) &
COLLABORATIONS WITH BOBBY COLE & LIONEL BART.

LIZA IS "FANTASTICK" ON THE ROAD IN
MINEOLA, MIAMI, & WESTPORT

MARK HERRON:
JUDY'S AMBITIOUS 4TH HUSBAND
HE ISN'T PERFECT, BUT NEITHER IS JUDY

MADNESS IN MELBOURNE:
AN AUDIENCE IN REVOLT.
JUDY'S SOGGY, DRUG-SOAKED RECOVERY IN
HONG KONG

INTRODUCING PETER ALLEN
KANGAROO HOPPING WITH THE BOY FROM OZ

"Being Judy Garland means I've been loved by the public, but you can't take John Q. Public home with you to warm your bed at night. I've also been ripped to pieces, completely shattered by the newspapers and the bastards who want to take me down. But I've survived the jerks, and I'll come back."

—Judy Garland

"My marriage to Mark Herron ended before it began. He left me right after our wedding to meet some commitment in Los Angeles. During our time together, I never knew where he was—even his friends didn't know. After he left, I was alone again; even though he hadn't been much company. I seem to attract people who need to destroy me just to stay alive themselves. If you're considered a living legend, some people just want to back away from you—not women, just men."

—Judy Garland

"I've never written a fan letter in my life, but I'm writing one to you tonight. Judy Garland. Your show has improved. You're bringing theater to Television."

—Mary Martin

"I've played Judy Garland's mother in films. I'm surprised she didn't burn out long ago, the way she lives in a world of booze and pills. But she bounces back, the Black Irish Witch herself. A cat has only nine lives... Judy at least twenty-seven."

—Mary Astor

As the New Year of 1964 arrived, Judy continued to star
in her TV series, defying predictions that her show would be taken off the air. She also fell in love, albeit temporarily, with Greg Bautzer, the "Don Juan of Hollywood," one of its most sought-after lawyers and lovers, even

though he was married to actress Dana Wynter, star of *The Invasion of the Body Snatchers* (1956).

Judy hired him, the town's most powerful and charismatic lawyer, for a retainer of $3,500 a month. She needed "someone to battle for me, as I was being sued by half the people on the planet."

Right after she retained him as her lawyer, Judy learned that he brought with him a fringe benefit: "He crawled into bed with me every night so I could sample his fat German sausage."

No lawyer in Hollywood ever achieved the movie star fame of Greg Bautzer. His seductions of A-list movie stars read like a *Who's Who:* Merle Oberon, Rita Hayworth, Marlene Dietrich, Ava Gardner, Peggy Lee, Dorothy Lamour, and Jane Wyman (the ex-Mrs. Ronald Reagan), among many others.

Like Judy herself, Bautzer was known for his drunken outbursts, often in public.

His biographer, James Gladstone, wrote: "A darker compulsion lurked below the surface. Bautzer was a confirmed alcoholic. When he drank, his personality changed from Dr. Jekyll to Mr. Hyde. He would start the evening as the most gracious, mannered gentleman in the room and end up an enraged bull."

Tearing herself away from the much-married Clark Gable, **Lana Turner,** in 1941, launched a torrid affair with **Greg Bautzer,** the most seductive attorney in the history of California.

His affair with Judy Garland lay in his future.

Here's **Joan Crawford** in a still from the trailer of her Oscar-winning *film noir* crime drama, *Mildred Pierce* (1945).

Of Bautzer's many movie star affairs, Crawford's was the longest, although their relationship was often argumentative and violent.

His longest-running affair was with Joan Crawford. As a couple, they became known for their violent confrontations, some of them in public.

As a lawyer, he was fiercely loyal to his clients, including Judy.

Bautzer's most lucrative client was Howard Hughes, the aviator, movie mogul and (at the time) the richest man in America. Bautzer plotted many of Hughes' business deals and also covered up the more sordid aspects of his private life. [*Hughes kept a harem of budding young starlets, and—as a bi-*

sexual—got into more than one scandal for his seductions of some of the leading (male) matinee idols of the day, too: Errol Flynn, Tyrone Power, Cary Grant, and Robert Taylor.]

Clients of Bautzer's burgeoning law practice included Rock Hudson, Marion Davies (mistress of William Randolph Hearst), Ingrid Bergman, Jack Benny, Kirk Douglas, Sophia Loren, Mickey Rooney, and studio chiefs Darryl F. Zanuck and Jack Warner.

Joan Crawford always maintained a surface friendship with Judy, but when she learned that she was dating Bautzer, she phoned Judy late one night and said, "Darling, you are so adorable, but I felt I must tell you that Greg belongs to me. He's just using you. He doesn't love you. Even worse, he's involved, business-wise, with David Begelman, and I hear they're robbing you blind. Watch out! And I think you should drop Greg at once—OR ELSE!"

"Or else *what?*" Judy asked.

"I could make serious trouble for you in this town."

Two views of "The Big Mouth" **Martha Raye** on *The Judy Garland Show.*

Upper photo: Proving that an "old gal" could still sing and dance in "Taking a Chance on Love."

Lower photo: With **Peter Lawford and Judy** in a comedy *schtick.*

"Too late, Joanie, old gal," Judy said. "Greg has already dropped me and moved on to younger stuff. I plan to keep him as my lawyer, however, perhaps for a couple more years." Then she gently put down the phone.

***

For the taping of her first TV episode of 1964, Judy began rehearsals on January 14 for a program scheduled for broadcast on the 26th. As her guest stars, she was joined by two old friends, Peter Lawford and Martha Raye.

Also on the bill were Ken Murray, with his ever-present cigar, and Rich Little, who would soon become famous for impersonations of celebrities that eventually earned him a nickname, "The Man of a Thousand Voices."

When Judy showed up three hours late for the first day of rehearsals, the crew noticed that she looked puffy and had put on some extra poundage—most of it derived from heavy drinking and lots of chocolates—over the Christmas holidays.

She found Lawford buried deep in his woes in the wake of the assassination of JFK. She and Lawford spent a lot of time talking about the aftereffects of the murder of their friend, some of which negatively affected

584

Lawford's relationship with his wife, Patricia Kennedy.

Judy saw that he'd been drinking hard and heavily, and virtually everyone—cast, crew, and director—complained when he took an astounding sixty takes before he got one segment right. Eventually, the crew was able to release "a pampered billionaire's rendition of "It's So Nice to Have a Man Around the House," and with Judy, a tongue-in-cheek version of "I'm Old Fashioned."

Martha Raye turned "Taking a Chance on Love" into a comedy sketch. At one point, Lawford put his hand over her famous "big mouth," and he yelled when she chomped down on his fingers. Mugging and shimmying, she made her way across the floor, at one point, butting in on Judy's close-up. Much of her footage ended up on the cutting room floor, as it was judged as too risqué.

Judy and Raye were at their best when they borrowed *Pennsylvania 6-5000,* one of Glenn Miller's Big Band Swing numbers. Lawford joined them for a reprised medley *(Hit Parade of 1964)* that incorporated that song.

Tormé was not satisfied with Judy's performance, finding both her and the show itself lackluster. After she'd wrapped it, he told her that he felt her rant against Louis B. Mayer was not appropriate. "Mayer is rotting away in his grave, and your viewers don't give a damn about how he tormented you in the 1930s."

At first, Judy had not wanted Rich Little on the show. But after she heard him impersonate James Mason as Norman Maine in *A Star Is Born,* she was won over. She also found it amusing when she called out the names of various stars, and, emulating their style, he performed a few bars of each of them singing *The Man That Got Away.*

Judy was not pleased at the end of the show, and she made that obvious. She had ended some of her previous episodes with a rendition of "Maybe I'll Come Back." But this time, she exited the stage without singing it, forcing the orchestra to play an (unaccompanied) rendition of it anyway.

After the show, Judy invited Raye, Lawford, and Bob Wynn, the episode's production consultant, to a late-night Mexican restaurant. Midway through it, Wynn complained, "This Mexican food is hard to digest."

"Kid, you don't know how to fart," Raye responded.

According to Wynn, "Judy and Martha then proceeded to teach me how to fart, and those ladies really stunk up the joint."

Lawford kept his head buried low, before pontificating, in a drunken voice, "Life is nothing but a bowl of shit."

The next day, the crew had to immediately begin setting up for a taping of the next show, this one to be taped on January 17 for an airing on February 2. This was a pivotal moment in the continuity of the series: CBS executives had flown in from New York to decide on its fate, with the understanding that they'd be sitting through a dress rehearsal.

The *Hollywood Reporter,* days before, had leaked a story that relayed how likely it was that the series would be canceled. That led to a barrage of mail from Judy's most devoted fans, enough to inaugurate a "Save Judy" campaign.

As it turned out, Episode 19 was a bad choice as a bellwether of the series, as it was one of the most lackluster. Her backup singers were the

Kirby Stone Four, an unfortunate choice. She described them as "an innocuous coven of middle-aged warblers. Any barber shop quartet could beat them." She also complained about her own performance, claiming that her throat was too dry to hit the high notes.

After its taping, she criticized Ken Murray and his semi-antique "home movies" for his second appearance in her series. "You're overstaying your welcome, showing your silly movies of stars doing silly things."

In spite of her displeasure, Murray would be invited back for two more episodes.

Judy had a comedy sketch that brought the most laughs. She started to sing "Smoke Gets in Your Eyes," as stage smoke billowed all around her. Suddenly, a group of firemen arrived and hauled her bodily off from the stage.

Her main guest star for that episode was the French heartthrob, Louis Jourdan, who, in a 1948 poll, had been voted the handsomest man in the world. He was

Judy found the Gallic charm of the debonaire French actor, **Louis Jourdan,** enchanting.

She asked him, "When my former husband, Vincente Minnelli, directed you in *Gigi* (1958), did he put you on the casting couch?"

He never answered her.

imbued with a certain Gallic charm, and Judy was powerfully attracted to him. That had been the case ever since she'd seen him in his "role of a lifetime" when her then-husband, Vincente Minnelli, had cast him in the Oscar-winning musical, *Gigi* (1958), with Leslie Caron.

Judy introduced Jourdan by singing "Paris is a Lonely Town." Then, after some banter, she performed *The Children's Song Medley* with him, a compilation that included "Popeye the Sailor Man." Their romantic song-and-dance number was "Some Day My Prince Will Come."

According to Judy, "When the taping was over, I invited him for a late-night supper But he had another engagement. That clown, Danny Kaye, arrived to steal him away into the night. What is it with that jerk? He's had this long-running thing with Larry Olivier, of all people, and now he's got something going with Jourdan, too."

***

During November of 1963, Liza had lived in Los Angeles with her mother. One night, she woke up in pain to find "my temperature boiling and my legs feeling like noodles."

Screaming for her mother, she lay in bed sobbing. Although it took some time for Judy to pull herself together, she called at once for an ambulance. Liza was rushed to a hospital, where she was diagnosed with a severe case of kidney stones.

Both of her parents visited her every day in the hospital. She made a rapid recovery, and when she was better, against Judy's wishes, flew on to New York. Her agent had gotten the then-seventeen-year-old a lead role in a road show revival of *Carnival!* — described as "an entertainment with magic, puppetry, aerial work, and a luxurious musical score" — during its tour of the U.S.'s Eastern Seaboard. She'd play Lili, an optimistic orphan who visits a carnival hoping to find a job.

Liza's involvement in **Carnival** began with one of its revivals. She appeared in it "everywhere except in Manhattan."

Here's the cover of the soundtrack for the original Broadway production

At first, she fights off a sexual assault, but is rescued by "Marco the Magnificent," a handsome magician with whom she falls in love. The musical, originally developed by David Merrick for a Broadway opening in 1961, had been based on the 1953 film, *Lili,* that had starred Leslie Caron and Mel Ferrer.

When the news reached Judy that Liza would be starring in a road-show revival of *Carnival!,* she became almost hysterical and set about to sabotage her gig, even threatening legal action, claiming that Liza at seventeen was far too young.

She called columnists to campaign against her daughter's continuing with the show's rehearsals. She told Dorothy Kilgallen, "Liza's in poor health and is risking her life. I'm protesting because I want to save her life, but she's defiant. I'll have to sue the producers to remove her from the show."

In one drunken phone call to Walter Winchell wherein she did her best to enlist him in getting Liza removed from the cast, Judy admitted, "If I can help it, I'll see that Liza never appears on the stage."

The fast-talking columnist reminded Judy that at one point, "Liza will come of age and can make her own decisions."

Pat Hipp, hired as one of the publicists for *Carnival!,* said, "Morale among the cast and crew was low. We didn't know if we'd have a show or not. Garland might shut us down. Night after night, I never knew if Liza were going to go on, or if we'd eventually face a court order. She was a skinny, insecure kid and a pain in the neck. It wasn't because of anything she did — she was very professional — but because of this wicked witch of a stage mother."

When lawyers descended into the fray, Liza became distraught. In the words of Hipp, "The poor girl was held together by snapping rubber bands instead of cartilage. She seemed hyperkinetic, but was fabulous in the role, however."

And then one day, the all-out assault from Judy stopped when Liza's father, Vincente Minnelli, intervened. Apparently, he informed Judy that

587

there was a lot of gossip about how she was hysterically jealous of a new star being born, and that she was doing everything in her power to sabotage her daughter, deliberately trying to block her fledgling career.

Liza opened as Lili in *Carnival!* at the Mineola Playhouse on Long Island on January 28, 1964. [*On February 11, it moved on to Millburn, New Jersey for an opening at the Paper Mill Playhouse.*]

At Mineola, at the very moment she went on stage, the audience heard the strident ringing of a phone backstage. A stagehand picked it up. Someone was calling from Los Angeles with an urgent message that Judy Garland had tried to commit suicide and had been rushed to a hospital. Even when the message was delivered between acts, Liza did not respond until the next day. By now, she was accustomed to these suicide attempts, never really believing that her mother was actually trying to commit suicide. "Judy desperately wanted attention," she was quoted as saying.

The opening night audience had applauded Liza throughout the show, especially after her rendition of "Love Makes the World Go Round." Before the curtain rose, she had been seen sobbing backstage. After she made her final exit from the stage, she told cast members standing by, "I'm not a clone of Judy Garland."

Michael McGrady, writing for *Newsday,* said, "The comparisons to Judy Garland were inevitable—the tremulous voice, the respect for the lyrics, the wide eyes, the clenching hands, the eyebrows never still. Yet, by the time she sings her second number, 'Yes, My Heart,' the applause belongs to her alone. From that point on, one forgets to make comparisons."

The road show version of *Carnival!* was a smash hit, and Liza continued as its star as it moved between venues along the Eastern Seaboard. Nothing further was heard from Judy, who boycotted all of her daughter's performances.

Liza was paid very little for her performances, and found herself in debt, owing five-thousand dollars. She was advised to declare bankruptcy. "Seventeen years old and bankrupt. This must be some sort of record."

A New York State surrogate judge ruled that all her future earnings as a performer would have to be paid directly to Judy. Her mother was then required to deposit the monies in a New York bank, with the understanding that. Liza could not draw upon her own earnings without permission from the court. To help in the control of her future earnings and to pay off her debts, an attorney was hired. That arrangement remained in effect until she turned twenty-one.

After finishing her stint in *Carnival!,* Liza moved on with her life and her career, with stardom predicted. Of course, she faced the anticipated assault from some of Judy's fans and from critics in the press. Most of it focused on her status as Judy Garland's daughter, and for trying to coast into stardom on her mother's reputation.

According to Liza, "There are two things I can't bear: They're pity and depression. I don't have time for either. I want to forge my own agenda, defying the odds."

***

On January 20, 1964, the memo from CBS that Judy had long dreaded arrived from New York. It announced that at the end of March, the studio would cancel *The Judy Garland Show,* freeing her to resume other engagements, perhaps returning to her career as a "freelance" concert artist. James Aubrey decided to give her "a saving grace" and made public her letter of resignation:

During his reign at CBS, **James Aubrey** was the most hated man in the business of television.

Gossip maven Liz Smith called him, "Mean, hateful, a truly scary, bad, *outré* guy."

"Firstly, I am most grateful for the support that I've had from CBS these past months. I have found my experience on weekly television a most gratifying one and a part of my career that I will always remember as exciting and fulfilling, as well as challenging. I have had to make the decision not to continue. I have found the involvement that I must give to production and performing these programs to be incompatible with the time and attention that I must give to family matters. My children's interests come before anything. I know this decision to be the right one. There will be many opportunities for us to work together in the coming years."

Lucille Ball, the reigning diva of television in the 1950s, called him "an S.O.B."

Danny Thomas, Red Skelton, Arthur Godfrey, and Jack Benny had words far worse to describe him.

Aubrey's response, perhaps not written by him, went like this:

Secretaries at CBS learned that when he ordered them to go to bed with him, they either did—or were shown the door.

"Although I can appreciate the compelling reason for Miss Garland's action, I would like to say how genuinely sorry all of us at the Network are that she has reached this decision. Judy's great talent and electrifying personality have added distinction to this television season, and we are proud that the CBS Television Network was able to provide, through this gifted artist, so many hours of heart-warming delight for the nation's viewers. We look forward to her return to television –hopefully on the CBS Network."

CBS didn't want to take the blame for the show's demise, knowing that it would provoke outrage among Judy's most devoted fans. Those "fake" letters from both her and Aubrey fooled no one, especially Lucille Ball, a star on CBS herself.

Ball went public with her outrage: "On Judy's show, she was given lines such as 'I'm a little old lady.' On another episode, there was talk about 'the next Judy Garland.' I bet she's glad the series is over. She's the best."

Harriet Von Horne in the *New York World Telegram and Star* weighed in with a strong opinion:

"After triumphing over the bureaucratic idiocy that sought to remake her personality, Judy Garland now faces a March cancellation of her TV series. However, ratings weren't that low if you consider the millions who watched her show. Of course, the ugly, violent, forever predictable Bonanza *continued to delight the masses."*

Photo shows **Diahann Carroll** as Nurse Baker in the CBS sitcom *Julia (1968-71)*, with **Fred Williamson.**

It was the first time an African-American woman was featured in a "non-stereotypical role" on a TV sitcom.

Carroll was good on television, and in the view of many network insiders, "television was good to her."

TV Guide had nothing but praise for Judy as an artist. In an unprecedented move, the little magazine ran a barrage of letters from outraged fans, denouncing CBS for the show's cancellation.

For the remainder of the series, director Bill Colleran and Judy decided that the final shows would focus on her singing without any particular emphasis on comedy sketches. They would include only a few all-star guests: Diahann Carroll, Jack Jones, and Vic Damone, and in one show, musical arranger Mel Tormé in a not-very-exciting sequence, making his *adieu*.

On January 24, Judy taped Episode 20, which included tributes to her three children. With all the comedians excised from the show, more musicians were hired by Mort Lindsey for his orchestra. Their members swelled to forty.

Relentlessly, Aubrey continued to harass Judy. Word soon reached her that he'd been telling CBS executives that "Judy Garland has lost whatever talent she originally had. For nostalgia reasons, she can still get applause from gay boys and middle-aged matrons or grandmothers who remember seeing her as Dorothy in *The Wizard of Oz.*"

On January 24, for airing on February 9, she videotaped Episode 20 with Lorna and Joey. "On most shows, I felt either like Queen Victoria or a complete ass. On this episode, I felt royal, with Lorna and Joey to cheer me on."

She was in top form when she opened with "Swing Low, Sweet Chariot," followed by a World War I medley, featuring such songs as "When Johnny Comes Marching Home" and "Give My Regards to Broadway."

She also sang tender songs to her children, opening her tribute with "Liza." To her son, she dedicated the song "Happiness Is a Thing Called Joe." He appeared with her on camera, and she hugged and kissed him.

Only Lorna didn't have a tune where her name didn't configure into the lyrics, but weeks before the show, she hired Johnny Mercer to dash off an original song, "Lorna." It included the lines, "I can shout it from the rooftops—Lorna Loves Me Too." As the cameras rolled, she and her youngest daughter warmly embraced.

The episode was a resounding success, ending with a beautiful rendition of "America the Beautiful."

The *Chicago Tribune* pronounced it "brilliant," citing Judy's "shining and electric personality."

The *New York Times* suggested that the show was so outstanding that "even the Cartwrights might watch it," a reference to the ranchers on *Bonanza*.

The *Hollywood Reporter* gave her a rave: "Miss Garland sure showed them she could carry any ol' show, anytime, anywhere—all by herself in spades in her solo slot."

Later, after looking back at the final concerts helmed by Bill Colleran, Judy remarked to musician Bobby Cole: "Filming those episodes were the highlight of my career."

The African American singer, Diahann Carroll, was brought back to appear with Judy in a videotape shot on the last day of January 1964. Episode 21 was broadcast on February 16.

For the episode with Carroll, Judy adopted a hairstyle inspired by Jacqueline Kennedy, a sort of "teased pompadour." Gowns—still created by Ray Aghayan—were the most stylish she'd ever worn. A highlight of the show was a Garland/Carroll medley of songs by Harold Arlen and Richard Rodgers, including "Any Place I Hang My Hat Is Home," and the Lena Horn standard, "Stormy Weather."

[Judy was long gone from the planet and wasn't around to see Vic Damone, her former lover, wed Carroll in 1987, the marriage lasting until 1996.

Before Damone, Carroll had been involved in a nine-year affair with Sidney Poitier beginning in 1959, and with TV talk show host David Frost (1970-1973).]

Tormé came on to sing "Stranger in Town," which Judy criticized later as "pretentious." He blatantly imitated Frank Sinatra by appearing in a trench coat draped over his shoulder. This was the last time he'd ever star with Judy on camera.

She ended that episode by singing "Don't Ever Leave Me" and "Great Day."

Judy and Colleran had a habit of watching the first airing of every episode of their show at her home on Rockingham Drive. By the time the show aired, the children had usually gone to bed, so, with Colleran, she sat in her living room, usually on the carpet in front of her TV set.

"Judy and I had fun watching her shows," Colleran said. "We drank a lot, and I was always amused by her sharp wit. There

The **Mineola** (Long Island) **Playhouse** was a theatrical venue with Manhattan-caliber performances in a way off-Broadway venue.

In the 1960s, it was part of a circuit—comprised of the Paper Mill Playhouse, the Bucks County Playhouse, and the Westport Country Playhouse—in which talented actors like Liza Minnelli thrived.

was one embarrassing moment, however:"

"She was high on champagne, and at one point, she reached over and unzipped my pants, taking out my cock."

Almost immediately, Colleran rose to his feet and hurriedly zipped up his trousers. "Judy, I'd love to but I'm a happily married man."

Then she, too, rose to her feet and headed for the doorway, where she stood, hand on her hip, glaring back at him. "No one, absolutely no one, wants to fuck a legend." *[She had used that same line previously with Frank Sinatra.]*

***

Before the next videotaping session, Judy, with Lorna and Joey, flew to New York for a one-week sojourn at the Sherry-Netherland Hotel.

Late the following afternoon, after some late-morning shopping, a limousine delivered them to the Mineola Playhouse on Long Island, where they had a reunion with Liza, who was starring in a play there that night.

The mother-daughter relationship had been strained since they'd feuded over Liza's involvement in *Carnival,* but all seemed forgiven at the time of their reunion.

That night, Judy, Lorna, and Joey saw her in *The Fantasticks,* an Off-Broadway play with music by Harvey Schmidt and lyrics by Tom Jones (no, not that one). The play ran for forty-two years, making it the longest-running musical in theater history, thanks in part to its hit song, "Try to Remember." *[It famously rhymed "remember" with "September", "December", and "so tender."]*

Liza played the lead female role of Luisa, singing a solo, "Much More," although mostly she sang in a duet or trio.

Her co-star was Elliott Gould, then married to Barbra Streisand. "Talk about living in the shadow of a star," Judy said.

Gould claimed, "Liza was all manic, wild, and unbelievable. She always had her heart out there. She wasn't selfish and was as interested in my role as her own. She had a most positive attitude."

On her first night

"THE FANTASTICKS"

Eclipsed by the memory of her famous mother, **the rich Off Broadway life of Liza** Minnelli often went unnoticed outside the inner sanctums of the entertainment industry and its players.

The right-hand photo shows the front cover of the program for a road show production of *The Fantasticks* in Coconut Grove, Florida. In it, she co-starred with **Elliott Gould,** later married to Barbra Streisand.

off, Liza took the train from Mineola to Manhattan, where she found that the electricity in her apartment had been turned off. "I am truly my mother's daughter, always late paying a bill."

Back within her hotel suite with Lorna and Joey, Judy slipped and fell, hitting her head so hard she suffered a concussion. Rushed to Manhattan's Mount Sinai Hospital, she was examined and treated by Dr. Kermit Osterman, who released her after an overnight stay.

Still wobbly on her feet, she popped pep pills the next day and invited Lorna and Joey to accompany her to CBS's Manhattan headquarters. There, they saw themselves in the footage of the episode of her TV show that had been taped on January 24. At its end, Judy kissed both of them, saying "Weren't we wonderful? We should tour the country."

When Liza's gig with *The Fantasticks* ended, she found more work in regional theater, this time starring in *Time Out for Ginger* opposite a fading matinee idol, Chester Morris. With his flat nose and furrowed brow, he had appeared in films about cops and robbers in the 1930s.

[The play had opened on Broadway in 1952 and later proved popular in regional theater. It was later made into a feature film, Billie *(1965), starring Patty Duke.]*

During the time she spent on the road with it, Liza phoned Judy whenever she could. By then, her mother had returned to Hollywood to tape the final episode of *The Judy Garland Show.*

In 1964, Liza was offered her first dramatic role, appearing on TV in an episode of *Mr. Broadway.* Its star, Craig Stevens, played a New York public relations specialist, Mike Bell, who helps launch an unknown singer, Minnie (Liza) in her career. "I needed all the help I could get," she said.

***

Judy was still in Manhattan when Peter Lawford phoned her suite and invited her to go for a night on the town "in the city that never sleeps."

She wanted to go to Jilly's for drinks and dinner. *[Jilly's was Frank Sinatra's favorite watering hole, and he'd taken her there. During her stopover there with Sinatra, Bobby Cole had performed at the piano. "I was entranced with him, especially when he joined Ol' Blue Eyes and me at table," she said.]*

When she showed up again, this time with Lawford, Cole spotted them and signaled. Later, during his break, he joined them at their table.

Liza, as she appeared in 1964 in her guest appearance as a struggling opera singer in "Nightingale for Sale," an episode in the CBS-TV series *Mr. Broadway.*

On the right is actor **Horace McMahon,** known for playing thugs, "heavies," and well-intentioned police detectives.

Broadcast on Saturdays, *Mr. Broadway* ran for 13 prime time episodes, after *Gilligan's Island* and before *Gunsmoke.*

Cole remembered Judy chicly dressed in a simple black dress in a style inspired by Coco Chanel and a black feather boa.

"Judy had a marvelous wit and I just adored her," Cole said. "I also found her sexy. So what if she were a decade older than me?"

At one point, the singer, Jack Jones, entered the club and joined Judy's table. Jones had already signed on as one of the guest stars on the next episode of Judy's show.

By 2AM, after the club had been emptied of its regular clients, Sinatra and Tony Bennett arrived with "two blonde bimbos" (Lawford's words). Sinatra had made a deal with the manager to keep Jilly's open until dawn broke over Manhattan.

"We drank we sang, and hung out until the roosters crowed, if such a thing exists in New York," Cole said. "When I wasn't at the piano, I had my arm around Judy."

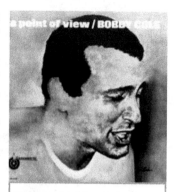

Musician **Bobby Cole** as he appeared on his record album, *Point of View.* After he and Judy bonded, he became her musical arranger.

In the beginning, they had an affair. He was still with her at her final concert.

At around 6AM, Sinatra's rented limousine hauled everyone back to their respective hotels. Judy invited Cole up to her suite at the Sherry Netherland. "He phoned his wife, but I don't care to know what he told her," Judy said later to Lawford.

According to Cole, "I took a sabbatical from my wife. The next day, Judy offered me a thousand bucks a week to become part of her TV series in Los Angeles. That was a hell of a lot better than the $150 I was pulling in at Jilly's. The next day, I was on a plane to L.A. with Judy and her brood."

Mel Tormé claimed, "Garland pranced into the CBS Studio Monday morning with this second-rate piano player she'd picked up in a sleazy Sinatra hangout in New York patronized by the Mafia. It was obvious to me that my days were numbered at CBS."

"After introducing me to this musical hustler, who I knew was sticking it to her, she gave me one of her imperial demands to create a medley for her to sing with Jack Jones."

For some reason, Judy wanted to sing songs from those late 1930s MGM musicals with Jeanette MacDonald and Nelson Eddy.

Tormé overheard her dissing MacDonald, a singer she often mocked on TV. "It's hard to believe this, considering how proper Jeanette looked on the screen, but she got her start as a high-class prostitute, servicing top politicians and tycoons of industry, not horny sailors on leave."

Then Tormé stormed off to assemble and tweak the medley she'd demanded. But when it came time to hear its rendition from Judy and Jones, he was shocked that his arrangement had been "rebuilt," he had no doubt, by Cole.

With Jones, Judy led off with a duet of "San Francisco." *[As it happened, that song had derived from a movie,* San Francisco *(1936), that MacDonald had*

594

made with Clark Gable and Spencer Tracy.]

From there, they moved into a delivery of "Lover Come Back to Me" and "I'll See You Again."

When Tormé confronted her about these radical changes to the lineup and the episode's content, they got into a bitter argument and crew members were shocked at the language Judy used to denounce Tormé.

"You're fired, you son of a bitch!" she shouted at him. "GET OUT!"

"I've got a contract!" he countered. "You'll have to see my lawyer."

"Up yours!" she yelled at him before turning her back on him and storming off to her dressing room.

In his office, Tormé agonized over what to do. Finally, because he needed the money and had no other offers, he decided he'd remain and try to run out his contract.

Then, however, Bill Colleran came to see him, warning him that if he stayed, Judy would call security to have him physically removed from the studio.

Mel Tormé remained furious and some said, vindictive, toward Judy for the rest of his life.

He was among the hundreds of performers whose material was partially destroyed in a warehouse fire in 2008 on the back lot of Universal Studios.

That certainly helped him make up his mind. He packed his possessions and moved out at around four that afternoon, telling Colleran to warn Judy that a lawsuit would be pending.

In retrospect, Tormé recalled, "I was with Judy Garland's show for nine months, and it was a fascinating experience, but a real ordeal. My feelings ranged from compassion to disgust, from admiration to loathing. Those late-night calls waking you up at three in the morning, hearing her drugged and drunken voice on the phone. I refused to be part of her so-called 'Dawn Patrol,' a group of crew members who sat up with her until the sun came up. To me, working with Judy was a case of cow manure hitting the fan."

"I was shocked by her truck driver tongue," Tormé continued. "Not only songs emerged from her golden throat, but the vilest words I ever heard, enough to peel the skin off a grape."

As it happened, Tormé had a solidly defensible contract which called for a payment of $3,500 a week, plus $4,500 for every appearance on the show with her.

On March 10, he filed a lawsuit against Judy and her Kingsrow Enterprises, demanding payment for the final weeks of his contract, plus three more appearances on her show, for which he'd been signed.

That April, she was summoned to give a deposition. She falsely claimed that Tormé had walked off the set and refused to work on her show with Jack Jones. As Tormé recalled, "She looked like Mother Courage holding up Planet Earth."

After she gave her deposition, and as she was leaving the building,

Tormé ran into her in the hall. She addressed him in a soft voice. "Goodbye, Mel, it's been great."

He saluted her. "Goodbye, Sadie."

"I hate that nickname you gave me. It's a whore's name."

He would never see Judy Garland again.

That afternoon, Tormé met with his attorney, who told him, "I've learned that Judy owes a mountain of bills, with the IRS likely to take precedent. Even if you sued and won a judgment, you'll have to wait in a long line of debtors who'll get nothing. Drop the suit. Write it off as a bad memory and get on with your career."

Tormé's ordeal with Judy led him to write a memoir, *The Other Side of the Rainbow,* released in 1991. In some quarters, the small book was praised, but it offered a very unflattering portrait of a star coming unglued. Many insiders claimed that Tormé exaggerated his role in the series. Judy's family unsuccessfully sued.

RAY STARK
BARBRA STREISAND · SYDNEY CHAPLIN
ORIGINAL BROADWAY CAST
Capitol

A NEW MUSICAL
JULE STYNE · BOB MERRILL
ISOBEL LENNART
by CAROL HANEY
by DANNY MEEHAN

Funny Girl

To Judy's distress, **Barbra Streisand's** rising star was eclipsing and upstaging even the formidable Judy Garland's.

***

As Judy began taping the last of her shows—each of them known as *Judy Garland in Concert*—she faced increasing speculation in the press about the possible cancellation of her series.

One day, as she was entering the CBS Studios in Los Angeles, a reporter from *Variety* approached her for a comment.

"If my ratings don't get better against *Bonanza,* I'll start watching it myself. Maybe I might even guest star on it. I could play a madam who runs a saloon and operates a bordello in the upstairs rooms."

Bobby Cole became not only her musical arranger, but her young lover, too. Each of them would eventually move on to other lovers, but for weeks, they'd be in bed together.

[Cole would remain her friend until the end of her life, in fact, being the conductor and musical director of her last concert. Because of his exposure on The Judy Garland Show, *he'd be in demand to play the Sands and Caesar's Palace in Las Vegas, and for singing gigs in Atlantic City and Miami Beach. His trademark song became "The Lady's in Love With You."]*

Judy encouraged him to release a solo album, *Point of View,* which he did in 1966. It sold well in New York City, where he was well known among a late-night crowd.

Cole and Judy had more in common that sex: Both of them were heavy drinkers and smokers. "I might as well smoke as I've spent most of my life in night clubs inhaling the smoke of others, second-hand."

It was not Judy's drinking but her drug habit that alarmed him. "How can a body survive taking forty Dexedrine tablets a day?" he asked the series' director Bill Colleran. "That's enough to keep a horse racing around the track for ten years. At night come the downers. She can't go to sleep without them. Seconal is like a narcotic sledgehammer to her, knocking her out cold."

Cast and crew on her TV series came and went, but Cole stuck with her until the very end, even appearing with her on camera in the next-to-last show, aired on March 22, 1964. He also arranged the music for her last taping on March 13.

"I've never seen Judy so afraid," Cole told Colleran. "She's afraid of everything. I try to comfort her, but it doesn't seem to do much good."

Only Judy's most diehard fans attended the taping of her last two shows, and they had to wait and wait—and wait some more—for her to go on. Finally, to the music of "Over the Rainbow," she appeared, to thunderous applause.

"For one of the tapings, she interrupted the rehearsals to enter the audience's seating area, pouring her fans glasses of champagne. The filming was to end with Judy taking a final bow as credits flashed across the TV screen. But right before taping, she stormed out, heading for her dressing room, where she barricaded herself inside. As she entered, she noticed an orchid plant, a gift from Hunt Stromberg, Jr., still the right-hand man of James Aubrey, the CBS president. A note read, "You were just great. Thanks a lot. You're through!"

She burst into tears, calling it, "The cruelest day of my life."

She finally allowed Colleran into her dressing room. He later claimed, "During our series, I had gone through hell and survived. I'd seen her despondent, depressed, and dejected, but nothing like what I encountered in her dressing room that night. She was fortifying herself with booze and those damn pills. I faced a woman who had hit rock bottom like it was the end of her life."

She demanded to see her managers, David Begelman and Freddie Fields. Colleran had to tell her that both of them had flown to New York for the opening of Barbra Streisand in *Funny Girl*. They had signed the emerging star as their latest client.

"She took the news real bad," Colleran said. "I mean REAL bad! I felt as soon as I left, an attempt at suicide was about to happen."

"I faced a roller coaster ride getting that show launched, having to draw upon segments taped for other shows but not used."

"We got her back out there, but she could hold out for only ten minutes before running back to that dressing room. Her most loyal fans in the audience, some of them, who had been there since afternoon, stuck with her, waiting for her to come back. She failed to get through 'Love Walks In,' but managed to sing a number like 'Carolina In the Morning.'"

At one point, she spotted Tony Bennett in the audience and called out to him. "Tony, if you have any class, you'll get your ass up here and help me out."

The singer would later say, "The reaction from critics and others were mostly negative about Judy's series at the time. Now, people rave about those shows."

She struggled to get through the final number but could not do it. She left the stage. By that time, only Judy Garland "fanatics" had remained in their seats, and now, they slowly filed out to face the dawn over Los Angeles.

Once again, she let Colleran, but not Bobby Cole, into her dressing room. She told him, "I can't go back out there. After tonight, I feel Judy Garland is no more."

When the series went on the air, Colleran subbed "When the Sun Comes Out," as her final number, which she'd previously taped for another episode, but which had not been used.

The next he heard of her was a news item on March 18 that she had been admitted to the Cedars of Lebanon Hospital, suffering from an acute attack of appendicitis, according to her doctor, Lee Siegel. It turned out to be a severe case of the flu.

After her release from the hospital, she and Cole flew to San Francisco where they attended the opening of a musical, *Firefly*. A local newspaper reported that Judy was considering acquiring the rights to it as a "comeback vehicle" for herself. The deal, like so many of her other projects, fell through.

The following night in her suite at the Fairmont, Judy confided to Cole what her dream was: She wanted to open a little gay bar in San Francisco, where he could entertain patrons at the piano while she stood at the door and greeted her fans. "At midnight, I'd sing 'Over the Rainbow' to them, my most devoted Friends of Dorothy."

On March 16, Judy was back in Los Angeles, heeding Colleran's call for her to return to the CBS Studio to tape a twelve-minute production of her "Born in a Trunk" number from *A Star Is Born*. He also wanted her to tape "A Farewell Song."

She struggled but could only get through the first four minutes. She seemed to be on the brink of collapse as she headed for her dressing room.

It was a hot night, and before her exit, a grip had called down from above the set, "Judy, it's hot as hell up here. We're broiling."

She glared up at him and called back, "I don't give a god damn if you fry." Then she stormed off the stage, never to return. For the episode's airing on March 29, Colleran had to rely on previous recordings not used up to now.

Despite the many uncomfortable events during the crafting of her final show, she received her most favorable appraisal from Terrence O'Flaherty writing for the *San Francisco Chronicle*, a newspaper that had always championed her:

"The final Judy Garland show has come crackling over the air. It was the most crisp and stylish musical series of the season. In fact, I cannot recall any in television's history where the production was so polished or where the star burned with any brighter intensity. For Garland fans —as well as viewers who seek showmanship and sophistication — the demise is a disaster.

"Despite saying in her letter of resignation that she was quitting 'to be able to give more attention to her children,' Miss Garland was actually dropped. But she walked out of CBS a bigger star than when she came in. She mastered the uneasy relationship between star and camera. She tackled new kinds of songs with moods and emotions difficult to sustain and managed to bring them off successfully. In my estimations, the creative elements backstage were superior at all times."

In spite of her many difficulties, the 15th annual poll of television critics and editors voted her "Best Female Vocalist of 1964," and her series received four Emmy nominations. Danny Kaye beat out both Judy and Streisand for Outstanding Performance in a Variety or Music Performance or Series.

"I put my hopes and dreams into that series, but I never saw a penny of that $24 million promised," Judy said.

"Far more than her wonderful MGM musicals, the series showed the best of Judy Garland in her finest role, playing herself," said Tony Bennett, who remained one of her most loyal fans.

On looking back, Judy said, "My TV series was a good thing that happened to me. I learned a great deal. But if I had known what I was in for, I would not have committed to a weekly show—no way, not ever!"

[By October of 1969, Judy had been dead for months before James Aubrey, "The Smiling Cobra," took over MGM, which had been run by Louis B. Mayer during Judy's heyday as a film star. His attorney, Greg Bautzer, Judy's former lover, had lobbied hard to get him appointed to the post.

Aubrey became MGM's third president that year, and he faced a studio going bankrupt. The story may be apocryphal—and no doubt was—but gossip went around Hollywood that

"SEASON'S BEST MUSICAL"

SHE LOVES ME!

Judy Garland was not the only megastar whose hopes and dreams were thwarted by James Aubrey.

After his departure from CBS-TV, during his wrenching stewardship of MGM (the studio which had "created" Judy Garland), he abruptly cut funding for two movies that superstar **Julie Andrews** had nurtured and in which she would have starred.

One was a film adaptation of the 1963 Broadway hit, **She Loves Me.** In 1967, it too, was sacrificed on the altar of Aubrey's obsession with entertainment that catered to "more youthful" (some said "dumber") audiences.

At the time, Andrews was a highly bankable star with a huge fan base. The left-hand photo shows her as Maria, an ex-nun and governess to the Von Trapp family in the spectacularly successful 1965 film adaptation of the 1959 Broadway hit, **The Sound of Music.**

She Loves Me, despite Aubrey's sabotage, went on to a wildly successful reprise in London's West End, and in 1998, it was the inspiration for a successful film adaptation (*You've Got Mail*) with Tom Hanks and Meg Ryan.

Aubrey's first act after taking office was to sell the Ruby Slippers she'd worn in The Wizard of Oz. *Although selling them wasn't his first act, he soon thereafter did sell the fabled slippers, finding them "of no intrinsic value other than for nostalgia buffs." At the same time, he also ordered the sale of the dresses and gowns Vivien Leigh had worn in MGM's Gone With the Wind (1939).*

Actually, Aubrey's first act as MGM president was to pull the plug on twelve MGM productions already being filmed or about to be made, including two Julie Andrews pictures, She Loves Me *and* Say It With Music.

In an even more dramatic move, he moved MGM's headquarters from Culver City to Manhattan, firing hundreds of employees in the process, and sold MGM's sprawling backlot, the site where Judy and Mickey Rooney had made all those Andy Hardy movies.

"Musicals, like those Garland used to make, have long gone out of style," Aubrey said. "The 1960s and the sexual revolution have arrived. No one is meeting in St. Louis. They're heading for San Francisco. It was time for Judy Garland to leave CBS, where before, that studio was swimming in red ink. That gal never knew what a budget was."

When a reporter from Variety *inquired about Judy, Aubrey asked "Judy? Judy who? Judy Holliday? Judy Canova?"*

"No, Judy Garland," the newsman said.

"During my time at CBS, I screwed Judy Garland, but at times she made me the screwee."]

As directed by corporate raider Kirk Kerkorian, Aubrey, during his stewardship of MGM, went on to sell off part of its legendary back lot, in this case, 38 acres in Culver City that had been the film location for many of MGM's (and Judy Garland's) most iconic postwar movies.

In 1970, even the sets for Judy's "breakthrough" hit, *Meet Me in St. Louis* (1944), fell to the wrecking ball. **Judy and Leon Ames**, the actor who played her stern but benevolent father, are distantly visible in the lower photo.

Aubrey didn't know it at the time, but some members of the "Judy cult" defined him as hell-bent on destroying the legacy and legend of Judy Garland, the actress who had made many millions of dollars for the studio that eventually fired her.

***

Judy had been in Los Angeles during the dying days of December 1963. She'd taken time out from her worries to attend a New Year's Eve party hosted by Ray Aghayan, her costume designer for her TV series. In would ring in the fateful year of 1964.

She was the last to arrive at a party that was already in full swing. She had come alone, having rented a chauffeur-driven limousine, wisely perceiving that Los Angeles was no place to drive, in her own drunken state, on a night when many other drivers would probably also be drinking heavily.

Although some strangers were present, she knew most of the revelers from CBS at the party. She had talked to at least eight people before she spotted Roddy McDowall coming her way with a handsome young man. She'd known the Londoner from her days at MGM when he'd co-starred with an eleven-year-old Elizabeth Taylor in *Lassie Come Home* (1943). The former child actor had gone on, when he grew up, to play snobs and eccentrics. He introduced her to his latest lover, aspirant actor Mark Herron, with whom he was living at the time.

Even during her *zaftig* period, **Judy** was beloved by **Roddy McDowall**, practically the leader of her gay cult followers.

McDowall had just returned from Rome, where he'd co-starred with Elizabeth Taylor and Richard Burton in *Cleopatra* (1963). He had many a juicy tale to tell about what had gone on behind the scenes. [*Much of what he had to reveal was published in 2012 in Blood Moon's biography of Elizabeth Taylor,* There Is Nothing Like a Dame.]

Mark Herron (in foreground) as a spa owner, "Bellemondo," a small role he played in the low-budget horror film, *Eye of the Cat (1969)*.

The *New York Times* reviewed it as "overstated, reworked, and all too familiar," with a climax "as hokey as it is horrible."

The *Los Angeles Times* called it "so unintentionally hilarious that one would be tempted to recommend it were not the price of theater admissions so high these days."

After a while, McDowall wandered off, and Judy found herself alone talking to Herron, finding him handsome, tall, slim, with brown hair and blue eyes. He still had "a hint of the magnolia" in his Southern accent. She soon learned that he was from Baxter, Tennessee, and was six years her junior. She was surprised to learn that he had grown up only miles from the boyhood home of her father, Frank Gumm.

At the party, shortly before midnight, art director Bob Kelly approached Herron and Judy. Dressed in drag, he wore a replica of her costume from her number, "Get Happy": a (tailored) men's tuxedo jacket and, down below, nylon stockings encasing his shapely (shaven) legs. When he'd gone, Judy revealed her quick wit to Herron: "There's one thing that bothers me about him," she said…"He's got better legs than mine."

When the New Year was rung in, she impulsively grabbed Herron and gave him a long, lingering kiss on the mouth before joining with the rest of the party to sing *Auld Lang Syne*. She stayed at the party until McDowall had to go home with his new lover. Before that, she invited Herron to arrange with Aghayan to come to the CBS studio to watch her rehearse for her TV series. He promised he would.

That was a promise he kept. When he showed up, she invited him to occupy a director's chair in the same spot where one of her previous lovers, Glenn Ford, had also sat watching her sing.

Her intimate involvement with Herron took a while to get going since he had to stand in line. She was still involved with Greg Bautzer. After he left her, she'd have a fling with Bobby Cole. But weeks later, when Cole returned to his wife, she was once again a free agent. Herron moved in to fill the vacuum.

In time, Roddy McDowall would dump Herron as his lover, taking instead with another young actor.

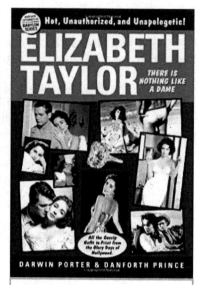

Hot, Unauthorized, and Unapologetic!

ELIZABETH TAYLOR

THERE IS NOTHING LIKE A DAME

All the Gossip Unfit to Print from the Glory Days of Hollywood

DARWIN PORTER & DANFORTH PRINCE

Even during Judy Garland's peak, **Elizabeth Taylor** thrived as hot competition for the role of Hollywood's most scandal-soaked Über-Diva.

Produced by Blood Moon in 2012, and eventually, one of its all-time best-sellers, this book reveals everything that Dame Elizabeth never wanted her public to know.

Soon, Herron was seen around town on dates with Judy, frequently showing up with her at Ciro's or at Cocoanut Grove. From the beginning, he got a bad press, referred to as a "gigolo," "a hustler," "a user," or "an actor dating Judy to advance his career."

One article called him "Judy Garland's new male nurse on a 24-hour suicide watch."

After several weeks, when she got to know him better, she asked him to move in with her at her home in Brentwood.

It was not a completely sexual liaison. As she admitted to Kay Thompson, "Mark doesn't seem to want to go beyond the heavy petting stage."

He met Lorna and Joey, and she claimed he was very friendly and nice to both of them. Their father, Sid Luft, had not met him yet.

Herron was frequently absent from the house, never explaining exactly where he was going or when he planned to return.

She learned a bit about this new man in her life, although he held back many of the details of his private life. Moving to California, he had enrolled in Los Angeles City College, specializing in drama. In 1952, the drama department designated him as "Best Actor of the Year." At the time, he was being supported by a "sponsor," a much older insurance executive

602

who paid all his bills and gave him a new Ford.

At the end of the term, he was among the select few to study with the noted British actor Charles Laughton, who was married to the noted eccentric, the English character actress Elsa Lanchester.

Laughton became enchanted with the young man and invited him to New York where he got him a role in the Broadway production of George Bernard Shaw's *Major Barbara*. Herron went into rehearsals as the stuffy brother of Major Barbara. At night he let Laughton "service" him, and for a brief time, he became his kept boy. He viewed this "degrading of myself" as his chance to get ahead in the theater. But after three weeks, he was fired before the opening of the production.

Gay and sometimes predatory, Academy Award-winning British homosexual, **Charles Laughton** ("*The Hunchback of Notre Dame;*" 1939) is shown here with his wife ("*The Bride of Frankenstein;*" 1935) **Elsa Lanchester,** during their promotional tour of Disneyland in 1956.

At a party in Manhattan, Laughton introduced him to the outspoken Tallulah Bankhead, the legendary stage actress. She told him that when she first went to Hollywood, she had co-starred with Laughton and Gary Cooper in *Devil and the Deep Sea* (1932).

"Both of us were vying for Cooper, 'The Montana Mule.' I got him and told Laughton that whereas Cooper was divine, he (Laughton) was 'a repulsive mass of glob.'"

Bankhead invited Herron home with her, but was very disappointed by his "performance," kicking him out the next day.

Soon after that, Herron met an Italian producer, who invited him to Rome, where he managed to get him a job dubbing Italian films into English. He also nabbed a walk-on role in Federico Fellini's *8½* (1963).

Judy apparently learned very few of these details from Herron himself, but rather

Flamboyant and outrageous, **Tallulah Bankhead** appreciated the charms of younger men.

She appears here as a predatory diva with **Tab Hunter** in a 1964 production of Tennessee Williams' *The Milk Train Doesn't Stop Here Anymore.*

Does Art, indeed, imitate Life?? Tallulah tested and later rejected Judy's future husband, Mark Herron, as "unsuitable, unsatisfying, and tedious."

from Roddy McDowall during one of the sessions when he photographed her. [*In addition to his work as an actor, McDowall was a noted photographer, too.*]

On one of the nights that Judy and Herron stayed home together, they concocted a fanciful whim that as an acting team, they'd become known as the new Alfred Lunt and Lynn Fontanne of the American theater. She had seen the 1962 film adaptation of Tennessee Williams' *Sweet Bird of Youth,* starring Geraldine Page and Paul Newman, and proposed it as the first of the vehicles they'd pursue, artistically. It relayed the story of a former movie queen, a has-been, shacked up with a handsome male hustler.

Geraldine Page, as a fading and deeply insecure movie star, appears here with **Paul Newman**, as a gigolo, in the 1962 film adaptation of Tennessee Williams's "decadent" 1959 stage play, *Sweet Bird of Youth.*

Judy, floundering and desperate for movie roles she could convincingly play, thought that she and Mark Herron should reprise it as a vehicle in which, as an acting team, each of them could shine.

Herron suggested that she reconsider *Sweet Bird of Youth,* lest someone interpret it as an (accurate) reflection of their own lives. "It's too close to home," he told her. In lieu of that, he endorsed Williams' more tender play, *The Glass Menagerie,* as a better vehicle for them. Judy would play the family's ferocious, semi-demented matriarch, a faded Southern belle. Herron would play Tom, her claustrophobic and fed-up son, and Liza would portray her lame and lonely daughter Laura.

When Judy pitched the proposal to some potential backers the following week, "I faced a blank wall of silence."

One night, Judy invited Herron to escort her to a black tie charity event at the Beverly Hills Hotel, a gala occasion widely reviewed by the Hollywood press. She and Herron were seated at a table when Robert Vaughn appeared, arriving "stag." Herron spotted him and beckoned him to join Judy and him at their table. Herron and Vaughn had been close friends when they attended college together.

Vaughn had met Judy before when she attended a party at his home, entertaining his guests with singing and with indiscreet late-night stories. He defined her as a raconteur *par excellence.*

Since Vaughn was clearly aware that Herron was gay, he'd been surprised to read in the paper that he had become romantically involved with Judy.

[*In the 1960s, Vaughn became known in the living rooms of America for his TV series, playing master spy Napoleon Solo, in the hit series The Man from U.N.C.L.E.*]

He soon discovered that both his friend and Judy "were well oiled with hooch."

The press was there and recorded the focus of attention for the evening:

the arrival of Elizabeth Taylor and Richard Burton. When she saw Taylor across the room, Judy, in a voice that carried to some of the tables nearby, exclaimed, "Here she comes, Miss MGM Tits! Look at the creep she's with—that no talented, nasal-voiced, pock-marked son of a bitch from Wales."

As people were milling around and being seated, the orchestra began to play some soft dance music. Judy almost demanded that Vaughn dance with her.

After only a few minutes of dancing with Judy cheek to cheek, the actor felt her left hand at his crotch. Her right one was bandaged, possibly from another suicide attempt. Then she unzipped him for an inspection just as a photographer snapped their picture. If that photograph still exists today, it would be a valuable collector's item.

Although Herron could never be defined as any woman's perfect mate, Judy was still drawn to him. She needed a man in her life for love and protection, and she also valued his congenial company. "Women over forty don't always get the perfect lover," she said. "You settle for what's out there on the hoof."

Also, she was in urgent need of an escort and helpmate during her upcoming and recently announced concert tour of Australia. David Begelman and Freddie Fields, who were now pursuing other, more bankable clients, would not be available to go with her.

Based on the exciting MGM-ARENA TV series

THE MAN FROM U.N.C.L.E.

an all-new adventure by Michael Avallone, as U.N.C.L.E.'s top enforcement officer fights a diabolical THRUSH plan for world domination.

BLAST FROM THE (Campy, Spy-Fiction) PAST

Here's **Robert Vaughn,** the fleeting object of Judy Garland's affection, as a suave super-cop in *The Man from U.N.C.L.E.*

As a tongue-in-cheek TV series on NBC, it ran from 1964-1968. Despite its mindless premise, it spawned a half-dozen spinoffs.

Thus, she proposed that Herron fly with her as her tour manager instead, with the understanding that she'd pay him $300 a week. Since he had only $86.17 in the bank (his words), he was more than willing to take her up on the offer.

But before breaching the borders of Australia, she decided she needed a week's vacation in Hawaii. They were seen leaving the Los Angeles Airport for Honolulu on May 2. Although they shared many long conversations over drinks and dinner, it quickly became obvious to both of them that their relationship lacked an important grace note: SEX.

In Honolulu, Judy, with Herron, boarded a plane for the long trip to Sydney, Australia.

***

After their arrival in Sydney, Judy faced a barrage of voracious reporters who peppered her with often embarrassing questions. Newsman Philip Scott said, "Sid Luft has claimed that you tried to commit suicide twenty-two times. Is that true?"

She turned to Herron and then asked the reporter, "Why don't you ask him?"

At first, Herron looked startled before quipping, "Who's counting?" That made Judy laugh.

Members of the press in Sydney seemed puzzled as to how they should identify the new man in her life. For the most part, they defined him as "a traveling companion." One newspaper, however, labeled him "a Hollywood homosexual."

Judy went through a rough time in customs, two agents searching her luggage thoroughly and confiscating her stash of pills. Back at her hotel, she complained to Herron, "I can't perform without my pills."

Through some unknown connection, she was put in touch with a Chinese abortion doctor who had links to the black market. By noon of the following day, a new set of drugs arrived in the form of pills manufactured in Europe. To Judy's distress, they did not have the desired effect that the American-made drugs had.

Although she was pleased with most of the news coverage of her arrival, she was deeply disturbed by one of them:

"It seems that American has-beens — take Marlene Dietrich, for example — come to appear on stage in Australia as a last resort to milk some final money out of a fading career. Judy Garland arrived yesterday with a young man to earn some badly needed cash. She's reported to be drowning in debt and is scheduled to give two concerts in Sydney and one in Melbourne. The question is, will she show up at all? It was obvious from her appearance yesterday at the airport that the sun has set on a fabled career."

For her three concerts, she expected to earn $52,000, the most money any entertainer had ever received for that limited time on a stage in the history of Australia.

Her concerts in Sydney (on May 13 and 16, 1964) were presented in a wrestling arena. Each drew an audience of 10,000, many of whom were dedicated Judy Garland fans. Both concerts were viewed as personal triumphs for her, even though her performance was riddled with mistakes, including her forgetting the lyrics to a song she'd sung a thousand times. During moments in each of the two concerts, she stopped and asked the orchestra leader, Mort Lindsey, to start all over again.

Nonetheless, each event generated thunderous applause, and reviews, for the most part, were favorable.

Variety reviewed her appearance in Sydney with: "Judy Garland won the greatest audience ovation in the history of Australian showbiz. She had the audience in the palm of her hand the moment she stepped at the rostrum."

The *Sydney Sunday Herald* wrote, "The Beatles may come and go, but the past week belongs to Judy Garland. That little figure under the lights conquered all."

Before leaving Sydney, she told a reporter, "I have had seven years of bad luck. In Australia, I hope to change all that."

For the second stage of their Australian tour, Herron and Judy decided to take the train from Sydney to Melbourne, although the press had been instructed to meet her at the airport. That miscommunication marked the beginning of what she later termed, "The most embarrassing disaster of my life."

Herron later recalled the condition of the woman he escorted to Melbourne. "She was taking an inordinate amount of amphetamines. Doctors had told her that both her liver and her kidneys were in danger, and she had awful problems with her colon. Yet she was carrying on bravely, although at times she stumbled and fell. This was very dangerous because she could hit her head and cause a concussion. Her days and nights were a living hell."

Her concert on May 20 attracted an audience of 7,000 to Melbourne's Festival Hall. The crowd was seated, hushed in anticipation at the concert's announced starting time of 8:30PM—but no Judy.

Dysfunctionally, she appeared on stage

Airport Jeers for Singer

Singer Judy Garland was hustled towards her aircraft at Melbourne airport last night amid jeers from a small crowd.

She was escorted past the crowd by a uniformed Department of Civil Aviation official and friend, actor Mark Herron. She gave two autographs but was then hurried toward the plane.

Miss Garland, accompanied by Mr. Herron and her manager Mr. Karl Brent, was driven directly to the airport's V.I.P. room and emerged to board the aircraft seconds before it took off.

When sections of the crowd started to jeer her,

est," and "Come back soon, Judy."

Last night the secretary of the Musicians' Union (Mr. J. D. Thomson) said Melbourne musicians employed at the Judy Garland concert were "screaming over the whole shocking affair."

"It was the most humiliating experience professional musicians have ever had to bear in Australia," he added.

"I doubt if I would give permission for any musician to work with her again in Melbourne."

JEERED OUT OF MELBOURNE

Judy Garland Forced on to Plane

(CP From Reuters-AP)

MELBOURNE, Australia—A struggling Judy Garland, who walked out on a concert here Wednesday night, was put aboard a plane for Sydney tonight by three airport officials and American actor Mark Herron.

She cried "no, no" as she was pulled across the tarmac to the plane's steps through a crowd of fans. She protested and tried to break free.

KEPT PROTESTING

Miss Garland continued to protest but her words were lost in the roar of the engines warming up.

Wednesday night, by the time the orchestra played "Over the Rainbow," the

audience was hooting and Miss Garland had stalked off the stage. Besieged by reporters at her hotel, she told them "I think you stink!"

Miss Garland and Herron, her constant companion since she arrived in Australia for a concert tour, arrived at the airport today 10 minutes before the plane was due to take off.

She stayed in the VIP room at Essendon Airport until officials insisted she go aboard.

Flanked by Herron and the officials as she walked to the plane, Miss Garland stopped to talk with about 50 fans lining a barrier, kissed a child and argued with her escort.

The sour notes didn't end with Miss Garland's concert Wednesday night.

ORCHESTRA HUMILIATED

The box office was besieged for refunds today and the head of the musicians' union said the Australian orchestra that accompanied the singer had never been so humiliated.

Miss Garland herself commented, "I didn't like it, did you?"

The American singer's travail began when she arrived an hour late. Her manager blamed it on a sore throat. "You're late" and "have another brandy," hecklers shouted.

Turn to Page 5—JUDY

JUDY GARLAND

Photo (top left) shows fans lining up in front of **Melbourne's Festival Hall** in 1964 for a different musical act, The Beatles.

But whereas the Fab Four were *feted*, applauded, and celebrated, Judy's audience there became enraged and punitive, heckling and booing her with venom —evident in the headlines replicated above.

two hours later. By that time, the audience had begun a series of loud, slow, vengeful claps to indicate that their patience had worn thin.

Finally, she stumbled out onto the stage. At all her previous concerts, her first appearance had brought loud applause, but not that night in Melbourne. She walked out on unsteady feet to greet a crowd that was already hostile. She took the baton from Mort Lindsey and playfully tapped him on the head. She looked bewildered, not remembering her opening song. "You're late!" a heckler shouted at her. She appeared to be drunk. Another heckler yelled at her "Have another brandy, Judy!"

She grew even more bewildered as the audience began to boo her. She responded by calling out, "I love all of you!" but that didn't work. She tried to rescue her act with banter, but no one laughed.

For forty-five minutes, she gave the worst performance of her life. She sang "When You're Smiling" and got through it. In her rendition of "San Francisco," she complained about her squeaky microphone. She suddenly departed from the stage and was gone for twenty-five minutes. At this point, most of the audience began to rise from their seats and headed out the door, many stopping at the box office, demanding a return of their ticket price.

Back on the stage, she stumbled through "Puttin' on the Ritz," stopping every now and then to complain about the mike. She got through "Rockabye Your Baby to a Dixie Melody." Then she tried to sing "By Myself," but had not alerted Lindsey's orchestra to the change in venue.

As more and more people rose to their feet and headed for the exits, she called out, imploring, "Don't go! Where are you going?"

One Aussie yelled back at her, "We're going home! Go back to America!"

At this point, she fled from the stage and into the protective arms of Herron. The abuse from the audience had shattered her already damaged nerves.

Even when she left Melbourne's airport the following morning for a flight to Hong Kong, she claimed, "Some two-hundred hecklers were waiting to ambush me." With Herron by her side, she fled to the plane, the sound of boos and loud denunciations ringing in her ears.

She didn't bother to read the reviews. One paper wrote, "Judy Garland appeared last night at Festival Hall, and the audience walked out on her. She was staggeringly drunk. She is no longer Dorothy. Never in the history of show business in this country has a major American entertainer delivered such an outrageously bad concert. It was not a concert at all, but a living disaster."

In local parlance, a reviewer wrote, "Judy Garland appeared at Festival Hall last night pissed out of her mind."

The next issue of *Variety* reported, "The legend of Judy Garland was sadly and brutally shattered in Melbourne."

The press was there to meet her at the Hong Kong airport when she arrived there with Herron on May 22. News had reached reporters that she'd had to flee from Melbourne. On newsman asked, "What went wrong?"

Her answer was simple: "Australia."

In an article written in 1967 for *McCall's* magazine, she reflected on her brief tour of Down Under:

"I didn't know that Sydney and Melbourne are like Los Angeles and San Francisco. If you're a success in Sydney, you've got to be killed in Melbourne. And vice versa. I just went and tried to sing. Sydney was a tremendous success. But the Melbourne crowds were brutish, and so was the press. At my hotel in Melbourne, the press bored holes through the walls to spy on me. They'd taken the suite next to my bathroom and bedroom. So I went around with Q-Tips and stuck them through the holes. I heard screams on the other end where I'd jab the peeper in the eye. I think that is one of the reasons the reporters got mad at me."

***

After their traumatized arrival in Hong Kong, Judy and Herron headed immediately for the Mandarin Hotel, where they were escorted to their suite on the 22nd floor.

Within the hour, Typhoon Viola slammed into the city with winds of ninety miles an hour. Judy was terrified of storms and clung to Herron, who offered what comfort he could. "That storm in Kansas swept me to Oz. Where in hell is this typhoon going to take us?"

They huddled together in bed. All the TV programs were in Chinese, so at the newsstand downstairs, he'd bought magazines for them to read, thinking they might be locked into their suite for hours. Regrettably, he bought a copy of the latest edition of *Time* magazine.

Its report asserted, "Judy Garland may have gone over the rainbow for the last time," followed by one of the most devastating reviews of her career, attacking her by now notorious performance in Melbourne.

In spite of the storm outside, Herron, exhausted from the flight and the events that preceded it, fell asleep. When he woke up, the storm and heavy rains and wind were pounding at the windows of the suite. It was 4AM, and Judy was nowhere to be seen.

He rushed into the bathroom and discovered Judy in a coma on the tiled floor, an empty bottle of Tuinal capsules beside her. He immediately summoned the night manager and porter, who helped him wrap her in a blanket and put her into a wheelchair.

Through the typhoon, the worst in Hong Kong's recorded modern history, he wheeled her to the Canossa Hospital, run by Catholic nuns, three blocks away.

There, she had her stomach pumped, but not much came up. Doctors told Herron that she may have already absorbed the pills into her blood stream. For the next fifteen hours, she remained in a coma in an oxygen tent.

Hours later, a night nurse examined her body and could find no pulse. Without waking the sleeping Herron, she went to a nearby phone and alerted the local newspaper. The newsroom sent a bulletin to the Associated Press, which was transmitted around the world in time for the front pages of newspapers everywhere. Radios were the first to broadcast the bulletin: JUDY GARLAND DIES IN HONG KONG.

"Second Coming" headlines were crafted and printed with her obituary, which most papers had ready and waiting. Then another bulletin came across the AP wires alerting newspapers that she had regained consciousness and emerged from her coma. Doctors claimed that she had been technically dead for five hours, if such a thing were medically possible. One headline read: DOROTHY COMES BACK FROM OVER THE RAINBOW.

A dire medical report looked grim. A tube had gone into her throat to pump her stomach; her vocal cords and her heart had been damaged; and she had pleurisy in both lungs.

With a deeply troubled **Mark Herron** at her side, Judy exits from Hong Kong's Canossa Hospital with a show-biz smile.

Prior to her stay there, she had ingested the contents of of a container of Tuinol capsules.

To the embarrassment of radio announcers worldwide, news outlets had already reported:

**JUDY GARLAND DIES
IN HONG KONG.**

Herron was told, "It is highly doubtful that Miss Garland will ever sing again."

In the meantime, her Los Angeles doctor, Lee Siegel, had been summoned, and he was on a plane headed to Hong Kong. With him was Karl Brent, her new manager. [*Actually, Siegel did not expect her to live. He had brought Brent along as the "escort" who would accompany her body back to L.A. and to plan her funeral rites.*]

***

Still In Hong Kong on June 10, as a celebration of her 42nd birthday, Herron hosted a small party for a select few. Judy was brought out to sit on a sofa. She told the gathering, "Being alive is birthday present enough." She also said that she might take a long ocean voyage with Herron so that she could recuperate slowly at sea.

The next day, Herron told her some news that he'd been holding back until she felt better. On May 26 in Las Vegas, her sister Suzanne had committed suicide with an overdose of sleeping pills. Judy sobbed for most of the afternoon, mourning the loss of her sister.

[*Judy's other sister, Jimmie, was still alive, but she would die at the age of fifty-nine, having lived longer than either of her siblings.*]

***

610

From her base in Hong Kong, in Herron's words, Judy underwent "history's most rapid recovery, though remaining in a weak condition." Even so, she asked Herron to marry her. She had been told that ship captains were legally empowered to perform marriage ceremonies, so he made arrangements for Captain Thorvald Norvick to marry them aboard his 18-ton cargo ship, *Bodø*, as it was anchored in Hong Kong Harbor.

[Later, Herron and Judy were advised that such ceremonies were legal and official only if a ship were three miles out to sea, far from any port, and that the ceremony aboard the Bodø *had been merely ceremonial—neither official nor legal.]*

Herron, perhaps acting manically to keep the romantic illusion alive, then arranged for them to be married by a Buddhist priest in a ceremony that included burning joss sticks, candles, flowers, meditation, and chants. News of their wedding leaked to the press.

Inconveniently, her divorce from Sid Luft had not yet been finalized. In Los Angeles, he issued a statement to the press: "This guy, Herron, and Judy must have been married on the *Good Ship Lollipop*. Their marriage is a fairy tale. Judy Garland is still Mrs. Sid Luft."

In Hong Kong, Herron issued declaration stating that Judy had obtained a divorce from Luft in Mexico, but that turned out to be incorrect.

Commenting on her most recent marriage, Judy said, "I've been alone in the world too long, facing the darkness by myself. My struggle has always been trying to climb the mountain but never reaching the top. With Mark at my side, the road will no longer be rougher and lonelier. I'm not alone any more."

Two days later, her publicist in California, Guy MacElwaine, denied reports of any marriage. "She's still wed to Luft. Judy was just joking."

[Judy would not be legally free of Luft until the autumn of 1965. "We survived the typhoon, but I feel I'm still living in a blizzard."

That comment led to some reporters asserting that there had been no marriage ceremony at all, either aboard a Norwegian cargo ship or as part of a Buddhist ceremony. One newsman said, "Those ceremonies existed only in Judy Garland's fertile mind."]

In the meantime, Herron was reading and censoring her fan mail. Over the years, most of her letters had been filled with either praise or sympathy. But he noticed a major change after all the recent negative publicity, especially that coming out of Australia.

He destroyed what he called "the poison pen letters." A typical one came in from an ex-Judy Garland fan in Chester, Pennsylvania: "Get rid of that faggot Mark Herron and return to Sid Luft, the father of your children. If you don't, you'll end up being delivered to the Gates of Hell. You're a rotten mother who has ruined her own life and is now setting out to destroy the lives of your children, too."

***

Back in her suite at the Hong Kong Mandarin, Judy struggled to recover from her recent collapse. She insisted that Herron stay by her side,

611

although he was clearly bored with his role as a nursemaid.

One morning, she suffered a relapse, and Herron summoned Dr. Siegel, her visiting doctor from Los Angeles, who had remained in Hong Kong for a while and was still a resident at the Mandarin Hotel. After ascertaining that she had a dangerously high fever, he had her transferred once again to the Canossa Hospital, this time for X-rays, thinking it best for her to remain in residence at the Canossa for at least three days for more tests. Something seemed seriously wrong with her body, which always seemed on the verge of breaking down.

Herron remained with her at the hospital until she fell asleep under sedation. Then he returned to his hotel, restless and itching to see the town. At least he wanted a few drinks in the downstairs bar. But the moment he entered the lobby, the manager spotted him and warned him that a lot of reporters were waiting for him in the bar. To escape from them, he was shown how to exit through the Mandarin's delivery entrance in back.

Outside in the open air, he wandered through the streets until he noticed a sign advertising "The Allen Brothers," a lounge act which was appearing at The Eagle's Nest, the penthouse-level nightclub atop the Hong Kong Hilton. He headed there, eager for some diversion and entertainment...perhaps an adventure.

The Allen Brothers topped the bill, their act backed up by a dancer, Adrienne Erdos, a blonde beauty who, as it turned out, was the girlfriend of Chris Bell.

Although billed as the Allen Brothers, Chris was not the biological brother of Peter Allen, whose real name was Peter Richard Woolnough. Born in small towns in New South Wales, Down Under, both young men had gained fame on the TV show, *Australian Bandstand,* a clone of Dick Clark's *American Bandstand.*

An immigrant to Australia from Hungary, Erdos was also an ice-skater and was put into the Allen Brothers' act as "eye candy" for tired businessmen staying at the Hilton.

Peter could hardly have known that he would meet Judy Garland's "husband" that night. As a devotee of MGM musicals of the 1940s, he had long been one of her most ardent fans. He had read about Judy's arrival in Hong Kong and her so-called marriage to Mark Herron.

So had the *maître d'* of the Eagle's Nest, who seated Herron at ringside—in fact, Peter even introduced him to the audience as a visiting celebrity.

After the show, Chris disappeared with his Budapest-born girlfriend, and Herron invited Peter to join him at his table. The two men bonded at once, each man finding the other alluring. At first, as was inevitable, their talk was of Judy, who was currently being sedated at the Canossa Hospital.

They chatted until the Eagle's Nest closed for the night. Then Peter invited Herron to his hotel room on a lower floor for a midnight cap. At this point, each man had figured out that the other was gay.

The men made love for a good part of the night before falling asleep before dawn. Herron had to get up to visit Judy at the hospital at 8AM. Before kissing Peter goodbye, he promised to see him that afternoon and to bring Judy to his club as soon as she was released from the hospital. "She'll love you guys!"

Back at the hospital, bleary-eyed and in rumpled clothes, Herron found Judy in a foul mood. She complained to him that she had placed multiple calls to the Mandarin, and that he had not been in. "Where in hell were you? Out somewhere having sex?"

"No, I'm too weak for that," he said. He explained about the Eagle's Nest at the Hilton and told her

"Pre-Judy" publicity shots of **Peter Allen and Chris Bell** as "The Allen Brothers."

They were about to enter the lives of Judy Garland and Mark Herron...and ultimately, Liza Minnelli, too.

that as soon as she was well, he wanted to take her there to hear The Allen Brothers from Australia.

"Don't you ever mention that country to me again," she snapped.

Then, Herron told her that he was going shopping while she rested in bed. He slipped into the Hilton to pay an afternoon visit to Peter in his bedroom. As he was leaving, he told his Aussie bloke that "If you keep making love like that, I'm going to fall in love with you."

Eventually, as Herron continued to rave about them, Judy changed her mind about going to hear the Allen Brothers. "Well, at least they loved me in Sydney, so I can forgive them."

When Judy made an entrance into the Eagle's Nest at the Hilton, she was clad in "Minnie Mouse" spiked heels, a white fedora, and a pearl choker that hid her black-and-blue neck bruises and her surgical scars. Instantly recognized by the Allen Brothers, she was given a standing ovation and shown to a ringside table.

Just like Herron, she found the brothers amazingly talented, especially in their rendition of "The Kangaroo Hop." To conclude the evening, Peter sat at the piano and began to play "Over the Rainbow." Judy rose from her table and joined him in a duet. When it was over, the patrons delivered thunderous applause.

She told Allen, "My doctors told me I would never sing again, and I wanted to show the bastards they were wrong."

Their act over, she suggested to Peter, "The night is still young. Perhaps you'll show Mark and me Hong Kong."

Chris excused himself and disappeared with his Hungarian girlfriend.

Peter, Judy, and Herron boarded a ferry from Hong Kong Island to the Kowloon Peninsula [*an integral part of Greater Hong Kong*], where they visited a late-night dive to play pool and drink beer. They stayed too late and missed the last ferry back to Hong Kong Island [*site of their hotels*]. Consequently, Herron "chartered" a piloted rowboat from an old Chinese man, who ferried them back across the channel.

In the rowboat, Herron sat watching as Judy and Peter Allen laughed, talked, joked, and bonded. Peter later told Herron, "When Judy laughs, I hear silver bells."

For the rest of their gig, Herron escorted Judy every night to the Eagle's Nest at the Hilton to hear the Allen Brothers romp their way through their cabaret/lounge act. During the afternoon, while Judy slept, Herron slipped away for sexual rendezvous with Peter in his hotel room, assuring him that "the sex gets better every time."

Judy eventually wore the men down, demanding that after each of Peter's performances with Chris and Adrienne, they hit the town. They visited club after club, settling on the King Kong Bar as their favorite late-night joint.

One night in her suite, Judy insisted that both Herron and Peter listen to her entire Carnegie Hall repertoire. Before she reached the final five numbers, an exhausted Peter dozed off. He was rewarded with her drink thrown in his face. Startled, he heard her say, "I know how to wake up my audience."

Fortunately, he wasn't offended, but took it as a "Judy Joke."

***

Father Bell, the manager of the Allen Brothers and the father of Chris, the "other" member of the group, had already booked them aboard the ocean liner *SS President Roosevelt*, en route at the time from Hong Kong to Tokyo. Herron booked Judy and himself into a suite aboard that ship so that they could sail onward with their new friends. *[Originally built by the U.S. Navy as a transport ship, the* USS General W. P. Richardson *during World War II; it served as a passenger ship, registered under a variety of names, including the* SS President Roosevelt *(1961–1970) before being sold for scrap in 2004.]*

Judy used this time at sea to learn more about her new friend, Peter Allen. He was born in a small town in New South Wales in 1944 as World War II was entering its final brutalizing months. He had been reared mainly by his mother, grandmother, and three aunts. His father had been a hopeless alcoholic and frequently battered him. "I became 'Bloody Nose Peter' since he bashed my face every chance he got. I didn't cry one bit when he took a shotgun, aimed it at his head, and committed suicide."

"One of my aunts taught me to dance and, as a boy, I worked the local tavern singing in blackface from an Al Jolson repertoire. My theme song was 'Mammy'. Those Outback Aussies nicknamed me 'Peter the Poufter Woolnough.'"

As he grew older, he sang and danced in casinos. In those days, Australia had more slot machines than Las Vegas.

"With the coming of the sexual revolution, everybody was fucking everybody else," he said. He felt free to tell her that one night, as he was leaving the club, three rough and tough Aussies grabbed him in the alley behind a tavern and brutally raped him, "leaving me a bloody pulp."

Eventually, he hooked up with Chris Bell, and they worked out a joint act as "The Allen Brothers." It led to their exposure on *Australian Bandstand* and made them quite well-known on their home turf.

Aboard the *SS. President Roosevelt*, where the Allen Brothers were the paid entertainers, Judy sometimes joined their act, singing along with them, or doing a solo every now and then. Her favorite number with Peter became "I Wish You Love."

Their fellow passengers were delighted. The captain said, "I hired the Aussies not knowing I'd get Judy Garland as part of the deal…and free!"

In Tokyo, the Olympic Games were underway, and the town was bustling with activity. Chris, Peter, Herron, and Judy checked into the Tokyo Hilton, where the Aussies performed nightly in its cabaret/lounge, The Star Club.

To Judy's amazement, Peter and Chris had learned to sing "Waltzing Matilda" in Japanese. Sometimes, Judy joined their act, giving her most extended performance in front of American servicemen off-duty but stationed in Japan. For it, she got a rave review in *Stars & Stripes.*

One night, Peter took Judy to one of Tokyo's leading gay bars, Mama San's, with Herron tagging along. She discovered that she had loyal fans even in Tokyo. Wearing a white sequined gown, she stood before a crowd of young gay men who sat on their haunches on the floor as she tenderly sang "Over the Rainbow" to them.

Later, she managed to get through a call to Liza in New York, telling her, "Boy, have I got a guy for you. When I can arrange it, I'm bringing him and his fellow performer, Chris Bell, to London, where I want you to fly over to perform with me. You'll really go for him. He's a helluva lot of fun."

Almost simultaneously, she told Peter, "Have I got a girl for you—my daughter, Liza Minnelli."

She didn't really heed his warning: "If you're into match-making, it's better that you set Liza up with Chris."

Before departing from Tokyo, Judy promised Peter and Chris that she'd send for them as soon as she could find engagements for them in London, perhaps appearing with her. She'd also send them tickets and arrange a place for them to stay.

At the airport, Peter hugged and kissed both Judy and Herron goodbye. After they had gone through the gate to board their plane, he turned to Chris and (incorrectly) predicted, "You and I will never see Judy Garland again."

***

As Judy and Mark Herron departed from Tokyo, she was met by reporters whom she called "news hounddogs." She had intensely disliked the press she'd received. Nevertheless, she spoke to them. "I've learned my lesson. All my troubles were caused by overwork. I plan to see that that doesn't happen to me again."

On June 26, their plane landed in Copenhagen, where she and Herron had an overnight stopover, spending their layover in a suite at the Royal Hotel. In the lobby, she faced at least eighteen members of the Danish press. As she clung to Herron's arm, she said, "I am very, very happy—in fact, the happiest I have ever been in my life."

"Are you legally married?" asked one of the more aggressive reporters.

"I can answer that question by quoting from that old 1942 movie, Bette Davis in *Now, Voyager*. To quote Bette, 'Why ask for the moon when we have the stars?'"

Arriving in London the next day, she and Herron were escorted by Karl Brent, her new on-site manager, in a limousine to a rented home in Chelsea. During a phone call to Liza, in California at the time, she told her, "Whether legally married or not, Mark and I will settle in for a while, living like a blissful couple."

If only that had been true.

As she would later confide to her friend, Noël Coward, "Mark and I are conducting our relationship from a moving telephone booth. He is gone all the time, showing up mainly to get his picture taken as he escorts me around town, where he seems to have alerted the press before I get there."

On July 20, 1964, headlines proclaimed: JUDY GARLAND SLITS WRISTS. She was reported to be lodged in a room at the St. Stephens Hospital.

Acting as her manager, Brent denied the report, explaining that she had accidentally injured herself as she was opening an old trunk. "Miss Garland was using a pair of scissors trying to cut steel wires and had an accident." No one believed him.

She bounced back quickly and only three nights later she entered the London Palladium on the arm of Herron as flashbulbs popped. She was attending a gala charity benefit, *Night of 100 Stars*, but only as a guest, not as a performer. Once she was recognized, her entrance was wildly applauded. Men and women rose to their feet as Herron and Judy walked to the footlights to take a bow.

Escorted to their seats, Judy was astonished that the patrons did not sit down but continued to applaud frantically for ten thunderous minutes. She rose and bowed several times, blowing kisses.

Though not part of the program, she was greeted with chants of "SING, JUDY, SING!" It went on and on until she figured she had to take the stage. And she did, singing "Swanee" and "Over the Rainbow." Each of her renditions received long and sustained applause.

It was later agreed in the press that she outshone every other act, including the new sensation known as The Beatles. [*The Fab Four performed "I'm Flying" from the musical,* Peter Pan.]

Sir Laurence Oliver and Kenneth More appeared onstage together in a drag act, and Burt Lancaster with his longtime friend, Kirk Douglas, did a song-and-dance number.

Shirley Bassey was a featured act, dedicating her songs to Judy and blowing kisses to her from the stage. Discreetly, Judy whispered to Herron, "Whenever I hear Shirley, I don't know if she's imitating Lena Horne or Eartha Kitt."

Judy's "Night of Nights," as she referred to it, was reviewed in the *London Listener*:

"Stars today have become devalued and it is tempting to dismiss them as merely a product of their publicity. So it is salutary to be reminded that a star

616

is a star, with an inexplicable magic which more than justifies the fame and the ballyhoo. Tears were in many eyes at what appeared to be a personal triumph over adversity, while Miss Garland's magnificent voice fully deserved the cheers which eclipsed any that had gone before in this genuinely starry show. This was an exceptional occasion which everyone present will remember forever."

Later, Judy expressed her own feelings about that amazing welcome at the Palladium. "How unlike Melbourne, where they threw kangaroo carcasses at me, arms from cadavers in the morgue, and the unflushed dumps in the stadium's latrines."

As she delivered the following statement, she teared up:

"Because these people were taking the trouble to show me that, to them, all the things that have happened in the past, all the things that have been said about me, didn't matter. They wanted me to know that they really cared. It was as if they were sending a great wave of love across to me. London has always been like home to me. Now, it's more than ever like home. I don't know what happened there at the Palladium, or why the people should have shown such emotion toward me. I guess it's something which just happened. And, believe me, it was the most exciting thing in the world."

At their (rented) home in Chelsea, Roddy McDowall showed up and had a reunion with Herron, his former lover. On many nights, he took them out to a round of parties and to gay bars. At the opening of one of them, Judy was designated as guest of honor, and received loud applause as she entered. At some of the private parties, McDowall escorted her to, Judy was the only female in the room.

A new club had opened in the center of London which was mobbed every night. Its star was Danny La Rue, a female impersonator, who detested that term, preferring to call himself "a comic in a frock." He came out to loud applause wearing a mammoth blonde wig, platform shoes, pink ostrich feathers, and huge plumed headdresses that made him look seven feet tall.

Judy found him to be "an adorable man, a darling of darlings. Behind all that finery, glitter, and glitz, beat a heart of pure gold."

His act began to attract celebrities, and on any given night, seated at a ringside table, you might see Zsa Zsa Gabor, Elizabeth Taylor, Marlene Dietrich, Princess Margaret, and even "The Iron Lady," Margaret Thatcher. Betty Grable became one of La Rue's most ardent fans, and Bob Hope called him "the most glamourous woman in the world."

Broadway producer David Merrick flew in from New York, hoping to get La Rue to replace Pearl Bailey in his stage production of *Hello, Dolly,* but he turned Merrick down. *[La Rue later defined that as "the biggest mistake of my life."]*

Judy and Herron became friends with both La Rue and his lover, Jack Hanson, a rugged ex-commando whom La Rue had met in an East End pub.

Often, after the show, La Rue and Hanson would go home with Judy and Herron, laughing and talking and drinking champagne until London woke up to another morning.

Marlene Dietrich was in town at the time, appearing at the Queens Theatre, where she was introduced by Noël Coward. *[He began his introduction of her to the audience (which included Judy and Herron) with, "God has a talent for creating exceptional women..."]*

Marlene Dietrich and **Noel Coward** were among the most sophisticated people in Europe

Here's a publicity photo associated with Dietrich's 1954 appearance at London's Cafe de Paris.

On Dietrich's night off, she and Coward showed up to dine with Judy and Herron. When Rex Harrison heard about their quartet, he quipped, "It was an evening of sexual ambiguity."

Herron told Dietrich and Coward, "I've never seen Judy look so happy, and it's thanks to me. I love her more and more as each day goes by."

When he excused himself to answer the phone, Judy said, "Mark conducts our relationship from a moving telephone booth when he calls in from time to time. He shows up when he has to escort me somewhere, and he tips off photographers in advance. "

One night, Rex Harrison showed up to meet and talk with Judy. She'd always found him to be suave and charismatic, although he often played characters who were aloof and snobbish. Virtually ignoring Herron, he spent much of the evening fantasizing about Judy and him appearing together in a revival of *My Fair Lady*. He predicted that she would be the "best Eliza Doolittle ever."

Since he was more or less ignored during Judy's reunion with Harrison, Herron excused himself and retired early. At the door, as Harrison was kissing Judy goodbye, he told her, "You could do so much better than this rent boy."

On another night, Judy and Herron were seen entering the Café Royal with the fabled ballet dancers, Rudolf Nureyev and Margot Fonteyn. As Herron later confessed to Roddy McDowall, "As Margot and Judy were chatting, that Russian stud took my hand and placed it on his ample crotch, which started to expand. A tablecloth can cover up many an indiscretion."

Vivien Leigh showed up one night with her new beau, Jack Merivale, who had replaced Laurence Olivier in her life. Out on the terrace, Merrivale told Herron, "You and I have found ourselves stuck with two of the most demented ladies in London. If you think you have troubles with Judy, wait until you hang out with Miss Scarlett O'Hara, who has a lot in common with Blanche DuBois."

***

On August 5, Judy showed up at the recording studio of EMI Records, an affiliate of Capitol Records. For her career, it was a historic moment, marking her last recording session, this time for a 45-rpm disc. The occasion also marked the end of her years-long association with Capitol Records, although the company would, as time went by, issue two more Judy Garland records based on earlier recording sessions.

After hearing the 45's soundtrack, EMI's brass interpreted it as something rather low-caliber and chose not to release it in America.

At the time, Judy became deeply involved with Lionel Bart, the British composer of pop music and musicals. He asked her to record four songs from his upcoming musical, *Maggie May,* a stage play based on a traditional ballad about a Liverpudlian [i.e., "from Liverpool"] prostitute who becomes romantically involved with a free-wheeling sailor. The musical would open at a theater in London's West End in September of 1964 and ran for 500 performances.

Judy recorded four songs from the not-yet-opened *Maggie May*: "The Land of Promises," "It's Yourself," "There's Only One Union," and the musical's theme song, "Maggie, Maggie May."

When Herron wasn't available, Judy often went out on the town with Bart, a closeted homosexual. There was speculation in the press that he had become her new beau, and that perhaps she had dumped Herron. They remained, however, platonic friends.

Bart had become famous in 1960 as the sole creator of the musical *Oliver!*. Andrew Lloyd Webber hailed Bart as "the father of modern British musicals."

In 1963, Bart had won a Tony for Best Original Score for *Oliver!* When it was made into a movie (1968), it won six Oscars, one as Best Picture. Bart's music was heard around the world when he wrote the theme song for the James Bond film, *From Russia With Love* (1963).

***

At the private dinner Judy had hosted for Vivien Leigh at her rented home in London's Chelsea district, the British actress had come up with a casting proposal that Judy found fascinating: a mother-daughter act at the London Palladium starring Judy Garland and Liza Minnelli.

"From what I hear, your daughter is incredibly talented, with a powerful voice in one so young. The two of you might make show

Hip, Swinging, and Liberated London

Upper photo: **Judy** with the writer and composer **Lionel Bart.**

Lower photo: A poster for his hit West End play, songs from which Judy recorded. Some critics define it as his "forgotten masterpiece."

business history at the Palladium."

After staying awake mulling it over all night, a sleepy Judy put through a call to Liza, finally reaching her in New York.

She found her daughter reluctant to agree to the gig. She was flattered, however, that her mother recognized her as a world-class performer even at her young age. But somehow, as Liza later told friends, "It didn't feel right."

She had heard alarming reports about Judy's fragile health, the Melbourne disaster, and the rumors she'd heard about some sort of "bug" she'd contracted in Hong Kong that she could not shake.

At the time, Liza was scrambling to get cast as the lead in a Broadway musical, and she didn't want to leave town, preferring to pursue her goal in New York. Although she didn't want to hurt her mother's feelings, she had to reject the proposal. *[At that point, there was also no certainty that the managers of the Palladium would okay the deal.]*

The London press was publishing items about other possible ventures for Herron and Judy. One was a projected ABC-TV comedy, *It's Better in the Dark,* to be shot in London. Yet another was a co-starring deal for them to appear in a play, *The Owl and the Pussycat.*

[In 1970, Barbra Streisand and George Segal starred in its film version.]

Somehow, some way, by early September, Judy at last persuaded her daughter to fly to London to spend a week with her and Herron. Both of them were waiting at the airport to greet her. Liza's new stepfather hugged her....or was he not her stepfather yet?

Mother-daughter in 1964. The boundaries between their respective roles sometimes got blurred.

SUICIDE & ARSON ATTEMPTS, DRUG ABUSE & SELF-MUTILATIONS

WIDELY PUBLICIZED ÜBER-DRAMAS
WITH PRINCESS MARGARET, PATRICIA KENNEDY, FRENEMIES FROM THE OLD DAYS, AND HAPPENSTANCE "OBJECTS OF HER INCREASINGLY ERRATIC AFFECTIONS"

UNHARMONIOUS DISCORDS WITH LIZA

A CALIFORNIA D-I-V-O-R-C-E FROM SID, &

A SPONTANEOUS (4TH) MARRIAGE AT A TACKY ALL-NIGHT CHAPEL IN VEGAS

"WEDDING BELL BLUES" (MORE ABOUT MARK)

JUDY! JUDY! JUDY!
GARFREAKS & THEIR MUSICOLOGICAL FEUDS

PROMISCUOUS RONDELAYS WITHIN JUDY'S ENTOURAGE
"But it's the '60s, dahling..."

IS IT THE BEGINNING OF THE END?
AS A SINGER, JUDY FLOPS IN CINCINNATI, THEN RECEIVES AN OFFER TO PORTRAY A "DEVOURING MOTHER" IN A BIOPIC OF JEAN HARLOW

FOR JUDY & LIZA: WHAT BECOMES A LEGEND MOST?
BLACKGAMA

"One minute she smiled at me. The next minute, she was like a lioness that owned the stage and suddenly somebody was invading her territory. The killer instinct of a performer came out in her."

—Liza Minnelli, on performing with her mother at the London Palladium

"During the bad days, I'm sure I would have perished without those wonderful audiences. Without that and a sense of humor, I would have died. I think there's something peculiar about me that I haven't died. It doesn't make sense, but I refuse to die."

—Judy Garland

"Although Peter Allen and Liza Minnelli were both in different worlds, their life histories, their mythologies, meshed. Their traumas were similar, and so were their wounds. Liza's story has always remained the saga of a child forever struggling to protect a parent's reputation, to hide the truth, and to remain loyal, no matter how deep the disgrace, no matter how dramatic the disintegration."

—Author Wendy Leigh

"The world is driving me crazy"

—Judy Garland

Judy and Liza were deep into rehearsals for their upcoming show at the London Palladium, but they took time out to ride in a limousine to Heathrow Airport to greet Peter Allen and Chris Bell, who had flown in from Sydney. Judy had invited seven members of the press to meet the Aussies upon their arrival, and she acted like their advance press agent.

"I discovered these two guys in Hong Kong and loved their act. Their appeal can be summed up in one word—TALENT!

"I predict that they're going places and soon will be traveling with me on my next concert tour in America. They are the best male duet I've ever seen perform, and I've seen the best."

After Peter and Chris had moved through British customs and immigration, Judy introduced them to Liza. "Peter, this is the girl I've wanted you to meet—Liza, my daughter… Liza, this is Peter Allen, the boy from Down Under I've been ranting about. Chris Bell here is not his biological brother. They just bill themselves as The Allen Brothers—it's less complicated that way."

At the time, Judy was chicly attired, but Liza was not. If Peter expected that Liza would also be a glamourous figure, he was mistaken. She looked like a typical high school girl, although her features, especially her large eyes, set her apart from coeds who might have been seen on any campus.

That night over a dinner that included both Judy and Herron, Peter became acquainted with Liza, finding her amusing, charming, and with a sharp wit inherited from her parents.

The following day, far away in the courthouse at Santa Monica, Judy's reputation came under fire as heavy artillery was aimed at her from her estranged husband, Sid Luft. Perhaps on the advice of his lawyers, he had held back until now, but this time, he had assembled a coven of cohorts and sympathizers—some of them no doubt paid—to attack Judy's character. His goal was to have the court declare her as an unfit mother for the rearing of Lorna and Joey. At the time, he had only limited visitation rights.

Although this edition of the French-language **Cinemonde** magazine didn't reach newsstands until 1970, the photo its editors put on the cover depicted Liza from several years before its publication, when she looked a bit more like a raw ingenue. Yet even then there was the suspicion, shared by many theatrical insiders, that Liza was hot, ready, and on the rise as serious competition, even for her celebrated mother.

None of that was lost on Judy…

Witness after witness took the stand, most of them former employees Luft had assembled. Each of them testified that Judy was "a hopeless drug addict and alcoholic," and that she had endangered the lives of Lorna and Joey with her reckless behavior.

Luft himself claimed, "My kids have become virtual vagabonds, dragged along from town to town, having been enrolled in at least eight schools. That's why their grades are so bad. They don't know a semblance of family life with Judy Garland, who's not only a terrible mother, but a reckless one."

One of their former housekeepers, Rhoda Chiolak, claimed, "Often at home she's drunk, not able to supervise her children…They sometimes exist on candy bars instead of a proper meal."

Luft associate Vern Alves, a former intimate of Judy, testified to numerous suicide attempts and heavy drug abuse. Alves went on to testify that once, in a hotel in Philadelphia, she pulled off all her clothes and was

Despite the charm of its cover, few other albums associated with the musical repertoire of Judy Garland were as "plagued" (in the words of the respected Judy scholar and musicologist **Lawrence Schulman**) as this one. This illustration shows the cover of the CD "remastering" of Judy and Liza's 1964 concert at the London Palladium. It was released in 2009 by DRG Records, after an earlier attempt to produce and distribute it by Collector's Choice Recordings had failed, on the 40th anniversary of Judy's death.

Could part of the dysfunction associated with the (troubled) soundtracks of this concert have been a reflection of the chaotic events (her recent fiasco in Melbourne, her deteriorating emotional and physical health) swirling around Judy at the time? Schulman, in the *Journal of the Association for Recorded Sound Collections* in 2009, raised a question: "Is it best to release a mediocre recording in its embarrassing entirety, or to cut it down to its best parts according to one or another individual's supposed good taste?"

According to Schulman, "Garland's 1964 Palladium shows pose the dilemma of what to do with a minor work by a major artist... Liza's voice was painfully young...a voice that is yet to flower....Judy herself was in painful vocal condition...her once-resplendent voice...a faded flower, here in ruin…the fun isn't funny, but pathetic... The glimmer is gone, the magic faded."

It was not the first recorded version of Judy and Liza's 1964 concert at The Palladium to be met with disapproval. A four-sided LP, a radically abbreviated (some said "mangled") version of the concert distributed in 1965 was condemned by Schulman and many others as "a confusing mess," with bad production values and without regard to the flows and ebbs of the songs in their order of appearance.

Another attempt (in 2002, by Capitol Records) to re-release 45 of the the (sometimes "doctored") sound tracks , along with rehearsal takes and phone interviews from Judy herself) was pulled out of circulation a few days before their pre-announced release. The album was the victim of ego-driven turf wars and objections from Judy's heirs about how best to preserve Judy's legacy and musical reputation. *[Regrettably for the profitability of the 2009 release, "pirated" versions of the (aborted) 2002 version had already proliferated across the internet.]*

As questioned by Shulman in his scholarly review, Lessons from Judy's 1964 event at The Palladium apply to other great performers, too: It's about what to do with "less-than-great last works that do not represent an artist at his or her peak."

seen running up and down the hallways naked. "At one time she threatened to jump to her death from a hotel window. Her kids often saw her drunk, drugged, and screaming obscenities at them."

Yet despite all the negative testimony, the judge gave Luft only a partial victory. Instead of visitation rights, he was granted joint custody. Perhaps to their long-term suffering that probably extended for years to come, Lorna and Joey sat through all that damaging testimony against their mother.

***

At the London Palladium, on the night of November 8, 1964, in a symbolic reprise of the theme of *A Star Is Born,* Judy Garland witnessed the end of her reign as a superstar. In contrast, it marked the emergence of Liza Minnelli as a world-class performer.

The show was formatted as a fifty-song concert, with Judy performing fifteen solo numbers, including such memorable renditions as "What Now, My Love?" alongside the songs most closely associated with her previous successes: "San Francisco," "The Man That Got Away," and, of course, "Over the Rainbow."

Liza was brought on as Judy sang "Well, Hello Liza!" to the tune of "Hello, Dolly!"

Although Judy had more or less exhausted herself during the long rehearsal of that afternoon, Liza came on like a bolt of lightning.

She did a brilliant rendition of "Who's Sorry Now?", at first sounding a bit like Ella Fitzgerald. But as the song progressed, Liza's delivery took on an eerie hostility that appeared to be directed at Judy. Out of her throat emerged the words, "You...you've had your way. Now you must pay." It received an ovation from the audience.

Their next number, a mother-daughter duet of "It All Depends on You," continued in somewhat the same vein. Liza's lyrics included "You're not to blame, Mother, for what I do." To some observers, her delivery seemed like a direct reprimand (some said "insult") to Judy.

As Judy recalled, "We opened the act as mother and daughter. We ended it as my loving child became my competitor."A headline the next morning read: JUDY & LIZA DUET BECOMES A DUEL.

It is not unknown in the history of humankind for a mother to be jealous of her daughter, Often, it has been a theme in movies, most notably in Joan Crawford's *Mildred Pierce* (1945), where her onscreen daughter, Ann Blyth, betrays her and steals her boyfriend, Zachory Scott.

One critic wrote, "By bringing her daughter, Liza Minnelli, on stage, Judy Garland opened a Pandora's Box. Before last night, she was the most notable high energy songbird, sitting on her throne. Her own daughter has now dethroned her. She upstaged her superstar mother."

Another critic weighed in with: "A polished performer at the age of nineteen, Liza Minnelli had The Palladium rocking last night, evocative of Judy Garland's long ago appearance on that same stage in April of 1951."

Yet another critic theorized, "At times, one had the incredible sensation of seeing and hearing Judy Garland twenty-five years ago when she was at the peak of her vocal power, not the frail little songbird we witnessed last night at The Palladium."

"Gary Cooper met his *High Noon* in that long ago western," wrote Sean Collins. "Last night, Judy faced high noon with her own daughter, who vanquished her on stage."

The Daily Mail was ecstatic:

> *"History was made last night at The Palladium, when Judy Garland and her daughter Liza Minnelli sang together for the first time on any stage. History was made, too, by a frenzied mob of fans who gave Judy the ovation of a lifetime...To talk about Judy Garland rationally is about as difficult as describing magic. Apart from still being the greatest of them all, through every routine it was apparent that she also is an accomplished actress. And if, to the very critical, the voice is no longer always what it used to be, she still has that elusive 'star quality,' which makes her the most-loved performer in the world today."*

***

A few nights after their engagement's final performance at The Palladium, Judy and Liza dined with Peter Allen and Mark Herron at Trader Vic's, a popular restaurant in the center of London. When Judy excused herself for a trip to the powder room, Peter looked into Liza's big eyes and asked her, "Will you go steady with me?"

Then Herron butted in: "Why don't you go a step farther and ask her to become engaged to you?"

"Good idea," Peter said. "How about it, babe?" Liza hesitated for only a moment before accepting. As he was putting a small diamond ring on her finger, Judy returned to the table. With her shrewd powers of observation, she instantly realized what had happened.

Seated again at table with them, Judy ordered champagne to toast the newly engaged couple. When it was poured, she held up her glass to Peter, telling him, "Welcome to the family, son-in-law."

"Don't rush things, mama," Liza cautioned.

Thanks to her acute radar, Judy must have known that Peter was gay, but perhaps concluded that he was bisexual. Probably because she'd been the matchmaker who had brought them together from the very beginning, she didn't seem too concerned with his sexual orientation. On a previous occasion, when she was intoxicated, she'd said, "Most women in Hollywood marry gay husbands. Why do they do that? Find just one actor in Hollywood who is completely straight—I dare you."

Herron had his own motive for wanting to define Peter as a member of the family. He had developed a powerful crush on him. Secretly, the men had booked and retained "daytime lodgings" at a B&B in the Earl's Court sector of London. *[The London press had already nicknamed Earl's Court as "Kangaroo Valley," because of the large numbers of Australia tourists staying in that neighborhood's dozens of cheap B&Bs.]* The staff there might have wondered why Peter and Herron visited their shared room only in the afternoon, rarely, if ever, spending a night there.

A few days after their engagement, Peter and Liza, as a couple, flew to Paris to meet with Vincente Minnelli. She wanted to introduce her new beau to her father.

Minnelli was in France shooting *The Sandpiper* (eventually released in 1965), starring Elizabeth Taylor and Richard Burton, at the time the most publicized couple in the world.

Their outdoor scenes, based on the plot, had to be filmed at Big Sur along the central California coast. For tax reasons, Burton and Taylor had demanded that interior shots be filmed outside the U.S.—in this case, in Paris. To qualify for the lower tax rate, IRS regulations at the time demanded that they could live within the United States for only a month of any fiscal year. Their time quota for 1964 had already been spent in the U.S., shooting outdoor scenes in Big Sur.

Vincente invited Peter and Liza to dine with Taylor and Burton. Taylor dominated the evening, telling amusing tales while Burton drank. "If anyone wants to see me in the nude, they should go see *The Sandpiper*. I pose nude for a sculptor. It will shock audiences."

Vincente said, "Elizabeth's original choice for the sculptor was Sammy Davis, Jr. That would sure have stirred up controversy. We had to settle instead for Charles Bronson."

The following evening, Peter and Liza attended a party for the cast of *What's New, Pussycat?*, which was also being shot in Paris. Peter later referred to that night "as my crash course in celebrity." Woody Allen was there, supervising the filming of his first screenplay.

Liza puts a loving hand on the shoulder of her father, **Vincente Minnelli**, as both gaze up at the stars entering the room. They are attending a screening of his latest film, *The Sandpiper*.

After watching it, Liza assured him, "You are without a doubt the finest director in Hollywood."

METRO-GOLDWYN-MAYER — FILMWAYS

ELIZABETH TAYLOR · RICHARD BURTON
EVA MARIE SAINT

· MARTIN RANSOHOFF'S PRODUCTION · *the Sandpiper*

The MGM film, **The Sandpiper**, was originally written for Kim Novak, but Elizabeth Taylor read the script and wanted it for Richard Burton and herself. It was released in 1965 at the peak of the Taylor/Burton tabloid frenzy.

On screen, they portrayed adulterous lovers, which they had been, but they were married in March of 1964 shortly before filming began.

Columnist Hedda Hopper found the casting ideal. "Tayor & Burton knew a lot about adultery. Just ask Eddie Fisher and the Welsh actress Sybil Williams."

At that party, Peter Allen met another Peter, Peter O'Toole, who had been cast as a fashion editor lusting after beautiful women. Four of them were at the party: Capucine, Romy Schneider, Paula Prentiss, and Ursula

Andress. Tom Jones, who sang *Pussycat's* theme song, was in Paris at the time. He showed up in pants so tight you could determine that he was uncut.

For Liza, the party was a milestone in that she was introduced to Peter Sellers, her future lover. In *Pussycat*, he was cast as a psychiatrist who was crazier than any of his patients. Sparks and bonfires did not ignite between them. *[That would come later.]*

Liza told guests at the party that she was engaged to Peter Allen, although no announcement of that had yet been communicated to the press. "I have found my sanctuary," she said. "The reason I love Peter is that he's a carbon copy of myself."

Somewhat snidely, O'Toole asked her, "Isn't that called self-love?"

When Woody Allen learned that Peter was headed for the States to accompany Judy on her concert tour, he asked, "But how will you cope with her mood swings?"

Peter answered, "There is nothing wrong with a little drama at the end of the day."

Can love conquer all? Before Liza's wedding to **Peter Allen**, rumors about his alleged bi- or homosexuality might have bothered Vincente Minnelli more than they did Liza herself.

But perhaps Allen's publicist, in approving this PR pic, really wanted to convey that, indeed, in many ways, Australians are less inhibited than their North American counterparts...and a lot more fun.

Liza wanted to know if her father approved of her upcoming marriage, and she met privately with him for lunch the following day.

"I like your young man," he told her. "But both of you are quite young and are just beginning your professional careers. No doubt, they'll drive you in different directions, perhaps to different continents. I know the rate of success for such unions is very small. I also know that you are very determined to enter into such a marriage, and I can't be your roadblock."

Later, through some source, Vincente learned a lot more about his future son-in-law. However, he did not share these revelations with Liza.

In his biography of Vincente Minnelli, Emanuel Levy wrote: "There were indications that even Judy was beginning to change her mind about Allen when she learned more about his gay lifestyle. Minnelli, too, was worried about the gossip that outed Allen as a flamboyant homosexual trying to pass in straight society as a bisexual as a means of promoting his career. Who better than Minnelli to understand the urge to do that? He had always been discreet about his own sexuality. But Allen belonged to a different generation, and he was known to frequent gay bathhouses in whatever city he was in and to attend all-night male orgies in every place he performed."

Liza and Peter were back in London when Judy held a press conference, announcing her daughter's engagement to Peter Allen. She explained who he was and how she had discovered him.

628

At that same confab, Herron told the visiting Hollywood columnist, Mike Connally, that he was abandoning his acting career to take over the management of Judy's.

Later that day, Peter and Judy went to Heathrow to see Liza board a flight to New York. She was returning to the U.S. to audition for an upcoming Broadway musical, *Flora, the Red Menace.*

***

At 6:30PM on the evening of December 19, 1964, Judy, Peter, and Chris Bell arrived in New York and were transferred by limousine to the Regency Hotel on Park Avenue. Liza was waiting there to greet them. When she saw him, she fell into Peter's arms.

Judy told the press that she had not yet decided whether she'd make her home in New York or Hollywood, and even suggested that she might settle permanently in London.

Then she was asked about the possibility of a double wedding—Judy & Mark Herron; Liza & Peter Allen.

Her answer? "Dream on."

***

Peter O'Toole

HELLRAISER | SEXUAL OUTLAW | IRISH REBEL

DARWIN PORTER & DANFORTH PRINCE

The also-very-flamboyant **Peter O'Toole** also had a LOT to say about Peter Allen, Judy Garland, Liza Minnelli and everyone else in the movie and theater arts.

For more about everything that the "occasionally mad" O'Toole did to surprise and shock the movie and theater-goers of his era, consider referencing Blood Moon's 2015 overview of his rakish charm, high-profile affairs, and spectacular eccentricities.

For the Christmas holidays of 1964, Sid Luft refused to transfer Lorna and Joey to New York. Because it was her officially sanctioned time to have her kids with her, Judy defined Luft's decision as "kidnapping." Lorna and Joey did fly cross-country to meet her on December 29th when Judy presented them, belatedly, with their Christmas presents.

For the final day of 1964, Judy and Herron attended a benefit for the Actors Studio which had been configured as a New Year's Eve party. They immediately encountered a flamboyantly intoxicated Shelley Winters. Although Winters trapped Herron in a corner, Judy managed to slip away from her to make the rounds.

"I've just flown in from the Coast, where I couldn't get a decent fuck," Winters said. "I hope my luck improves in New York. Oh, how I miss the good old days in Hollywood: Clark Gable, Burt Lancaster, Marlon Brando, Sean Connery, Errol Flynn, even Howard Hughes....You wanna be next?"

"Sorry, Miss Winters, but I'm the exclusive property of Miss Judy Garland."

"You'll get over that soon enough," Winters said. "Welcome to New

York, where everybody fucks everybody else."

Before the stroke of midnight, Herron escaped from Winters' clutch to make his way to Judy, where he took her in his arms and gave her a long, lingering kiss.

It was at that moment that a bell rang. It was midnight. Judy joined with the rest of the party singing *Auld Lang Syne* with her fellow actors.

***

Much later, in an interview with *Good Housekeeping*, Liza said, "When I was a little girl and jumped up on stage with mother to dance while she sang, it was unrehearsed, amateurish, and spontaneous. Working with her at The Palladium was a different thing. I'll never be afraid to appear again with any topnotch performer—say, Frank Sinatra. I've had my baptism of fire. Mother became very competitive with me. I was not her daughter, but another woman vying with her under those harsh lights."

Their second concert, on November 15, more or less confirmed what the opening night critics had already stated, but also received rave, self-standing reviews of its own. The critic for *The Viewer* wrote:

"Down the aisles ran the so-called unemotional British—balding, middle-aged men in dinner jackets and long-haired youths jostling to get to Judy's outstretched hands—and to kiss them. It was a fantastic sight to climax a fantastic night."

After the final show, Judy and Herron invited Liza, Peter, and Chris Bell to join them at the late-night disco, Ad Lib, which at the time was one of the trendiest in London, the favorite of visiting celebrities. They were greeted by Jackie Collins, the manager, who later moved to Hollywood and became a best-selling author turning out potboilers.

The following night, they were collectively invited to the country home of actor George Sanders for a birthday celebration. The spontaneous entertainment by the guests should have been recorded, especially when Judy and Vivien Leigh sang a duet.

By now, Judy had realized that it was a bad time to have teamed up with her daughter for a joint appearance at The Palladium. She was in poor health and at one point prior to the show, signed up for a brief rest cure in a London nursing home.

Not wanting another scandal, she later trivialized her stay there to the press, calling its reason as "a mere stomach ache." Actually, she'd been suffering from acute abdominal pain, perhaps deriving from her kidneys and liver.

***

Judy faced the New Year of 1965 with almost no money in her bank account, but she managed to get Bank of America to lend her $25,000 to keep her afloat.

By mid-January, she and Mark Herron were back in Los Angeles, which she had not seen since early May of the previous year. Waiting for her at the airport, Lorna and Joey rushed to meet her, and it was a lovefest of hugging and kissing.

After she settled in and went out on the town with Herron, they showed up at Daisy, a chic nightclub. What surprised celebrity-spotting reporters that night was that their guests included her ex-husband, Vincente Minnelli, and his wife, Denise.

Her first gig did not come until the first of February, when she showed up at CBS-TV, the studio from which she'd been fired. For an appearance on their show, *On Broadway Tonight,* she taped six songs. That was not unusual for her. What was, was that the taping marked her first recording with Peter Allen and Chris Bell, singing "I Wish You Love." Liza sat in the audience, taking it all in.

When the show was aired, it was reviewed by the *New York Daily News,* among other newspapers: "When Judy Garland came onto the TV screen, she lit it up like a glittering Broadway marquee. Judy Garland is back!"

She was paid $7,500 for her appearance.

In a rare move that month, Judy, through her lawyer and former lover, Greg Bautzer, managed to suppress the publication of an unauthorized biography, entitled *Judy,* written by Charles Samuels. She had received an advance copy and had found it embarrassingly revelatory, in part because of its allegations of lesbianism.

"I WISH YOU LOVE"—**Judy with Peter Allen** on the CBS-TV show, *On Broadway Tonight.*

She would be surprised one day when he married her daughter.

She'd be even more surprised when she found out he was sleeping with her husband.

[Pre-announced by Putnam for a per-unit price of $4.95 and scheduled for release in February of 1965, and then delayed till late June of the same year, its publication was eventually canceled altogether. Customers who had pre-ordered it were sent postcards informing them that it had been canceled, and refunds were issued to those who had pre-paid. There appears to be only two reasons why Bautzer was able to get it suppressed: He either paid Samuels not to publish it, or else he threatened a million-dollar libel suit against its author and /or publisher if it were.]

Judy's next gig was in Toronto, but she stopped first with Herron in New York. They stayed for a short time in the townhouse owned by Miriam Hopkins, a blonde-haired, spectacularly stubborn screen diva who had reached the peak of her career in the 1930s.

Judy and Herron arrived in Canada with Peter Allen and Chris Bell. They had signed on as an opening act for Judy's show at the O'Keefe Center. She had been booked for a week-long engagement. Actually, she was a last-minute replacement for Nat King Cole, who had come down with a severe flu.

The Allen Brothers charmed the audience in Toronto with numbers that included "Waltzing Matilda" and "The Kangaroo Twist." They were followed by comedian Nipsy Russell, who did a sketch and a high energy dance routine.

At last, Judy appeared onstage. Accompanied by Mort Lindsey's Orchestra, she paced her way through numbers that included "Swanee" and "Chicago", and ending with "Over the Rainbow". As part of the show, she and Peter sang and danced "The Toreador." Her voice was weaker than usual because she was feeling the onslaught of the flu.

On the second night of her gig in Toronto, she was in a weakened condition, and at times coughing. She didn't include "Over the Rainbow" in that night's repertoire, in spite of the dozens of requests for it yelled to her from the audience.

On February 10, she canceled both the matinee and evening performances because of the flu, yet she was back on stage the following night.

On the final night of her gig in Toronto, Liza flew in from New York to watch the show. When it was over, Judy received a check for $98,000, money she desperately needed.

Variety reviewed the show, writing, "In truth, Miss Garland's voice was like sandpaper grinding, often missing the notes completely. Laryngitis kept her out of both shows one day. Although she was seldom on key throughout the one-week engagement, audiences did not seem to mind."

Her trials and tribulations seemed but a memory when Judy and Herron flew into the Miami Airport. A limousine was waiting to take them to her lavish suite at the Fontainebleau Hotel on Miami Beach. At a press conference, she made a startling and untrue statement to the press: "There is nothing tragic about my life."

In a voice that was powerful at times, tender at others, and always on key, she wowed her audience, most of whom were "snowbird" visitors from the Northeast.

Her concert at the Fontainebleau was another triumph. *The Miami Herald* defined it as, "The best show ever presented in Florida. Her voice danced."

Liza flew into Miami to see her mother's show and to celebrate her nineteenth birthday with Peter and Judy. Herron tossed an elaborate party for her.

When Judy had finished her gig at the Fontainebleau, she had to rush over to its competitor, the Eden Roc, to fill in for Debbie Reynolds, whose show had ground to a halt after she'd been stricken with the flu. Judy told the press, "And you guys call me unreliable."

***

In the history of Hollywood, competing studios have often devised, more or less simultaneously, parallel plots and themes for equivalent movies. Such was the case with two virtually simultaneous but competing biopics, each released in 1965, about Jean Harlow, Hollywood's platinum blonde bombshell of the 1930s.

[The idea of a biopic on Harlow had always fascinated the creative teams of

Hollywood. A movie based on her life had first been raised in the 1950s yet didn't come to immediate fruition. In 1964, Irving Shulman wrote a best-selling book about Harlow. Joseph E. Levine, through Paramount, acquired the screen rights for its film adaptation. Around the same time, in a kind of "Harlow craze," Columbia considered a film starring Cleo Moore as Harlow, and 20th Century Fox thought Jayne Mansfield might be ideal as the tragic blonde, but neither was ever started. A screenplay was then fashioned for Marilyn Monroe, but she died before production could begin.]

Finally, at Paramount, filming based on the ideas nailed down in Schulman's book began on *Harlow*. Released in June of 1965, it was directed by Gordon Douglas and starred Carroll Baker in the title role. Angela Lansbury, only six years older than Baker, played her greedy mother, "Mama Jean." Rounding out the cast were Raf Vallone as Harlow's big-spending stepfather; and Peter Lawford playing Paul Bern, who marries Harlow, proves himself impotent, beats her, and eventually commits suicide.

After an overview of Harlow's failed relationships and alcoholism, the Paramount version ends with Harlow's death from kidney failure at the age of twenty-six.

At around the same time, the low-budget Magna Corporation, in a move interpreted as predatory and cynical, also began the rushed filming of a feature film with the same name: *Harlow*. Shot in only eight fre-

Blondes, blondes, everyone's a blonde...**Ginger Rogers**, depicted above in 1933, had been a jealousy-inducing thorn in Judy's side since her adolescence.

Lower photo shows **Jean Harlow**, the jazz age sex symbol who "legitimatized" peroxide and, according to her critics, "easy virtue."

netic days, it was released in May of 1965, about five weeks in advance of its better-funded competitor. Slapdash and hasty, it was filmed in cost-saving black-and-white format known as "electrovision," a photographic technique later relegated to television. On a very limited budget, producer Bill Sargent and director Alex Segal cast Carol Lynley as Harlow (the similarity of the leading actresses' names added to the confusion of viewing audiences), with Judy Garland set to play "Mama Jean," her devouring, tyrannical mother. Rounding out the cast were Efrem Zimbalist, Jr., Barry Sullivan, Hurd Hatfield, Hermione Baddeley (as Marie Dressler), and Audrey Totter, that 1940s *film noir* blonde.

Disillusioned and disgusted after only two days on the set, Judy withdrew from the project, telling Lynley, "Honey, I'm not drunk, and I'm not on drugs, but this picture is a piece of junk. I'm out of here!"

Although Eleanor Parker was immediately hired to replace her, she, too, bolted after only two days.

Eventually, the role of Mama Jean went to Ginger Rogers, who slogged on to finish the picture with Lynley. *[Replacing Judy in a film role certainly wasn't anything novel for Rogers. She had previously stepped in to replace her in* The Barclays of Broadway *(1949) opposite Fred Astaire.]* One of the greatest stars of Hollywood, Rogers' involvement in this picture cast a sad and dismal light on the end of her film career.

Both *Harolow* movies flopped at the box office.

***

On April 5, 1965, Judy was seen by millions of people when she made a surprise appearance at the Academy Awards presentations. In the aftermath, Rex Harrison (for *My Fair Lady*) and Julie Andrews (for *Mary Poppins*) would walk off with the gold.

Joe Pasternak, who produced the show for ABC-TV, selected Judy to appear, but soon realized that she might not be up to the task. Gene Kelly introduced her for a medley of songs by Cole Porter, as arranged by Roger Edens. He'd been her musical mentor for years, but this was the last time they'd work together, as he died in 1970.

Judy walked onto the stage with a microphone on a long cord, which she casually flipped over her shoulder. For once, and perhaps for the only time, everybody in the intensely competitive audience of her peers wanted her to succeed.

Her conductor, Johnny Green, actually shed a tear when he realized that she was not in top form. She later admitted, "My voice was off, but I felt love from the audience. All was forgiven. I was back in their good graces, at least for that night."

She did not get good reviews, one critic claiming, "Last night *tout* Hollywood saw Judy Garland go over the rainbow. But the only thing she found at the end was a film career in twilight."

***

After her less-than-stellar performance at the Academy Awards, Judy needed a vacation, so along with Herron, Lorna, and Joey, she flew to Hawaii, arriving there on April 9. They were driving to a bungalow on Diamond Head Road on Oahu.

As they were checking in, Steve McQueen appeared at the door to welcome

Too Many Damn Rainbows

Although other (younger) actors received Oscars that night, **Judy,** as part of the stage show, was the star of **the 37th Annual Oscar ceremony** (1965).

them, as he was booked into the cottage next door.

At first, the vacation seemed idyllic, but after two days it turned ugly. Lorna and Joey slept in the same bed in the room next to Herron and Judy's. Late at night, the children were awakened by a raging fight between Judy and Herron in their small living room.

Lorna opened her bedroom door slightly to witness a scene of horror. Judy was screaming at Herron and striking him, and he was slugging her back. He was stark naked, and Judy was clad only in panties. As Lorna remembered in a memoir, "Both of them were covered in blood."

When Herron spotted Lorna, he retreated to his bedroom, hurriedly dressed, and stormed out of the house. Judy had hired an assistant to help around the cottage and to look after the children. The assistant suddenly emerged and began to put ice on Judy's swollen eye, ordering Lorna to mop up the blood.

Judy retreated to her bedroom, and when Lorna and Joey got up the next morning, the assistant told them not to disturb their mother, who would be sleeping in all day.

After breakfast, they headed for the beach for the day, returning at around 4PM. Judy was sitting in front of the cottage in a lounge chair, sunning herself, something they had never seen her do because of her delicate

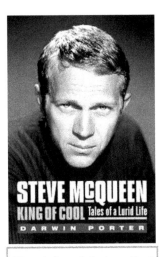

STEVE McQUEEN
KING OF COOL Tales of a Lurid Life
D A R W I N   P O R T E R

After Judy set (yet another) house on fire, this time something she'd rented for a holiday with her children in Oahu, **Steve McQueen,** "the King of Cool," offered to put out the flames.

Wanna read more about McQueen and how he appeared cool even when he wasn't?

Check out Blood Moon's award-winning biography, **Steve McQueen, King of Cool**, for stories about his almost unimaginably lurid life.

porcelain skin. She was wearing a two-piece blue bathing suit and large sunglasses, hiding her black eye. Herron was nowhere to be seen.

From Judy's bedroom, Lorna and Joey noticed smoke billowing out. Lorna shouted, "Fire! Fire!" But Judy ordered her not to go inside and remained perfectly calm. "I've called the fire department. I set Mark's clothes on fire myself."

At this point, McQueen rushed into the yard clad in his jockey shorts. He'd come to try to help put out the fire, but she ordered him to sit down.

"Don't be a hero, McQueen," she said. "This isn't a damn movie. The firemen are on the way."

After putting out the fire, the firefighters asked for Judy's autograph. When she was allowed to go inside, she and Lorna discovered she had also ruined her own wardrobe. What remained of Judy and Herron's closets had been linked by a ventilation shaft, and all her clothes had been ruined by the soot and smoke.

The next morning, Joey and Lorna were hustled aboard a plane headed back to Los Angeles. Judy remained behind. When she returned to L.A., it was obvious that she had made up with Herron, who accompanied her and moved back into their home. No mention was ever made of the fire.

***

After their disastrous holiday in Hawaii, Judy and Herron flew to Charlotte, North Carolina, for a gig, on April 22, at the Charlotte Coliseum. At the Red Carpet Motor Inn, she held a small press conference, holding onto Herron's arm. As she smiled into his face, she said, "I can't go on forever getting by with 'Over the Rainbow'. Mark here is forcing me to learn new songs."

When a reporter asked her what new songs she planned to introduce the following night, she said, "Hush...Hush, Sweet Charlotte," a reference to the film, released in 1964, that Bette Davis had made with Olivia de Havilland after Joan Crawford dropped out.

Perhaps she was joking, because she did not sing that number, sticking instead to such tried and true songs as "The Trolley Song" and "Over the Rainbow." The Allen Brothers opened the show. Judy's appearance lasted for only forty minutes before she abruptly exited from the stage. She was paid $29,000 for her engagement.

***

Back in New York, Judy and Herron had a "gay old time" attending a party Andy Warhol threw for Rudolf Nureyev at his studio, The Factory.

Escorting Judy and Herron were the gay actor, Montgomery Clift, and the gay playwright, Tennessee Williams. Clift was intoxicated, and Williams was drugged.

Half-jokingly, Judy suggested to Clift that the two of them should co-star in a remake of *Sunset Blvd.* (1950). [*Clift had originally been offered the role of the gigolo, Joe Gillis, opposite Gloria Swanson, playing the faded screen star of yesterday, Norma Desmond, but rejected the role because of pressure exerted by his notorious "sponsor" at the time, torch singer Libby Holman. In reference to her own possible casting as the older lover of a younger man, Judy said, "I'd be perfect typecast as a legendary screen has-been."*]

Then, in a separate conversation with Tennessee Williams and still angling for possible roles, Judy suggested that she be cast in a revival of his play, *A Streetcar Named Desire.* "The part of the demented Blanche DuBois would require very little acting on my part."

En route back to their hotel, Herron told her that Williams, drunk and high, had sexually propositioned him during the dinner party. "He told me I'd be perfect in the role of Chance Wayne, the hustler in *Sweet Bird of Youth.*"

"I wonder what gave him that idea," Judy said provocatively.

***

In the spring of 1965, Judy was trying to establish residency in Nevada so that she could finally divorce Sid Luft.

636

But according to Luft, "I decided I would outsmart her and I brought charges in Santa Monica, since California has much better community property laws than Nevada. I wasn't going to let her get away with any property or money that I felt was owed to me or coming to me in the future. In other words, I beat her to the punch."

Judy appeared in court in Santa Monica on May 19. As she was entering the courthouse, she told a reporter, "It's about time I divorced Luft the Lug. I've always felt that it's better to cut out completely when two people can't get along and are always fighting over money."

Luft had already filed charges against her in Las Vegas, alleging that she had concealed two million dollars in earnings that were owed to him as part of their joint business enterprises. In court, he also alleged that he had been denied royalties from her films *Gay Purr-ee, A Child is Waiting,* and *I Could Go On Singing.* He also claimed that royalties from Columbia Records should have been split with him. Frustrated that his legal challenges had failed in Vegas, he decided to renew them in California.

In his battle for custody of Lorna and Joey, Luft once again introduced testimony that she was

D-I-V-O-R-C-E

Reno—and the rest of Nevada, too—has been called "The divorce capital of the world."

Judy maneuvered, unsuccessfully, for a divorce from Luft in Nevada, but to her chagrin, the venue was changed to California, where Community Property laws would tend to benefit the less wealthy survivor of the (estranged) marriage (i.e., Sid Luft).

LET'S ASK THE WIZARD:
SHOULD JUDY ('OUR DOROTHY') HAVE COLLABORATED WITH ATTEMPTS TO CAST HER AS THE DEMENTED HAS-BEEN "COUGAR," **NORMA DESMOND?**

In the mid-60s, when other film roles had dried up, Judy began scheming, maneuvering, and dreaming of casting herself as Norma Desmond in a remake (co-starring Montgomery Clift as the gigolo) of *Sunset Blvd.*?

The photo on the left shows **Sunset Blvd.**'s original cast members, **William Holden** as the "play for pay" hustler, Joe Gillis, and **Gloria Swanson** as the crazed has-been from the (silent) Silver Screen.

As an aging actress familiar with the seductive charms of younger men, Judy would probably have been brilliant. One thing is certain: EVERYBODY would have seen it.

an unfit mother, "drugged every day of her life, even setting fires in her house, and endangering the lives of her children."

Judy countered that she was a loving mother, fervently protective of Lorna and Joey. She counter-charged that Luft had a violent temper and frequently attacked her, even injuring her. She further claimed that he conducted numerous adulterous affairs with Hollywood starlets. "My children and I feared him every time he walked through the door. And he never contributed to the support of our kids."

Judy won, and although it would not become final until September, the divorce was granted. She was awarded full custody of Lorna and Joey, and the judge ordered Luft to pay $300 a month in child support.

Outside the courthouse, she announced her victory. "I am going to marry Mark Herron. My three children adore him. So at long last, with Mark, I am happy for the first time."

Richard Brody, writing in *The New Yorker,* said, "Sid Luft recognized Judy's intellectual powers, her vast and protean personality, her theatrical talents, her artistic imagination, her sheer human force. He laments the end of their romance and the dissolution of their marriage, but he laments all the more the neglect and abuse of one of the great artists of the time. Garland came off as a production of the studio system which both created and destroyed her."

*****

At the time of her divorce from Luft, Judy—as always—was besieged by debt, especially from the IRS, and numerous bill collectors. Lawsuits from former co-workers were piling up, too.

She continued her custom of checking in and out of hotels without paying the bill. On such occasions, she had her children put on all the clothes they could wear, and then escape in the middle of the night.

The actress, Hermione Gingold, once described a scene she'd witnessed when her taxi came to a stop in Manhattan on 57ᵗʰ Street. "Judy and her children were standing in front of a hotel. Apparently, she had been turned out of the hotel for not paying her bill. She was shouting at the doorman, who would not release her luggage. I didn't know whether to get out of the taxi and help her or not. I feared that if I did, it would be awfully embarrassing for her, so I rode on feeling nothing but pity for a star who had made millions for other people."

Judy continued with her concert tours and accepted almost any gig offered. She made that claim, but then qualified it: "The only deals I turned down were to appear in a lesbian bar in Skunk, Oklahoma; a bar catering to child molesters in Shitsville, Nebraska; and a tavern attracting panty sniffers in Farts Village, Montana."

As Judy was dumping Luft in California, her older daughter, Liza Minnelli, was starring on

WOMEN WE LOVE

Hermione Gingold— an embarrassed witness to a street scene debacle involving a destitute Judy Garland.

638

Broadway in *Flora, the Red Menace*. In vivid contrast, Judy would end her "memorable but deplorable" month of May by taking Herron to Cincinnati, where she was set to present a concert at Cincinnati Gardens, for which she was to be paid $20,000. The concert turned out to be one of the low points of her singing career.

Her performance was choreographed with two acts separated by an intermission, but she managed to go on only for the first one. Backstage, she took ill and had to leave. Management announced she would not appear again, much to the disappointment of the audience. Most of the 4,500 patrons that night felt that they'd been cheated.

As it turned out, she was running a temperature of 102° and was suffering from a virus infection.

Judy was almost violently ill during the flight from Ohio back to Los Angeles. There, she checked into the Neuropsychiatric Institute of UCLA. It seemed that all the medication she'd been massively ingesting had damaged her internal organs and put her life in danger.

In memorializations of this once-enormous entertainment and sports complex in Ohio (built in 1949, demolished in 2017), mention is often made of The Beatles and Elvis.

Less of a fuss is made, however, about Judy Garland's appearance in 1965.

It was evaluated at the time as something that irritated many members of the audience, who left feeling cheated.

Her appearance here in the Buckeye State was not her finest, by far.

Once again, she underwent a miraculous recovery. A few days after her release, she and Herron were photographed at the Cocoanut Grove, showing up for a concert that featured Jack Jones .

The next day, she taped an interview for *The World of Showbusiness*, which was broadcast on the Armed Forces Radio and Television Services overseas.

For her forty-third birthday on June 10, her longtime friend, Peter Lawford, began organizing a party for her, secretly inviting some of her friends and admirers. Like so many previous occasions, the lavish "surprise" party unfolded horribly.

In the days leading up to it, Herron had spent several hours with Lawford planning the guest list, the entertainment, the venue, and the food. Judy interpreted his time with Lawford (a notoriously promiscuous bisexual) as "suspicious." With absolutely no advance knowledge about the party being planned in her honor, she suspected Herron was having an affair with him.

At first, furious, she refused to go to Lawford's home, forcing Herron to reveal that all the time, they had been planning this surprise party for her.

Chastised, but still convinced that Lawford had already seduced her boyfriend, she agreed to get dressed and go.

At the party, as the night wore on, Judy was drinking an excessive amount of champagne, and still furious at Lawford, despite his good intentions in his planning and hosting of the "surprise" birthday party in her

639

honor. At one point, fully intoxicated, she turned on him: "You know, Peter, you never could act worth shit. You were the worst actor in the MGM stable. Mayer only hired you because many of his male stars were in the service during the war."

He did not fight back, but sat calmly in his chair, listening to her tirade. In her frustration at his lack of response, she hit him over the head with her purse. Then she stormed out of the party without saying goodbye to anybody. Inside her car with Herron, she ordered him to take her back to the medical clinic at UCLA, where she was admitted once again as a patient.

[On December 17, about six months after her spectacularly disastrous "surprise" party, Judy read in Variety *that Lawford and his wife, Patricia Kennedy, had filed for a legal separation. Feeling that it was time for her to make up with him, she wrote him a note, expressing regret that his marriage to JFK's sister had not worked out. She also apologized to him for "my outrageous behavior at your party—please forgive me. I was half out of my mind because of these damn pills I've been taking. The world is driving me crazy"]*

When she was released from the clinic, Judy and Herron flew to Las Vegas for a two-week engagement (June 15 to the 28th) at The Thunderbird Hotel. Backed up by a thirty-one piece orchestra, her show was designed to outdraw every other act along the glittery Strip.

Once again, the Allen Brothers were her opening act. The Aussies had been success-

Happier times: Snapped after their wedding in 1954, here's **Peter Lawford**, an actor who was "long on charm" and usually "short of funds."

It was snapped a few minutes after his "fêted-in-the-society-pages" marriage to **Patricia Kennedy**, sister of JFK, RFK, and Teddy Kennedy.

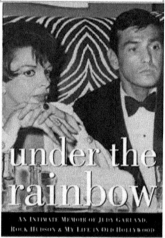

under the rainbow

AN INTIMATE MEMOIR OF JUDY GARLAND, ROCK HUDSON & MY LIFE IN OLD HOLLYWOOD

john carlyle

Many friends and/or lovers who knew Judy turned their experiences with her into memoirs. Such was the case with the handsome gay actor, **John Carlyle**.

During the optimistic early years of his career as a newcomer, his agent (Henry Willson) had tried to promote him as "the new Montgomery Clift", but the campaign wasn't successful.

Near the end of his life, he authored *Under the Rainbow*. After some legal and editorial wrangling (and censorship) It was published in 2006. Having died in May of 2003 from lung cancer, he never saw his book in print.

In it, he "dished sympathetic dirt on Judy's peccadilloes," mused about his affairs with, among others, Tom Drake ("the boy next door" in MGM's *Meet Me in St. Louis)*, and reflected on the obstacles he confronted as a Hollywood wannabe in an era of homophobia.

ful in every previous appearance they'd made with Judy.

When it was over, back in Los Angeles, Judy, Herron, and Peter Allen attended a party at the home of her close friend, John Carlyle, with whom she had formed a relationship ever since he had had a minor role in *A Star Is Born*.

At the party, Carlyle introduced her, along with Herron and Peter Allen, to his latest acquisition, his then-boyfriend, actor Craig Hill.

[Not long after the party, Carlyle informed Judy that his affectionate relationship with Hill had ended one night when Carlyle brought home a hustler for paid sex. A huge fight began when Hill returned from a trip two days earlier than expected and discovered Carlyle "in flagrante delicto." In the aftermath, the relationship ended and Hill moved out.

Judy also learned that Hill had been the former lover of Rock Hudson.

After walking out on Carlyle, Hill appeared in Las Vegas, living with Marlene Dietrich in Billy Wilder's vacation home.

But soon, Dietrich dumped Hill to take up with the English actor, Michael Wilding, who had previously been married to Elizabeth Taylor.

These roundelays of sexual deception continued flagrantly: Unknown to Judy at the time, and consistent with the sexual revolution then consuming America and Southern California in particular, her friend, Carlyle complicated the dynamic by slipping around and having an affair with Herron. Around the same time, in Las Vegas, Peter Allen began an affair with Craig Hill after Hill was "evicted" by Dietrich.

Judy knew about the Hill/Allen affair because the two performers made it rather obvious. Peter was still engaged to her daughter, but it is not known if this revelation caused Judy to endure any sleepless nights. She seemed amazingly tolerant of Peter's homosexual liaisons while he was touring with her.

Peter's interlude with Hill did not survive their time together in Las Vegas. The last news anyone in Judy's entourage heard at the time was that Hill had moved to Spain to make "spaghetti Westerns."]

Craig Hill was one of the "pretty boys" being hyped by the gay talent agent, Henry Willson.

Willson's bevy of beefcake included Rock Hudson, Robert Wagner, Tab Hunter, Troy Donahue, James Darren, and Rory Calhoun.

Hill had made his screen debut in 1950 with a mere walk-on part in *All About Eve*, starring Bette Davis and Anne Baxter.

In Las Vegas, at the Thunderbird on opening night, it was a wonder that Judy was able to go onstage at all. By 3PM that afternoon, she had ingested so many pills that she went into convulsions. But she recovered before nightfall and was not only able to go on, but she got rave reviews in the papers the next day. *Variety* wrote, "Judy Garland hit a home run with the bases loaded." A Vegas newspaper, *The Sun*, called her "the most exciting performer in the history of show business."

***

At this point in her life, it seemed that every triumph was followed by a disaster of one sort or another. After her opening night in Las Vegas, her divorce lawyers the next day legally attached, through a lien, the fee she received from the Thunderbird, with the understanding that it would be diverted to pay her legal fees.

She said, "If it's not a lawsuit taking away my salary, it's the damn IRS. Don't those bastards know that I have to make a living and feed my kids, not to mention my boyfriend."

In spite of her frail physical condition, she was able to complete the Thunderbird gig with no more breakdowns.

Over the course of his career, **Andy Williams** would record forty-three albums, fifteen of them gold certified, and sell more than 100 million records worldwide.

His most famous song became "Moon River" by Johnny Mercer and Henry Mancini. From 1962 to 1971, he hosted his own TV show, winning new fans every year.

Here, Judy "makes up" with him through over-applications of cosmetics as a guest on his NBC-TV Show.

But when the booking was over, she'd been back for only two days when firemen were summoned to her residence to put out a blaze in her bedroom. She claimed that a malfunctioning air conditioner had set her draperies on fire, and that the fire had spread to the contents of her closet. Speculation became rampant that for one reason or another, she might have set the fire herself, as she had done in the past.

After the fire, word reached Judy that she was wanted for a guest appearance on *The Andy Williams Show* for NBC-TV on July 9th. She eagerly accepted, since Andy Williams was one of her favorite singers.

Opening with Williams, Judy sang "On a Wonderful Day Like Today," and performed a medley with her host. On camera, she looked fairly healthy, but one critic wrote that her voice was "sluggish and slurry."

In mid-July, Judy was spotted escorting Lorna and Joey to see Liza perform on Broadway in *Flora, the Red Menace.*

After the show, Judy and Herron went to Arthur's, at the time the most chic and sought-after disco in Manhattan, a hip and glittering venue patronized by the political and cultural elite.

There, she ran into, and spent time with, the widowed Jacqueline Kennedy, who was escorted by her brother-in-law, Robert Kennedy. Their trio, which was later joined by Rudolf Nureyev, comprised the most-watched, most gossiped-about, most notorious quartet at the club that night. At one point, Nureyev invited the former First Lady onto the dance floor, and they danced together. Then, to Judy's surprise, Nureyev asked the former attorney general to dance with him, too, and he accepted.

Judy later recalled, "It was the 1960s and Arthur's was the most sophisticated joint in town. I loved watching them."

Judy and Herron were joined by Sybil Burton, the divorced wife of Richard Burton, who had abandoned her for Elizabeth Taylor. They also met her handsome and much younger boyfriend, Jordan Christopher, a member of the club's "house band." As he bantered with Herron, Sybil whispered to Judy, "You have your Mark, and I have my Chris, and it's wonderful when older women like us can snare young stuff."

Rudolf Nureyev was the greatest male ballet dancer of his generation. His was the first defection of a Soviet artist during the Cold War, and it created an international sensation.

He appears here as Romeo in Sergei Prokofiev's ballet based on William Shakespeare's play.

During this sojourn in New York, on July 17 at the Forest Hills Stadium in Forest Hills, Judy also scored one of her greatest concert tour triumphs. She received what was hailed in the news as "the longest standing ovation in the history of show business." It lasted for thirty minutes.

Before a seemingly devoted crowd of 10,000 fans, she performed for ninety minutes with Mort Lindsey conducting his thirty-piece orchestra. She went through the familiar repertoire of some of her long-established favorites (i.e., "For Me and My Gal" and "This Can't Be Love", and "Over the Rainbow")

For her effort, she received rave reviews, *Billboard* claiming: "Judy Garland is simply one of the rare artists who can transfix an audience by sheer personal magnetism."

Variety wrote, "Slim, confident, and buoyant, Judy Garland could have gotten away with singing 'The Internationale' in Russian."

The New York Times called her "a fascinating phenomenon of modern show business." At the end of the show, her orchestra leader, Mort Lindsey, hugged and kissed her, telling her, "Gal, you really went over the rainbow tonight."

***

After her concert triumph in Forest Hills, Judy and Herron transferred coasts, showing up in San Francisco, perhaps her alltime favorite city, home of many of her most ardent fans. For a much-needed vacation, they headed for a retreat outside the city, occasionally venturing into town. Such was the occasion when they arrived at Basin Street West to hear Duke Ellington. She joined him onstage, singing two numbers.

In late August, she videotaped an appearance on *The Gypsy Rose Lee Show,* chatting with America's most famous stripper. [*Two years after its pub-*

lication, her 1957 memoir was adapted into and opened as the long-running hit Broadway musical, Gypsy. *Off camera, Gypsy Rose Lee and Judy animatedly discussed starring together in a revival of that musical.]*

On camera, Judy told an amusing but bittersweet story about her last day at MGM: "I had been fired from *Annie Get Your Gun,* and I showed up at the [MGM] gate the next day to pick up my personal possessions in my dressing room. For years, I had waved at the old gatekeeper, who must have been a hundred years old. But on this morning, he told me I was not on the list, and he would not permit me to go inside. I was turned away and never retrieved my possessions."

The Beatles were in San Francisco performing at the Cow Palace at the time of Judy's visit. At a press conference, she was asked about the group. "I hear they're great guys. I also hear that they *own* Liverpool."

Privately, she told Herron, "I think it would take two Beatles to make one decent-sized cock."

"You're not jealous, are you?" Herron quipped.

When a reporter asked her about her large and devoted following of gay men, she responded sharply, "I sing to people. I don't ask about their sexual orientation. Next question?"

On the last day of August, Herron drove her to San Carlos, lying about halfway between San Francisco and San Jose. She was set to appear at The Circle Star Theater, where many noted artists had presented shows, including Richard Pryor. It was later torn down and turned into office buildings.

That night marked Judy's first performance on a stage "in the round." She later said, "I felt I was on a merry-go-round, and it made me dizzy and nervous."

For two nights during her engagement, Lorna and Joey joined her on the stage, her daughter singing "Zing! Went the Strings of My Heart," and with her son accompanying her on the drums. For eight performances, she was paid $105,000.

***

Back in Los Angeles, Herron was often away, somewhere. With no work in sight, Judy soon tired of the role of housewife and mother. "I loved Lorna and Joey, but not twenty-four hours a day. I'm very fond of adult pleasures."

Judy was delighted when the actress, Janet Leigh, phoned and invited her to a party in honor of Patricia Kennedy Lawford, who had separated from her husband, Peter.

Before going to the party, Judy swallowed some new pills she'd been given by "this quack doctor" (her words). She was soon to learn what affect they had on her.

A handyman had been hired as part of a two-day commitment to repair leaks on the roof of her house, and she asked him to take off from work to drive her to Janet Leigh's party, and to wait outside for her until it was over. She had a slightly dizzy feeling.

At the party, the hostess, Leigh, welcomed her warmly, but seemed to

644

sense that something was wrong. She offered Judy some champagne, and Judy drank more than a few glasses of it, obviously not thinking of the effect that alcohol would have when combined with the pills she'd swallowed.

At one point during the party, Leigh huddled with her: "I've always wanted to ask you something about the times when Tony and I sometimes got invited to Rat Pack gatherings." *[Leigh was referring to her husband, Tony Curtis.]* "Did you and Tony ever make it?" Leigh asked her.

"Not at all," Judy answered. "Your husband preferred Rock Hudson."

Patricia Kennedy Lawford stood at the far corner of the living room, and the guests dutifully filed over to greet her, as if in a receiving line. Judy was the last to approach her, a woman she had known for years through her friendship with Peter Lawford.

With humor, as they "explained away'" some of Judy's most horrifying social embarrassments, her staunchest fans always maintained that "she doesn't throw champagne at just anybody."

Depicted on the left in the photo is **Patricia Kennedy Lawford**, sister of **JFK,** standing near the podium as the future President addresses the Democratic National Convention in 1960 in Los Angeles.

"I'm sorry to hear that your marriage to Peter didn't work out," Judy said. "I felt it was doomed from the beginning. I never thought Peter was husband material. Not only that, but my friend, George Cukor, and I agreed he was a lousy lay."

Deeply embarrassed, Patricia did not respond and turned away, perhaps hoping to be rescued by the hostess.

"I also hear you've switched parties, and that you've become a god damned Republican," Judy said. At that point, she took her champagne glass and emptied it onto Patricia's back. Then she staggered out of the party.

[Patricia, the sister of JFK, RFK, and Teddy Kennedy, was the sixth of Rose and Joseph P. Kennedy Sr.'s nine children. Often cited as the most introverted but most sophisticated of her five sisters, she harbored ambitions of becoming a film producer and an enduring fascination with the business of show-business. After her divorce, in 1966, she worked as a production assistant on patriotic and religious productions, often for NBC-TV. In an ironic twist of fate, Judy gave birth to her son Joseph at the same hospital and on the same day Kennedy gave birth to her son Christopher.

After her divorce, horrified by Peter Lawford's infidelities and increasing drug addiction, she never remarried, and—in reference to Judy's accusation that she'd "joined the Republicans"—never showed any serious signs of abandoning her family's deeply entrenched links to the Democratic Party.]

The next day, when an embarrassed and disgruntled Janet Leigh

645

phoned Judy to discuss the incident at her party, Judy said, "I swear, I don't remember doing that to Patricia. It doesn't sound like me at all. I just can't believe I would do something like that. My doctor has me on this new medication. It's driving me wild."

She was still ingesting that same medication (and still ingesting it with alcohol) when she and Herron dined together in Beverly Hills at a chic restaurant known as The Bistro.

At the time, Princess Margaret and Antony Armstrong-Jones, 1st Earl of Snowdon, were on a barnstorming tour of America, including being fêted by President Lyndon B. Johnson in Washington, D.C. At the time, they were the toast of Los Angeles, and seemingly everyone in town was treating Margaret as if she were the Queen of England.

Her Royal Highness The **Princess Margaret**, Countess of Snowdon, in 1965.

Insulting her in public one afternoon at a drunken luncheon in Los Angeles, to the horror of everyone present, Judy called her "a nasty, rude little princess," and a "stuck-up bitch."

No one was amused.

The Princess was sitting far away, on the opposite side of the restaurant's dining room, from Judy. In a corner of the restaurant was an area where singers—backed up by a trio of musicians—could entertain the restaurant's patrons.

Spotting Judy at the far end of the room, the Princess sent the *maître d'* over to ask Judy to sing three songs for her, specifically naming "I Left My Heart in San Francisco," "Chicago," and "The Man That Got Away."

Overly medicated, Judy was offended, and retorted, "You go and tell that nasty, rude little Princess that we've known each other long enough and gabbed together in the ladies' room long enough that she should skip this ho-hum arrogance and just pop her ass over here and ask me to sing herself. Go tell the stuck-up bitch that I'll sing if she'll go and christen a ship!"

In spite of this vulgar and public display of hostility, Judy did get up and sing the numbers she'd requested. Princess Margaret never came over to her table, but her husband did.

Lord Snowdon was a noted photographer, who had not only photographed the Queen, but Marlene Dietrich, Elizabeth Taylor, Princess Grace, Laurence Olivier, and a wide selection of other prominent celebrities.

He conveyed the thanks of Princess Margaret and also requested that he wished to photograph Judy. She agreed to that, and Herron gave him her contact information. Snowdon promised to call the next day.

Actually, he phoned that very night after Judy had gone to bed. Herron took the call and left the house shortly thereafter. He did not return home until 8AM the next morning, when he faced an angry Judy, who accused him of having had a sexual rendezvous with Margaret's husband. She may have been right.

In London society, the Earl of Snowdon was known as England's most famous bisexual, engaging in numerous affairs with both men and women. Margaret herself was known for her adulterous affairs, too. Snowdon once told a reporter, "I never fell in love with boys, but a few men have fallen in love with me."

Snowdon was known for his late-night partying and undisguised sexual profligacy. "If it moves, he'll go after it," said one of his close friends.

Writers of memoirs, both male and female, sometimes confessed to their affairs with Snowdon, who finally divorced Margaret in 1978. Biographer Sarah Bradford claimed that Snowdon once wrote the Princess a note, concealing it within the pages of a book she was reading at the time, with the expectation that she'd find it. It read: "You look like a Jewish manicurist, and I hate you!"

Still in Los Angeles, Judy admitted, "I was just sitting around waiting for the next earthquake when the phone rang."

It was an offer for a week-long gig at The Greek Theatre, a 5,900-seat outdoor music venue located in L.A.'s Griffith Park, the site of one of her biggest and best-reviewed musical venues of 1957. With Mort Lindsey conducting, she was guaranteed at least $35,000 for the week, plus 65% of the gross over $70,000. It was a fee she considered generous.

She began rehearsing immediately. She didn't want to try anything too experimental and therefore decided to stick to the songs that had made her famous, including (of course) "Over the Rainbow."

From the local press, including the *Hollywood Reporter* and the *Los Angeles Times,* she received rave reviews. "My battered ego was restored with the love I felt flowing my way on September 13."

The course of Judy's life had been filled with "triumph and tragedy" (her words), which she said would be the title of the memoirs she was always threatening to write. But whereas she experienced a triumph September 13th, a tragedy occurred the following day, when she tripped over her dog, breaking her arm in two places, and tearing all the ligaments in her forearm, too.

In great pain and heavily medicated, she decided to go on stage that night with her arm in a sling. She called on old friends, Mickey Rooney and Martha Raye, to help her, and also brought in one of her favorite singers, the velvet-voiced Johnny Mathis.

At that day's second show, she began to weaken and Rooney filled in for her. Although she was desperate for money, she knew she could not fill out the week's commitment, so the remaining shows were canceled. She checked into a hospital the next day.

Variety reviewed her second performance within the now-cancelled week-long booking. "There is no arguing with a broken arm. But the long-time effects of the occurrence will unfortunately compound the impression that exists in the minds of some producers and fans that Miss Garland cannot be relied upon to completely fill an engagement."

Although Judy still had her arm in a sling, heavy medication had eased the pain. That is why she accepted a guest appearance on *The Ed Sullivan Show,* which was broadcast on CBS-TV. She removed the sling temporarily for her segment's taping at Television City in Hollywood, then put it back on when it was over.

She stuck to the songs she knew so well, including "Come Rain Or Come Shine." She was praised for her vocal power and was seen by millions of Americans that night in their family living rooms.

Judy was added to the list of performers Sullivan booked on his weekly show. Established in 1948 during the early days of television, Sullivan's prime-time variety program endured as a staple until 1971. Guests had included Maria Callas, Sammy Davis, Jr., Ella Fitzgerald, and Joan Sutherland.

For **Judy Garland and her spontaneous late-night wedding,** "What Happened in Vegas Didn't Stay Quiet, Unnoticed, and Unpublicized in Vegas."

Here, looking like an standardized, run-of-the-mill snapshot that's included automatically in the all-inclusive cost of a marriage at a late-night wedding chapel in Nevada, is a nuptial photo of the bride kissing her groom—in this case, **Mark Herron**.

One of Judy's most successful TV appearances that year was videotaped on October 15, when she was a guest hostess on ABC-TV's *The Hollywood Palace.*

On its set, she was reunited with her former lover, singer Vic Damone, who performed a medley with her, singing such songs as "Tonight." As her opener, she selected "Just Once in a Lifetime." For a change, she was in fine voice, moving through such numbers as "Some of These Days," a song made famous by Sophie Tucker.

After the taping, she asked Damone to go to dinner with her, but he declined.

***

On the Strip in Las Vegas, at 1:30AM, Judy took Mark Herron as her fourth husband in a fast and standardized ceremony at the neon-lit Little Church of the West, a venue known for all-night marriage ceremonies. Presiding was David Howe, an officiant in the Church of Religious Science. The best man was Judy's publicist, Guy McElwiane, and her matron of honor was his wife, Pamela Austin. When the ceremony was over, a reporter from *The Sun* asked Judy how she felt.

"I feel like I am Mrs. Mark Herron, and I'm the happiest I've ever been in my life."

648

Following the ceremony, Eddie Fisher, her former lover, and a group of Vegas friends headed for Don Rickles' late night show. His routine methodologies involved mocking people, and he didn't hesitate taking on any celebrity. Herron and Judy were his obvious targets for abuse that night.

Sarcastically, and with tinges of cruelty, Rickles called out from the stage to his audience, "When this Herron fag first saw Judy's overused twat, he screamed hysterically that there was no penis, calling out in panic, 'You've been castrated!'"

As his performance that night grew more vicious and more homophobic, Judy rose and Herron followed her to the door. Seeing them leaving, Rickles called out, "When you have to do the dirty deed, Herron, I'm warning you, it smells like Camembert cheese. Just close your eyes and pretend she's Rock Hudson."

The newlyweds took the next week off to honeymoon in San Francisco with two nights spent in Carmel.

While they were away, Lorna and Joey were under the care of a "Mrs. Chapman," their nanny, whom both kids despised.

Judy couldn't have chosen a worse nanny than Mrs. Chapman, who—for Lorna and Joey—evoked the Wicked Witch of the West.

Here's **Cloris Leachman** in 1972, holding her "Best Supporting Actress" award for her performance as a desperately lonely spinster in Peter Bogdanovich's *The Last Picture Show.*

Lorna Luft always cited Leachman for her extraordinary kindness to her whenever Judy, who lived next door at the time, was indisposed. .

Joey and Lorna often escaped from their house to find refuge at the home of Judy's neighbor, Cloris Leachman, and her husband, George Englund. "I adored her," Lorna said. "The kind of mom we saw on TV."

Leachman and Englund seemed like the kind of parents Lorna longed for. However, even that happy home crumbled when Cloris found her husband having an affair with the sultry British star, Joan Collins.

One night, Mrs. Chapman became the target of one of Judy's rages. After a bitter argument, the nanny was fired. She was ordered from the house, but instead, she rushed to her bedroom, where she bolted the door. Judy lit a pack of matches and stuck them under her door, threatening to burn her out. All she managed to do was set a throw rug on fire.

In the meantime, Mrs. Chapman had packed her bag and escaped through a ground-floor window. Seeing her leaving, Judy rushed into the kitchen and emerged with a large butcher knife, which would have been useful for splitting a calf's head. Wielding the knife, Judy shouted at the departing woman, "I'll kill you, you bitch."

Fortunately, Mrs. Chapman was already in her car, and had rolled up its windows. In reaction, Judy threw the knife at the driver's side window, shattering the glass. In her car, Mrs. Chapman roared down the driveway and out onto the road to freedom.

After that, Lorna, aged thirteen at the time, was assigned the duties of running the household and taking care of her brother whenever Judy was incapacitated, which was most of the time.

Often, they were short of money, and the refrigerator was bare. To their rescue came Dr. Marc Rabwin, who, as a young man, had been the lover of Judy's father, Frank Gumm. He would arrive with hamburgers, pizza, and bags of groceries. Having known Judy for forty-five years, he was like a grandfather to her children.

***

After settling in briefly on home turf, Judy and Herron were back on the road again, prepping for her upcoming appearance at The Sahara on the Strip in Las Vegas, scheduled for an opening on November 30. She was to be paid $100,000 for a two-week engagement.

Backed by a thirty-piece Louis Basil Orchestra, Judy sang only songs she'd sung before, but adding "He's Got the Whole World in His Hands." Lorna, on occasion, also got up on stage to sing, "Hello, Lorna!" *[The song was an odd choice for the little girl, as it should have been sung by her mother.]*

On Judy's closing night, she sang "Hello, Liza!" in recognition that her daughter would follow her act at The Sahara with an act of her own.

Judy's show was presented in the main showroom of the mammoth, 1,600-room hotel whose club had been extensively rebuilt and remodeled after a fire that had started on the roof. The waters that had extinguished the fire had flooded the showroom below. Management always tried to book big name acts such as Frank Sinatra, Marlene Dietrich, Barbra Streisand, Jack Benny, Martha Raye, Donald O'Connor, or Judy Garland.

Writing in the Las Vegas *Sun,* Paul Rice said, "The appearance of Judy Garland may well have been the most fabulous night in show business history, and I've never been that much of a fan of hers."

Another big booking came in from Houston, Texas before the end of 1965. Herron and Judy flew there for Judy's appearance at the Astrodome. Having opened in April of that year, it made Judy the first show-biz artist to ever star within that venue. She would be paid $43,000 for a one-time show. This time, her opening act was not The Allen Brothers, who at the time were appearing elsewhere.

Diana Ross and The Supremes opened the show. In the 1960s, they became the most commercially successful of Motown's acts. When they appeared with Judy in the mid-1960s, they rivaled The Beatles in worldwide popularity, and Judy was amazed that they were her opening act and not the star attraction. They sang their big hit, "Where Did Our Love Go?" followed by "Stop in the Name of Love" and "Baby Love," which that year was nominated for the Grammy Award for Best R&B song. *Time* magazine referred to them as "The Three Thrushes."

Houston's Astrodome was the world's first multi-purpose, domed sports arena. It could hold a staggering 45,000 spectators, but only 15,000 fans came to hear Judy and The Supremes. After meeting all its expenses, including Judy's salary, the Astrodome suffered a big loss.

Judy and her entourage spent Christmas that year within her Brentwood home. Herron, Judy, Lorna, and Joey celebrated it like a family. Then, they all flew to Las Vegas to catch Liza's opening act at The Sahara.

A week later, for New Year's Eve, Herron and Judy showed up at the home of Pamela Mason. Judy and Pamela had become friends during the filming of *A Star Is Born,* when she had witnessed her husband, James Mason, working through his scenes with Judy.

After hugging and kissing Herron at midnight, and singing *Auld Lang Syne,* Judy said to him, "Welcome to 1966. The New Year! What new humiliations will it bring?"

***

At the time, *Publimetrix* was an enterprise that measured the amount of publicity a celebrity received in any given year. Shortly after the debut of the new year, it announced that the winners, with Judy coming in fifth, for 1965, after Frank Sinatra, Julie Andrews, Bob Hope, and Elizabeth Taylor. Trailing Judy were Dorothy Malone (a surprise), Richard Burton, Marlon Brando, Patricia Neal, and Rex Harrison.

DIVAS THREE
Glam, Very Glam, and Über-Glam

For notes on these "Touches of Minx" please refer to the caption on the next page

WHAT BECOMES A LEGEND MOST?
JUDY, LIZA, AND BLACKGAMA

In the late 1960s, two Manhattan-based ad executives, Jane Trahey and Peter Rogers, developed a campaign to resuscitate lagging sales of "ranch-bred mink," linking the then-fashionable fur to *haute* photographic portraits of very famous celebrities and the brand name "Blackgama." To that end, they enlisted major league photographers (Richard Avedon, Bill King, and Rocco Laspata) in the creation of something akin to a "National Portrait Gallery" of the *Überglams*.

It was later praised as one of the most instantly recognizable and glamorous ad campaigns in American history. Beginning in 1980, many of the models weren't paid, nor did their names appear on the ads (everyone assumed at the time that each would be instantly recognizable, even without their names), but they each received a coat of their choice.

Although the ads that focused on **Judy, Liza,** and their contemporary, *[a woman we love,* **Debbie Reynolds]** are depicted above, equivalent ads, always with the same tagline ("What Becomes a Legend Most") were devised with Lillian Gish, Marlene Dietrich, Brigitte Bardot, Gloria Swanson, Bette Davis, Joan Crawford, Helen Hayes, Janet Jackson, Lucille Ball, Diana Ross, Audrey Hepburn, Elizabeth Taylor, Barbra Streisand, Maria Callas, and a host of supermodels, always with the (probably correct) premise that many women certainly feel (and look) powerful and sexy when wrapped in fur.

A cultural phenomenon like this was hard not to lampoon: Katharine Hepburn, Dolly Parton, and Jackie Onassis each turned down repeated offers to star in the campaign, and late-night TV hosts included it as a part of their ongoing *schticks*.

Three of the models (Liza Minnelli, Lillian Hellman and Bette Davis) posed with lit cigarettes. Carol Burnett famously rejected the idea of being compensated with a mink coat and became one of the few celebrities who asked for her compensation to be donated to charity instead.

More than any other luminary in the campaign, Judy Garland's portrait gained a kind of longevity that the others never achieved: Andy Warhol, an undying fan who was keen on identifying *Zeitgeist* trends, got into the act, adapting her Blackgama ad into a series of colored silkscreens snapped up by collectors and today worth millions.

With the increasing visibility of animal rights activists, especially, PETA (*People for the Ethical Treatment of Animals; look them up at* **PETA.org**), Blackgama's campaign (and fur itself) eventually became the focus of protest and ridicule. In 1984 Joan Rivers released a comedy album on whose cover she posed as a Blackgama model with the slogan *"What Becomes a Semi-Legend Most?"*

Comedienne Amy Sedaris positioned herself as the centerpiece for a lampoon of the Blackgama campaign, grimacing into a camera while asking, *"What Becomes a Loser Most? When you wear fur, people laugh at you, not with you."* And activist artists such as Mark Verabioff factored graffiti-covered renditions of individual portraits from the campaign (including the depictions of Judy and Liza wearing mink) into metaphors for violence and degradation.

What's the takeaway from all this?

Fur is no longer fashionable, but the legacy of Judy (and to a lesser extent, Liza) endure.

652

LIZA BECOMES A RED MENACE ONSTAGE,
A CABARET SENSATION AT THE PLAZA,
A RECORDING STAR (LIZA! LIZA! LIZA!)
AND A COMPETITIVE THREAT TO HER MOTHER.
JUDY CONSIDERS SUING HER WHEN THEIR BATTLES ESCALATE.

JUDY SCREENS *THE WIZARD OF OZ* FOR HER CHILDREN:
"I think it's too scary for kids."

JOHN CARLYLE GOES UNDER THE RAINBOW WITH JUDY
BEFORE SEDUCING HER HUSBAND

GOSSIPY CHITCHAT & SOCIAL HORROR
WITH HEDY LAMARR, CHRISTOPHER ISHERWOOD, ANGELA
LANSBURY, & THE EX-HUSBAND OF LANA TURNER.

MEANWHILE, PETER ALLEN (NOW, LIZA'S HUSBAND & JUDY'S
SON-IN-LAW) BECOMES A PIANO-PLAYING STAPLE AT
THE PLAYBOY CLUBS

HELL HATH NO FURY
LIKE A PILL ADDICTED MEGA-DIVA SCORNED
JUDY TRASHES HER DRESSING ROOM (AGAIN)

THE I.R.S. GETS RED, WHITE, & BLUE WITH JUDY

MARK HERRON FINDS LOVE AT LAST
BUT AFTER MULTIPLE FIST FIGHTS, IT ISN'T WITH JUDY.

LOVE IS PAIN
THE SAD AND TAWDRY SAGA OF TOM GREEN

THE VALLEY OF THE DOLLS
PRETENTIOUS, UNFUNNY, AND TRASHY, IT'S
ANOTHER NAIL IN JUDY'S PROFESSIONAL COFFIN

"Judy Garland's lovers came in all shapes, sizes—and all sexes. As a proud gay man, it was my turn in line to have an affair with her. I was one busy boy, as I had to slip around a satisfy her husband, Mark Herron, as well."
—Actor John Carlyle

"Am I tired of 'Over the Rainbow?' Listen, that would be like getting tired of breathing. The whole premise of the song is a question. A quest. At the end, it isn't. Well, I've found my world, and I am a success—and you and I will be together. The lyric is having little bluebirds fly over the rainbow. 'Why, oh why, can't I?' it represents everyone's wondering why things can't be a little better."
—Judy Garland in the summer of 1967

"I've heard 'How difficult' it is to be with Judy Garland. And for me to live with me? I've had to do it—and what more unkind life can you think of than the one I've lived? I'm told I'm a legend. Fine. But I don't know what that means. I certainly did not ask to be a legend, and I was totally unprepared for it."
—Judy Garland (*McCalls*, August 1967)

As Judy was desperately searching for her next gig,

Liza Minnelli was starring on Broadway in *Flora, The Red Menace,* a Hal Prince musical, a kind of spoof on communism. It opened at the Alvin Theatre in May of 1965, marking the debut of Liza in the title role.

The book was by George Abbott and Robert Russell, with music by John Kander and lyrics by Fred Ebb. This marked the first collaboration between Kander and Ebb, who would later write such Broadway and Hollywood hits as *Cabaret* and *Chicago*. Each of them would become a music mentor for Liza, playing key roles in her career.

Initially, Ebb was not impressed with Liza. "I remember this shy, awkward girl coming into the room. She looked awful, like a Raggedy Ann. Everything was just a little torn and a little soiled. She just sat there and stared at me, and I stared back."

She would later refer to Ebb as "My Svengali."

He said, "If one day she writes her own autobiography, it should be entitled *Rage to Live.*"

Liza almost lost out on the role, but she persisted. At first, Russell saw it as a vehicle for Barbra Streisand (she wisely chose *Funny Girl* instead) and Abbott promoted the casting of Eydie Gormé, the wife of singer Steve Lawrence.

Both Judy and Vincente Minnelli showed up for its sold-out opening. At the cast party that followed, Judy hugged and kissed her daughter. "Tonight you were standing in stardust," Judy told the emerging actress.

Reviews were mixed, *Time* magazine heaping praise on her: "At nineteen, Liza Minnelli is a star-to-be, a performer of arresting presence, who does not merely occupy the stage, but fills it." In contrast, its rival, *Newsweek,* had the opposite view: "The voice of Liza Minnelli is thin, her movements swift, her presence wobbly and uncertain."

The New York Times claimed, "The voice of Miss Minnelli is not yet distinctive. She is going to be a popular singer, all right. *Flora* has the appearance of being pasted together with bits and pieces. A promising idea has not been enlivened by a creative spark."

Norman Nadel of the *New York World Telegram and Sun* said, "The girl has the face of a startled rabbit—wide, watchful eyes and an apprehensive upper lip. There is something charmingly *gauche* about her toes-in stance and the way she charges into situations as if her physical momentum would overcome her inner trepidation. The aspect of her blinded innocence makes her perfect as the girl who can be talked into joining the Communist Party and eventually strong-arming her way out."

In the *Herald Tribune,* Walter Kerr wrote: "Liza Minnelli, who no longer needs to be identified as Judy Garland's daughter, has many a fetching way about her. Her smile, for instance, is marvelously unsteady, always eager to shoot for the moon, always on the verge of wrinkling down to half-mast. She does lyrics extremely well."

The public did not rush to fill up the 1,344 seats of the theater, and the show closed on July 16, having lasted only eleven weeks, losing its

At the age of nineteen, **Liza Minnelli** became the youngest star ever to win a Best Actress Tony Award.

She played "Flora Meszaros," a young fashion illustrator in love with a communist (Bob Dishy), against the backdrop of the Great Depression.

Newsday called her "a wonder, a magic, and a doll."

estimated $400,000 investment. After it became clear that its popularity had waned, Ebb met with Prince to reflect, labeling *Flora, the Red Menace* as "a disaster," and blaming Abbott.

Nevertheless, Liza won a Tony Award as Best Actress in a Musical, becoming the youngest person (at age nineteen) to do so.

[At the Tony Awards ceremony, Liza's win was presented to her by Bert Lahr, who had co-starred as the Cowardly Lion alongside her mother in The Wizard of Oz.*]*

On the night of the Tony Awards in Los Angeles, Judy was said to have experienced "an emotional upset" and was rushed to the Cedars of Lebanon Hospital.

[The spring of 1965 ("the season of flopping musicals") was one of the most dismal in the history of Broadway. Other plays that failed that season included the otherwise well-recommended What Makes Sammy Run? *and* Baker Street.*]*

Ironically, at *Flora's* closure, producer Hal Prince was working on a new idea for a musical in collaboration with Kander and Ebb. It was called *Cabaret,* and for its opening on November 20, 1966 at Manhattan's Broadhurst Theater, it would need a "hot" female star. Prince told Ebb and Kander, "I want a strong but charming English stage star."

***

Judy began 1966 by sitting at home beside the TV with Lorna and Joey to watch *The Wizard of Oz* during its January 9 telecast. Afterward, in an interview with reporter Richard Kleiner, Judy said, "I had to spend most of the broadcast trying to keep my children from crying. I had to assure them that the Munchkins were only little boys and wouldn't harm me. Actually, I think my picture is too scary for kids."

Judy's first gig of 1966 was an engagement (February 2-10) at the Diplomat Hotel in Miami Beach. *[Originally, Robert Goulet had been scheduled to fill that slot, but a conflict emerged within his overbooked scheduled and Judy was hired as his replacement.]*

The Miami News asserted that "Judy Garland's rainbow glowed at The Diplomat. In the Crystal Café, she's not so far away that she looks like a pygmy standing in front of a 26-piece orchestra. We're close to her and that's what we want."

The *Hollywood Sun-Tatler [a newspaper serving Hollywood, Florida, and Southern Broward County]* interpreted her performance as "electrifying, with enough current to lift the audience out of their seats. Her voice was never better."

Ironically, the very next day, a false rumor spread across South Florida that Judy had died. The fake news was broadcast during the pre-dawn hours on two radio stations. In an attempt to either confirm or deny it, a reporter from *The Miami Herald* got through to Herron in their suite at The Diplomat. "Miss Garland is very much alive," Herron assured the newsman. None of those (false) rumors about her death ever made the newspapers, and they quickly died.

From Miami, Judy flew with Herron to New York and checked into the Plaza Hotel. On February 20, she appeared for a videotaping of *The*

Kraft Music Hall for NBC-TV in Brooklyn.

She was greeted by its host, Perry Como, who introduced her to Bill Cosby, the show's other featured guest. This gig became one of Judy's finest appearances—perhaps the best—of 1966. New York's *Daily News* found both Como and Judy at the peak of their powers as entertainers.

The *Philadelphia Enquirer* gave each of them rave reviews for their medley of duets, with special praise aimed at her for giving musical answers to Cosby's clue-seeking questions.

California's *Oakland Tribune* praised her for her good voice and for her glamourous appearance, swathed as she was in a cluster of black feathers.

Later that night, Judy and Herron, accompanied by Sammy Davis, Jr., dropped into the Plaza's chic nightclub, *The Persian Room*, for Liza's opening. Every ticket had been sold, and she was a hit with

In tandem with this photo and their logo, the Plaza Hotel in Midtown Manhattan took out this spectacular ad in *The New York Times:*

"She's faster than a speeding bullet.

Leaps tall buildings in a single bound. Conquered Broadway in just one year. From February 9 to March 8 (1966), mild-mannered Liza Minnelli will sing, dance, and stop speeding trains in the Persian Room.

Mark Monte and Burt Farber will provide supermusic for dancing.

Quick, Lois, a reservation! PL 9-3000."

The Plaza

both patrons and critics. Her costumes ranged from a backless gown to sexy tights.

Leonard Harris in the *World Telegram and Sun* wrote: "Liza proved she could sock the stuffings out of a song, dance beautifully for a singer—and even sing pretty for a dancer."

Once again, the reviewer for *Newsweek* was critical. "All the slick Vegas arrangements couldn't get Liza Minnelli to sing 'He's My Guy' or 'They

Liza! Liza! morphed into hefty competition for her mother for record sales, and soon began inspiring vivid comparisons to **Barbra! Barbra!**

During Judy's career decline, and during the early days of his marriage to Liza, **Peter Allen** (left photo above) got consistent bookings at franchises of the fast-expanding **PLAY-BOY CLUBS**, appearing as a live entertainer at multiple Playboy Clubs during the period of its greatest expansion.

Wanna know more about Hugh Hefner, his rocky road to success, and his battles for survival in the culture and censorship wars? Check out Blood Moon's award-winning 2018 overview, **PLAYBOY'S HUGH HEFNER, EMPIRE OF SKIN** of a then-incendiary career that by today's standards, seems congenial and tame.

Wouldn't Believe Me' as if she meant it. A girl has got to have lived a little to sing about the steamy side of life and love."

From there, Liza moved on to perform in Washington, D.C., at the Shoreham Hotel in Rock Creek Park. Other bookings followed, including at the Cocoanut Grove in Los Angeles and the Deauville on Miami Beach.

Her successes had already generated recording contracts from Capitol Records for the production of three albums: *Liza! Liza!* (1964); *It Amazes Me* (1965), and *There Is a Time* (1966). Combining pop standards with show tunes, they sparked taglines which defined her as "Barbra Streisand's Little Sister."

Although still engaged to each other, Liza and Peter saw little of each other in those days. He and Chris Bell often appeared at one of Hugh Hefner's Playboy Clubs. When he wasn't otherwise working, Peter pursued an active gay life, having developed a fondness for American men and boys. By now, both he and Liza had become sophisticated at dealing with Judy and her "quirks and eccentricities."

Each of them had rejected Judy's invitations to attend her wedding to Herron. Liza cabled her regrets: "Sorry, mama, I can't come to your wedding, but I promise you I'll come to the next one."

When Peter was on the road, Liza was seen with a number of men, including the French singer Charles Aznavour, who described his relationship with Liza to the press: "It's less than sexual, but more than platonic."

Before her departure from New York, Judy made an appearance on *The Sammy Davis Show,* whose taping occurred at the NBC-TV Studios in Brooklyn on February 23. With Davis, she delivered some of her best-known songs. For their rendition of "The Lady is a Tramp," each was clad in a tramp costume.

The show was so successful that Davis asked her to return on March 6, when, as a duo, they sang "Let Us Entertain You" and "April Showers." The New York Daily News praised their act, labeling it "a sparkling medley."

On March 7, Judy boarded a flight to Los Angeles with Mark Herron. Her marriage to him was on the rocks with only weeks to live. But when reporters plied her with questions, it was no longer about her relationship with Herron, but about her daughter's engagement to Peter Allen. Most of them queried her for some comment about his rumored gay life. Judy had a standard response: "Who wouldn't like men?"

***

In the spring of 1966, actor John Carlyle came back into Judy's life stronger than ever before. Actually, they'd been friends ever since he'd had a brief cameo in her film *A Star Is Born* (1954),

Since both of them worshipped **Judy Garland**, **John Carlyle** (left) and **Mark Herron** (right) discovered that they had more in common than sexual attraction.

No one was more shocked than Carlyle when he learned that Judy and Herron had become "an item," as reported in the gossip columns. Carlyle referred to the couple as "the road show version of Elizabeth Taylor and Richard Burton."

According to Carlyle, as discussed with his friends, "Knowing Mark as well as I did, I doubt if he ever actually plugged Judy. Maybe some heavy petting, but I think he was more her caretaker."

even though its footage had been cut from its final versions. Since then, she'd seen him on and off, sometimes visiting for parties at his home on Norma Place in West Hollywood. She was fully aware that he'd already had a string of gay lovers.

Carlyle had first met Herron in the early 1950s when each of them had vied for the lead in *The Sleeping Prince,* a production at the Pasadena Playhouse. *[The role went to Herron.]*

They didn't meet again until 1962, when Robert Osborne *[who later became the primary host at Turner Classic Movies]* brought Herron as his guest to a party at Carlyle's house.

Even after the passage of all those intervening years, Carlyle and Herron were still attracted to each other, and (casually) resumed their intermittent, long-dormant affair.

Sometimes, Judy would arrive unannounced on Carlyle's doorstep, "looking like a wounded bluebird." He was always there for her, talking and listening to her until it was almost dawn before tucking her into bed and listening to the sounds of her sounding like "a snoring chipmunk."

Since she had a volatile temper and most often was drunk or drugged, disputes, even fights, with Herron were commonplace. She would storm out of his house and threaten to never return.

His feelings toward her also underwent various shifts. At the Hillside Coffee Shop, he told fellow actor John Dall, "Judy causes me sleepless nights. She's completely unreasonable. She's a madwoman. I never want to see her again. It's over!"

Judy called Carlyle at three o'clock the next morning, begging to come over "or else I'll kill myself." Within the hour, with his approval, she arrived at his door for a 24-hour sleepover.

More and more frequently, Carlyle became Judy's escort, making the rounds of Hollywood parties. At one event, Judy shared a reunion with Hedy Lamarr, who had co-starred with her and Lana Turner in *Ziegfeld Girl* (1941).

Carlyle had been amused to hear their exchange of stories, including "comparing notes about what it was like to go to bed with John F. Kennedy." Judy had had too much champagne that night and wandered into forbidden territory. She asked Lamarr what it was also like to go to bed with Adolf Hitler, a friend a Hedy's first husband, the Austrian munitions magnate Fritz Mendl.

Judy: "I hear Hitler had the world's smallest penis and a testicle that never descended—poor Eva Braun."

At that point, Carlyle and Judy saw Lamarr's back as she spun around and walked away.

Often, they would end their evenings together in a gay bar, where Judy's most devoted fans hovered around her. Sometimes, they dined at Por Favor, a gay bar attached to a Mexican restaurant. "This South of the Border stuff makes me fart," she said.

She liked to be taken to the movies. One night, they went to see *Morgan!* (1966) for a view of Vanessa Redgrave in her film debut. In this offbeat drama, David Warner played her "bordering-on-insanity" husband. In the middle of the screening, Judy said in a too-loud voice, "Her father, Sir Michael Redgrave, likes to be flagellated."

Sometimes when both of them were drunk, Judy demanded that Carlyle take her to the home of someone she knew, even though she almost never telephoned in advance. Such was the case when he knocked, at her bidding, on the door of the English author, Christopher Isherwood. When he opened the door, he was clad only in pajamas, as he was getting ready to retire with his

Christopher Isherwood and **Don Bachardy** evolved into one of the most sought-after and stylish couples in Hollywood.

During one of her late-night highs, Judy thought it would be fun to "pop in" on them, with Mark Herron in tow, for giggles and gossip.

Irritated and sleepy, and in no mood to either party or put up with her antics, Isherwood closed the door in their faces.

Ironically, it would be Isherwood's *Berlin Stories* that morphed into the film, *Cabaret* (1972), starring Liza Minnelli.

660

young lover, Don Bachardy. Seeing who it was, he shut the door in their faces.

Judy liked to visit the restaurant run by Steve Crane in the 9000 Sunset Building since he never presented them with a check for meals they'd consumed. Crane had once been married to Lana Turner, and the two of them had produced a lesbian daughter, Cheryl Crane, who became involved in the stabbing death, in her mother's bedroom, of the mobster, Johnny Stompanato.

Judy and Herron constantly either encountered celebrities or invited them over. One night, actress Jean Peters (Mrs. Howard Hughes) arrived. During the course of that evening, Judy pleaded with her to persuade her husband to finance a movie starring her and based on the turbulent life of Aimee Semple McPherson, America's most famous and controversial evangelist.

Carlyle's life with Judy had its highs and lows. A high was when he got to swim nude with Robert F. Kennedy at Peter Lawford's home on the beach in Santa Monica. It had once been owned by Louis B. Mayer.

At a party they once attended there, guests appeared in masquerade, Troy Donahue, dressed as a nun, showing up with Rock Hudson, who appeared as a Roman gladiator, his heavy genitals encased in a gold *lamé* jockstrap. As the evening wore on, a drunken Hudson denounced Donahue for "having a cock that is too god damn small."

Once, Carlyle appeared on a popular TV show, *The Dating Game.* The winner, among other awards, got to have a date, part of it televised, with stars Juliet Prowse and Chita Rivera, starring at the time in Las Vegas in *Sweet Charity.*

As Carlyle, the winner, recalled, "Juliet took my hand and placed it under the table, where the sun don't shine. I felt territory often invaded by Frank Sinatra."

Then the inevitable happened one night when Judy invited him to her home in Brentwood. They had spent most of the evening with Lana Turner at the Polo Lounge at the Beverly Hills Hotel. It was very late, and Lorna and Joey were asleep.

July excused herself to go to her bedroom while he mixed drinks. She emerged after a few minutes wearing a pink chiffon *peignoir* with a strong scent of White Shoulders perfume.

As quoted by Carlyle in his memoirs:

"The sound of that voice sighing endearments while I gave her pleasure was the stimulation that enabled me to have one of my only successful times with a woman. My lifelong fixation manifested itself physically, to my relief and to my delight. My tongue and my mouth and loins belonged to someone new. Her noises and her body that had no limits for me were astonishing. She wanted me to stay by her when we were finished. When she drifted off to sleep. I slipped out through the bedroom's sliding glass doors. I felt bashful about being seen by Joey and Lorna. I was puffed with pride at her infinite, tactile capacity to make me feel like the number one, indispensable male in her universe...God knows that moment became the heterosexual height of my life."

Sid Luft had once told him that, "The only thing Judy can do right is sing a song."

"Sid was wrong," Carlyle said. "She could get a gay man to fuck her."

"During her short marriage to Mark Herron, he wasn't giving Judy any," Carlyle claimed. "He turned to me for that pleasure, and I don't think Judy ever found out."

"When she was drunk and drugged, she always asked the same question: 'Are you in love with me?'"

His answer was always the same: "I've loved you all my life, even as a boy. But I don't know if I am in love with you."

Some nights when she felt insecure around him and not trusting his love, she would attack him physically as he slept. Such was the case when she seriously injured him one night by tossing a big crystal ashtray directly into his sleeping face.

"Sometimes, we'd be naked in bed, and she'd get mad at me and chase after me with some dangerous object," he said. "I just hoped Joey and Lorna would not open their door onto such a scene."

On many a night, she made the same threat while he was driving. "You're not going to get rid of me."

"I knew she meant it, curled beside me in the Hillman Minx that had replaced my Oldsmobile as we twisted out Sunset toward her home at Rockingham."

***

In Los Angeles, Judy faced the worst financial crisis of her life, as the Internal Revenue Service was cracking down, demanding immediate payment of $400,000, which, of course, she did not have.

Although she needed every penny she could earn, she was forced to cancel another appearance on *The Andy Williams Show,* since she was suffering another case of laryngitis, an affliction that plagued her frequently. She lost the $7,500 fee he would have paid her, although that would have been only a token of the money she needed to cover her mountain of debts and expenses. Her new business manager, Morgan Maree, Jr., arrived on her doorstep to give her the bad news. At present, she had 120 creditors demanding immediate payment. She was notified that the sheriff was going to place a lien on her house for her failure to keep up with mortgage payments.

Among the many payments she owed was $3,000 a month to Sid Luft as part of their divorce settlement. She was already five months in arrears with him. She had $12,000 in the bank but saw that going fast. Lorna and Joey were growing out of their clothes; food had to be purchased, and her dwindling staff had to have money to run their own households.

On top of all that, she and Herron flew to Acapulco, hoping that a brief vacation would restore her health and help her get over her latest tangle with the flu.

During her stay (May 16-23) in Mexico, she learned the depressing results of a *Billboard* contest: In its poll of 2,500 college students as to whom was their favorite singer, Judy ranked 19th on the list of 25 artists.

Back in Los Angeles on March 27, she began rehearsals for her next gig as hostess on *The Hollywood Palace* for ABC-TV. Her guest would be her friend and former co-star, Van Johnson.

Over lunch, each of them shared details about their personal career and romantic concerns: "You and I are no longer the sweethearts of MGM," she said. "Actually, it was our pal, June Allyson, who was America's sweetheart in those pictures you made with that little nymph."

She and Johnson opened their show singing "Mr. and Mrs. Clown."

She confessed to him, "My finances are in shambles, and my marriage is coming unglued. Some fucking marriage! Mark Herron was more of a gay traveling companion than a husband. Maybe I should assign him to you."

"Not a bad idea," Johnson said. "These days, I'm reduced to paying for it. I ask their measurements on the phone, and the hustlers always exaggerate by two inches."

During the first week of April, she was constantly complaining of a sore throat, and the taping of her show with Johnson did not go well. Gripped with anxiety and refusing to come out of her dressing room until very late, she had the crew working one early morning until 3AM.

When she finally emerged from seclusion, it was after midnight and she flubbed several takes of the song, "By Myself." At the end of the taping, she said, "By Myself—that's how I felt, deserted by my kids, my husband, my friends, and my fans."

To compound matters, she received depressing news. She was informed that ABC-TV would never again employ her, even as a guest. "I was blacklisted," she complained. In the days ahead, she learned the extent of that, as NBC and CBS let it be known that she was never to be offered another guest appearance. As if that weren't enough, Capitol Records sent word that they would not renew her contract.

For Judy, it was just too much disappointment. In her rage and fury, she began trashing her dressing room before her eviction. She had been smoking heavily, and she emptied the contents of her ashtrays into the spaces between the keys of her dressing room's piano before moving on to vandalize the bathroom.

There, she stuffed a towel down the toilet and flushed it again and again so that water flooded over its edges. Then she plugged the bathtub's drain so that it copiously overflowed and flooded onto the tiled floor. Then, moving on to the living room, she slashed three of its oil paintings with a knife and shattered all of its mirrors. As she was preparing to set fire to the place, a security guard was alerted and entered. When he saw what she was doing, he summoned his colleague. The two burly men practically dragged her to the gate, dumping her outside. In the pre-dawn hours, she pounded on the gate, screeching obscenities before a squad car arrived. It was clear that she was in no condition to drive, so—in the back seat of their police vehicle—they drove her back to her home.

Word of her vandalization and ejection from ABC spread across the Hollywood grapevine. The question was, would any other studio ever employ her again?

"No one wants Judy Garland anymore," she lamented. "This is the lowest period of my life. I fucked up everything, and I've had a lot of help from the bastards surrounding me, especially that damn hustler, Mark Herron. He just used me."

Lorna recalled, "Mark had tried to look after Joey and me, but he couldn't compete with an old pro like Judy Garland. Her medication intake skyrocketed, and her rapid mood swings worsened."

In the closing weeks of his marriage, Herron became more open about his gay life. Handsome young men, including Tab Hunter and Troy Donahue, showed up to go off with him.

Arguments with Judy over this turned into violent, hard-hitting scratch- and fistfights. Lorna later said, "Mark could not change his sexual orientation."

Late at night, Judy would descend into screaming rages, even banging herself against the walls. "I can't take it anymore," she shouted.

Mark responded with "I know it's a *cliché*, but with Judy, it was always darkest before the dawn. After a night of horror, she would finally drift into a coma-like sleep and remain in bed for most of the rest of the day.'

Somehow, she had managed to accumulate $30,000 in cash and had hidden it away in an emergency stash. [*Apparently, she'd requested cash as payment for some of her performances, knowing that if a studio gave her a check, it would be confiscated by either the IRS or one of her creditors suing her for payment.*]

One drunken night, she needed money, but couldn't remember where she'd hidden it. She accused Mark of stealing it, telling him that she'd call the police and demand his arrest. As it happened, a maid went to clean her room, which looked like a hurricane had demolished it. She found the money in a purse stashed beneath her bed.

Peace returned temporarily. Accompanied by George Cukor, the gay director of *A Star Is Born,* Judy attended one of Herron's performances at the Ivar Theatre in Hollywood. Herron was starring in Noël Coward's *Private Lives* opposite Kathie Browne.

Cukor hosted an after-the-show party at Marroni's Bistro, where Judy sang "Somewhere I'll Find You" and other numbers with singer Marti Stevens, who had attended that night's performance, too. The other honored guest at the party was the aging actress, Hermione Gingold.

Only three days later, Judy turned on Herron again, attacking him with a butcher knife, screaming that she wanted to kill him. He knocked it out of her hand and raced toward the exit, never to return.

After he stormed out, Judy became hysterical. In her living room, she broke the glass in the frames holding photographs of her children and some of her friends, including JFK. Then she tore up the photos before shredding the upholsteries of her furniture with a kitchen knife, tossing the stuffings around the room. Anything made of glass was thrown against the walls and shattered. One of the few staff members remaining in her household managed to subdue her and persuade her to return to her bedroom.

On May 4, Judy had her new attorney, Herbert Schwab, announce to the press that she and Herron had begun a trial separation. By August 16, he sued for divorce. On December 3, she amended her own divorce petition, changing it to a petition for annulment, justifying it with the assertion that her marriage to Herron had never been consummated.

[Whatever happened to Judy's fourth husband? Mark Herron became a footnote in Hollywood history. During his sham marriage to Judy, he had fallen in love with another actor, Henry Brandon, who was sixteen years his senior.

After leaving Judy's Brentwood home, Herron moved in with him, not returning even to gather his clothing. Brandon volunteered to buy him a new wardrobe so that he could avoid further dangers and begin his life anew.

Born in Berlin in 1912, Brandon (his original name was Heinrich von Kleinbach) emigrated with his parents to America when he was an infant. As he matured, he attended Stanford University and later appeared in stage productions at the Pasadena Playhouse. That led to a career in the movies, his output spanning six decades and some one-hundred films. He never evolved into a star but worked steadily in character parts. He could play almost any role: A Native American; the Chinese villain Fu Manchu; an African tribal chieftain in Tarzan and the Sea Devil *(1953). At six feet four, he was taller than Errol Flynn in* Edge of Darkness *(1943), where he played Major Ruck, a British secret agent disguised as an SS officer.*

In 1941, Brandon had married Dolores Dorn, and the couple produced a son.

With Herron, he found his true love. They lived together for the rest of Brandon's life until his death at the age of 77. Herron would survive for another six years before dying of cancer on January 13, 1996, at the age of 67.]

***

After her breakup with Herron, Judy entered a deep depression as her life spiraled downward. She appealed to Liza for money and called her so many times that her daughter refused to come to the phone.

The last time she spoke to her before a later reconciliation, she said, "If you don't send me money, Lorna, Joey, and I will be out on the street. Peter is making money. He'll take care of you if you could bail me out."

Liza did not respond and temporarily cut her mother off.

Enraged at being dropped by Liza, Judy phoned her lawyer and ordered him to launch a million-dollar lawsuit against her. "I've spent that much on the selfish bitch already, raising her, and she owes me."

The lawyer did not file such a hopeless suit, as it was bound to be tossed out of court.

Then she called Sid Luft, telling him, "I'm broke, absolutely penniless. I need help—and I need it now. I've got to take care of Lorna and Joey, your children."

He came over that afternoon and—because her weight had dropped to about ninety pounds—he was shocked by her appearance and gaunt condition. "She looked more like the mother of Judy Garland," he said.

"No one in Hollywood will give me a job!" she said. "I call friends for money, people like Ethel Merman and Andy Williams, but members of their household have been instructed to tell me that they're not at home."

Before that afternoon ended, Luft had convinced Judy to file a multi-million-dollar lawsuit against the company she had formed with David Begelman and Freddie Fields.

When news of it broke in *Variety,* Luft started to get late-night phone calls from the Mafia, warning him that he was going "to be taken on a ride." In another call, a male voice threatened to kidnap Lorna and Joey.

He phoned Judy to alert her of the potential danger. "How am I supposed to end this drama like they do in the movies?" she asked. "Should I walk into the ocean like James Mason did in *A Star Is Born?* I'd do that, but I fear I wouldn't be camera-ready when I washed up on shore. Did you see that picture of Marilyn Monroe taken after her autopsy in the morgue? I'm afraid I'd look even worse."

Then she put down the phone.

***

After Mark Herron had settled into his new life with his male lover, Judy longed to find another man of her own. He appeared in the handsome, charming form of Tom Green, a twenty-six-year-old New Englander. He had found employment with Guy McElwaine, Judy's publicist. Green had begun working for the agency in the spring of 1966 for a salary of $500 a week.

At one point, Green asked his boss why he'd been assigned a star as big as Judy in spite of his relative inexperience. He was told, "She is yesterday's news. She's broke, not even keeping up with our monthly charges. We represent high-grossing stars. She's our charity case."

When Green first met Judy, he was delighted to find her so warm and hospitable to him, since he'd heard stories from the agency that she was "a temperamental bitch."

One of his first assignments for her back then involved drafting a statement to the press—a response to Mark Herron's expressing, to a reporter a few weeks before his filing for a divorce, his hopes for a reconciliation.

His public statement, issued with Judy's approval, read: "Mark Herron's public and private behavior, which has been distasteful and untenable, makes any reconciliation impossible."

Still in dire need of money, she plotted, once again, to sell her autobiography to a major publisher.

[In the past, she'd accepted an advance from Bennett Cerf of Random House, but after ago-

A handsome, dashing, and young New Englander, **Tom Green**, was hired as Judy's publicist but soon became her lover. He moved in with her when she tried once again to dictate her memoirs, morphing him into its author.

Her flow of words was sometimes interrupted when she used her throat for other purposes, as he soon found out when she came over and unzipped his pants.

nizing delays and multiple complaints, had delivered only the beginning of any-
thing publishable. As such, she was emphatically aware that neither Random
House or any of its affiliates would be interested or amused by this new spin on a
book deal.]

As a means to getting her autobiography crafted, she gave Green his
first literary assignment: to write it. To that effect, with a tape recorder,
pencils, and notebooks, he showed up, as she had instructed, at 2PM one
afternoon. *[She was pleased that afternoon visits were convenient for him, as she
usually slept till very late every morning. He had no wife or girlfriend and no family in California to otherwise distract him, and he expressed enthusiasm for the
project.]*

Green proceeded to interview her as she recollected her early life as
"Baby Frances" Gumm on the vaudeville circuit. She expressed nothing
but praise for her father, Frank, but delivered scathing condemnations of
her "witch mother," Ethel.

She told Green, "I'm going to tell it all, everything from all forty-four
years of my god damn, marvelous, failing, successful, hopelessly tragic,
and sorrowful life. The doomed love affairs, the betrayals, the brutal, even
savage attacks on me, the lies. The embezzlement of all my money. How
I've been insulted, slandered, humiliated."

After only a week, Judy developed a strong emotional dependency on
Green. She suggested that since they often worked until the early hours,
he should move into her house for convenience. She also told him that after
Joey and Lorna went to bed, he could use her pool at any time he might
want to take a cooling dip—"swimsuit optional."

When Green met Lorna and Joey, Judy introduced him as her "personal publicist."

Lorna interpreted that to mean somebody her mother wanted to have
around the house all the time.

In her memoirs, Lorna claimed that, "My mother had always needed
a man in her life pretty much on a daily basis. She was tired, increasingly
sick, and insecure about the toll her illness was taking on her looks. She
was also lonely, and she needed someone to give her constant affection
and emotional support."

In his looks and demeanor, Lorna noted that Green was not "a macho-
type guy" like her father, Sid Luft. She may have been taken aback by
Green's makeup, claiming, "He wore green eye shadow. It was discreetly
applied along the edges of his lashes, but clearly visible. He also wore lip
gloss a decade or so before American men even used hair spray."

His makeup made some people assume he was gay. Judy's third husband, Vincente Minnelli, on occasion, especially early in his career, had
worn red lipstick.

Within a week of working with Judy, Green also became her escort.
He flew with her to Las Vegas, where she performed as a replacement for
Martha Raye (she had fallen ill) in the Casbah Room of the Sahara Hotel.

He may (or may not) have been surprised when Judy booked them
into the same suite. After the first night of her gig, she seduced him, and
apparently found him satisfactory as a lover. Back at her home in Brentwood, she would sometimes stop his recording of anecdotes from her

childhood, unzip his trousers, and perform oral sex on him.

Faced with no offers for performances in the United States, Judy accepted a gig South of the Border. On August 14, she and Green flew to Mexico City, where they checked into the Marco Polo Suite at the Maria Isabel Hotel.

Then she faced the Mexican press, telling them she was free of Capitol Records—"the bastards fired me"—and that she'd be launching her own recording company, hoping to sign such artists as Eddie Fisher. She was also planning to release albums of her own with a completely new roster of songs. None of those dreams came true.

She had signed to appear at Mexico City's *El Patio* Nightclub, as part of a twelve-night booking. For fourteen shows, she'd be paid $17,500. She asked that her compensation be secret and in cash, as she was afraid that her creditors would confiscate whatever money she was paid if it were made more public. For her appearance in Mexico, she had learned the Spanish-language translation of "The Party's Over."

On the night of her debut, she sang twenty-one songs, appearing onstage for ninety minutes with a huge orchestra overcrowded with ninety-one musicians.

El Heraldo de México claimed, "An artist of the soul and the heart, and physically fragile, she was strong in spirit and electrified the audience, which stomped their feet and received her with an ovation."

Cine Mundial called Judy "a celebrity among celebrities, a star of immortal fame that will never disappear for centuries and centuries."

Éxito, a newspaper then flourishing in Mexico City, interpreted her performance as "glorious, extraordinary, electrifying, and magnetic. She is a little giant. She is a great artist and a great woman."

The next day, she developed a severe case of laryngitis, but went on with her performance anyway, singing with a scratchy voice. After the show, her throat grew worse, and she had Green cancel the remaining performances of her gig in Mexico City, and boarded a night flight back to Los Angeles.

Ironically, management of *El Patio* hurriedly replaced her with Betty Hutton, the actress and singer who had been her (unhappy) substitute in the film version of *Annie Get Your Gun,* way back in 1950.

By mid-September, Judy and Green were seen visiting San Francisco, where she always liked to make appearances at the leading gay bars. Any time she walked in the door of a tavern the young men gave her a standing ovation.

Rumors of a romance between Judy and Green made all the gossip columns. He escorted her around Los Angeles to events such as the opening of the Yellow Brick Road Art Gallery, or to Jack Carter's debut at the Cocoanut Grove. Her gay friend, John Carlyle, joined Judy and Green that night, although she feared he'd make a play for Green himself. She was delighted to be with the two men, on each of whom she had already bestowed her sexual (often oral) favors.

Rumors spread that Judy, already casual about sexual mores, had evolved into a more aggressive player, asking for (or demanding it) in settings that were increasingly inappropriate and/or potentially embarrassing and dangerous. Such was the case in an incident relayed by author Nigel Cawthorne: "Judy disappeared under the table at a Santa Monica restaurant and performed oral sex on Green while he 'nibbled' his hors d'oeuvres. They passed on the entrée and went home for the main course."

As the gossip columnists noted, Judy and Green became an "item," showing up together at fashionable Hollywood parties, and seen frequently together in the Polo Lounge of the Beverly Hills Hotel talking with Tony Bennett, Van Johnson, Gene Kelly, and Bing Crosby.

***

On the first day of September in 1966, Judy announced to the press that she was abandoning her six-year association with CMA (Creative Management Agency), run by David Begelman and Freddie Fields. Privately, she referred to them as "those god damn embezzlers who stole all my money."

Urged on by Sid Luft, Judy, on October 11, filed a lawsuit against her former partners, seeking $3 million in damages. Her charge alleged that for years, her agents had been cheating her, which she referred to as "embezzlement, extortion, and fraud, withholding monies meant for me. They gave me the ten percent agent's fee while they gobbled up the rest. Instead of paying my taxes to the Internal Revenue Service, they put the money in their own private accounts."

The case would drag out, long and expensively, for months.

***

For the holidays that marked the end of 1966, Judy, with Tom Green, took the train East, stopping first in Chicago, where they were seen dining in the chic Pump Room of the Ambassador East Hotel. Then it was on for a holiday in his hometown of Lowell, Massachusetts, about twenty miles north of Boston.

Over the "holidays, he not only introduced Judy to his upper-middle-class family but presented her with an engagement ring.

For reading material during the eastbound train ride, she had brought along a suitcase filled with recent fan letters from her public. Whereas in the past, it had been almost always favorable, this batch was different, containing a lot of poisonously critical letters. One woman from Winston-Salem, North Carolina, wrote: "Remember when we loved you, our beloved Dorothy in *The Wizard of Oz*? She has nothing to do with the drunken, drugged, Judy Garland we read about today."

During the holidays, Green promised Judy that he would do anything in his power to help her reclaim her former life. Looking back on that comment years later, he said, "How stupid, how naïve I was."

His family was very Catholic, and all of them wanted to attend mass on Christmas Eve. Green phoned Cardinal Cushing to ask if it would be all right with the Church if he brought Judy Garland. *[Cushing was the charismatic and relatively lenient Archbishop of Boston (1944-1970). He had been a cardinal of the Roman Catholic Church since 1958. Diplomatic, hardworking, and gifted as an "intermediary" to politicians and the non-Catholic public, he was credited with "spinning" the Democratic Party's candidate for President (JFK) into something that was acceptable to the general American population at the time.]*

Cushing responded with "Of course... God loves everybody, even Judy Garland, although she does try my patience from time to time."

Alienated from Liza at the time, Judy praised, to anyone who would listen, the talents of her younger daughter Lorna. She had attended one of Lorna's performances in a school production of *The Unsinkable Molly Brown.* "Lorna has more talent than either Liza or me. She'll be the one who pays the rent."

Liza had recently released another of her albums, and Green made it a point to play it for Judy. "What do you think?" he asked, when it was over.

"It will take time, but she'll get better."

Green and Judy also journeyed to Dartmouth College in Hanover, New Hampshire, Green's *Alma Mater.* She told the editor of the school newspaper that Dartmouth was the most beautiful campus she'd ever seen. "I'm thinking of retiring with Tom Green after we're married. We're considering settling down here in Hanover."

***

Judy spent most of January, 1967, in Manhattan with Green, whom she wanted to introduce to Liza Minnelli. She hoped to have a reconciliation with her estranged daughter, who had rented an apartment there with Peter Allen, having made plans to marry him in March.

The mother and daughter were friends again as each of them, in spite of their differences, deeply loved the other.

Judy also had a reunion with Peter. He was still working the Playboy Club circuit with Chris Bell and they were still being billed as "The Allen Brothers." Judy was very complimentary about the three recordings that the two Aussies had made for ABC Paramount Records, even though they had not sold well.

Judy was anxious to see Liza's first movie, *Charlie Bubbles,* which had been shot in England with Albert Finney, its co-star and director. Called "a kitchen sink drama," it was a depiction of working class England. In it, Liza had been cast in a secondary role, playing the American secretary of the Finney character, with whom she has an adulterous relationship.

As her director, Finney told her, "You have a face that registers everything. But it's not veiled enough. Do just half of what you're doing."

When Sid Luft was informed of Liza's upcoming marriage to Peter Allen, he told friends, "Liza is following a family tradition. "Her grandmother, Ethel Gumm, married a homosexual. So did Judy—in fact, two of them. Now Liza wants to marry an Aussie fag."

Luft also claimed that he'd heard that when Peter and Chris Bell weren't working for Hugh Hefner on the Playboy Club circuit, that they starred in revues at gay clubs in various cities. "I'm told that this Allen guy does a wicked impersonation of Judy dressed in full drag."

In Manhattan, Judy was eager to show off her handsome and much

670

younger new beau, Tom Green. Liza found he was good-looking and full of grace and charm. Peter seemed very attracted to him, and the two men bonded, a bit too amicably for Judy, who was jealous whenever Green showed attention to anybody else. Peter and Liza were seen coming and going from Judy's suite at the Waldorf Astoria. Later, Judy and Green checked out, transferring into another suite at the Drake Hotel, six blocks uptown.

The happy foursome was seen on several occasions at Jilly's, where one night, they talked to Frank Sinatra. Judy's former lover, Bobby Cole, was appearing there at the piano with a trio of other musicians. After Judy sang a number with him, she promised, "We'll work together again real soon."

Twice, once with Liza and Peter, Judy attended a production of *Mame,* starring Angela Lansbury. All of them came backstage to greet the English star. Secretly, Judy wanted to play Mame in that play's film adaptation but would lose the role to Lucille Ball.

Liza and Peter were still sharing an apartment in Manhattan, but except for rare instances, they weren't in it together, as they appeared with their respective acts in widely different towns and cities.

Judy, Green, and Liza hugged and kissed Peter goodbye, as he set out for Chicago. Then, as a trio, they migrated back to Los Angeles, where Judy was scheduled for a videotaping of the then-popular prime-time variety show, *The Hollywood Palace,* on which she had performed before.

Mame, the female lead of a musical comedy that swept Broadway in the 60s, was a plum role that any middle-aged actress would have killed for, including Judy Garland.

It became so famous that **Angela Lansbury**, playing the jazz-age hoofer, made the cover of *Life* magazine for the way she handled it.

Judy Garland, to no avail and with some degree of personal humiliation, valiantly lobbied to either replace Lansbury on stage or to star in its film adapataion, weaving her spells as only a "Black Irish Witch" (*her term*) could do.

But it was all to no avail. The producers, including its composer, Jerry Herman, considered her a bad risk, and that whatever version she was in would be just too much **JUDY JUDY JUDY.**

News awaited Judy in Los Angeles: Sid Luft had renewed his friendship with her, and once again, was trying to be a guiding force in her fast-fading, "in need of a resurrection" [*Luft's words*] career. [*"Didn't Christ pull that off?" she jokingly quipped. "Don't ask me," Luft answered. "I'm a Jew."*]

During her absence from L.A., Luft had hired an agent, John E. Dugan, and he had come up with a deal to have Judy cast in the movie adaptation—eventually released in 1967—of Jacqueline Susann's best-selling novel, *Valley of the Dolls.* Judy was to be paid $75,000 for eight week's work, money she desperately needed.

***

Judy flew into New York on March 1, 1967, with plans to attend the wedding of Liza Minnelli to Peter Allen the following day. She checked into the St. Regis Hotel and later gave a press conference in its Versailles Room.

She appeared before the press with Susann, the controversial author of *Valley of the Dolls*. *[Even the novel's title — a reference to mood-altering pills — was controversial.]* It was on its way to becoming the best-selling novel of all time. Some seventeen million copies of this potboiler about

Publishing industry insiders cited **Jacqueline Susann**'s press and PR efforts as virtually "superhuman." With her hard-hitting husband, Irving Mansfield, Susann (*depicted above*) made it a point to greet everyone in the nation's book supply chains—from store managers to the drivers who delivered the cartons— at the time of its release.

What was it? It was *Valley of the Dolls*, a bad, even terrible book that was made into a campy but deadly serious and absolutely terrible movie that everybody read and everybody went to see.

the decadent personalities pulling strings within show-biz had already been sold. *[By 2020, it had sold more than 31 million copies.]*

Judy had not read the book yet, although she must have been aware of the cyclones of gossip whirling around it. One of its main characters, Neely O'Hara, had obviously been inspired by Judy herself. In a book sometimes interpreted as a "nihilistic tsunami of show-biz decadence and despair," the young actress interprets stardom as "too many minks, too many pills, and too many men."

Whereas it was clear that Judy was far too old to play the embittered *ingénue* (Neely), Mark Robson, the director of the upcoming film adaptation wanted her in the role of Helen Lawson, a character obviously based on the life of Broadway diva Ethel Merman. *[Susann, the book's author, had originally envisioned Bette Davis for that role.]*

Robson instructed Judy to portray the character of Helen Lawson as a brilliant but utterly ruthless legend. *[When a reporter asked Susann — based on the harsh light which she'd thrown over Merman — whether Merman was still speaking to her, Susann replied, "Merman wasn't speaking to me even before the book was written."]*

Liza had read *Valley of the Dolls* and urged her mother not to accept the role. "They're only using you and your name to exploit you for maximum publicity. My God, I recognized you in the character of Neely O'Hara. You and Merman should sue for libel."

Liza found one scene particularly revolting, that is when Neely confronts Lawson in the women's toilet, rips off her wig, and tries to flush it down the toilet, "It made me shudder," said Liza. "Your fans will be horrified to see you in such a role. It will cheapen your image."

"This is show biz," Judy said, countermanding her, "and besides, I need the dough. It's not that I'm being swamped with movie roles these days. I can handle a meaty part like this, and I might even win the Oscar that was denied me for *A Star Is Born.*"

At the press conference at the St. Regis, Judy reaffirmed her dedication to the role. "I think there's a good chance I'm going to sing one song. Yet I don't have to depend on my singing. I like to act, too, so I think it's going to be good. I hope I'm good in it. Let's face it. The role calls for an old pro. It's been some time since I played Dorothy in *The Wizard of Oz.* It's a challenging role, but I want you to know this: The character of Helen Lawson is not based on my life."

She also ignored the gossip that a younger Judy Garland had been Susann's inspiration for Neely O'Hara.

Susann claimed, "It's all right for Judy to play what might seem like an unsympathetic character, a brutal portrait of a star. But it's not. It shows how unhappy a star is up there with all the encroachments of success. It's a sad commentary, and there are many stars who get all these telegrams inviting them

Two views of **Patty Duke** portraying a character (Neely O'Hara) whose ambition, drug addiction, violent outbursts, and raw talent were inspired by the real-life history of Judy Garland.

Judy, of course, was horrified, and couldn't say enough negative things about Patty.

Top photo shows a histrionic Patty Duke, as Neely or a desperate Judy, reaching for her pills.

Lower photo shows an out-of-control **Patty or Neely or Judy** being restrained in a psychiatric ward by her nurses.

Judy was not amused.

to every opening, every place, and then there's a mad scramble of 'Where do I get an escort?'"

"In other words, it's lonely at the top," Judy chimed in.

A reporter who was covering the story wanted to "out" Judy as a pill-popper. He asked, "The book deals with pills which Miss Susann calls 'dolls.' Have you found pill-popping prevalent in show business?"

"Well," Judy quipped. "I've found it prevalent among newspaper people."

[After Valley of the Dolls *had already become a movie (without Judy), she sat down and read the novel. "Susann wrote about my life, a fictional disguise that made me seem like a comic book caricature. In fact, she ripped off my story and made millions for herself at a time I was losing my home in Brentwood, the last home I would ever own. As for starring in the film, I got kicked out on my ass.*

There is just no justice in life."]

***

It was March 3, 1967, the day after Judy and Susann had faced the press, when Vincente Minnelli was awakened at 6AM. It was Judy Garland calling his hotel suite in Manhattan. As a team, they planned to attend the wedding that day of Liza, their daughter, to Peter Allen. They each had reservations about her selection of a groom, wondering where his true sexual interests lay, but as parents, they were committed to putting up a brave and supportive front.

Judy was very blunt with her ex-second husband: "If you had any class, you'd escort me to the wedding."

"Where is Tom Green?" he asked.

"Who knows what young men do when mama is out of town?" She gave him the details, and he agreed to be in a limousine waiting for her in front of the St. Regis Hotel in time for them to attend the wedding.

The ceremony was at the Manhattan apartment of Stevie Phillips, once known as "Judy Garland's shadow" when she had both lived and worked with her. *[Philips had later accused her then-employer of lesbian advances.]*

Right before the ceremony, Judy made a flamboyant entrance, as if to divert attention away from the bride.

Lorna and Joey were already there. Judy had not seen them since the day before. Lorna always remembered her mother emerging in a rainbow-colored coat over a sunflower yellow sheath, with a matching pillbox hat. "Bright as a daffodil," as Lorna described her. All eyes turned to look at Judy, who at least appeared to be virtually upstaging the bride.

Dropping Vincente shortly after she entered the room, she headed over to greet Sid Luft, and was almost flirtatious with him in spite of their many widely publicized court battles. In the far corner of the room stood David Begelman and Freddie Fields. Judy was furious at Liza for inviting them, knowing that she planned to sue them in the weeks ahead. During the wedding and later at the reception, too, Luft and Judy remained on opposite sides of the room from Begelman and Fields.

Before the ceremony began, Peter Allen came over to kiss and hug Judy and to shake hands with Luft. "Our daughter is marrying a real flamer," Luft whispered into Judy's ear.

At the altar stood Judge Joseph A Macchia, flanked by the Best Man, Paul Jasmin, and the Matron of Honor, Pamela Reinhardt. Nearby were Peter's sister and mother, who had flown in

Portrait of an Unconventional Wedding

Left to right: **Lorna, Vincente Minnelli** (half-hidden), **Judy, Liza, Peter Allen, Joey Luft** and (right side) **Peter's sister and mother**, just arrived from Australia.

from Sydney. Judy had not yet met them.

When the bride appeared, her wedding outfit could hardly compete with Judy's flamboyant attire. Vincente himself had designed Liza's clothing: a white blouse in Parisian lace over a straight skirt crafted from ivory-colored wool. She carried a bouquet. He gave the bride away.

The ceremony over, Liza entered her first marriage just a few days before her 20th birthday on March 12. Allen would be the first of her four husbands, oddly mirroring the marital record of her mother, who, before she died, would have five.

The wedding was followed by a lavish reception in the apartment of Martin Bragman (Liza's business manager) on Central Park West.

Judy circulated freely among the guests, hugging and kissing Van Johnson, and greeting Tony Bennett, John Kander, Diahann Carroll, Gwen Verdon, Bob Fosse, and Phil Silvers. She embraced her daughter and Peter, too, telling him, "Welcome to our family. We're a bit stuffy at times, too conservative to be much fun, but always sweet, punctual, and reliable."

"Yeah, right!," Peter quipped.

She had a reunion with Yul Brynner ("The King of Siam"), who had once been one of the "loves of my life." He hugged and kissed her, and whispered in her ear, "You are the best of them all, my dear, divine lady."

George Muir, one of Liza's biographers, wrote, "Discomfort could not begin to cover what Liza must have felt when it turned out that she was in competition with her husband's new gay lover. Peter spent his wedding night with him, not Liza."

Another of Liza's biographers, Wendy Leigh, wrote:

"Ostensibly, Liza and Peter's union had all the hallmarks of young love ever after. Seeing the ecstatic couple, an onlooker may well have sighed enviously, anticipating the marital bliss that awaited them. The reality, however, was very different. (A confidential source who was very close to Liza and to whom she revealed the information) has claimed that the marriage to Peter wasn't consummated on the wedding night because he was out having sex with a gay lover."

The biographer of Vincente Minnelli, Emanuel Levy, put a different spin on it: "Just as Judy surprised Vincente when she found him in bed with another man, so now, only weeks into her marriage, Liza caught Allen in a compromising position. Judy's friends testified that, barely a year into her daughter's marriage, she cried over Liza's suffering for repeating her pattern of marrying a gay man."

In a biography of Peter Allen, *The Boy From Oz*, another scenario emerged: The couple did not embark on an immediate honeymoon. Instead, Liza and Peter began immediately setting up future arrangements with their agents. Within three weeks of her wedding, she was said to have returned to their apartment early one afternoon and found her husband in bed with an attractive male model who looked like he had stepped out of a Calvin Klein underwear ad. The betrayal was huge, and Liza was devastated.

As the model fled from their apartment, Peter had a lot of excuses, claiming, "I had too much to drink. I'll never do it again. This was the first time ever. I was curious to see what it was like."

He was to follow this pattern of betrayal and deceit throughout the rest of their ill-fated marriage. As his popularity and visibility grew in America, so did his wider choice of ready, willing, and able young men who often sought him out.

In the wake of all the publicity generated by the Allen/Minnelli wedding, Johnny Carson invited Peter and Chris Bell for an appearance on *The Tonight Show*. Liza insisted they sing one of her mother's standards, "Come Rain Or Come Shine." Watched by thirty million TV viewers, they were a sensation, inspiring Carson to book them for twelve more appearances.

"The phone didn't stop ringing with requests for me, and not so much for Liza," Peter said.

Columnist Earl Wilson wrote, "The two boys captured the late-night audience as no other singers ever had. Perhaps they will bridge the gap between the teeny-boppers, the rock 'n' rollers, and even the senior citizens who watch *The Lawrence Welk Show*."

***

Three days after her daughter's wedding, Judy agreed to be interviewed by an up-and-coming reporter, Barbara Walters. When Walters arrived in Judy's suite at the St. Regis, the star kept her waiting for four hours. Feeling thwarted, and as she was packing up to leave, Judy entered from her bedroom. "She was adorable, all was forgiven," Walters said. "My first question to her was, 'did you give Liza any advice about marriage?'"

"No, I don't think I'm qualified to do that," Judy answered. "I've not been successful myself when it comes to marriage. When I first got married, I was six months old. I think that is too young to marry."

Her interview was filled with both humor and sadness. She related stories of her early days at MGM when she and Mickey Rooney often worked seventy-two hours straight. "That's why both of us ended up as Munchkins."

She spoke of the bad headlines she was getting in the press, citing a recently generated headline: JUDY GARLAND ADMITS SHE'S BROKE.

"The press says I'm addicted to carpets or drinking or pills. I wouldn't have time to learn a song if I'd be as sick as printed most of the time. And temperamental...I can't afford to be temperamental."

Walters did not rank it among her best interviews.

Before flying back to California, Judy granted one final interview with reporter John Gruen, who published it in the *World Journal Tribune Magazine*. He called her "The Sob Queen of All Time," and noted that she was in town to attend the wedding of her daughter, and also to publicize her film role in *Valley of the Dolls*. [He went on to describe the novel on which it was based as "drug-drenched and sex-besotted."

Midway through the interview, three calls came in for Judy from Los Angeles. Based on what Gruen overheard, he surmised that banks were foreclosing on her home in Brentwood.

After she put down the phone, she continued with the interview, telling Gruen, "After today, I'll have to pitch a tent in front of the Beverly

676

Hills Hotel. I'll get Lorna to earn money to buy food by singing gospel hymns."

In reference to losing her house, she said, "It was too big anyway, too costly, required servants. Good riddance, I say. It was more suited to Gloria Swanson during her heyday on the silent screen."

She discussed *Valley of the Dolls*: "I play an older woman, but not an ancient crone. The press already has me walking off the set, and the sets aren't even built yet."

"I will forever be associated with my role of Dorothy in *The Wizard of Oz*. My character was a symbol of heartbreak and bittersweet joy."

She also lamented the trouble she was having trying to find "a mate for Judy Garland, the living legend. My last husband, Mark Herron, married me strictly for business reasons. You know he bats for the other team."

That last line was not published.

Gruen described Judy in his article as "a paragon of survival and show-biz glitz and glamour."

***

As Peter Allen moved into married life with Liza, friends noted that he seemed like a brother to her instead of a husband, a companion and disco-hopper more than a lover. He always treated his mother-in-law with great respect, and on occasion, when he could afford it, he paid some of Judy's bills.

Lorna was fifteen at the time, Joey thirteen. Peter and Liza often had to play the roles of father and mother to them when Judy was incapacitated, especially when she went into one of her frequent rages, breaking everything in whatever rooms she occupied and often injuring herself.

As she moved deeper into her marriage, Liza became increasingly independent and could no longer "drop everything" and come to the rescue of her mother. Sometimes, when Judy phoned from California, Liza "instructed" Peter to tell Judy that she was not at home.

On her final night in Manhattan, Judy remained inside her suite at the St. Regis Hotel, where Joey and Lorna noticed that their mother seemingly was coming "unglued." She had run out of Ritalin, it was way past midnight, and she did not know who to call. Judy was so nervous, so distraught, and so desperate that she appeared on the brink of suicide.

To rescue her mother, Lorna put through a call to John Carlyle in Hollywood. She was aware that he was resourceful, and that he had a number of "connected" friends in Manhattan.

Lorna reached Carlyle on the phone as he was retiring to bed for the night, and, indeed, he did know a possible source for Ritalin. He called his close friend, musician Charlie Cochran. Carlyle had long known that many musicians, often playing in clubs until dawn, took Ritalin to keep them awake and alert through their hard-working pre-dawn performance gigs.

Carlyle also placed a call to Mickey Deans, who had replaced Bobby Cole at the piano at Jilly's. Indeed, Deans had a supply on hand, and—with Cochran—maneuvered his way late, late at night to Judy's suite at the St. Regis. When Lorna ushered them inside to meet the (very distraught) Judy, Cochran introduced Mickey as "Dr. Deans, who's come to look after Judy."

Deans went into her bedroom to deliver the pills and emerged after only five minutes. Judy could not have been aware that she had just met her fifth and final husband.

After sleeping for most of the next day, she rose from her bed and got ready to take a night flight to Los Angeles. Both Lorna and Joey were on the plane with her. So was Sid Luft.

***

During the flight to California, Judy settled back in her seat and read, for the first time, the filmscript of *Valley of the Dolls*. Its plot focused on three young women. *[Actresses for those roles had already been cast: Barbara Parkins as the hardworking career girl Anne Welles; Patty Duke as the brilliantly talented and "onstage charismatic" singer Neely O'Hara; and Sharon Tate as the spectacularly beautiful but not-particularly-talented Jennifer North.]* In the movie, the trio become friends, sharing the bonds of ambition and a tendency to fall in love with the wrong men.

Judy was shocked that episodes in the script associated with the character of Neely (Patty Duke), the scenes seemed directly derived from her (Judy's) own life, and that much of that character's dialogue "seemed to have been uttered by my own desperate throat."

Judy's character of Helen Lawson was the archetype of "a legendary star who had already reached the top—and had the claws to stay there." The filmscript depicted her as a vile, brutal, egomaniacal, and easy-to-dislike character. Judy searched, perhaps frantically, for some redeeming value...and found none. As a brittle and venomous character with a relatively small (but crucial) part, Lawson seemed to take pleasure in destroying any young aspiring competitor. Judy hoped that she could prevail upon the scriptwriters, Helen Deutsch and Dorothy Kingsley, for a rewrite. "If only there could be some revelation that made Helen Lawson the bitter character she was in this screenplay....if only..." Judy pondered.

After her arrival in L.A., one of the first friends to return Judy's call was John Carlyle. As usual, he was filled with gossip, much of which he had

**VALLEY GIRLS
(Dolls Who Play with Dolls)**

Left to right: **Sharon Tate** (victim of multiple stab wounds two years after filming, by members of the Charles Manson cult); **Barbara Parkins** (already a daytime soap opera star from her key role in more than 500 episodes of *Peyton Place*); and **Patty Duke**, spectacularly famous for her Broadway and film depictions of Helen Keller in *The Miracle Worker* five years before.

learned from his close friend, Robert Osborne, "who seemed to know whenever a cockroach crossed Hollywood Boulevard."

He shocked Judy with his news. *[Having lived in Hollywood for so long, she did not shock easily.]* According to Carlyle, Ethel Merman, the basis for the character of Helen Lawson, had once had a lesbian affair with Susann. Their association had become the insider gossip of Broadway. Their liaison had ended bitterly, and there was, perhaps, a measure of revenge in Susann's portrayal of Merman through the character of Helen Lawson.

[Judy was relieved that Carlyle did not have the bad taste to bring up those long-ago rumors that she, too, had had a lesbian affair with the bisexual Ethel Merman.]

***

Before reporting to work on the set of *Valley of the Dolls,* Judy met with John Cohan, known in the Entertainment Industry as "the Celebrity Psychic to the Stars." His predictions for the year ahead have appeared annually for many years in Cindy Adams' column in the *New York Post.*

Over the years, many in show-biz have turned to him for insights during their crises and for guidance for their futures. Cohan played an influential role in the lives of Elizabeth Taylor, Inger Stevens, Nicole Brown Simpson and Sandra Dee, whom he defines as having been "The Love of My Life."

"John is a great man to know during one's darkest hours," said Danforth Prince. "He's kind, he's generous, he's deeply spiritual, he has valuable insights into the agonies of 'the celebrity experience,' and he's an emotionally intelligent and very positive guiding force for anyone barging a path through the insecurities and doubts of a career in show-biz."

In a memoir, Cohan once wrote: "My gift is something that has been with me since I was born. Most of my adolescence, I spent time and energy ignoring or suppressing my psychic ability, because I didn't know what it was that possessed me. Finally, I did grasp hold of it and actually embraced my talent."

Judy had been an occasional friend of Cohan. She wanted his views on her acceptance of the role of Helen Lawson in *Valley of the Dolls.* He had always been a good choice for her to turn to, because his advice had always been on target.

For his reunion with Judy, he was in a unique position. Cohan was also a psychic advisor to Jacqueline Susann.

Cohan was acutely aware that the novelist had based the character of Neely O'Hara on Judy herself. "She'd be in the awkward position of working in a film that starred Patty Duke in a role ripped off from the tormented saga of Judy's own life."

Judy confessed to Cohan that she detested the role of Helen Lawson "as written in the screenplay," and that she wanted her agent to demand a rewrite from Fox. Cohan was doubtful if Fox would make such a concession, and indeed, the studio refused. In reference to one of the film's (younger) stars, Barbara Parkins, Judy told him, "That girl from Vancouver twirls in her own orbit."

Cohan advised her not to accept the role, fearing that it would be a disaster for her, generating more negative press coverage. "I felt she was not physically or mentally up to it. Her role was clearly based on Ethel Merman, who was a tough show-biz survivor. Judy wasn't that tough, as she was far more vulnerable, almost like a time bomb that could go off at any minute."

A savvy show-biz pro like Cohan knew that the role should have been assigned to a younger actress, perhaps an emotional equivalent of Barbara Stanwyck, Joan Crawford, or Bette Davis, if such an actress existed at the time, which he doubted.

Judy read to Cohan some of the lines from the script she'd been assigned. According to Cohan, "They were so unlike Judy's own image of herself. She found it difficult even to say the lines."

In the spring of 1969, Cohan spoke to Judy for the last time. She told him she was heading off to London with the new man in her life, Mickey Deans.

"You need someone with you at all times," he advised, "in case you should have a panic attack."

Here's a scene from **Valley of the Dolls** that Judy's psychic advisor, John Cohan, thought would be particularly bad for her image if she had continued in the part.

Patty Duke (left figure above, playing Neely O'Hara, the role inspired by the eccentricities of Judy Garland), has just humiliated Helen Lawson, the imperious diva whose portrayal Judy might have played if she hadn't been fired, by flushing her wig down the toilet.

Susan Hayward, depicted on the right, filled in for Judy after she was dismissed. Insiders cited Ethel Merman as the inspiration for Helen.

Confusing? Indeed, yes. But insiders within the cult of "the Valley Girls" found all of it mesmerizings, and ratings went through the ceiling.

Many of **John Cohan**'s insights and revelations have been published in *Catch a Falling Star*, a startling overview of his life as a psychic to show-biz celebrities.

Cohan frequently warned his friends and clients, including Judy Garland, to expect disappointment in marriage and love, and the importance of not becoming bitter and disillusioned.

Advice from the Celebrity Seer? "I've been disappointed but never pessimistic. True love is the one infallible shield against all the ugly and harsh things in the world. Once you find it, hold onto it and cherish it carefully, forever."

She hugged and kissed him, saying, "You've already seen what happens to me when I don't listen to you."

Cohan later said, "I had a feeling of impending doom for her. It frightened me. Dark shadows seemed to be creeping into her life."

He would never hear the sound of Judy's distinctive voice again, a voice that had brought joy to people around the globe. In London, she'd face the doom that Cohan sensed was lurking in her near-term future.

***

On March 27, 1967, Judy showed up for the first day of work at 20th Century Fox, where she submitted to hair, wardrobe, and makeup tests. A chestnut-colored wig was fitted onto her head, and she was provided with a sequin-studded pants suit designed by Bill Travilla. It became her all-time favorite outfit.

She also pre-recorded her solo, "I'll Plant My Own Tree," which she evaluated, musically, as "weak lemonade." She planned to approach the director, Mark Robson, for permission to sing an alternate number, "Get Off Looking Good," by her ever-faithful Bobby Cole.

A few nights later, she showed up drunk at a dinner honoring Marcella Rabwin, the wife of Dr. Mark Rabwin, a family friend since her childhood in Minnesota, when Frank Gumm had brought him home for introductions to the Gumm family. Both of them cringed as Judy made a drunken spectacle of herself, ruining the evening's tribute to Marcella. The couple was horribly embarrassed for Judy and saw that she got home safely and put to bed.

During that period, Lorna would sometimes call Dr. Rabwin, and he would arrive with groceries to stock the bare refrigerator.

Three days later, Judy appeared at a courthouse, rushing past reporters waiting on the steps. It was a big moment in her life. Not only was her divorce from Mark Herron granted, but she officially changed her name to "Judy Garland." *[Prior to that, her legal name had been Frances Ethel Gumm Rose Minnelli Luft Herron.]*

***

David Hartnell (MNZM) is New Zealand's "Number One" celebrity gossip columnist on television, radio, and print. As is said of him, his visits to Hollywood established his credentials until he became a living encyclopedia of trivia and scandal about the rich and famous.

His lifetime of pursuing the glitter and glamour of showbiz is delightfully captured in his *Memoirs of a Gossip Columnist* published in 2011. That same year, he was recognized by Her Majesty, Queen Elizabeth II as a Member of the New Zealand Order of Merit for his services to the entertainment industry.

David met Mark Herron in 1989 at a dinner party in Los Angeles. "I was amazed to find out that he was still cashing in on Judy Garland. He was selling some of Judy's stage costumes and casual clothing to collectors.

But the thing I found most bizarre was that he was selling sets of false eyelashes once used by Judy. A devotee of Judy could have picked up a pair for about fifty dollars."

***

Judy arrived at 7:30AM at the gates of 20th Century Fox, ready to shoot her first scene for *Valley of the Dolls*. Nervous with anticipation, but irritable and groggy from a sleepless night, she met three wardrobe and makeup people, two women and a man, in her dressing room.

A wig was positioned carefully and added to her *coiffe*, and she underwent makeup and wardrobe fittings. The director, Mark Robson, kept sending messages that he was ready for her first scene, one with Barbara Parkins, a native of Vancouver who was four years older than Liza.

[At this point in her career, Parkins was already a huge star on daytime TV, having made a name for herself in a key role (the small-town bad girl, Betty Anderson), in 514 episodes (1964-1969) of TV's first prime-time soap opera, Peyton Place. When asked about her character's contribution to the plot devices in that TV series, she'd defined it as "the salt and pepper in the stew."

Parkins was well aware of the politics and emotional labyrinths associated with her role within the screenplay. In Susann's novel, Parkins' character of Anne Welles, "the good girl with the million-dollar face and all the bad breaks," had been partly autobiographical, based as it was on the author's own life.]

"I'm ready for my 'face-off' with Judy Garland," Parkins told Robson, her director. "Bring her on."

Lunch time came and went—and still no Judy. Parkins spent the (otherwise wasted) time talking to Robson about her character and its contribution to the film. She seemed delighted to be working with her fellow

A GATHERING OF THE CLAN
(Photo courtesy of David Hartnell)

Left to right, **Mark Herron** (Judy Garland's fourth husband); gossip columnist **David Hartnell**; **Matthew West** (a New Zealand-born publicist who had arranged the details of Judy's marriage to Mickey Deans and later handled the publicity for her gig at Talk of the Town), and **Marc Christian**, the former lover of Rock Hudson.

The photo was snapped in Los Angeles in 1989, shortly after Hartnell had put down the phone after a conversation with Peter Ford, a senior producer of *Good Morning Australia*. Ford had asked Hartnell to use his influence to sign Christian for a world exclusive TV interview.

Herron and Christian were hustlers, Herron with Judy, Christian with Hudson. But there was a difference:

Whereas Judy's ex was forced, late in life, to hustle dubious artifacts belonging to the (long-deceased) Judy, Christian made off with $5 million. He was the recent beneficiary of a lawsuit he'd filed, wherein he claimed that the (deceased in 1985) Hudson had had sex with him without telling him he was afflicted with AIDS.

682

Canadian. He had directed the feature film version of *Peyton Place* in 1957, and he had recently won an Oscar nomination for his direction of *Von Ryan's Express* (1965), starring Frank Sinatra.

As Robson and Parkins were seated together and talking, word reached them that Judy had fallen ill and left the lot for the day, and that she'd report for filming the following day.

The next day (the second day of her scheduled shooting), Judy showed up late again as Robson and Parkins once again waited and waited. Before lunch, a messenger reported that although, indeed, she had appeared briefly on the set, she hadn't been able to work and had already returned to her home.

Judy appeared on the third day, but word soon reached Robson because of a recent "disaster" she'd suffered, she wouldn't be available for filming. She could not locate the caps for her front teeth. Stumbling her way through a solution, she had frantically called on John Carlyle to commission the fabrication of a new set of false teeth from her dentist.

When Judy, much later, did show up for work, she faced hostile stares from both Robson and Parkins. In the scene they wanted to shoot, the naïve newcomer (Parkins) was to deliver contracts to Lawson (Judy), who is belligerent, hostile, and lashes into her before tearing the (unsigned) contracts to shreds. According to Judy, "In other words, I was supposed to be a god damn harridan on the screen—and that's not the role I wanted to play."

Robson tried to direct the scene anyway, but Judy refused to embody any of his directives, doing the scene her way, which to him was "the wrong way" and a defiant challenge to his authority.

After she departed that day, he complained to *Valley of the Doll's* producer David Weisbart, "Garland is sabotaging her role, perhaps her career, too."

Parkins had a comment, too: "So *that* was the legendary Judy Garland that I've always read so much about? With that wig, I didn't recognize her at first. Neely O'Hara is supposed to rip it off in an upcoming scene. Then we'll get to see the real Judy Garland."

Reports about these dysfunctions reached all the ways to the top, eventually arriving at the desk of the Fox Studio's dreaded honcho, Darryl F. Zanuck in New York, who was counting on *Valley of the Dolls* to make millions for Fox.

He fired off a phone call to Robson: "Fire the bitch! I've got the ideal replacement: Susan Hayward. We know her well. She's another bitch but she'll understand Helen Lawson to her left tit."

Meanwhile, Judy had been chatting in her dressing room with a budding young actress, Sharon Tate. Judy found her, a former model from Dallas, Texas, to be both beautiful and endearing. She confided to Tate that in her opinion, Patty Duke was dreadfully miscast and completely wrong as Neely O'Hara. "A young Judy Garland could have pulled it off simply by acting like ME. Duke is way off the mark, way wrong for the part. The press is gonna DESTROY her."

Judy's death sentence soon arrived from Fox executive Owen McLean, who was very blunt (some said "savage") in his delivery: "We're tired of your foolishness, and we're not going to put up with it. YOU'RE FIRED!

Please pack up your belongings and leave the studio by two o'clock this afternoon."

Tate watched in horror as Judy reacted. "She went wild, breaking anything that was breakable. When Fox heard that she liked to play pool, they even brought in a pool table for her. She took a piece of jagged glass and cut into its green felt covering. She was like a raging monster, and I fled the scene, fearing I'd be seriously injured, maybe facially scarred by all this shattered glass."

Actually, Fox was generous with the terms of Judy's departure, giving her $40,000 of her agreed-upon fee, plus the $5,000 sequin-covered pants suit, which she'd wear at every concert performance for the rest of her life.

As anticipated, her creditors moved in, the IRS making off with $23,000. By the time her agent got his commission and some other deductions were subtracted, she received only $10,000.

Before summoning a press conference, Judy put through a (probably enraged) phone call to the producer, David Weisbart. He refused to talk to her. So did the film's director, Robson. She even tried to reach Zanuck in New York, but he, too, refused to accept her call.

News of her firing hit the press like a tornado. Judy told reporters, "Fox has released the news that I have withdrawn from *Valley of the Dolls* for personal reasons. That is a god damn lie. I did not resign. I was fired. I was up before dawn this morning to report to work on time. I was ready and waiting for Mark Robson to call me before the camera. I waited and waited and sent word to him to let me know when he wanted me. I didn't hear from him. All I got was a letter from the top brass that I was canned. Out on my ass! Fired! Kicked out! It's shocking the way I was treated. No respect. The script was horrible. The woman I was to play was vulgar and coarse, shouting all the time. I was to play a dirty old lady. My first line to a young girl was, 'Who in hell are you?'"

Tom Green was by her side at the time. He said, "The first day we got to the set, they were shooting a nude scene! Right then I knew it wasn't the type of film for Judy. She is, after all, America's Sweetheart. Families go to see her movies. Miss Garland can't be a glittering bitch in a Hollywood film that looks to me like porn."

Judy continued her rant: "I was fired because I think that filthy son of a bitch, Darryl F. Zanuck, thinks he's Louis B. Mayer. He once fired me, too. I can't use vulgar language on the screen. People who saw me in *The Wizard of Oz* don't want to see me like that. I took the part only for the money, not because I had any respect for the script. It's pure sleaze. I detested the role. It'll make a terrible picture. I loathed the part of Helen Lawson. Ethel Merman should sue. I think the fact that I can gross $110,000 for a concert is more important than this bloody damn movie. Judy Garland is back on the road again, where a gal who was born in a trunk in a vaudeville theater belongs."

Her friend, Roddy McDowall, had his own reaction: "Judy's pursuit of the role of Helen Lawson was like scratching and clawing one's way to board the *Titanic* on its maiden voyage."

In the wake of her firing, Judy was alleged to have put through a call to the mogul, Howard Hughes, inviting him over. Once there, face to face, she pleaded with the decrepit billionaire to purchase 20th Century Fox. "That way, I can fire all the cast and crew associated with *Valley of the Dolls,* even Zanuck himself."

Hughes, with plenty of problems of his own during that period of his decline, denied her request.

***

When *Valley of the Dolls* was released, the reviews were devastating, but it made money, generating a box office of $50 million, having been made on a budget of $4.6 million.

Harsh appraisals called it "a melodramatic mishmash...a piece of trash...lowest rating possible...unbelievably hackneyed...inept...inane... tasteless...dirty...filthy...one of the most stupefying films ever made..." and so forth. One critic wrote, "It has no more sense of its own ludicrousness than a village idiot stumbling in cow manure."

One of its most insightful reviews was not posted by critics in New York or Los Angeles, but by "Anonymous:"

"In Hollywood, however, only the box office matters and Valley of the Dolls, *in spite of its vicious critical reception, became a box office sensation, in fact, it was no less than the biggest non-roadshow grossing film in the history of Twentieth Century Fox up to that time. Today,* Valley of the Dolls *has been given a new lease on life. In the succeeding years it has begun to build momentum and is frequently revived and appreciated by a whole new generation of filmgoers who were too young to have seen it originally. But why would anyone want to revive a bad movie? Quite simply because* Valley of the Dolls *is no run of the mill bad movie. Anyone with a camera and a roll of film can make a bad movie, but it takes a certain talent to make a really bad movie. And* Valley of the Dolls *is a really bad movie. It is truly, deeply, and completely bad. In fact, it is perfectly bad. And what makes it so bad in addition to its inept script, direction and acting, is the deadly seriousness by which it takes itself. This film was not made as a parody even though it contains virtually every old show business cliché in existence. No, the makers of this film thought they were creating a masterpiece. And this celluloid monstrosity was made not by a cheap sleaze ball operation or an Ed Wood-type director but was a major motion picture from a major motion picture studio with a top flight producer, director and cast. And it was based not only on a best-selling book, but on what was the best-selling novel of all time. Now, that is special!"*

***

[Jacqueline Susann, like Judy herself, would face a tragic ending, dying of cancer in the autumn of 1974 at the age of fifty-six.

She would see Judy one final time, and that was at a chance meeting as she was leaving her apartment house in Manhattan. She spotted a distraught woman wearing a T-shirt and slacks, who called out to her: "Hey, author! Hey author!"

At first, the novelist did not recognize Judy until she came face to face with her. She looked desperate and was not made up. "She was in horrible shape," Su-

sann said.

"I've been kicked out of my hotel," she said. "They won't let me into my room to get my clothes and stuff unless I pay up. I don't have any money."

"How much do you owe?" Susann asked.

"I'm not sure."

Susann invited her to go with her upstairs to her apartment. When they got there, Susann went into her bedroom and returned with eight one-hundred dollar bills, handing them to Judy.

She accepted the money but warned, "I don't know when I can pay you back."

"Who said anything about paying me back?" the writer replied.

She noticed Judy eyeing her liquor cabinet but felt this was not an occasion for Judy to get drunk in her apartment. Susann showed her to the door and took her hand. "Goodbye, Judy. Take care of yourself."

"Thank you very much," Judy said.

Susann stood in her doorway, watching Judy get on the elevator. She waved her final goodbye. She would never see her again.]

***

Postscript: In 1968, Barbara Parkins flew to London to be a bridesmaid at the wedding of Sharon Tate to director Roman Polanski. Parkins liked the atmosphere and traditions of London and decided to settle there permanently.

By June of 1969, Judy herself had settled into London, but never lived to see what happened in Hollywood on the night of August 9. Polanski was away and his wife, Sharon Tate, hosted a party for intimate friends.

During the party, deranged members of the bloodthirsty Charles Manson gang burst into her home and killed Tate and her guests. She was eight-and-a-half months pregnant, and was stabbed sixteen times, mostly in her visibly swollen stomach.

***

After Judy's dismissal from *Valley of the Dolls,* Luft managed to sell Judy's Brentwood home for $130,000, far below its market value of one million dollars. The IRS took a good hunk of the proceeds.

"I put everything Judy owned into storage," Luft said, "and immediately set about arranging a concert tour for her."

For the remainder of her short life, Judy became a self-styled vagabond, wandering from town to town, often with Lorna and Joey. She left a string of unpaid hotel bills in her wake. Home life became nonexistent.

She even wrote a poem:

"Oh, to go home…
But where?
I never yet was there."

686

OVERMEDICATED, EXHAUSTED, & MENTALLY UNSTABLE, JUDY STAYS CAMERA-READY FOR CLOSEUPS

AT CONCERT GIGS IN WESTBURY (LONG ISLAND), THE PALACE (NYC), CAMDEN (NJ), BOSTON (TWICE), COLUMBIA (MD), CHICAGO, CLEVELAND, DETROIT, INDIANAPOLIS, LAS VEGAS, HOLMDEL (NJ), & (WITH HORRIBLE AFTER-EFFECTS) **BALTIMORE**

SAUCY AND SOPHISTICATED: TALK-TV INTERVIEWS WITH

DICK CAVETT, MERV GRIFFIN, MIKE DOUGLAS, & JOHNNY CARSON
"ON THE AIR, SHE'S THE FEMALE EQUIVALENT OF DEAN MARTIN... WHEN HE'S DRUNK"

"GARLAND'S ONSTAGE PIZZAZ STILL HOLDS"
UNTIL IT DOESN'T

"SHE'S A SCHEMING, INCOHERENT MESS."

AFTER ANOTHER ABORTED STAB AT FINDING A WRITER
FOR HER MEMOIRS, JUDY UNLEASHES NEW HORRORS ON TOM GREEN,
& CALLS IN AN ANONYMOUS BOMB THREAT TO A BROADWAY THEATER.

THE MILE-HIGH CLUB: JUDY'S BRAWL AT 30,000 FEET

NINETEEN EXPENSIVE & EMBARRASSING HOURS OF IN-FLIGHT MISERY

FAMILY, FAMILY, FAMILY

JUDY LASHES OUT AT HER CHILDREN

HEARTBREAKER: TWO MONTHS WITH JOHN MEYER.
IN LONDON, JUDY BECOMES **THE TALK OF THE TOWN**

THE MAN WHO WANTED TO GET AWAY, BUT COULDN'T
MICKEY DEANS

DEATH OF AN ICON
"JUDY GARLAND WAS A STAR IN HER FINAL ROLE"
—NY DAILY NEWS

"Nagging question is how long Judy Garland can keep it up. How long does she want to? Audience affection and good will are there, but there can be a limit to how long folks watch a well-loved champ gamble with her talent."

—Variety

"The playwright, Arthur Miller, never understood Marilyn Monroe. Tom Green, my current beau, says he wants to marry me, but I fear he does not understand me."
—Judy Garland

"I'm always asked to write the story of my life, and I have started it, sometimes with a ghost writer. But when you've lived the life I have, when you've loved and suffered and been really happy and desperately sad— well, that's when you realize you will never be able to get it all down. Maybe you'd rather die first."

—Judy Garland

"I can live without money, but I cannot live without love."

—Judy Garland

"Judy Garland keeps being reincarnated, but somehow manages to come back every time as herself. So, Judy, carry on. Give the lie to mortality. If anybody can live forever, it's going to be you."

—**The Chicago Daily News** (September, 1967)

For years, doctors had sounded alarms about Judy's deteriorating health.

By 1969 (right photo), they diagnosed her emaciated, drug-ravaged, and deeply depressed survival as a miraculous triumph.

At this dark period at the end of her rainbow, Judy was sustained mainly by her memories of happier times.

In the first week of May (1967), Judy made her last prime-time television appearance. A Jack Paar special, *A Funny Thing Happened to Me on the Way to Hollywood,* was telecast over NBC-TV in color.

Escorted by Tom Green (her lover) and Sid Luft, (her ex-husband), she showed up at NBC's Rockefeller Center Studio in midtown Manhattan. She seemed lively and in good spirits as she chatted with the show's producer, Jack Haley, Jr. *[Although she would not live to attend his marriage ceremony to Liza, he would in time become her son-in-law. She was already well acquainted with his father, Jack Haley, Sr., as he had played "The Tin Man" in* The Wizard of Oz *way back in the late 1930s.]*

As the cameras were rolling, Judy and Paar engaged in some fascinating banter, but some of the best clips never made it into the final broadcast. In one segment, she discussed an incident where she was in a car driven by Paar, and they stopped at a red light. As they waited for the light to change, Elvis Presley, piloting a late-model pink Cadillac convertible, pulled up beside them.

"Hey, Judy!" he called out to her. "You're my favorite gal singer. I'm my favorite male singer." When the light changed, he abruptly stepped on the accelerator and sped away without acknowledging Paar.

For another sequence of Paar's show, it was understood that Judy would belt out a rendition of "God Bless America," aiming it at a female model representing the Statue of Liberty. Unknown to Judy or anyone else behind the scenes, the model had had too much to drink, and in the middle of Judy's song, she crash-landed from her pedestal, falling down drunk, flat on her face.

A few days later, Judy met with a possible ghost writer that Luft had met, prompting her to make another attempt at dictating her autobiography. His name was Sanford Dody. He had made a name for himself as the ghost writer who had previously labored alongside Bette Davis in the drafting of her autobiography, *The Lonely Life,* published by Putnam in 1962.

As it turned out, Dody spent only one session with Judy, when she talked and talked until seven that morning. He wrote

The upper photo depicts **Jack Haley, Jr.**, and his bride, **Liza Minnelli,** who were married from 1974 to 1979. Judy met her future son-in-law when he produced a TV special on which she appeared. She never lived to attend the wedding.

The lower photos depict **Jack Haley, Sr.**, who played The Tin Man in *The Wizard of Oz.*

689

about their session in his 1980 autobiography, *Giving Up the Ghost.*

Tom Greene was in the room at the time and silent for the most part. His task involved replenishing the drinks, and he eventually excused himself to go to bed to read *The Boston Strangler.*

To the ghostwriter, Judy relayed stories from her early childhood, presenting the two horrors of her life, Ethel Gumm and Louis B. Mayer, continuing on, maniacally, till dawn

By 7AM, Dody was falling asleep, but she urged him to stay awake. "Wait till I tell you about Clark Gable, Greta Garbo, and Mickey Rooney. Wait until you hear about that crazy Deanna Durbin."

Dody later claimed that he found Judy "insatiable and vampiric," but quite charming. As he was leaving, heading off into the bright morning, she almost wanted a compliment from him. "Isn't it remarkable that with all the horror of my life, all that I've been through, that I never drifted into booze or pills?

After that (ridiculous) declaration, Dody knew he was not the writer to choreograph and produce Judy's autobiography. He had to leave, as he was due at 10AM at the apartment of Helen Hayes to hear her dictate her autobiography, too.

As he bid Judy goodbye, he planned to never see her again.

Sanford Dody, Ghostwriter to the Stars: He penned "autobiographies" of Bette Davis, Dagmar Godowsky, and Helen Hayes, and became noted for his abilities to cope with the rambling, often self-indulgent recollections of *Über-divas.*

But after an extended headache-inducing session listening to the disjointed life saga of Judy Garland, he gathered up his pencils and recording devices, and vowed that the project and its subject were "not his scene," leaving an overview of the life of Judy Garland to other contenders, including Darwin Porter.

*　　*　　*

As Judy was nearing the end of her life, she turned to Sid Luft to manage her career. Once again, he promised to arrange a cross-country string of concert bookings, virtually guaranteeing her "a cool million." She had heard forecasts like that before, but agreed to go along with his elaborate plans anyway.

In June of 1967, he urged her to sign a contract for the establishment of a corporation known as "Group Five." She was falsely told that it would be governed by a board of directors comprised of herself, Luft, and her three children.

But when its final version was presented to her for signature, its major stockholders included Ray Filiberti, a former Wall Street broker, who had spent time in Federal prison for carrying stolen securities across state lines. The other stockholders (and signatories) were Filiberti's shadowy friends, each of whom had Mob connections. And in vivid contradiction to the original concept, Luft and Judy were configured as employees (not owners), and she would be paid only $1,500 (always in cash) per concert. An armada of confusing tax-avoidance provisions—each designed to prevent seizure of funds by the IRS— were built into its charter.

It was agreed—with the intention of hiding her taxable income—that Group Five would pay all her living expenses, including household support for Joey and Lorna, plus hotel and medical expenses, train and air travel, wardrobe, and entertainment costs. Considering the massive bills she ran up for those categories of expenses, the deal seemed to synch with her needs—that is, if Filiberti would actually honor such an agreement as it applied to Judy's "spendthrift" expenses.

Despite her bitter complaints about the ill treatment she received at the hands of Group Five, her management paid for her lodgings at **8 East 63rd Street** in this since-renovated townhouse.

In 2020, it was being marketed as one of the top-notch real estate investments in Manhattan at an asking price of more than $30 million.

Judy's Group Five contract contained one of the most bizarre stipulations ever written into a business deal: With built-in penalties if she violated it, she was compelled to notify the stockholders twenty-four hours in advance of her death.

Luft told her that, based on the terms of the contract, that he and her children would often travel with her from city to city, from concert to concert.

She interpreted that to mean that he planned to resume sexual relations with her—in fact, she invited him to go to bed his first night back with her. He declined, partly because he was involved at the time in an affair with a beautiful young actress named Marianna Hill.

"What's the matter, Sid?" she asked. "Turned fag on me?"

Included in the terms of the Group Five contract were clauses that covered whatever home she'd occupy—in this case, a rented townhouse at 8 East 63rd Street in Manhattan, around the corner from Central Park. Judy, Lorna, and Joey would define it as "home" until early in 1968.

Lorna remembered moving in when she was fourteen years old and already five inches taller than her mother. She likened it to "a cross between a French bordello and a mausoleum. No expense had been spared by its owner to make it truly hideous. It was the ugliest place I've ever seen in my life."

She was referencing its owner, Dr. Murray Banks, who had a unique taste in décor. For example, on each side of Judy's four-poster bed were two hanging antique lamps, each fashioned from World War I helmets, each with decorative strings of red horsehair dangling from the top of each helmet to the floor. After two nights, Judy gave the lamps a haircut.

Another room within the house contained whips, chains, and other instruments of medieval torture, everything laid out for the sexual pleasure of aficionados in a style inspired by the Marquis de Sade.

Judy launched her most recent concert tour at the Music Fair in Westbury, New York, for a run from June 13 to 18. But it almost never came off.

A few hours before she'd been scheduled to walk out on stage, she complained of a sore throat telling Luft that he'd have to cancel her appearance. "Oh, no, not again!" he moaned. "How many sore throats can a singer get in a year?"

When he placed a call about it to Filiberti in Manhattan, he was met with a blast from the promoter. "This is the first day of our launch, and the bitch is already sick...*again!*"

Frantically, Luft contacted a throat specialist and—at great expense—persuaded him to ride with him in a chauffeur-driven limousine from Manhattan to Westbury.

Rushing to Judy's bedside, the doctor examined her throat. "For a throat specialist, you have bad breath," Judy informed him. "So did my beloved dog, Toto, in *The Wizard of Oz.*"

In his diagnosis, the doctor told Luft, "Her throat is raw. She admitted to me she's on Ritalin...lots and lots of it. Ritalin dries out the throat. And from what I gathered, she's taken enough to kill three people."

Right before the concert, Judy announced she was going on. After each number, she would disappear into the wings for a throat spray from the doctor.

Judy dragged Lorna onstage with her, and she was given an ovation, followed by Judy singing with her new son-in-law, Peter Allen.

After their joint rendition of "Swanee," Judy walked off the stage. When the doctor went to spray her throat for a final time, she said, "Who needs you? Listen at that applause!" Rejecting him and his ministrations, she maneuvered her way back to center stage to deliver a powerful rendition of "Over the Rainbow."

For her six performances at Westbury, Judy grossed $70,000.

Variety claimed, "Her once magnificent voice is virtually shattered." But *Billboard* noted that, "Even hoarse, Miss Garland gives a song more meaning, more vitality, than many a healthy performer."

The New York Times stated that "hundreds and hundreds rose to their feet shouting love, and the place was in an uproar."

After Westbury, Judy and Green flew to Los Angeles, where she entered the Cedars of Lebanon Hospital, telling reporters, "It's only for a routine check-up, so I'm sure you guys will write that it's another suicide attempt."

Rushing back to New York after her hospital stint, she and Green stopped off in Chicago and checked into the Ambassador East. In its elegant Pump Room downstairs, she celebrated her forty-fifth birthday. The hotel kitchen was flooded that night, so the chef emerged from the rear with a grill and cooked their dinner beside their table.

While Luft remained in New York lining up Judy's return to The Palace, Green went with her for an engagement at the Storrowtown Music Festival (June 26 -July 1) at West Springfield, Massachusetts.

A critic for the *Berkshire Eagle* found that, "Her voice has the same pulsations it did when she was riding the comeback waves at The Palace in New York of the 1950s. *The Springfield News* cited her for having "a certain magic on stage."

Beginning on July 10, she was booked for nearly a week at the Camden Music Fair in Haddonfield, New Jersey. The *Woodbury Evening News* found her voice "as clear as a trumpet." The *Trenton Evening News* wrote, "Her rhythm is perfect; her small right foot keeps time as body and voice combine to make each song her own."

It was at Camden that Judy told the press, "Lorna has more talent than all of us put together." Liza did not appreciate that critique. She had Lorna sing "Singin' in the Rain" from the hit musical starring Debbie Reynolds and Gene Kelly. Judy had sung the song in her 1940 film, *Little Nelly Kelly.*

Back in Manhattan, on July 20, Judy was seen entering the Nola Studios on West 57th Street to begin rehearsals. For her return engagement at The Palace (July 31-August 26), she appeared nightly on stage to a standing ovation. It marked her third—and final—concert there. It became part of the Judy Garland legend.

Both Lorna and Joey appeared with her, her son on the drums and Lorna singing the Petula Clark hit, "Don't Sleep in the Subway."

Vincent Canby of *The New York Times* wrote: "That magnetic talent is alive once again in New York, and so is one of the most remarkable personalities of the contemporary entertainment scene. Miss Garland was in fine fettle last night. She wrestles with a mike that looks like the Loch Ness monster and calms an overly exuberant balcony clique that behaves like a coven of elderly Beatles fans. All in all, it's an evening of spectacular showmanship." [*That "balcony clique" was a reference to screaming hordes of gay men.*]

The *Daily News'* Lee Silver found her "looking slim, lovely, and vibrant. Her voice was richer, stronger, and truer than ever."

The *Rhode Island Journal* in Providence found her show "a celebration of survival."

A record company wanted to sign her. ABC Records recorded her first three nights at The Palace. *Billboard* called it "a must for Judy Garland fans."

Her salary was $225,000, but whether she would receive any of that money from Group Five was highly unlikely.

At the end of her gig, she announced, "I am a very contented, healthy woman."

Before she made that announcement, Tom Green told the press that, "My engagement to Miss Garland is off. She is probably the finest, kindest, and most morally responsible person I have ever seen. Her most outstanding fault is her listening to the wrong people and taking their advice, which has often resulted in great personal loneliness and unhappiness."

The Tom Green/Judy Garland saga had not ended, however. There was more to come in the weeks ahead—a tawdry drama, in fact.

***

On August 30, Judy, with Lorna and Joey, arrived by train in the city of Boston for her appearance the following evening at The Boston Commons. There, she played to a staggering audience of 108,000 people backed up by the orchestral music of her former lover, Bobby Cole.

She walked out onto a twenty-four foot runway that extended deep into the audience's seating area. As the event neared its end, the Mayor of Boston presented her with a silver bowl. "Miss Garland, we've taken you to our hearts. I think that is the sentiment of all of us. God bless you!"

Boston's *Evening Globe* claimed, "Judy Garland is all Earth Mother, Soul Sister, and Living Legend." Its counterpart, the *Evening Globe* defined her voice as "as biting crisp as burnished brass."

***

Next were twin concerts (September 8 and 9) planned for the recently opened Merriweather Post Pavilion, a venue fraught with disappointment and drama since its opening in 1967. *[One of the centerpieces for the ambitious "planned community" in Columbia, Maryland, midway between Baltimore and Washington, D.C., it had originally been planned as the summer home for the National Symphony Orchestra. A year after its disastrous inauguration in 1967 (a rainstorm flooded the orchestra pit), the orchestra went bankrupt the following year, and mega-heiress Marjorie Merriweather Post withdrew her support. Its venue changed to focus on political rallies and popular music from artists like Judy Garland, Janis Joplin, The Doors, and Led Zeppelin.]*

Accompanied by Sid Luft, back in the fray once again, Judy and their two kids arrived in Columbia to face a swirling disaster that seemed consistent with many of the other controversies associated with that unlucky venue. All of their luggage (thirty-two pieces) had been lost, and, with some highly agitated rancor, they left the railway station for their hotel with just the small items they'd carried with them. Their baggage arrived the next day.

Later, at a press conference on eve of her gig, Judy claimed, "I'm not afraid anymore. I can't wait to go on stage, where I am the happiest."

She filled the 3,000-seat Merriweather Post Pavilion for a gross of $45,000. She told her audience, "You know I wouldn't leave you. I'd die first, and I'm not going to die. When my number is up, I want a new one."

The *Washington Post* wrote, "The voice is ragged, but it's been ragged for years. Her rhythm is catching, even when she throws it around. Her diction is a model of clarity. The evening wound up as a love affair."

As the weeks went by, Judy began to regret signing that contract with Group Five, claiming "those hoodlums owned me body and soul. I made the mistake of my life signing with them, and I've made quite a few mistakes. I should have known by now that no woman should ever put her trust in a man. I agree with Susan Hayward: All men should be boiled in deep fat."

Flying into Chicago in September, Judy told the press at the Ambassador West Hotel, "It's so good to be back home again." Her always faithful Bobby Cole was on hand to hug and kiss her and to conduct a twenty-five piece orchestra for her gig there (September 14 to 16).

She opened at the Civic Opera House, running through her familiar

694

songs. What made it different was when she sang (as a duet with Lorna) "Jamboree Jones" and later, "Together" (as a trio with Lorna and Joey).

The *Chicago Tribune* wrote, "The low notes, always husky, are brittle now. The top notes are an amplified howl. But they applaud. They start applauding at the first note and stand to applaud at the last. Never has such a mutual admiration society convened at the Civic Opera House."

The *Chicago Daily News* claimed, "Judy Garland keeps being reincarnated, but somehow manages to come back every time as herself. So, Judy, carry on. Give the lie to mortality. If anybody can live forever, it's going to be you."

Perhaps in honor of her midwestern roots, Judy made a one-night stopover in Cleveland to appear at the Public Auditorium. She held a small press conference for local reporters and appeared on local TV.

Her TV host, Dorothy Fuldhelm, said, "Her face is gaunt and her eyes enormous, like her daughter's. She is rail-thin. Gone is that plump look she had when married to Sid Luft. Meeting her is like getting shocked by an electric bolt. She is that magnetic. She has gone Over the Rainbow into the Valley of the Dolls to entertain the people of Cleveland."

She left Cleveland by train, heading for St. Louis, Missouri, to take her show to the Kiel Auditorium on September 27. Her concert was a success and generated a sensitive review by John Brod Peters in the *St. Louis Globe-Democrat:*

> *"Judy Garland's secret is that she knows how to provoke and foster involvement. She tears herself open—she's basically a sweet waif wanting love. She says what others dare not say for fear of embarrassment, for fear of being hurt: 'I Love You. I want you to like me, to love me. I need your love.' The pleading of this button-eyed waif of a celebrity—pleading to you and me—is utterly irresistible and she's saying openly and boldly what the rest of us all our lives only say indirectly—when we say it at all. The experience of a Judy Garland performance may not turn everyone into a true believer, but it cannot fail to leave one utterly moved."*

For a one-night stand on September 29 at the Cobo Arena in Detroit, Bob Carr in the *Detroit News* wrote:

> *"What is left is nostalgia—with enough of the special magic to make an evening with Judy Garland an unbelievable experience. It would be easy to say the magic was all in the minds of the beholders. But even the most hardened cynic might wonder if he hadn't caught a twinkle of it himself from this capricious leprechaun on stage."*

Shirley Eder, in the *Detroit Free Press,* wrote, "Judy, do you realize how much love there is for you in this world? Bask in it, bake in it, and blossom in it, and please be happy in it."

She also reported that "Judy and her older daughter, Liza Minnelli, have become very close again after a slight rift for a while."

Before her return to New York, Judy had two more stopovers, the first on October 1-2 at the Clowes Memorial Hall in Indianapolis. She filled

4,000 of the auditorium's 4,400 seats, grossing $34,000. At this point, her grueling schedule had taken its toll, and she arrived looking exhausted after a sleepless night.

Nonetheless, the critic for the *Indianapolis Star* wrote: "She has a voice like an organ. When she cuts loose with a crescendo, it makes people want to stand up and cheer."

Her final stopover on October 7 was for a concert at the Veterans Memorial Hospital in Columbus, Ohio. She looked worn out and tired, but when she came out onstage, the love from the audience seemed to revive her.

Critic Donald Blake said, "She faltered on three opening songs before coming back strong, where she sang on key. Her singing voice has been called brassy, powerful, effortless, and resonant, often demonstrating a tremulous, powerful vibrato."

On October 11, Judy boarded what she later claimed to be "the most disastrous airplane flight of my life." *En route* to London for a much-needed vacation, she was seated in first class with Sherwin Filiberti, the "atomic blonde beauty" and wife of Raymond Filiberti, the president of Group Five, the company that managed Judy's career…and her money, especially her money.

Reportedly, Sherwin had never liked Judy, and so-called friends reported to her that she'd referred to Judy as "an over-the-hill bitch," and claimed, "The hag is over fifty, if she's a day." [*Judy was forty-five.*]

As they flew over the site where the *Titanic* went to its watery grave, the heavily medicated singer could take Sherwin's "blabber" no more and told her to "shut your flapping mouth."

Sherwin didn't take insults lightly, and soon, the two women got into a hair-pulling catfight—Judy tossed her vodka into the woman's face when Sherwin called her "a worn-out old hag."

The co-pilot rushed from his cockpit into the first-class cabin to break up the ensuing brawl and to change their seats.

When the plane arrived at Heathrow, Judy booked a seat on the next flight back to New York. Round-trip, the transit wasted nineteen hours of her traumatic life, fifteen of which were misspent aboard airplanes.

Relations with Group Five, never good, went steadily downhill after that epic slugfest in the sky.

***

Back in America, Judy made a brief trip to California to meet with executives from NBC. Sid went with her as he pitched a possible Judy Garland TV series, conceived as something different from her failed CBS series. They, along with the concept, were dismissed. Judy later claimed, "I'm still blacklisted."

Back on the East Coast again, she headed for a two-night engagement (October 20 and 21) at the Bushnell Auditorium in Hartford, Connecticut. Bobby Cole was on hand to hug and kiss her once again and to direct her and to conduct a 26-piece orchestra. Lorna and Joey went on stage to round out the show with her.

Barbara Carlson of the *Hartford Courant* commented on how movingly she sang "Old Man River" and continued with:

> *"What other tiny, feminine woman, who never toted a barge or lifted a bale, could make it sound as if she knew what it meant. None but Judy. In a husky voice, she sang 'Over the Rainbow' to end the concert. It sent shivers down one's spine."*

After that, Judy flew to Las Vegas to perform at Caesar's Palace. She had signed to do a midnight show (November 30 to December 16).

John Carlyle, accompanied with two friends, flew in from Los Angeles for the opening, meeting her in her hotel suite before the show, hugging and kissing her. She chastised him, asking, "Why don't you marry me?"

He answered: "Because I'm a card-carrying homosexual."

"That's the poorest excuse I've ever heard," she said.

After her opening, he said, "That Garland pizzaz still held."

He attended the lackluster party in Judy's suite that followed her concert, spending time talking with Sid Luft: "Yawning, he told me to take good care of Judy, who was his meal ticket. I promised I would."

After a night of partying in Las Vegas, he collapsed on her "oceanic bed" and woke up the following morning with a hangover. She held his head as he vomited into her toilet bowl. Recovering after four cups of black coffee, he bid her farewell before he headed back to L.A. "As always, it was one hell of a blast," he told her.

In its review of her Vegas act, *Variety* claimed, "Whether in voice or not, there is always a super-charged authority present in the sometimes awkward, always disturbing, yet never dull or lackadaisical delivery of anything, ballad or uptempo."

Days later, Carlyle read in *Variety* that Bert Lahr, the beloved Cowardly Lion in *The Wizard of Oz,* had died. Reportedly, Judy was so grief-stricken that she canceled her December 4 show.

Lorna suggested another reason she might have canceled: "Her reaction might have something to do with the fact that Dad showed up with Patti Hemingway. My mom was livid. She might not want him back as a husband, but that didn't mean anyone else could have him. He was *hers.* The result was another huge blowup, and another concert performance down the drain. It was an endless, hopeless downward spiral."

Tom Green flew in from Boston, arriving the day after her glittering opening. The once-estranged couple had a reunion and "hit the sack" (her words) within the hour.

To end the year with a Christmas show, Group Five got her a booking from Christmas to New Year's Eve at the Felt Forum at Madison Square Garden. On her opening night, Tony Bennett appeared onstage with her to sing a Christmas song as Mort Lindsey conducted the orchestra. Green had been trying to keep her pills away from her, but, as he slept, she made a connection with a dealer who delivered her "medication" to her downstairs in her hotel's lobby.

After that, her condition deteriorated, and she missed three performances.

The engagement grossed $75,000, but she could have doubled that amount if she hadn't missed three of her six concerts. Green, Luft, and Group Five were all losing patience with her.

***

As 1967 came to an end, the "unreliable" Judy had performed an amazing total of eighty concerts with only four illness-related cancellations. Her overall gross was one million dollars, and she had come to suspect that the "coven of gangsters" who ran Group Five were robbing her.

Her greatest joy that year was her realization that the concert tour had introduced her to a new generation of fans.

She faced 1968 with a sense of impending doom. "The Black Irish Witch," as she described herself, seemed terrified that it would evolve into something genuinely horrible.

Yet despite her deep, perhaps paranoic fears, assessments had been coming in about her voice and her decades-long career. Record producer Ronald O'Brien claimed that "Judy Garland's combination of natural phrasing, elegant delivery, mature pathos, and powerful dynamics she brings to song make her renditions the definitive interpretations."

Other critics such as Jonathan Riggs weighed in, too: "Garland has a tendency to imbue her vocals with a paradoxical combination of fragility and resilience that eventually became a signature trademark of hers."

Cary O'Dell wrote, "Garland's raps and occasional quiver only upped the emotional quotient of many of her numbers, particularly in her signature songs of 'Over the Rainbow' and 'The Man That Got Away.'"

In the *Washington Post*, Louis Bayard called her voice "throbbing, capable of connecting with audiences in a way that no other voice does. Listeners find it hard to disentwine the sorrow in her voice from the sorrow that dogged her life."

The New York Times concluded that "Garland, intentionally or not, brought with her all the well-publicized phantoms of her emotional breakdown, her career collapses and comebacks. Her voice changed and lost some of its quality as she aged, although she retained much of her personality."

***

In the early morning hours of January 5, 1968, a desperate call was directed from New York to singer Tony Bennett at his home in Los Angeles. Rather sleepily, he answered the phone to hear the voice of a frantic Judy Garland on the other end of the line.

Overloaded with pills and booze, she sounded unhinged and unglued: "I didn't know who to turn to, so I phoned you, Tony. Sid Luft is threatening to kill me and even harm our kids, Lorna and Joey. He's crazed. I hate to call the police and cause a big scandal in the papers."

Bennett listened to her tale of woe and told her he'd get back to her soon. After he put down the phone, not knowing what to do, he called Frank Sinatra, who had plenty of connections in New York. Ol' Blue Eyes responded immediately: "I always told Judy that that bum would be nothing but bad luck for her. Call her and tell her that protection will arrive soon at her doorstep."

True to his word, before dawn broke over Manhattan, two policemen and four detectives were at her door. At the time, Judy was living in a brownstone, which, because of its spooky décor, she called "The Dracula House." As the day moved on, the force diminished until only one policeman remained to guard her throughout the following night.

In the meantime, policemen in faraway Los Angeles grilled Luft. He convinced them that he hadn't been anywhere near her and that she was under heavy medication and prone to "all sorts of demons and fears."

Thus, Judy launched herself into 1968, her final full year on Earth.

Just to show his concern, Sinatra called her every night for a week, and each time, she thanked him for "loving and protecting me and Lorna, too, and my dear boy, Joey, who plays your records all the time."

"Judy spent most of the year out of her mind," said John Carlyle, her close friend. "Every night, her active brain, fueled by Ritalin, created a spider web of fantasy. She began to fear that the mob was plotting to have her murdered like it did Marilyn Monroe. At one point, she didn't even trust her little Joey. On one drunken night, she accused Lorna of plotting against her. Can you imagine?"

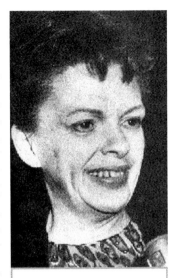

Judy Garland wasn't even fifty years old, but her face reflected the ravages of time.

According to her close friend, actor John Carlyle, "I came to realize that she was so emotionally damaged that at this point in her life, there would be no turning back."

"She was on the road to self-destruction. Let me rephrase that: She was on the road to Hell. None of us who loved her could save her."

"In some ways, she was still Dorothy in *The Wizard of Oz,*" he said. "Those were the times she was loving, even cuddly, filled with devotion to her friends and her kids. At other times, she was a scheming, devouring woman, out of her mind with all that heavy drug intake. On those horrible nights, she lashed out at all those around her and even at the entire world, damning practically everybody who had been close to her."

***

As a performer, 1968 was a year of tragedy and triumph for Judy, even though it came nowhere near the success of 1967. She would have some peak moments on stage, but her voice was hardly what it was at its pinnacle (1945 to 1955).

She had on-stage disasters, where even some of her fans walked out on her performances. And twice, she suffered devastating embarrassments when she appeared onstage in a daze, seemingly not known what city she was in.

She told her on-again, off-again beau, Tom Green, "Sometimes, in my deepest despair, I know that even though I'm in the pits of Hell, I'll come back. You're talking to the Queen of Comebacks!"

"I didn't really believe she'd come back," Green said. "Oh, maybe she'd pull herself together and present some aura of the Judy Garland of long ago that we cherished and loved. But she was too far gone. I knew in my heart she would never grow old. Not with her diet of Ritalin and too much Dexamyl, along with those four packages of cigarettes a day that turned her into a smoke stack." *[Widely abused, Dexamyl is no longer manufactured.]*

Around this time, Judy settled her lawsuit against David Begelman and Freddie Fields for only $8,000. This horrified Luft, who had instigated the legal action, claiming that "Leopold & Loeb," *[notorious thrill killers of the 1920s]* had embezzled a fortune from her."

"I don't think I've ever been so pissed off at Judy," Luft said. "She sure must have needed the money. For my part, I would continue to go after the asses of those two crooks."

On top of all her other troubles, the IRS appeared ready to move in on her at any moment. The back taxes and interest she owed them had by now skyrocketed to half a million dollars.

Recovering slightly, she still held onto her dream of replacing Angela Lansbury on Broadway in the hit musical, *Mame*. She had seen it more than once, but the last time she went, she had objected to the location of her seat, and was determined to seek revenge.

In the lobby, she phoned the police station, disguising her voice, claiming that a bomb was set to go off in fifteen minutes unless the theater was emptied. The police believed her, and in minutes, they showed up in force, ordering the audience, the cast, and the backstage crew out of the theater. Then a bomb squad almost tore the theater apart but found no explosives.

The police never knew that the anonymous caller was the one, the only, Judy Garland.

At her rented Manhattan brownstone, composer Jerry Herman arrived with three of *Mame's* financial backers. The men had already been invited inside, served drinks, and were seated in the living room listening to Gene Palumbo, a young musician, playing

It was Judy's career desire to replace **Angela Lansbury** on Broadway as the flamboyant **Mame**. At a performance she attended, she objected to the seat she was assigned, saying to the usher, "This is no way to treat a star."

In her drug-fueled madness, she sought revenge by disguising her voice and phoning in an anonymous bomb scare to the police.

the score of *Mame*. Suddenly, Judy descended the townhouse's curved Victorian stairs dressed as the play's female lead, attired in a lookalike for the most flamboyant costume Lansbury had ever worn on stage.

Even Herman admitted, "She did a good job, but I feared that my show would not be about Mame but about Judy Garland. Also, the backers determined that she was too unreliable to trust with our baby."

***

On February 18, Green escorted Judy to Baltimore to co-star with Tony Bennett, her favorite male singer [*"Eat your heart out, Frankie!" she had said in reference to her stated preference*] at the Civic Center.

Earlier, she had eaten "poisonous shrimp" and was suffering from acute stomach pains and vomiting. She should not have gone onstage, but she valiantly tried.

Nearly 10,000 people saw Bennett perform Act One with his usual smooth style. In glaring contrast, the act that followed him [*Judy*] was a mess. She couldn't remember the words to two songs she'd sung for years, and at one point, she dropped the microphone.

Horrified, Lorna was in the audience that night. "I didn't know what to do. Call an ambulance? Get my daddy to go up and carry her off? Ring down the curtain? No one knew what to do. I felt my mother was a pathetic figure up there, exposing herself to the world. Was it real food poisoning or had she overly medicated in her dressing room?"

Judy's voice sounded like a croak, and even some of her devoted fans began exiting from their seats and leaving the theater. From the stage, Judy pleaded with them: "PLEASE COME BACK! DON'T LEAVE ME NOW! I NEED YOU."

Luft, too, was in the audience. "She was humiliating herself. I wanted to rush the stage, grab her, and carry her off."

Her young pianist hurried toward her with a stool for her to sit on. As she struggled through her medley, he held her arm to keep her from falling off the stool. Responding to her crisis, her gay fans in Baltimore rushed to the foot of the stage, shouting "WE LOVE YOU, JUDY! GO GIRL, GO!"

In the audience was the deeply embarrassed father of John Carlyle. He later said, "Her songs were mumbled, slurred, not really sung. At some point, I got up and walked out. I could never figure what my beautiful son saw in this broken-down relic, a holdover from yesterday."

Critics cited this performance as "worse than Melbourne," not that any of them had actually attended her performance there.

In spite of the Baltimore fiasco, on February 25, she staged one of her comebacks for an evening at Philharmonic Hall in Manhattan's Lincoln Center. She later told the press, "I received such a warm reception that it was like a great big heating pad on a cold winter's night. I truly had love for those New Yorkers who turned out on a cold night to welcome me back home. I gave them my blood last night!"

***

Judy claimed that she was bored in her spooky brownstone, so she moved with Joey and Lorna into the St. Moritz Hotel. She and Green had broken up, but he suddenly came back to her. She'd phoned him: "Darling, I've decided I can't live without you. Please come back and take me in your strong arms." After he heeded her calls, they jointly announced to reporters that they planned to be married in May of 1968.

On March 18, Judy slipped in her bathtub at the St. Moritz and had to be rushed to the hospital with an injured shoulder. She was given Demerol to stop the pain.

She needed money to pay immediate bills. Green had already borrowed thousands from his father, but even that had evaporated with the never-ending expenses.

In her drugged state, she instructed him to pawn her two most valuable rings, one of them a diamond and jade ring acquired in Hong Kong; another crafted from diamonds and cultured pearls. Their value was estimated at $110,000, but at the Provident Loan Society on Park Avenue, he got only $1,000 for both of them.

The next time she appeared in public was on March 30 as she and Green took Joey to the Tin Lizzie Restaurant in Manhattan to celebrate his thirteenth birthday. She and Green gave every appearance of being a loving, well-functioning couple.

Yet on April 2, Judy was trying out "some new type of pills." Green was gone that day. Extremely agitated, she told Lorna, "That bastard Green has stolen my two most valuable rings from my jewelry case." She immediately phoned the nearest (West 54th Street) police precinct. A day later, she also filed a report with the F.B.I.

When he learned what Judy had done, Green wrote a letter to Luft, claiming that Judy told him to pawn the rings to pay the bills. Since he got so little for them, he pawned all of his own jewelry, too, accumulating another $3,000 to pay immediate bills—not only Judy's, but to help support Lorna and Joey, too. "I only wanted to help her. God damn it. In spite of the nonsense, I still love her very much."

On April 8, Judy continued to press her case against Green and had him arrested, although the night before, she had been very loving with him, leading him to think "that damn mess is over."

She appeared in night court to press her charges against him. An hour later, two policemen were waiting in the lobby of the St. Moritz Hotel, where they arrested him, handcuffed him, hustled him into a squad car, and hauled him off to a jail in Lower Manhattan.

He shared a cell with eight other men, some of whom had long criminal records. During the course of that long, terrifying night, after enduring many taunts of "pretty boy," two burly men held him down with the intention of gang raping him. He fought back, and the noise (at last) alerted a security guard.

Green was placed in solitary confinement for his own safety. The following morning, Nancy Barr, a devoted fan of Judy's, bailed him out of jail. When Judy learned of that, she ordered Barr out of her life forever.

Amazingly, Green didn't leave Judy, but returned to the St. Moritz for a reconciliation. When his court case came up, his lawyer testified that he had "physically, emotionally, and financially sustained Judy for three years." Charges were dropped.

Back at the hotel, Judy accepted him back again into her suite, where she was being warned of an immediate eviction unless she paid a $1,800 hotel bill.

When she learned that the case against Green had been closed, she told him, "I'm a god damn movie star—and I don't want you to forget that. I'm adored by millions of fans. But where are they? I need their help now. If they love me, why don't they come and save me?"

Then she started to wreck her suite, breaking objects. He packed his two suitcases and fled from the St. Moritz. He could no longer endure her taunts, and he had never really forgiven her for having him arrested.

For deserting her, she plotted a diabolical revenge. She phoned the front desk and learned that he was having his mail forwarded to the Alrae Hotel. *[Built in 1927 in Manhattan on East 64th Street between Madison and Park Avenues, it was gutted and reopened as the Plaza Athenée Hotel in 1984.]* Judy phoned the front desk of the Alrae and confirmed that, indeed, he had recently registered there.

She told Lorna, "I know how to get even with the bastard." She phoned Bellevue Hospital's emergency unit: "This is Judy Garland," she sobbed into the telephone. "You've got to help me. I've secretly married a young man named Tom Green, who has checked into the Alrae Hotel. He's just phoned me from his room. He's taken an entire bottle of sleeping pills, hoping to commit suicide. You've got to get to him and rush him to your hospital to have his stomach pumped. He'll deny he took those pills, and he'll put up a fight. If you believe him, he'll die. His death will be on your hands."

Later, it was reported that Lorna had said, "My mother didn't win an Oscar for *A Star Is Born,* but she sure deserved one that night, as she sobbed

Histrionics from "The Judy Show"

Contrary to her "usual" crises, where Judy needed the urgent attention of medical technicians, in April of 1968, the emergency she reported was a fake.

In her most calculated histrionics, she notified the emergency team at **Bellevue Hospital** about a (nonexistent) suicide attempt by Tom Green, her estranged boyfriend with whom she had recently quarreled.

Tearfully identifying herself as a distraught Judy Garland, she vengefully demanded that Bellevue send, "because he's going to die," an ambulance to forcibly pump out his stomach.

Very few mortals could resist a hysterical appeal from the world's greatest diva...and so they did.

And, as might be expected, in the aftermath, Tom Green became yet another "MAN THAT GOT AWAY."

her heart out over the phone."

It was later learned that an ambulance, with dome lights flashing, rushed to Green's hotel and forcibly dragged him from his room and into the lobby, out onto the street, and into the ambulance, where he was strapped down.

At the hospital, two doctors pumped his stomach, causing an injury to his vocal cords that would last for the rest of his life.

As she told Lorna, "Judy Garland knows how to get rid of a man."

Another young man would soon emerge. His name was Mickey Deans.

***

During less troubled times with Tom Green, Judy had cultivated some semblance of a family life whenever she and her beau, sometimes accompanied by Lorna and Joey, visited the apartment of Peter Allen and Liza.

They'd gather around the piano and join in a sing-along, with Peter providing the music. Liza would cook dinner, although, after leaving, Judy would tell Green, "I'm a much better cook, as I'm sure you know after tasting Liza's cuisine."

But those nights were rare. What was more common was Judy acting out her terror of the future, her crumbling romantic involvements, and her increasing financial hardships, usually through the lens of her growing dependence on pills. At times during her ensuing rages, Lorna and Joey were terrified.

Friends from yesterday began to desert her in droves. At times, she was left with only her children around her, and, in spite of her love for them, she often turned on them, probably only because they seemed the only ones left in the aftermath of Green's (horrifying) departure. She always needed a man in her life, and now that he was gone, even she—in her moments of clarity—had to admit that it was she who drove him away. "I guess he just couldn't take me anymore," she told Lorna.

After all those years of fighting with Sid Luft for custody of their children, she now had custody—and wasn't at all certain that that was what she wanted after all. One wild, overly medicated night, she didn't seem to know who Joey was. As related by biographer Gerald Clarke, "She chased him around the room until he leaped out the door and stumbled down the stairs. She hurled a butcher knife at him, aiming well enough that it narrowly sailed past his hair."

Dressed only in pajama bottoms, the terrified boy ran out and into the snowy streets of Manhattan. In his bare feet, he raced down the streets for four blocks to the hotel where his father was staying. There, he was warmly welcomed and put to bed.

In time, Lorna would be the last of Judy's children to leave her, eventually opting to live with her father in Los Angeles. She would return on occasion, even appearing with her mother on stage. But the mother-daughter relationship was changing. Lorna continued to grow up and mature, breaking some of their (severely damaged) maternal bonds and cultivating her own friends and interests.

Judy made a new friend in Mickey Deans, the night manager of Arthur, at the time the hippest disco in Manhattan. It had been opened by Sybil Burton with money she had obtained from her divorce with Richard Burton. *[He had dumped her in Rome to pursue his co-star, Elizabeth Taylor, in Cleopatra (1963) the film being (disastrously and expensively) crafted and the subject of almost obsessive public scrutiny at the time.]*

Sybil became so impressed with Deans' social and organizational skills as a nightclub host that she promoted him to night manager of Arthur.

Judy became a frequent visitor, and a friendship de-

Mickey Deans (right), who evolved into Judy's fifth and final husband, was a man with a past, chapters of which involved strong women (such as his employer, **Sybil Burton** (left), owner of the disco that employed him) and lots and lots of gay men.

Sybil ran Arthur, the then "Must Visit" NYC disco that EVERYBODY wanted to see, including Judy, who made it "my regular."

As its night manager, Mickey got to meet every VIP who visited Manhattan, Judy included.

veloped between them. In time, it would evolve into an affair and even marriage. But that lay in their futures. In the meantime, she turned to four—"maybe five"—other men for her sexual flings. In reference to one or another of them, on some occasion or another, she announced, "This is the new man in my life. There will be wedding bells."

Whenever Judy was in town, she made Arthur her favorite hangout. Sometimes she and Deans, along with friends, would remain on the premises long after the disco had closed. She also began to pay visits to Deans' apartment, which he shared with a gifted musician, Charlie Cochran, his best friend.

Often, dawn found them singing around Deans' in-house piano.

One night, she confessed to him what she thought of her perennial standard, "Over the Rainbow."

"That damn song has plagued me for most of my life. You know, it's hard to be remembered for a song you first sang thirty years ago. It's like seeing a grandmother in pigtails."

Deans was well-known among the jet-setters who frequented Arthur, but outside of that, he was hardly known at all. She would, in the months ahead, morph him into a tabloid staple.

He was born Michael DeVinko, Jr. in September of 1934 in Garfield, New Jersey, which made him twelve years younger than Judy.

As a teenager, he'd developed a love of the piano. Working at odd jobs, he saved up enough money to purchase an old, broken-down piano.

By the time he was sixteen, he was making a meager living playing piano at various dives in New Jersey, leading a nomadic existence from place to place. After time in the U.S. Army, he attended Emerson College in Boston.

After graduation, he moved to Manhattan to "try to make it there."

Eventually, he landed a job at Jilly's, Frank Sinatra's favorite hangout. He and Cochran alternated as the club's piano player. Sometimes, gathered near Deans' piano, would be Sinatra, Sammy Davis, Jr., Dean Martin, and perhaps Sarah Vaughan.

At Arthur, Deans developed a friendship with Judy months before their affair began.

One night, after a late-night sleepover at the apartment of Deans and Cochran, she returned to the St. Moritz, where she discovered she had left three eight-months-old kittens. The manager presented her with a bill, demanding immediate payment, which she did not have. *[Up until then, Raymond Filiberti had been picking up her mounting hotel tabs, but he had suddenly derailed the money train.]*

At the time, Luft was looking after Joey and Lorna, and she found herself alone and out on the street, with her clothing and costumes held as "collateral and hostage." She found a welcoming refuge at the apartment of Deans and Cochran.

Group Five at the time filed a hopeless lawsuit for $250,000 against Madison Square Garden, claiming that management did not provide Judy with a mike and proper lighting, leading her to become "sick, lame, and in need of medical assistance."

More unhappy and complicated news followed. On May 17, Judy learned that Group Five had sold her contract for $18,750. Taking it over were Leon Greenspan and Howard Harper, the latter having a police record.

On May 23, Judy reunited with Lorna and Joey, who agreed to appear on stage with her in Boston the following night. The trio checked into a suite at the Sheraton Plaza to prepare for the event at the decaying 5,000-seat Back Bay Theater. Judy would be the last artist performing live on stage there before its closing in June, 1968, a few weeks later.

Lorna noted, with happiness, that the audience rose to its feet many times to give her mother standing ovations. Her voice seemed adequate, and reviews, for the most part, were kind.

Trouble began the following night. The day before, she had visited the Chelsea Naval Hospital, going from bed to bed to greet the wounded, the crippled, and the paraplegic, many of them injured in conflicts in Vietnam, singing renditions of 'Over the Rainbow" to them at various floors as a piano was wheeled around to accompany her. She then invited all of them to the Back Bay Theater for her final performance.

But as late as 7PM the following night, from her dressing room, she alerted management that she was not going on. She wasn't technically sick, yet was "too exhausted to perform."

That led to a bitter fight with the theater's management, which involved Sid Luft, who had flown in from New York. He could not persuade Judy to appear, so he enlisted help from both Joey and Lorna.

The boy pleaded with her to go on, but she slammed down the phone on him. Finally, Lorna got on the phone, citing all the wounded warriors who had shown up, many at her invitation.

"Well, if you wheeled them in, you can wheel them out," she snapped. Then she slammed down the phone.

***

After that disaster, Judy managed to pull herself together for her next gig at the opening of The Garden State Arts Center in Holmdel, New Jersey. From July 25 to 29, she was booked as the first entertainer to perform at this new $10 million indoor-outdoor theater.

Johnathon Kwinty reviewed her performance for the *Evening News:* "Judy Garland still has it! Last night, she was on stage for an hour and thirty-five minutes and sang nineteen songs, many of her old favorites. She still can sing the words of those tired old songs as if any one of them could break her heart."

Around the time of her appearance, she launched an affair with Wesley M. Fuller, a professor of music at Clark University (in Worcester, Massachusetts) who took over as her musical director. He was an intelligent, quietly spoken, fine-looking divorced man with a small daughter. Judy went to live with him and his parents.

She bonded with him at once, and the two of them could be seen walking along the boardwalk early in the morning, hand in hand. She told friends, "I have fallen in love with Wes. Sooner or later, I plan to become Mrs. Wesley M. Fuller. One afternoon, she turned to him and looked into his eyes. "I need a man, and that man is you, Wes."

Of course, that marriage never happened.

With Fuller waiting in the wings, rooting for her, she pulled off a second night at the Garden State Arts Center. Trouble seemed to follow her on the third night of her concert. Offstage, Fuller knew at once that something was wrong when she struggled to get through "The Trolley

The upper photo shows **Judy** signing the plaster cast of a wounded soldier during her tour of the Chelsea Naval Hospital in Boston in May of 1968

Although her mission of mercy was remembered years later as a spectacular success by the sailors, her no-show at the Back Bay concert that night left a residual anger with many of her fans in Boston who were furious at her last-minute cancellation.

That didn't prevent the hotel that had housed her (The Lenox) from inaugurating—on the 50th anniversary of her stay—**The Judy Garland Brunch** at their in-house restaurant.

Menu items inspired by its brush with mega-fame? "Ruby Slipper cocktails," "Chicken Under a Yellow Brick," and "Emerald City Waffles."

707

Song" and "Chicago." Her voice was weak, and she stumbled over a word or two. Then it happened as she began her third song. She faltered with the opening of "Zing! Went the Strings of My Heart." Her voice was weak until almost no sound came out at all. Then she put her hand over her own heart before collapsing on stage, falling to the floor, face down.

The curtain was not pulled, and the audience looked on in horror as two men arrived with a stretcher to haul her off into the night. She was taken for examinations and an overnight stay at the nearby Monmouth (New Jersey) Medical Center. The next day, she embarked on a long (and certainly very expensive) ambulance transfer to the LeRoy Medical Center near Rochester, New York.

There, it was predetermined that she needed a long rest and recuperation at the Peter Brent Brigham Hospital in Boston, where she would undergo care to try to help her break her dependence on "dolls," in the vernacular of novelist Jacqueline Susann.

She'd been in and out of this hospital before. When she arrived, the director came down to the entrance to greet her with "Welcome home, Judy."

At this point in his life, Sid Luft was ready to move on. He could take her no more, and he packed that night to move out of her life forever. He flew to Los Angeles, taking his boy with him. Lorna soon followed.

According to Luft: "Ever since she turned nine, Lorna had been her mother's caretaker. But the time had come for her to move on, too. I remember her phone call from back East where she told me, 'Daddy, I can't take it. I want to come and live with you.'"

"I knew that Judy, though granted custody, could not take care of our kids anymore. She couldn't take care of herself. It was time for all of us to move on like Liza had already done. We had our lives to live, and so did Judy."

***

For the first time in years, Judy, after her release from the hospital in Boston, seemed free from her dependence on drugs. Regrettably, it would be only a temporary reprieve. She embarked on a historic moment in her career, her last concert in the United States.

On July 20, she appeared on stage at the J.F.K. Stadium in Philadelphia with the Count Basie Band. There would be a certain irony here, as it was in Philadelphia that she'd been the centerpiece of first concert (in July of 1943), bringing joy to fans mired in the gloom and doom of World War II.

Back again in Philadelphia, she was in top shape with a strong, powerful voice as she sang her old favorites such as "What Now, My Love?." The stadium was packed with 20,000 people, who gave her entrance a standing ovation.

The *Philadelphia Inquirer* referred to Judy as "her old self, holding the audience in the palm of her hand. Her voice had its distinctive throb and resonance, and she sang with practiced ease. It was a love affair from the first to the last."

She was backed up by musicians Wesley Fuller and Gene Palumbo, with whom she was allegedly having affairs.

708

***

On the last day of July, with her Pennsylvania concert behind her, Judy flew to California for a brief reunion with her kids, Joey and Lorna, who were living in an apartment with Sid Luft.

John Carlyle picked her up at the airport and drove her to live with him at his residence on Norma Place in West Hollywood. *En route,* Judy looked out as they passed the gates of MGM, which was in decline, its sets unused as the studio struggled to survive, its memory of a Golden Age fading. She told Carlyle, "I'd rather forget what happened to me there."

When she called Luft, he told her that he didn't know where Lorna had gone, but that he'd allow her to come by to take Joey to dinner. Before her designated time of arrival, she devised a scheme to kidnap Joey, but Carlyle talked her out of it.

Hugging and kissing Joey, she had a tense meeting with Luft. Joey got dressed in preparation for his dinner with his mother and Carlyle. He drove to one of her favorite haunts, the gay-bar-with-Mexican-restaurant, Por Favor.

Present that night was Diahann Carroll, who had appeared on Judy's TV series. At the time, she was starring in a hit TV hospital drama/sitcom, *Julia* (1968-71), and Judy asked her to use her influence to get her an appearance on it. Although Carroll promised that she would, nothing ever came of it.

After their meal, Judy wanted to take her son to the fashionable disco, The Factory, even though Carlyle warned that they had to get Joey home early because it was a school night.

It was on the dance floor of The Factory that Judy was seen dancing with her son for the first and last time. In the car with Carlyle, driving Joey back to Luft's apartment, Judy promised Joey that she'd take him the following night to hear Tony Bennett at the Cocoanut Grove.

When she said goodbye to Joey that night, Judy was in tears. She would not keep her promise to take him out again. The night marked the last time she would ever see her son.

The following night, she asked Carlyle to drive her to the Los Angeles Airport where she took a 10:30PM flight to Boston, telling him that she planned to make her new home in that city.

After resting up in an apartment she'd rented, she next appeared in Philadelphia for a videotaping of *The Mike Douglas Show*. It was shot in color at the KWY-TV Studio on August 9.

The co-host of the show was Peter Lawford, her long-time friend and former lover. Both of them assured the other that they were looking wonderful, although that was not the case for either of them. Judy looked puffy and Lawford had aged quite a lot since Judy had last seen him.

After banter with Douglas and Lawford, she sang, by request, "Over the Rainbow" and then did a duet with Lawford of "Blue Skies." After that, she returned to Boston and spent most of the dying days of summer with Wesley Fuller, her musician lover.

709

***

As autumn came to New England and the leaves turned to red and gold, Judy decided to leave Boston and move to Manhattan once again. It was there that she met the new man in her life, a piano player and songwriter named John Meyer.

Meyer played the piano in cafes around town. Although he knew Judy for only two months, he managed to make her the centerpiece of a 300-page memoir entitled *Heartbreaker,* published in 1983, four years after her death.

It was during this period of her life that no hotel would take her in. When she tried to check into the Americana, she was asked to leave the lobby. The manager even had one of the bellhops escort her to the entrance opening onto the street.

Meyer had been introduced to Judy on October 8 in the Carnegie Hall apartment of Richard Stryker, who ran a small company, Institute of Sound, a recording service. He augmented his living by selling records from his vast archive.

Heartbreaker

TWO MONTHS WITH JUDY

JOHN MEYER

Somewhere along the way, he'd met "a homeless and penniless" Judy and had taken her to live with him in his cramped, filthy, and stuffed-to-the-ceiling apartment, a duplex which witnesses claimed usually looked like it had been recently ravaged by a hurricane. Meyer had written a song called, "I'd Like to Hate Myself in the Morning," and Stryker thought it would be ideal for Judy, for whom he was preparing a new act filled with songs she'd never sung before.

When Meyer entered Stryker's apartment, Judy was still on its upper level, which was accessible via a spiral stair. Stryker suggested that music suitable for her descent from the upper level would be "Blue Moon," a recording of which he played to "accessorize" her entrance. Singing the lyrics as she descended, and clad in a black dress, she looked frail and fragile.

The three of them spent the rest of the day laughing, talking, trading stories, and enjoying the food Stryker ordered from a local deli.

Meyer and Judy became instant friends. "The chemistry was right," he said. "I visited her every day. One afternoon, Stryker was gone, and we ended up on the sofa, kissing and kissing some more. I wonder how I, as a kisser, compared to such men as Gene Kelly, Robert Walker, David Rose, even Vincente Minnelli. I

During his brief encounter with Judy as her lover, secretary, and business manager, the author of this book (**John Meyer**) experienced up close and "in his face" the reality of domestic life with "The Lady."

Everyday life included pills, all-night partying, suicide attempts, fan mail, and battles to get an increasingly crazy and virtually homeless Judy back in business. For a while, it seemed worthwhile and in some ways, fulfilling.

But after sixty days of explosive dysfunction, he abruptly realized that it wasn't.

just knew I didn't stack up very well against Sid Luft. But she seemed to enjoy me."

In a few days, Judy agreed to escape from the filth of Stryker's apartment, and she moved in with Meyer's parents at Park Avenue and 84th Street. Meyer referred to his mother and father as "Park Avenue Jewish chic."

When Meyer agreed to house her, he learned that she had only five dollars in her purse. So he got her a job at "Three," a gay and lesbian piano bar on East 72nd Street near Second Avenue. The manager, singer/actress Mary McCarty, was a big fan of Judy's and agreed to give her $100 a night every weekend. When word reached the gay community that Judy Garland was singing there, fans began packing in every night she appeared.

Meyer soon became aware of Judy's dependence on pills. She had tried to cure herself of her addiction during her hospitalization in Boston, but as her troubles engulfed her, she resumed her consumption.

Meyer's parents were kind and considerate, but Judy was a rather disruptive element within their personal spaces, and consistently trashed their guest room. After her 3AM raids on their refrigerator, she left the perishables on the countertops, where they spoiled.

Meyer's grandfather lived in the large apartment, too, and he asked his grandson "You could have any number of pretty chicks, so why this aging Floradora Girl?"

Meyer didn't take his grandfather's advice, and on October 28, he popped the question: "Judy, will you marry me?"

She gave a brief and immediate answer: "Yes!"

On November 2, Tom Green showed up in Manhattan and had somehow managed to track her down. This time, it was not for love-making or a reconciliation. Instead, he presented her with an itemized bill for $58,815.62, which he claimed was for expenses he'd paid for her out of his own pocket. *[Actually the money had come from his father.]* He threatened that if she didn't borrow the money from one of her friends, perhaps Meyer, that he'd haul her into court. He left that day but never filed a lawsuit. She never heard from him again.

Meyer went to work trying to come up with a gig for Judy at one of Manhattan's major nightclubs but was rejected. He also met resistance from all the record companies he contacted.

On November 1, she did make a guest appearance at Lincoln Center in a tribute to Harold Arlen, singing "Last Night When We Were Young." She told Meyer, "New Yorkers will at the very least know that Judy Garland is still alive."

In the weeks ahead, Judy's lifestyle took its toll on Meyer. He found his thwarted attempts to find work for her humiliating. Her return to massive pill consumption led to rapid mood swings, and she was in and out of hospitals.

She would break off her relationship with him, then reconcile. Although he played a key role in her life, it was of short duration, and for that reason, most of Judy's biographers ignored him.

Finally, it became a severe case of the "Hong Kong flu" (his, not hers) that separated them.

It was based on those circumstances that she ended her physical relationship with Meyer and then shifted her focus to Mickey Deans. She continued visiting him at Arthur, where he was still the night manager.

Before her "farewell to America," she appeared as a guest on three nationally televised TV talk shows hosted, respectively, by Dick Cavett, Johnny Carson, and Merv Griffin.

On December 13, she was a guest on *The Dick Cavett Show*, which was shot in color at the ABC-TV Studio in Manhattan and aired on the morning edition of Cavett prior to his moving to a late-night lineup. She appeared alongside actor Lee Marvin, who was suffering from a hangover. On the air, he was blunt in his assessment of her. "Honey chile', I don't know who looks worse, me or you?"

She and Cavett indulged in bemused banter, and she sang two songs, one of which had racist overtones. "You Lousy Jippy Jippy Japs." She also sang a song that Meyer had written, "Prayer," but introduced it as the work of "Johnny Meyers," incorrectly adding an "s" to the end of his name. Critic Rex Reed defined her appearance as "an unmitigated disaster."

Cavett later told *The New York Times*, "Judy is a real comedian—garrulous, witty, and wickedly funny. She made me feel like an old friend while keeping me in stiches."

After the taping, Judy headed to Arthur to see Mickey Deans, and shortly thereafter, moved into his apartment on East 88th Street, the one he shared with musician Charlie Cochran, later that same night.

In the epilogue of his memoir, Meyer evaluated his whirlwind romance with "The Legend":

"Judy took my heart, my talent, my wit, and validated them for me. In going to bat for her, I found myself stretched beyond my limits. I was as powerful and effective as I'd ever been in my whole life. But in the midst of this terrific blossoming, she let me down, goddamit, and really blew it for me. She was crazy, a fucking lunatic. And then she was gone."

On December 17, Judy was back on familiar turf as she made a return to *The Tonight Show* hosted by Johnny Carson at a videotaping in color at NBC-TV Studio in Manhattan. On the show, she announced her upcoming appearance at the Town & Country Nightclub. [*She meant to say, "The Talk of the Town."*] She sang two songs, both part of her "new repertoire" composed by Meyer: "It's All for You" and "Till After the Holidays."

Her appearance with Carson was the last known taping of a television appearance by Judy that still exists.

On December 19, Judy made her last TV appearance in America on *The Merv Griffin Show*, although it would not be aired until January 6, 1969. No known tape of that show is believed to exist. She walked out to an ovation from the live audience and a reunion with her longtime director, Mort Lindsey. She warned Griffin that she was running a temperature of 102°, but she sang three songs anyway.

She spoke with the gay host about her origins with the Gumm Sisters in vaudeville: "We were really bad. We've not only gone out of style, we were never in style. I started the act when I was two with my two ugly sisters. They were really ugly. They were not only ugly but mean, and my mother was really a wreck. There is no reason for me to try to be Dorothy Adorable. My sisters were terrible."

Griffith invited Judy to be the host of his show for her return engagement on December 23 while he was on vacation with a handsome young man. He asked her to select guests she wanted on the show. In response to her invitations, James Mason and Burt Lancaster turned her down.

"I was amazed at the virulence with which these two former co-stars rejected Judy," Griffin said. She also requested Liza Minnelli but was told that she was out of town.

She then invited Margaret Hamilton, who had co-starred with her as the Wicked Witch of the West. She had aged quite a lot, and both of them swapped tales of making the classic *Wizard of Oz*.

Judy also invited the African American comedian, the aging Moms Mabley onto the show. "She was more outrageous than I was." She also had a reunion with her longtime friend, the gay actor Van Johnson.

The critic, Rex Reed, was also on the show. At time, he had been critical of Judy, but on the TV show, he praised her, telling her she should have won the Oscar for *A Star Is Born.*

"Oh, let the princess have it," Judy quipped.

It was at this time that columnist Earl Wilson leaked the news that Judy was engaged to Mickey Deans.

As December entered its final hours, Judy, with Deans seated beside her, lifted off from the tarmac at Kennedy Airport, flying to a new life in London.

***

It was a foggy day in London as Judy and Deans arrived at Heathrow Airport at 7:30AM on December 28 for an engagement scheduled to begin two days later. Deans had assumed that at that early hour, there would be no newsmen or photographers. How wrong he was. An unruly mob was waiting for them.

Crews from three major TV news channels were there, as well as a dozen reporters from the Fleet Street newspapers, plus a coven of freelance photographers with about a hundred of her most devoted fans, especially young males.

As Deans was making his way toward customs, with an arm protectively guiding Judy along, a strange man stepped forward and handed him a brown envelope. Imagining that it was a gift from a fan, he opted to open it later.

Judy and Deans managed to escape from the airport in a limousine that had been arranged in advance. She told Deans, "Those vultures were hovering to feed off my flesh.:"

At the Ritz Hotel, a suite was waiting for them, but Judy was disappointed, as she had requested that a piano be part of her accommodations.

As they settled in, a bellhop delivered a number of urgent messages. The first envelope Deans opened was the one presented to him by the stranger at Heathrow. It had been channeled through a private detective,

Keith Cockerton, and it had originated at the law firm of Lawford and Company, the English solicitors for Greenspan and Harper, the management group that had bought Judy's contract from the notorious Group Five. As Judy's new business agents, they had not authorized her appearance at London's Talk of the Town, that 1,000-seat night club—the big-ticket equivalent of the Copacabana in New York City—off Leicester Square.

Lawford and Company was seeking a restraining order that would prevent Judy's performance there. It became clear that she'd have to hire a local attorney and appear in court to defend her right to appear there.

There was more trouble. Someone (the name was not revealed) was in possession of her musical arrangements and was holding them "hostage" unless Judy forked over $35,000, money she did not have.

Immediately, Deans began "lifting" the scores of the arrangements from previous recordings.

The next telegram he opened was from Arthur, the disco he'd worked at in Manhattan. Sybil Burton had fired him for leaving his job.

The next day, Judy appeared before Judge Justice Magarty. The peppery judge read Judy's contract and then declared, "It is one I would not use to enjoin a dog." Then he tossed the case out of his court.

Outside the courthouse, Judy turned to Deans. "I will loathe Sid Luft until the day I die. He's the culprit who got me involved with those crooks."

Her court victory was announced only five hours before she was to go on stage at the nightclub.

Throughout her engagement at Talk of the Town, Judy would be assisted by its resident makeup artist, Vivian Martyne, whom Judy referred to as "my lady-in-waiting."

Martyne was waiting as Judy was ushered into her dressing room. It contained more flowers that a florist shop. After the makeup artist asked Judy if she wanted some of the flowers removed, Judy answered, "I want you to keep all of them here. I hope there are this many flowers at my funeral."

Then a distressed Burt Rhodes, her conductor, arrived. He was a nervous wreck, deeply distressed that Judy had not arrived at least three days earlier for rehearsals.

That marked the beginning of the ongoing conflicts they endured throughout the course of her five-week engagement at Talk of the Town. Without prior notice, Judy would regularly switch the order, the tempo, or the musical config-

Judy's last concert in London attracted many of her "to the death' fans—one of whom is reaching up to touch her.

Regrettably, a lot of the initial good will she generated evaporated as her attendance record deteriorated.

714

urations of her songs. Almost nightly, they departed from what had been previously decided.

Judy was to be paid $7,000 a week for a late-night show beginning at 11PM which was prefaced with warm-up numbers by other entertainers. On her opening night, she began her carefully choreographed, widely publicized act fifteen minutes late.

Seated near the front were visiting celebrities from Hollywood, notably Ginger Rogers, who migrated backstage after the show to meet with Judy in her dressing room, but was refused entry by Deans. [*The fading star had replaced Judy in* The Barclays of Broadway *(1949), and Judy had never forgiven her.*]

Zsa Zsa Gabor was in the opening night audience too, as was Danny LaRue, London's most famous female impersonator. The TV star David Frost showed up, seated next to the singer Johnnie Ray, who was soon to hook up with Judy as part of her act in later bookings in Scandinavia.

Judy opened with a new number, "I Belong to London," which went over well. Deans stood in the wings watching her as "she wielded the mike cord like a lion tamer's whip."

After her most famous numbers, she sat on the edge of the stage to sing "Over the Rainbow." Before she did, she told the audience "I'm not licked yet. I'm still searching for that bluebird." The concert ended with a standing ovation.

After greeting a horde of well-wishers, an exhausted Judy headed back in a chauffeur-driven limousine to the serenity of their hotel suite. She cuddled next to Deans: "I'm not alone anymore, am I, darling?"

"You'll never be alone again, my baby," he assured her. "Even before our marriage vows of 'till death do us part,' we'll be together."

The next morning, newspapers were delivered to their suite, and Deans went over them first, finding only six out of two dozen unfavorable.

The *Financial Times* claimed, "Judy Garland is the Maria Callas of popular music. Her voice still holds its tremendous charge of suppressed excitement."

The *Stage* wrote, "There are few artists who create an emotionalism—almost amounting to hysteria—moments before they actually set foot on stage. Of these, probably the greatest is Judy Garland."

Variety noted, "She had too many errors to satisfy any purist. But those who are not abashed by genuine nostalgia and who can rise to the peculiar alchemy that makes a woman a personality will have a very good time."

One reviewer from Manchester commented on her frail body—"the toothpick legs, the tiny little baby face, a flame fluttering in the wind like a piece of paper—in all, a bluebird who flew Over the Rainbow."

The critic, James Green, compared her to someone who looks like Peter Pan even at the age of forty-six. "Judy still has punch, star quality, and magnetism. She may no longer be the little girl crying for the rainbow. The voice many waver and the notes come harder; show business may eat its young, but the former Frances Ethel Gumm retains most of the magic given to her by *The Wizard of Oz.*"

As 1969 arrived, Judy continued her performances at The Talk of the Town, and she decided to marry Deans. On January 9, she and Deans were married in a secret ceremony at the chapel in St. Marylebone Parish Church by the Rev. Peter Delancey.

[Judy selected this church because it had been the setting for the marriage of Elizabeth Barrett to Robert Browning on September 12, 1846.]

The only person who broke the news to the press was columnist Arthur Helliwell. Judy told him, "I love Mickey Deans. Loving him means I no longer have to love the lights and the applause." The next day, when Godfrey Issac, her Los Angeles attorney, heard the news, he phoned Judy at the Ritz in London and told her that according to California law, a divorce was not legal until both parties had picked up the final divorce papers. Mark Herron had not done so.

As soon as he was notified of this, Deans phoned the actor, Henry Brandon, in Hollywood. Brandon, who had resumed his love affair with Judy's ex, told him, "I'll see that my boy picks up those papers today. No one wants him to be divorced from that hag more than I do. She left a scar on Mark's life, but he's mine now...for life."

On January 19, Judy made her last appearance at the London Palladium. It was also the last time she'd appear on a TV show. The occasion was *Sunday Night at the Palladium,* in which she was summoned at the last minute to replace Lena Horne, who had taken ill. She showed up only ten minutes before going on the air and sang three songs, including "I Belong to London."

Derek Jones filed this review for *The Sunday Times:*

> "Time has ravaged her singing voice. Within a certain range of scale, tone, and volume, it survives—most beautifully in a downbeat arrangement of 'Just in Time." Outside that range, the vibrato is wild and uncontrolled, the pitch uncertain. At times, she needs to sing very artfully indeed to disguise the flaws."

As the days went by, Judy became unreliable, making her audience at Talk of the Town wait a long time before she came on stage. On January 20, she was an hour late, making the patrons irate. The following day, Deans took her to hear Johnnie Ray perform at a venue known as *Cabaret at Caesar's Palace* in Luton, about thirty miles northwest of London.

From his stance onstage, Ray invited Judy to appear on stage with him, and she did, singing a duet with him. That collaboration blossomed into a friendship. "We practically adopted Johnnie as our mascot," Deans said. "In time, he would tour with Judy and me."

She arrived late that night for her own gig and was reported to be "fighting the flu." She told Deans, "I'm going on anyway."

Since Judy was never on time, for the remainder of her scheduled gig, the management of Talk of the Town began formally defining her starting time as 11:30PM, delaying it a half-hour from its previously announced time of 11PM. Even so, on January 22, she didn't arrive at the club until 12:40AM in their rented Rolls Royce Silver Cloud.

The following night, January 23, evolved into her most disastrous performance. Burt Rhodes had to wait until 1:05AM to begin her overture. By this time, the audience had grown belligerent and was clapping ominously.

716

When Judy finally appeared, she did not get an ovation, but a scattering of boos.

Suffering from yet another bout of the flu, she seemed way off-key, her voice giving out at times. Members of the audience began to throw objects at her on the stage, including packages of cigarettes. Since it was a dinner club, some members of the audience tossed bread rolls at her. One drunk hurled a glass, which shattered near her feet.

A red-haired Irishman from Dublin jumped up onto the stage and wrestled the mike from her frail hands. "If you can't show up on time, why show up at all?" Two stagehands emerged from the wings to carry him off.

Finally, Judy could take the taunts no more. She fled from the stage in tears, falling into Deans' arms.

[As a footnote to that night, the English composer Andrew Lloyd Webber was in the audience, watching Judy go through her horror. Back at his hotel, he composed "Don't Cry for Me, Argentina" for his up-and-coming musical, Evita.]

Judy struggled on night after night, trying to rescue her reputation with the club. She finally gave her last performance there on February 1, telling newsman Michael Dove, "Mickey and I are planning to settle in London after we get married. We're going to open a little night club, perhaps in the Haymarket area off Piccadilly Circus. We'll invite visiting stars from Hollywood, and I'll sing every night."

It was two in the morning when she left the Talk of the Town for the last time. At the stage door, a devoted young man was waiting with a photograph of her which he wanted autographed. She looked closely at it before signing her name. "I see that my mouth is smiling but there are tears in my eyes," she told him. Then she headed off with Deans into the pre-dawn.

***

Almost every day, Deans was on the phone, trying to arrange future bookings for her. He even tried to find backers for a possible documentary on her troubled life. He came up with the idea of getting backers to finance a string of Judy Garland theaters across America. But nothing came through until some club owners in Sweden and Denmark wanted Judy.

At the time, he and Judy were seeing Johnnie Ray almost nightly. He was years beyond his heyday as a singer, but both Judy and Deans wanted him to appear with her as part of a double bill in future bookings, even as Judy's drug ingestion increased.

It was during this period that Deans and Ray began an affair that would continue throughout the months ahead.

On July 25, Judy and Deans went to hear Ray perform again at Caesar's Palace, the cabaret in Luton. He had been a major popular singer in the 1950s when he achieved his greatest success, as noted by *Billboard,* with two numbers: "Cry" and "The Little White Cloud That Cried." He'd appeared in only one movie *There's No Business Like Show Business,* starring Ethel Merman and Marilyn Monroe, in 1954.

After 1957, his career went into decline and his record label dropped him. After having been a prime target for teen hysteria in the pre-Elvis

Presley days, he was outed as a homosexual on several occasions, the first in 1951 in Detroit, when he was arrested for soliciting an undercover vice squad police officer in the toilet of the Stone Theatre, a burlesque house.

***

In London, beginning in early February, Deans went house hunting, since they planned to settle there permanently. He found a modest, six-room mews house *[the British name for rows of usually antique houses built in the 19th century as stables with accommodations for servants upstairs]* on the border of Belgravia and Chelsea. It was a bit dilapidated, but he felt it could be fixed up. He took Judy to see it, and she pronounced it "medicinal looking," but agreed to settle in.

Johnnie Ray in happier times, 1955, his heyday. By the time he began hanging out with Deans, he was WAY past his prime, the target of ongoing allegations of drug abuse and drunken embarrassments that included multiple arrests by vice squads in men's toilets.

Since the weather was cold and rainy at that time of year in London, they depended on central heating, a gas-fueled little furnace which didn't always work.

Deans recalled what married life with Judy was like: "She lost out on that role in *The Three Faces of Eve [released in 1957, it brought an Oscar to Joanne Woodward]* but she showed three faces to me. She was the wildly unreasoning, polarized star; the scared, guilt-ridden, immature little girl; and the warm, glowing, mature woman who was my wife-to-be."

After they moved out of the Ritz Hotel, Judy was notified by her attorney, Godfrey Issac, that her divorce from Mark Herron was now final, and that she was free to marry again.

In early March, Judy received news from Los Angeles that suggested that her financial problems might forever be solved. A New York investment group was considering the construction of a chain of small movie houses across the United States that would become known as "The Judy Garland Cinemas." Each theater would have no more than 350 seats, since attendance in the TV age wasn't what it used to be. All Judy would have to do was give interviews and make promotional appearances at the opening of each theater, and, supposedly, receive payments for the licensing of her name.

Despite Judy's objections, Deans began packing for a flight to New York. They got into a bitter argument when she claimed, "You're deserting me. I can't live without you. You'll be back in the arms of your lover," a reference to Charles Cochran, the musician who had been his roommate in Manhattan.

He flew away anyway for a separation of ten days, during which Judy consumed more drugs and almost died when their gas heater started spewing out toxic fumes, and she felt too sick to escape from the house. Finally, after she summoned help, two firemen opened the windows to the bitter night, and the furnace was repaired.

In New York, Deans had several meetings with potential backers of the Judy Garland chain of mini-theaters. He phoned her three times from Manhattan, informing her that the deal looked very good, but the "money boys" had to give it more consideration, and that they wanted to meet with her in New York before committing themselves. They wanted to make sure she had the physical stamina to make appearances at the openings of so many theaters in towns stretching from Florida to Washington State.

With the deal still pending, Deans flew back to London, where he found Judy in "dire condition. She seemed to have aged five years since I went away."

On March 15, Judy took Mickey Deans as her fifth husband at the Chelsea Registry Office, not far from the St. Marylebone Parish Church where that had been (inconclusively and not legally) married before. Once again, their friend, the Rev. Peter Delancey, performed the marriage ceremony. Johnnie Ray was designated as Deans' Best Man. In most reports, no maid or matron of honor was mentioned.

Mickey Deans wooing Judy Garland: The illusion of gaiety and all the signs of "Too Many Damn Rainbows."

Clint Hirschhorn, who wrote for the *Sunday Express,* attended the wedding reception at Quaglino's Restaurant, a chic dining venue.

Judy had invited a star-studded list of guests, topped by Bette Davis, who was in London at the time. She also invited James Mason, who cabled his regrets. Also rejecting her invitation were Eva Gabor, Albert Finney, Margaret Leighton, Laurence Olivier, Veronica Lake, Peter Finch, and Laurence Harvey.

Peace and Love at the Chelsea (UK) Registry Office, left to right: **Johnnie Ray, Judy** looking tired and gaunt and wearing a pillbox hat in a style made famous by Jacqueline Kennedy, and **Mickey Deans.**

"None of those distinguished guests showed up," Hirschhorn said. "I stood by Judy in the fall-out of her stardust."

The headline in the *Express* the next day read—JUDY WEDS BUT STARS STAY AWAY.

At the reception, Judy spoke of her hopes for the marriage:

"I mean it this time. I'm going to make it work for both of us—if it's the last thing I ever do in my whole life. There's too much at stake for it to fail. I see it as my very last bid for real peace of mind and contentment. I've suffered too much, and I've been unhappy too often. With Mickey I feel reborn. We're going to settle in London, you know. I don't know if London still needs me, but I certainly need it! It's good and kind to me. I feel at home here. The people understand me, and I'm not aware of the cruelty I've so often felt in the States. I've reached a point in my life where the most precious thing is compassion—and I get this here."

The Royal Borough of Kensington and Chelsea

CADOGAN LANE, S.W.1

Although some of its neighbors considered it an architecturally mangled eyesore within the posh and very glamorous neighborhood that contained it, **Number 4 Cadogan Lane** became a (dysfunctional) love nest for Judy and the only man in her life who didn't get away.

Her early death prevented it.

To Johnnie Ray, Deans gave a different assessment: "Judy and I have a co-dependency on each other. Of course, we fight, loud, angry, *Taming of the Shrew* battles, sometimes epic. She tries to dominate me, and I try to control her. We often emerge with bruises before a compromise is reached."

James Mason, her co-star in her greatest film, casually made an offhanded remark at the Savoy Grill, which was overheard and published in a tabloid: "I didn't go to Judy's wedding because I sensed this marriage was even more ill-advised than her unions with Vincente Minnelli and Mark Herron."

For their honeymoon, Judy and Deans flew to Paris, where they stayed in a suite at the swanky George V. They really didn't have the money to pay for it, so Judy, on the day of their anticipated checkout, left without paying the bill. They had gradually removed their clothing and possessions, storing them at a nearby facility so that on the morning of their departure, they didn't arouse suspicions.

Deans always recalled waking up on the morning of the first day of their honeymoon. She emerged from the bathroom singing one of her favorite lyrics:

Fame if you win it,
Comes and goes in a minute.
Where's the real stuff in life to cling to?
Love is the answer.
Someone to love is the answer.

***

After their honeymoon, Judy and Deans, along with Johnnie Ray, embarked on a four-city concert tour of Sweden and Denmark. For each appearance, she was to be paid $2,500 and fifty percent of the box gross gross.

First stop, Stockholm, where they stayed in a suite at the Apollonia Hotel. On the afternoon of their arrival, the designer Bridget Johansson, appeared in their suite with an assistant. She brought two costumes to show to Judy, winning her approval. Judy told her, "I'm sorry your marriage didn't work out." She was referring to her divorce from Ingmar Johannson, the former heavyweight boxing champion of the world.

During her city tour of Stockholm, she asked to see the neighborhood where Greta Garbo had lived as a child.

Then Deans devised a plan that he hoped to capitalize off Judy's fame. He met with producers and pitched the idea of making a documentary about his wife's day-by-day existence during her time in Sweden. A crew would not only film her concert, but Judy in her suite, Judy in her dressing room, and Judy visiting some of the landmarks of Stockholm. The movie would be called *A Day in the Life of Judy Garland*.

On camera during its filming, Judy was often very candid. "Some of my critics are calling this concert tour my last hurrah. But what the hell! I don't care. I'm married now and my husband will take care of me. One of my favorite lines in a song goes, 'For once in my life, I have someone who needs me.'"

After filming the documentary, its producer, Arne Stivell, head of the Music Artists of Europe, sent his footage for development and processing to London "for technical reasons."

[After Deans returned to London, the laboratory alerted him that some of the footage revealed Judy nude in her dressing room. Legal action had to be taken, and he filed, in London, an injunction against the filmmakers. Although the British court ruled against him, he hired a lawyer in Stockholm who found some old (Swedish) copyright law that prevailed, thereby preventing the release of what Judy termed "my last humiliation."]

In spite of Judy's physical deterioration, her appearance at Stockholm's Concert Hall was a success.

A local critic, Dagene Myheter, wrote: "You could pick your favorite Garland song, because she did all of them in her special and great way." He did, however, complain about the malfunctioning loudspeakers.

The reviewer for *Expressen* found Judy "fabulous, full of warmth, intensity, and drama. When it came time for the applause for the last time, it was like when Sweden wins a football game."

Regrettably, Judy was so exhausted at the end of the concert, she had

Deans notify the managers in Gothenburg, site of her next concert, that she'd be unable to appear.

On March 23, Judy appeared on stage at the King Kroner Club in Malmö, Sweden. One reporter wrote, "Miss Garland arrived in our city looking shockingly frail. From out of nowhere, she made a pronouncement that she was considering becoming a Catholic, like her husband."

In spite of some technical problems, the concert was viewed as a success. One of the critics for the local newspaper wrote: "Judy Garland is a legend and is to be revered, although she mocks her own legend. Dorothy's road to Oz has been a terrifying journey for her, filled with mishaps along the way, including suicide attempts. Yet, through it all, she still evokes all those Andy Hardy movies with Mickey Rooney, the MGM musicals of the 1940s, records of early Sinatra, the nostalgia of a time long gone by. She certainly doesn't look like that plump matron when married to Sid Luft. Her frail body is encased in a pants suit, and she evokes a somewhat urchin *gaucherie*, but she received a rapturous reception here in Malmö."

For the final leg of her Scandinavian tour, Judy and Deans flew to Copenhagen. It would be the setting for the last concert of a fabled career. She was photographed with her latest husband checking into the Kong Frederick Hotel. There, they were assigned rooms previously occupied on separate occasions by Marlene Dietrich and Sammy Davis, Jr.

Being among fun-loving Danes, even though the city was cold and bleak, she seemed to be full of renewed energy, no doubt to some degree from her intake of pills. Fueled with pep pills, she and Deans hit the late-night taverns, sometimes stumbling out, exhausted and into pinkish dawns as the rest of the city was waking up.

Sleeping for most of the next day, she appeared that night before 1,100 Danes at the *Falkoner Centret*. Patrons had paid $18 a ticket, the highest price ever for a concert there, equaled only by the appearance of opera diva Maria Callas.

Of all her Scandinavian concerts, this one was the most heavily reviewed. Herbert Steinthal, in *Politiken*, wrote:

"How was she then? Before Judy Garland's long-awaited first appearance in Copenhagen the air was thick with rumors that the star was no longer a star, that she had lost not only her voice but also that she could no longer even get through her program at all. And so she stood suddenly there on Falkoner Centret's enormous stage and disproved all the rumors in the world. After only a few minutes she held the entire hall in the palm of her hand. The little woman immediately filled the air with electricity. She was slim and gracious in her red pants suit under a flowing feather-trimmed robe. The great brown eyes sparkled in the little gamin face. Chatting, while ruffling her hair with small, quick movements, relaxed and nonchalant in manner, concentrating on her show program—that is Judy Garland as we know her from her films."

Knud Voeler in *Kruelt* posted his impression, too:

"She was herself. Her distinctive personality was intact. Judy Garland's talent, vigorous as before. Her microphone technique is dazzling, her mode of delivery

strong and glowing, her personal charm indisputable. She was dressed in a simple fire-red but not gaudy pants suit without an elaborate hairdo: She was just herself—without anything not belonging to her type. She flung her hit songs into the microphone in a way that produced dramatic and brilliant effects, or she chatted quietly and intimately, apparently aware, a little awkwardly, uncertain, but at the same time witty, warm, and winning all hearts. There were the old standbys—'Just In Time,' 'Over The Rainbow,' 'San Francisco.' The applause was long and persistent."

Virtus Schade in the *Frederiksberg Bladet* found her appeal a question of radiance:

"There is something that comes through that makes people enthusiastic. The audience went wild. People streamed down the side aisles to applaud as near to the star as possible. These were a collection of old chestnuts, a collection of rehearsed gestures used time and time again on other stages and in other connections. In any event, they achieved their purpose—one felt part of a cult ceremony. The public seeks a star, an idol, and if one has neither the age nor the temperament to admire The Beatles, Judy Garland can fill the need. One sees how a star like this is reborn each time, taking form for each spectator's eyes, and that is suspenseful."

On March 26, Judy delivered the last radio interview of her life on Radio Denmark in a program hosted by Hans Vangkilde. He would always remember his one and only encounter with her: "I could see she was in no position to be giving concerts. She was very frail, completely emaciated and jittery, almost boiling over into hysteria. Yet Deans was talking of future concert dates, including a big one he was trying to line up for her in Paris."

On the air, she said, "My career, my life, has been a roller coaster. I'm either an enormous success or a down-and-out failure. Every star finds life at the top lonely and cold, knowing that our days there are numbered. If you're lucky, you'll find a person to live with. I have found him."

She was sitting behind Deans, who was holding her delicate hand. "Here he is, and I am the blushing bride. He makes me feel young again."

***

After Denmark, Deans flew Judy to Málaga, the capital of Spain's Costa del Sol. From there, he rented a limousine to take them to the emerging resort of Torremolinos, where he had booked a suite for them. He thought the warm weather would make a thoroughly exhausted and weakened Judy well again. However, on their first night there, she slipped and fell in the bathroom, injuring herself and causing a sustained great pain. Deans summoned a local doctor, who switched her from Ritalin, which she was regularly ingesting in large doses, to a less dangerous substance, Longacton.

Her condition did not improve, and he decided to fly her back to London where, if needed, she could get better medical care. He had hired a new public relations agent, Matthew West, and he asked him, via phone from Málaga, to meet Judy and him when they landed at Heathrow.

West, a New Zealander, had migrated to London in the mid-1960s, where he opened an entertainment agency representing stars. It was West who had organized Judy's wedding to Deans.

Regrettably, the flight from Málaga landed at London's Gatwick airport, not Heathrow. West was waiting, fruitlessly, at the wrong airport until he got the news of the change. In the meantime, Deans rented a car (without a driver) and he drove it, with Judy and their mountains of luggage, back to their mews cottage.

West had called Deans "a bit of a scalawag, a party animal, but lovable."

Privately, Deans complained to him, "Judy demands my attention twenty-four hours a day. I have to get away at times. London is filled with beautiful young men who also demand my attention."

En route back to London, Deans found Judy irrational. "She didn't seem to know where she was. I began to think she was out of her mind. All those falls might have led to brain damage—surely not."

Once at home in their cottage, he put her to bed, and with West, began to plot a more ambitious concert tour for when she recovered. At that point, he was absolutely convinced that she would indeed get better.

He envisioned a spectacular globe-trotting tour, with performances in South Africa, Spain, Switzerland, and at several locations in Italy that included Milan, Naples, and Rome.

As Judy began to recover, West invited Deans and her to spend a week or much longer at a 16th-Century thatched cottage in the West Sussex town of Haslemere. West lived there at the time with his partner, Brian Southcombe.

Judy would sing as Deans played the piano; they would watch old movies on television, and she would read a lot. Every day, they took long walks through scenic countryside which seemed little changed since the days of Shakespeare.

Returning to London, Deans and Judy planned to fly to New York on May 21, her final trip to America. She would remain there until June 17. The backers of the venture that would build a chain of Judy Garland cinemas wanted to meet with her in their Manhattan offices to determine if she'd be able to make all those personal appearances in nearly every big city in America. With alarm, they'd read newspaper accounts of her declining health.

Judy and Deans accepted an invitation to return to the apartment on East 88th Street which Deans had previously shared with Charlie Cochran, with the understanding that it was now also occupied by the singer, Anita O'Day. *[Judy had presented O'Day with the Best Jazz Singer of the Year Award way back in 1944.]* To accommodate this ersatz *ménage* of show-biz veterans, Cochran graciously relinquished his apartment and went to live with a friend, dropping in every day to see to the needs of his guests.

O'Day and Judy bonded and formed a fast friendship. Known as "The Jezebel of Jazz," she had a drug-addicted life, and had served time in jail for the possession of marijuana and heroin.

One night, Deans drove Judy to Garfield, New Jersey, to introduce her to his parents, Michael and Mary DeVinko, finding them living in a modest, one-story bungalow.

Her final birthday, her 47th, on June 10, 1969, was spent alone in bed in Cochran's apartment. Deans had forgotten it was her birthday, and he and Cochran were away somewhere. Harold Arlen heard of her whereabouts, and he remembered the occasion, sending flowers.

Five days later, on the evening of June 15, O'Day invited Deans and Judy to the Half Note Club in Greenwich Village, where she was singing. Entering the club wearing a large picture hat and Coco Chanel's "Little Black Dress," Judy received a standing ovation from an audience comprised mostly of gay men.

At one point, O'Day invited Judy to join her onstage and sing, which she did, choosing "Day In, Day Out" and "Over the Rainbow." Those were followed with O'Day and Judy's duet rendition of "April Showers." The venue marked Judy's last appearance, ever, on a stage.

The next day, she and Deans met with the would-be backers of the Judy Garland cinemas. Once they were inside their office, the president of the investment firm delivered the bad news: The investors were not going through with their original plan, and they were no longer interested.

En route back to Cochran's apartment, Judy burst into uncontrollable sobbing. "There goes our dream," Deans told her, holding her in his arms.

At Cochran's apartment, Judy had her final meeting with Liza. Her daughter was surprised to see her mother sitting in the far corner of the living room, wearing granny glasses and reading a book, *Judy: the Films and Career of Judy Garland,* which had just been published.

As Liza recalled, "Mama looked like a middle-aged lady, perhaps an aging Midwestern housewife. We talked, and she even asked me if I knew about Teflon." [*Teflon, a tough synthetic, resin, controversial at the time for suspected health-related side effects, had recently been introduced by an affiliate of DuPont. Defined as the "polymerization" of tetrafluoroethylene, it was/is chiefly used to coat nonstick cooking utensils and to make seals and bearings.]*

Judy concealed from Liza her bitter disappointment over losing the deal that might have generated financial security for life.

As they talked, and as the hours went by, Liza became keenly aware of how much her mother's health had deteriorated since their last visit. "All the

Judy Garland sang "Over the Rainbow" for the last time when she was invited onto a stage by the jazz artist **Anita O'Day** during her late-night gig in New York's Greenwich Village.

Like Judy, O'Day had a history of booze and drug addiction. But unlike Judy, O'Day's drug of choice was heroin, which led to a series of arrests and a prison sentence.

troubles I had with Liza seemed buried, as dead as yesterday," Judy later told Deans.

Peter Allen showed up later, and he invited Liza, Deans, and Judy to a nightclub called *Aux Puces*. There, he sang "Simon," dedicating it to Judy and aiming it directly at her. It was the first time she would hear him sing one of his original compositions. When it was over, she hugged and kissed him, telling him how proud she was to have him as a son-in-law.

On June 17, Judy and Deans boarded a plane that flew them back to London. That morning marked the last time she'd set foot on American soil.

Judy had gone ahead of him in line at the airport as Deans remained behind for a brief conversation with Cochran. "Take good care of Judy," he said to his longtime friend. "You and I both know she's dying."

***

On June 20, Matthew West, Judy's publicist in London, dropped in for lunch and was somewhat surprised when she served him only two sugared doughnuts and a glass of cold milk.

With Deans present, they discussed making another comeback, perhaps either a television special or a global concert tour. There was talk of her reappearing again at the Olympia Theatre in Paris, or perhaps recording another album for Blue Records.

She spoke of her desire to send for Lorna and Joey, hoping that Luft would allow them to spend a month with her in London. The composer, Jerry Herman, had also offered her the use of his summer cottage on Fire Island.

West also brought some bad news: At the Monmouth County Courthouse in New Jersey, Sid Luft had been charged with passing bad checks. Upon hearing this, Judy's concern was mostly for Lorna and Joey, hoping that these charges and bad publicity would not affect their lives.

Early that evening, Judy and Deans showed up at a dinner and birthday party for their new friend, the Rev. Peter Delancey.

When it was over, back in their cottage, Judy experienced two sleepless nights in a row. She took pills to put her to sleep. Deans urged caution. Both of them felt they were coming down with another bout with the flu.

Matthew West had invited them to the last performance of Danny LaRue, their friend, a female impersonator, but Deans phoned him, telling him they did not feel well and could not make it.

Judy had to go to bed, but Deans stayed up to greet Philip Roberge, described as a "very close friend" of his from Manhattan. He stayed at the mews house for about two hours, during which time he and Deans fried some hamburgers. Judy remained upstairs.

A messenger boy arrived from Dr. Traherne with plastic bottles of penicillin tablets for each of them. Later that night, Deans retreated upstairs, where he decided to join Judy in bed, since each of them already had the flu.

As he recorded in a memoir, "I crawled into bed and held her close, kissing her on the cheek. She curled up with her legs against my back. I was awakened by the shrill insistent ringing of the phone downstairs." Then he reached for Judy but found her side of the bed empty.

It was a drunken Charlie Cochran who had flown to California. Feeling cheerful and wanting to wish Judy a delayed happy birthday, he was staying with John Carlyle on Norma Place in West Hollywood. Deans told Cochran he'd have to check on Judy and that he'd get back to him.

Deans tried the bathroom door, finding it locked. This was not unusual. Judy often went into the bathroom and stayed there, behind locked doors for hours.

But when she refused to answer his alarmed calls, he exited onto the building's roof from a second-floor window and walked across to the bathroom's exterior windowsill. From the outside, he raised the window, after which he could see her sitting on the toilet, slumped over. When she still didn't answer him, he managed to crawl in through the narrow opening.

As he reported, "I went over and said. 'Hon. . . . ' I picked her up. I noticed that her skin was discolored, with both a red and bluish tinge, and that her face was dreadfully distorted. Blood came from her nose and mouth, and the air escaping from her mouth sounded like a low moan. 'Oh. my God, no! Oh, my God, no!'"

In a memoir, Deans wrote: "The shock of her death is something that I cannot even describe. I put her back gently into the same position, rested her head on her hands, and then ran down the stairs and picked up the telephone. I couldn't remember the emergency number, but I finally summoned the police and an ambulance which arrived right away."

To prevent pictures from being taken of Judy's corpse, she was draped over an attendant's arm like a folded coat and covered with a blanket. That was the way she was removed from the house and delivered to Westminster Hospital for an autopsy.

Scotland Yard found her body unmarked, and foul play was ruled out. An autopsy was performed Sunday afternoon, the day after her death, on Judy's 47-year-old body. It was discovered that massive doses of Seconal had been slowly consumed over a considerable period of time, thereby ruling out suicide. Judy had been addicted to Seconal for years.

The London coroner later ruled that the fading star had died of an accidental overdose of sleeping pills. "There is no evidence at all of a deliberate action by Miss Garland, and I want to make that absolutely clear," said Gavin Thursdon at a brief inquest. "I shall consider the cause of death to be an incautious self over-dosage of the sleeping drug Seconal."

Deans announced that he was "taking Miss Garland's body to New York," where it would be placed on public view, with the funeral and burial scheduled for the following Friday.

And so it was.

***

For all the world to see, a heavily made up Judy was displayed in a glass-topped steel coffin lined with blue velvet. "WE LOVE YOU JUDY!" said the inscription on a rainbow-shaped spray of multi-hued carnations. Under threatening skies, thousands of Judy's most loyal fans, including tribes of gay men, made their way to Campbell's Funeral Home at Madison Avenue and 81st Street in Manhattan, where Rudolph Valentino had lain in state some 43 years before.

Thousands filed past the bier. Over the sounds of the morning rush hour of Madison Avenue could be heard Judy singing "Over the Rainbow." She was surrounded with yellow chrysanthemums and daisies. Her eyelids were shadowed in blue, and she wore the long silver *lamé* gown in which she'd married Deans three months before. Her famous mouth from which had emerged all those songs was painted an orange hue. Wearing a single belt of pearls, Judy had had her hands clasped over a prayer book.

James Mason, with whom Judy had co-starred in one of her most famous films, *A Star Is Born,* delivered the eulogy. Having flown in from London, the Rev. Delancy presided over the service.

Mason told the assembled guests, "Judy Garland could sing so that it would break your heart." He also quoted Liza: "It was my mother's love of life which carried her through everything. The middle of the road was never for her. It bored her. She wanted the pinnacle of excitement. If she was happy, she wasn't just happy, she was ecstatic. And when she was sad, she was sadder than anyone."

Frank Sinatra offered to pay the funeral expenses, but his offer was not accepted.

Although all three of her children attended, Vincente Minnelli was the only former husband who showed up at the funeral.

The only person there who had known Frances Gumm since birth was Dr. Marc Rabwin, Frank Gumm's long-ago best friend and a family friend of Judy.

In London, during her gig at Talk of the Town, **Judy Garland** posed for her last glamourous photo with her publicist, **Matthew West**. The photo is from the collection of his long-term friend, Rex A. McClenaghan.

Matthew was the first person Mickey Deans called after he discovered Judy, lifeless that early Sunday, in their bathroom. It was he who helped report her death to the police, and it was he who helped Deans dress her body at the mortuary after her autopsy. When they'd finished, Matthew was given the nightgown she'd been wearing at the moment of her death.

In ill health, West returned to his native New Zealand in 2006, keeping the nightgown wrapped in tissue paper in a small flat box. Knowing that he didn't have long to live, he burned it a few days before his own death.

His friend, the celebrity columnist David Hartnell, said, "He didn't want it to fall into the ghoulish hands of some demented fan or end up in a Hollywood museum as a bit of kitsch memorabilia."

JUDY GARLAND DIES IN LONDON

Husband Finds Body in Home

JUDY WAS STAR IN FINAL ROLE

Hundreds Linger After Funeral

Letting the good times roll—however forced.

Photo shows **Judy with Mickey Deans** sometime during their residency in what would be her final home.

Mickey Rooney also attended her funeral. In Deans' words, he looked "more like Andy Hardy's grandfather than Andy Hardy himself."

Other honored guests included Katharine Hepburn, Lauren Bacall, Jack Benny, Sammy Davis, Jr., Dean Martin, Lana Turner, Freddie Bartholomew, Otto Preminger, Patricia Lawford, Cary Grant, Ray Bolger, Alan King, and the Mayor of New York, John Lindsay.

Liza had the last word: "My mother was a beautiful flower that withered and died."

***

Judy's remains were sent to Ferncliff Cemetery in Hartsdale, New York at a cost of $37,000. But Liza was nearly broke. Consequently, Judy was placed in temporary storage, actually just a hole in a wall.

Eventually, Liza paid the

Judy's funeral in New York on June 27, 1969, was legendary, drawing 22,000 fans, including hundreds of gay men. At Campbell's Funeral Chapel, her emaciated body was placed in an open coffin so fans could get a final look at her

During the early morning hours of the next day, Saturday, June 28, gay men—spearheaded by a phalanx of drag queens—launched the Stonewall riots. Was Judy responsible? Had she, in fact, been the catalyst that brought on the Gay Revolution?

money and the official burial took place on November 4, 1970, a year or so after Judy's death. A plaque on the polished marble of the vault read: JUDY GARLAND 1922-1969. Any reference to Deans was removed.

[On June 10, 2017, the anniversary of Judy Garland's 95th birthday, her remains were moved to the Judy Garland Pavilion at the Hollywood Forever Cemetery in Los Angeles, the final resting place of everyone from Cecil B. DeMille to George Harrison of The Beatles.

Attending the memorial service were Lorna and Joey Luft and Liza Minnelli. Judy's older daughter said it was their desire to "bring Mama home to Hollywood." She also thanked millions of fans for their constant and ongoing love and support.

Before his death in 2005, Sid Luft said: "My family never got over the tragedy of Judy's death. My former wife and the mother of my two children was a very rare mix of shattered nerves and insecurities, self-destructiveness, and suicidal tendencies — but also a true genius, the greatest talent who ever lived."]

After Judy's death, Deans, with Ann Pinchot, wrote a memoir, *Weep No More, My Lady*. In the years to come, he drifted to Ohio, where he opened a gay bar.

Deans lived until July 11, 2003, when he died of congestive heart failure in Cleveland. He was not interred with Judy at Ferncliff. Instead, his ashes were sent to a private individual in Florida.

The day Judy died, as legend has it, there was a tornado in Kansas.

DARWIN PORTER

As a precocious nine-year-old, **Darwin Porter** *began meeting entertainers through his mother, Hazel, a charismatic Southern girl whose husband had died in World War II. Migrating from the Depression-ravaged valleys of western North Carolina to Miami Beach during its most ebullient heyday, Hazel became a personal assistant to the vaudeville comedienne* **Sophie Tucker**, *the kind-hearted "Last of the Red Hot Mamas."*

Loosely supervised by his mother, Darwin was regularly dazzled by the likes of **Judy Garland, Dinah Shore, Frank Sinatra, Ronald Reagan** *(at the time near the end of his Hollywood gig), and* **Marilyn Monroe**. *Each of them made it a point, whenever they were in Miami (either on or off the record), to visit and pay their respects to "Miss Sophie."*

At the University of Miami, Darwin edited the school newspaper, raising its revenues, through advertising and public events, to unheard-of new levels. He met and interviewed **Eleanor Roosevelt** *and later invited her, as part of a sponsored event he crafted, to spend a day ("Eleanor Roosevelt Day") at the university, and to his delight, she accepted. Years later, in Manhattan, during her work as a human rights activist, he escorted her, at her request, to many public functions.*

After his graduation, Darwin, in a graceful transition from his work as editor of the University's newspaper and his sponsorship by **Wilson Hicks** *(Photo Editor and then Executive Editor of* Life *magazine) became a Bureau Chief of The Miami Herald (the youngest in that publication's history) assigned to its branch in Key West. At the time the island outpost was an avant-garde literary mecca and — thanks to the Cuban missile crisis — an flash point of the Cold War.*

Key West had been the site of Harry S Truman's "Winter White House" and Truman returned a few months before his death for a final visit. He invited young Darwin for "early morning walks" where he used the young emissary of The Miami Herald to "set the record straight."

Through Truman, Darwin was introduced and later joined the staff of **Senator George Smathers** *of Florida. His best friend was a young senator,* **John F. Kennedy.** *Through "Gorgeous George," as Smathers was known in the Senate, Darwin got to meet Jack and Jacqueline in Palm Beach. He later wrote two books about them—The Kennedys, All the Gossip Unfit to Print, and one of his all-time bestsellers, Jacqueline Kennedy Onassis—A Life Beyond Her Wildest Dreams.*

Buttressed by his status as The Miami Herald's Key West Bureau Chief, Darwin met, interviewed, and often befriended **Tennessee Williams. Ernest Hemingway, Tallulah Bankhead, Gore Vidal, Truman Capote, Carson McCullers,** *and a gaggle of other internationally famous writers and entertainers:* **Cary Grant, Rock Hudson, Marlon Brando, Montgomery Clift, Susan Hayward, Warren Beatty, Christopher Isherwood, Anne Bancroft, Angela Lansbury, and William Inge.**

731

Eventually transferred to Manhattan, Darwin worked for a decade in television advertising with the producer and arts-industry socialite **Stanley Mills Haggart.** In addition to some speculative ventures associated with Marilyn Monroe, they also jointly produced TV commercials that included testimonials from **Joan Crawford** (then feverishly promoting Pepsi-Cola); **Ronald Reagan** (General Electric); and **Debbie Reynolds** (Singer sewing machines). Other personalities they promoted, each delivering televised sales pitches, included **Louis Armstrong, Lena Horne, Rosalind Russell, William Holden,** and **Arlene Dahl,** each of them hawking a commercial product.

Beginning in the early 1960s, Darwin joined forces with the then-fledgling **Arthur Frommer** organization, playing a key role in researching and writing more than 50 titles and defining the style and values that later emerged as the world's leading travel guidebooks, *The Frommer Guides.* Darwin's particular journalistic expertise on Europe, New England, California, and the Caribbean eventually propelled him into authorship of (depending on the era and whatever crises were brewing at the time), between 70 and 80% of their titles. Even during the research of his travel guides, he continued to interview show-biz celebrities, discussing their triumphs, feuds, and frustrations. At this point in their lives, many were retired and reclusive. Darwin either pursued them (sometimes though local tourist offices) or encountered them randomly as part of his extensive travels. **Ava Gardner, Lana Turner, Hedy Lamarr, Ingrid Bergman, Ethel Merman, Andy Warhol, Elizabeth Taylor, Marlene Dietrich, Bette Davis,** and **Paul Newman** were particularly insightful.

Porter's biographies—at this writing, they number in the mid-fifties— have won thirty first prize or "runner-up to first prize" awards at literary festivals in cities or states which include New England, New York, Los Angeles, Hollywood,

Yesterday, when he was young,

Darwin Porter

A social historian feverishly fascinated by biographies
and the ironies of The American Experience

San Francisco, Florida, California, and Paris.

Darwin, also a magazine columnist, can be heard at regular intervals as a radio and television commentator, reviewing the ironies of celebrities, pop culture, politics, and scandal.

A resident of New York City, where he spent years within the social orbit of the Queen of Off-Broadway (the eccentric and very temperamental philanthropist, **Lucille Lortel)**, Darwin is currently at work on biographies of **Lucille Ball and Desi Arnaz** (available everywhere in the spring of 2021); the dysfunctionally fascinating father/daughter team of **Henry Fonda** and his rebellious daughter, **Jane;** and the avant-garde playwright some critics define as the greatest lover in the history of Hollywood in the '20s and '30s, **Mercedes De Acosta.**

DANFORTH PRINCE

A graduate of Hamilton College and a native of Easton and Bethlehem, Pennsylvania, he's president and founder (in 1983) of the Porter and Prince Corporation, the entity that produced the original texts and updates for dozens of key titles of **THE FROMMER GUIDES**—travel "bibles" for millions of readers during the travel industry's go-go years in the 80s, 90s, and early millennium.

He also founded, in 1996, the Georgia Literary Association, precursor to what morphed, in 2004, into **Blood Moon Productions**, the corporate force behind this biography of **Judy Garland and Liza Minnelli.** Its vaguely apocalyptic name was inspired by one of Darwin Porter's popular early novels, **Blood Moon**, a thriller about the false gods of power, wealth, and physical beauty. In 2011, he was named "Publisher of the Year" by a consortium of literary critics and marketers spearheaded by the J.M. Northern Media Group.

Prince has electronically documented his stewardship of Blood Moon in at least 50 videotaped documentaries, book trailers, public speeches, and TV or radio interviews. Most of these are available on **YouTube.com** and **Facebook** (keyword: "Danforth Prince"); on **Twitter** (#BloodyandLunar); or by clicking on **BloodMoonProductions.com**.

Hearkening back to his days as a travel writer, Prince is also an innkeeper, maintaining and managing a historic bed & breakfast, **Magnolia House (www.MagnoliaHouseSaintGeorge.com)**. Affiliated with AirBnb, and increasingly sought out by filmmakers as an evocative locale for moviemaking, it lies in St. George, at the northern tip of Staten Island, the "sometimes forgetten" Outer Borough of New York City. A landmarked building, it lies in the heart of a historic neighborhood closely linked to Henry James, Theodore Dreiser, the Van-derbilts, and key moments in America's colonial history.

Set in a terraced garden with views of nearby Manhattan, it's been visited by literary and show-biz stars who have included **Tennessee Williams, Gloria Swanson, Jolie Gabor** (*mother of Zsa Zsa, Eva, and Magda*), *soap opera queen* **Ruth Warrick**, *the Viennese chanteuse* **Greta Keller,** *and many of the luminaries of Broadway. It lies within a twelve-minute walk from the ferries sailing at frequent intervals to Manhattan.*

Publicized as "a reasonably priced celebrity-centric bed & breakfast with links to the book trades," and the beneficiary of rave ("superhost") reviews (including "New York's most fascinating B&B") from hundreds of previous guests, **Magnolia House** is loaded with furniture and memorabilia that Prince collected from around the world during his decades as a travel journalist for the Frommer Guides. **Since the onset of the Covid Crisis, social distancing and regular decontamination regimens have been rigorously enforced**. For photographs, testimonials from previous guests, and more information, click on

www.AirBNB.com/h/Magnolia-House

In reference to Magnolia House, your host, **Danforth Prince**, says, "Come with your friends for the night and stay for breakfast. Even with social distancing, Covid cautiousness, and a lot more 'scrub-a-dub-dubbing,' it's about healing, recuperation, razzmatazz, show-biz, Classic Hollywood, and sightseeing in the greatest city in the world."

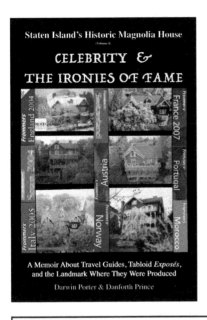

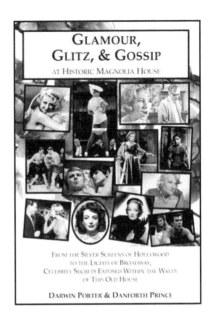

As depicted above, Volumes One and Two of Blood Moon's Magnolia House Series were conceived as affectionate testimonials to a great American monument, **MAGNOLIA HOUSE,** a nurturing and very tolerant historic home in NYC with a raft of stories to tell—some of them about how it adapted to America's radically changing tastes, times, circumstances, and values.

VOLUME ONE (ISBN 978-1-936003-65-5) focuses on its construction by a prominent lawyer during the booming (Northern) economy before the Civil War; its Gilded-Age purchase by the widow of the Surgeon General of the Confederate States of America; and later, its role as a branch office for dozens of travel titles during the heyday of THE FROMMER GUIDES, with detailed insights into the celebrity secrets their reporters (privately, until now) unveiled.

VOLUME TWO (ISBN 978-1-936003-73-0) is an *haute* celebrity romp through the half-century of Broadway, Hollywood, and publishing scandals swirling around Magnolia House's visitors and their frenemies…a "Reporters' Notebook" with everything that arts industry publicists didn't want fans and critics to know about at the time.

Each of these books is a celebration of the fast-disappearing
PRE-COVID AMERICAN CENTURY.

And both are available now through internet purveyors worldwide.

BLOOD MOON PRODUCTIONS
Historically Authentic Entertainment about
America's Legends, Icons, & Celebrities

One of the 20th Century's most fascinating woman was sired by one of its most widely heralded movie stars. As a precocious but love-starved child raised amid the bizarre abnormalities of Hollywood, Jane Fonda admitted, "I sometimes did naughty things to attract my father's attention."

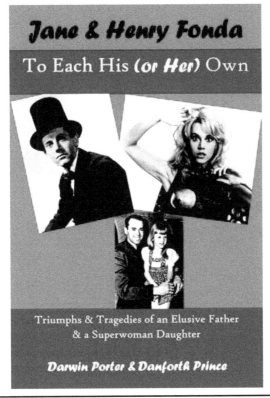

In a release scheduled for the Spring of 2021, Hollywood's leading biographers turn klieg lights on two emotionally intertwined Oscar winners, the lanky and boyish American hero, Henry Fonda, and his beautiful daughter Jane, a political activist and superstar beloved by millions despite her formerly poisonous reputation as "Hanoi Jane."

This book, unlike any other previously published, reflects the private agonies of a father and daughter engulfed by the divisions of their respective generations and the ironies of The American Experience.

JANE AND HENRY FONDA
To Each His (or Her) Own

Available Everywhere in March, 2021
ISBN 978-1-936003-77-8

CPSIA information can be obtained
at www.ICGtesting.com
Printed in the USA
LVHW022238050820
662515LV00001B/5